www.wadsworth.com

www.wadsworth.com is the World Wide Web site for Thomson
Wadsworth and is your direct source to dozens
of online resources.

At *www.wadsworth.com* you can find out about supplements,
demonstration software, and student resources.
You can also send email to many of our authors and
preview new publications and exciting new technologies.

www.wadsworth.com
Changing the way the world learns®

VOLUME A: TO 1500

SIXTH EDITION

WESTERN CIVILIZATION

JACKSON J. SPIELVOGEL

The Pennsylvania State University

THOMSON

WADSWORTH

Australia • Canada • Mexico • Singapore • Spain
United Kingdom • United States

THOMSON

WADSWORTH

Publisher *Clark Baxter*

Senior Development Editor *Margaret McAndrew Beasley*

Assistant Editor *Paul Massicotte*

Editorial Assistant *Anne Gittinger*

Technology Project Manager *Melinda Newfarmer*

Marketing Manager *Lori Grebe Cooke*

Marketing Assistant *Mary Ho*

Advertising Project Manager *Laurel Anderson*

Project Manager, Editorial Production *Kimberly Adams*

Art Director *Maria Epes*

Print/Media Buyer *Judy Inouye*

Permissions Editor *Sarah Harkrader*

Production Service *Dovetail Publishing Services*

Text Designer *tani hasagawa*

Photo Researcher *Image Quest*

Copy Editor *Bruce Emmer*

Illustrator *Maps.com*

Cover Designer *tani hasagawa*

Cover Image *Wall painting in Anhour Khaou's tomb, Thebes, Egypt.*
© *Erich Lessing/Art Resource, NY*

Cover Printer *Transcontinental Printing/Interglobe*

Compositor *Lachina Publishing Services*

Printer *Transcontinental Printing/Interglobe*

Printed in Canada

2 3 4 5 6 7 09 08 07

For more information about our products, contact us at:
Thomson Learning Academic Resource Center
1-800-423-0563
For permission to use material from this text or product, submit a request online at
http://www.thomsonrights.com.
Any additional questions about permissions can be submitted by email to
thomsonrights@thomson.com.

Library of Congress Control Number: 2004117058

Student Edition: ISBN-13: 978-0-534-64605-9
ISBN-10: 0-534-64605-0

Thomson Higher Education
10 Davis Drive
Belmont, CA 94002-3098
USA

Asia (including India)
Thomson Learning
5 Shenton Way
#01-01 UIC Building
Singapore 068808

Australia/New Zealand
Thomson Learning Australia
102 Dodds Street
Southbank, Victoria 3006
Australia

Canada
Thomson Nelson
1120 Birchmount Road
Toronto, Ontario M1K 5G4
Canada

UK/Europe/Middle East/Africa
Thomson Learning
High Holborn House
50–51 Bedford Road
London WC1R 4CR
United Kingdom

Latin America
Thomson Learning
Seneca, 53
Colonia Polanco
11560 Mexico
D.F. Mexico

Spain (including Portugal)
Thomson Paraninfo
Calle Magallanes, 25
28015 Madrid, Spain

ABOUT THE AUTHOR

*J*ACKSON J. SPIELVOGEL is associate professor emeritus of history at The Pennsylvania State University. He received his Ph.D. from The Ohio State University, where he specialized in Reformation history under Harold J. Grimm. His articles and reviews have appeared in such journals as *Moreana, Journal of General Education, Catholic Historical Review, Archiv für Reformationsgeschichte,* and *American Historical Review.* He has also contributed chapters or articles to *The Social History of the Reformation, The Holy Roman Empire: A Dictionary Handbook,* the *Simon Wiesenthal Center Annual of Holocaust Studies,* and *Utopian Studies.* His work has been supported by fellowships from the Fulbright Foundation and the Foundation for Reformation Research. At Penn State, he helped inaugurate the Western civilization courses as well as a popular course on Nazi Germany. His book *Hitler and Nazi Germany* was published in 1987 (fifth edition, 2005). He is the coauthor (with William Duiker) of *World History,* first published in 1998 (fourth edition, 2004), and *The Essential World History* (second edition, 2005). Professor Spielvogel has won five major universitywide teaching awards. He held the Penn State Teaching Fellowship, the university's most prestigious teaching award, in 1988–89. In 1996 he won the Dean Arthur Ray Warnock Award for Outstanding Faculty Member and in 2000 the Schreyer Honors College Excellence in Teaching Award.

To Diane,
whose love and support
made it all possible

BRIEF CONTENTS

DETAILED CONTENTS

DOCUMENTS

This page constitutes an extension of the copyright page. We have made every effort to trace the ownership of all copyrighted material and to secure permission from copyright holders. In the event of any question arising as to the use of any material, we will be pleased to make the necessary corrections in future printings. Thanks are due to the following authors, publishers, and agents for permission to use the material indicated.

MAPS

CHRONOLOGIES

PHOTO CREDITS

PREFACE

E ARE OFTEN REMINDED how important it is to understand today's world if we are to deal with our growing number of challenges. And yet that understanding will be incomplete if we in the Western world do not comprehend the meaning of Western civilization and the role Western civilization has played in history. Despite modern progress, we still greatly reflect our religious traditions, our political systems and theories, our economic and social structures, and our cultural heritage. I have written this history of Western civilization to assist a new generation of students in learning more about the past that has helped create them and the world in which they live.

At the same time, for the sixth edition, as in the fifth, I have added considerable new material on world history to show the impact other parts of the world have made on the West. Certainly, the terrorist attacks on the World Trade Center Towers and the Pentagon on September 11, 2001, have made clear the intricate relationship between the West and the rest of the world. In this sixth edition, I have attempted to show not only how Western civilization has affected the rest of the world but also how it has been influenced and even defined since its beginnings by contacts with other peoples around the world.

Another of my goals was to write a well-balanced work in which the political, economic, social, religious, intellectual, cultural, and military aspects of Western civilization have been integrated into a chronologically ordered synthesis. I have been especially aware of the need to integrate the latest research on social history and women's history into each chapter of the book rather than isolating it either in lengthy topical chapters, which confuse the student by interrupting the chronological narrative, or in separate sections that appear at periodic intervals between chapters.

Another purpose in writing this history of Western civilization has been to put the *story* back in history. That story is an exciting one; yet many textbooks fail to capture the imagination of their readers. Narrative history effectively transmits the knowledge of the past and is the form that best aids remembrance. At the same time, I have not overlooked the need for the kind of historical analysis that makes students aware that historians often disagree on their interpretations of the past.

To enliven the past and let readers see for themselves the materials that historians use to create their pictures of the past, I have included in each chapter primary sources (boxed documents) that are keyed to the discussion in the text. The documents include examples of the religious, artistic, intellectual, social, economic, and political aspects of Western life. Such varied sources as a Renaissance banquet menu, a student fight song in nineteenth-century Britain, letters exchanged between a husband on the battle front and his wife in World War I, the Declaration of the Rights of Woman and the Female Citizen in the French Revolution, and a debate in the Reformation era all reveal in a vivid fashion what Western civilization meant to the individual men and women who shaped it by their activities.

Each chapter has a lengthy introduction and conclusion to help maintain the continuity of the narrative and to provide a synthesis of important themes. Anecdotes in the chapter introductions convey more dramatically the major theme or themes of each chapter. Detailed chronologies reinforce the events discussed in the text, while timelines, now with thumbnail images illustrating major events and figures, at the end of each chapter enable students to review at a glance the chief developments of an era. Many of the timelines also show parallel developments in different cultures or nations. An annotated bibliography at the end of each chapter reviews the most recent literature on each period and also gives references to some of the older, "classic" works in each field.

Updated maps and extensive illustrations serve to deepen the reader's understanding of the text. Map captions are designed to enrich students' awareness of the importance of geography to history, and numerous "spot maps" enable readers to see at a glance the region or subject being discussed in the text. To facilitate understanding of cultural movements, illustrations of artistic works discussed in the text are placed near the discussions. Throughout the text, illustration captions have been revised and expanded to further our understanding of the past. Chapter outlines and focus questions, including critical thinking questions, have been combined in a new format at the beginning of each chapter to help students with an overview and guide them to the main subjects of each chapter. A glossary of important terms (now bold-faced in the text when they are introduced and defined) and a pronunciation guide are provided at the back of the book to maximize reader comprehension.

As preparation for the revision of *Western Civilization,* I reexamined the entire book and analyzed the comments and reviews of many colleagues who have found the book to be a useful instrument for introducing their students to the history of Western civilization. In making revisions for the sixth edition, I sought to build on the strengths of the first five editions and, above all, to maintain the balance, synthesis, and narrative qualities that characterized those editions. To keep up with the ever-growing body of historical scholarship, new or revised material has been added throughout the book on many topics, including Paleolithic painting; Jericho; the Hittites and Sea Peoples; rise to power of Assyria; the Hanging Gardens of Babylon; the development of democracy in Athens; Sparta; Greek interaction with India; the Celts and their threat to the Hellenistic kingdoms; Vestal Virgins and Pontifex Maximus; Greek influence on the Romans; Carthaginian political institutions; crises in third-century Rome; accomplishments of the five "good emperors"; childbirth in ancient Rome; Germans during the Late Roman Empire; Christianity, especially monastic missionaries and the development of Christianity; Late Antiquity; Empress Theodora; the cultural shift brought by the conversion of Europe to Christianity; *jihad* in Islam; Muslim libraries and intellectual life; Alfred the Great and Anglo-Saxon England; cross-cultural contacts between western and eastern translators and scholars; Maimonides; aristocratic women; the reconquest of Spain; Hildegard of Bingen; the Hundred Years' War; the Great Schism; the Serb-Ottoman conflict in the fourteenth century; the expansion of the Ottoman Empire and the fall of Constantinople; Brunelleschi and the Florentine Duomo; Zwingli; the theology of the Anabaptists; the Council of Trent; the clergy under Henry VIII; Jesuit missionaries in Asia; the triangular trade in the Atlantic economy; the Ming decline; the conquest of the Aztecs; European ideas of cultural superiority; the Danish phase of the Thirty Years' War; Denmark, Sweden, and Poland in early modern Europe; the art of Rubens and of Judith Leyster; chemistry in the Scientific Revolution; the marquise du Châtelet; social divisions in the American Revolution; the revolt in Saint Domingue; the life, career, and military conquests of Napoleon; Germaine de Staël; Chartism; Napoleon III's imperialistic adventure in Mexico; Vera Zasulich; the spread of industrialization to Japan; the political history of Britain, Italy, Austria-Hungary, and Russia; political history in general from 1894 to 1914; causal factors in the rise of imperialism; more background on Africa and Asia before imperialism; the new imperialism; World War I as a global conflict and a new kind of warfare; the Schlieffen Plan; the Spanish Civil War; the Stalinist era; the Japanese home front in World War II; the Berlin Wall; European opposition to American involvement in Vietnam; the Middle East, including the Suez Crisis; background and causes of decolonization; the Cold War; French artist Jean Dubuffet; politics since 1989; the reunification of Germany; the disintegration of Yugoslavia; and art and music, varieties of religious life, and science and popular culture since the 1970s. Throughout the revising process, I rewrote some sections and added many new subheadings to facilitate comprehension of the content of the chapters.

Chapters 6 and 7 were reorganized; Chapter 6 now focuses on the Roman Empire to 284, and Chapter 7 is a mostly new chapter on late antiquity and the emergence of the medieval world. The post–World War II material in Chapters 28 and 29 was reorganized to make the chapters chronologically consistent. Chapter 29 was also expanded and updated. New sections were added to a number of chapters: "Transformation of the Roman World: Crises in the Third Century" in Chapter 6; "The Spread of Industrialization to Japan" in Chapter 23; "The Casualties of War" in Chapter 25; "European States and the World: The Colonial Empires" in Chapter 26; "The Path to War in Asia" and "The New Order in Asia" in Chapter 27; "Decolonization and Cold War Rivalries" in Chapter 28; and "The West and Islam," "The Unification of Europe," and "Postmodern Thought" in Chapter 29. The "Suggestions for Further Reading" at the end of each chapter were updated, and new illustrations were added to every chapter.

The enthusiastic response to the primary sources (boxed documents) led me to evaluate the content of each document carefully and add new documents throughout the text, including "Respect for Women" in ancient Egypt; "Disaster in Sicily" in the Peloponnesian War; "The Vestal Virgins"; "The Eruption of Mount Vesuvius"; "The Qur'an: The Pilgrimage"; "The Vikings Invade England"; "An Italian Banker Discusses Trading Between Europe and China"; "A Feminist Heroine: Christine de Pizan on Joan of Arc"; "The Childhood of Catherine the Great"; "Soldier and Peasant Voices" in the Russian Revolution; and "Grandmaster Flash and the Furious Five: 'The Message.'"

Because courses in Western civilization at American and Canadian colleges and universities follow different chronological divisions, a one-volume edition, two two-volume editions, a three-volume edition, and a volume covering events since 1300 are being made available to fit the needs of instructors. Teaching and learning ancillaries include the following:

For the Instructor

Instructor's Manual with Test Bank   Prepared by Eugene Larson, Los Angeles Pierce College. This expanded, new, and improved manual has many new features, including chapter outlines, chapter summaries, suggested lecture topics, and discussion questions for the maps and artwork as well as the documents in the text. World Wide Web sites and resources, video collections, a Resource Integration Guide, and suggested student activities are also included. Exam questions include essays, true-false, identifications, and multiple-choice questions. Available in two volumes.

NEW! *Music of Western Civilization CD*   Available free to adopters and for a small fee to students, this CD contains many of the musical selections highlighted in the text and provides a broad sampling of the important musical pieces of Western civilization.

Instructor's Resource CD-ROM with ExamView®   Includes the Instructor's Manual, Resource Integration Grid, ExamView testing, and PowerPoint® slides with lecture outlines and images that can be used as offered or customized by importing personal lecture slides or other material. It also includes a correlation guide to the music CD. ExamView allows instructors to create, deliver, and customize tests and study guides (both print and online) in minutes via an easy-to-use assessment and tutorial system. Instructors can build tests with as many as 250 questions using up to twelve question types. Using ExamView's complete word-processing capabilities, they can enter an unlimited number of new questions or edit existing ones.

Full-Color Map Acetate Package   Fully revised for this edition of the text. Includes many maps from the text and other sources. More than one hundred images. Map commentary is provided by James Harrison, Siena College.

Lecture Enrichment Slides   Prepared by George Strong and Dale Hoak, College of William and Mary. These one hundred slides contain images of famous paintings, statues, architectural achievements, and interesting photos. The authors provide commentary for each individual slide.

History Video Library   A completely new selection of videos for this edition, from *Films from the Humanities & Sciences* and other sources. More than fifty titles to choose from, with coverage spanning from "Egypt: A Gift to Civilization" to "Children of the Holocaust." Available to qualified adoptions.

CNN Today Videos: Western Civilization   Organized by topics covered in a typical course, these videos are divided into one- to five-minute segments—perfect for introducing key concepts.

Sights and Sounds of History   Prepared by David Redles, Cuyahoga Community College. Short, focused video clips, photos, artwork, animations, music, and dramatic readings are used to bring life to historical topics and events that are most difficult for students to appreciate from a textbook alone. For example, students will experience the grandeur of Versailles and the defeat felt by a German soldier at Stalingrad. The video segments average four minutes in length and make excellent lecture launchers.

◢ For the Student

Study Guide   Prepared by James Baker, Western Kentucky University. Includes chapter outlines, chapter summaries, and six different types of questions for each chapter. Available in two volumes.

NEW! *Gregory, Documents of Western Civilization*   Contains a broad selection of carefully chosen documents accompanied by thought-provoking discussion questions. Available in two volumes.

NEW! *HistoryNow Western Civilization*   HistoryNow is a Web-based study system that saves time for students and instructors by providing a complete package of diagnostic quizzes, a personalized study plan, multimedia elements, and a grade book for instructors. HistoryNow uses an intelligent and pedagogically accurate system to help students devise a personalized study plan based on their current understanding of course material. This plan combines testing with interactions and documents to help students master the key concepts of the chapter they have just read. Professors can track their students' progress via a grade book, which is compatible with WebCT and Blackboard course management systems.

Map Exercise Workbook   Prepared by Cynthia Kosso, Northern Arizona University. Thoroughly revised and upgraded. Over twenty maps and exercises ask students to identify important cities and countries. Available in two volumes.

MapTutor CD-ROM   This interactive map tutorial helps students learn geography by having them locate geographical features, regions, cities, and sociopolitical movements. Each map exercise is accompanied by questions that test their knowledge and promote critical thinking. Animations vividly show movements such as the conquests of the Romans, the spread of Christianity, invasions, medieval trade routes, and the spread of the Black Death.

Document Exercise Workbook   Prepared by Donna Van Raaphorst, Cuyahoga Community College. A collection of exercises based around primary sources. Available in two volumes.

The Journey of Civilization CD-ROM   Prepared by David Redles, Cuyahoga Community College. This CD-ROM takes the student on eighteen interactive journeys through history. Enhanced with QuickTime movies, animations, sound clips, maps, and more, the journeys allow students to engage in history as active participants rather than as readers of past events.

History: Hits on the Web   Revised for 2005, Hits on the Web (HOW) is an exciting, class-tested product specially designed to help history students use the Internet for studying, conducting research, and completing assignments. HOW is approximately eighty pages of valuable teaching tools that can be bundled with any Wadsworth textbook at a very affordable price. Available through Thomson Custom Publishing.

Exploring the European Past: Text and Images   A new Custom Reader for Western civilization. Written by leading educators and historians, this fully customizable reader of primary and secondary sources is enhanced with an online module of visual sources, including maps, animations, and interactive exercises. Each reading also comes with an introduction and a series of questions. To learn more, visit http://etep.thomsonlearning.com or call Thomson Learning Custom Publishing at (800) 355-9983.

Magellan Atlas of Western Civilization   Available to bundle with any Western civilization text; contains forty-four full-color historical maps, including "The Conflict in Afghanistan, 2001" and "States of the World, 2001."

InfoTrac® College Edition   A Wadsworth exclusive. When InfoTrac College Edition is packaged with this text, students receive four months of real-time access to InfoTrac College Edition's online database of continuously updated, full-length articles from more than nine hundred journals and periodicals. By doing a simple keyword search, users can quickly generate a powerful list of related articles from thousands of possibilities and then select relevant articles to explore or print out for reference or further study. For professors, InfoTrac articles offer opportunities to ignite discussions or augment their lectures with the latest developments in the discipline. For students, InfoTrac's virtual library allows Internet access to sources that extend their learning far beyond the pages of a text.

Wadsworth History Resource Center and Book Companion Website

http://history.wadsworth.com

Both instructors and students will enjoy the chapter-by-chapter resources for *Western Civilization,* Sixth Edition, with access to the Wadsworth History Resource Center at http://www.history.wadsworth.com. Text-specific content for students includes interactive maps and timelines, tutorial quizzes, glossary, hyperlinks, InfoTrac College Edition exercises, and Internet activities. Instructors also have access to the Instructor's Manual and PowerPoint slides (access code required). The newly enhanced Wadsworth History Resource Center features such resources as documents and links to online readings correlated to specific periods in Western civilization, and photos that provide visual connections to events, places, and people covered in a Western civilization course.

Acknowledgments

I began to teach at age five in my family's grape arbor. By the age of ten, I wanted to know and understand everything in the world, so I set out to memorize our entire set of encyclopedia volumes. At seventeen, as editor of the high school yearbook, I chose "patterns" as its theme. With that as my early history, followed by many rich years of teaching, writing, and family nurturing, it seemed quite natural to accept the challenge of writing a history of Western civilization as I approached that period in life often described as the age of wisdom. Although I see this writing adventure as part of the natural unfolding of my life, I gratefully acknowledge that without the generosity of many others, it would not have been possible.

David Redles gave generously of his time and ideas, especially for Chapters 28 and 29. Chris Colin provided research on the history of music, while Laurie Batitto, Alex Spencer, Stephen Maloney, Shaun Mason, Peter Angelos, and Fred Schooley offered valuable editorial assistance. I deeply appreciate the valuable technical assistance provided by Dayton Coles. I am deeply grateful to John Soares for his assistance in preparing the map captions and to Charmarie Blaisdell of Northeastern University for her detailed suggestions on women's history. Daniel Haxall and Kathryn Spielvogel of The Pennsylvania State University provided valuable assistance with materials on postwar art, popular culture, and Postmodern art and thought. I am also thankful to the thousands of students whose questions and responses have caused me to see many aspects of Western civilization in new ways.

My ability to undertake a project of this magnitude was in part due to the outstanding European history teachers that I had as both an undergraduate and a graduate student. These included Kent Forster (modern Europe) and Robert W. Green (early modern Europe) at The Pennsylvania State University and Franklin Pegues (medieval), Andreas Dorpalen (modern Germany), William MacDonald (ancient), and Harold J. Grimm (Renaissance and Reformation) at The Ohio State University. These teachers provided me with profound insights into Western civilization and also taught me by their examples that learning only becomes true understanding when it is accompanied by compassion, humility, and open-mindedness.

I would like to thank the many teachers and students who have used the first five editions of my *Western Civilization.* Their enthusiastic response to a textbook that was intended to put the story back in history and capture the imagination of the reader has been very gratifying. I especially thank the many teachers and students who made the effort to contact me personally to share their enthusiasm. Thanks to Thomson Wadsworth's comprehensive review process, many historians were asked to evaluate my manuscript and review each edition. I am grateful to the following people for their innumerable suggestions over the course of the first five editions, which have greatly improved my work:

Paul Allen
University of Utah

Gerald Anderson
North Dakota State University

Susan L. H. Anderson
Campbell University

Letizia Argenteri
University of San Diego

Roy A. Austensen
Illinois State University

James A. Baer
Northern Virginia Community College–Alexandria

James T. Baker
Western Kentucky University

Patrick Bass
Morningside College

John F. Battick
University of Maine

Frederic J. Baumgartner
Virginia Polytechnic Institute

Phillip N. Bebb
Ohio University

Anthony Bedford
Modesto Junior College

F. E. Beemon
Middle Tennessee State University

Leonard R. Berlanstein
University of Virginia

Douglas T. Bisson
Belmont University

Charmarie Blaisdell
Northeastern University

Stephen H. Blumm
Montgomery County Community College

Hugh S. Bonar
California State University

Werner Braatz
University of Wisconsin–Oshkosh

Alfred S. Bradford
University of Missouri

Maryann E. Brink
College of William & Mary

Blaine T. Browne
Broward Community College

J. Holden Camp, Jr.,
Hillyer College, University of Hartford

Jack Cargill
Rutgers University

Martha Carlin
University of Wisconsin–Milwaukee

Elizabeth Carney
Clemson University

Eric H. Cline
Xavier University

Robert Cole
Utah State University

William J. Connell
Rutgers University

Nancy Conradt
College of DuPage

Marc Cooper
Southwest Missouri State

Richard A. Cosgrove
University of Arizona

David A. Crain
South Dakota State University

Michael A. Crane, Jr. (student)
Everett Community College

Luanne Dagley
*Pellissippi State Technical Community
College*

Michael F. Doyle
Ocean County College

James W. Ermatinger
University of Nebraska–Kearney

Porter Ewing
Los Angeles City College

Carla Falkner
Northeast Mississippi Community College

Steven Fanning
University of Illinois–Chicago

Ellsworth Faris
California State University–Chico

Gary B. Ferngren
Oregon State University

Mary Helen Finnerty
Westchester Community College

A. Z. Freeman
Robinson College

Marsha Frey
Kansas State University

Frank J. Frost
University of California–Santa Barbara

Frank Garosi
California State University–Sacramento

Richard M. Golden
University of North Texas

Manuel G. Gonzales
Diablo Valley College

Amy G. Gordon
Denison University

Richard J. Grace
Providence College

Hanns Gross
Loyola University

John F. Guilmartin
Ohio State University

Jeffrey S. Hamilton
Gustavus Adolphus College

J. Drew Harrington
Western Kentucky University

James Harrison
Siena College

A. J. Heisserer
University of Oklahoma

Betsey Hertzler
Mesa Community College

Robert Herzstein
University of South Carolina

Shirley Hickson
North Greenville College

Martha L. Hildreth
University of Nevada

Boyd H. Hill Jr.
University of Colorado–Boulder

Michael Hofstetter
Bethany College

Donald C. Holsinger
Seattle Pacific University

Frank L. Holt
University of Houston

W. Robert Houston
University of South Alabama

Paul Hughes
Sussex County Community College

Richard A. Jackson
University of Houston

Fred Jewell
Harding University

Jenny M. Jochens
Towson State University

William M. Johnston
University of Massachusetts

Jeffrey A. Kaufmann
Muscatine Community College

David O. Kieft
University of Minnesota

Patricia Killen
Pacific Lutheran University

William E. Kinsella, Jr.
*Northern Virginia Community College–
Annandale*

James M. Kittelson
Ohio State University

Doug Klepper
Santa Fe Community College

Cynthia Kosso
Northern Arizona University

Clayton Miles Lehmann
University of South Dakota

Diana Chen Lin
Indiana University, Northwest

Ursula W. MacAffer
Hudson Valley Community College

Harold Marcuse
University of California–Santa Barbara

Mavis Mate
University of Oregon

T. Ronald Melton
Brewton Parker College

Jack Allen Meyer
University of South Carolina

Eugene W. Miller Jr.
*The Pennsylvania State University–
Hazleton*

David Mock
Tallahassee Community College

John Patrick Montano
University of Delaware

Rex Morrow
Trident Technical College

Thomas M. Mulhern
University of North Dakota

Pierce Mullen
Montana State University

Frederick I. Murphy
Western Kentucky University

William M. Murray
University of South Florida

Otto M. Nelson
Texas Tech University

Sam Nelson
Willmar Community College

John A. Nichols
Slippery Rock University

Lisa Nofzinger
Albuquerque Technical Vocational Institute

Chris Oldstone-Moore
Augustana College

Donald Ostrowski
Harvard University

James O. Overfield
University of Vermont

Matthew L. Panczyk
Bergen Community College

Kathleen Parrow
Black Hills State University

Carla Rahn Phillips
University of Minnesota

Keith Pickus
Wichita State University

Linda J. Piper
University of Georgia

Janet Polasky
University of New Hampshire

Thomas W. Porter
Randolph-Macon College

Charles A. Povlovich
California State University–Fullerton

Nancy Rachels
Hillsborough Community College

Charles Rearick
University of Massachusetts–Amherst

Jerome V. Reel, Jr.
Clemson University

Joseph Robertson
Gadsden State Community College

Jonathan Roth
San Jose State University

Constance M. Rousseau
Providence College

Julius R. Ruff
Marquette University

Richard Saller
University of Chicago

Magdalena Sanchez
Texas Christian University

Jack Schanfield
Suffolk County Community College

Roger Schlesinger
Washington State University

Joanne Schneider
Rhode Island College

Thomas C. Schunk
University of Wisconsin–Oshkosh

Kyle C. Sessions
Illinois State University

Linda Simmons
*Northern Virginia Community College–
Manassas*

Donald V. Sippel
Rhode Island College

Glen Spann
Asbury College

John W. Steinberg
Georgia Southern University

Paul W. Strait
Florida State University

James E. Straukamp
California State University–Sacramento

Brian E. Strayer
Andrews University

Fred Suppe
Ball State University

Roger Tate
Somerset Community College

Tom Taylor
Seattle University
Jack W. Thacker
Western Kentucky University
Thomas Turley
Santa Clara University
John G. Tuthill
University of Guam
Maarten Ultee
University of Alabama

Donna L. Van Raaphorst
Cuyahoga Community College
Allen M. Ward
University of Connecticut
Richard D. Weigel
Western Kentucky University
Michael Weiss
Linn-Benton Community College
Arthur H. Williamson
California State University–Sacramento

Katherine Workman
Wright State University
Judith T. Wozniak
Cleveland State University
Walter J. Wussow
University of Wisconsin–Eau Claire
Edwin M. Yamauchi
Miami University

The following individuals contributed suggestions for the sixth edition:

Anne J. Aby
Minnesota West Community and Technical College, Worthington Campus
Gerald D. Anderson
North Dakota State University
James T. Baker
Western Kentucky University
John Bohstedt
University of Tennessee–Knoxville
Janet Brantley
Texarkana College
Jerry Brookshire
Middle Tennessee State University
Daniel Patrick Brown
Moorpark College
Gregory S. Brown
University of Nevada–Las Vegas
Kevin W. Caldwell
Blue Ridge Community College
Susan Carrafiello
Wright State University
Robert G. Clouse
Indiana State University
John Davies
University of Delaware
Joseph J. Eble
Burlington County College
Jennifer E. Forster
Lakeland Community College
Laura Gellott
University of Wisconsin–Parkside
Charlotte M. Gradie
Sacred Heart University

Candace Gregory
California State University–Sacramento
Katherine Gribble
Highline Community College
Doina Pasca Harsanyi
Central Michigan University
Jay Hatheway
Edgewood College
Michael C. Hickey
Bloomsburg University
Michael W. Howell
College of the Ozarks
David Hudson
California State University–Fresno
Paul J. L. Hughes
Sussex County Community College
Ed Krzemienski
The Citadel
Paul E. Lambert
Nichols College
Paul Douglas Lockhart
Wright State University
Priscilla McArthur
Troy State University–Dothan
David B. Mock
Tallahassee Community College
Wyatt S. Moulds
Jones County Junior College
Kenneth Mouré
University of California–Santa Barbara
Kathleen A. Parrow
Black Hills State University
Kathleen Paul
University of South Florida

Jody Peterson
Centralia College
Penne L. Prigge
Rockingham Community College
Nancy Rachels
Hillsborough Community College
Norman G. Raiford
Greenville Technical College
Roger Reese
Texas A&M University
William Roba
Scott Community College
Beverly J. Rowe
Texarkana College
Geraldine Ryder
Ocean County College
Linda J. Simmons
Northern Virginia Community College
Stuart J. Smyth,
Berkshire Community College
Heath A. Spencer
Seattle University
Robert P. Stephens
Virginia Tech
Emily Teipe
Fullerton College
David Tengewall
Anne Arundel Community College
J. Barry Vaughn
University of Alabama
Daniel Woods
Ferrum College
Robert W. Young
Carroll Community College

The editors at Thomson Wadsworth Publishing Company have been both helpful and congenial at all times. I especially wish to thank Clark Baxter, whose clever wit, wisdom, gentle prodding, and good friendship have added much depth to our working relationship. Margaret Beasley thoughtfully, wisely, efficiently, and pleasantly guided the overall development of the sixth edition. I also thank Kim Adams, production project manager; Mindy Newfarmer, technology project manager; and Paul Massicotte, assistant editor. I also want to express my gratitude to Jon Peck, whose good humor, well-advised suggestions, and generous verbal support made the production process such a delight.

Bruce Emmer, an outstanding copy editor, taught me much about the fine points of the English language.

Above all, I thank my family for their support. The gifts of love, laughter, and patience from my daughters, Jennifer and Kathryn; my sons, Eric and Christian; my daughters-in-law, Liz and Laurie; and my son-in-law, Daniel, were enormously appreciated. My wife and best friend, Diane, contributed editorial assistance, wise counsel, good humor, and the loving support that made it possible for me to accomplish a project of this magnitude. I could not have written the book without her.

INTRODUCTION TO STUDENTS OF WESTERN CIVILIZATION

*C*IVILIZATION, as historians define it, first emerged between five and six thousand years ago when people in different parts of the world began to live in organized communities with distinct political, military, economic, and social structures. Religious, intellectual, and artistic activities assumed important roles in these early societies. The focus of this book is on Western civilization, a civilization that many people identify with the continent of Europe.

Defining Western Civilization

Western civilization itself has evolved considerably over the centuries. Most historians trace the origins of Western civilization to the classical world of Rome and Greece and even farther back to the Mediterranean basin, including lands in North Africa and the Middle East. Nevertheless, people in these civilizations viewed themselves as subjects of states or empires, not as members of Western civilization. Later, with the rise of Christianity, peoples in Europe began to identify themselves as part of a civilization different from others, such as that of Islam, leading to a concept of a Western civilization different from other civilizations. In the fifteenth century, Renaissance intellectuals began to identify this civilization not only with Christianity but also with the intellectual and political achievements of the ancient Greeks and Romans.

Important to the development of the idea of a distinct Western civilization were encounters with other peoples. Between 700 and 1500, encounters with the world of Islam helped define the West. But after 1500, as European ships began to move into other parts of the world, encounters with peoples in Asia, Africa, and the Americas not only had an impact on the civilizations found there but also affected how people in the West defined themselves. At the same time, as they set up colonies, Europeans began to transplant a sense of Western identity to other areas of the world, especially North America and parts of Latin America, that have come to be considered part of Western civilization.

As the concept of Western civilization has evolved over the centuries, so have the values and unique features associated with that civilization. Science played a crucial role in the development of modern Western civilization. The societies of the Greeks, the Romans, and medieval Europeans were based largely on a belief in the existence of a spiritual order; a dramatic departure to a natural or material view of the universe occurred in the seventeenth-century Scientific Revolution. Science and technology have been important in the growth of today's modern and largely secular Western civilization, although antecedents to scientific development also existed in Greek and medieval thought and practice, and spirituality remains a component of the Western world today.

Many historians have viewed the concept of political liberty, belief in the fundamental value of every individual, and a rational outlook based on a system of logical, analytical thought as unique aspects of Western civilization. Of course, the West has also witnessed horrendous negations of liberty, individualism, and reason. Racism, slavery, violence, world wars, totalitarian regimes—these, too, form part of the complex story of what constitutes Western civilization.

The Dating of Time

In our examination of Western civilization, we need also to be aware of the dating of time. In recording the past, historians try to determine the exact time when events occurred. World War II in Europe, for example, began on September 1, 1939, when Hitler sent German troops into Poland, and ended on May 7, 1945, when Germany surrendered. By using dates, historians can place events in order and try to determine the development of patterns over periods of time.

If someone asked you when you were born, you would reply with a number, such as 1985. In the United States, we would all accept that number without question because it is part of the dating system followed in the Western world (Europe and the Western Hemisphere). In this system, events are dated by counting backward or forward from the birth of Jesus Christ (assumed to be the year 1). An event that took place four hundred years before the birth of Christ would be dated 400 B.C. (before Christ). Dates after the birth of Christ are labeled A.D. These letters stand for the Latin words *anno Domini,* which mean "in the year of the Lord." Thus an event that took place two hundred years after the birth of Christ is written A.D. 200, or in the year of the Lord 200. It can also be written as 200, just as you would not give your birth year as A.D. 1985, but simply as 1985. Historians also make use of other terms to refer to time. A *decade* is ten years, a *century* is one hundred years, and a *millennium* is one thousand years. Thus "the fourth century B.C." refers to the fourth period of one hundred years counting backward from 1, the assumed date of the birth of Christ. Since the first century B.C. would be the years 100 B.C. to 1 B.C., the fourth century B.C. would be the years 400 B.C. to 301 B.C. We could say, then, that an event in 350 B.C. took place in the fourth century B.C.

"The fourth century A.D." refers to the fourth period of one hundred years after the birth of Christ. Since the first period of one hundred years would be the years 1 to 100, the fourth period or fourth century would be the years 301 to 400. We could say, then, that an event in 350 took place in the fourth century. Likewise, the first millennium B.C. refers to the years 1000 B.C. to 1 B.C.; the second millennium A.D. refers to the years 1001 to 2000. Some historians now prefer to use the abbreviations B.C.E. ("before the Common Era") and C.E. ("Common Era") instead of B.C. and A.D. This is especially true of world historians, who prefer to use symbols that are not so Western- or Christian-oriented. The dates, of course, remain the same. Thus 1950 B.C.E. and 1950 B.C. would be the same year. In keeping with current usage by many historians of Western civilization, this book uses the terms B.C. and A.D.

The dating of events can also vary from people to people. Most people in the Western world use the Western calendar, also known as the Gregorian calendar after Pope Gregory XIII, who refined it in 1582. The Hebrew calendar uses a different system in which the year 1 is the equivalent of the Western year 3760 B.C., considered to be the date of the creation of the world according to the Bible. Thus the Western year 2005 is the year 5765 on the Hebrew calendar. The Islamic calendar begins year 1 on the day Muhammad fled Mecca, which is the year 622 on the Western calendar.

SIXTH EDITION

WESTERN CIVILIZATION

CHAPTER

1

THE ANCIENT NEAR EAST: THE FIRST CIVILIZATIONS

CHAPTER OUTLINE AND FOCUS QUESTIONS

The First Humans

● Where did the Neolithic agricultural revolution occur, and how did it affect the lives of men and women?

The Emergence of Civilization

● What are the characteristics of civilization, and what are some explanations for why early civilizations emerged?

Civilization of Mesopotamia

● How are the chief characteristics of civilization evident in ancient Mesopotamia?

Egyptian Civilization: "The Gift of the Nile"

● What are the basic features of the three major periods of Egyptian history? What elements of continuity are there in the three periods? What are their major differences?

On the Fringes of Civilization

● What is the significance of Indo-European-speaking peoples?

CRITICAL THINKING

● In what ways were the civilizations of Mesopotamia and Egypt alike? In what ways were they different?

Ruins of the ancient Sumerian city of Uruk

© Nik Wheeler/CORBIS

IN 1849, A DARING YOUNG Englishman made a hazardous journey into the deserts and swamps of southern Iraq. Moving south down the banks of the Euphrates River while braving high winds and temperatures that reached 120 degrees Fahrenheit, William Loftus led a small expedition in search of the roots of civilization. As he said, "From our childhood we have been led to regard this place as the cradle of the human race."

Guided by native Arabs into the southernmost reaches of Iraq, Loftus and his small group of explorers were soon overwhelmed by what they saw. He wrote, "I know of nothing more exciting or impressive than the first sight of one of these great piles, looming in solitary grandeur from the surrounding plains and marshes." One of these piles, known to the natives as the mound of Warka, contained the ruins of Uruk, one of the first cities in the world and part of the world's first civilization.

Southern Iraq, known to ancient peoples as Mesopotamia, was one area in the world where civilization began. Western civilization can be traced back to the ancient Near East, where people in Mesopotamia and Egypt developed organized societies and created the ideas and institutions that we associate with civilization. The later Greeks and Romans, who played such a crucial role in the development of Western civilization, were themselves nourished and influenced by these older societies in the Near East. It is appropriate, therefore, to begin our story of Western civilization in the ancient Near East with the early civilizations of Mesopotamia and Egypt. Before considering them, however, we must briefly examine humankind's prehistory and observe how human beings made the shift from hunting and gathering to agricultural communities and ultimately to cities and civilization.

The First Humans

Historians rely primarily on documents to create their pictures of the past, but no written records exist for the prehistory of humankind. In their absence, the story of early humanity depends on archaeological and, more recently, biological information, which anthropologists and archaeologists use to formulate theories about our early past. Although modern science has given us more precise methods for examining prehistory, much of our understanding of early humans still relies on conjecture.

The earliest humanlike creatures—known as hominids—existed in Africa as long as three to four million years ago. Known as Australopithecines, they flourished in East and South Africa and were the first hominids to make simple stone tools.

A second stage in early human development occurred around 1.5 million years ago when *Homo erectus* ("upright human being") emerged. *Homo erectus* made use of larger and more varied tools and was the first hominid to leave Africa and move into both Europe and Asia.

Around 250,000 years ago, a third—and crucial—stage in human development began with the emergence of *Homo sapiens* ("wise human being"). By 100,000 B.C., two groups of *Homo sapiens* had developed. One type was the Neanderthal, whose remains were first found in the Neander valley in Germany. Neanderthal remains have since been found in both Europe and the Middle East and have been dated to between 100,000 and 30,000 B.C. Neanderthals relied on a variety of stone tools and were the first early people to bury their dead.

The first anatomically modern humans, known as *Homo sapiens sapiens* ("wise, wise human being"), appeared in Africa between 200,000 and 150,000 years ago. Recent evidence indicates that they began to spread outside Africa around 100,000 years ago. Map 1.1 shows probable dates for different movements, although many of these are still controversial. By 30,000 B.C., *Homo sapiens sapiens* had replaced the Neanderthals, who had largely become extinct, and by 10,000 B.C., members of the *Homo sapiens sapiens* species could be found throughout the world. By that time, it was the only human species left. All humans today, whether they are Europeans, Australian Aborigines, or Africans, belong to the same subspecies of human being.

The Hunter-Gatherers of the Old Stone Age

One of the basic distinguishing features of the human species is the ability to make tools. The earliest tools were made of stone, and the term **Paleolithic** (Greek for "old stone") **Age** is used to designate this early period of human history (c. 2,500,000–10,000 B.C.).

For hundreds of thousands of years, humans relied on hunting and gathering for their daily food. Paleolithic peoples had a close relationship with the world around them, and over a period of time, they came to know which animals to hunt and which plants to eat. They did not know how to grow crops or raise animals, however. They gathered wild nuts, berries, fruits, and a variety of wild grains and green plants. Around the world, they hunted and consumed various animals, including buffalo, horses, bison, wild goats, and reindeer. In coastal areas, fish were a rich source of nourishment.

The hunting of animals and the gathering of wild plants no doubt led to certain patterns of living. Archaeologists and anthropologists have speculated that Paleolithic people lived in small bands of twenty or thirty people. They were nomadic (they moved from place to place) since they had no choice but to follow animal migrations and vegetation cycles. Hunting depended on careful observation of animal behavior patterns and required a group effort to achieve success. Over the years, tools became more refined and more useful. The invention of the spear, and later the bow and arrow, made hunting considerably easier. Harpoons and fishhooks made of bone increased the catch of fish.

Both men and women were responsible for finding food—the chief work of Paleolithic people. Since women bore and raised the children, they generally stayed close to the camps, but they played an important role in acquiring food by gathering berries, nuts, and grains. Men hunted the wild animals, an activity that took them far from camp. Because both men and women played important roles in providing for the band's survival, scientists have argued that a rough equality existed between men and women. Indeed, some speculate that both men and women made the decisions that affected the activities of the Paleolithic band.

Some groups of Paleolithic people, especially those who lived in cold climates, found shelter in caves. Over time, they created new types of shelter as well. Perhaps the most common was a simple structure of wood poles or sticks covered with animal hides. Where wood was scarce, Paleolithic hunter-gatherers might use the bones of mammoths to build frames that were then covered with animal hides. The systematic use of fire, which archaeologists believe began around 500,000 years ago, made it possible for the caves and human-made structures to have a source of light and heat. Fire also enabled early humans to cook their food, making it taste better, last longer, and,

Australopithecines	Flourished c. 2–4 million years ago
Homo erectus	Flourished c. 100,000–1.5 million years ago
Homo sapiens:	
Neanderthals	Flourished c. 100,000–30,000 B.C.
Homo sapiens sapiens	Emerged c. 200,000 B.C.

in the case of some plants, such as wild grain, easier to chew and digest.

The making of tools and the use of fire—two important technological innovations of Paleolithic peoples—remind us how crucial the ability to adapt was to human survival. But Paleolithic peoples did more than just survive. The cave paintings of large animals found in southwestern France and northern Spain bear witness to the cultural activity of Paleolithic peoples. A cave discovered in southern France in 1994 (known as the Chauvet cave after the leader of the expedition that found it) contains more than three hundred paintings of lions, oxen, owls, panthers, and other animals. Most of these are animals that Paleolithic people did not hunt, which suggests to some scholars that the paintings were made for religious or even decorative purposes. The discoverers were overwhelmed by what they saw: "There was a moment of ecstasy. . . . They overflowed with joy and emotion in their turn. . . . These were moments of indescribable madness."[1]

The Neolithic Revolution (c. 10,000–4000 B.C.)

The end of the last ice age around 10,000 B.C. was followed by what is called the **Neolithic Revolution**, a significant change in living patterns that occurred in the New Stone Age (the word *neolithic* is Greek for "new stone"). The name New Stone Age is misleading, however. Although Neolithic peoples made a new type of polished stone ax, this was not the major change that occurred after 10,000 B.C.

An Agricultural Revolution   The biggest change was the shift from hunting animals and gathering plants for sustenance to producing food by systematic agriculture. The planting of grains and vegetables provided a regular supply of food, while the taming of animals, such as goats, cattle, pigs, and sheep, added a steady source of meat, milk, and fibers such as wool for clothing. Larger animals could also be used as beasts of burden. The growing of crops and the taming of food-producing animals created a new

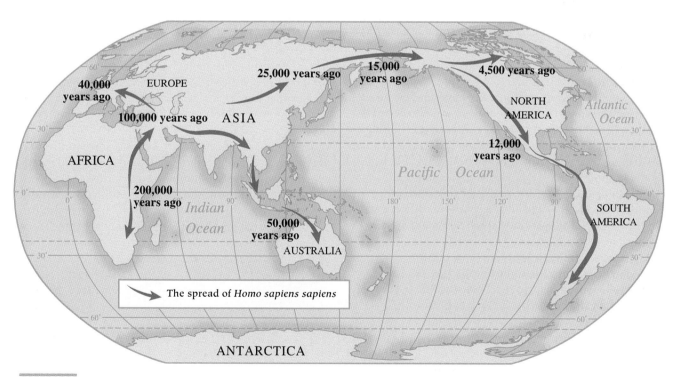

MAP 1.1   The Spread of *Homo sapiens sapiens*. *Homo sapiens sapiens* spread from Africa beginning about 100,000 years ago. Living and traveling in small groups, these anatomically modern humans were hunter-gatherers. Although groups of people advanced beyond their old hunting grounds at a rate of only 2 or 3 miles per generation, this was enough to populate the world in some tens of thousands of years. ❓ Given that some diffusion of humans occurred during ice ages, how would such climate change affect humans and their movements, especially from Asia to Australia and Asia to North America? ✎ **View an animated version of this map or related maps at** http://history.wadsworth.com/spielvogel06/

AP/Wide World Photos

Paleolithic Cave Painting: The Chauvet Cave. Cave paintings of large animals reveal the cultural creativity of Paleolithic peoples. This scene is part of a mural in a large underground chamber at Vallon-Pont-d'Arc, France, discovered in December 1994. It dates from around 30,000–28,000 B.C. and depicts aurochs (long-horned wild oxen), horses, and rhinoceroses. To make their paintings, Paleolithic artists used stone lamps in which they burned animal fat to illuminate the cave walls and combined powdered mineral ores with animal fat to create red, yellow, and black pigments. Some artists even made brushes out of animal hairs with which to apply the paints.

relationship between humans and nature. Historians like to speak of this as an agricultural revolution. Revolutionary change is dramatic and requires great effort, but the ability to acquire food on a regular basis gave humans greater control over their environment. It also allowed them to give up their nomadic way of life and begin to live in settled communities.

Systematic agriculture probably developed independently between 8000 and 7000 B.C. in four different areas of the world. In each of these areas, different plants were cultivated: wheat, barley, and lentils in the Near East, rice and millet in southern Asia, millet and yams in western Africa, and beans, potatoes, and corn (maize) in the Americas. In the Near East as elsewhere, the Neolithic agricultural revolution needed a favorable

environment. The upland areas above the Fertile Crescent (present-day northern Iraq and southern Turkey) were initially more conducive to systematic farming than the river valleys. This region received the necessary rainfall and was the home of two wild plant (barley, wheat) and four wild animal (pigs, cows, goats, sheep) species that humans eventually domesticated for their use.

Neolithic Farming Villages The growing of crops on a regular basis gave rise to more permanent settlements, which historians refer to as Neolithic farming villages or towns. One of the oldest known agricultural villages was Jericho, in Palestine near the Dead Sea. Jericho existed by 8000 B.C. and by 7000 B.C. covered several acres. It had a wall several feet thick that enclosed houses made of sun-dried bricks.

Çatal Hüyük, located in modern-day Turkey, was an even larger community. Its walls enclosed 32 acres, and its population probably reached six thousand inhabitants during its high point from 6700 to 5700 B.C. People lived in simple mudbrick houses that were built so close to one another that there were few streets. To get to their homes, people had to walk along the rooftops and then enter the house through a hole in the roof.

Archaeologists have discovered twelve cultivated products in Çatal Hüyük, including fruits, nuts, and three kinds of wheat. People grew their own food and stored it in storerooms in their homes. Domesticated animals, especially cattle, yielded meat, milk, and hides. Food surpluses also made it possible for people to do things other than farming. Some people became artisans and made weapons and jewelry that were traded with neighboring peoples.

Religious shrines housing figures of gods and goddesses have been found at Çatal Hüyük, as have a number of female statuettes. Molded with noticeably large breasts and buttocks, these "earth mothers" perhaps symbolically represented the fertility of both "our mother" earth and human mothers. Both the shrines and the statues point to the growing role of religion in the lives of these Neolithic people.

Statues from Ain Ghazal. These life-size statues made of plaster and bitumen dating from 6500 B.C. were discovered in 1984 in Ain Ghazal, an archaeological site near Amman, Jordan. They are among the oldest known statues of the human figure. Although they appear lifelike, their features are considered generic rather than portraits of individual faces. The purpose and meaning of these sculptures may never be known.

Courtesy of the Hashemite Kingdom of Jordan, Dept. of Antiquities

Consequences of the Neolithic Revolution   The Neolithic agricultural revolution had far-reaching consequences. Once people settled in villages or towns, they built houses for protection and other structures for the storage of goods. As organized communities stored food and accumulated material goods, they engaged in far greater trade than nomadic peoples did. People also began to specialize in certain crafts, and a division of labor developed. Pottery was made from clay and baked in a fire to make it hard. The pots were used for cooking and to store grains. Woven baskets were also used for storage. Stone tools became refined as flint blades were developed to make sickles and hoes for use in the fields. In the course of the Neolithic Age, many of the food plants still in use today began to be cultivated. Moreover, vegetable fibers from such plants as flax were used to make thread that was woven into cloth.

The change to systematic agriculture in the Neolithic Age also had consequences for the relationship between men and women. Men assumed the primary responsibility for working in the fields and herding animals, jobs that kept them away from the home. Although women also worked in the fields, many remained behind, caring for the children and weaving clothes, making cheese from milk, and performing other tasks that required considerable labor in one place. In time, as work outside the home was increasingly perceived as more important than work done at home, men came to play the more dominant role in society, a basic pattern that would persist until our own times.

Other patterns set in the Neolithic Age also proved to be enduring elements of human history. Fixed dwellings, domesticated animals, regular farming, a division of labor, men holding power—all of these are part of the human story. For all our scientific and technological progress, human survival still depends on the growing and storing of food, an accomplishment of people in the Neolithic Age. The Neolithic Revolution was truly a turning point in human history.

Between 4000 and 3000 B.C., significant technical developments began to transform the Neolithic towns. The invention of writing enabled records to be kept, and the use of metals marked a new level of human control over the environment and its resources. Already before 4000 B.C., craftspeople had discovered that metal-bearing rocks could be heated to liquefy metals, which could then be cast in molds to produce tools and weapons that were more useful than stone instruments. Although copper was the first metal to be used in producing tools, after 4000 B.C., craftspeople in western Asia discovered that a combination of copper and tin produced bronze, a much harder and more durable metal than copper. Its widespread use has led historians to call the period from around 3000 to 1200 B.C. the Bronze Age; thereafter, bronze was increasingly replaced by iron.

Harappa and Mohenjo-Daro

At first, Neolithic settlements were hardly more than villages. But as their inhabitants mastered the art of farming, more complex human societies emerged. As wealth increased, these societies began to develop armies and to build walled cities. By the beginning of the Bronze Age, the concentration of larger numbers of people in the river valleys of Mesopotamia and Egypt was leading to a whole new pattern for human life.

The Emergence of Civilization

As we have seen, early human beings formed small groups that developed a simple culture that enabled them to survive. As human societies grew and developed greater complexity, a new form of human existence—called civilization—came into being. A **civilization** is a complex culture in which large numbers of human beings share a variety of common elements. Historians have identified a number of basic characteristics of civilization. These include (1) an urban focus: cities became the centers of political, economic, social, cultural, and religious development; (2) a distinct religious structure: the gods were deemed crucial to the community's success, and professional priestly classes, as stewards of the gods' property, regulated relations with the gods; (3) new political and military structures: an organized government bureaucracy arose to meet the administrative demands of the growing population, and armies were organized to gain land and power; (4) a new social structure based on economic power: while kings and an upper class of priests, political leaders, and warriors dominated, there also existed a large group of free people (farmers, artisans, craftspeople) and at the very bottom, socially, a class of slaves; (5) the development of writing: kings, priests, merchants, and artisans used writing to keep records; and (6) new forms of significant artistic and intellectual activity: for example, monumental architectural structures, usually religious, occupied a prominent place in urban environments.

The civilizations that developed in Mesopotamia and Egypt, the forerunners of Western civilization, will be examined in detail in this chapter. But civilizations also developed independently in other parts of the world. Between 3000 and 1500 B.C., the valleys of the Indus River in India supported a flourishing civilization that extended hundreds of miles from the Himalayas to the coast of the Arabian Sea. Two major cities—Harappa and Mohenjo-Daro—were at the heart of this civilization in India. Many written records of this Indus valley civilization exist, but their language has not yet been deciphered. This Indus valley civilization carried on extensive trade with city-states in Mesopotamia.

The Yellow River, China

Another river valley civilization emerged along the Yellow River in northern China about 4,000 years ago. Under the Shang dynasty of kings, which ruled from 1750 to 1122 B.C., this civilization contained impressive cities with huge outer walls, royal palaces, and large royal tombs. A system of irrigation enabled early Chinese civilization to maintain a prosperous farming society ruled by an aristocratic class whose major concern was war.

Scholars have believed for a long time that civilization emerged only in four areas, in the fertile river valleys of the Tigris and Euphrates, the Nile, the Indus, and the Yellow River—that is, in Mesopotamia, Egypt, India, and China. Recently, however, archaeologists have discovered two other early civilizations. One of these flourished in Central Asia (in what are now the republics of Turkmenistan and Uzbekistan) around 4,000 years ago. People in this civilization built mudbrick buildings, raised sheep and goats, had bronze tools, used a system of irrigation to grow wheat and barley, and had a writing system.

Central Asian Civilization

Another early civilization was discovered in the Supe River valley of Peru. At the center of this civilization was the city of Caral, which flourished around 2600 B.C. It contained buildings for officials, apartment houses, and grand residences, all built of stone. The inhabitants of Caral also developed a system of irrigation by diverting a river more than a mile upstream into their fields.

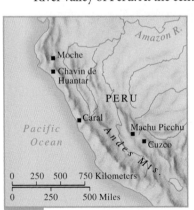

Caral, Peru

Why early civilizations developed remains difficult to explain. Since civilizations developed independently in different parts of the world, can general causes be identified that would explain why all of these civilizations emerged? A number of possible explanations of the beginning of civilization have been suggested. A theory of challenge and response maintains that challenges forced human beings to make efforts that resulted in the rise of civilization. Some scholars have adhered to a material explanation. Material forces, such as the growth of food surpluses, made possible the specialization of labor and development of large communities with bureaucratic organization. But the area of the Fertile Crescent, in which Mesopotamian civilization emerged (see Map 1.2), was not naturally conducive to agriculture. Abundant food could be produced only with a massive human effort to carefully manage the water, an effort that created the need for organization and bureaucratic control and led to civilized cities. Some historians have argued that nonmaterial forces, primarily religious, provided the sense of unity and purpose that made such organized activities possible. Finally, some scholars doubt that we are capable of ever discovering the actual causes of early civilization.

Civilization in Mesopotamia

The Greeks spoke of the valley between the Tigris and Euphrates Rivers as Mesopotamia, the land "between the rivers." The region receives little rain, but the soil of the plain of southern Mesopotamia was enlarged and enriched over the years by layers of silt deposited by the two rivers. In late spring, the Tigris and Euphrates overflow their banks and deposit their fertile silt, but since this flooding depends on the melting of snows in the upland mountains where the rivers begin, it is unpredictable and sometimes catastrophic. In such circumstances, farming could be done only when people built irrigation and drainage ditches. A complex system was required to control the flow of the rivers and produce the crops. Large-scale irrigation made possible the expansion of agriculture in this region, and the abundant food provided the material base for the emergence of civilization in Mesopotamia.

The City-States of Ancient Mesopotamia

The creators of Mesopotamian civilization were the Sumerians, a people whose origins remain unclear. By 3000 B.C., they had established a number of independent cities in southern Mesopotamia, including Eridu, Ur, Uruk, Umma, and Lagash. As the cities grew larger, they came to exercise political and economic control over the surrounding countryside, forming city-states. These city-states were the basic units of Sumerian civilization.

Sumerian Cities Sumerian cities were surrounded by walls. Uruk, for example, occupied an area of approximately 1,000 acres encircled by a wall 6 miles long with defense towers located every 30 to 35 feet along the wall. City dwellings, built of sun-dried bricks, included both the small flats of peasants and the larger dwellings of the civic and priestly officials. Although Mesopotamia had little stone or wood for building purposes, it did have plenty of mud. Mudbricks, easily shaped by hand, were left to bake in the hot sun until they were hard enough to use for building. People in Mesopotamia were remarkably inventive with mudbricks, inventing the arch and constructing some of the largest brick buildings in the world. Mudbricks are still used in rural areas of the Middle East today.

The most prominent building in a Sumerian city was the temple, which was dedicated to the chief god or goddess of the city and often built atop a massive stepped tower called a **ziggurat**. The Sumerians believed that the gods and goddesses owned the cities, and much wealth was used to build temples as well as elaborate houses for the priests and priestesses who served the gods. Priests and priestesses, who supervised the temples and their property, had great power. In fact, historians believe that in the early stages of the city-states, priests and priestesses played an important role in ruling. The Sumerians believed that the gods ruled the cities, making the state a **theocracy** (government by a divine authority). Eventually, however, ruling power was shared with worldly figures known as kings.

Kingship   Sumerians viewed kingship as divine in origin—kings, they believed, derived their power from the gods and were the agents of the gods. As one person said in a petition to his king: "You in your judgment, you are the son of Anu [god of the sky]; your commands, like the word of a god, cannot be reversed; your words, like rain pouring down from heaven, are without number."[2] Regardless of their origins, kings had power—they led armies, initiated

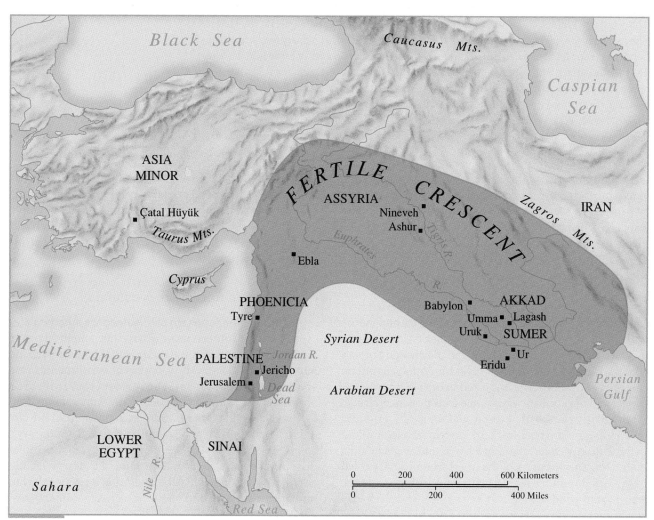

MAP 1.2   The Ancient Near East.   The Fertile Crescent encompassed land with access to water. Employing flood management and irrigation systems, the peoples of the region established civilizations based on agriculture. These civilizations developed writing, law codes, and economic specialization. ❓ What geographical aspects of the Mesopotamian city-states made conflict between them likely? 🌐 **View an animated version of this map or related maps at** http://history.wadsworth.com/ spielvogel06/

The "Royal Standard" of Ur. This detail is from the "Royal Standard" of Ur, a box dating from around 2700 B.C. that was discovered in a stone tomb from the royal cemetery of the Sumerian city-state of Ur. The scenes on one side of the box depict the activities of the king and his military forces. Shown in the bottom panel are four Sumerian battle chariots. Each chariot held two men, one who held the reins and the other armed with a spear for combat. A special compartment in the chariot held a number of spears. The charging chariots are seen defeating the enemy. In the middle band, the Sumerian soldiers round up the captured enemies. In the top band, the captives are presented to the king, who has alighted from his chariot and is shown standing above all the others in the center of the panel.

legislation, supervised the building of public works, provided courts, and organized workers for the irrigation projects on which Mesopotamian agriculture depended. The army, the government bureaucracy, and the priests and priestesses all aided the kings in their rule. Befitting their power, Sumerian kings lived in large palaces with their wives and children.

Economy and Society The economy of the Sumerian city-states was primarily agricultural, but commerce and industry became important as well. The people of Mesopotamia produced woolen textiles, pottery, and metalwork. Foreign trade, which was primarily a royal monopoly, could be extensive. Royal officials imported luxury items, such as copper and tin, aromatic woods, and fruit trees, in exchange for dried fish, wool, barley, wheat, and the goods produced by Mesopotamian metalworkers. Traders traveled by land to the eastern Mediterranean in the west and by sea to India in the east. The invention of the wheel around 3000 B.C. led to the development of carts with wheels that made the transport of goods easier.

Sumerian city-states contained three major social groups: nobles, commoners, and slaves. Nobles included royal and priestly officials and their families. Commoners included the nobles' clients who worked for the palace and temple estates and other free citizens who worked as farmers, merchants, fishers, scribes, and craftspeople. Probably 90 percent or more of the population were farmers.

They could exchange their crops for the goods of the artisans in free town markets. Slaves belonged to palace officials, who used them mostly in building projects; temple officials, who used mostly female slaves to weave cloth and grind grain; and rich landowners, who used them for farming and domestic work.

Empires in Ancient Mesopotamia

As the number of Sumerian city-states grew and the states expanded, new conflicts arose as city-state fought city-state for control of land and water. During the Early Dynastic Age (3000–2340 B.C.), the fortunes of various cities rose and fell over the centuries. The constant wars, with their burning and sacking of cities, left many Sumerians in deep despair, as is evident in this Sumerian poem from the city of Ur: "Ur is destroyed, bitter is its lament. The country's blood now fills its holes like hot bronze in a mold. Bodies dissolve like fat in the sun. Our temple is destroyed, the gods have abandoned us, like migrating birds. Smoke lies on our city like a shroud."

Sargon's Empire Located on the flat, open land of Mesopotamia, the Sumerian city-states were also vulnerable to invasion. To the north of the Sumerian city-states were the Akkadians. We call them a Semitic people because of the language they spoke (see Table 1.1). Around 2340 B.C., Sargon, leader of the Akkadians, overran the Sumerian city-

TABLE 1.1 **Some Semitic Languages**

Akkadian	*Canaanitic*
Arabic	Hebrew
Aramaic	*Phoenician*
Assyrian	*Syriac*
Babylonian	

Note: Languages in italic type are no longer spoken.

Hammurabi's Empire

states and established a dynastic empire. Sargon's empire, including all of Mesopotamia as well as lands westward to the Mediterranean, inspired generations of Near Eastern leaders to emulate his accomplishment. Even in the first millennium B.C. Sargon was still remembered in chronicles as a king of Akkad who "had no rival or equal, spread his splendor over all the lands, and crossed the sea in the east. In his eleventh year, he conquered the western land to its furthest point, and brought it under his sole authority."[3] Despite a period of economic growth, prosperity, and cultural flowering, Sargon's successors were ultimately unable to preserve his empire, however. Attacks from neighboring hill peoples caused the Akkadian empire to fall by 2100 B.C.

The end of the Akkadian empire brought a return to independent city-states in Mesopotamia until Ur-Nammu of Ur succeeded in reunifying much of Mesopotamia. The Third Dynasty of Ur (c. 2112–2000 B.C.) that he established witnessed a final flowering of Sumerian culture. The economy flourished, and new temples and canals were built. Invasion by nomadic tribes, a perennial problem in Mesopotamian history, proved disastrous for the Third Dynasty of Ur, however. After a lengthy period of fighting and confusion, the sixth king of the Amorite dynasty, Hammurabi, managed to establish power. Under Hammurabi, the Amorites or Old Babylonians, a large group of Semitic-speaking seminomads, created a new empire.

Hammurabi's Empire Hammurabi (1792–1750 B.C.) had a well-disciplined army of foot soldiers who carried axes, spears, and copper or bronze daggers. He learned to divide his opponents and subdue them one by one. Using such methods, he gained control of Sumer and Akkad and reunified Mesopotamia almost to the old borders established by Sargon. After his conquests, Hammurabi called himself "the sun of Babylon, the king who has made the four quarters of the world subservient," and established a new capital at Babylon.

Hammurabi, the man of war, was also a man of peace. He followed in the footsteps of previous conquerors by assimilating Mesopotamian culture with the result that Sumerian ways continued to exist despite the end of the Sumerians as a political entity. A collection of his letters, found by archaeologists, reveals that the king took a strong interest in state affairs. He built temples, defensive walls, and irrigation canals; encouraged trade; and brought about an economic revival. Indeed, Hammurabi saw himself as a shepherd to his people: "I am indeed the shepherd who brings peace, whose scepter is just. My benevolent shade was spread over my city. I held the people of the lands of Sumer and Akkad safely on my lap."[4] Hammurabi left his dynasty strong enough that it survived until the 1550s B.C. when the Kassites from the northeast took over.

The Code of Hammurabi

Hammurabi is best remembered for his law code, a collection of 282 laws. For centuries, laws had regulated people's relationships with one another in the lands of Mesopotamia, but only fragments of these earlier codes

Stele of Hammurabi (Code of Hammurabi, King of Babylonia). Although the Sumerians compiled earlier law codes, Hammurabi's code was the most famous in early Mesopotamian history. The upper part of the stele depicts Hammurabi standing in front of the seated sun god Shamash. The king raises his hand in deference to the god, who gives Hammurabi the power to rule and orders the king to record the law. The lower portion of the stele contains the actual code.

THE CODE OF HAMMURABI

*H*AMMURABI'S CODE is the most complete Mesopotamian law code, although not the earliest. It was inscribed on a stone stele topped by a bas-relief picturing Hammurabi receiving the inspiration for the law code from the sun god Shamash, who was also the god of justice. The law code emphasizes the principle of "an eye for an eye" and punishments that vary according to social status. The following examples illustrate these concerns.

The Code of Hammurabi

25. If fire broke out in a freeman's house and a freeman, who went to extinguish it, cast his eye on the goods of the owner of the house and has appropriated the goods of the owner of the house, that freeman shall be thrown into that fire.

129. If the wife of a freeman has been caught while lying with another man, they shall bind them and throw them into the water. If the husband of the woman wishes to spare his wife, then the king in turn may spare his subject.

131. If a freeman's wife was accused by her husband, but she was not caught while lying with another man, she shall make affirmation by god and return to her house.

196. If a freeman has destroyed the eye of a member of the aristocracy, they shall destroy his eye.

198. If he has destroyed the eye of a commoner or broken the bone of a commoner, he shall pay one mina of silver.

199. If he has destroyed the eye of a freeman's slave or broken the bone of a freeman's slave, he shall pay one-half his value.

209. If a freeman struck another freeman's daughter and has caused her to have a miscarriage, he shall pay ten shekels of silver for her fetus.

210. If that woman has died, they shall put his daughter to death.

211. If by a blow he has caused a commoner's daughter to have a miscarriage, he shall pay five shekels of silver.

212. If that woman has died, he shall pay one-half mina of silver.

213. If he struck a freeman's female slave and has caused her to have a miscarriage, he shall pay two shekels of silver.

214. If that female slave has died, he shall pay one-third mina of silver.

survive. Although many scholars today view Hammurabi's collection less as a code of laws and more as the attempt of Hammurabi to portray himself as the source of justice to his people, the code still gives us a glimpse of the Babylonian society of his time (see the box above).

The Code of Hammurabi reveals a society with a system of strict justice. Penalties for criminal offenses were severe and varied according to the social class of the victim. A crime against a member of the upper class (a noble) was punished more severely than the same offense against a member of the lower class. Moreover, the principle of "an eye for an eye, a tooth for a tooth" was fundamental to this system of justice. This meant that punishments should fit the crime: "If a freeman has destroyed the eye of a member of the aristocracy, they shall destroy his eye." Hammurabi's code also had an impact on legal ideas in southwestern Asia for hundreds of years, as the following verse from the Hebrew Bible (Leviticus 24:19–20) demonstrates: "If anyone injures his neighbor, whatever he has done must be done to him: fracture for fracture, eye for eye, tooth for tooth. As he has injured the other, so he is to be injured."

Hammurabi's code took the responsibilities of public officials very seriously. The governor of an area and city officials were expected to catch burglars. If they failed to do so, officials in the district where the crime was committed had to replace the lost property. If murderers were not found, the officials had to pay a fine to the relatives of the murdered person. Soldiers were likewise expected to fulfill their duties and responsibilities for the order and mainte-

nance of the state. If a soldier hired a substitute to fight for him, he was put to death, and the substitute was given control of his estate.

The law code also furthered the proper performance of work with what virtually amounted to consumer protection laws. Builders were held responsible for the buildings they constructed. If a house collapsed and caused the death of the owner, the builder was put to death. If the collapse caused the death of the son of the owner, the son of the builder was put to death. If goods were destroyed by the collapse, they had to be replaced and the house itself reconstructed at the builder's expense.

The number of laws in Hammurabi's code dedicated to land tenure and commerce reveal the importance of agriculture and trade in the Mesopotamian economy. Laws concerning land use and irrigation were especially strict, an indication of the danger of declining crop yields if the land was used incompetently. If landowners and tenants failed to keep dikes in good repair or to control water flow properly and thus caused damage to others' crops, they were required to pay for the grain that was destroyed. If they could not pay, they were sold into slavery and their goods sold and the proceeds divided among the injured parties.

Commercial activity was carefully regulated. Rates of interest on loans were watched closely. If the lender raised the interest rate after a loan was made, he lost the entire amount of the loan. The Code of Hammurabi even specified the precise wages of laborers and artisans, such as brickmakers and jewelers.

Sumerian city-states: Early Dynastic Age	c. 3000–2340 B.C.
Sargon's empire	c. 2340–2100 B.C.
Third Dynasty of Ur	c. 2112–2000 B.C.
Hammurabi's reign	1792–1750 B.C.
Invasion by Kassites	c. 1550 B.C.

The largest number of laws in the code focused on marriage and the family. Parents arranged marriages for their children. After marriage, the parties involved signed a marriage contract; without it, no one was considered legally married. While the husband provided a bridal payment, the woman's parents were responsible for a dowry to the new husband.

As in many patriarchal societies, women possessed far fewer privileges and rights in the married relationship than men. A woman's place was in the home, and failure to fulfill her expected duties was grounds for divorce. If she was not able to bear children, her husband could divorce her, but he did have to return the dowry to her family. If his wife tried to leave home to engage in business, thus neglecting her house, her husband could divorce her and did not have to repay the dowry. Furthermore, if his wife was a "gad-about, . . . neglecting her house [and] humiliating her husband," she could be drowned. We do know that in practice not all women remained at home. Some worked in the fields and others in business, where they were especially prominent in running taverns.

Women were guaranteed some rights, however. If a woman was divorced without good reason, she received the dowry back. A woman could seek divorce and get her dowry back if her husband was unable to show that she had done anything wrong. In theory, a wife was guaranteed the use of her husband's legal property in the event of his death. A mother could also decide which of her sons would receive an inheritance.

Sexual relations were strictly regulated as well. Husbands, but not wives, were permitted sexual activity outside marriage. A wife and her lover caught committing adultery were pitched into the river, although if the husband pardoned his wife, the king could pardon the guilty man. Incest was strictly forbidden. If a father committed incestuous relations with his daughter, he would be banished. Incest between a son and his mother resulted in both being burned.

Fathers ruled their children as well as their wives. Obedience was duly expected: "If a son has struck his father, they shall cut off his hand." If a son committed a serious enough offense, his father could disinherit him, although fathers were not permitted to disinherit their sons arbitrarily.

The Culture of Mesopotamia

A spiritual worldview was of fundamental importance to Mesopotamian culture. To the peoples of Mesopotamia, the gods were living realities who affected all aspects of life. It was crucial, therefore, that the correct hierarchies be observed. Leaders could prepare armies for war, but success really depended on a favorable relationship with the gods. This helps explain the importance of the priestly class and is the reason why even the kings took great care to dedicate offerings and monuments to the gods. The records of these dedications are among our earliest historical documents.

The Importance of Religion   The Mesopotamians viewed their city-states as earthly copies of a divine model and order. Each city-state was sacred because it was linked to a god or goddess. Hence Nippur, the earliest center of Sumerian religion, was dedicated to Enlil, the god of wind. Moreover, located at the heart of each major city-state was a temple complex. Occupying several acres, this sacred area consisted of a ziggurat with a temple at the top dedicated to the god or goddess who owned the city. The temple complex was the true center of the community. The main god or goddess dwelt there symbolically in the form of a statue, and the ceremony of dedication included a ritual that linked the statue to the god or goddess and thus supposedly harnessed the power of the deity for the city's benefit. Considerable wealth was poured into the construction of temples and other buildings used for the residences of priests and priestesses who served the gods. Although the gods literally owned the city, the temple complex used only part of the land and rented out the remainder. The temples dominated individual and commercial life, an indication

Ziggurat at Ur. This ziggurat, located at Ur, is rectangular, not square like later ones. Built around 2100 B.C., the ziggurat had a base of mud bricks that was 50 feet high. Shown here is the northeastern facade, with steps that have been restored. Three stairways of one hundred steps each led to a gateway flanked by two towers. From the gateway, a central staircase led to a temple at the top, which no longer exists. This temple was dedicated to the god believed to own the city.

A Creation Myth: "Let Man Carry the Labor-Basket of the Gods"

*T*HIS SELECTION is taken from *Atrahasis*, a Mesopotamian poem probably composed early in the second millennium B.C. It is a myth that relates the creation, destruction, and regeneration of the human race. In this excerpt, the gods create human beings to do the physical labor—digging canals—that they have grown to detest.

Atrahasis

When the gods, like man,
  bore the work, carried the labor-basket—
  the labor-basket of the great gods—
  the work was heavy, much was the distress. . . .
Forty more years
  they bore the labor night and day.
They wearied, complained,
  grumbled in the workpits.
"Let us confront the throne-bearer
  that he may remove from us our heavy labor.
Come on, let us confuse him in his dwelling,
Enlil, the counselor of the gods, the hero,
  come on, let us confuse him in his dwelling. . . ."

[After the lesser gods who are digging the canals rebel against Enlil, who rules the surface of the earth, he agrees to create human beings to do the physical labor for the lesser gods.]

"While [Nintu the birth-goddess] is present,
  let the birth-goddess create the offspring,
  let man bear the labor-basket of the gods."

They called the goddess and asked her,
  the midwife of the gods, wise Mami:
"You are the birth-goddess, creatress of man.
Create lullu-man, let him bear the yoke.
Let him bear the yoke, the work of Enlil;
  let man carry the labor-basket of the gods. . . ."
At the new moon, the seventh day, and the full moon,
  he set up a purifying bath.
We-ila, who had rationality,
  they slaughtered in their assembly.
With his flesh and blood
Nintu mixed the clay.
Till the end of days they hear the drum [heartbeat].
From the flesh of the god there was spirit.
She proclaimed "alive" as its sign.
For the sake of not-forgetting there was a spirit.
After she had mixed the clay,
  she called the Anunnaki, the great gods.
The Igigi, the great gods,
  cast their spittle on the clay.
Mami opened her mouth
  and said to the great gods,
"You commanded me a task—
I have completed it.
You slaughtered a god together with his rationality.
I have removed your heavy labor,
  have placed your labor-basket on man.
You raised a cry for mankind;
I have loosened your yoke, have established freedom."

---

of the close relationship between Mesopotamian religion and culture.

The physical environment had an obvious impact on the Mesopotamian view of the universe. Ferocious floods, heavy downpours, scorching winds, and oppressive humidity were all part of the Mesopotamian climate. These conditions and resulting famines easily convinced Mesopotamians that this world was controlled by supernatural forces and that the days of human beings "are numbered; whatever he may do, he is but wind," as *The Epic of Gilgamesh* laments (see "Mesopotamian Literature" later in this chapter). In the presence of nature, Mesopotamians could easily feel helpless, as this poem relates:

The rampant flood which no man can oppose,
shakes the heavens and causes earth to tremble,
In an appalling blanket folds mother and child,
Beats down the canebrake's full luxuriant greenery,
And drowns the harvest in its time of ripeness.

Rising waters, grievous to eyes of man,
All-powerful flood, which forces the embankments
And mows down mighty trees,
Frenzied storm, tearing all things in massed confusion
With it in hurtling speed.[5]

The Mesopotamians discerned cosmic rhythms in the universe and accepted its order but perceived that it was not completely safe because of the presence of willful, powerful cosmic forces that they identified with gods and goddesses.

With its numerous gods and goddesses animating all aspects of the universe, Mesopotamian religion was **polytheistic**. The four most important deities were An, Enlil, Enki, and Ninhursaga. An was the god of the sky and hence the most important force in the universe. Since his basic essence was authority, he was also viewed as the source or active principle of all authority, including the earthly power of rulers and fathers alike. In one myth, the gods address him thus:

What you have ordered comes true!
The utterance of prince and lord is but what you have
  ordered, do agree with.
O An! your great command takes precedence, who could
  gainsay it?
O father of the gods, your command, the very foundations
  of heaven and earth, what god could spurn it?[6]

Enlil, god of wind, was considered the second greatest power of the visible universe. In charge of the wind and thus an expression of the legitimate use of force, Enlil became the symbol of the proper use of force on earth as well. Enki was the god of the earth. Since the earth was the source of life-giving waters, Enki was also the god of rivers, wells, and canals. More generally, he represented the waters of creativity and was responsible for inventions and crafts. Ninhursaga began as a goddess associated with soil, mountains, and vegetation. Eventually, however, she was worshiped as a mother goddess, a "mother of all children," who manifested her power by giving birth to kings and conferring the royal insignia on them.

Human beings' relationship with their gods was based on subservience since, according to Sumerian myth, human beings were created to do the manual labor the gods were unwilling to do for themselves (see the box on p. 12). Moreover, humans were insecure because they could never be sure what the gods would do. But humans did make attempts to circumvent or relieve their anxiety by discovering the intentions of the gods and by trying to influence them as well; these efforts gave rise to the development of the arts of **divination**.

Divination took a variety of forms. A common form, at least for kings and priests who could afford it, involved killing animals, such as sheep or goats, and examining their livers or other organs. Supposedly, features seen in the organs of the sacrificed animals foretold events to come. Thus one handbook states that if the animal organ has shape *x*, the outcome of the military campaign will be *y*. Private individuals relied on cheaper divinatory techniques. These included interpreting patterns of smoke from burning incense or the pattern formed when oil was poured into water.

The Mesopotamian arts of divination arose out of the desire to discover the purposes of the gods and goddesses. If people could decipher the signs that foretold events, the events would be predictable and humans could act wisely. But the Mesopotamians also developed cultic arts to influence good powers (gods and goddesses) whose decisions could determine human destiny and to ward off evil powers (demons). These cultic arts included ritualistic formulas, such as spells against evil spirits, and prayers or hymns to the gods to win their positive influence. Since only the priests knew the precise rituals, it is not hard to understand the important role they exercised in a society dominated by a belief in the reality of spiritual powers.

Writing The realization of writing's great potential was another aspect of Mesopotamian culture. The oldest Mesopotamian texts date to around 3000 B.C. and were written by the Sumerians, who used a **cuneiform** ("wedge-shaped")

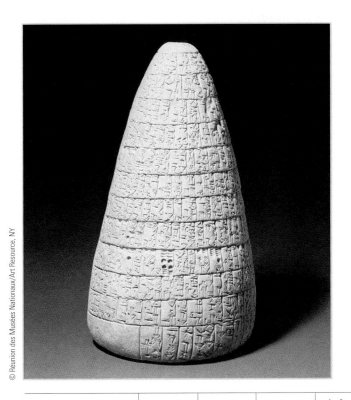

© Réunion des Musées Nationaux/Art Resource, NY

The Development of Cuneiform. Pictured here is the cone of Uruinimgina, an example of cuneiform script from an early Sumerian dynasty. The inscription announces reductions in taxes. The table shows the evolution of writing from pictographic signs to cuneiform script.

Pictographic sign, c. 3100 B.C.									
Interpretation	star	?sun over horizon	?stream	ear of barley	bull's head	bowl	head + bowl	lower leg	?shrouded body
Cuneiform sign, c. 2400 B.C.									
Cuneiform sign c. 700 B.C. (turned through 90°)									
Phonetic value*	dingir, an	u_4, ud	a	še	gu_4	nig_2, ninda	ku_2	du, gin, gub	lu_2
Meaning	god, sky	day, sun	water, seed, son	barley	ox	food, bread	to eat	to walk, to stand	man

*Some signs have more than one phonetic value and some sounds are represented by more than one sign; for example, u_4 means the fourth sign with the phonetic value *u*.

From Cultural Atlas of Mesopotamia & the Ancient Near East by Michael Roaf/Andromeda Oxford Limited, Oxford, England

THE ANCIENT NEAR EAST: THE FIRST CIVILIZATIONS **13**

A SUMERIAN SCHOOLBOY

THIS DOCUMENT is a Sumerian essay narrating the daily activities of a schoolboy, written by a teacher as a copying exercise for pupils. The schoolboy experiences numerous trials and tribulations, including being beaten ("caned") for improper behavior. Scribal schools came into being in Sumer around 2500 B.C.

A Sumerian Essay for Schoolboys

"Schoolboy, where did you go from earliest day?"
"I went to school."
"What did you do in school?"
"I read my tablet, wrote it, finished it; then my prepared lines were prepared for me and in the afternoon, my hand copies were prepared for me."
Upon the school's dismissal, I went home, entered the house, there was my father sitting. I spoke to my father of my hand copies, then read the tablet to him, and my father was pleased; truly I found favor with my father.
"I am thirsty, give me drink, I am hungry, give me bread, wash my feet, set up the bed, I want to go to sleep; wake me early in the morning, I must not be late, or my teacher will cane me."
When I awoke early in the morning, I faced my mother, and said to her: "Give me my lunch, I want to go to school. . . ."
My mother gave me two "rolls," I went to school.
In the tablet-house, the monitor said to me: "Why are you late?" I was afraid, my heart beat fast. I entered before my teacher, took my place.

My "school-father" read my tablet to me, said "The . . . is cut off," caned me. . . .
Who was in charge of drawing said "Why when I was not here did you stand up?" caned me.
Who was in charge of the gate said "Why when I was not here did you go out?" caned me. . . .
My teacher said "Your hand is not good," caned me.

[At this point, the student decides he needs help and suggests to his father that he invite his teacher home for dinner. The father does so, thanks the teacher, and treats him to a feast and gifts. The teacher now responds to the student.]

Young man, because you did not neglect my work, did not forsake it,
May you reach the pinnacle of the scribal art, achieve it completely
Because you gave me that which you were by no means obliged to give,
You presented me with a gift over and above my earnings, have shown me great honor, may Nidaba, the queen of the guardian deities, be your guardian deity.
May she show favor to your fashioned reed,
May she take all evil from your hand copies.
Of your brothers, may you be their leader,
Of your companions, may you be their chief,
May you rank the highest of all the schoolboys.

system of writing. Using a reed stylus, they made wedge-shaped impressions on clay tablets, which were then baked or dried in the sun. Once dried, these tablets were virtually indestructible, and the several hundred thousand that have been found so far have provided a valuable source of information for modern scholars. Sumerian writing evolved from pictures of concrete objects to simplified and stylized signs, leading eventually to a phonetic system that made possible the written expression of abstract ideas.

Sumerian was the chief spoken and written language of Mesopotamia in the third millennium, but it was replaced in the second millennium by Akkadian. After 2500 B.C., Sumerian cuneiform was adapted by Semitic-speaking peoples (as seen in Old Akkadian) for their own written languages. Eventually, two dialects of Old Akkadian were used in Mesopotamia, Assyrian in the north and Babylonian in the south.

Mesopotamian peoples used writing primarily for record keeping. The most common cuneiform tablets record transactions of daily life: tallies of cattle kept by cowherds for their owners, production figures, lists of taxes and wage payments, accounts, contracts, and court deci-

sions dealing with business matters. There are also monumental texts, documents that were intended to last forever, such as inscriptions etched in stone on statues and royal buildings.

Still another category of cuneiform inscriptions includes a large body of basic texts produced for teaching purposes (see the box above). Schools for scribes were in operation by 2500 B.C. They were necessary because considerable time was needed to master the cuneiform system of writing. The primary goal of scribal education was to produce professionally trained scribes for careers in the temples and palaces, the military, and government service. Pupils were male and primarily from wealthy families. Gradually, the schools became important centers for culture because Mesopotamian literature was used for instructional purposes. Moreover, new literary productions came out of the scribal schools.

Mesopotamian Literature Writing was important because it enabled a society to keep records and maintain knowledge of previous practices and events. Writing also made it possible for people to communicate ideas in new ways,

THE GREAT FLOOD

HE GREAT EPIC POEM of Mesopotamian literature, *The Epic of Gilgamesh,* includes an account by Utnapishtim (a Mesopotamian version of the later biblical Noah), who had built a ship and survived the flood unleashed by the gods to destroy humankind. This selection recounts how the god Ea advised Utnapishtim to build a boat and how he came to land his boat at the end of the flood. In this section, Utnapishtim is telling his story to Gilgamesh.

The Epic of Gilgamesh

"In those days the world teemed, the people multiplied, the world bellowed like a wild bull, and the great god was aroused by the clamor. Enlil heard the clamor and he said to the gods in council, 'The uproar of mankind is intolerable and sleep is no longer possible by reason of the babel.' So the gods agreed to exterminate mankind. Enlil did this, but Ea [Sumerian Enki, god of the waters] because of his oath warned me in a dream . . . 'tear down your house and build a boat, abandon possessions and look for life, despise worldly goods and save your soul alive. Tear down your house, I say, and build a boat. . . . Then take up into the boat the seed of all living creatures. . . .' [Utnapishtim did as he was told, and then the destruction came.]

"For six days and six nights the winds blew, torrent and tempest and flood overwhelmed the world, tempest and flood raged together like warring hosts. When the seventh day dawned the storm from the south subsided, the sea grew calm, the flood was stifled; I looked at the face of the world and there was silence, all mankind was turned to clay. The surface of the sea stretched as flat as a rooftop; I opened a hatch and the light fell on my face. Then I bowed low, I sat down and I wept, the tears streamed down my face, for on every side was the waste of water. I looked for land in vain, but fourteen leagues distant there appeared a mountain, and there the boat grounded; on the mountain of Nisir the boat held fast, she held fast and did not budge. . . . When the seventh day dawned I loosed a dove and let her go. She flew away, but finding no resting-place she returned. Then I loosed a swallow, and she flew away but finding no resting-place she returned. I loosed a raven, she saw that the waters had retreated, she ate, she flew around, she cawed, and she did not come back. Then I threw everything open to the four winds, I made a sacrifice and poured out a libation on the mountain top."

---

which is especially evident in Mesopotamian literary works. The most famous piece of Mesopotamian literature was *The Epic of Gilgamesh.* This epic poem, Sumerian in origin but preserved in Akkadian, records the exploits of a legendary king of Uruk. Gilgamesh, wise, strong, and perfect in body, part man, part god, abused the citizens of Uruk:

> "Gilgamesh sounds the tocsin for his amusement," the people complained, "his arrogance has no bounds by day or night. No son is left with his father, for Gilgamesh takes them all, even the children. . . . His lust leaves no virgin to her lover, neither the warrior's daughter nor the wife of the noble. . . ."[7]

The citizens asked the gods to send a competitor to oppose Gilgamesh and keep him busy. The gods comply and send a hairy, barbaric beast named Enkidu whom Gilgamesh tries to weaken by sending a prostitute to seduce him. When Enkidu finally comes to Uruk, he and Gilgamesh engage in a fierce struggle that neither can win. The two become fast friends and set off in pursuit of heroic deeds. Ishtar (Sumerian Inanna), the goddess of love, attempts to seduce Gilgamesh, but he refuses her advances. In anger, she convinces her father Anu (Sumerian An) to send the Bull of Heaven to kill Gilgamesh and Enkidu. They manage to kill the bull instead, and the gods decide that in return one of them must die. Enlil, the god of wind, rules for Enkidu, and he falls ill and dies, much to the prolonged grief of Gilgamesh. Gilgamesh experiences the pain of mor-

tality and enters upon a search for the secret of immortality. He finds the man who had been granted "everlasting life" by the gods, Utnapishtim. The latter tells him the story of how he survived the Great Flood sent by the gods to destroy humankind (see the box above). Regretting what they had done, the gods bestowed immortality on Utnapishtim, who now instructs Gilgamesh to dive to the bottom of a river and find a certain plant that gives the power to grow younger. Although Gilgamesh finds the plant, a snake snatches it away before he can eat it. Gilgamesh remains mortal. The desire for immortality, one of humankind's great searches, ends in frustration. "Everlasting life," as this Mesopotamian epic makes clear, is only for the gods.

Mathematics and Astronomy People in Mesopotamia made outstanding achievements in mathematics and astronomy. In math, the Sumerians devised a number system based on 60, using combinations of 6 and 10 for practical solutions. They used the processes of multiplication and division and compiled tables for the computation of interest. Geometry was used for practical purposes, such as measuring fields and building projects. In astronomy, the Sumerians made use of units of 60 and charted the chief heavenly constellations. Their calendar was based on twelve lunar months and was brought into harmony with the solar year by adding an extra month from time to time.

SIGNIFICANCE OF THE NILE RIVER AND THE PHARAOH

WO OF THE most important sources of life for the ancient Egyptians were the Nile River and the pharaoh. Egyptians perceived that the Nile River made possible the abundant food that was a major source of their well-being. This *Hymn to the Nile*, probably from the nineteenth and twentieth dynasties in the New Kingdom, expresses the gratitude Egyptians felt for the Nile.

Hymn to the Nile

Hail to you, O Nile, that issues from the earth and comes to keep Egypt alive! . . .

He that waters the meadows which Re created, in order to keep every kid alive.

He that makes to drink the desert and the place distant from water: that is his dew coming down from heaven. . . .

The lord of fishes, he who makes the marsh-birds to go upstream. . . .

He who makes barley and brings emmer [wheat] into being, that he may make the temples festive.

If he is sluggish, then nostrils are stopped up, and everybody is poor. . . .

When he rises, then the land is in jubilation, then every belly is in joy, every backbone takes on laughter, and every tooth is exposed.

The bringer of food, rich in provisions, creator of all good, lord of majesty, sweet of fragrance. . . .

He who makes every beloved tree to grow, without lack of them.

The Egyptian king, or pharaoh, was viewed as a god and the absolute ruler of Egypt. His significance and the gratitude of the Egyptian people for his existence are evident in this hymn from the reign of Sesotris III (c. 1880–1840 B.C.).

Hymn to the Pharaoh

He has come unto us that he may carry away Upper Egypt; the double diadem [crown of Upper and Lower Egypt] has rested on his head.

He has come unto us and has united the Two Lands; he has mingled the reed with the bee [symbols of Lower and Upper Egypt].

He has come unto us and has brought the Black Land under his sway; he has apportioned to himself the Red Land.

He has come unto us and has taken the Two Lands under his protection; he has given peace to the Two Riverbanks.

He has come unto us and has made Egypt to live; he has banished its suffering.

He has come unto us and has made the people to live; he has caused the throat of the subjects to breathe. . . .

He has come unto us and has done battle for his boundaries; he has delivered them that were robbed.

Egyptian Civilization: "The Gift of the Nile"

Although contemporaneous with Mesopotamia, civilization in Egypt evolved along somewhat different lines. Of central importance to the development of Egyptian civilization was the Nile River. That the Egyptian people recognized its significance is apparent in this *Hymn to the Nile* (see the box above): "The bringer of food, rich in provisions, creator of all good, lord of majesty, sweet of fragrance. . . . He who . . . fills the magazines, makes the granaries wide, and gives things to the poor. He who makes every beloved tree to grow."[8] Egypt, like Mesopotamia, was a river valley civilization.

The Impact of Geography

The Nile is a unique river, beginning in the heart of Africa and coursing northward for thousands of miles. It is the longest river in the world. Thanks to the Nile, an area several miles wide on both banks of the river was capable of producing abundant harvests. The "miracle" of the Nile was its annual flooding. The river rose in the summer from rains in Central Africa, crested in Egypt in September and October, and left a deposit of silt that enriched the soil. The Egyptians called this fertile land, dark from the silt and the lush crops that grew on it, the "Black Land." Beyond these narrow strips of fertile fields lay the deserts (the "Red Land").

Unlike the floods of Mesopotamia's rivers, the flooding of the Nile was gradual and usually predictable, and the river itself was seen as life-enhancing, not life-threatening. Although a system of organized irrigation was still necessary, the small villages along the Nile could make the effort without the massive state intervention that was required in Mesopotamia. Egyptian civilization consequently tended to remain more rural, with many small population centers congregated along a narrow band on both sides of the Nile. About 100 miles before it empties into the Mediterranean, the river splits into two major branches, forming the delta, a triangular-shaped territory called Lower Egypt to distinguish it from Upper Egypt, the land upstream to the south (see Map 1.3). Egypt's important cities developed at the tip of the delta. Even today, most of Egypt's 65 million people are crowded along the banks of the Nile River.

The surpluses of food that Egyptian farmers grew in the fertile Nile valley made Egypt prosperous. But the Nile also served as a unifying factor in Egyptian history. In

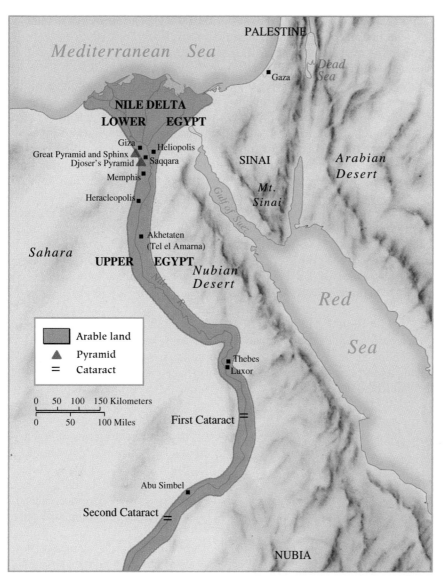

MAP 1.3 **Ancient Egypt.** Egyptian civilization centered on the life-giving water and flood silts of the Nile River, with most of the population living in Lower Egypt, where the river splits to form the Nile delta. Most of the pyramids, built during the Old Kingdom, are clustered at the entrance to the delta. ❓ How did the lands to the east and west of the river make invasions of Egypt difficult? 🐾 **View an animated version of this map or related maps at** http://history.wadsworth.com/spielvogel06/

ancient times, the Nile was the fastest way to travel through the land, making both transportation and communication easier. Winds from the north pushed sailboats south, and the current of the Nile carried them north. Often when they headed downstream (north), people used long poles or paddles to propel their boats forward.

Unlike Mesopotamia, which was subject to constant invasion, Egypt was blessed by natural barriers that protected it from invasion and gave it a sense of security. These barriers included the deserts to the west and east; the cataracts (rapids) on the southern part of the Nile, which made defense relatively easy; and the Mediterranean Sea to the north. These barriers, however, did not prevent the development of trade. Indeed, there is evidence of very early trade between Egypt and Mesopotamia.

In essence, Egyptian geography and topography played important roles in the early history of the country. The regularity of the Nile floods and the relative isolation of the Egyptians created a sense of security that was accompanied by a feeling of changelessness. To the ancient Egyptians, when the Nile flooded each year, "the fields laugh and people's faces light up." Unlike people in Mesopotamia, Egyptians faced life with a spirit of confidence in the stability of things. Egyptian civilization was characterized by a remarkable degree of continuity over thousands of years. It was no accident that Egyptians believed in cyclical rather than linear progress. Just as the sun passed through its daily cycle and the Nile its annual overflow, Egyptian kings reaffirmed the basic, unchanging principle of justice at the beginning of each new cycle of rule.

🎐 The Old and Middle Kingdoms

The basic framework for the study of Egyptian history was provided by Manetho, an Egyptian priest and historian who lived in the early third century B.C. He divided Egyptian history into thirty-one dynasties of kings. On the basis of Manetho's and other king lists, modern historians have divided Egyptian history into three major periods known as the Old Kingdom, the Middle Kingdom, and the New Kingdom. These were periods of long-term stability characterized by strong monarchical authority, competent bureaucracy, freedom from invasion, much construction of temples and pyramids, and considerable intellectual and cultural activity. But between the periods of stability were ages of political chaos known as the Intermediate Periods, which were characterized by weak political structures and rivalry for leadership, invasions, a decline in building activity, and a restructuring of society.

The Old Kingdom   According to the Egyptians' own tradition, their land consisted initially of numerous populated areas ruled by tribal chieftains. Around 3100 B.C., during the Early Dynastic Period, the first Egyptian royal dynasty, under a king called Menes, united both Upper and Lower Egypt into a single kingdom. Henceforth, the king would be called "King of Upper and King of Lower Egypt," and the royal crown would be a double diadem, signifying the unification of all Egypt. Just as the Nile served to unite Upper and Lower Egypt physically, kingship served to unite the two areas politically.

The Old Kingdom encompassed the third through sixth dynasties of Egyptian kings, lasting from around 2686 to 2125 B.C. It was an age of prosperity and splendor, made visible in the construction of the greatest and largest pyramids in Egypt's history. The capital of the Old Kingdom was located at Memphis, south of the delta.

Kingship was a divine institution in ancient Egypt and formed part of a universal cosmic scheme (see the box on p. 16): "What is the king of Upper and Lower Egypt? He is a god by whose dealings one lives, the father and mother of all men, alone by himself, without an equal."[9] In obeying their king, subjects helped maintain the cosmic order. A breakdown in royal power could only mean that citizens were offending divinity and weakening the universal structure.

Pair Statue of King Menkaure and His Queen. During the Old Kingdom, kings (eventually called pharaohs) were regarded as gods, divine instruments who maintained the fundamental order and harmony of the universe and wielded absolute power. Seated and standing statues of kings were commonly placed in Egyptian royal tombs. Seen here are the standing portraits of King Menkaure and his queen, Khamerernebty, from the fourth dynasty. By artistic convention, kings and their queens were shown in a rigid pose, reflecting their timeless nature. Husband and wife show no emotion but are seen looking out into space.

Pair Statue of King Mycerinus and His Queen; From Giza, Dynasty IV, 2599– 1571 B.C., Slate Schist, 54 1/2 in. Harvard MFA Expedition. Courtesy Museum of Fine Arts, Boston.

Among the various titles of Egyptian kings, that of pharaoh (originally meaning "great house" or "palace") eventually came to be the most common.

Although they possessed absolute power, Egyptian kings were supposed to rule not arbitrarily but according to set principles. The chief principle was called *Ma'at,* a spiritual precept that conveyed the idea of truth and justice, especially right order and harmony. To ancient Egyptians, this fundamental order and harmony had existed throughout the universe since the beginning of time. Pharaohs were the divine instruments who maintained it and were themselves subject to it.

Although theoretically absolute in their power, in practice Egyptian kings did not rule alone. Initially, members of the king's family performed administrative tasks, but by the fourth dynasty, a bureaucracy with regular procedures had developed. Especially important was the office of vizier, "steward of the whole land." Directly responsible to the king, the vizier was in charge of the bureaucracy, with its numerous departments, including police, justice, river transport, and public works. Agriculture and the treasury were the most important departments. Agriculture was, of course, the backbone of Egyptian prosperity, and the treasury collected the taxes, which were paid in kind. A careful assessment of land and tenants was undertaken to establish the tax base.

For administrative purposes, Egypt was divided into provinces or nomes, as they were later called by the Greeks—twenty-two in Upper and twenty in Lower Egypt. A governor, called by the Greeks a nomarch, was head of each nome and was responsible to the king and vizier. Nomarchs, however, tended to build up large holdings of land and power within their nomes, creating a potential rivalry with the pharaohs.

The Middle Kingdom   Despite the theory of divine order, the Old Kingdom eventually collapsed, ushering in an Intermediate Period of chaos c. 2125– 2055 B.C.). A so-called prophet named Nefer-Rohu (Neferti) described the scene:

> This land is so damaged that there is no one who is concerned with it, no one who speaks, no one who weeps. . . . The sun disc is covered over. It will not shine so that people may see. . . . The rivers of Egypt are empty, so that the water is crossed on foot. Men seek for water for the ships to sail on it. . . . This land is helter-skelter, and no one knows the result that will come about, which is hidden from speech, sight, or hearing.[10]

Early Dynastic Period (dynasties 1–2)	c. 3100–2686 B.C.
Old Kingdom (dynasties 3–6)	c. 2686–2125 B.C.
First Intermediate Period (dynasties 7–10)	c. 2125–2055 B.C.
Middle Kingdom (dynasties 11–12)	c. 2055–1650 B.C.
Second Intermediate Period (dynasties 13–17)	c. 1650–1550 B.C.
New Kingdom (dynasties 18–20)	c. 1550–1070 B.C.
Postempire Egypt (dynasties 21–31)	1070–30 B.C.

During this First Intermediate Period of chaos, new centers of power established rival dynasties, such as those at Heracleopolis near Lower Egypt and Thebes in Upper Egypt. Finally, the king of Thebes, Mentuhotep, defeated the ruler of Heracleopolis and achieved the reunification of all Egypt, thus beginning the Middle Kingdom, a new period of stability lasting from around 2055 to 1650 B.C.

Much of the Middle Kingdom's history centered around the twelfth dynasty founded by Amenemhet I, a vizier who established himself and his successors as pharaohs. Egyptians later portrayed the Middle Kingdom as a golden age, a clear indication of its stability. Several factors contributed to its vitality. The nome structure was reorganized. The boundaries of each nome were now settled precisely, and the obligations of the nomes to the state were clearly delineated. Nomarchs were confirmed as hereditary officeholders but with the understanding that their duties must be performed faithfully. These included the collection of taxes for the state and the recruitment of labor forces for royal projects, such as stone quarrying.

The Middle Kingdom was characterized by a new concern on the part of the pharaohs for the people. In the Old Kingdom, the pharaoh had been viewed as an inaccessible god-king. Now he was portrayed as the shepherd of his people with the responsibility to build public works and provide for the public welfare. As one pharaoh expressed it: "He [a particular god] created me as one who should do that which he had done, and to carry out that which he commanded should be done. He appointed me herdsman of this land, for he knew who would keep it in order for him."[11]

As confirmation of its newfound strength, Egypt embarked on a period of expansion. Lower Nubia was conquered, and fortresses were built to protect the new southern frontier. The government also sent military expeditions into Palestine and Syria. Although they did not remain there, this campaign marks the beginning of Egyptian imperialism in those areas.

Society and Economy in Ancient Egypt

Egyptian society had a simple structure in the Old and Middle Kingdoms; basically, it was organized along hierarchical lines with the god-king at the top. The king was surrounded by an upper class of nobles and priests who participated in the elaborate rituals of life that surrounded the pharaoh. This ruling class ran the government and managed its own landed estates, which provided much of its wealth.

Below the upper classes were merchants and artisans. Merchants engaged in active trade up and down the Nile as well as in town and village markets. Some merchants also engaged in international trade; they were sent by the king to Crete and Syria, where they obtained wood and other products. Expeditions traveled into Nubia for ivory and down the Red Sea to Punt for incense and spices. Egyptian artisans displayed unusually high standards of craftsmanship and physical beauty and produced an incredible variety of goods: stone dishes; beautifully painted boxes made of clay; wooden furniture, especially of Lebanon cedar; gold, silver, and copper tools and containers; paper and rope made of papyrus; and linen clothes.

The largest number of people in Egypt simply worked the land. In theory, the king owned all the land but granted portions of it to his subjects. Large sections were in the possession of nobles and the temple complexes. Most of the lower classes were serfs, common people who were bound to the land and cultivated the estates. They paid taxes in the form of crops to the king, nobles, and priests; lived in small villages or towns; and provided military service and labor for building projects.

The Culture of Egypt

Egypt produced a culture that dazzled and awed its later conquerors. The Egyptians' technical achievements alone, especially visible in the construction of the pyramids, demonstrated a measure of skill unique to the world of that time. To the Egyptians, all of these achievements were part of a cosmic order suffused with the presence of the divine.

Spiritual Life in Egyptian Society   The Egyptians had no word for religion because it was an inseparable element of the world order to which Egyptian society belonged. Egypt was part of the universal cosmic scheme, and the pharaoh was the divine being whose function was to maintain its stability within that cosmic order.

The Egyptians possessed a remarkable number of gods associated with heavenly bodies and natural forces. Two groups, sun gods and land gods, came to have special prominence, hardly unusual in view of the importance to Egypt's well-being of the sun, the river, and the fertile land along its banks. The sun was the source of life and hence worthy of worship. A sun cult developed, especially at Heliopolis, now a suburb of modern Cairo. The sun god took on different forms and names, depending on his specific function. He was worshiped as Atum in human form and as Re, who had a human body but the head of a falcon. The pharaoh took the title "Son of Re" because he was regarded as the earthly embodiment of Re.

River and land deities included Osiris and Isis with their child Horus, who was related to the Nile and to the sun as well. Osiris became especially important as a symbol of resurrection. A famous Egyptian myth told of the struggle between Osiris, who brought civilization to Egypt, and his evil brother Seth, who killed him, cut his body into fourteen parts, and tossed them into the Nile. Osiris' faithful wife Isis found the pieces and, with help from other gods, restored Osiris to life. As a symbol of resurrection and as judge of the dead, Osiris took on an important role for the Egyptians. By identifying with Osiris, one could hope to gain new life, just as Osiris had done. The dead, embalmed and mummified, were placed in tombs (in the case of kings, in pyramidal tombs), given the name of Osiris, and by a process of magical identification became Osiris. Like Osiris, they could then be reborn. The flood of the Nile and the new life it brought to Egypt were symbolized by Isis gathering all of Osiris' parts together and were celebrated each spring in the festival of the new land.

Later Egyptian spiritual practice began to emphasize morality by stressing Osiris' role as judge of the dead. The dead were asked to give an account of their earthly deeds to show whether they deserved a reward. Other means were also employed to gain immortality. As seen in the *Book of the Dead,* magical incantations were used to ensure a favorable journey to a happy afterlife. Specific instructions explained what to do when confronted by the judge of the dead. These instructions had two aspects. The negative confession gave a detailed list of what one had not done:

> What is said on reaching the Broad-Hall of the Two Justices [the place of the next-world judgment], absolving X [the name and title of the deceased] of every sin which he had committed, . . .

I have not committed evil against men.
I have not mistreated cattle. . . .
I have not blasphemed a god. . . .
I have not done violence to a poor man. . . .
I have not defamed a slave to his superior.
I have not made anyone sick.
I have not made anyone weep.
I have not killed. . . .
I have not caused anyone suffering. . . .
I have not had sexual relations with a boy.
I have not defiled myself. . . .
I have not driven cattle away from their pasturage.[12]

Later the supplicant made a speech listing his good actions: "I have done that which men said and that with which gods are content. . . . I have given bread to the hungry, water to the thirsty, clothing to the naked, and a ferry-boat to him who was marooned. I have provided divine offerings for the gods and mortuary offerings for the dead."[13]

At first the Osiris cult was reserved for the very wealthy, who could afford to take expensive measures to preserve the body after death. During the Middle Kingdom, however, the cult became "democratized," extended to all Egyptians who aspired to an afterlife.

The Pyramids One of the great achievements of Egyptian civilization, the building of pyramids, occurred in the time of the Old Kingdom. Pyramids were not built in isolation but as part of a larger complex dedicated to the dead—in effect, a city of the dead. The area included a large pyramid for the king's burial, smaller pyramids for his family, and

Osiris as Judge of the Dead. According to the *Book of the Dead,* after making a denial of offenses (the "negative confession"), the deceased experienced the "weighing of the heart." Shown here is a judgment scene from the *Book of the Dead* of Hunefer, a royal scribe who died around 1285 B.C. Hunefer's heart is placed on one side of a balance scale; on the other side is the feather of Ma'at, the goddess of truth. For Hunefer, heart and feather are of equal weight, so the god Anubis ushers him into the presence of Osiris, seated on his throne at the right. A "Swallowing Monster," a hybrid creature of crocodile, lion, and hippopotamus, stood ready at the scale to devour the deceased if he failed the test.

mastabas, rectangular structures with flat roofs, as tombs for the pharaoh's noble officials. The tombs were well prepared for their residents. The rooms were furnished and stocked with numerous supplies, including chairs, boats, chests, weapons, games, dishes, and a variety of foods. The Egyptians believed that human beings had two bodies, a physical one and a spiritual one, which they called the *ka*. If the physical body was properly preserved (that is, mummified) and the tomb furnished with all the various objects of regular life, the *ka* could return and continue its life despite the death of the physical body.

To preserve the physical body after death, the Egyptians practiced mummification, a process of slowly drying a dead body to prevent it from rotting. Special workshops, run by priests, performed this procedure, primarily for the wealthy families who could afford it. According to Herodotus, an ancient Greek historian (see Chapter 3) who visited Egypt around 450 B.C., "The most refined method is as follows: first of all they draw out the brain through the nostrils with an iron hook. . . . Then they make an incision in the flank with a sharp Ethiopian stone through which they extract all the internal organs."[14] The liver, lungs, stomach, and intestines were then placed in four special jars that were put in the tomb with the mummy. The priests then covered the corpse with a natural salt that absorbed the body's water. Later, they filled the body with spices and wrapped it with layers of linen soaked in resin. At the end of the process, which took about seventy days, a lifelike mask was placed over the head and shoulders of the mummy, which was then sealed in a case and placed in its tomb.

Pyramids were tombs for the mummified bodies of pharaohs. The first pyramid was built in the third dynasty during the reign of King Djoser. The architect Imhotep, a priest of Heliopolis, the center dedicated to the sun cult, was responsible for the step pyramid at Saqqara. Beginning with Djoser, wives and immediate families of the kings were buried in pyramids, nobles and officials in mastabas.

The first real pyramid, with each side filled in to make an even surface, was constructed in the fourth dynasty around 2600 B.C. by King Snefru, who built three pyramids. But the largest and most magnificent of all was built under Snefru's son Khufu. Constructed at Giza around 2540 B.C., the famous Great Pyramid covers 13 acres, measures 756 feet at each side of its base, and stands 481 feet high. Its four sides are almost precisely oriented to the four points of the compass.

The building of the Great Pyramid was an enormous construction project that used limestone blocks as well as granite from Upper Egypt. Herodotus reported that it took 100,000 Egyptians twenty years to build the Great Pyramid. But Herodotus wrote two thousand years after the event, and considerable controversy and speculation still surround the construction of the Great Pyramid, especially in view of the precision with which it was built. The stone slabs on the outside of the pyramid, for example, fit so closely side by side that a hair cannot be pushed into the joints between them. The Great Pyramid still stands as a

© Digital Vision/Getty Images

The Pyramids at Giza. The three pyramids at Giza, across the Nile River from Cairo, are the most famous in Egypt. At the rear is the largest of the three pyramids—the Great Pyramid of Khufu. Next to it is the pyramid of Khafre. In the foreground is the smaller pyramid of Menkaure standing behind the even smaller pyramids for the pharaohs' wives. Covering almost 13 acres, the Great Pyramid of Khufu is immense. It is estimated that the Great Pyramid contains 2.3 million stone blocks, each weighing about 2.5 tons.

symbol of the power of Egyptian kings of the Old Kingdom. No later pyramid ever matched its size or splendor. But an Egyptian pyramid was not just the king's tomb; it was also an important symbol of royal power. It could be seen for miles away as a visible reminder of the glory and might of the ruler, a living god on earth.

Art and Writing Commissioned by kings or nobles for use in temples and tombs, Egyptian art was largely functional. Wall paintings and statues of gods and kings in temples served a strictly spiritual purpose. They were an integral part of the performance of ritual, which was thought necessary to preserve the cosmic order and hence the well-being of Egypt. Likewise, the mural scenes and sculptured figures found in the tombs had a specific function. They were supposed to aid the journey of the deceased into the afterworld.

Egyptian art was also formulaic. Artists and sculptors were expected to observe a strict canon of proportions that determined both form and presentation. This canon gave Egyptian art a distinctive appearance for thousands of years. Especially characteristic was the convention of combining the profile, semiprofile, and frontal views of the human body in relief work and painting in order to represent each part of the body accurately. This fashion created an art that was highly stylized yet still allowed distinctive features to be portrayed.

Writing emerged in Egypt during the first two dynasties. It was the Greeks who later labeled Egyptian writing

hieroglyphics, meaning "priest-carvings" or "sacred writings." Hieroglyphs were signs that depicted objects and had a sacred value at the same time. Although hieroglyphs were later simplified for writing purposes into two scripts, they never developed into an alphabet. Egyptian hieroglyphs were initially carved in stone, but later the two simplified scripts were written on papyrus, a paper made from the papyrus reed that grew along the Nile. Most of the ancient Egyptian literature that has come down to us was written on papyrus rolls and wooden tablets.

Chaos and a New Order: The New Kingdom

The Middle Kingdom came to an end in the midst of another period of instability. An incursion into the delta region by a people known as the Hyksos initiated this second age of chaos. The Hyksos, a Semitic-speaking people, infiltrated Egypt in the seventeenth century B.C. and came to dominate much of Egypt during the Second Intermediate Period. However, the presence of the Hyksos was not entirely negative for Egypt. They introduced Bronze Age technology, teaching the Egyptians how to make bronze for use in new agricultural tools and weapons. More significantly, the Hyksos brought new aspects of warfare to Egypt, including the horse-drawn war chariot, a heavier sword, and the compound bow. Eventually, the Egyptians made use of their new weapons to throw off Hyksos domination.

The Egyptian Empire   It was the pharaoh Ahmose I who managed to defeat and expel the Hyksos from Egypt. He reunited Egypt, founded the eighteenth dynasty, established the New Kingdom (c. 1550–1070 B.C.), and launched the Egyptians along a new militaristic and imperialistic path. A more professional army was developed. Viziers, who were in charge of the state bureaucracy, were now chosen only from the ranks of military commanders.

During the period of the New Kingdom, Egypt became the most powerful state in the ancient Near East (see Map 1.4). Thutmosis I (c. 1524–1518) expanded Egypt's border to the south by conquering the African kingdom of Nubia. Thutmosis III (c. 1480–c. 1450 B.C.) led seventeen military campaigns into Palestine and Phoenicia. The Egyptians occupied these lands but permitted local native princes to rule. Egypt, no longer content to remain in isolation, now pursued an active political and diplomatic policy.

The new Egyptian imperial state reached its height during the reign of Amenhotep III (c. 1412–1375 B.C.),

MAP 1.4 The Egyptian and Hittite Empires.   The Hittite empire was the dominant power north of Egypt for roughly two centuries (see pp. 27–28). It assimilated important linguistic, political, and religious aspects of the peoples it conquered and thus helped transmit Mesopotamian culture to the eastern Mediterranean. **?** What made both the Hittite and Egyptian empires vulnerable to invasion?

View an animated version of this map or related maps at http://history.wadsworth.com/spielvogel06/

Nubians in Egypt. During the New Kingdom, Egypt expanded to the north, into Palestine and Syria, and to the south, into the African kingdom of Nubia. Nubia had first emerged as an African kingdom around 2300 B.C. Shown here in a fourteenth-century B.C. painting from an Egyptian official's tomb in Nubia are Nubians arriving in Egypt with bags and rings of gold. Nubia was a rich source of gold for the Egyptians.

the great-grandson of Thutmosis III. The achievements of the empire were made visible in the construction of magnificent new buildings and temples. Especially famous were the temple centers at Karnak and Luxor and the 70-foot-high statues of Amenhotep III in front of the mortuary temples along the Nile.

By the end of his reign, Amenhotep III faced a growing military challenge from a people known as the Hittites (see "The Impact of the Indo-Europeans" later in this chapter). His son, Amenhotep IV (c. 1364–1347 B.C.), proved even less able to deal with this threat, a failure that was due in large part to a religious upheaval that he had initiated in Egypt.

Akhenaten and Religious Change Amenhotep introduced the worship of Aten, god of the sun disk, as the chief god (see the box on p. 24) and pursued his worship with great enthusiasm. Changing his own name to Akhenaten ("it is well with Aten"), the pharaoh closed the temples of other gods and especially endeavored to lessen the power of the priesthood dedicated to the god Amon-Re at Thebes, which had become the chief landowner in Egypt. Akhenaten strove to reduce the priests' influence by replacing Thebes as the capital of Egypt with Akhetaten ("dedicated to Aten"), a new city located near modern Tel el Amarna, 200 miles north of Thebes.

Akhenaten's attempt at religious change failed. It was too much to ask Egyptians to ignore their traditional ways and beliefs, especially since they saw the destruction of the old gods as subversive of the very cosmic order on which Egypt's survival and continuing prosperity depended. Moreover, the priests at Thebes were unalterably opposed to the changes, which diminished their influence and power. At the same time, Akhenaten's preoccupation with religion caused him to ignore foreign affairs and led to the loss of both Syria and Palestine. Akhenaten's changes

were soon undone after his death by those who influenced his successor, the boy-pharaoh Tutankhamen (1347–1338 B.C.). Tutankhamen returned the government to Thebes and restored the old gods. The Aten experiment had failed to take hold, and the eighteenth dynasty itself came to an end with the rise to power of a military officer and vizier, Horemhab, who assumed the kingship in 1333 B.C.

The End of the Empire The nineteenth dynasty managed to restore Egyptian power one more time. Under Rameses II (c. 1279–1213 B.C.), the Egyptians regained control of Palestine but were unable to reestablish the borders of their earlier empire. New invasions in the thirteenth century by the "Sea Peoples," as the Egyptians called them, destroyed Egyptian power in Palestine and drove the Egyptians back within their old frontiers. The days of Egyptian empire were ended, and the New Kingdom itself expired with the twentieth dynasty in 1070 B.C. For the next thousand years, despite periodic revivals of strength, Egypt was dominated by Libyans, Nubians, Assyrians, Persians, and finally Macedonians after the conquest of Alexander the Great (see Chapter 4). In the first century B.C., Egypt became a province in Rome's mighty empire.

Daily Life in Ancient Egypt

Ancient Egyptians had a very positive attitude toward daily life on earth and followed the advice of the wisdom literature, which suggested that people marry young and establish a home and family. Monogamy was the general rule, although a husband was allowed to keep additional wives if his first wife was childless. Pharaohs were entitled to harems; the queen was acknowledged, however, as the Great Wife, with a status higher than that of the other wives. The husband was master in the house, but wives were very much respected and in charge of the household and education of

THE ANCIENT NEAR EAST: THE FIRST CIVILIZATIONS

MENHOTEP IV, more commonly known as Akhena-ten, created a religious upheaval in Egypt by intro-ducing the worship of Aten, god of the sun disk, as the chief god. Akhenaten's reverence for Aten is evident in this hymn. Some authorities have noted a similarity in spirit and wording to the 104th Psalm of the Old Testament.

Hymn to Aten

Your rays suckle every meadow.
When you rise, they live, they grow for you.
You make the seasons in order to rear all that you have
*   made,*
The winter to cool them,
And the heat that they may taste you.
You have made the distant sky in order to rise therein,
In order to see all that you do make.
While you were alone,
Rising in your form as the living Aten,
Appearing, shining, withdrawing or approaching,
You made millions of forms of yourself alone.

Cities, towns, fields, road, and river—
Every eye beholds you over against them,
For you are the Aten of the day over the earth. . . .
The world came into being by your hand,
According as you have made them.
When you have risen they live,
When you set they die.
You are lifetime your own self,
For one lives only through you.
Eyes are fixed on beauty until you set.
All work is laid aside when you set in the west.
But when you rise again,
Everything is made to flourish for the king . . .
Since you did found the earth
And raise them up for your son,
Who came forth from your body: the King of Upper
*   and Lower Egypt, . . . Akh-en-Aten, . . . and the*
Chief Wife of the King . . . Nefert-iti, living and
*   youthful forever and ever.*

---

the children (see the box on p. 25). From a book of wise sayings (which the Egyptians called "instructions") came this advice:

> If you are a man of standing, you should found your household and love your wife at home as is fitting. Fill her belly; clothe her back. Ointment is the prescription for her body. Make her heart glad as long as you live. She is a profitable field for her lord. You should not contend with her at law, and keep her far from gaining control. . . . Let her heart be soothed through what may accrue to you; it means keeping her long in your house.[15]

Women's property and inheritances remained in their hands, even in marriage. Although most careers and public offices were closed to women, some women did operate businesses. Peasant women worked long hours in the fields and at numerous domestic tasks, especially weaving cloth. Upper-class women could function as priestesses, and a few queens even became pharaohs in their own right. Most famous was Hatshepsut in the New Kingdom. She initially served as regent for her stepson Thutmosis III but assumed the throne for herself and remained in power until her death.

Hatshepsut's reign was a prosperous one, as is espe-cially evident in her building activity. She is most famous for the temple dedicated to herself at Deir el Bahri on the west bank of the Nile at Thebes. As pharaoh, Hatshepsut sent out military expeditions, encouraged mining, fostered

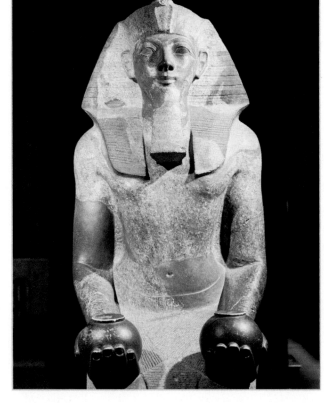

Statue of Hatshepsut. Wife of Thutmosis II, Hatshepsut served as regent for her stepson Thutmosis III after her husband's death. In 1473 B.C., however, she proclaimed herself pharaoh: "I myself am a god. That which happens is meant. Nothing I say is erroneous." Numerous statues of her were constructed at the temple dedicated to her at Deir el Bahri. Many of them were shattered after her death by her stepson. This red granite statue of Hatshepsut, pieced together from fragments, shows her as a man, dressed in the royal male headdress and bearded like a king. She is seen kneeling, making an offering to the sun god.

agriculture, and sent a trading expedition up the Nile. Because pharaohs were almost always male, Hatshepsut's official statues show her clothed and bearded like a king. She was addressed as "His Majesty." That Hatshepsut was aware of her unusual position is evident from an inscription she had placed on one of her temples. It read: "Now my heart turns to and fro, in thinking what will the people say, they who shall see my monument in after years, and shall speak of what I have done."

Marriages were arranged by parents. The primary concerns were family and property, and the chief purpose of marriage was to produce children, especially sons (see the box on p. 26). Only sons could carry on the family name. Daughters were not slighted, however. Numerous tomb paintings show the close and affectionate relationship parents had with both sons and daughters. Although marriages were arranged, some of the surviving love poems from ancient Egypt would indicate an element of romance in some marriages. Here is the lament of a lovesick boy for his "sister" (lovers referred to each other as "brother" and "sister," although some scholars believe that the practice of brother-sister marriage in the Egyptian royal family probably reached down into the general population as well):

Seven days to yesterday I have not seen the sister,
 And a sickness has invaded me;
My body has become heavy,
 And I am forgetful of my own self.
If the chief physicians come to me,
 My heart is not content with their remedies. . . .
What will revive me is to say to me: "Here she is!"
 Her name is what will lift me up. . . .
My health is her coming in from outside:
 When I see her, then I am well.[16]

Marriages could and did end in divorce, which was allowed, apparently with compensation for the wife. Adultery, how-

ever, was strictly prohibited, and punishments were severe, especially for women, who could have their noses cut off or be burned at the stake.

Under normal circumstances, Egypt was blessed by a material abundance that not only kept its entire population fed but also enabled its upper classes to lead a life of gracious leisure. These wealthy families had attractive homes located on walled estates. Much energy was devoted to the garden, which contained fruit trees and vegetables, as well as tree-lined paths and pools for the family's leisure time.

Tomb paintings indicate that the upper classes participated in numerous banquets where guests were lavishly fed and entertained. Although some people obviously got drunk, a collection of "instructions" advises more circumspect behavior:

If you are one of those sitting at the table of one greater than yourself, take what he may give, when it is set before your nose. You should gaze at what is before you. . . . Let your face be cast down until he addresses you, and you should speak only when he addresses you. Laugh after he laughs, and it will be very pleasing to his heart and what you may do will be pleasing to the heart.[17]

The same collection of "instructions" warns that when one has been invited to a party, "beware of approaching the women. It does not go well with the place where that is done."[18]

Entertainment, especially music, was a regular feature of parties. The Egyptians used an astonishing variety of instruments: drums, tambourines, flutes, trumpets, and stringed instruments that were plucked rather than played with a bow. Singers, accompanying themselves on lute or harp, presented songs in praise of the host's generosity and of enjoying life.

Judging from the paintings in their tombs, the upper classes found a myriad of ways to entertain themselves

A FATHER'S ADVICE

*U*PPER-CLASS EGYPTIANS enjoyed compiling collections of wise sayings to provide guidance for leading an upright and successful life. This excerpt is taken from *The Instruction of the Vizier Ptah-hotep* and dates from around 2450 B.C. The vizier was the pharaoh's chief official. In this selection, Ptah-hotep advises his son on how to be a successful official.

The Instruction of the Vizier Ptah-hotep

Then he said to his son:

Let not your heart be puffed-up because of your knowledge; be not confident because you are a wise man. Take counsel with the ignorant as well as the wise. The full limits of skill cannot be attained, and there is no skilled man equipped to his full advantage. Good speech is more hidden than the emerald, but it may be found with maid-servants at the grindstones. . . .

If you are a leader commanding the affairs of the multitude, seek out for yourself every beneficial deed, until it may be that your own affairs are without wrong. Justice is great, and its appropriateness is lasting; it has been disturbed since the time of him who made it, whereas there is punishment for him who passes over its laws. It is the right path before him who knows nothing. Wrongdoing has never brought its undertaking into port. It may be that it is fraud that gains riches, but the strength of justice is that it lasts. . . .

If you are a man of intimacy, whom one great man sends to another, be thoroughly reliable when he sends you. Carry out the errand for him as he has spoken. Do not be reserved about what is said to you, and beware of any act of forgetfulness. Grasp hold of truth, and do not exceed it. Mere gratification is by no means to be repeated. Struggle against making words worse, thus making one great man hostile to another through vulgar speech. . . .

If you are a man of standing and found a household and produce a son who is pleasing to god, if he is correct and inclines toward your ways and listens to your instruction, while his manners in your house are fitting, and if he takes care of your property as it should be, seek out for him every useful action. He is your son, . . . you should not cut your heart off from him.

But a man's seed often creates enmity. If he goes astray and transgresses your plans and does not carry out your instruction, so that his manners in your household are wretched, and he rebels against all that you say, while his mouth runs on in the most wretched talk, quite apart from his experience, while he possesses nothing, you should cast him off: he is not your son at all. He was not really born to you. Thus you enslave him entirely according to his own speech. He is one whom god has condemned in the very womb. . . .

as well. Fowling in the stands of papyrus reeds that grew along the riverbanks was a favorite pastime. Using a reed skiff, the huntsman used a boomerang to bring down his prey, much to the delight of his family, who accompanied him. Once the waterfowl was downed, Egyptian families used trained retriever cats to swim out into the water and bring back the birds. The hunting of animals was only for the men. The hunters rode in chariots and used dogs to pursue antelope, gazelles, and other creatures who were shot with bows and arrows. Indoor activities included board games among other things. The earliest known board games in the world have been found in Egyptian

A Hunting Scene. A favorite pastime of the Egyptian upper classes was hunting waterfowl in the stands of papyrus reeds that grew along the riverbanks. Shown here is a hunting scene from the eighteenth-dynasty tomb of Nebamun in Thebes. Nebamun, a nobleman, is seen standing in his boat using his throwstick to hunt birds. He holds three in his right hand while a cat retrieves two in its claws and holds the wings of another in its teeth. Also in the picture are Nebamun's wife and daughter, who are gathering lotuses.

© Werner Forman/Art Resource, NY

tombs. Many are made of wood decorated with ivory or ebony. The games played on them involved moving pieces on the boards according to the roll of the dice.

On the Fringes of Civilization

Our story of the beginnings of Western civilization has been dominated so far by Mesopotamia and Egypt. But significant developments were also taking place on the fringes of these civilizations. Farming had spread into the Balkan peninsula of Europe by 6500 B.C., and by 4000 B.C. it was well established in southern France, central Europe, and the coastal regions of the Mediterranean. Although migrating farmers from the Near East may have brought some farming techniques into Europe, historians now believe that the Neolithic peoples of Europe domesticated animals and began to farm largely on their own.

One outstanding feature of late Neolithic Europe was the building of megalithic structures. *Megalith* is Greek for "large stone." Radiocarbon dating, a technique that allows scientists to determine the age of objects, shows that the first megalithic structures were built around 4000 B.C., more than a thousand years before the great pyramids were built in Egypt. Between 3200 and 1500 B.C., standing stones placed in circles or lined up in rows were erected throughout the British Isles and northwestern France. Other megalithic constructions have been found as far north as Scandinavia and as far south as the islands of Corsica, Sardinia, and Malta. Some archaeologists have demonstrated that the stone circles were used as observatories to detect not only such simple astronomical phenomena as the midwinter and midsummer sunrises but also such sophisticated observations as the major and minor standstills of the moon.

By far the most famous of these megalithic constructions is Stonehenge in England. Stonehenge consists of a series of concentric rings of standing stones. Its construction sometime between 2100 and 1900 B.C. was no small accomplishment. The eighty bluestones used at Stonehenge weigh 4 tons each and were transported to the site from their original source 135 miles away. Like other megalithic structures, Stonehenge indicates a remarkable awareness of astronomy on the part of its builders, as well as an impressive coordination of workers.

The Impact of the Indo-Europeans

For many historians, both the details of construction and the purpose of the megalithic structures of Europe remain a mystery. Also puzzling is the role of the Indo-European

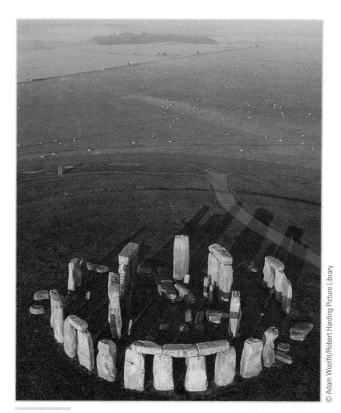

Stonehenge. The Bronze Age in northwestern Europe is known for its megaliths, large standing stones. Between 3200 and 1500 B.C., standing stones that were placed in circles or lined up in rows were erected throughout the British Isles and northwestern France. By far the most famous of these megalithic constructions is Stonehenge in England.

Stonehenge and Other Megalithic Sites in Europe

people. The term *Indo-European* refers to people who used a language derived from a single parent tongue. Indo-European languages include Greek, Latin, Persian, Sanskrit, and the Germanic languages (see Table 1.2). It has been suggested that the original Indo-European-speaking peoples were based somewhere in the steppe region north of the Black Sea or in southwestern Asia, in modern Iran or Afghanistan. Although there had been earlier migrations, around 2000 B.C. they began major nomadic movements into Europe (including present-day Italy and Greece), India, and the Near East. The Indo-Europeans who moved into Asia Minor and Anatolia (modern Turkey) coalesced with the native peoples to form the first Hittite kingdom, known as the Old Kingdom (c. 1700–1400 B.C.), with its capital at Hattusas (Bogazkoy in modern Turkey).

The Hittite Empire The Hittites began to spread outward around 1600 B.C., but it was not until around two hundred years later that a new line of kings created the Hittite

TABLE 1.2 **Some Indo-European Languages**

Subfamily	Languages
Indo-Iranian	*Sanskrit*, Persian
Balto-Slavic	Russian, Serbo-Croatian, Czech, Polish, Lithuanian
Hellenic	Greek
Italic	*Latin*, Romance languages (French, Italian, Spanish, Portuguese, Romanian)
Celtic	Irish, Gaelic
Germanic	Swedish, Danish, Norwegian, German, Dutch, English

Note: Languages in italic type are no longer spoken.

New Kingdom or Hittite Empire. Especially notable was Suppiluliumas I (c. 1370–1330 B.C.), one of the strongest rulers of the era, who established Hittite control from western Turkey to northern Syria. He destroyed the power of the Mitanni kingdom, which had been established in the sixteenth century B.C. by a people known as the Hurrians from the mountainous northern border of Mesopotamia. Suppiluliumas formed an alliance with the Egyptians and then conquered Syria. The Hittites were the first of the Indo-European peoples to make use of iron, enabling them to construct weapons that were stronger and cheaper to make because of the widespread availability of iron ore.

TIMELINE

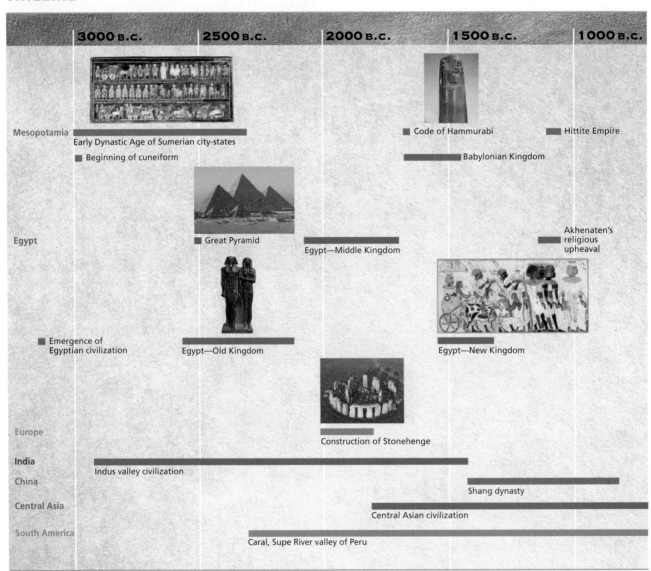

	3000 B.C.	2500 B.C.	2000 B.C.	1500 B.C.	1000 B.C.

Mesopotamia
Early Dynastic Age of Sumerian city-states
Beginning of cuneiform
Code of Hammurabi
Hittite Empire
Babylonian Kingdom

Egypt
Great Pyramid
Egypt—Middle Kingdom
Akhenaten's religious upheaval
Emergence of Egyptian civilization
Egypt—Old Kingdom
Egypt—New Kingdom

Europe
Construction of Stonehenge

India
Indus valley civilization

China
Shang dynasty

Central Asia
Central Asian civilization

South America
Caral, Supe River valley of Peru

For the next hundred years, the Hittites were in conflict with Egypt until the Egyptian pharaoh Rameses II made a remarkable nonaggression treaty that stabilized relations between Egypt and the Hittites. The end of Hittite power came in part from internal problems but also as a result of attacks by the Sea Peoples from the west around 1200 B.C. and by a group of aggressive tribespeople known as the Gasga, who raided Hittite cities. By 1190 B.C., Hittite power had come to an end.

During its heyday, however, the Hittite Empire was one of the great powers in western Asia. The Hittite ruler, known as the "Great King," controlled the core areas of the kingdom but in western and southern Anatolia and Syria allowed local rulers to swear allegiance to him as his vassals. Constant squabbling over succession to the throne, however, tended to weaken the royal authority at times.

During its height, the Hittite Empire also demonstrated an interesting ability to assimilate other cultures into its own. In language, literature, art, law, and religion, the Hittites borrowed much from Mesopotamia as well as from the native peoples they had subdued. Their law code, for example, though less harsh, reflected the influence of Mesopotamia. Hittite religion combined Indo-European deities and Mesopotamian gods, such as An and Ishtar. Recent scholarship has stressed the important role of the Hittites in transmitting Mesopotamian culture, as they transformed it, to later Western civilization in the Mediterranean area, especially to the Mycenaean Greeks (see Chapter 3).

CONCLUSION

$\mathcal{A}$LTHOUGH EARLY CIVILIZATIONS emerged in different parts of the world, the foundations of Western civilization were laid by the Mesopotamians and the Egyptians. They developed cities and struggled with the problems of organized states. They developed writing to keep records and created literature. They constructed monumental architecture to please their gods, symbolize their power, and preserve their culture. They developed new political, military, social, and religious structures to deal with the basic problems of human existence and organization. These first literate civilizations left detailed records that allow us to view how they grappled with three of the fundamental problems that humans have pondered: the nature of human relationships, the nature of the universe, and the role of divine forces in that cosmos. Although later peoples in Western civilization would provide different answers from those of the Mesopotamians and Egyptians, it was they who first posed the questions, gave answers, and wrote them down. Human memory begins with these two civilizations.

By the middle of the second millennium B.C., much of the creative impulse of the Mesopotamian and Egyptian civilizations was beginning to wane. The invasion of the Sea Peoples around 1200 B.C. ushered in a whole new pattern of petty states and new kingdoms that would lead to the largest empires the ancient Near East had seen.

NOTES

1. Jean-Marie Chauvet et al., *Dawn of Art: The Chauvet Cave* (New York, 1996), pp. 49–50.
2. Quoted in Amélie Kuhrt, *The Ancient Near East, c. 3000–330 B.C.* (London, 1995), vol. 1, p. 68.
3. Quoted in Marc van de Mieroop, *A History of the Ancient Near East, ca. 3000–323 B.C.* (Oxford, 2004), p. 69.
4. Quoted in ibid., p. 106.
5. Quoted in Thorkild Jacobsen, "Mesopotamia," in Henri Frankfort et al., *Before Philosophy* (Baltimore, 1949), p. 139.
6. Quoted in Thorkild Jacobsen, *The Treasures of Darkness: A History of Mesopotamian Religion* (New Haven, Conn., 1976), p. 97.
7. *The Epic of Gilgamesh*, trans. N. K. Sandars (London, 1972), p. 62.
8. James B. Pritchard, *Ancient Near Eastern Texts*, 3d ed. (Princeton, N.J., 1969), p. 372.
9. Quoted in Milton Covensky, *The Ancient Near Eastern Tradition* (New York, 1966), p. 51.
10. Pritchard, *Ancient Near Eastern Texts*, p. 445.
11. Quoted in B. G. Trigger, B. J. Kemp, D. O'Connor, and A. B. Lloyd, *Ancient Egypt: A Social History* (Cambridge, 1983), p. 74.
12. Pritchard, *Ancient Near Eastern Texts*, p. 34.
13. Ibid., p. 36.
14. Quoted in Rose-Marie Hagen and Rainer Hagen, *Egypt: People, Gods, Pharaohs* (Cologne, 2002), p. 148.
15. Pritchard, *Ancient Near Eastern Texts*, p. 413.
16. Quoted in John A. Wilson, *The Culture of Ancient Egypt* (Chicago, 1956), p. 264.
17. Pritchard, *Ancient Near Eastern Texts*, p. 412.
18. Ibid., p. 413.

SUGGESTIONS FOR FURTHER READING

For a beautifully illustrated introduction to the ancient world, see **Past Worlds: The Times Atlas of Archaeology** (Maplewood, N.J., 1988), written by an international group of scholars. A detailed history of the ancient world with chapters written by different specialists is available in the twelve volumes of **The Cambridge Ancient History,** now in its third edition. A less detailed but sound survey can be found in **L. De Blois and R. J. van der Spek, *An Introduction to the Ancient World,*** trans. S. Mellor (London, 1997). The following works are of considerable value in examining the prehistory of humankind: **M. N. Cohen, *The Food Crisis in Prehistory: Overpopulation and the Origins of Agriculture*** (New Haven, Conn., 1977); **R. Leakey, *The Making of Mankind*** (London, 1981); **R. J. Wenke, *Patterns in Prehistory: Humankind's First Three Million Years,*** 4th ed. (New York, 1999); **P. Mellars and C. Stringer, *The Human Revolution*** (Edinburgh, 1989); and **D. O. Henry, *From Foraging to Agriculture*** (Philadelphia, 1989).

For a study of the role of women in early human society, see **E. Barber,** ***Women's Work: The First 20,000 Years*** (New York, 1994).

Excellent reference tools on the ancient Near East can be found in **P. Bienkowski and A. Milward, eds.,** ***Dictionary of the Ancient Near East*** (Philadelphia, 2000), and **G. Leick,** ***Who's Who in the Ancient Near East*** (London, 1999). General surveys of Mesopotamia and Egypt include **A. B. Knapp,** ***The History and Culture of Ancient Western Asia and Egypt*** (Chicago, 1987); **W. von Soden,** ***The Ancient Orient: An Introduction to the Study of the Ancient Near East*** (Grand Rapids, Mich., 1994); and **H. J. Nissen,** ***The Early History of the Ancient Near East, 9000–2000 B.C.*** (Chicago, 1988). For a detailed survey, see **A. Kuhrt,** ***The Ancient Near East, c. 3000–330 B.C.,*** 2 vols. (London, 1995). A brief recent survey can be found in **M. van de Mieroop,** ***A History of the Ancient Near East, ca. 3000–323 B.C.*** (Oxford, 2004). **H. W. F. Saggs,** ***Babylonians*** (Norman, Okla., 1995), and **G. Leick,** ***The Babylonians*** (London, 2003), provide an overview of the peoples of ancient Mesopotamia. On the economic and social history of the ancient Near East, see **D. C. Snell,** ***Life in the Ancient Near East*** (New Haven, Conn., 1997).

General works on ancient Mesopotamia include **J. N. Postgate,** ***Early Mesopotamia: Society and Economy at the Dawn of History*** (London, 1992), and **A. L. Oppenheim,** ***Ancient Mesopotamia,*** 2d ed. (Chicago, 1977). A beautifully illustrated survey can be found in **M. Roaf,** ***Cultural Atlas of Mesopotamia and the Ancient Near East*** (New York, 1996). The world of the Sumerians has been well described in **S. N. Kramer,** ***The Sumerians*** (Chicago, 1963) and ***History Begins at Sumer*** (New York, 1959). See also the summary of the historical and archaeological evidence by **H. Crawford,** ***Sumer and the Sumerians*** (Cambridge, 1991). The fundamental work on the spiritual perspective of ancient Mesopotamia is **T. Jacobsen,** ***The Treasures of Darkness: A History of Mesopotamian Religion*** (New Haven, Conn., 1976). For a reference work on daily life, see **S. Bertman,** ***Handbook to Life in Ancient Mesopotamia*** (New York, 2003).

For a good introduction to ancient Egypt, see the beautifully illustrated works by **M. Hayes,** ***The Egyptians*** (New York, 1997), and **D. P. Silverman, ed.,** ***Ancient Egypt*** (New York, 1997). Other general surveys include **I. Shaw, ed.,** ***The Oxford History of Ancient Egypt*** (New York, 2000); **N. Grant,** ***The Egyptians*** (New York, 1996); and **N. Grimal,** ***A History of Ancient Egypt,*** trans. I. Shaw (Oxford, 1992). On Akhenaten and his religious changes, see **D. Redford,** ***Akhenaten: The Heretic King*** (Princeton, N.J., 1984). Egyptian religion is covered in **S. Quirke,** ***Ancient Egyptian Religion*** (London, 1992), and **E. Hornung,** ***Conceptions of God in Ancient Egypt: The One and the Many*** (Ithaca, N.Y., 1982). On Egyptian culture in general, see **J. A. Wilson,** ***The Culture of Ancient Egypt*** (Chicago, 1956). An important study on women is **G. Robins,** ***Women in Ancient Egypt*** (Cambridge, Mass., 1993). Daily life can be examined in **E. Strouhal,** ***Life of the Ancient Egyptians*** (Norman, Okla., 1992).

On the Sea Peoples, see the standard work by **N. Sandars,** ***The Sea Peoples: Warriors of the Ancient Mediterranean*** (London, 1978). Surveys on the Hittites can be found in **O. R. Gurney,** ***The Hittites,*** rev. ed. (Harmondsworth, England, 1990), and **T. Bryce,** ***The Kingdom of the Hittites*** (Oxford, 1998). See also **T. Bryce,** ***Life and Society in the Hittite World*** (Oxford, 2002).

History Now™

Enter *HistoryNow* using the access card that is available for *Western Civilization*. *HistoryNow* will assist you in understanding the content in this chapter with lesson plans generated for your needs. In addition, you can read the following documents, and many more, online:

Enuma Elish

Herodotus, History, Book 2, Chapters 124–127

INFOTRAC SEARCH TERMS

 For additional reading, go to InfoTrac College Edition, your online research library at http://infotrac.thomsonlearning.com

Subject Guide Search	Key Term Search
antiquities	Mesopotamia
archaeology	
Egypt history	

WESTERN CIVILIZATION RESOURCES

Visit the *Western Civilization* Companion Web site for resources specific to this book:

http://history.wadsworth.com/spielvogel06/

For a variety of tools to help you succeed in this course, visit the Western Civilization Resource Center at

http://history.wadsworth.com/western/

Included are quizzes; images; documents; interactive simulations; maps and timelines; movie explorations; and a wealth of other sources.

THE ANCIENT NEAR EAST: PEOPLES AND EMPIRES

CHAPTER OUTLINE AND FOCUS QUESTIONS

The Hebrews: "The Children of Israel"

● In what ways was the Jewish faith unique in the ancient Near East, and how did it evolve over time?

The Neighbors of the Israelites

● Who were the neighbors of the Israelites, and what was their significance?

The Assyrian Empire

● What methods and institutions did the Assyrians use to amass and maintain their empire?

The Neo-Babylonian Empire

● What was the significance of the Neo-Babylonian Empire?

The Persian Empire

● What methods and institutions did the Persians use to amass and maintain their empire, and how did these differ from those of the Assyrians?

CRITICAL THINKING

● What is the relationship between the political history of the Israelites and the evolution of their religious beliefs?

A medieval Italian manuscript version of the judgment of Solomon

© Alinari/Regione Umbria/Art Resource, NY

AROUND 970 B.C., Solomon came to the throne of Israel, a small state in western Asia. He was lacking in military prowess but excelled in many other ways. Through trade and a series of foreign alliances, he created a strong, flourishing state. But he was especially famed for another of his qualities. When confronted with two women who each claimed that the child before them was her natural child, Solomon ordered his servant to cut the child in half and give half to each woman. The first woman objected: "Please, my lord, give her the living baby! Don't kill him!" The second woman replied, "Neither I nor you shall have him. Cut him in two!" Then Solomon rendered his judgment: "Give the living baby to the first woman. Do not kill him; she is his mother." According to the biblical account, "when all Israel heard the verdict the king had given, they held the king in awe, because they saw that he had wisdom from God to administer justice." After Solomon's death, Israel's power began to crumble. But how had such a small nation been able to survive for as long as it did in a Near East dominated by mighty empires?

The destruction of the Hittite kingdom and the weakening of Egypt around 1200 B.C. temporarily left a power vacuum in the Near East, allowing a patchwork of petty kingdoms and city-states to emerge, especially in Syria and Palestine. One of these small states, the nation of Israel, has played a role in Western civilization completely disproportionate to its size. The Israelites were a minor factor in the politics of the ancient Near East, but their spiritual heritage—the Judeo-Christian values—is one of the basic pillars of Western civilization.

The small states did not last, however. Ever since the first city-states had arisen in the Near East around 3000 B.C., there had been a movement toward the creation of larger territorial states with more sophisticated systems of control. This process reached a high point in the first millennium B.C. with the appearance of empires that embraced the entire Near East. Between 1000 and 500 B.C., the Assyrians, Chaldeans, and Persians all created empires that encompassed most or all of the ancient Near East. Each had impressive and grandi-ose capital cities that emphasized the power and wealth of its rulers. Each brought peace and order for a period of time by employing new administrative techniques. Each eventually fell to other conquerors. In the long run, these large empires had less impact on Western civilization than the Hebrew people of Israel did. In human history, the power of ideas is often more significant than the power of empires.

The Hebrews: "The Children of Israel"

The Hebrews were a Semitic-speaking people who had a tradition concerning their origins and history that was eventually written down as part of the Hebrew Bible, known to Christians as the Old Testament. Describing themselves originally as nomads organized into clans, the Hebrews' tradition states that they were descendants of the patriarch Abraham, who had migrated from Mesopotamia to the land of Palestine, where they became identified as the "Children of Israel." Again according to tradition, a drought in Palestine caused many Hebrews to migrate to Egypt, where they lived peacefully until they were enslaved by pharaohs who used them as laborers on building projects. They remained in bondage until Moses led his people out of Egypt in the well-known Exodus, which some historians have estimated would have occurred in the first half of the thirteenth century B.C. According to the biblical account, the Hebrews then wandered for many years in the desert until they entered Palestine. Organized into twelve tribes, they became embroiled in conflict with the Philistines, a people who had settled in the coastal area of Palestine but were beginning to move into the inland areas.

Many scholars today doubt that the early books of the Hebrew Bible reflect the true history of the early Israelites. They argue that the early books of the Bible, written centuries after the events described, preserve only what the Israelites came to believe about themselves and that recent archaeological evidence often contradicts the details of the biblical account. Some of these scholars have even argued that the Israelites were not nomadic invaders but indigenous peoples in the Palestinian hill country. What is generally agreed, however, is that between 1200 and 1000 B.C., the Israelites emerged as a distinct group of people, possibly organized into tribes or a league of tribes, who established a united kingdom known as Israel.

The United Kingdom

The first king of the Israelites was Saul (c. 1020–1000 B.C.), who initially achieved some success in the ongoing struggle with the Philistines. But after his death in a disastrous battle with this enemy, a brief period of anarchy ensued until one of Saul's lieutenants, David (c. 1000–970 B.C.), reunited the Israelites, defeated the Philistines, and established control over all of Palestine (see Map 2.1). According to the biblical account, some of his conquests led to harsh treatment for the conquered people: "David also defeated the Moabites. He made them lie down on the ground and measured them off with a length of cord. Every two lengths of them were put to death, and the third length was allowed to live. So the Moabites became subject to David and brought tribute."[1] Among David's conquests was the city of Jerusalem, which he made the capital of a united kingdom. David centralized Israel's political organization and accelerated the integration of the Israelites into a settled community based on farming and urban life.

Solomon David's son Solomon (c. 970–930 B.C.) did even more to strengthen royal power. He expanded the political and military establishments and was especially active in extending the trading activities of the Israelites. Solomon is best known for his building projects, of which the most famous was the Temple in Jerusalem. The Israelites viewed the Temple as the symbolic center of their religion and hence of the kingdom of Israel itself. The Temple now housed the Ark of the Covenant, a holy chest containing the sacred relics of the Hebrew religion and, symbolically, the throne of the invisible God of Israel. Under Solomon, ancient Israel was at the height of its power, but his efforts to extend royal power throughout his kingdom led to dissatisfaction among some of his subjects.

The Divided Kingdom

After Solomon's death, tensions between the northern and southern tribes in Israel led to the establishment of two separate kingdoms—the kingdom of Israel, composed of the ten northern tribes, with its capital eventually at Samaria, and the southern kingdom of Judah, consisting of two tribes, with its capital at Jerusalem. The northern kingdom of Israel, especially under King Ahab (869–850 B.C.), joined with some small Syrian states to temporarily stop the onslaught of the Assyrians, who had consolidated their

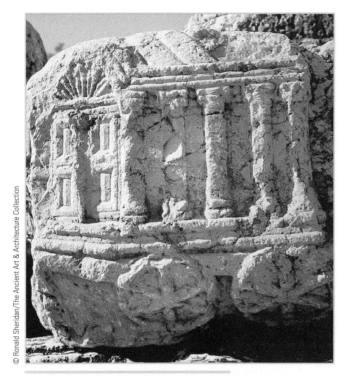

A Representation of the Ark of the Covenant. The most famous project carried out under King Solomon was the building of the Temple of Jerusalem, in which the Israelites placed the Ark of the Covenant, a holy chest containing the sacred relics of the Hebrew faith. The Ark was also considered the throne of the invisible God on earth. This representation of the Ark, believed to be one of the earliest, is from a second-century A.D. synagogue at Capernaum.

The King of Israel Pays Tribute to the King of Assyria. By the end of the ninth century B.C., the kingdom of Israel had been forced to pay tribute to the Assyrian Empire. The Assyrians overran the kingdom in 722 or 721 B.C. and destroyed the capital city of Samaria. In this scene from a black obelisk, Jehu, king of Israel, is shown paying tribute to the king of Assyria.

MAP 2.1 Palestine in the first Millennium B.C. United under Saul, David, and Solomon, greater Israel split into two states—Israel and Judah—after the death of Solomon. With power divided, the Israelites could not resist invasions that dispersed many Jews from Palestine. Some, such as the "ten lost tribes," never returned. Others were sent to Babylon but were later allowed to return under the rule of the Persians. ❓ Why was Israel more vulnerable to the Assyrian Empire than Judah was? 🌐 **View an animated version of this map or related maps at** http://history.wadsworth.com/spielvogel06/

kingdom to the northeast (see "The Assyrian Empire" later in this chapter). But the power of Israel declined after Ahab, and by the end of the ninth century, the kingdom of Israel was forced to pay tribute to Assyria. In the next century, Israel itself was destroyed. The Assyrians overran the kingdom, destroyed the capital of Samaria in 722 or 721 B.C., and deported many Israelites to other parts of the Assyrian Empire. These dispersed Israelites (the "ten lost tribes") merged with neighboring peoples and gradually lost their identity.

The southern kingdom of Judah was also forced to pay tribute to Assyria but managed to survive as an independent state as Assyrian power declined. A new enemy, however, appeared on the horizon. The Chaldeans first demolished Assyria and then, under King Nebuchadnezzar II, conquered Judah and completely destroyed Jerusalem in 586 B.C. Many upper-class people from Judah were

Saul—first king	c. 1020–1000 B.C.
King David	c. 1000–970 B.C.
King Solomon	c. 970–930 B.C.
Northern kingdom of Israel destroyed by Assyria	722 or 721 B.C.
Southern Kingdom of Judah falls to Chaldeans; destruction of Jerusalem	586 B.C.
Return of exiles to Jerusalem	538 B.C.

sent to Babylonia in exile, the memory of which is still evoked in the stirring words of Psalm 137:

> By the rivers of Babylon, we sat and wept when we remembered Zion. . . .
> How can we sing the songs of the Lord while in a foreign land?
> If I forgot you, O Jerusalem, may my right hand forget its skill.
> May my tongue cling to the roof of my mouth if I do not remember you, if I do not consider Jerusalem my highest joy.[2]

But the Babylonian captivity of the people of Judah did not last. Upon the destruction of the Chaldean kingdom by a new set of conquerors, the Persians, the people of Judah were allowed to return to Jerusalem and rebuild their city and the Temple, although Judah remained under Persian control until the conquests of Alexander the Great in the fourth century B.C. The people of Judah survived, eventually becoming known as the Jews and giving their name to Judaism, the religion of Yahweh, the Jewish God.

The Spiritual Dimensions of Israel

The spiritual perspective of the Israelites evolved over time. Early Israelites probably worshiped many gods, including nature spirits dwelling in trees and rocks. For some Israelites, Yahweh was the chief god of Israel, but many, including kings of Israel and Judah, worshiped other gods as well. It was among the Babylonian exiles in the sixth century B.C. that Yahweh—the God of Israel—came to be seen as the *only* God. After the return of these exiles to Judah, their point of view eventually became dominant, and pure **monotheism,** or the belief that there is only one God for all peoples, came to be the major tenet of Judaism.

"I Am the Lord Your God": Ruler of the World   According to the Jewish conception, there is but one God, whom the Jews called Yahweh. God is the creator of the world and everything in it. Indeed, Yahweh means "he causes to be." To the Jews, the gods of all other peoples were idols. The Jewish God ruled the world; he was subject to nothing. All peoples were his servants, whether they knew it or not. This God was also transcendent. He had created nature but was not in nature. The stars, moon, rivers, wind, and other natural phe-

nomena were not divinities or suffused with divinity, as other peoples of the ancient Near East believed, but were God's handiwork. All of God's creations could be admired for their awesome beauty but not worshiped as gods.

This omnipotent creator of the universe was not removed from the life he had created, however, but was a just and good God who expected goodness from his people. If they did not obey his will, they would be punished. But he was also a God of mercy and love: "The Lord is gracious and compassionate, slow to anger and rich in love. The Lord is good to all; he has compassion on all he has made."[3] Despite the powerful dimensions of God as creator and sustainer of the universe, the Jewish message also emphasized that each person could have a personal relationship with this powerful being. As the psalmist sang: "My help comes from the Lord, the Maker of heaven and earth. He will not let your foot slip—he who watches over you will not slumber."[4]

The chief source of information about Israel's spiritual conceptions is the Hebrew Bible, which is the Old Testament of the Christian Bible. Its purpose was to teach the essential beliefs about the God of Israel after the Babylonian captivity of the Jews and their dispersal. During and after the Babylonian exile, the Jews recorded many of their traditions in order to preserve their identity. These writings became the core of the Hebrew Bible. The first five books (known as the **Pentateuch**), which cover the time from the beginning of the world until the Israelites' arrival in Palestine, constitute the **Torah,** or law code, governing the lives of worshipers and their relations to one another and to the non-Jewish population. The Hebrew Bible focuses on one basic theme: the necessity for the Jews to obey their God.

"You Only Have I Chosen": Covenant and Law   Three aspects of the Jewish religious tradition had special significance: the covenant, the law, and the prophets. The Israelites believed that during the Exodus from Egypt, when Moses supposedly led his people out of bondage into a land of plenty promised to them by Yahweh, a special event occurred that determined the Jewish experience for all time. According to tradition, God entered into a covenant or contract with the tribes of Israel, who believed that Yahweh had spoken to them through Moses (see the box above). The Israelites promised to obey Yahweh and follow his law. In return, Yahweh promised to take special care of his people, "a peculiar treasure unto me above all people."

This covenant between Yahweh and his chosen people could be fulfilled, however, only by obedience to the law of God. Law became a crucial element of the Jewish world and had a number of different dimensions. In some instances, it set forth specific requirements, such as payments for offenses. Most important, since the major characteristic of God was his goodness, ethical concerns stood at the center of the law. Sometimes these took the form of specific standards of moral behavior: "You shall not murder. You shall not commit adultery. You shall not steal."[5] But these concerns were also expressed in decrees that regulated the economic, social, and political life of the community, for God's

THE COVENANT AND THE LAW: THE BOOK OF EXODUS

*A*CCORDING TO the biblical account, it was during the Exodus from Egypt that the Israelites supposedly made their covenant with Yahweh. They agreed to obey their God and follow his law. In return, Yahweh promised to take special care of his chosen people. These selections from the Book of Exodus describe the making of the covenant and God's commandments to the Israelites.

Exodus 19:1–8

In the third month after the Israelites left Egypt—on the very day—they came to the Desert of Sinai. After they set out from Rephidim, they entered the Desert of Sinai, and Israel camped there in the desert in front of the mountain. Then Moses went up to God, and the Lord called to him from the mountain, and said, "This is what you are to say to the house of Jacob and what you are to tell the people of Israel: 'You yourselves have seen what I did to Egypt, and how I carried you on eagles' wings and brought you to myself. Now if you obey me fully and keep my covenant, then out of all nations you will be my treasured possession. Although the whole earth is mine, you will be for me a kingdom of priests and a holy nation.' These are the words you are to speak to the Israelites." So Moses went back and summoned the elders of the people and set before them all the words the Lord had commanded him to speak. The people all responded together, "We will do everything the Lord has said." So Moses brought their answer back to the Lord.

Exodus 20:1–17

And God spoke all these words, "I am the Lord your God, who brought you out of Egypt, out of the land of slavery. You shall have no other gods before me. You shall not make for yourself an idol in the form of anything in heaven above or on the earth beneath or in the waters below. You shall not bow down to them or worship them; for I, the Lord your God, am a jealous God, punishing the children for the sin of the fathers to the third and fourth generation of those who hate me, but showing love to a thousand generations of those who love me and keep my commandments. You shall not misuse the name of the Lord your God, for the Lord will not hold anyone guiltless who misuses his name. Remember the Sabbath day by keeping it holy. Six days you shall labor and do all your work, but the seventh day is a Sabbath to the Lord your God. On it you shall not do any work, neither you, nor your son or daughter, nor your manservant or maidservant, nor your animals, nor the alien within your gates. For in six days the Lord made the heavens and the earth, the sea, and all that is in them, but he rested on the seventh day. Therefore the Lord blessed the Sabbath day and made it holy. Honor your father and your mother, so that you may live long in the land the Lord your God is giving you. You shall not murder. You shall not commit adultery. You shall not steal. You shall not give false testimony against your neighbor. You shall not covet your neighbor's house. You shall not covet your neighbor's wife, or his manservant or maidservant, his ox or donkey, or anything that belongs to your neighbor."

laws of morality applied to all areas of life. These laws made no class distinctions and emphasized the protection of the poor, widows, orphans, and slaves.

The Prophets The Israelites believed that certain religious leaders or holy men, called prophets, were sent by God to serve as his voice to his people. In the ninth century B.C., the prophets were particularly vociferous about the tendency of the Israelites to accept other gods, chiefly the fertility and earth gods of other peoples in Palestine. They warned of the terrible retribution that Yahweh would exact from the Israelites if they did not keep the covenant to remain faithful to him alone and just in their dealings with one another (see the box on p. 36).

The golden age of prophecy began in the mid-eighth century and continued during the time when the people of

Hebrew Law. Because of the supposed covenant between Yahweh and the Israelites, law became an important part of Jewish life. Seen here is a twelfth-century manuscript page of the *Mishneh Torah*, a fourteen-volume study of all of Jewish law by Moses Maimonides, the foremost Jewish philosopher of the Middle Ages.

THE HEBREW PROPHETS: MICAH, ISAIAH, AND AMOS

THE HEBREW PROPHETS warned the Israelites that they must obey God's commandments or face punishment for breaking their covenant with God. These selections from the prophets Micah, Isaiah, and Amos make clear that God would punish the Israelites for their sins. Even the Assyrians, as Isaiah indicated, would be used as God's instrument to punish them.

Micah 6:9–16

Listen! The Lord is calling to the city—and to fear your name is wisdom—"Heed the rod and the One who appointed it. Am I still to forget, O wicked house, your ill-gotten treasures . . . ? Shall I acquit a man with dishonest scales, with a bag of false weights? Her rich men are violent; her people are liars and their tongues speak deceitfully. Therefore, I have begun to destroy you, to ruin you because of your sins. You will eat but not be satisfied; your stomach will still be empty. You will store up but save nothing, because what you save I will give to the sword. You will plant but not harvest; you will press olives but not use the oil on yourselves, you will crush grapes but not drink the wine. . . . Therefore I will give you over to ruin and your people to derision; you will bear the scorn of the nations."

Isaiah 10:1–6

Woe to those who make unjust laws, to those who issue oppressive decrees, to deprive the poor of their rights and withhold justice from the oppressed of my people, making widows their prey and robbing the fatherless. What will you do on the day of reckoning, when disaster comes from afar? To whom will you run for help? Where will you leave your riches? Nothing will remain but to cringe among the captives or fall among the slain. Yet for all this, his anger is not turned away, his hand is still upraised. "Woe to the Assyrian, the rod of my anger, in whose hand is the club of my wrath! I send him against a godless nation, I dispatch him against a people who anger me, to seize loot and snatch plunder, and to trample them down like mud in the streets."

Amos 3:1–2

Hear this word the Lord has spoken against you, O people of Israel—against the whole family I brought up out of Egypt: "You only have I chosen of all the families of the earth; therefore, I will punish you for all your sins."

Israel and Judah were threatened by Assyrian and Chaldean conquerors. These "men of God" went through the land warning the Israelites that they had failed to keep God's commandments and would be punished for breaking the covenant: "I will punish you for all your iniquities." Amos prophesied the fall of the northern kingdom of Israel to Assyria; twenty years later, Isaiah said the kingdom of Judah too would fall.

Out of the words of the prophets came new concepts that enriched the Jewish tradition and ultimately Western civilization, including a notion of universalism and a yearning for social justice. Although the Jews' religious practices gave them a sense of separateness from other peoples, the prophets transcended this by embracing a concern for all humanity. All nations would someday come to the God of Israel: "All the earth shall worship you." A universal community of all people under God would someday be established by Israel's effort. This vision encompassed the elimination of war and the establishment of peace for all the nations of the world. In the words of the prophet Isaiah: "He will judge between the nations and will settle disputes for many people. They will beat their swords into plowshares and their spears into pruning hooks. Nation will not take up sword against nation, nor will they train for war anymore."[6]

The prophets also cried out against social injustice. They condemned the rich for causing the poor to suffer, denounced luxuries as worthless, and threatened Israel with prophecies of dire punishments for these sins. God's command was to live justly, share with one's neighbors, care for the poor and the unfortunate, and act with compassion. When God's command was not followed, the social fabric of the community was threatened. These proclamations by Israel's prophets became a source for Western ideals of social justice, even if they have never been perfectly realized.

Although the prophets ultimately developed a sense of universalism, the demands of the Jewish religion—the need to obey their God—encouraged a separation between the Jews and their non-Jewish neighbors. Unlike most other peoples of the Near East, Jews could not simply be amalgamated into a community by accepting the gods of their conquerors and their neighbors. To remain faithful to the demands of their God, they might even have to refuse loyalty to political leaders.

The Social Structure of the Hebrews

Originally, the Israelites had been organized along tribal lines, but a new social structure had evolved by the time of the monarchy as the Israelites settled in towns and villages. Although historians warn that the Israelites did not develop social classes in the modern sense of self-conscious groups opposed to one another, there were conspicuous "divisions of the population."

Social Patterns The "men of rank and influence" formed a special group of considerable importance in Hebrew society. This group included officials of the king, military officers, civil officials, and governors. Although simply servants to the kings, they held a privileged position in the society at large. The common people, sometimes called "people of the land," remained a body of free people having basic civil rights. Their livelihood came mostly from the land and from various crafts. These peasants and artisans sold their own produce and products directly to buyers in markets in their local town or village squares, thus eliminating intermediaries or traders. There was no real merchant class in ancient Israel. Commerce was carried on by foreigners, such as the Phoenicians. Not until the **Diaspora,** when Jews became scattered throughout the ancient world after their exile to Babylon, did they become merchants.

Family The family was the central social institution in Hebrew life and consisted of individuals connected by common blood and a common living place. A family living in one house could comprise husband and wife, married sons and their wives, and their children. The Hebrew family was **patriarchal.** The husband-father was master of his wife and possessed absolute authority over his children, including the power of life and death.

Marriage and Women Marriage was an important aspect of Hebrew family life. In ancient Israel, under the monarchy, polygamy was an accepted form of marriage, especially for kings and wealthier citizens. Hebrew law limited kings to eighteen wives and citizens to four. In practice, only kings could afford a large harem. When others had more than one wife, it was usually because they desired more children; the first wife, for example, might be unable to have children or have produced only daughters.

Many Hebrews, however, believed that monogamy was the preferred form of marriage. Wives were honored for their faithfulness and dedication to their husbands. The Book of Proverbs in the Hebrew Bible provides a picture of what Hebrews considered a perfect wife:

> *A wife of noble character who can find? She is worth far*
> *more than rubies.*
> *Her husband has full confidence in her and lacks nothing*
> *of value.*
> *She brings him good, not harm, all the days of her life.*
> *She selects wool and flax and works with eager hands.*
> *She is like the merchant ships, bringing her food from*
> *afar.*
> *She gets up while it is still dark; she provides food for her*
> *family and portions for her servant girls.*
> *She considers a field and buys it; out of her earnings she*
> *plants a vineyard.*
> *She sets about her work vigorously; her arms are strong*
> *for her tasks.*
> *She sees that her trading is profitable, and her lamp does*
> *not go out at night.*
> *In her hand she holds the distaff and grasps the spindle*
> *with her fingers.*
> *She opens her arms to the poor and extends her hands to*
> *the needy. . . .*

> *She makes linen garments and sells them, and supplies*
> *the merchants with sashes.*
> *She is clothed with strength and dignity; she can laugh at*
> *the days to come.*
> *She speaks with wisdom, and faithful instruction is on*
> *her tongue.*
> *She watches over the affairs of her household, and does*
> *not eat the bread of idleness.*
> *Her children arise and call her blessed; her husband also,*
> *and he praises her.*[7]

Women were greatly valued, but their work was obviously never done.

Although the Hebrew Bible, a male-edited work, reveals a society dominated by men, it also includes stories of women who played heroic roles in the early history of Israel. Deborah, for example, played a prominent role in the defeat of the Canaanites at Mount Tabor. After the same battle, Jael killed Sisera, the leader of the Canaanites. According to the Song of Deborah, "Most blessed of women be Jael, . . . most blessed of tent-dwelling women. . . . Her hand reached for the tent peg, her right hand for the workman's hammer. She struck Sisera, she crushed his head, she shattered and pierced his temple. At her feet he sank, he fell; there he lay."[8]

But these accounts are not the norm. In the Hebrew Bible, women are mostly dependent on men. It should not surprise us, then, to learn that a married woman was subject to her husband's authority. Unlike the Mesopotamians, the Hebrews did not develop the custom of a dowry from the bride's parents. They did, however, have a practice whereby the bridegroom's family paid a sum of money to the bride's family, not as a purchase price as such, but apparently as compensation to the family for the loss of their daughter. A married woman left her parents' home, lived with her husband's family, and became a member of their clan. Her children also belonged to the husband's clan.

Since boys and girls were married at a relatively young age, parents took the responsibility for matchmaking. Although marriages occurred between persons of different families and even with foreign women, it was customary to find marriage partners within one's own clan or extended family. Wives were expected to remain faithful to their husbands, an ideal that would later have an impact on Christian attitudes toward women.

The primary goal of marriage was to produce children. They were the "crown of man," and sons, in particular, were desired. Daughters would eventually leave the family house, but sons carried on the family line. Mothers were in charge of the early education of children, especially in regard to basic moral principles. As boys matured, their fathers took over responsibility for their education, which remained largely informal. This included religious instruction as well as general education for life. The rod was not spared as a matter of principle. Since trades were usually hereditary, fathers also provided their sons' occupational education. As one rabbi (a Jewish teacher) warned, "He who does not teach his son a useful trade is bringing him up to be a thief."[9] Additional education for boys came from priests, whose sacred mission was to instruct people in the Torah. An organized school system was not established until much later, possibly in the second century B.C. The only education girls received was from their mothers, who taught them the basic fundamentals of how to be good wives, mothers, and housekeepers.

The Neighbors of the Israelites

The Israelites were not the only people living in Palestine. The Philistines, who invaded from the sea, established five towns on the coastal plain of the region. They settled down as farmers and eventually came into conflict with the Israelites. The Phoenicians had resided in Palestine for some time but now found themselves with a new independence. A Semitic-speaking people, the Phoenicians resided along the Mediterranean coast on a narrow band of land 120 miles long. They had rebuilt their major cities, Byblos, Tyre, and Sidon, after destruction by the Sea Peoples. Their newfound political independence helped the Phoenicians expand the trade that was already the foundation of their prosperity. In fact, Byblos had been the principal distribution center for Egyptian papyrus outside Egypt (the Greek word for book, *biblos,* is derived from the name Byblos).

All three chief cities of Phoenicia were seaports, but they also served as distribution centers for the lands to the east in Mesopotamia. The Phoenicians themselves produced a number of goods for foreign markets, including purple dye, glass, wine, and lumber from the famous cedars of Lebanon. In addition, the Phoenicians improved their ships and became great international sea traders. They charted new routes, not only in the Mediterranean but also in the Atlantic Ocean, where they sailed south along the west coast of Africa. The Phoenicians established a number of colonies in the western Mediterranean, including settlements in southern Spain, Sicily, and Sardinia. Most of the Phoenician colonies were trading stations, not permanent settlements. A major exception was Carthage, the Phoenicians' most famous colony, located on the North African coast.

Culturally, the Phoenicians are best known as transmitters. Instead of using pictographs or signs to represent whole words and syllables as the Mesopotamians and Egyptians did, the Phoenicians simplified their writing by using twenty-two different signs to represent the sounds of their speech. These twenty-two characters or letters could be used to spell out all the words in the Phoenician language. Although the Phoenicians were not the only people to invent an alphabet, theirs would have special signifi-

Phoenician Plaque. The Phoenicians were a Semitic-speaking people dwelling in ancient Palestine who became the predominant sea traders of the ancient Near East. Ivory was one of the favorite materials of Phoenician artists of the ninth and eighth centuries B.C. This ivory plaque inlaid with glass stones shows a lioness attacking a slave boy.

cance because it was eventually passed on to the Greeks. From the Greek alphabet was derived the Roman alphabet that we still use today (see Table 2.1). The Phoenicians achieved much while independent, but they ultimately fell subject to the Assyrians, Chaldeans, and Persians.

The Assyrian Empire

Independent states in Palestine flourished in the power void that followed the destruction of the Hittite kingdom and the weakening of the Egyptian empire. But this state of affairs did not last; new empires soon came to dominate vast stretches of the ancient Near East. The first of these empires emerged in Assyria, an area whose location on the upper Tigris River brought it into both cultural and political contact with southern Mesopotamia.

Although part of Mesopotamia, Assyria, with its hills and adequate, if not ample, rainfall, had a different terrain and climate. The Assyrians were a Semitic-speaking people; for much of their early history, they were vassals of foreign rulers, including Sargon of Akkad, the Third Dynasty of Ur, and the Babylonian King Hammurabi. From about

Phoenician Colonies and Trade Routes, c. 800 B.C.

TABLE 2.1 A Comparison of the Phoenician, Greek, and Latin Alphabets (Letters *A–F*)

Phoenician			Greek			Latin	
Phoenician	*Phoenician Name*	*Modern Symbol*	*Early Greek*	*Classical Greek*	*Greek Name*	*Early Latin*	*Classical Latin*
⟨	'aleph	'	△	A	alpha	A	A
◁	beth	b	৪	B	beta		B
⟨	gimel	g	1	Γ	gamma		C
◁	daleth	d	△	△	delta	◁	D
⇥	he	h	ⅎ	E	epsilon	ⅎ	E
Y	waw	w	ⅎ		digamma	ⅎ	F

Source: Andrew Robinson, *The Story of Writing* (London: Thames & Hudson, 1995), p. 170.

1650 to 1360 B.C., the Hurrian kingdom of Mitanni dominated Assyria (see Chapter 1). The Assyrians finally became independent when the Hittites destroyed Mitanni; we read in Hittite documents from about 1360 B.C. of the emergence of the "king of the land of Assyria." For the next 250 years, the Assyrians experienced alternating expansion and decline until the reassertion of Assyrian power under Tiglath-Pileser I (1114–1076 B.C.), a brutal conqueror whose policy of deliberate terror set a pattern for later Assyrian rulers.

The Assyrian Empire created by Tiglath-Pileser was unable to maintain its strength after his death. A new phase of expansion did not begin until the ninth century with the conquests of Shalmaneser III (858–824 B.C.), who marched westward into Palestine and southward into Babylonia. Yet

Assyrian power did not go unchallenged. The almost continuous warfare on these new frontiers did not end until the reigns of Tiglath-Pileser III (744–727 B.C.) and Sargon II (721–705 B.C.), who waged military campaigns almost every year, reestablishing control over Mesopotamia and completely subduing Palestine. The conquered territories were then incorporated into the empire as provinces. By 700 B.C., the Assyrian Empire had reached the height of its power and included Mesopotamia, sections of Asia Minor, Syria, Palestine, and Egypt down to Thebes (see Map 2.2).

Ashurbanipal (669–626 B.C.) was one of the strongest Assyrian rulers, but it was already becoming apparent during his reign that the Assyrian Empire was greatly overextended. Internal strife intensified as powerful Assyrian nobles gained control of vast territories and waged their

MAP 2.2 **The Assyrian and Neo-Babylonian Empires.** The Assyrian Empire expanded in large part due to its brutal military methods. It maintained its rule through use of a common language and religion, along with extremely violent suppression of internal revolts. It was overthrown by Chaldeans in Babylonia, leading to the Neo-Babylonian Empire epitomized by Nebuchadnezzar. **?** Why was control of Babylonia crucial to both empires? 🖱 **View an animated version of this map or related maps at** http://history.wadsworth.com/spielvogel06/

Ashurbanipal Destroys an Elamite City. Assyria was the first great empire to gain control over the ancient Near East in the first millennium B.C. The Assyrians had a highly efficient and well-organized military machine, capable of fighting under a variety of conditions. This relief depicts the army of King Ashurbanipal sacking an Elamite city in 647 B.C. Shown at the top are Assyrian soldiers destroying the city walls while below soldiers carry off the spoils of war.

© Erich Lessing/Art Resource, NY

own private military campaigns. Moreover, subject peoples greatly resented Assyrian rule. The hatred that the Babylonians felt after the brutal Assyrian sack of the city of Babylon in 689 B.C., for example, led them to rebel during the reign of Ashurbanipal. Soon after Ashurbanipal's death, the Assyrian Empire began to disintegrate. The capital city of Nineveh fell to a coalition of Chaldeans and Medes (see "The Neo-Babylonian Empire" later in this chapter) in 612 B.C., and in 605 B.C., the Neo-Babylonian Empire took over the rest of the empire.

Organization of the Empire

At its height, the Assyrian Empire was ruled by kings whose power was considered absolute. Under their leadership, the empire became well organized. By eliminating governorships held by nobles on a hereditary basis and instituting a new hierarchy of local officials directly responsible to the king, the Assyrian kings gained greater control over the resources of the empire. The Assyrians also developed an efficient system of communication to administer their empire more effectively. A network of posting stages was established that used relays of horses (mules or donkeys in mountainous terrain) to carry messages throughout the empire. The system was so effective that a provincial governor anywhere in the empire (except Egypt) could send a question and receive an answer from the king in his palace within a week.

The Assyrian Military Machine

The ability of the Assyrians to conquer and maintain an empire derived from a combination of factors. Through years of practice, the Assyrians developed effective military leaders and fighters. They were able to enlist and deploy troops numbering in the hundreds of thousands, although most campaigns were not on such a large scale. In 845 B.C., Shalmaneser III led an army of 120,000 men across the Euphrates on a campaign. Size alone was not decisive, however. The Assyrian army was extremely well organized and disciplined. It included a standing army of infantry as its core, accompanied by cavalry and horse-drawn war chariots that were used as mobile platforms for shooting arrows. Moreover, the Assyrians had the advantage of having the first large armies equipped with iron weapons. The Hittites (see Chapter 1) had been the first to develop iron metallurgy, but iron came to be used extensively only after new methods for hardening it came into common use after 1000 B.C.

Another factor in the army's success was its ability to use different kinds of military tactics (see the box on p. 41). The Assyrian army was capable of waging guerrilla warfare in the mountains and set battles on open ground as well as laying siege to cities. The Assyrians were especially renowned for their siege warfare. They would hammer a city's walls with heavy, wheeled siege towers and armored battering rams while sappers dug tunnels to undermine the walls' foundations and cause them to collapse. The besieging Assyrian armies learned to cut off supplies so effectively that if a city did not fall to them, the inhabitants could be starved into submission.

A final factor in the effectiveness of the Assyrian military machine was its ability to create a climate of terror as an instrument of warfare. The Assyrians became famous for their terror tactics, although some historians believe their policies were no worse than those of other Near Eastern conquerors. As a matter of regular policy, the Assyrians laid waste the land in which they were fighting, smashing dams, looting and destroying towns, setting crops on fire, and cutting down trees, particularly fruit trees. The Assyrians were especially known for committing atrocities on their captives. King Ashurnasirpal recorded this account of his treatment of prisoners:

> 3000 of their combat troops I felled with weapons.... Many of the captives taken from them I burned in a fire. Many I took

THE ASSYRIAN MILITARY MACHINE

HE ASSYRIANS won a reputation for having a mighty military machine. They were able to use a variety of military tactics and were successful whether they were employing guerrilla warfare, fighting set battles, or laying siege to cities. In these three selections, Assyrian kings describe their military conquests.

King Sennacherib (704–681 B.C.) Describes a Battle with the Elamites in 691

At the command of the god Ashur, the great Lord, I rushed upon the enemy like the approach of a hurricane. . . . I put them to rout and turned them back. I transfixed the troops of the enemy with javelins and arrows. . . . I cut their throats like sheep. . . . My prancing steeds, trained to harness, plunged into their welling blood as into a river; the wheels of my battle chariot were bespattered with blood and filth. I filled the plain with the corpses of their warriors like herbage. . . . As to the lords of the Chaldeans, panic from my onslaught overwhelmed them like a demon. They abandoned their tents and fled for their lives, crushing the corpses of their troop as they went. . . . In their terror they passed scalding urine and voided their excrement into their chariots.

King Sennacherib Describes His Siege of Jerusalem (701 B.C.)

As to Hezekiah, the Jew, he did not submit to my yoke, I laid siege to 46 of his strong cities, walled forts and to the countless small villages in their vicinity, and conquered

them by means of well-stamped earth-ramps, and battering-rams brought thus near to the walls combined with the attack by foot soldiers, using mines, breeches as well as sapper work. I drove out of them 200,150 people, young and old, male and female, horses, mules, donkeys, camels, big and small cattle beyond counting, and considered them booty. Himself I made a prisoner in Jerusalem, his royal residence, like a bird in a cage. I surrounded him with earthwork in order to molest those who were leaving his city's gate.

King Ashurbanipal (669–626 B.C.) Describes His Treatment of Conquered Babylon

I tore out the tongues of those whose slanderous mouths had uttered blasphemies against my god Ashur and had plotted against me, his god-fearing prince; I defeated them completely. The others, I smashed alive with the very same statues of protective deities with which they had smashed my own grandfather Sennacherib—now finally as a belated burial sacrifice for his soul. I fed their corpses, cut into small pieces, to dogs, pigs, . . . vultures, the birds of the sky and also to the fish of the ocean. After I had performed this and thus made quiet again the hearts of the great gods, my lords, I removed the corpses of those whom the pestilence had felled, whose leftovers after the dogs and pigs had fed on them were obstructing the streets, filling the places of Babylon, and of those who had lost their lives through the terrible famine.

alive; from some of these I cut off their hands to the wrist, from others I cut off their noses, ears, and fingers; I put out the eyes of many of the soldiers. . . . I burned their young men and women to death.

After conquering another city, the same king wrote: "I fixed up a pile of corpses in front of the city's gate. I flayed the nobles, as many as had rebelled, and spread their skins out on the piles. . . . I flayed many within my land and spread their skins out on the walls."[10] (Obviously, this was not a king to play games with!) Note that this policy of extreme cruelty to prisoners was not used against all enemies but was reserved primarily for those who were already part of the empire and then rebelled against Assyrian rule.

Assyrian Society and Culture

Unlike the Hebrews, the Assyrians were not fearful of mixing with other peoples. In fact, the Assyrian policy of deporting many prisoners of newly conquered territories to Assyria created a polyglot society in which ethnic differences were not very important. It has been estimated that over a period of three centuries, between four and five million people were deported to Assyria, resulting in a popu-

lation that was racially and linguistically mixed. What gave identity to the Assyrians themselves was their language, although even that was akin to that of their southern neighbors in Babylonia. Religion was also a cohesive force. Assyria was literally "the land of Ashur," a reference to its chief god. The king, as the human representative of the god Ashur, served as a final unifying focus.

Agriculture formed the principal basis of Assyrian life. Assyria was a land of farming villages with relatively few significant cities, especially in comparison to southern Mesopotamia. Unlike the river valleys, where farming required the minute organization of large numbers of people to control irrigation, Assyrian farms received sufficient moisture from regular rainfall.

Trade was second to agriculture in economic importance. For internal trade, metals, such as gold, silver, copper, and bronze, were used as a medium of exchange. Various agricultural products also served as a form of payment or exchange. Because of their geographical location, the Assyrians served as intermediaries and participated in an international trade in which they imported timber, wine, and precious metals and stones while exporting textiles produced in palaces, temples, and private villas.

King Ashurbanipal's Lion Hunt. This relief, sculptured on alabaster as a decoration for the northern palace in Nineveh, depicts King Ashurbanipal engaged in a lion hunt. Lion hunts were not done in the wild but under controlled circumstances. The king and his retainers faced lions released from cages in an arena. The purpose of the scene was to glorify the king as a conqueror of the king of beasts. Relief sculpture, one of the best-known forms of Assyrian art, reached its zenith under Ashurbanipal at about the time that the Assyrian Empire began to disintegrate.

The culture of the Assyrian Empire was a hybrid. The Assyrians assimilated much of Mesopotamian civilization and saw themselves as guardians of Sumerian and Babylonian culture. Ashurbanipal, for example, amassed a large library at Nineveh that included the available works of Mesopotamian history. Assyrian religion reflected this assimilation of other cultures as well. Although the Assyrians considered their own national god, Ashur, their chief deity, they recognized virtually all of the Mesopotamian gods and goddesses as well.

Among the best-known objects of Assyrian art are the relief sculptures found in the royal palaces in three of the Assyrian capital cities, Nimrud, Nineveh, and Khorsabad. These reliefs, which were begun in the ninth century and reached their high point in the reign of Ashurbanipal in the seventh century, depicted two different kinds of subject matter: ritual or ceremonial scenes revolving around the person of the king and scenes of hunting and war. The latter show realistic action scenes of the king and his warriors engaged in battle or hunting animals, especially lions. These reliefs depict a strongly masculine world where discipline, brute force, and toughness are the enduring values, indeed, the very values of the Assyrian military monarchy.

The Neo-Babylonian Empire

The Chaldeans, a Semitic-speaking people, had gained ascendancy in Babylonia by the seventh century and came to form the chief resistance to Assyrian control of Mesopotamia. The Chaldean king Nabopolassar (625–605 B.C.), who joined forces with the Medes to capture the Assyrian capital Nineveh in 612 B.C., was responsible for establish-

ing a new Babylonian monarchy. But it was his son Nebuchadnezzar II (605–562 B.C.) who achieved the final defeat of the Assyrian Empire. Under his rule, the Chaldeans defeated Egypt to gain control of Syria and Palestine, destroyed Jerusalem, carried the people of Judah into exile in Babylon, and in the process regained for Babylonia a position as the leading power in the ancient Near East (see Map 2.2).

During Nebuchadnezzar's reign, Babylonia was renowned for a prosperity based on lush agricultural lands, lucrative trade routes, and industries, especially textiles and metals. Nebuchadnezzar rebuilt Babylon as the center of his empire, giving it a reputation as one of the great cities of the ancient world. Babylon was surrounded by towering walls, 8 miles in length, encircled by a moat filled by the Euphrates River. The Ishtar Gate opened onto the Triumphal Way, which led to the sacred precincts of Marduk, the chief Babylonian god. Babylon was adorned with temples and palaces; most famous of all were the Hanging Gardens, known as one of the Seven Wonders of the ancient world. These were supposedly built to satisfy Nebuchadnezzar's wife, a princess from the land of Media, who missed the mountains of her homeland. A series of terraces led to a plateau, an artificial mountain, at the top of which grew the lush gardens irrigated by water piped to the top. According to the account of a first-century A.D. author, the impression of the gardens from a distance was quite remarkable:

On the top of the citadel are the hanging gardens, a wonder celebrated in the tales of the Greeks. . . . Columns of stone were set up to sustain the whole work, and on these was laid a floor of squared blocks, strong enough to hold the earth which is thrown upon it to a great depth, as well as the water with which

Ishtar Gate of Babylon. Nebuchadnezzar rebuilt Babylon as the center of his empire and adorned it with such architectural wonders as the Ishtar Gate, which was built of blue glazed bricks and opened onto the Triumphal Way. The bricks were made separately and then assembled on the gate walls. figures of the dragon of Marduk (patron god of the city of Babylon, whose sacred animal was the dragon) and the bull of Adad (god of storms, whose sacred animal was the bull) alternate on the surfaces of the gate. Ishtar was the Babylonian goddess of war and sexual love. This picture shows the Ishtar Gate as it was rebuilt in the Pergamum Museum in Berlin.

they irrigate the soil; and the structure supports trees of such great size that the thickness of their trunks equals a measure of eight cubits [about 12 feet]. They tower to a height of fifty feet, and they yield as much fruit as if they were growing in their native soil. . . . To those who look upon the trees from a distance, real woods seem to be overhanging their native mountains.[11]

The splendor of the Neo-Babylonian Empire proved to be short-lived. Nabonidus (555–539 B.C.) was the last king of the Chaldean dynasty. He had a great interest in history and encouraged scholars to collect Sumerian texts and study the Sumerian language. But his policies aroused considerable internal dissent. Among other things, Nabonidus neglected the cult of Marduk, instead worshiping the moon god, Sin. When Babylon fell to the Persian conqueror Cyrus in 539 B.C., the Babylonians welcomed him as a liberator.

CHRONOLOGY   The Empires

The Assyrians

Tiglath-Pileser I	1114–1076 B.C.
Shalmeneser II	858–824 B.C.
Tiglath-Pileser III	744–727 B.C.
Sargon II	721–705 B.C.
Ashurbanipal	669–626 B.C.
Capture of Nineveh	612 B.C.
Assyrian Empire destroyed	605 B.C.

The Chaldeans

Ascendancy in Babylonia	600s B.C.
Nabopolassar establishes Neo-Babylonian monarchy	625–605 B.C.
Height of empire under king Nebuchadnezzar II	605–562 B.C.
Fall of Babylon	539 B.C.

The Persians

Unification of Persians	600s B.C.
Conquests of Cyrus the Great	559–530 B.C.
Cambyses II and conquest of Egypt	530–522 B.C.
Reign of Darius	521–486 B.C.

The Persian Empire

The Persians were an Indo-European-speaking people who lived in southwestern Iran. Primarily nomadic, the Persians were organized into tribes or clans led by petty kings assisted by a group of warriors who formed a class of nobles. At the beginning of the seventh century, the Persians became unified under the Achaemenid dynasty, based in Persis in southern Iran. One of the dynasty's members, Cyrus (559–530 B.C.), created a powerful Persian state that rearranged the political map of the ancient Near East (see Map 2.3).

Cyrus the Great

In 550 B.C., Cyrus established Persian control over Media, making it the first Persian **satrapy** (province). Three years later, Cyrus defeated the prosperous Lydian kingdom in western Asia Minor, and Lydia became another Persian satrapy. Cyrus' forces then went on to conquer the Greek city-states that had been established on the Ionian coast. Cyrus then turned eastward, subduing the eastern part of the Iranian plateau, Sogdia, and even western India. His eastern frontiers secured, Cyrus entered Mesopotamia in 539 and captured Babylon (see the box on p. 44). His treatment of Babylonia showed remarkable restraint and wisdom. Babylonia was made into a Persian province under a Persian **satrap,** or governor, but many government officials

THE FALL OF BABYLON

UNDER THE CHALDEANS, Babylon became the center of an empire and gained a reputation as one of the great cities of the ancient world. But the Neo-Babylonian Empire did not last, and Babylon fell to the Persian forces under King Cyrus in 539 B.C. In his history of the Persian Wars, the ancient Greek historian Herodotus described how Cyrus supposedly captured Babylon.

Herodotus, *The Persian Wars*

Cyrus, with the first approach of the ensuing spring, marched forward against Babylon. The Babylonians, encamped without their walls, awaited his coming. A battle was fought at a short distance from the city, in which the Babylonians were defeated by the Persian king, whereupon they withdrew within their defenses. Here they shut themselves up, and made light of his siege, having laid in a store of provisions for many years in preparation against this attack; for when they saw Cyrus conquering nation after nation, they were convinced that he would never stop, and that their turn would come at last.

Cyrus was now reduced to great perplexity, as time went on and he made no progress against the place. In this distress, either some one made the suggestion to him, or he thought himself of a plan, which he proceeded to put in execution. He placed a portion of his army at the point where the river enters the city and another body at the back of the place where it issues forth, with orders to march into the town by the bed of the stream, as soon as the water became shallow enough: he then himself drew off with the unwarlike portion of his host, and made for the place where Nitocris [supposedly a queen of Babylon] dug the basin for the river, where he did exactly what she had done formerly: he turned the Euphrates by a canal into the basin, which was then a marsh, on which the river sank to such an extent that the natural bed of the stream became fordable. Hereupon the Persians who had been left for the purpose at Babylon by the river-side, entered the stream, which had now sunk so as to reach about midway up a man's thigh, and thus got into the town. Had the Babylonians been apprised of what Cyrus was about, or had they noticed their danger, they would not have allowed the entrance of the Persians within the city, which was what ruined them utterly, but would have made fast all the street-gates which gave upon the river, and mounting upon the walls along both sides of the stream, would so have caught the enemy as it were in a trap. But, as it was, the Persians came upon them by surprise and so took the city. Owing to the vast size of the place, the inhabitants of the central parts (as the residents at Babylon declare) long after the outer portions of the town were taken, knew nothing of what had chanced, but as they were engaged in a festival, continued dancing and reveling until they learned the capture but too certainly. Such, then, were the circumstances of the first taking of Babylon.

were kept in their positions. Cyrus took the title "King of All, Great King, Mighty King, King of Babylon, King of the Land of Sumer and Akkad, King of the Four Rims (of the Earth), the Son of Cambyses the Great King, King of Anshan"[12] and insisted that he stood in the ancient, unbroken line of Babylonian kings. By appealing to the vanity of the Babylonians, he won their loyalty. Cyrus also issued an edict permitting the Jews, who had been brought to Babylon in the sixth century B.C., to return to Jerusalem with their sacred temple objects and to rebuild their Temple as well.

From 538 to 530 B.C., Cyrus consolidated his empire. Among other things, he constructed forts, especially in the northeast, to protect against nomadic incursions. It was there that he undertook his last campaign. In 530 B.C., he marched from Sogdia into the territory of the Massagetae, where he was killed in battle.

To his contemporaries, Cyrus the Great was deserving of his epithet. The Greek historian Herodotus recounted that the Persians viewed him as a "father," a ruler who was "gentle, and procured them all manner of goods."[13] Cyrus must have been an unusual ruler for his time, a man who demonstrated considerable wisdom and compassion in the conquest and organization of his empire. Cyrus obtained the favor of the priesthoods in his conquered lands by restoring temples and permitting religious toleration. He won approval by using not only Persians but also native peoples as government officials in their own states. He allowed Medes to be military commanders. Unlike the Assyrian rulers of an earlier empire, he had a reputation for mercy. Medes, Babylonians, and Jews all accepted him as their legitimate ruler. Some peoples portrayed him as a great leader and peacemaker. Indeed, a Hebrew prophet regarded him as the anointed one of God: "I am the Lord who says of Cyrus, 'He is my shepherd and will accomplish all that I please'; he will say of Jerusalem, 'Let it be rebuilt'; and of the temple, 'Let its foundations be laid.' This is what the Lord says to his anointed, to Cyrus, whose right hand I take hold of to subdue nations before him."[14] Cyrus had a genuine respect for ancient civilizations—in building his palaces, he made use of Assyrian, Babylonian, Egyptian, and Lydian practices. Indeed, Cyrus believed that he was creating a "world empire" that included peoples who had ancient and venerable traditions and institutions.

Expanding the Empire

Upon Cyrus' death in 530 B.C., his son Cambyses II assumed power as the Great King. Four years later, Cam-

MAP 2.3 **The Persian Empire at the Time of Darius.** Cyrus the Great united the Persians and led them in successful conquest of much of the Near East. By the time of Darius, the Persian Empire was the largest the world had yet seen. The Persians allowed a high degree of religious tolerance and gave some government positions to natives of conquered territories. ❓ How did Persian policies attempt to overcome the difficulties of governing far-flung provinces?

🌐 **View an animated version of this map or related maps at** http://history.wadsworth.com/spielvogel06/

byses undertook the invasion of Egypt, the only kingdom in the Near East not yet brought under Persian control. Aided by the Phoenician fleet, he defeated and captured the pharaoh and the Egyptian forces. Egypt was made into a satrapy with Memphis as its capital. In the summer of 525 B.C., Cambyses took the title of pharaoh.

After the death of Cambyses in 522, Darius emerged as Great King after a year of intense civil war. Once in charge, Darius (521–486 B.C.) turned to the task of strengthening the empire. He codified Egyptian law and built a canal to link the Red Sea and the Mediterranean. A campaign into western India led to the creation of a new Persian province that extended to the Indus River. Darius also moved into Europe proper, conquering Thrace and making the Macedonian king a vassal. A revolt of the Ionian Greek cities in 499 B.C. resulted in temporary freedom for these communities in western Asia Minor. Aid from the Greek mainland, most notably from Athens, led to a brief invasion of Lydia by the Ionians and the burning of Sardis, center of the Lydian satrapy. This event led to Darius' involvement with the mainland Greeks. After reestablishing control of the Ionian Greek cities, Darius undertook an invasion of the Greek mainland, which culminated in the famous Athenian victory in the Battle of Marathon in 490 B.C. (see Chapter 3).

Governing the Empire

By the reign of Darius, the Persians had created the largest empire the world had yet seen. It not only included all the old centers of power in the Near East, Egypt, Mesopotamia, and Assyria but also extended into Thrace and Asia Minor in the west and into India in the east.

For administrative purposes, the empire had been divided into approximately twenty provinces called satrapies. Each province was ruled by a governor or satrap, literally a "protector of the kingdom." Although Darius had not introduced the system of satrapies, he did see that it was organized more rationally. He created a sensible system for calculating the tribute that each satrapy owed to the central government and gave satraps specific civil and military duties. They collected tributes, were responsible for justice and security, raised military levies, and normally commanded the military forces within their satrapies. In terms of real power, the satraps were miniature kings who established courts imitative of the Great King's.

From the time of Darius on, satraps were men of Persian descent. The major satrapies were given to princes of the king's family, and their position became essentially hereditary. The minor satrapies were placed in the hands of Persian nobles. Their offices, too, tended to pass from

Like the Assyrians, the Persians established staging posts equipped with fresh horses for the king's messengers.

The Great King

In this vast administrative system, the Persian king occupied an exalted position. Although not considered a god like the Egyptian pharaoh, he was nevertheless the elect one or regent of the Persian god Ahuramazda (see "Persian Religion" later in this chapter). All subjects were the king's servants, and he was the source of all justice, possessing the power of life and death over everyone. Persian kings were largely secluded and not easily available. They resided in a series of splendid palaces. Darius in particular was a palace builder on a grand scale. His description of the construction of a palace in the chief Persian capital of Susa demonstrated what a truly international empire Persia was:

> This is the . . . palace which at Susa I built. From afar its ornamentation was brought. . . . The cedar timber was brought from a mountain named Lebanon; the Assyrians brought it to Babylon, and from Babylon the Carians and Ionians brought it to Susa. Teakwood was brought from Gandara and from Carmania. The gold which was used here was brought from Sardis and from Bactria. The stone—lapis lazuli and carnelian—was brought from Sogdiana. . . . The silver and copper were brought from Egypt. The ornamentation with which the wall was adorned was brought from Ionia. The ivory was brought from Ethiopia, from India, and from Arachosia. The stone pillars were brought from . . . Elam. The artisans who dressed the stone were Ionians and Sardians. The goldsmiths who wrought the gold were Medes and Egyptians. . . . Those who worked the baked brick [with figures] were Babylonians. The men who adorned the wall were Medes and Egyptians. At Susa here a splendid work was ordered; very splendid did it turn out.[15]

But Darius was unhappy with Susa. He did not really consider it his homeland, and it was oppressively hot in the summer months. He built another residence at Persepolis, a new capital located to the east of the old one and at a higher elevation.

The policies of Darius also tended to widen the gap between the king and his subjects. As the Great King himself said of all his subjects, "What was said to them by me, night and day it was done."[16] Over a period of time, the Great Kings in their greed came to hoard immense quantities of gold and silver in the various treasuries located in the capital cities. Both their hoarding of wealth and their later overtaxation of their subjects are seen as crucial factors in the ultimate weakening of the Persian Empire (see the box on p. 47).

In its heyday, however, the empire stood supreme, and much of its power depended on the military. By the time of Darius, the Persian monarchs had created a standing army of professional soldiers. This army was truly international, composed of contingents from the various peoples who made up the empire. At its core was a cavalry force of ten thousand and an elite infantry force of ten thousand Medes and Persians known as the Immortals because they were never allowed to fall below ten thousand

Darius, the Great King. Darius ruled the Persian Empire from 521 to 486 B.C. He is shown here on his throne in Persepolis, a new capital city that he built. In his right hand, Darius holds the royal staff. In his left hand, he grasps a lotus blossom with two buds, a symbol of royalty.

father to son. The hereditary nature of the governors' offices made it necessary to provide some checks on their power. Consequently, some historians think that there were officials at the satrapal courts, such as secretaries and generals in charge of the garrison, who reported directly to the Great King, keeping him informed of what was going on within the various satrapal governments. It is also possible that an official known as the "king's eye" or "king's messenger" made annual inspections of each satrapy.

An efficient system of communication was considered crucial to sustaining the Persian Empire. Well-maintained roads facilitated the rapid transit of military and government personnel. One in particular, known as the Royal Road, stretched from Sardis, the center of Lydia in Asia Minor, to Susa, the chief capital of the Persian Empire (see Map 2.3).

A DINNER OF THE PERSIAN KING

THE PERSIAN KINGS lived in luxury as a result of their conquests and ability to levy taxes from their conquered subjects. In this selection, we read a description of how a Persian king dined with his numerous guests.

Athenaeus, *The Deipnosophists,* 4:145–146

Heracleides of Cumae, author of the *Persian History,* writes in the second book of the work entitled *Equipment:* "All who attend upon the Persian kings when they dine first bathe themselves and then serve in white clothes, and spend nearly half the day on preparations for the dinner. Of those who are invited to eat with the king, some dine outdoors, in full sight of anyone who wishes to look on; others dine indoors in the king's company. Yet even these do not eat in his presence, for there are two rooms opposite each other, in one of which the king has his meal, in the other the invited guests. The king can see them through the curtain at the door, but they cannot see him. Sometimes, however, on the occasion of a public holiday, all dine in a single room with the king, in the great hall. And whenever the king commands a symposium [drinking-bout following the dinner] which he does often, he has about a dozen companions at the drinking. When they have finished dinner, that is the king by himself, the guests in the other room, these fellow-drinkers are summoned by one of the eunuchs; and entering they drink with him, though even they do not have the same wine; moreover, they sit on the floor, while he reclines on a couch supported by feet of gold, and they depart after having drunk to excess. In most cases the king breakfasts and dines alone, but sometimes his wife and some of his sons dine with him. And throughout the dinner his concubines sing and play the lyre; one of them is the soloist, the others sing in chorus. And so, Heracleides continues, the 'king's dinner,' as it is called, will appear prodigal to one who merely hears about it, but when one examines it carefully it will be found to have been got up with economy and even with parsimony; and the same is true of the dinners among other Persians of high station. For one thousand animals are slaughtered daily for the king; these comprise horses, camels, oxen, asses, deer, and most of the small animals; many birds are also consumed, including Arabian ostriches—and the creature is large—geese, and cocks. And of all these only moderate portions are served to each of the king's guests, and each of them may carry home whatever he leaves untouched at the meal. But the greater part of these meats and other foods are taken into the court-yard for the body-guard and light-armed troopers maintained by the king; there they divide all the half-eaten remnants of meat and bread and share them in equal portions. . . ."

in number. When one was killed, he was immediately replaced. The Persians made effective use of their cavalry, especially for operating behind enemy lines and breaking up lines of communication. The Persian navy consisted of ships from subject states, including the Phoenicians, Egyptians, Anatolians, and Ionian Greeks.

Persian Religion

Of all the Persians' cultural contributions, the most original was their religion. Before the advent of **Zoroastrianism** in the sixth century, the popular religion of the Iranians focused on the worship of the powers of nature, such as the sun, moon, fire, and winds. Mithra was an especially popular god of light and war who came to be viewed as a sun god. The people worshiped and sacrificed to these powers of nature with the aid of priests, known as Magi.

Archers of the Persian Guard. One of the main pillars supporting the Persian Empire was the military. This frieze, composed of enameled brick, depicts members of the famous infantry force known as the Immortals, so called because their number was never allowed to drop below ten thousand. Anyone killed would be replaced immediately. They carry the standard lance and bow and arrow of the infantry.

Zoroaster was a semilegendary figure who, according to Persian tradition, was born in 660 B.C. After a period of wandering and solitude, he experienced revelations that caused him to be revered as a prophet of the "true religion." It is difficult to know what Zoroaster's original teachings were, since the sacred book of Zoroastrianism, the *Zend Avesta*, was not written down until the third century A.D. Scholars believe, however, that the earliest section of the *Zend Avesta*, known as the *Yasna*, consisting of seventeen hymns or *gathas*, contains the actual writings of Zoroaster. This enables us to piece together his message.

Zoroaster did not introduce a new god but taught that Ahuramazda, who had long been one of the Iranians' deities, was the only God and that his religion was the only perfect one. Ahuramazda (the "Wise Lord") was the supreme deity who brought all things into being:

> *This I ask of You, O Ahuramazda; answer me well:*
> *Who at the Creation was the first father of Justice?—*
> *Who assigned their path to the sun and the stars?—*
> *Who decreed the waxing and waning of the moon, if it*
>   *was not You?— . . .*
> *Who has fixed the earth below, and the heaven above*
>   *with its clouds that it might not be moved?—*
> *Who has appointed the waters and the green things upon*
>   *the earth?—*
> *Who has harnessed to the wind and the clouds their*
>   *steeds?— . . .*
> *Thus do I strive to recognize in You, O Wise One,*
> *Together with the Holy Spirit, the Creator of all things.*[17]

According to Zoroaster, Ahuramazda also possessed abstract qualities or states that all humans should aspire to, such as Good Thought, Right, and Piety. Although Ahuramazda was supreme, he was not unopposed. Right is opposed by the Lie, Truth by Falsehood, Life by Death. At the beginning of the world, the good spirit of Ahuramazda was opposed by the evil spirit (in later Zoroastrianism identified with Ahriman). Although it appears that Zoroaster saw it as simply natural that where there is good there will be evil, later followers had a tendency to make these abstractions concrete and overemphasize the reality of an evil spirit. Humans also played a role in this cosmic struggle between good and evil. Ahuramazda, the creator, gave all humans free will and the power to choose between right and wrong. The good person chooses the right way of Ahuramazda. Zoroaster taught that there would be an end to the struggle between good and evil. Ahuramazda would eventually triumph, and at the last judgment at the end of the world, the final separation of good and evil would occur. Zoroaster also provided for individual judgment as well. Each soul faced a final evaluation of its actions. A person who had performed good deeds would achieve paradise, the "House of Song" or the "Kingdom of Good Thought"; the soul of a person who had performed evil deeds would be thrown into an abyss, the "House of Worst Thought," where it would experience future ages of darkness, torment, and misery.

The spread of Zoroastrianism was due to its acceptance by the Great Kings of Persia. The inscriptions of Darius make clear that he believed Ahuramazda was the only God. Although Darius himself may have been a monotheist, dramatic changes occurred as the kings and Magi of Persia propagated Zoroaster's teachings on Ahuramazda. Zoroastrianism lost its monotheistic emphasis, and the old nature worship resurfaced. Soon Persian religion had returned to polytheism, with Ahuramazda the chief of a number of gods of light. Mithra, the sun god, became a helper of Ahuramazda and later, in Roman times, the source of another religion. Persian kings were also very tolerant of other religions, and gods and goddesses of those religions tended to make their way into the Persian pantheon. Moreover, Zoroaster's teachings, as frequently happens to the ideas of founders of religions, acquired concrete forms that he had never originally intended. The struggle between good and evil was taken beyond the abstractions of Zoroaster into a strong ethical dualism. The spirit of evil became an actual being who had to be warded off by the use of spells and incantations. Descriptions of the last judgment came to be filled with minute physical details. Some historians believe that Zoroastrianism, with its emphasis on good and evil, a final judgment, and individual judgment of souls, had an impact on Christianity, a religion that eventually surpassed it in significance.

CONCLUSION

*A*ROUND 1200 B.C., THE DECLINE of the Hittites and the Egyptians left a power vacuum that allowed a number of small states to emerge and flourish temporarily in the Near East. All of them were eventually overshadowed by the rise of the great empires of the Assyrians, Chaldeans, and Persians. The Assyrian Empire was the first to unite almost all of the ancient Near East. Far larger was the empire of the Great Kings of Persia.

Although it owed much to the administrative organization created by the Assyrians, the Persian Empire had its own peculiar strengths. Persian rule was tolerant as well as efficient. Conquered peoples were allowed to keep their own religions, customs, and methods of doing business. The many years of peace that the Persian Empire brought to the region facilitated trade and the general well-being of its peoples. Many Near Eastern peoples expressed gratitude for being subjects of the Great Kings of Persia.

The Hebrews were one of these peoples. They created no empire and were dominated by the Assyrians, Chaldeans, and Persians. Nevertheless, they left a spiritual legacy that influenced much of the later development of Western civilization. The evolution of Hebrew monotheism created in Judaism one of the world's greatest religions; it influenced the development of both Christianity and Islam. When we speak of the Judeo-Christian heritage of Western civilization, we refer not only to the concept of monotheism but also to ideas of law, morality, and social justice that have become important parts of Western culture.

On the western fringes of the Persian Empire, another relatively small group of people, the Greeks, were creating cultural and political ideals that would also have an important impact on Western civilization. It is to the Greeks that we now turn.

TIMELINE

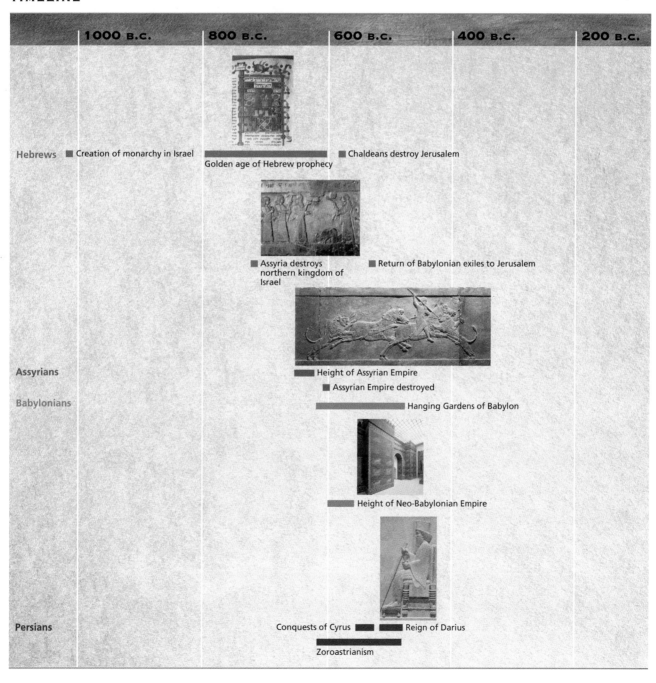

| | 1000 B.C. | 800 B.C. | 600 B.C. | 400 B.C. | 200 B.C. |

Hebrews ■ Creation of monarchy in Israel — Golden age of Hebrew prophecy ■ Chaldeans destroy Jerusalem

■ Assyria destroys northern kingdom of Israel ■ Return of Babylonian exiles to Jerusalem

Assyrians ■ Height of Assyrian Empire ■ Assyrian Empire destroyed

Babylonians Hanging Gardens of Babylon

Height of Neo-Babylonian Empire

Persians Conquests of Cyrus ■ ■ Reign of Darius

Zoroastrianism

NOTES

1. 2 Samuel 8:2.
2. Psalms 137:1, 4–6.
3. Psalms 145:8–9.
4. Psalms 121:2–3.
5. Exodus 20:13–15.
6. Isaiah 2:4.
7. Proverbs 31:10–20, 24–28.
8. Judges 5:24–27.
9. Quoted in Roland de Vaux, *Ancient Israel: Its Life and Institutions* (New York, 1961), p. 49.
10. Quoted in H. W. F. Saggs, *The Might That Was Assyria* (London, 1984), pp. 261–262.
11. John C. Rolfe, trans., *Quintus Curtius I* (Cambridge, Mass., 1971), pp. 337–339.
12. Quoted in John M. Cook, *The Persian Empire* (New York, 1983), p. 32.
13. Herodotus, *The Persian Wars*, trans. George Rawlinson (New York, 1942), p. 257.
14. Isaiah 44:28, 45:1.
15. Quoted in Albert T. Olmstead, *History of the Persian Empire* (Chicago, 1948), p. 168.
16. Quoted in Cook, *The Persian Empire*, p. 76.
17. Yasna 44:3–4, 7, as quoted in A. C. Bouquet, *Sacred Books of the World* (Harmondsworth, England, 1954), pp. 111–112.

SUGGESTIONS FOR FURTHER READING

For an excellent general survey of the material covered in this chapter, see **A. Kuhrt,** *The Ancient Near East, c. 3000–330 B.C.,* vol. 2 (London, 1995), and **M. van de Mieroop,** *A History of the Ancient Near East, ca. 3000–323 B.C.* (Oxford, 2004). There is an enormous literature on ancient Israel. Two good studies on the archaeological aspects are **A. Mazar,** *Archaeology of the Land of the Bible* (New York, 1992), and **A. Ben-Tor, ed.,** *The Archaeology of Ancient Israel* (New Haven, Conn., 1992). For historical narratives, see especially **J. Bright,** *A History of Israel,* 3d ed. (Philadelphia, 1981), a fundamental study; **J. M. Miller and J. H. Hayes,** *A History of Ancient Israel and Judah* (Philadelphia, 1986); **M. Grant,** *The History of Ancient Israel* (New York, 1984); and **H. Shanks,** *Ancient Israel: A Short History from Abraham to the Roman Destruction of the Temple* (Englewood Cliffs, N.J., 1988). For a new perspective, see **N. P. Lemche,** *Ancient Israel: A New History of Israelite Society* (Sheffield, England, 1988). On the origins of the Israelites, see **W. G. Dever,** *Who Were the Early Israelites and Where Did They Come From?* (Grand Rapids, Mich., 2003). A brief summary of Hebrew history and thought can be found in **J. H. Hexter,** *The Judaeo-Christian Tradition* (New York, 1966). **R. de Vaux,** *Ancient Israel: Its Life and Institutions* (New York, 1961), is especially good on the social institutions of ancient Israel. On women in ancient Israel, see **C. Meyers,** *Discovering Eve: Ancient Israelite Women in Context* (New York, 1988).

For general studies on the religion of the Hebrews, see **R. Albertz,** *A History of Israelite Religion in the Old Testament Period* (Louisville, Ky., 1994), and **W. J. Doorly,** *The Religion of Israel* (New York, 1997). The role of the prophets is examined in **J. Lindblom,** *Prophecy in Ancient Israel* (Oxford, 1962), and is given a new interpretation in **N. Podhoretz,** *The Prophets* (New York, 2002).

For a good account of Phoenician domestic and overseas expansion, see **D. Harden,** *The Phoenicians,* rev. ed. (Harmondsworth, England, 1980). See also **M. E. Aubet,** *The Phoenicians and the West: Politics, Colonies and Trade* (Cambridge, 1993), and **G. Markoe,** *Phoenicians* (London, 2000), on Phoenician society.

A detailed account of Assyrian political, economic, social, military, and cultural history is **H. W. F. Saggs,** *The Might That Was Assyria* (London, 1984). **A. T. Olmstead,** *History of Assyria* (Chicago, 1975), is a basic survey of the Assyrian Empire. The Neo-Babylonian Empire can be examined in **J. Oates,** *Babylon* (London, 1979), and **H. W. F. Saggs,** *Babylonians* (Norman, Okla., 1995).

The classic work on the Persian Empire is **A. T. Olmstead,** *History of the Persian Empire* (Chicago, 1948), but **J. M. Cook,** *The Persian Empire* (New York, 1983), provides new material and fresh interpretations. Also of value is **J. Curtis,** *Ancient Persia* (Cambridge, Mass., 1990). On the history of Zoroastrianism, see **R. C. Zaehner,** *The Dawn and Twilight of Zoroastrianism* (London, 1961), and **S. A. Nigosian,** *The Zoroastrian Faith: Tradition and Modern Research* (New York, 1993).

History Now™

Enter *HistoryNow* using the access card that is available for *Western Civilization. HistoryNow* will assist you in understanding the content in this chapter with lesson plans generated for your needs. In addition, you can read the following documents, and many more, online:

Book of Ezra (Old Testament)

Baal Myth of Ugarit

INFOTRAC SEARCH TERMS

 For additional reading, go to InfoTrac College Edition, your online research library at http://infotrac.thomsonlearning.com

Key Terms Search

Assyrian	Phoenician
Babylonian	Persian

WESTERN CIVILIZATION RESOURCES

Visit the *Western Civilization* Companion Web site for resources specific to this book:

http://history.wadsworth.com/spielvogel06/

For a variety of tools to help you succeed in this course, visit the **Western Civilization Resource Center** at

http://history.wadsworth.com/western/

Included are quizzes; images; documents; interactive simulations; maps and timelines; movie explorations; and a wealth of other sources.

3

THE CIVILIZATION
OF THE GREEKS

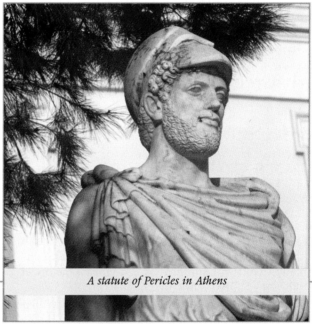

A statute of Pericles in Athens

akg-images/John Hios

IN 431 B.C., WAR ERUPTED in Greece as two very different Greek city-states—Athens and Sparta—fought for domination of the Greek world. The people of Athens felt secure behind their walls and in the first winter of the war held a public funeral to honor those who had died in battle. On the day of the ceremony, the citizens of Athens joined in a procession, with the relatives of the dead wailing for their loved ones. As was the custom in Athens, one leading citizen was asked to address the crowd, and on this day it was Pericles who spoke to the people. He talked about the greatness of Athens and reminded the Athenians of the strength of their political system. "Our constitution," he said, "is called a democracy because power is in the hands not of a minority but of the whole people. When it is a question of settling private disputes, everyone is equal before the law. Just as our political life is free and open, so is our day-to-day life in our relations with each other. . . . Here each individual is interested not only in his own affairs but in the affairs of the state as well."

In this famous Funeral Oration, Pericles gave voice to the ideal of democracy and the importance of the individual. It was the Greeks who created the intellectual foundations of our Western heritage. They asked some basic questions about human life that still dominate our own intellectual pursuits: What is the nature of the universe? What is the purpose of human existence? What is our relationship to divine forces? What constitutes a community? What constitutes a state? What is true education? What are the true sources of law? What is truth itself, and how do we realize it? Not only did the Greeks provide answers to these questions, but they created a system of logical, analytical thought to examine them. This rational outlook has remained an important feature of Western civilization.

The story of ancient Greek civilization is a remarkable one that begins with the first arrival of the Greeks around 2000 B.C. By the eighth century B.C., the characteristic institution of ancient Greek life, the *polis* or city-state, had emerged. Greek civilization flourished and reached its height in the classical era of the fifth century B.C., which has come to be closely identified with the achievements of Athenian democracy.

Early Greece

Geography played an important role in the evolution of Greek history. Compared to the landmasses of Mesopotamia and Egypt, Greece occupied a small area, a mountainous peninsula that encompassed only 45,000 square miles of territory, about the size of the state of Louisiana. The mountains and the sea played especially significant roles in the development of Greek history. Much of Greece consists of small plains and river valleys surrounded by mountain ranges 8,000 to 10,000 feet high. The mountainous terrain had the effect of isolating Greeks from one another. Consequently, Greek communities tended to follow their own separate paths and develop their own way of life. Over a period of time, these communities became attached to their independence and were only too willing to fight one

another to gain advantage. No doubt the small size of these independent Greek communities fostered participation in political affairs and unique cultural expressions, but the rivalry among these communities also led to the bitter warfare that ultimately devastated Greek society.

The sea also influenced the evolution of Greek society. Greece had a long seacoast, dotted by bays and inlets that provided numerous harbors. The Greeks also inhabited a number of islands to the west, the south, and particularly the east of the Greek mainland. It is no accident that the Greeks became seafarers who sailed out into the Aegean and Mediterranean Seas, first to make contact with the outside world and later to establish colonies that would spread Greek civilization throughout the Mediterranean region.

Greek topography helped determine the major territories into which Greece was ultimately divided. South of the Gulf of Corinth was the Peloponnesus, virtually an island connected to the mainland by a narrow land bridge (see Map 3.1). Consisting mostly of hills, mountains, and small valleys, the Peloponnesus was the location of Sparta, as well as the site of Olympia, where athletic games were held. Northeast of the Peloponnesus was the Attic peninsula (or Attica), the home of Athens, hemmed in by mountains to the north and west and surrounded by the sea to the south and east. Northwest of Attica was Boeotia in central Greece, with its chief city of Thebes. To the north of Boeotia was Thessaly, which contained the largest plains and became a great producer of grain and horses. To the north of Thessaly lay Macedonia, which was not of much importance in Greek history until 338 B.C., when a Macedonian king, Philip II, conquered the Greeks.

Minoan Crete

The earliest civilization in the Aegean region emerged on the large island of Crete, southeast of the Greek mainland. A Bronze Age civilization that used metals, especially bronze, in making weapons had been established there by 2800 B.C. This civilization was discovered at the turn of the

The Minoan Sport of Bull Leaping. Minoan bull games were held in the great palaces on the island of Crete. As seen in this fresco from the east wing of the palace at Knossus, women and men acrobats (the man in red) somersaulted over the back of the bull. Another person waited behind the bull to catch the leapers.

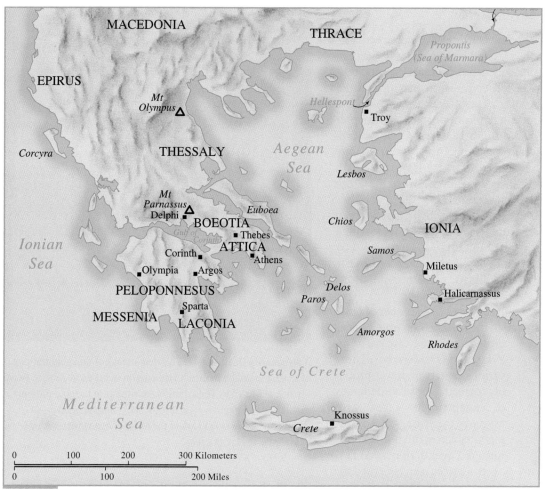

MAP 3.1 **Ancient Greece (c. 750–338 B.C.).** Between 750 and 500 B.C., Greek civilization witnessed the emergence of the city-state as the central institution in Greek life and the Greeks' colonization of the Mediterranean and Black seas. Classical Greece lasted from about 500 to 338 B.C. and encompassed the high points of Greek civilization in arts, science, philosophy, and politics, as well as the Persian Wars and the Peloponnesian War. **?** How does the geography of Greece help explain the rise and development of the Greek city-state? 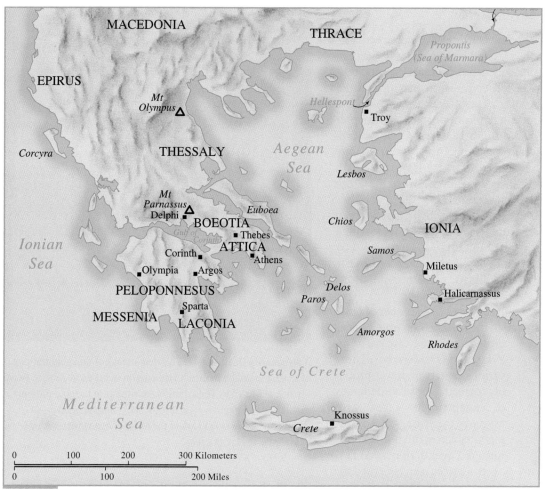 **View an animated version of this map or related maps at** http://history.wadsworth.com/spielvogel06/

twentieth century by the English archaeologist Arthur Evans, who named it "Minoan" after Minos, a legendary king of Crete. In language and religion, the Minoans were not Greek, although they did have some influence on the peoples of the Greek mainland.

Evans's excavations on Crete led to the discovery of an enormous palace complex at Knossus, near modern Heracleion. The remains revealed a rich and prosperous culture with Knossus as the likely center of a far-ranging "sea empire," probably largely commercial. We know from archaeological remains that the people of Minoan Crete were accustomed to sea travel and had made contact with the more advanced civilization of Egypt. Egyptian products have been found in Crete and Cretan products in Egypt. Minoan Cretans also made contact with and exerted influence on the Greek-speaking inhabitants of the Greek mainland.

The Minoan civilization reached its height between 2000 and 1450 B.C. The palace at Knossus, the royal seat

of the kings, demonstrates the prosperity and power of this civilization. It was an elaborate structure built around a central courtyard and included numerous private living rooms for the royal family and workshops for making decorated vases, small sculptures, and jewelry. Even bathrooms, with elaborate drains, formed part of the complex. The rooms were decorated with frescoes in bright colors showing sporting events and naturalistic scenes that have led some observers to conclude that the Cretans had a great love of nature. Storerooms in the palace held enormous jars of oil, wine, and grain, presumably paid as taxes to the king.

The centers of Minoan civilization on Crete suffered a sudden and catastrophic collapse around 1450 B.C. The cause of this destruction has been vigorously debated. Some historians believe that a tsunami triggered by a powerful volcanic eruption on the island of Thera was responsible for the devastation. Most historians, however, maintain that the destruction was the result of invasion and pillage by mainland Greeks known as the Mycenaeans.

The First Greek State: Mycenae

The term *Mycenaean* is derived from Mycenae, a remarkable fortified site first excavated by the amateur German archaeologist Heinrich Schliemann. Mycenae was one center in a Mycenaean Greek civilization that flourished between 1600 and 1100 B.C. The Mycenaean Greeks were part of the Indo-European family of peoples (see Chapter 2) who spread from their original Central Asian location into southern and western Europe, India, and Iran. One group entered the territory of Greece from the north around 1900 B.C. and managed to gain control of the Greek mainland and develop a civilization.

Mycenaean civilization reached its high point between 1400 and 1200 B.C. It is especially noted for its fortified palace-centers, which were built on hills surrounded by gigantic stone walls. The royal families lived within the walls of these complexes, while the civilian populations lived in scattered locations outside the walls.

Mycenaean civilization consisted of a number of powerful monarchies centered in the palace complexes, such as those found at Mycenae, Tiryns, Pylos, and Orchomenos. These various centers of power probably formed a loose confederacy of independent states, with Mycenae the strongest. According to tablets written in an early form of Greek script called Linear B, a Mycenaean king used the title of *wanax*. Next in importance to the king were commanders of the army, priests, and bureaucrats who kept careful records. The free citizenry included peasants, soldiers, and artisans, with the lowest rung of the social ladder consisting of serfs and slaves.

Minoan Crete and Mycenaean Greece

The Mycenaeans were above all a warrior people who prided themselves on their heroic deeds in battle. Archaeological evidence also indicates that the Mycenaean monarchies developed an extensive commercial network. Mycenaean pottery has been found throughout the Mediterranean basin, in Syria and Egypt to the east and Sicily and southern Italy to the west. But some scholars believe that the Mycenaeans, led by Mycenae itself, also spread outward militarily, conquering Crete and making it part of the Mycenaean world. Some of the Aegean islands also fell subject to Mycenaean control. The most famous of all the Mycenaeans' supposed military adventures has come down to us in the epic poetry of Homer (discussed in the next section). Did the Mycenaeans, led by Agamemnon, king of Mycenae, sack the city of Troy on the northwestern coast of Asia Minor around 1250 B.C.? Scholars have debated this question ever since Schliemann began his excavations in 1870. Many believe that Homer's account does have a basis in fact, even if the details have become shrouded in mystery.

A Mycenaean Death Mask. This death mask of thin gold was one of several found by Heinrich Schliemann in his excavation of Grave Circle A at Mycenae. These masks are similar to the gold mummy mask used in Egyptian royal tombs. Schliemann claimed—incorrectly—that he had found the mask of Agamemnon, king of Mycenae in Homer's *Iliad*.

By the late thirteenth century, Mycenaean Greece was showing signs of serious trouble. Mycenae itself was torched around 1190 B.C., and other Mycenaean centers show similar patterns of destruction as new waves of Greek-speaking invaders moved into Greece from the north. By 1100 B.C., the Mycenaean culture was coming to an end, and the Greek world was entering a new period of considerable insecurity.

The Greeks in a Dark Age (c. 1100–c. 750 B.C.)

After the collapse of the Mycenaean civilization, Greece entered a difficult period in which population declined and food production dropped. Because of the difficult conditions and our lack of knowledge about the period, historians refer to it as the Dark Age. Not until 850 B.C. did farming revive. At the same time, some new developments were forming the basis for a revived Greece.

During the Dark Age, large numbers of Greeks left the mainland and migrated across the Aegean Sea to various islands and especially to the southwestern shore of Asia Minor, a strip of territory that came to be called Ionia. Based on their dialect, the Greeks who resided there were called Ionians. Two other major groups of Greeks settled in established parts of Greece. The Aeolian Greeks, located in northern and central Greece, colonized the large island of Lesbos and the adjacent territory on the northwestern coast of Asia Minor. The Dorians established themselves in southwestern Greece, especially in the Peloponnesus, as well as on some of the southern Aegean islands, including Crete and Rhodes.

Other important activities occurred in this Dark Age as well. Greece saw a revival of some trade and some economic activity besides agriculture. Iron replaced bronze in the construction of weapons, making them affordable for more people. And farming tools made of iron helped reverse the decline in food production. At some point in the eighth century B.C., the Greeks adopted the Phoenician alphabet to give themselves a new system of writing. By reducing all words to a combination of twenty-four letters, the Greeks made learning to read and write simpler. Finally, near the end of this Dark Age appeared the work of Homer, who has come to be viewed as one of the great poets of all time.

Homer and Homeric Greece

The *Iliad* and the *Odyssey*, the first great epic poems of early Greece, were based on stories that had been passed on from generation to generation. It is generally assumed that early in the eighth century B.C., Homer made use of these oral traditions to compose the *Iliad*, his epic of the Trojan War. The war was caused by an act of Paris, a prince of Troy. By kidnapping Helen, wife of the king of the Greek state of Sparta, he outraged all the Greeks. Under the leadership of the Spartan king's brother, Agamemnon of Mycenae, the Greeks attacked Troy. Ten years later, the Greeks finally won and sacked the city.

But the *Iliad* is not so much the story of the war itself as it is the tale of the Greek hero Achilles and how the "wrath of Achilles" led to disaster. As is true of all great literature, the *Iliad* abounds in universal lessons. Underlying them all is the clear message, as one commentator has observed, that "men will still come and go like the generations of leaves in the forest; that [man] will still be weak, and the gods strong and incalculable; that the quality of a man matters more than his achievement; that violence and recklessness will still lead to disaster, and that this will fall on the innocent as well as on the guilty."[1]

The *Odyssey*, Homer's other masterpiece, is an epic romance that recounts the journeys of one of the Greek heroes, Odysseus, after the fall of Troy, and his ultimate return to his wife. But there is a larger vision here as well: the testing of the heroic stature of Odysseus until, by both cunning and patience, he prevails. In the course of this testing, the underlying moral message is "that virtue is a better policy than vice."[2]

Although the *Iliad* and the *Odyssey* supposedly deal with the heroes of the Mycenaean age of the thirteenth century B.C., many scholars believe that they really describe the social conditions of the Dark Age. According to the Homeric view, Greece was a society based on agriculture in which a landed warrior-aristocracy controlled much wealth and exercised considerable power. Homer's world reflects the values of aristocratic heroes.

Homer's Enduring Importance

This, of course, explains the importance of Homer to later generations of Greeks. Homer did not record history; he made it. The Greeks regarded the *Iliad* and the *Odyssey* as authentic history as recorded by one poet, Homer. These masterpieces gave the Greeks an ideal past with a cast of heroes and came to be used as standard texts for the education of generations of Greek males. As one Athenian stated, "My father was anxious to see me develop into a good man . . . and as a means to this end he compelled me to memorize all of Homer."[3] The values Homer taught were essentially the aristocratic values of courage and honor (see the box on p. 56). A hero strives for excellence,

The Slaying of Hector. This scene from a late-fifth-century B.C. Athenian vase depicts the final battle between Achilles and the Trojan hero Hector. Achilles is shown lunging forward with his spear to deliver the fatal blow to the Trojan prince, a scene taken from Homer's *Iliad*. The *Iliad* is Homer's masterpiece and was important to later Greeks as a means of teaching the aristocratic values of courage and honor.

HOMER'S IDEAL OF EXCELLENCE

THE *ILIAD* AND THE *ODYSSEY*, epics that the Greeks believed were written by Homer, were used as basic texts for the education of Greeks for hundreds of years in antiquity. This passage from the *Iliad*, describing a conversation between Hector, prince of Troy, and his wife, Andromache, illustrates the Greek ideal of gaining honor through combat. At the end of the passage, Homer also reveals what became the Greek attitude toward women: women are supposed to spin and weave and take care of their households and their children.

Homer, *Iliad*

Hector looked at his son and smiled, but said nothing. Andromache, bursting into tears, went up to him and put her hand in his. "Hector," she said, "you are possessed. This bravery of yours will be your end. You do not think of your little boy or your unhappy wife, whom you will make a widow soon. Some day the Achaeans [Greeks] are bound to kill you in a massed attack. And when I lose you I might as well be dead. . . . I have no father, no mother, now. . . . I had seven brothers too at home. In one day all of them went down to Hades' House. The great Achilles of the swift feet killed them all. . . .

"So you, Hector, are father and mother and brother to me, as well as my beloved husband. Have pity on me now; stay here on the tower; and do not make your boy an orphan and your wife a widow. . . ."

"All that, my dear," said the great Hector of the glittering helmet, "is surely my concern. But if I hid myself like a coward and refused to fight, I could never face the Trojans and

the Trojan ladies in their trailing gowns. Besides, it would go against the grain, for I have trained myself always, like a good soldier, to take my place in the front line and win glory for my father and myself. . . ."

As he finished, glorious Hector held out his arms to take his boy. But the child shrank back with a cry to the bosom of his girdled nurse, alarmed by his father's appearance. He was frightened by the bronze of the helmet and the horsehair plume that he saw nodding grimly down at him. His father and his lady mother had to laugh. But noble Hector quickly took his helmet off and put the dazzling thing on the ground. Then he kissed his son, dandled him in his arms, and prayed to Zeus and the other gods: "Zeus, and you other gods, grant that this boy of mine may be, like me, pre-eminent in Troy; as strong and brave as I; a mighty king of Ilium. May people say, when he comes back from battle, 'Here is a better man than his father.' Let him bring home the bloodstained armor of the enemy he has killed, and make his mother happy."

Hector handed the boy to his wife, who took him to her fragrant breast. She was smiling through her tears, and when her husband saw this he was moved. He stroked her with his hand and said: "My dear, I beg you not to be too much distressed. No one is going to send me down to Hades before my proper time. But Fate is a thing that no man born of woman, coward or hero, can escape. Go home now, and attend to your own work, the loom and the spindle, and see that the maidservants get on with theirs. War is men's business; and this war is the business of every man in Ilium, myself above all."

---

which the Greeks called *arete*. In the warrior-aristocratic world of Homer, *arete* is won in a struggle or contest. Through his willingness to fight, the hero protects his family and friends, preserves his own honor and that of his family, and earns his reputation.

In the Homeric world, aristocratic women, too, were expected to pursue excellence. Penelope, for example, the wife of Odysseus, the hero of the *Odyssey*, remains faithful to her husband and displays great courage and intelligence in preserving their household during her husband's long absence. Upon his return, Odysseus praises her for her excellence: "Madame, there is not a man in the wide world who could find fault with you. For your fame has reached heaven itself, like that of some perfect king, ruling a populous and mighty state with the fear of god in his heart, and upholding the right."[4] Homer gave the Greeks a model of heroism, honor, and nobility. But in time, as a new world of city-states emerged in Greece, new values of cooperation and community also transformed what Greeks learned from Homer.

The World of the Greek City-States (c. 750–c. 500 B.C.)

In the eighth century B.C., Greek civilization burst forth with new energies, beginning the period that historians have called the Archaic Age of Greece. Two major developments stand out in this era: the evolution of the *polis*, or city-state, as the central institution in Greek life and the Greeks' colonization of the Mediterranean and Black Seas.

The *Polis*

The Greek *polis* (plural, *poleis*) developed slowly during the Dark Age but by the eighth century B.C. had emerged as a unique and fundamental institution in Greek society. In a physical sense, the *polis* encompassed a town or city or even a village and its surrounding countryside. But the town or city or village served as the focus or central point where the citizens of the *polis* could assemble for political, social, and religious activities. In some *poleis*, this central meeting point was a hill, which could serve as a place of refuge during an attack and later in some locales came to be the religious center where temples and public monuments were erected. Below this *acropolis* would be an *agora,* an open space that served both as a place where citizens could assemble and as a market.

Poleis varied greatly in size, from a few square miles to a few hundred square miles. The larger ones were the product of consolidation. The territory of Attica, for example, had once had twelve *poleis* but eventually became a single *polis* (Athens) through a process of amalgamation. The population of Athens grew to about 250,000 by the fifth century B.C. Most *poleis* were much smaller, consisting of only a few hundred to several thousand people.

Although our word *politics* is derived from the Greek term *polis,* the *polis* itself was much more than just a political institution. It was, above all, a community of citizens in which all political, economic, social, cultural, and religious activities were focused. As a community, the *polis* consisted of citizens with political rights (adult males), citizens with no political rights (women and children), and noncitizens (slaves and resident aliens). All citizens of a *polis* possessed rights, but these rights were coupled with responsibilities. The Greek philosopher Aristotle argued

that the citizen did not just belong to himself: "We must rather regard every citizen as belonging to the state." The unity of citizens was important and often meant that states would take an active role in directing the patterns of life. However, the loyalty that citizens had to their *poleis* also had a negative side. *Poleis* distrusted one another, and the division of Greece into fiercely patriotic sovereign units helped bring about its ruin. Greece was not a united country but a geographical location. The cultural unity of the Greeks did not mean much politically.

A New Military System: The Hoplites   As the *polis* developed, so did a new military system. In earlier times, wars in Greece had been fought by aristocratic cavalry soldiers—nobles on horseback. These aristocrats, who were large landowners, also dominated the political life of their *poleis.* But at the end of the eighth century, a new military order came into being that was based on **hoplites,** heavily armed infantrymen who wore bronze or leather helmets, breastplates, and greaves (shin guards). Each carried a round shield, a short sword, and a thrusting spear about 9 feet long. Hoplites advanced into battle as a unit, shoulder to shoulder, forming a **phalanx** (a rectangular formation) in tight order, usually eight ranks deep. As long as the hoplites

The Hoplite Forces.   The Greek hoplites were infantrymen equipped with large round shields and long thrusting spears. In battle, they advanced in tight phalanx formation and were dangerous opponents as long as this formation remained unbroken. This vase painting from the seventh century B.C. shows two groups of hoplite warriors engaged in battle. The piper on the left is leading another line of soldiers preparing to enter the fray.

kept their order, were not outflanked, and did not break, they either secured victory or, at the very least, suffered no harm. The phalanx was easily routed, however, if it broke its order. The safety of the phalanx thus depended on the solidarity and discipline of its members. As one seventh-century B.C. poet noted, a good hoplite was "a short man firmly placed upon his legs, with a courageous heart, not to be uprooted from the spot where he plants his legs."[5]

The hoplite force, which apparently developed first in the Peloponnesus, had political as well as military repercussions. The aristocratic cavalry was now outdated. Since each hoplite provided his own armor, men of property, both aristocrats and small farmers, made up the new phalanx. Initially, this created a bond between the aristocrats and peasants, which minimized class conflict and enabled the aristocrats to dominate their societies. In the long run, however, those who could become hoplites and fight for the state could also challenge aristocratic control.

Colonization and the Growth of Trade

Greek expansion overseas was another major development of the Archaic Age. Between 750 and 550 B.C., large numbers of Greeks left their homeland to settle in distant lands.

Poverty and land hunger created by the growing gulf between rich and poor, overpopulation, and the development of trade were all factors that led to the establishment of colonies. Some Greek colonies were simply trading posts or centers for the transshipment of goods to Greece. Most were larger settlements that included good agricultural land taken from the native populations found in those areas. Each colony was founded as a *polis* and was usually independent of the mother *polis* (*metropolis*) that had established it.

In the western Mediterranean, new Greek settlements were established along the coastline of southern Italy, including the cities of Tarentum (Taranto) and Neapolis (Naples) (see Map 3.2). So many Greek communities were established in southern Italy that the Romans later called it *Magna Graecia* ("Great Greece"). An important city was founded at Syracuse in eastern Sicily in 734 B.C. by the city-state of Corinth, one of the most active Greek states in establishing colonies. Greek settlements were also established in southern France (Massilia—modern Marseilles), eastern Spain, and northern Africa west of Egypt.

To the north, the Greeks set up colonies in Thrace, where they sought good agricultural lands to grow grains. Greeks also settled along the shores of the Black Sea and

MAP 3.2 Greece and Its Colonies in the Archaic Age. Impelled by overpopulation and poverty, Greeks spread out from their homelands during the Archaic Age, establishing colonies in many parts of the Mediterranean. The colonies were independent city-states that traded with the older Greek city-states. **?** What aspects of the colonies' locations facilitated trade between them and city-states in Greece? 🌐 **View an animated version of this map or related maps at** http://history.wadsworth.com/spielvogel06/

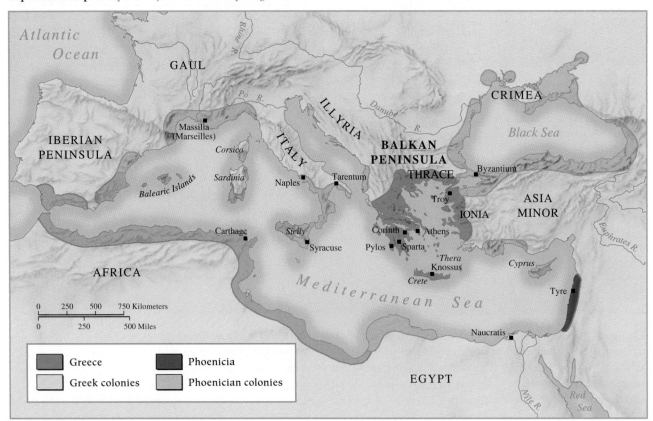

secured the approaches to it with cities on the Hellespont and Bosporus, most notably Byzantium, site of the later Constantinople (Istanbul). A trading post was established in Egypt, giving the Greeks access to both the products and the advanced culture of the East.

The Effects of Colonization   The establishment of these settlements over such a wide area had important effects. For one thing, they contributed to the diffusion of Greek culture throughout the Mediterranean basin. The later Romans had their first contacts with the Greeks through the settlements in southern Italy. Furthermore, colonization helped the Greeks foster a greater sense of Greek identity. Before the eighth century, Greek communities were mostly isolated from one another, leaving many neighboring states on unfriendly terms. Once Greeks from different communities went abroad and encountered peoples with different languages and customs, they became more aware of their own linguistic and cultural similarities.

Colonization also led to increased trade and industry. The Greeks sent their pottery, wine, and olive oil to these areas; in return, they received grains and metals from the west and fish, timber, wheat, metals, and slaves from the Black Sea region. The expansion of trade and industry created a new group of rich men in many *poleis* who desired political privileges commensurate with their wealth but found them impossible to gain because of the power of the ruling aristocrats. The desire for change on the part of this group soon led to political crisis in many Greek states.

Tyranny in the Greek *Polis*

When the *polis* emerged as an important institution in Greece in the eighth century, monarchical power waned, and kings virtually disappeared in most Greek states or survived only as ceremonial figures with little or no real power. Instead, political power passed into the hands of local aristocracies. But increasing divisions between rich and poor and the aspirations of newly rising industrial and commercial groups in Greek *poleis* opened the door to the rise of **tyrants** in the seventh and sixth centuries B.C. They were not necessarily oppressive or wicked, as our word *tyrant* connotes. Greek tyrants were rulers who seized power by force and who were not subject to the law. Support for the tyrants came from the new rich, who made their money in trade and industry, as well as from poor peasants, who were in debt to landholding aristocrats. Both groups were opposed to the domination of political power by aristocratic oligarchies.

Tyrants usually achieved power by a local coup d'état and maintained it by using mercenary soldiers. Once in power, they built new marketplaces, temples, and walls that created jobs, glorified the city, and also enhanced their own popularity. Tyrants also favored the interests of merchants and traders by encouraging the founding of new colonies, developing new coinage, and establishing new systems of weights and measures. In many instances, they added to the

prosperity of their cities. By their patronage of the arts, they encouraged cultural development.

The Example of Corinth   One of the most famous examples of tyranny can be found in Corinth. During the eighth and early seventh centuries B.C., Corinth had become one of the most prosperous states in Greece under the rule of an oligarchy led by members of the Bacchiad family. Their violent activities, however, made them unpopular and led Cypselus, a member of the family, to overthrow the oligarchy and assume sole control of Corinth.

Cypselus was so well liked that he could rule without a bodyguard. During his tyranny, Corinth prospered by exporting vast quantities of pottery and founding new colonies to expand its trade empire. Cypselus' son, Periander, took control of Corinth after his father's death but ruled with such cruelty that shortly after his death in 585 B.C., his own son, who succeeded him, was killed, and a new oligarchy soon ruled Corinth.

As in Corinth, tyranny elsewhere in Greece was largely extinguished by the end of the sixth century B.C. The children and grandchildren of tyrants, who tended to be corrupted by their inherited power and wealth, often became cruel and unjust rulers, making tyranny no longer seem such a desirable institution. Its very nature as a system outside the law seemed contradictory to the ideal of law in a Greek community. Tyranny did not last, but it played a significant role in the evolution of Greek history. The rule of narrow aristocratic oligarchies was destroyed. Once the tyrants were eliminated, the door was opened to the participation of more people in the affairs of the community. Although this trend culminated in the development of democracy in some communities, in other states expanded oligarchies of one kind or another managed to remain in power. Greek states exhibited considerable variety in their governmental structures; this can perhaps best be seen by examining the two most famous and most powerful Greek city-states, Sparta and Athens.

Sparta

The Greeks of Sparta and Athens spoke different dialects and developed different political systems. The Spartans sought stability and conformity and emphasized order. The Athenians allowed for individual differences and stressed freedom. Although the two states shared a common heritage, their differences grew so large in their own minds that they were ultimately willing to engage in a life-and-death struggle to support their separate realities. When they did so, the entire Greek world was the real loser.

Located in the southeastern Peloponnesus, in an area known as Laconia, the Spartans had originally occupied four small villages that eventually became unified into a single *polis* (a fifth soon joined the others). This unification made Sparta a strong community in Laconia and enabled the Spartans to conquer the neighboring Laconians. Many Laconians became **perioikoi,** free inhabitants but

THE LYCURGAN REFORMS

TO MAINTAIN THEIR CONTROL over the helots, the Spartans instituted the reforms that created their military state. In this account of the lawgiver Lycurgus, the Greek historian Plutarch discusses the effect of these reforms on the treatment and education of boys.

Plutarch, *Lycurgus*

Lycurgus was of another mind; he would not have masters bought out of the market for his young Spartans, . . . nor was it lawful, indeed, for the father himself to breed up the children after his own fancy; but as soon as they were seven years old they were to be enrolled in certain companies and classes, where they all lived under the same order and discipline, doing their exercises and taking their play together. Of these, he who showed the most conduct and courage was made captain; they had their eyes always upon him, obeyed his orders, and underwent patiently whatsoever punishment he inflicted; so that the whole course of their education was one continued exercise of a ready and perfect obedience. The old men, too, were spectators of their performances, and often raised quarrels and disputes among them, to have a good opportunity of finding out their different characters, and of seeing which would be valiant, which a coward, when they should come to more dangerous encounters. Reading and writing they gave them just enough to serve their turn; their chief care was to make them good subjects, and to teach them to endure pain and conquer in battle. To this end, as they grew in years, their discipline was proportionately increased; their heads were close-clipped, they were accustomed to go barefoot, and for the most part to play naked.

After they were twelve years old, they were no longer allowed to wear any undergarments, they had one coat to serve them a year; their bodies were hard and dry, with but little acquaintance of baths and unguents; these human indulgences they were allowed only on some few particular days in the year. They lodged together in little bands upon beds made of the rushes which grew by the banks of the river Eurotas, which they were to break off with their hands with a knife; if it were winter, they mingled some thistledown with their rushes, which it was thought had the property of giving warmth. By the time they were come to this age there was not any of the more hopeful boys who had not a lover to bear him company. The old men, too, had an eye upon them, coming often to the grounds to hear and see them contend either in wit or strength with one another, and this as seriously . . . as if they were their fathers, their tutors, or their magistrates; so that there scarcely was any time or place without some one present to put them in mind of their duty, and punish them if they had neglected it.

[Spartan boys were also encouraged to steal their food.] They stole, too, all other meat they could lay their hands on, looking out and watching all opportunities, when people were asleep or more careless than usual. If they were caught, they were not only punished with whipping, but hunger, too, being reduced to their ordinary allowance, which was but very slender, and so contrived on purpose, that they might set about to help themselves, and be forced to exercise their energy and address. This was the principal design of their hard fare.

not citizens who were required to pay taxes and perform military service for Sparta. Other Laconians became known as **helots** (derived from a Greek word for "capture"). They were bound to the land and forced to work on farms and as household servants for the Spartans.

When the land in Laconia proved unable to maintain the growing number of Spartan citizens, the Spartans looked for land nearby and, beginning around 730 B.C., undertook the conquest of neighboring Messenia despite its larger size and population. Messenia possessed a spacious, fertile plain ideal for growing grain. After its conquest, which was not completed until the seventh century B.C., the Messenians were made helots and forced to work for the Spartans. To ensure control over their conquered Laconian and Messenian helots, the Spartans made a conscious decision to create a military state.

Sometime between 800 and 600 B.C., the Spartans instituted a series of reforms that are associated with the name of the lawgiver Lycurgus (see the box above). Although historians are not sure that Lycurgus ever existed, there is no doubt about the result of the reforms that were made: Sparta was transformed into a perpetual military camp.

The New Sparta The lives of Spartans were now rigidly organized. At birth, each child was examined by state officials who decided whether it was fit to live. Those judged unfit were exposed to the elements and left to die. Boys were taken from their mothers at the age of seven and put under control of the state. They lived in barracks, where they were subjected to harsh discipline to make them tough and given an education that stressed military training and obedience to authority. At twenty, Spartan males were enrolled in the army for regular military service. Although allowed to marry, they continued to live in the barracks and ate their meals in public dining halls with their fellow soldiers. Meals were simple; the famous Spartan black broth consisted of a piece of pork boiled in blood, salt, and vinegar, causing a visitor who ate in a public mess to remark that he now understood why Spartans were not afraid to die. At thirty, Spartan males were recognized as mature and allowed to vote in the assembly and live at home, but they remained in the army until the age of sixty.

While their husbands remained in military barracks until age thirty, Spartan women lived at home. Because of this separation, Spartan women had greater freedom of movement and greater power in the household than was common for women elsewhere in Greece. They were encouraged to exercise and remain fit to bear and raise healthy children. Like the men, Spartan women engaged in athletic exercises in the nude. At solemn feasts, the young women would march naked in processions, and in the presence of the young men, they would sing songs about those who had showed special gallantry or cowardice on the battlefield. Many Spartan women upheld the strict Spartan values, expecting their husbands and sons to be brave in war. The story is told that as a Spartan mother was burying her son, an old woman came up to her and said, "You poor woman, what a misfortune." "No," replied the other, "because I bore him so that he might die for Sparta and that is what has happened, as I wished."[6] Another Spartan woman saw her son off to war by telling him to come back carrying his shield or carried on it.

The Spartan social structure was rigidly organized. At the summit were the *Spartiates*—full Spartan citizens. Each Spartan citizen owned a piece of land, worked by the helots, to provide economic sustenance. With their material needs provided for them, Spartan citizens could dedicate themselves to their duties as a ruling class. Below the Spartiates were the *perioikoi*. Though free, they did not possess the privileges of citizenship and served as small merchants and artisans. They were subject to military duty, however. At the bottom of the social scale were the helots, perpetually bound to the land. They were assigned to the lands of the Spartan citizens. The helots farmed the land and gave their masters half of the produce. According to one seventh-century Spartan poet, helots worked "like donkeys exhausted under heavy loads." A secret police force lived among them and was permitted to kill any helot considered dangerous. To legalize this murder, the state officially declared war on the helots at the beginning of each year.

The Spartan State   The so-called Lycurgan reforms also reorganized the Spartan government, creating an **oligarchy.** Two kings from different families were primarily responsible for military affairs and served as the leaders of the Spartan army on its campaigns. Moreover, the kings served as the supreme priests within the state religion and had some role in foreign policy.

The two kings shared power with a body called the *gerousia*, a council of elders. It consisted of twenty-eight citizens over the age of sixty, who were elected for life, and the two kings. The primary task of the *gerousia* was to prepare proposals that would be presented to the *apella,* an assembly of all male citizens. The assembly did not debate but only voted on the proposals put before it by the *gerousia;* rarely did the assembly reject these proposals. The assembly also elected the *gerousia* and another body known as the *ephors.*

To balance the power of the kings and the *gerousia*, the Spartan state created a college of five *ephors*. Elected annually (all males over the age of thirty were eligible), their duties included convening the *gerousia* and supervising the education of youth and the conduct of all citizens. They also served as judges in all civil cases and could even bring charges against a king for wrongdoing.

To make their new military state secure, the Spartans deliberately turned their backs on the outside world. Foreigners, who might bring in new ideas, were discouraged from visiting Sparta. Nor were Spartans, except for military reasons, encouraged to travel abroad where they might pick up new ideas. Trade and commerce were likewise minimized. Spartan citizens were discouraged from pursuing philosophy, literature, the arts, or any subject that might foster novel thoughts dangerous to the stability of the state. The art of war and ruling was the Spartan ideal. All other arts were frowned on.

In the sixth century, Sparta used its military might and the fear it inspired to gain greater control of the Peloponnesus by organizing an alliance of almost all the Peloponnesian states. Sparta's strength enabled it to dominate this Peloponnesian League and determine its policies. By 500 B.C., the Spartans had organized a powerful military state that maintained order and stability in the Peloponnesus. Raised from early childhood to believe that total loyalty to the Spartan state was the basic reason for existence, the Spartans viewed their strength as justification for their militaristic ideals and regimented society.

Athens

By 700 B.C., Athens had established a unified *polis* on the peninsula of Attica. Although early Athens had been ruled by a monarchy, by the seventh century B.C., it had fallen under the control of its aristocrats. They possessed the best land and controlled political and religious life by means of a council of nobles called the Areopagus, assisted by a board of nine archons. Since the archons served only one year and entered the Areopagus afterward, the latter body held the real power. Although there was an *ecclesia* or assembly of full citizens, it possessed few powers.

Near the end of the seventh century B.C., Athens faced political turmoil because of serious economic problems. Many Athenian farmers found themselves sold into slavery when they were unable to repay the loans they had borrowed from their aristocratic neighbors, pledging themselves as collateral. Over and over, there were cries to cancel the debts and give land to the poor. Athens seemed on the verge of civil war.

The Reforms of Solon   Hoping to avoid tyranny, the ruling Athenian aristocrats responded to this crisis by choosing Solon, a reform-minded aristocrat, as sole archon in 594 B.C. and giving him full power to make reforms. Solon canceled all current land debts, outlawed new loans based on humans as collateral, and freed people who had fallen into slavery for debt. He refused, however, to carry out the redistribution of the land and hence failed to deal with the basic cause of the economic crisis.

Like his economic reforms, Solon's political measures were also a compromise. Though by no means eliminating the power of the aristocracy, they opened the door to the participation of new people, especially the nonaristocratic wealthy, in the government. Wealth instead of birth now qualified people for holding political office, thus creating upward political mobility. Solon now divided all Athenian citizens into four classes on the basis of wealth. Only men in the first two classes (the wealthiest classes) could hold the archonship and be members of the Areopagus. Men in the third class could be elected to a new council of four hundred called the *boule,* whose function was to prepare the agenda for the assembly. The fourth (and poorest) class, though not allowed to hold any political offices, could now vote in the assembly. Male citizens of all four classes could also sit in the new popular court (the *heliaea*) instituted by Solon to hear appeals from cases tried before the archons. Moreover, any male citizen could bring to the new court charges against any magistrate suspected of a crime. Government officials were now answerable to all citizens. Indeed, Solon's laws created the principle that Athens would be directed by citizens working together, and in effect, Solon defined a citizen as a person who is involved in public affairs. This, however, did not include women.

The Move to Tyranny   Solon's reforms, though popular, did not solve Athens's problems. Aristocratic factions continued to vie for power, and the poorer peasants resented Solon's failure to institute land redistribution. Internal strife finally led to the very institution Solon had hoped to avoid—tyranny. Pisistratus, an aristocrat and a distant relative of Solon, seized power in 560 B.C. and made himself a tyrant.

Pisistratus did not tamper very much with the constitution. The assembly, councils, and courts continued to function while he made sure that his supporters were elected as magistrates and council members. Pisistratus curried favor with small farmers by offering land and loans to the needy. His ambitious building program, aimed at beautifying the city, also created jobs. Pursuing a foreign policy that aided Athenian trade, Pisistratus also maintained the support of the mercantile and industrial classes. Pisistratus' mild tyranny was popular with many Athenians, but the policies of his son Hippias (527–510 B.C.) eventually produced a reaction, and the Athenians sent Hippias into exile and ended the tyranny. Although the aristocrats attempted to reestablish an aristocratic oligarchy, Cleisthenes, an aristocratic reformer, opposed this plan and, with the backing of the Athenian people, gained the upper hand in 508 B.C. The reforms of Cleisthenes now established the basis for Athenian democracy.

The Reforms of Cleisthenes   A major aim of Cleisthenes' reforms was to weaken the power of traditional localities and regions, which had provided the foundation for aristocratic strength. He made the *demes,* the villages and townships of Attica, the basic units of political life. Cleisthenes enrolled all the citizens of the demes in ten new

CHRONOLOGY   Archaic Greece: Sparta and Athens

Sparta	
Conquest of Messenia	c. 730–710 B.C.
Beginning of Peloponnesian League	c. 560–550 B.C.
Athens	
Solon's reforms	594–593 B.C.
Tyranny of Pisistratus	c. 560–556 and 546–527 B.C.
Deposition of Hippias—end of tyranny	510 B.C.
Cleisthenes' reforms	c. 508–501 B.C.

tribes, each of which contained inhabitants located in the country districts of Attica, the coastal areas, and Athens. The ten tribes thus contained a cross section of the population and reflected all of Attica, a move that gave local areas a basic role in the political structure. Each of the ten tribes chose fifty members by lot each year for a new Council of Five Hundred, which was responsible for the administration of both foreign and financial affairs and prepared the business that would be handled by the assembly. This assembly of all male citizens had final authority in the passing of laws after free and open debate; thus Cleisthenes' reforms strengthened the central role of the assembly of citizens in the Athenian political system.

The reforms of Cleisthenes laid the foundations for Athenian democracy. More changes would come in the fifth century when the Athenians themselves would begin to use the word *democracy* (from the Greek words *demos,* "people," and *kratia,* "power"; thus, power to the people) to describe their system. By 500 B.C., Athens was more united than it had been and was about to assume a more important role in Greek affairs.

Greek Culture in the Archaic Age

The period after the Dark Age witnessed a revitalization of Greek life that is also evident in Greek art and literature. Some aspects of Archaic Greek culture, such as pottery and sculpture, were especially influenced by the East. Greek sculpture, particularly that of the Ionian Greek settlements in southwestern Asia Minor, demonstrates the impact of the considerably older Egyptian civilization. There we first see the life-size stone statues of young male nudes known as *kouros* figures. The *kouros* bears considerable resemblance to Egyptian statues of the New Kingdom. The figures are not realistic but stiff, with a slight smile; one leg is advanced ahead of the other, and the arms are held rigidly at the sides of the body.

Greek literature of the seventh century is perhaps best known for its lyric poetry. The lyric is considerably shorter than epic poetry (such as Homer's) and focuses on personal emotions, usually the power of love and its impact on human lives. Later Greeks acknowledged Sappho as their greatest female lyric poet (see the box on p. 64). Born in the seventh century, Sappho lived on the island of Lesbos in the Aegean Sea, where she taught music and poetry to her young charges. Many of her poems are love songs to her female students. Our word *lesbian* is derived from Sappho's island of Lesbos. Sappho, like many upper-class Greeks, accepted that homosexual and heterosexual feelings could exist in the same individual. Sappho was a wife and a mother who also wrote poems about love between men and between women.

Archaic Greece is also known for poets who reflected the lifestyles of both aristocrats and peasants. A wide gulf, however, separated the wealthy aristocrat with his large landed estates from the poor peasants and small farmers who eked out their existence as best they could. Hesiod, a poet from Boeotia in central Greece who lived around 700 B.C., wrote a lengthy epic poem titled *Works and Days*. Himself a farmer, Hesiod distrusted aristocrats and looked down on what he considered the aristocratic emphasis on pride and war. One of his aims was to show that the gods punished injustice and that the way to success was to work: "Famine and blight do not beset the just, who till their well-worked fields and feast. The earth supports them lavishly." *Works and Days* is the first known paean to work in Western literature.

Hesiod emphasized the importance of two things to the farmer's success. It depended, first of all, on proper respect for and treatment of divine forces: "Please the gods with incense and libations, when you go to bed, and when the holy light returns, that they may favor you, with gracious hearts and spirits, so that you may buy the lands of other men, and they may not buy yours." But success depended on more than prayer; therefore:

> . . . you must learn to organize your work
> So you may have full barns at harvest time.
> From working, men grow rich in flocks and gold
> And dearer to the deathless gods. In work
> There is no shame; shame is in idleness.
> And if you work, the lazy man will soon
> Envy your wealth: a rich man can become
> Famous and good. No matter what your luck,
> To work is better; turn your foolish mind
> From other men's possessions to your own,
> And earn your living, as I tell you to.[7]

To Hesiod, hard work and honesty were the keys to success.

Theognis of Megara described a way of life considerably different from Hesiod's. Theognis was an aristocrat who lived and wrote primarily in the sixth century B.C. Because of revolutionary upheaval, he, like other aristocrats in sixth-century *poleis,* lost his position and probably his wealth. Sent into exile, he became a bitter man. In his

Kouros. On the left is a statue of a young male nude from around 600 B.C., making it an early example of Greek *kouros* sculpture. Such statues, which were placed in temples along with companion figures of clothed young women, known as *korai,* were meant to be representations of the faithful dedicated to the gods. At right is an early-seventh-century B.C. statue of an Egyptian nobleman that shows the influence of Egyptian sculpture on Greek art. Unlike the Egyptians, Greek sculptors preferred depicting nude male figures.

poetry, he portrayed aristocrats as the only good people who are distinguished from others by their natural intelligence, virtue, honor, and moderation. The lower classes or common people were by nature bad and debased:

> Only a fool does favors for the base;
> You'd do as well to sow the gray salt sea.
> No crop of corn would come up from the deep,
> No gratitude, no favors from the base.
> The scum are never sated. If you slip,
> Just once, their former friendship melts away.
> But put a gentleman once in your debt,
> You have a friend for life; he won't forget.

Aristocrats, then, should associate only with other aristocrats: "Avoid low company, mix only with the better sort of men. . . . From them you will learn goodness. Men of little worth will spoil the natural beauty of your birth."[8] The poems of Theognis reveal the political views and biases of a typical sixth-century aristocrat.

THE LYRIC POETRY OF SAPPHO

THESE LOVE POEMS are examples of the work of Sappho of Lesbos, regarded as one of Greece's greatest lyric poets. She wrote directly about her personal world of emotions. Sappho is an unusual figure, an independent woman in a world dominated by males. Her attitude toward the Trojan War, as seen in the poem "To Anaktoria," is quite different from that found in Homer's *Iliad*.

Sappho, "To Anaktoria, Now a Soldier's Wife in Lydia"

Some say cavalry and some would claim
infantry or a fleet of long oars
is the supreme sight on the black earth.
   I say it is

the girl you love. And easily proved.
Did not Helen, who was queen of mortal
beauty, choose as first among mankind
   the very scourge

of Trojan honor? Haunted by Love
she forgot kinsmen, her own dear child
and wandered off to a remote country.
   O weak and fitful

woman bending before any man:
so Anaktoria, although you are
far, do not forget your loving friends.
   And I for one

would rather listen to your soft step
and see your radiant face—than watch
all the dazzling horsemen and armored
   hoplites of Lydia.

"To Atthis"

So I shall never see Atthis again,
and really I long to be dead,
although she too cried bitterly

when she left and she said to me,
"Ah, what a nightmare we've suffered.
Sappho, I swear I go unwillingly."

And I answered, "Go, and be happy.
But remember me, for surely you
know how I worshiped you. If not,

then I want you to remember all
the exquisite days we too shared;
how when near me you would adorn

your hanging locks with violets and
tiny roses and your sapling throat
with necklets of a hundred blossoms;

how your young flesh was rich with kingly
myrrh as you leaned near my breasts on
the soft couch where delicate girls

served us all an Ionian could desire;
how we went to every hill, brook,
and holy place, and when early spring

filled the woods with noises of birds
and a choir of nightingales—we two
in solitude were wandering there."

The High Point of Greek Civilization: Classical Greece

Classical Greece is the name given to the period of Greek history from around 500 B.C. to the conquest of Greece by the Macedonian king Philip II in 338 B.C. It was a period of brilliant achievement, much of it associated with the flowering of democracy in Athens under the leadership of Pericles. Many of the lasting contributions of the Greeks occurred during this period. The age began with a mighty confrontation between the Greek states and the mammoth Persian Empire.

The Challenge of Persia

As Greek civilization grew and expanded throughout the Mediterranean region, it was inevitable that it would come into contact with the Persian Empire to the east. In his play *The Persians*, the Greek playwright Aeschylus reflected what some Greeks perceived to be the essential difference between themselves and the Persians. The Persian queen, curious to find out more about the Athenians, asks: "Who commands them? Who is shepherd of their host?" The chorus responds: "They are slaves to none, nor are they subject."[9] Thus at least some Greeks saw the struggle with the Persians as a contest between freedom and slavery. To the Greeks, a person was a citizen of the state, not a subject.

The Ionian Greek cities in southwestern Asia Minor had already fallen subject to the Persian Empire by the midsixth century B.C. (see Chapter 2). But the Greek cities were restless under Persian control, and a revolt of the Ionian cities, led by Miletus, broke out against the Persians in 499 B.C. The Athenians sent twenty ships to aid the revolt and helped the Milesians capture and burn Sardis, the Persian capital of the Lydian satrapy. The success was temporary, however, and the Persians managed to sack Miletus and reestablish control. By 494 B.C., the rebellion had been suppressed. The Persian ruler Darius now decided to attack the mainland Greeks, in part, no doubt, to gain revenge for the Athenian action but also to expand his empire westward. In 490 B.C., a Persian expedition was sent to Greece.

The First Persian Attack The Persians sailed across the Aegean, captured Eretria (which had also aided the Ionian rebels) on the island of Euboea across from Attica, and then transferred their army to the plain of Marathon, only 26 miles from Athens (see Map 3.3). The Athenians, aided by the Plataeans (from a neighboring town in Boeotia), confronted the Persians without additional assistance. The two armies were quite different. The Persians, with their light-armed troops, were more mobile and flexible and relied heavily on missiles; the Greek hoplites were armed with heavy shields and relied on spear thrusts at close range. The Athenians and Plataeans were clearly outnumbered, but led by Miltiades, one of the Athenian leaders who insisted on attacking, the Greek hoplites charged across the plain of Marathon and crushed the Persian forces (see the box on p. 66). The Persians did not mount another attack against mainland Greece for ten years.

In the meantime, Athens had acquired a new leader, Themistocles, who persuaded his fellow citizens to pursue a new military policy, namely, the development of a navy. The Athenians used a new vein of silver from Laurium to finance the construction of ships and new port facilities. By 480 B.C., Athens had produced a navy of about two hundred vessels, primarily triremes (ships with three banks of oars).

A revolt in Egypt, compounded by the death of Darius in 486 B.C., kept the Persians from mounting another attack on Greece. Xerxes, the new Persian monarch, was bent on revenge and expansion, however. Some of the Greeks prepared by forming a defensive league under Spartan leadership, although many Greek states remained neutral; some even fought on the Persian side.

The Invasion of Xerxes The Persians under Xerxes mounted their invasion in 480 B.C. Their military forces were massive: close to 150,000 troops, almost seven hundred naval ships, and hundreds of supply ships to feed their large army. The Persians crossed the Hellespont by forming a bridge of ships and then moved through Thrace and Macedonia on their way into Greece. The Greek plan, as it evolved, was to fight a holding action at the pass of Thermopylae along the main road from Thessaly into Boeotia, probably to give the Greek fleet of three hundred ships at Artemisium, off northern Euboea, the chance to fight the

MAP 3.3 **The Persian Wars.** The Athenians defeated Persia in 490 B.C. at Marathon. Athens later led a coalition of Greek city-states that decisively defeated Xerxes' navy at the Battle of Salamis in 480 B.C., leading Xerxes to withdraw most of his troops back to Asia. ⚡ How far did the Persian army have to walk to get to Athens, and through what types of terrain? 🌐 **View an animated version of this map or related maps at** http://history.wadsworth.com/spielvogel06/

THE BATTLE OF MARATHON

HE BATTLE OF MARATHON (490 B.C.) was an important event in the struggle between the Greeks and the Persians. The defeat of the mighty Persians gave Athenian confidence a tremendous boost. In *The Persian Wars,* the Greek historian Herodotus gave an account of this momentous battle.

Herodotus, *The Persian Wars*

So when the battle was set in array, and the victims showed themselves favorable, instantly the Athenians, so soon as they were let go, charged the barbarians at a run. Now the distance between the two armies was little short of a mile. The Persians, therefore, when they saw the Greeks coming on at speed, made ready to receive them, although it seemed to them that the Athenians were bereft of their senses, and bent upon their own destruction; for they saw a mere handful of men coming on at a run without either horsemen or archers. Such was the opinion of the barbarians; but the Athenians in close array fell upon them, and fought in a manner worthy of being recorded. They were the first of the Greeks, so far as I know, who introduced the custom of charging the enemy at a run, and they were likewise the first who dared to look upon the Median garb, and to face men clad in that fashion. Until this time the very name of the Medes had been a terror to the Greeks to hear.

The two armies fought together on the plain of Marathon for a length of time; and in the mid battle, where the Persians themselves and the Sacae had their place, the barbarians were victorious, and broke and pursued the Greeks into the inner country; but on the two wings the Athenians and the Plataeans defeated the enemy. Having so done, they suffered the routed barbarians to fly at their ease, and joining the two wings in one, fell upon those who had broken their own center, and fought and conquered them. These likewise fled, and now the Athenians hung upon the runaways and cut them down, chasing them all the way to the shore, on reaching which they laid hold of the ships and called for fire. . . .

After the full of the moon 2,000 Lacedaemonians [Spartans] came to Athens. So eager had they been to arrive in time, that they took but three days to reach Attica from Sparta. They came, however, too late for the battle; yet, as they had a longing to behold the Medes, they continued their march to Marathon and there viewed the slain. Then, after giving the Athenians all praise for their achievement, they departed and returned home.

The Greek Trireme. The trireme became the standard warship of ancient Greece. Highly maneuverable, fast, and outfitted with metal prows, Greek triremes were especially effective at ramming enemy ships. The bas-relief shows a fifth-century B.C. Athenian trireme. The photo shows the *Olympias,* a trireme reconstructed by the Greek navy.

Courtesy of William M. Murray

© The Art Archive/Acropolis Museum Athens/Dagli Orti

Persian fleet. The Greeks knew that the Persian army depended on the fleet for supplies. A Greek force numbering close to nine thousand, under the leadership of the Spartan king Leonidas and his contingent of three hundred Spartans, held off the Persian army at Thermopylae for two days. The Spartan troops were especially brave. When told that Persian arrows would darken the sky in battle, one Spartan warrior supposedly responded, "That is good news. We will fight in the shade!" Unfortunately for the Greeks, a traitor told the Persians of a mountain path they could use to outflank the Greek force. King Leonidas and the three hundred Spartans fought to the last man.

The Athenians, now threatened by the onslaught of the Persian forces, decided to abandon Athens and evacuated the population of Attica to the offshore island of Salamis.

Meanwhile, the Greek fleet remained in the straits off Salamis while the Persians sacked Athens. The Peloponnesians wanted the Greeks to retreat to the Peloponnesus and the Greek ships to move to the isthmus as well. Themistocles' refusal and his threat to withdraw the Athenian ships altogether if a fight was not made forced the ships to remain and set up the naval Battle of Salamis. Although

Persian control of Greek cities in southwestern Asia Minor	By 540s B.C.
Rebellion of Greek cities in Asia Minor	499–494 B.C.
Battle of Marathon	490 B.C.
Xerxes invades Greece	480–479 B.C.
Battles of Thermopylae and Salamis	480 B.C.
Battles of Plataea and Mycale	479 B.C.

the Greeks were outnumbered, they managed to outmaneuver the Persian fleet (mostly Phoenicians and Ionians) and decisively defeated them. The Persians still had their army and much of their fleet intact, but Xerxes, frightened at the prospect of another Ionian revolt, decided to return to Asia. He left a Persian force in Thessaly under his general, Mardonius.

Early in 479 B.C., the Greeks formed the largest Greek army seen up to that time. The Athenians forced the Spartans to move north of the Peloponnesus and take on the Persians at Plataea, northwest of Athens, where the Greek forces decisively defeated the Persian army. The remnants of the Persian forces returned to Asia. At the same time, the Greeks destroyed much of the Persian fleet in a naval battle at Mycale in Ionia. The Greeks were overjoyed at their victory but remained cautious. Would the Persians try again?

The Growth of an Athenian Empire

After the defeat of the Persians, Athens stepped in to provide new leadership against the Persians by forming a confederation called the Delian League. Organized in the winter of 478–477 B.C., the Delian League was dominated by the Athenians from the beginning. Its main headquarters was the island of Delos, sacred to the Ionian Greeks, but its chief officials, including the treasurers and commanders of the fleet, were Athenians. Athens also provided most of the league's three hundred ships. While the larger states in the league, such as Lesbos, Samos, and Chios, contributed ships, the smaller communities made payments in money.

Under the leadership of the Athenians, the Delian League pursued the attack against the Persian Empire. Virtually all of the Greek states in the Aegean were liberated from Persian control, and the Persian fleet and army were decisively defeated in 469 B.C. in southern Asia Minor. Arguing that the Persian threat was now over, some members of the Delian League wished to withdraw. Naxos did so in 470 and Thasos in 465 B.C. The Athenians responded vigorously. They attacked both states, destroyed their walls, took over their fleets, eliminated their liberty, and forced them to pay tribute. "No secession" became Athenian policy. The Delian League was rapidly becoming an instrument of Athenian imperialism and the nucleus of an Athenian empire.

The Age of Pericles   At home, Athenians favored the new imperial policy, especially in the 450s B.C., when an aristocrat named Pericles began to play an important political role. Under Pericles, Athens embarked on a policy of expanding democracy at home while severing its ties with Sparta and expanding its new empire abroad. This period of Athenian and Greek history, which historians have subsequently labeled the Age of Pericles, witnessed the height of Athenian power and the culmination of its brilliance as a civilization.

In the age of Pericles, the Athenians became deeply attached to their democratic system. The sovereignty of the people was embodied in the assembly (*ecclesia*), which consisted of all male citizens over eighteen years of age. In the 440s, that was probably a group of about 43,000. Meetings of the assembly were held on the hillside of the Pnyx, east of the Acropolis. Not all could attend, and the number present seldom exceeded six thousand, which was the capacity of the Pnyx. The assembly passed all laws and

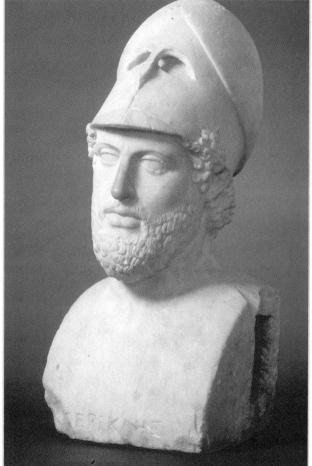

Pericles: Roman Copy of Fifth-Century Bronze Original. Pericles dominated Athenian politics from 461 to 429 B.C. In addition to increasing the Athenians' participation in their own democratic system, he pursued an imperialistic policy, expanding the Athenian empire both on the Greek mainland and abroad. It is reported that Pericles possessed a somewhat elongated skull, which the sculptor sought to conceal by adding the helmet to Pericles' head.

ATHENIAN DEMOCRACY: THE FUNERAL ORATION OF PERICLES

*I*N HIS *History of the Peloponnesian War,* the Greek historian Thucydides presented his reconstruction of the eulogy given by Pericles in the winter of 431–430 B.C. to honor the Athenians killed in the first campaigns of the Great Peloponnesian War. It is a magnificent, idealized description of the Athenian democracy at its height.

Thucydides, *History of the Peloponnesian War*

Our constitution is called a democracy because power is in the hands not of a minority but of the whole people. When it is a question of settling private disputes, everyone is equal before the law; when it is a question of putting one person before another in positions of public responsibility, what counts is not membership of a particular class, but the actual ability which the man possesses. No one, so long as he has it in him to be of service to the state, is kept in political obscurity because of poverty. And, just as our political life is free and open, so is our day-to-day life in our relations with each other. We do not get into a state with our next-door neighbor if he enjoys himself in his own way, nor do we give him the kind of black looks which, though they do no real harm, still do hurt people's feeling. We are free and tolerant in our private lives; but in public affairs we keep to the law. This is because it commands our deep respect.

We give our obedience to those whom we put in positions of authority, and we obey the laws themselves, especially those which are for the protection of the oppressed, and those unwritten laws which it is an acknowledged shame to break. . . . Here each individual is interested not only in his own affairs but in the affairs of the state as well: even those who are mostly occupied with their own business are extremely well-informed on general politics—this is a peculiarity of ours: we do not say that a man who takes no interest in politics is a man who minds his own business; we say that he has no business here at all. We Athenians, in our own persons, take our decisions on policy or submit them to proper discussions: for we do not think that there is an incompatibility between words and deeds; the worst thing is to rush into action before the consequences have been properly debated. . . . Taking everything together then, I declare that our city is an education to Greece, and I declare that in my opinion each single one of our citizens, in all the manifold aspects of life, is able to show himself the rightful lord and owner of his own person and do this, moreover, with exceptional grace and exceptional versatility. And to show that this is no empty boasting for the present occasion, but real tangible fact, you have only to consider the power which our city possesses and which has been won by those very qualities which I have mentioned.

made final decisions on war and foreign policy. Although anyone could speak, usually only respected leaders did so, a feat that required considerable speaking ability in such a large crowd.

The reforms of Cleisthenes had introduced the Council of Five Hundred, elected by lot from the ten tribes. It prepared the agenda for the assembly and made recommendations for action. Thus the council served as a control on the assembly. The council was divided into ten smaller groups of fifty called *prytanies.* Each prytany held office for one-tenth of the year to supervise the execution of the laws passed by the assembly.

Routine administration of public affairs was handled by a large body of city magistrates, usually chosen by lot without regard to class and usually serving only one-year terms. This meant that many male citizens held public office at some time in their lives. A board of ten officials known as generals (*strategoi*) were elected by public vote to guide affairs of state, although their power depended on the respect they had attained. Generals were usually wealthy aristocrats, even though the people were free to select otherwise. The generals could be reelected, enabling individual leaders to play an important political role. Pericles' frequent reelection (fifteen times) as one of the ten generals made him one of the leading politicians between 461 and 429 B.C.

All public officials were subject to scrutiny and could be deposed from office if they lost the people's confidence. After 488 B.C., the Athenians occasionally made use of a tactic called *ostracism.* This practice enabled the members of the assembly to write on a broken pottery fragment (*ostrakon*) the name of the person they most disliked or considered most harmful to the *polis.* Frequently, this was a person whose policy, approved at first by the assembly, had failed. A person who received a majority (if at least six thousand votes were cast) was exiled for ten years, although the practical Athenians often recalled a man from exile if they needed him.

Pericles expanded the Athenians' involvement in democracy, which was by now what Athenians had come to call their form of government (see the box above). Power was in the hands of the people: male citizens voted in the assemblies and served as jurors in the courts. Lower-class citizens were now eligible for public offices formerly closed to them. Pericles also introduced state pay for officeholders, including the widely held jury duty. This meant that even poor citizens could hold public office and afford to participate in public affairs. Nevertheless, although the Athenians developed a system of government that was unique in its time in which citizens had equal rights and the people were the government, aristocrats continued to hold the most important offices, and many people, including women, slaves, and foreigners residing in Athens, were not given the same political rights.

Athenian Imperialism   The Athenian pursuit of democracy at home was coupled with increasing imperialism abroad as Athens attempted to create both a land empire in Greece and a maritime empire in the Aegean. As we have seen, after 470 B.C., Athenian policies had the effect of converting the voluntary allies of the Delian League into the involuntary subjects of an Athenian naval empire. After 462 B.C., Athens attempted to expand its empire on the Greek mainland as well. The creation of a land empire, however, overextended the Athenians and involved them in a series of skirmishes with Sparta and its allies known as the First Peloponnesian War (c. 460–445 B.C.). After a series of defeats in 445 B.C., the land empire of Athens disintegrated, and Athens agreed to a thirty years' peace with the Spartans in the following year. Athens consented to give up most of its land empire, and in return, Sparta recognized the existence of Athens' maritime empire.

While building its land empire, Athens continued its offensive against Persia and at the same time tightened its control over the Delian League. Citing the threat of the Persian fleet in the Aegean, the Athenians moved the treasury of the league from the island of Delos to Athens itself, possibly in 454 B.C. Members were, in effect, charged a fee (tribute) for the Athenian claim of protection. Pericles also used the treasury money of the league, without the approval of its members, to build new temples in Athens, a clear indication that the Delian League had become the Athenian empire. Henceforth, any protest by a league state against the tribute imposed by Athens could be heard only before an Athenian court. However, Athenian imperialism, pursued both in Greece and abroad, took its toll. Pericles recognized the dangers of Athenian exhaustion and sought a lull. After peace was made with Sparta in 445 B.C., the Athenians had a breathing space in which to beautify Athens and enjoy the fruits of empire, but it was not long before all of Greece was plunged into a new and prolonged struggle.

The Great Peloponnesian War (431–404 B.C.)

In the decades that followed the defeat of the Persians, the Greek world divided into two major camps: Sparta and its Peloponnesian League and the Athenian maritime empire.

In his classic *History of the Peloponnesian War,* the great Greek historian Thucydides pointed out that the fundamental, long-range cause of the war was the fear that Athens and its empire inspired in Sparta. The Spartans were especially concerned that Athens would use its superior naval power to weaken Sparta's control of the Peloponnesian League. The immediate causes of the war involved conflicts between Corinth and Athens and between Athens and Megara. When these two allies of Sparta threatened to

withdraw from the Peloponnesian League if Sparta did not back them, the Spartans sent an ultimatum to Athens: if the Athenians did not back down in their disputes with Corinth and Megara, it would mean war. The Athenians refused to compromise when Pericles convinced them that if they accepted Sparta's ultimatum, they would be admitting that Sparta was the dominant power in Greece.

At the beginning of the war in 431 B.C., both sides believed they had winning strategies. The Athenian plan was based on the navy. The citizens of Attica would be brought in behind the protective walls of Athens and the port of Piraeus, while the overseas empire and the navy would keep them supplied (see Map 3.4). Pericles knew perfectly well that the Spartans and their allies could beat the Athenians in pitched battles, which, of course, formed the focus of the Spartan

Piraeus and Athens

strategy. The Spartans and their allies invaded Attica and ravaged the fields and orchards, hoping that the Athenians would send out their army to fight beyond the walls. But Pericles was convinced that Athens was secure behind its walls and retaliated by sending out naval excursions to ravage the seacoast of the Peloponnesus. In the second year of the war, however, a plague devastated the crowded city of Athens and wiped out possibly one-third of the population. Pericles himself died the following year (429 B.C.), a severe loss to Athens. Dominance now passed to Cleon, leader of the war party, who was opposed by Nicias, head of a conservative faction that favored peace. Despite the losses from the plague, the Athenians fought on in a struggle that witnessed numerous instances of futile destruction. Cleon achieved some successes for the Athenians; Brasidas came to be a dynamic general for the Spartans. At the Battle of Amphipolis in 422 B.C., both generals were killed, and the new Athenian leader, Nicias, negotiated the Peace of Nicias (421 B.C.). Although both parties agreed to keep the peace for fifty years, the truce did not solve the problems that had caused the war in the first place.

A second phase of the war began only six years after the fifty-year truce began. This phase was initiated by Alcibiades, a nephew of Pericles. Elected to the generalship in 420 B.C., he proved to be a poor choice because of his recklessness and self-seeking. In 415 B.C., he convinced the Athenians to invade the island of Sicily, arguing that its conquest would give the Athenians a strong source of support to carry on a lengthy war. But the expedition was ill-fated. Alcibiades himself was removed from leadership of the expedition on a charge of profaning the religious mysteries. Rather than stand trial, he fled to Sparta and advised the Spartans how to defeat Athens by getting help from Persia and assembling a navy with ships and money supplied by the Persians. The Spartans later followed his advice.

DISASTER IN SICILY

*A*T THE BEGINNING OF his *History of the Peloponnesian War,* the Greek historian Thucydides wrote, "The Peloponnesian War . . . not only lasted for a long time, but throughout its course brought with it unprecedented suffering for Greece. Never before had so many cities been captured and then devastated, . . . never had there been so many exiles; never such loss of life." The greatest defeat for Athens came in Sicily in 413 B.C. In his history, Thucydides described what happened to the captured Athenians.

Thucydides, *History of the Peloponnesian War*

The Syracusans and their allies now brought their forces together into one, took up the spoils and as many of the prisoners as they could, and went back to their city. They put the Athenian and allied prisoners whom they had taken into the stone quarries, thinking that this was the safest way of keeping them. . . .

Those who were in the stone quarries were treated badly by the Syracusans at first. There were many of them, and they were crowded together in a narrow pit, where, since there was no roof over their heads, they suffered first from the heat of the sun and the closeness of the air; and then, in contrast, came on the cold autumnal nights, and the change in temperature brought disease among them.

Lack of space made it necessary for them to do everything on the same spot; and besides there were the bodies all heaped together on top of one another of those who had died from their wounds or from the change of temperature or other such causes, so that the smell was insupportable. At the same time they suffered from hunger and from thirst. During eight months the daily allowance for each man was half a pint of water and a pint of corn. In fact they suffered everything which one could imagine might be suffered by men imprisoned in such a place. For about ten weeks they lived like this all together; then, with the exception of the Athenians and any Greeks from Italy or Sicily who had joined the expedition, the rest were sold as slaves. It is hard to give the exact figure, but the whole number of prisoners must have been at least 7,000.

This was the greatest Hellenic action that took place during this war, and, in my opinion, the greatest action that we know of in Hellenic history—to the victors the most brilliant of successes, to the vanquished the most calamitous of defeats; for they were utterly and entirely defeated; their sufferings were on an enormous scale; their losses were, as they say, total; army, navy, everything was destroyed, and, out of many, only few returned. So ended the events in Sicily.

In the meantime, the Athenians pursued the Sicilian policy. A "great expedition" consisting of five thousand Athenian hoplites was sent out in 415 B.C. and reinforced two years later by an even larger army of Athenians and allies. All was in vain. The Athenians failed to take Syracuse and were captured during their retreat. All of the Athenians were killed or sold into slavery (see the box above). These heavy losses at Syracuse had immediate domestic repercussions. The democracy was weakened, and an aristocratic oligarchy was temporarily established (411–410 B.C.).

Despite the disaster, the Athenians refused to give up; they raised new armies and sent out new fleets. The final crushing blow came, however, in 405 B.C., when the Athenian fleet was destroyed at Aegospotami on the Hellespont. Athens was besieged and surrendered the next year. Its walls were torn down, the navy was disbanded, and the Athenian empire was dissolved. The great war was finally over.

The Decline of the Greek States (404–338 B.C.)

The next seventy years witnessed continuing warfare among the Greeks, with the leading roles shifting among Sparta, Athens, and a new Greek power, the city-state of Thebes. After the defeat of Athens in 404 B.C., the Spartans established their own control over Greece. The Athenian empire was no more. Oligarchies, headed by local *decarchies*

(ten-man boards) in cooperation with Spartan garrisons, were placed in control of the states "liberated" from Athenian imperialism. But oligarchical control proved ineffective, especially in Athens, where the ruling oligarchical faction of thirty, set up by the Spartans, earned the nickname of "Thirty Tyrants" by executing about fifteen hundred of their democratic opponents. This led to a reaction in which the Athenians were able to reestablish their democracy in 403 B.C. They also rebuilt their navy and again became an important force in the Greek world.

To maintain its newly organized leadership in Greek affairs, Sparta encouraged a Panhellenic crusade against the Persians as a common enemy. The Persians had taken advantage of the Greeks' internal struggle to reimpose their control over the Greek states in western Asia Minor. The Spartans, under King Agesilaus, led a Greek expedition into Asia Minor in 396 B.C. But the Persians had learned the lessons of Greek politics and offered financial support to Athens, Thebes, and other Greek states to oppose Spartan power within Greece itself, thus beginning a new war, the Corinthian War (395–386 B.C.). The war ended when the Greek states, weary of the struggles, accepted the King's Peace, dictated by the Great King of Persia.

The city-state of Thebes, in Boeotia north of Athens, now began to exert its influence. Under their leader Epaminondas, the Thebans dramatically defeated the Spartan army at the Battle of Leuctra in 371 B.C. Spartan power declined, to be replaced by the ascendancy of the Thebans.

But Theban power was short-lived. After the death of Epaminondas in the Battle of Mantinea in 362 B.C., the Thebans could no longer dominate Greek politics. And yet the Greek states continued their petty wars, seemingly oblivious to the growing danger to the north, where King Philip II of Macedonia was developing a unified state that would finally end the destructive fratricide of the Greek states by imposing Macedonian authority.

Culture and Society of Classical Greece

Classical Greece saw a period of remarkable intellectual and cultural growth throughout the Greek world. Historians agree, however, that Periclean Athens was the most important center of Classical Greek culture. Indeed, the eighteenth-century French philosopher and writer Voltaire listed the Athens of Pericles as one of four happy ages "when the arts were brought to perfection and which, marking an era of the greatness of the human mind, are an example to posterity."[10]

The Writing of History

History as we know it, the systematic analysis of past events, was a Greek creation. Herodotus (c. 484–c. 425 B.C.), a Dorian Greek from Asia Minor, was the author of *The Persian*

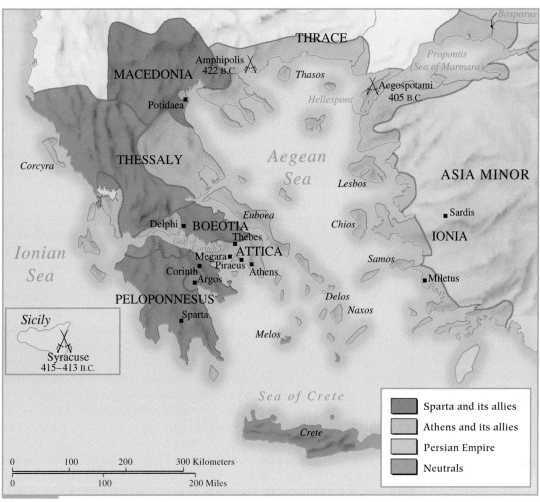

MAP 3.4 **The Great Peloponnesian War (431–404 B.C.): Alliances and Battles.** During much of the fifth century B.C., Athens sought to dominate Greece and the Aegean Sea. The Peloponnesian War ultimately saw Sparta and the Peloponnesian League defeat Athens and its allies, culminating in the destruction of Athens's navy and the dismantling of its empire in 404 B.C. ❓ How did Athens use its proximity to the ocean to forge and maintain its empire and to conduct the war? 🌐 **View an animated version of this map or related maps at** http://history.wadsworth.com/spielvogel06/

Wars, a work commonly regarded as the first real history in Western civilization. The Greek word *historia* (from which we derive our word *history*) means "research" or "investigation," and it is in the opening line of Herodotus' work that we find the first recorded use of the word:

Here are presented the researches (*historiae*) carried out by Herodotus of Halicarnassus. The purpose is to prevent the traces of human events from being erased by time, and to preserve the fame of the important and remarkable achievements produced by both Greeks and non-Greeks; among the matters covered is, in particular, the cause of the hostilities between Greeks and non-Greeks.[11]

The central theme of Herodotus' work is the conflict between the Greeks and the Persians, which he viewed as a struggle between Greek freedom and Persian despotism. Herodotus traveled widely for his information and was dependent for his sources on what we today would call oral history. Although he was a master storyteller and sometimes included considerable fanciful material, Herodotus was also capable of exhibiting a critical attitude toward the materials he used. Regardless of its weaknesses, Herodotus' history is an important source of information on the Persians and our chief source on the Persian Wars themselves.

Thucydides Thucydides (c. 460–c. 400 B.C.) was by far the better historian; in fact, modern historians consider him the greatest of the ancient world. Thucydides was an Athenian and a participant in the Peloponnesian War. He had been elected a general, but a defeat in battle led the Athenian assembly to send him into exile. In *History of the Peloponnesian War,* he described his activities:

I lived through the whole of it, being of an age to understand what was happening, and I put my mind to the subject so as to get an accurate view of it. It happened, too, that I was banished from my country for twenty years after my command at Amphipolis [422 B.C.]; I saw what was being done on both sides, particularly on the Peloponnesian side, because of my exile, and this leisure gave me rather exceptional facilities for looking into things.[12]

Unlike Herodotus, Thucydides was not concerned with underlying divine forces or gods as explanatory causal factors in history. He saw war and politics in purely rational terms, as the activities of human beings. He examined the long-range and immediate causes of the Peloponnesian War in a clear, methodical, objective fashion. Thucydides placed much emphasis on accuracy and the precision of his facts. As he stated:

And with regard to my factual reporting of the events of the war I have made it a principle not to write down the first story that came my way, and not even to be guided by my own general impressions; either I was present myself at the events which I have described or else I heard of them from eyewitnesses whose reports I have checked with as much thoroughness as possible.[13]

Thucydides also provided remarkable insight into the human condition. He believed that human nature was a constant: "It will be enough for me, however, if these words of mine are judged useful by those who want to understand clearly the events which happened in the past and which (human nature being what it is) will, at some time or other and in much the same ways, be repeated in the future."[14] He was not so naive as to believe in an exact repetition of events but felt that political situations recur in similar fashion and that the study of history is of great value in understanding the present.

Greek Drama

Drama as we know it was created by the Greeks and was clearly intended to do more than entertain. It was used to educate citizens and was supported by the state for that reason. Plays were presented in outdoor theaters as part of religious festivals. The form of Greek plays remained rather stable. Three male actors who wore masks acted all the parts. A chorus, also male, spoke the important lines that explained what was going on. Action was very limited because the emphasis was on the story and its meaning. Content was generally based on myths or legends that the audience already knew.

Aeschylus The first Greek dramas were tragedies, plays based on the suffering of a hero and usually ending in disaster. Aeschylus (525–456 B.C.) is the first tragedian whose plays are known to us. Although he wrote ninety tragedies, only seven have survived. As was customary in Greek tragedy, his plots are simple. The entire drama focuses on a single tragic event and its meaning. Greek tragedies were sometimes presented in a trilogy (a set of three plays) built around a common theme. The only complete trilogy we possess, called the *Oresteia,* was composed by Aeschylus. The theme of this trilogy is derived from Homer. Agamemnon, the king of Mycenae, returns a hero from the defeat of Troy. His wife, Clytemnestra, avenges the sacrificial death of her daughter Iphigenia by murdering Agamemnon, who had been responsible for Iphigenia's death. In the second play of the trilogy, Agamemnon's son Orestes avenges his father by killing his mother. Orestes is now pursued by the avenging Furies, who torment him for killing his mother. Evil acts breed evil acts, and suffering is one's lot, suggests Aeschylus. But Orestes is put on trial and acquitted by Athena, the patron goddess of Athens. Personal vendetta has been eliminated, and law has prevailed.

Sophocles Another great Athenian playwright was Sophocles (c. 496–406 B.C.), whose most famous play is *Oedipus the King.* The oracle of Apollo foretells that a man (Oedipus) will kill his own father and marry his mother. Despite all attempts at prevention, the tragic events occur. Although it appears that Oedipus suffered the fate determined by the gods, Oedipus also accepts that he himself as a free man must bear responsibility for his actions: "It was Apollo, friends, Apollo, that brought this bitter bitterness, my sor-

Greek Tragedy: *The Eumenides*. The Greek artist Python depicted this detail on a fourth-century B.C. vase. Shown is a scene from *The Eumenides,* the third play of the *Oresteia* trilogy written by Aeschylus. In this play, Orestes is acquitted by Athena of the crime of killing his mother to avenge his father's death. The Furies, who had been pursuing Orestes for killing his mother, now become the Eumenides—the "Kindly Ones."

rows to completion. But the hand that struck me was none but my own."[15]

Euripides   The third outstanding Athenian tragedian, Euripides (c. 485–406 B.C.), moved beyond his predecessors in creating more realistic characters. His plots also became more complex, reflecting a greater interest in real-life situations. Perhaps the greatest of all his plays is *The Bacchae,* which deals with the introduction of the hysterical rites associated with Dionysus, god of wine. Euripides is often seen as a skeptic who questioned traditional moral and religious values. Euripides was also critical of the traditional view that war was glorious. He portrayed war as brutal and barbaric and expressed deep compassion for the women and children who suffered from it.

Greek tragedies dealt with universal themes that are still relevant in our day. They probed such problems as the nature of good and evil, the conflict between spiritual values and the demands of the state or family, the rights of the individual, the nature of divine forces, and the nature of human beings. Over and over again, the tragic lesson was repeated: humans were free and yet could operate only within limitations imposed by the gods. The real task was to cultivate the balance and moderation that led to awareness of one's true position. But the pride in human accomplishment and independence is real. As the chorus chants in Sophocles' *Antigone:* "Is there anything more wonderful on earth, our marvellous planet, than the miracle of man?"[16]

Greek Comedy   Greek comedy developed later than tragedy. The plays of Aristophanes (c. 450–c. 385 B.C.), who used both grotesque masks and obscene jokes to entertain the Athenian audience, are examples of Old Comedy. But comedy in Athens was also more clearly political than tragedy. It was used to attack or savagely satirize both politicians and intellectuals. In *The Clouds,* for example, Aristophanes characterizes the philosopher Socrates as the operator of a thought factory where people could learn deceitful ways to handle other people. Later plays give up the element of personal attack and feature contemporary issues. Of special importance to Aristophanes was his opposition to the Peloponnesian War. *Lysistrata,* performed in 411 B.C., at a time when Athens was in serious danger of losing the war, has a comic but effective message against the war (see the box on p. 74).

The Arts: The Classical Ideal

The artistic standards established by the Greeks of the Classical Period have largely dominated the arts of the Western world. Classical Greek art did not aim at experimentation for experiment's sake but was concerned with expressing eternally true ideals. Its subject matter was basically the human being, expressed harmoniously as an object of great beauty. The Classical Style, based on the ideals of reason, moderation, symmetry, balance, and harmony in all things, was meant to civilize the emotions.

In architecture, the most important form was the temple dedicated to a god or goddess. Since Greek religious ceremonies were held at altars in the open air, temples were not used to enclose the faithful, as modern churches are. At the center of Greek temples were walled rooms that housed the statues of deities and treasuries in which gifts to the gods and goddesses were safeguarded. These central rooms were surrounded by a screen of columns that make Greek temples open structures rather than closed ones. The columns were originally made of wood but changed to limestone in the seventh century and to marble in the fifth century B.C. The most significant formal element in Greek temples was the shape and size of the columns in combination with the features above and below the column.

Some of the finest examples of Classical Greek architecture were built in fifth-century Athens. The development of Athenian architecture was aided tremendously by the massive rebuilding program funded from the treasury of the Delian League and instituted almost a half-century after the Persians destroyed Athens in the Persian Wars. New buildings were erected in the agora, but especially important was a series of constructions on the Acropolis begun in 448 B.C., which included a monumental entrance gate, a temple to Athena Nike (the Bringer of Victory), and the Erechtheum, a multilevel temple. These temples honored the gods and heroes who protected Athens.

The most famous building, regarded as the greatest example of the Classical Greek temple, was the Parthenon, built between 447 and 432 B.C. The master builders Ictinus and Callicrates directed the construction of this temple, which was consecrated to Athena, the patron goddess of Athens. The Parthenon typifies the principles of Classical architecture: the search for calm, clarity, and freedom from superfluous detail. The individual parts of the temple were constructed in accordance with certain mathematical ratios found in nature. The concern of the architects with these laws of proportion is paralleled by the attempt of Greek philosophers to understand the general laws of nature.

Greek sculpture also developed a Classical style that differed significantly from the artificial stiffness of the *kouros* figure of the Archaic Period. Statues of the male nude, the favorite subject of Greek sculptors, now exhibited more relaxed attitudes; their faces were self-assured, their bodies flexible and smooth-muscled. Although the figures possessed natural features that made them lifelike, Greek sculptors sought to achieve not realism but a standard of ideal beauty. Polyclitus, a fifth-century sculptor, wrote a treatise (now lost) on a canon of proportions that he illustrated in a work known as the *Doryphoros*. His theory maintained that the use of ideal proportions, based on mathematical ratios found in nature, could produce an ideal human form, beautiful in its perfected and refined features. This search for ideal beauty was the dominant feature of the Classical standard in sculpture.

Doric, Ionic, and Corinthian Orders. The size and shape of a column constituted one of the most important aspects of Greek temple architecture. The Doric order, with plain capitals and no base, developed first in the Dorian Peloponnesus and was rather simple in comparison to the slender Ionic column, which had an elaborate base and spiral-shaped capitals, and the Corinthian column, which featured leaf-shaped capitals.

© Art Resource, NY

The Parthenon. The arts in Classical Greece were designed to express the eternal ideals of reason, moderation, symmetry, balance, and harmony. In architecture, the most important form was the temple, and the classic example of this kind of architecture is the Parthenon, built between 447 and 432 B.C. Located on the Acropolis in Athens, the Parthenon was dedicated to Athena, the patron goddess of the city, but it also served as a shining example of the power and wealth of the Athenian empire.

The Greek Love of Wisdom

Philosophy is a Greek word that literally means "love of wisdom." Early Greek philosophers were concerned with the development of critical or rational thought about the nature of the universe and the place of divine forces and souls in it.

Much of early Greek philosophy focused on the attempt to explain the universe on the basis of unifying principles. Thales of Miletus, an Ionian Greek who lived around 600 B.C., postulated the unity of the universe. All things were linked by water as the basic substance. Another Ionian Greek, Pythagoras (c. 580–c. 490 B.C.), taught that the essence of the universe could be found in music and number. These early Greek philosophers may have eliminated the role of the gods as they were portrayed in Greek myths, but they did not eliminate divinity itself from the world, tending instead to identify it with the underlying, unchanging forces that govern the universe.

Many Greeks, however, were simply not interested in speculations on the nature of the universe. The **Sophists** were a group of philosophical teachers in the fifth century who rejected such speculation as foolish; they argued

Doryphoros. This statue, known as the *Doryphoros,* or spear carrier, is a Roman copy of the original work by the fifth-century B.C. sculptor Polyclitus, who believed it illustrated the ideal proportions of the human figure. Classical Greek sculpture moved away from the stiffness of the *kouros* figure but retained the young male nude as the favorite subject matter. The statues became more lifelike, with relaxed poses and flexible, smooth-muscled bodies. The aim of sculpture, however, was not simply realism but rather the expression of ideal beauty.

that understanding the universe was beyond the reach of the human mind. It was more important for individuals to improve themselves, so the only worthwhile object of study was human behavior. The Sophists were wandering scholars who sold their services as professional teachers to the young men of Greece, especially those of Athens. The Sophists stressed the importance of **rhetoric** (the art of persuasive speaking) in winning debates and swaying an audience, a skill that was especially valuable in democratic Athens. To the Sophists, there was no absolute right or wrong—what was right for one individual might be wrong for another. True wisdom consisted of being able to perceive one's own good and to pursue its acquisition. Many people, however, viewed the Sophists as harmful to the traditional values of society and especially dangerous to the values of young people.

In Classical Greece, Athens became the foremost intellectual and artistic center. Its reputation is perhaps strongest of all in philosophy. After all, Socrates, Plato, and Aristotle raised basic questions that have been debated for more than two thousand years; these are still largely the same philosophical questions we wrestle with today.

Socrates Socrates (469–399 B.C.) left no writings, but we know about him from his pupils, especially his most famous one, Plato. By occupation, Socrates was a stonemason, but his true love was philosophy. He taught a number of pupils, but not for pay, because he believed that the goal of education was only to improve the individual. He made use of a teaching method that is still known by his name. The **Socratic method** employs a question-and-answer technique to lead pupils to see things for themselves using their own reason. Socrates believed that all real knowledge is within each person; only critical examination was needed to call it forth. This was the real task of philosophy, since "the unexamined life is not worth living."

Socrates' questioning of authority and public demonstrations of others' lack of knowledge led him into trouble. Athens had had a tradition of free thought and inquiry, but its defeat in the Peloponnesian War had created an environment intolerant of open debate and soul-searching. Socrates was accused and convicted of corrupting the youth of Athens by his teaching, and an Athenian jury sentenced him to death.

Plato One of Socrates' disciples was Plato (c. 429–347 B.C.), considered by many scholars the greatest philosopher of Western civilization. Unlike his master Socrates, who wrote nothing, Plato wrote a great deal. In his dialogues, he used Socrates as his chief philosophical debater.

Plato's philosophical thought focused on the essence of reality and was centered in the concept of Ideas or ideal Forms. According to Plato, a higher world of eternal, unchanging Ideas or Forms has always existed. To know these Forms is to know truth. These ideal Forms constitute reality and can be apprehended only by a trained mind, which, of course, is the goal of philosophy. The objects that we perceive with our senses are simply reflections of the ideal Forms. Hence they are shadows, while reality is found in the Forms themselves.

Plato's ideas of government are set out in a dialogue titled *The Republic*. Based on his experience in Athens, Plato had come to distrust the workings of democracy. It was obvious to him that individuals could not attain an ethical life unless they lived in a just and rational state. This insight led him to construct an ideal state in which the population was divided into three basic groups. At the top was an upper class, a ruling elite, the famous philosopher-kings: "Unless either philosophers become kings in their countries or those who are now called kings and rulers come to be sufficiently inspired with a genuine desire for wisdom; unless, that is to say, political power and philosophy meet together . . . there can be no rest from troubles . . . for states, nor yet, as I believe, for all mankind."[17] The second group consisted of the courageous; they would be the warriors who protected the society. All the rest made up the masses, essentially people driven not by wisdom or courage but by desire for material things. They would be the producers of society—the artisans, tradesmen, and farmers.

In Plato's ideal state, each group fulfilled its assigned role, creating a society that functioned harmoniously. The needs of the community, rather than the happiness of the individual, were Plato's concern, and he focused on the need for the guardians or rulers, above all, to be removed from any concerns for wealth or prestige so that they could strive for what was best for the community. To rid the guardians of these desires, Plato urged that they live together, forgoing both private property and family life. Plato believed that women, too, could be rulers; in this he departed radically from the actual practices of the Greek states.

Aristotle Plato established a school at Athens known as the Academy. One of his pupils, who studied there for twenty years, was Aristotle (384–322 B.C.), who later became a tutor to Alexander the Great. Aristotle differed significantly from his teacher in that he did not accept Plato's theory of ideal Forms. He, like Plato, believed in universal principles, but he believed that form and matter were inseparable. By examining individual objects, we can perceive their form and arrive at universal principles, but they do not exist as a separate higher world of reality beyond material things; rather they are a part of things themselves. Aristotle's interests, then, lay in analyzing and classifying things based on thorough research and investigation. His interests were wide-ranging, and he wrote treatises on an enormous number of subjects: ethics, logic, politics, poetry, astronomy, geology, biology, and physics.

Like Plato, Aristotle wished for an effective form of government that would rationally direct human affairs. Unlike Plato, he did not seek an ideal state based on embodiment of an ideal Form of justice; he tried to find the best form of government by a rational examination of existing governments. For his *Politics* (see the box on p. 77), Aristotle examined the constitutions of 158 states and arrived at general categories for organizing governments. He identified three

THE POLITICS OF ARISTOTLE

*A*RISTOTLE WAS one of the great philosophers of ancient Athens. His philosophical and political ideas would play an important role in the evolution of Western thought during the Middle Ages. In this selection from his *Politics*, Aristotle examines the nature of political community and of the *polis*.

Aristotle, *Politics*

From these considerations it is evident that the *polis* belongs to the class of things that exist by nature, and that man is by nature an animal intended to live in a *polis*. He who is without a *polis*, by reason of his own nature and not of some accident, is either a poor sport of being, or a being higher than man: he is the man of whom Homer wrote in denunciation: "Clanless and lawless and heartless is he." The man who is such by nature [unable to join in the society of a *polis*] at once plunges into a passion for war; he is in the position of a solitary advanced piece in a game of [checkers].

The reason why man is a being meant for political association, in a higher degree than bees or other gregarious animals can ever associate, is evident. Nature, according to our theory, makes nothing in vain; and man alone of the animals is furnished with the faculty of language. The mere making of sounds serves to indicate pleasure and pain, is thus a faculty that belongs to animals in general: their nature enables them to attain the point at which they have perceptions of pleasure and pain, and can signify those perceptions to one another. But language serves to declare what is advantageous and what is the reverse, and it therefore serves to declare what is just and what is unjust. It is the peculiarity of man, in comparison with the rest of the animal world, that he alone possesses perception of good and evil, of the just and the unjust, and of other similar qualities; and it is association in [a common perception of] these things which makes a family and a *polis*.

We now proceed to add that [though the individual and the family are prior in the order of time] the *polis* is prior in the order of nature to the family and the individual.

good forms of government: monarchy, aristocracy, and constitutional government. But based on his examination, he warned that monarchy can easily turn into tyranny, aristocracy into oligarchy, and constitutional government into radical democracy or anarchy. He favored constitutional government as the best form for most people.

Aristotle's philosophical and political ideas played an enormous role in the development of Western thought during the Middle Ages (see Chapter 10). So did his ideas on women. Aristotle believed that marriage was meant to provide mutual comfort between man and woman and contributed to the overall happiness of a community: "The community needs both male and female excellences or it can only be half-blessed." Nevertheless, Aristotle maintained that women were biologically inferior to men: "A woman is, as it were, an infertile male. She is female in fact on account of a kind of inadequacy." Therefore, according to Aristotle, women must be subordinated to men, not only in the community but also in marriage: "The association between husband and wife is clearly an aristocracy. The man rules by virtue of merit, and in the sphere that is his by right; but he hands over to his wife such matters as are suitable for her."[18]

Greek Religion

Greek religion was intricately connected to every aspect of daily life; it was both social and practical. Public festivals, which originated from religious practices, served specific functions: boys were prepared to be warriors, girls to be mothers. Since religion was related to every aspect of life, citizens had to have a proper attitude toward the gods. Religion was a civic cult necessary for the well-being of the state. Temples dedicated to a god or goddess were the major buildings of Greek society.

Homer gave an account of the gods that provided a definite structure to Greek religion. Over a period of time, most Greeks came to accept a common religion based on twelve chief gods who supposedly lived on Mount Olympus, the highest mountain in Greece. Among the twelve were Zeus, the chief deity and father of the gods; Athena, goddess of wisdom and crafts; Apollo, god of the sun and poetry; Aphrodite, goddess of love; and Poseidon, brother of Zeus and god of the seas and earthquakes.

The twelve Olympian gods were common to all Greeks, who thus shared a basic polytheistic religion. Each *polis* usually singled out one of the twelve Olympians as a guardian deity of its community. Athena was the patron goddess of Athens, for example. But each *polis* also had its own local deities who remained important to the community as a whole, and each family had patron gods as well. Because it was desirable to have the gods look favorably on one's activities, ritual assumed enormous proportions in Greek religion. Prayers were often combined with gifts to the gods based on the principle "I give so that you, the gods, will give in return." Some prayers directly reflected this mutual benefit: "Protect our city. I believe that what I say is in our common interest. For a flourishing city honors the gods." Ritual meant sacrifices, whether of animals or agricultural products. Animal victims were burned on an altar in front of a temple or on a small altar in front of a home.

Festivals were also developed as a way to honor the gods and goddesses. Some of these (the Panhellenic celebrations) were important to all Greeks and were held at

An Animal Sacrifice. Animal sacrifice was a regular part of Greek religious ritual. This painted wooden tablet, which was found in a cave near Corinth and dates from the sixth century B.C., depicts the beginning stage of an animal sacrifice performed at a small altar. After the sacrifice, the meat of the animal was cooked and shared by the participants.

special locations, such as those dedicated to the worship of Zeus at Olympia, to Poseidon at the Isthmus of Corinth, and to Apollo at Delphi. The great festivals incorporated numerous events in honor of the gods, including athletic competitions to which all Greeks were invited. According to tradition, the first such games were held at the Olympic festival in 776 B.C. and then held every four years thereafter to honor Zeus. Initially, the Olympic contests consisted of foot races and wrestling, but later, boxing, javelin throwing, and various other contests were added. Competitions were always between individuals, not groups.

As another practical side of Greek religion, Greeks wanted to know the will of the gods. There were seers who obtained omens from dreams, the flight of birds, or the entrails of sacrificial animals. But perhaps the most famous method of divining the will of the gods was the use of the *oracle,* a sacred shrine dedicated to a god or goddess who revealed the future. The most famous was the oracle of Apollo at Delphi, located on the side of Mount Parnassus, overlooking the Gulf of Corinth. At Delphi, a priestess listened to questions while in a state of ecstasy that was believed to be induced by Apollo. Her responses were interpreted by the priests and given in verse form to the person asking questions. Representatives of states and individuals traveled to Delphi to consult the oracle of Apollo. States might inquire whether they should undertake a military expedition; individuals might raise such questions as "Heracleidas asks the god whether he will have offspring from the wife he has now." Responses were often enigmatic and could be interpreted in more than one way. Croesus, the king of Lydia in Asia Minor who was known

for his incredible wealth, sent messengers to the oracle at Delphi, asking whether he should go to war with the Persians. The oracle replied that if Croesus attacked the Persians, a mighty empire would be destroyed. Overjoyed to hear these words, Croesus made war on the Persians but was crushed by his enemy. A mighty empire was indeed destroyed—Croesus' own.

Greek religion, centered in ritual and a formal relationship with the gods, tended to lack a strong emotional component. It also offered no hope of life after death for most people. As a result, the Greeks sometimes turned to **mystery religions,** which included initiation into secret rites that promised a more emotional involvement with spiritual forces and a greater hope of immortality. The most important mysteries were those of the Eleusinian cult connected with the myth of Demeter. This was a fertility cult in which participants felt reborn and gained some hope for life after death. The Orphic cultists, who considered themselves followers of the legendary singer Orpheus, believed in cycles of reincarnation since the human soul had become trapped in the physical body. Their aim was to liberate the soul from its confinement.

Daily Life in Classical Athens

The Greek city-state was, above all, a male community: only adult male citizens took part in public life. In Athens, this meant the exclusion of women, slaves, and foreign residents, or roughly 85 percent of the total population of Attica. In the fifth century, Athens had the largest population of all the Greek city-states. There were probably

150,000 citizens, of whom about 43,000 were adult males who exercised political power. Resident foreigners, known as **metics,** numbered about 35,000 and received the protection of the laws, but they were also subject to some of the responsibilities of citizens, namely, military service and the funding of festivals. The remaining social group, the slaves, numbered around 100,000.

Slavery and the Economy Slavery was a common institution in the ancient world. Economic necessity dictated the desirability of owning at least one slave, although the very poor in Athens did not own any. A soldier on campaign usually took along one slave to carry his armor. The really wealthy might own large numbers of slaves, but those who did usually employed them in industry. Most often slaves in Athens performed domestic tasks as cooks and maids or worked in the fields. Few peasants could afford more than one or two. Other slaves worked as unskilled and skilled laborers. Slaves who worked in public construction were paid the same as metics or citizens.

The Athenian economy was largely agricultural but highly diversified. Athenian farmers grew grains, vegetables, and fruit for local consumption; cultivated vines and olives for wine and olive oil, which were exportable products; and raised sheep and goats for wool and milk products. Given the size of the population in Attica and the lack of abundant fertile land, Athens had to import between 50 and 80 percent of its grain, a staple in the Athenian diet. Trade was thus very important to the Athenian economy. The building of the port at Piraeus and the Long Walls (a series of defensive walls 4 1/2 miles long connecting Athens and Piraeus) created the physical conditions that made Athens the leading trade center in the fifth-century Greek world.

Athens did not have large numbers of artisans, but those it had were important to the economy. Athens was the chief producer of high-quality painted pottery in the fifth century. Other crafts had moved beyond the small workshop into the factory through the use of slave labor.

A Simple Lifestyle The Athenian lifestyle was basically simple. Athenian houses were furnished with necessities bought from artisans, such as beds, couches, tables, chests, pottery, stools, baskets, and cooking utensils. Wives and slaves made clothes and blankets at home. The Athenian diet was rather plain. Basic foods consisted of barley, wheat, millet, lentils, grapes, figs, olives, almonds, bread made at home, vegetables, eggs, fish, cheese, and chicken. Olive oil was widely used, not only for eating but also for lighting lamps and for rubbing on the body after washing and exercise. Owners of country houses kept animals for reasons other than their flesh: oxen for plowing, sheep for wool, and goats for milk and cheese. Meat was consumed only on special occasions, such as festivals, when animals were sacrificed, cooked, and then eaten.

Family and Relationships The family was an important institution in ancient Athens. It was composed of husband, wife, and children (a nuclear family), although other dependent relatives and slaves were regarded as part of the family because of its economic unity. The family's primary social function was to produce new citizens. Strict laws of the fifth century had stipulated that a citizen must be the offspring of a legally acknowledged marriage between two Athenian citizens. By law, property was divided by lot among all the surviving sons; as a result, marriages were usually sought within a close circle of relatives so as to preserve the family property. The family also served to protect and enclose women.

Women were citizens who could participate in most religious cults and festivals but were otherwise excluded from public life. They could not own property beyond personal items and always had a male guardian: if unmarried, a father or male relative; if married, a husband; if widowed, a son or male relative.

Women in the Loom Room. In Athens, women were considered citizens and could participate in religious cults and festivals, but they were barred from any political activity. Women were thought to belong in the house, caring for the children and the needs of the household. A principal activity of Greek women was the making of clothes. This vase shows two women working on a warp-weighted loom.

HOUSEHOLD MANAGEMENT AND THE ROLE OF THE ATHENIAN WIFE

IN CLASSICAL ATHENS, a woman's place was in the home. She had two major responsibilities: bearing and raising children and managing the household. In his dialogue on estate management, Xenophon relates the instructions of an Athenian to his new wife.

Xenophon, *Oeconomicus*

[Ischomachus addresses his new wife:] For it seems to me, dear, that the gods with great discernment have coupled together male and female, as they are called, chiefly in order that they may form a perfect partnership in mutual service. For, in the first place that the various species of living creatures may not fail, they are joined in wedlock for the production of children. Secondly, offspring to support them in old age is provided by this union, to human beings, at any rate. Thirdly, human beings live not in the open air, like beasts, but obviously need shelter. Nevertheless, those who mean to win stores to fill the covered place, have need of someone to work at the open-air occupations; since plowing, sowing, planting and grazing are all such open-air employments; and these supply the needful food. . . .

For he made the man's body and mind more capable of enduring cold and heat, and journeys and campaigns; and therefore imposed on him the outdoor tasks. To the woman, since he had made her body less capable of such endurance, I take it that God has assigned the indoor tasks. And knowing that he had created in the woman and had imposed on her the nourishment of the infants, he meted out to her a larger portion of affection for newborn babes than to the man. . . .

Your duty will be to remain indoors and send out those servants whose work is outside, and superintend those who are to work indoors, and to receive the incomings, and distribute so much of them as must be spent, and watch over so much as is to be kept in store, and take care that the sum laid by for a year be not spent in a month. And when wool is brought to you, you must see that cloaks are made for those that want them. You must see too that the dry corn is in good condition for making food. One of the duties that fall to you, however, will perhaps seem rather thankless: you will have to see that any servant who is ill is cared for.

The function of the Athenian woman as wife was very clear. Her foremost obligation was to bear children, especially male children who would preserve the family line. The marriage formula that Athenians used put it succinctly: "I give this woman for the procreation of legitimate children." A wife was also expected to take care of her family and her house, either doing the household work herself or supervising the slaves who did the actual work (see the box above).

Women were kept under strict control. Since they were married at fourteen or fifteen, they were taught about their responsibilities at an early age. Although many managed to learn to read and play musical instruments, they were often cut off from any formal education. And women were expected to remain at home out of sight unless they attended funerals or festivals, such as the women's festival of Thesmophoria. If they left the house, they were to be accompanied. A woman working alone in public was either poverty-stricken or not a citizen.

Women in Athens served males in other ways as well. Prostitution flourished in Classical Athens. Most female prostitutes were slaves in brothels run as a business or trade by an Athenian citizen. Another class of prostitutes in Athenian society occupied a more favorable position; these more refined courtesans were known as *hetairai*, literally "female companions." Usually ex-slaves or foreigners, these women were more sophisticated than ordinary prostitutes and were known for their intellectual and musical achievements as well as their physical ones. Athenian males continued the aristocratic practice of the *symposium*, a sophisticated drinking party, where *hetairai* were often present. Symposia were held in the men's dining rooms, and wives were not present. *Hetairai* danced, played musical instruments, and provided entertainment, including sex. Some *hetairai* achieved fortune and considerable renown. Aspasia was the most famous. A friend of Socrates and known for her learning, she was the mistress of Pericles and eventually became his wife.

Male homosexuality was also a prominent feature of Classical Athens. It was widely practiced and tolerated. Athenian law disfranchised a citizen who had prostituted his body to another male, but nothing was done to males who engaged in homosexual love with male prostitutes or other adult males for love or pleasure. The law did not eliminate male prostitution but ensured that male prostitutes would be foreigners, not Athenian citizens.

The Greek homosexual ideal was a relationship between a mature man and a young male. It is likely that this was primarily an aristocratic ideal. While the relationship was frequently physical, the Greeks also viewed it as educational. The older male (the "lover") won the love of his "beloved" by his value as a teacher and by the devotion he demonstrated in training his charge. In a sense, this love relationship was seen as a way of initiating young males into the male world of political and military dominance. The Greeks did not feel that the coexistence of homosexual and heterosexual predilections created any special problems for individuals or their society.

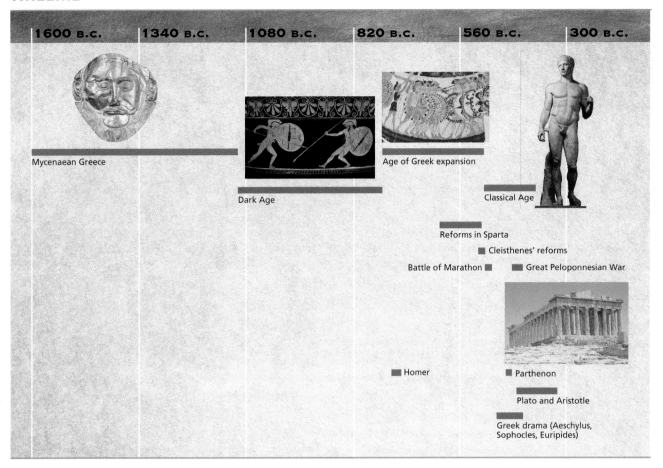

1600 B.C.	1340 B.C.	1080 B.C.	820 B.C.	560 B.C.	300 B.C.

Mycenaean Greece

Age of Greek expansion

Classical Age

Dark Age

Reforms in Sparta

Cleisthenes' reforms

Battle of Marathon ■   ■ Great Peloponnesian War

■ Homer   ■ Parthenon

Plato and Aristotle

Greek drama (Aeschylus, Sophocles, Euripides)

CONCLUSION

*T*HE CIVILIZATION OF THE ANCIENT GREEKS was the fountainhead of Western culture. Socrates, Plato, and Aristotle established the foundations of Western philosophy. Herodotus and Thucydides created the discipline of history. Our literary forms are largely derived from Greek poetry and drama. Greek notions of harmony, proportion, and beauty have remained the touchstones for all subsequent Western art. A rational method of inquiry, so important to modern science, was conceived in ancient Greece. Many political terms are Greek in origin, and so are our concepts of the rights and duties of citizenship, especially as they were conceived in Athens, which gave the idea of democracy to the Western world. Especially during the Classical Period, the Greeks raised and debated fundamental questions about the purpose of human existence, the structure of human society, and the nature of the universe that have concerned Western thinkers ever since.

All of these achievements came from a group of small city-states in ancient Greece. And yet Greek civilization also contains an element of tragedy. For all of their brilliant accomplishments, the Greeks were unable to rise above the divisions and rivalries that caused them to fight each other and undermine their own civilization. Luckily, their contributions to Western civilization survived their political struggles.

NOTES

1. H. D. F. Kitto, *The Greeks* (Harmondsworth, England, 1951), p. 64.
2. Homer, *Odyssey*, trans. E. V. Rieu (Harmondsworth, England, 1946), p. 337.
3. Xenophon, *Symposium*, trans. O. J. Todd (Cambridge, Mass., 1968), 3.5.
4. Homer, *Odyssey*, pp. 290–291.
5. Quoted in Thomas R. Martin, *Ancient Greece* (New Haven, Conn., 1996), p. 62.

6. These words from Plutarch are quoted in Elaine Fantham et al., *Women in the Classical World* (New York, 1994), p. 64.

7. Hesiod, *Works and Days,* trans. Dorothea Wender (Harmondsworth, England, 1973), pp. 77, 69, 71, 68.

8. Theognis, *Elegies,* trans. Dorothea Wender (Harmondsworth, England, 1973), pp. 118, 100.

9. Aeschylus, *The Persians,* in *The Complete Greek Tragedies,* vol. 1, ed. David Grene and Richmond Lattimore (Chicago, 1959), p. 229.

10. Voltaire, *The Age of Louis XIV,* trans. Martyn Pollack (London, 1926), p. 1.

11. Herodotus, *The Persian Wars,* trans. Robin Waterfield (New York, 1998), p. 3.

12. Thucydides, *History of the Peloponnesian War,* trans. Rex Warner (Harmondsworth, England, 1954), p. 24.

13. Ibid.

14. Ibid.

15. Sophocles, *Oedipus the King,* trans. David Grene (Chicago, 1959), pp. 68–69.

16. Sophocles, *Antigone,* trans. Don Taylor (London, 1986), p. 146.

17. Plato, *The Republic,* trans. F. M. Cornford (New York, 1945), pp. 178–179.

18. Quotations from Aristotle are from Sue Blundell, *Women in Ancient Greece* (London, 1995), pp. 106, 186.

SUGGESTIONS FOR FURTHER READING

A standard one-volume reference work for Greek history is **J. B. Bury and R. Meiggs,** *A History of Greece to the Death of Alexander the Great,* 4th ed. (New York, 1975). For a beautifully illustrated introduction, see **F. Durando,** *Ancient Greece: The Dawn of the Western World* (New York, 1997). For a brief illustrated introduction, see **J. Camp and E. Fisher,** *The World of the Ancient Greeks* (London, 2002). Other good general introductions to Greek history include *The Oxford History of the Classical World,* ed. **J. Boardman, J. Griffin, and O. Murray** (Oxford, 1986), pp. 19–314; **T. R. Martin,** *Ancient Greece* (New Haven, Conn., 1996); **P. Cartledge,** *The Cambridge Illustrated History of Ancient Greece* (Cambridge, 1998); and **W. Donlan et al.,** *Ancient Greece: A Political, Social, and Cultural History* (New York, 1998). Hoplite warfare is well covered in **V. D. Hanson,** *Hoplites: The Classical Greek Battle Experience* (New York, 1991).

Early Greek history is examined in **O. Murray,** *Early Greece,* 2d ed. (Cambridge, Mass., 1993); **M. I. Finley,** *Early Greece: The Bronze and Archaic Ages,* 2d ed. (New York, 1982); and **J. L. Fitton,** *The Discovery of the Greek Bronze Age* (Cambridge, 1995). On Homer and his world, see the modern classic by **M. I. Finley,** *The World of Odysseus,* 2d ed. (New York, 1979).

General works on Archaic Greece include **A. M. Snodgrass,** *Archaic Greece* (London, 1980), and **M. Grant,** *The Rise of the Greeks* (London, 1987). Economic and social history of the period is covered in **C. Starr,** *The Economic and Social Growth of Early Greece, 800–500 B.C.* (Oxford, 1977). On colonization, see **J. Boardman,** *The Greeks Overseas,* rev. ed. (Baltimore, 1980). On tyranny, see **J. F. McGlew,** *Tyranny and Political Culture in Ancient Greece* (Ithaca, N.Y., 1993). On the culture of Archaic Greece, see **W. Burkert,** *The Orientalizing Revolution: Near Eastern Influence on Greek Culture in the Early Archaic Age* (Cambridge, Mass., 1992). The best histories of Sparta are **W. Forrest,** *A History of Sparta, 950–121 B.C.,* 2d ed. (London, 1980), and **P. A. Cartledge,** *Sparta and Laconia: A Regional History, 1300–362 B.C.* (London, 1979). See also **P. A. Cartledge,** *Spartan Reflections* (Berkeley, Calif., 2001) and *The Spartans* (New York, 2003). On early Athens, see the still valuable **A. Jones,** *Athenian Democracy* (London, 1957), and **R. Osborne,** *Demos* (New York, 1985). The Persian Wars are examined in **P. Green,** *The Greco-Persian Wars* (Berkeley, Calif., 1996).

A general history of Classical Greece can be found in **S. Hornblower,** *The Greek World, 479–323 B.C.* (London, 1983), and **J. K. Davies,** *Democracy and Classical Greece,* 2d ed. (Cambridge, Mass., 1993). Valuable works on Athens include **D. Kagan,** *Pericles of Athens and the Birth of Democracy* (New York, 1991); **C. Farrar,** *The Origins of Democratic Thinking: The Invention of Politics in Classical Athens* (Cambridge, 1988); **C. W. Fornara and L. J. Samons II,** *Athens from Cleisthenes to Pericles* (Berkeley, Calif., 1991); and **D. Stockton,** *The Classical Athenian Democracy* (Oxford, 1990). An interesting work on the intellectual and political history of Athens in the late fifth century B.C. is **M. Munn,** *The School of History: Athens in the Age of Socrates* (Berkeley, Calif., 2000). On the development of the Athenian empire, see **R. Meiggs,** *The Athenian Empire* (Oxford, 1975), and **M. F. McGregor,** *The Athenians and Their Empire* (Vancouver, 1987). The best way to examine the Great Peloponnesian War is to read the work of **Thucydides,** *History of the Peloponnesian War,* trans. **R. Warner** (Harmondsworth, England, 1954). An excellent recent history is **D. Kagan,** *The Peloponnesian War* (New York, 2003). On fourth-century Athens, see **M. H. Hansen,** *The Athenian Democracy in the Age of Demosthenes* (Oxford, 1991).

For a comprehensive history of Greek art, see **M. Robertson,** *A History of Greek Art,* 2 vols. (Cambridge, 1975). On sculpture, see **A. Stewart,** *Greek Sculpture: An Exploration* (New Haven, Conn., 1990). A basic survey of architecture is **H. W. Lawrence,** *Greek Architecture,* rev. ed. (Harmondsworth, England, 1983). On Greek drama, see the general work by **J. De Romilly,** *A Short History of Greek Literature* (Chicago, 1985). For sound studies of Greek history writing, see **J. A. S. Evans,** *Herodotus* (Boston, 1982), and **K. Dover,** *Thucydides* (Oxford, 1973). On Greek philosophy, a detailed study is available in **W. K. C. Guthrie,** *A History of Greek Philosophy,* 6 vols. (Cambridge, 1962–81).

On Greek religion, see **J. N. Bremmer,** *Greek Religion* (Oxford, 1994); **W. Burkert,** *Greek Religion,* trans. J. Raffan (Cambridge, Mass., 1985); and **R. Garland,** *Religion and the Greeks* (New York, 1994). On athletic competitions, see **S. G. Miller,** *Ancient Greek Athletics* (New Haven, Conn., 2004).

On the family and women, see **C. B. Patterson,** *The Family in Greek History* (New York, 1998); **M. Golden,** *Children and Childhood in Classical Athens* (Baltimore, 1990); **S. B. Pomeroy,** *Goddesses, Whores, Wives, and Slaves: Women in Classical Antiquity* (New York, 1975); **E. Fantham et al.,** *Women in the Classical World* (New York, 1994); and **S. Blundell,** *Women in Ancient Greece* (London, 1995). On slavery, see **Y. Garlan,** *Slavery in Ancient Greece* (Ithaca, N.Y., 1988), and **N. R. E. Fisher,** *Slavery in Classical Greece* (New York, 1995). On homosexuality, see **K. J. Dover,** *Greek Homosexuality* (London, 1978), and **E. Cantarella,** *Bisexuality in the Ancient World* (New Haven, Conn., 1992).

History Now™

Enter *HistoryNow* using the access card that is available for *Western Civilization*. *HistoryNow* will assist you in understanding the content in this chapter with lesson plans generated for your needs. In addition, you can read the following documents, and many more, online:

Tyrtaeus, A War Song

Aeschylus, selection from the end of *Agamemnon*

Sophocles, excerpts from *Oedipus the King*

Euripides, excerpt from *Medea*

Plato, excerpts from *Apology* and *Republic*

INFOTRAC SEARCH TERMS

For additional reading, go to InfoTrac College Edition, your online research library at http://infotrac.thomsonlearning.com

Subject Guide Search
Greek mythology

Key Terms Search
Greek history
Peloponnesian War

WESTERN CIVILIZATION RESOURCES

 Visit the *Western Civilization* Companion Web site for resources specific to this book:

http://history.wadsworth.com/spielvogel06/

For a variety of tools to help you succeed in this course, visit the Western Civilization Resource Center at

http://history.wadsworth.com/western/

Included are quizzes; images; documents; interactive simulations; maps and timelines; movie explorations; and a wealth of other sources.

4

THE HELLENISTIC WORLD

CHAPTER OUTLINE AND FOCUS QUESTIONS

Macedonia and the Conquests of Alexander

● How was Alexander able to amass his empire, and what might his rule have been like if he had lived longer?

The World of the Hellenistic Kingdoms

● What were the main features of the political and military organization of the Hellenistic kingdoms, and how did the new political systems differ from those of the Greek city-states?

Hellenistic Society

● What were the main social developments in the Hellenistic world?

Culture in the Hellenistic World

● What achievements in literature, art, science, medicine, and philosophy occurred during the Hellenistic period?

Religion in the Hellenistic World

● Which religions were prominent during the Hellenistic period, and what does their popularity suggest about Hellenistic society?

CRITICAL THINKING

● How was the Hellenistic period different from the Greek Classical Age?

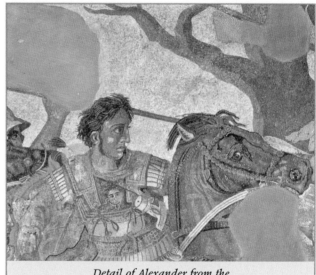

Detail of Alexander from the Battle of Issus mosaic in Pompeii

© Scala/Art Resource, NY

IN 334 B.C., ALEXANDER THE GREAT led an army of Greeks and Macedonians into western Asia to launch his attack on the Persian Empire. Years of campaigning resulted in the complete defeat of the Persians, and in 327 B.C., Alexander and his troops pushed eastward into India. But two more years of fighting in an exotic and difficult terrain exhausted his troops, who rebelled and refused to go on. Reluctantly, Alexander turned back, leading his men across the arid lands of southern Persia. Conditions in the desert were appalling; the blazing sun and lack of water led to thousands of deaths. At one point, when a group of his soldiers found a little water, they scooped it up in a helmet and gave it to Alexander. Then, according to Arrian, an ancient Greek historian, Alexander, "with a word of thanks for the gift, took the helmet and, in full view of his troops, poured the water on the ground. So extraordinary was the effect of this action that the water wasted by Alexander was as good as a drink for every man in the army." Ever the great military leader, Alexander had found yet another way to inspire his troops.

Alexander the Great was the son of King Philip II of Macedonia, who in 338 B.C. defeated the Greeks and established his control over the Greek penin-sula. After Philip's death, Alexander became king and led the Macedonians and Greeks on a spectacular conquest of the Persian Empire, opening the door to the spread of Greek culture throughout the ancient Near East. Greek settlers poured into these lands as bureaucrats, traders, soldiers, and scholars. Alexander's triumph created a new series of kingdoms that blended the achievements of the eastern world with the cultural outlook and attitudes of the Greeks. We use the term **Hellenistic** to designate this new order. The Hellenistic world was the world of Greeks and non-Greek easterners, and it resulted, in its own way, in a remarkable series of accomplishments that are sometimes underestimated. They form the story of this chapter.

Macedonia and the Conquests of Alexander

While the Greek city-states were busy fighting each other, to their north a new and ultimately powerful kingdom was emerging. Its people, the Macedonians, were viewed as barbarians by their southern neighbors, the Greeks. The Macedonians were mostly rural folk and were organized into tribes rather than city-states. Not until the end of the fifth century B.C. did Macedonia become an important kingdom. But when King Philip II (359–336 B.C.) took control, he turned Macedonia into the chief power of the Greek world.

≋ Philip and the Conquest of Greece

Philip had spent three years as a hostage in Thebes, where he had gained a great admiration for Greek culture and absorbed the latest Greek military developments. Philip understood the importance of having an efficient army if Macedonia was to be a strong state. Philip used Macedonian countrymen, sturdy peasants and shepherds, as the core of his phalanx of infantrymen. From the gold mines of Mount Pangaeus, he obtained the wealth to pay these soldiers and establish a standing professional army. The Macedonian phalanx was also armed with long thrusting spears and supported by strong cavalry contingents that served to break the opposing line of battle and create disorder in the enemy's ranks. Philip's new army defeated the Illyrians to the west and the Thracians to the north and east and was then drawn into the Greeks' interstate conflicts.

The Greeks had mixed reactions to Philip's growing strength. Many Athenians, especially the orator Demosthenes, came to have a strong distrust of the Macedonian leader's intentions. Demosthenes delivered a series of orations, known as the *Philippics,* in which he portrayed Philip as ruthless, deceitful, treacherous, and barbaric and called on the Athenians to undertake a struggle against him (see the box on p. 86). Other Athenians, such as Isocrates, a teacher of rhetoric, viewed Philip as a savior who would rescue the Greeks from themselves by uniting them and organizing the entire Greek world in a crusade against the common enemy, the Persians.

Demosthenes' repeated calls for action, combined with Philip's rapid expansion, finally spurred Athens into action. Allied with Thebes and some other smaller states, Athens fought the Macedonians at the Battle of Chaeronea, near Thebes, in 338 B.C. The Macedonian army crushed the Greek allies, and Philip was now free to consolidate his control over the Greek peninsula. While Thebes was punished severely, Athens was treated leniently out of respect for its past and expected cooperation in the future. The Greek states were joined together in an alliance that we call the Corinthian League because they met at Corinth. All members took an oath of loyalty: "I swear by Zeus, Earth, Sun, Poseidon, Athena, Ares, and all the gods and goddesses. I will abide by the peace, and I will not break the agreements with Philip the Macedonian, nor will I take up arms with hostile intent against any one of those who abide by the oaths either by land or by sea."[1]

Though based on the principle of self-governing, independent states, the league did have an army and a council. Philip of Macedon was recognized as *hegemon* (leader) of the league and its army. Although Philip allowed the Greek city-states autonomy in domestic affairs, he retained the general direction of their foreign affairs. Many Greeks still objected to being subject to the less civilized master from the north, but Philip insisted that the Greek states end their bitter rivalries and cooperate with him in a war against Persia.

Before Philip could undertake his invasion of Asia, however, he was assassinated, leaving the task to his son Alexander. Although Alexander justly deserves credit for the destruction of the Persian Empire, it was Philip who really paved the way for the conquest. He had unified Macedonia, created a powerful military machine, and subdued the Greeks.

≋ Alexander the Great

Alexander was only twenty when he became king of Macedonia. In the next twelve years, he achieved so much that he has ever since been called Alexander the Great. The illustrious conqueror was in many ways groomed for kingship by his father, who had taken Alexander along on military campaigns and at the important Battle of Chaeronea had given him control of the cavalry. After his father's assassination, Alexander moved quickly to assert his authority, securing the Macedonian frontiers and smothering a rebellion in Greece. He then turned to his father's dream, the invasion of the Persian Empire.

Alexander's Conquests There is no doubt that Alexander was taking a chance in attacking the Persian Empire. Although weakened in some respects, it was still a strong state. Alexander's fleet was inferior to the Persian navy, which drew its ships from the Phoenicians and other coastal peoples of western Asia, and his finances were shaky at best. His army would have to live off the countryside and win quick victories to gain the resources needed to continue the struggle. In the spring of 334 B.C., Alexander

Demosthenes Condemns Philip of Macedonia

*A*MONG THE GREEKS, Demosthenes reacted most strongly to the growing strength and expansionary policies of the Macedonian king Philip II. Demosthenes delivered a series of orations to the Athenian assembly in which he portrayed Philip as a ruthless and barbaric man. This excerpt is from the *Third Philippic,* delivered around 341 B.C.

Demosthenes, *The Third Philippic*

I observe, however, that all men, and you first of all, have conceded to him something which has been the occasion of every war that the Greeks have ever waged. And what is that? The power of doing what he likes, of calmly plundering and stripping the Greeks one by one, and of attacking their cities and reducing them to slavery. Yet your hegemony in Greece lasted seventy-three years, that of Sparta twenty-nine, and in these later times Thebes too gained some sort of authority after the battle of Leuctra. But neither to you nor to the Thebans nor to the Spartans did the Greeks ever yet, men of Athens, concede the right of unrestricted action, or anything like it. On the contrary, when you, or rather the Athenians of that day, were thought to be showing a want of consideration in dealing with others, all felt it their duty, even those who had no grievance against them, to go to war in support of those who had been injured. . . . Yet all the faults committed by the Spartans in those thirty years, and by our ancestors in their seventy years of supremacy, are fewer, men of Athens, than the wrongs which Philip has done to the Greeks in the thirteen incomplete years in which he has been coming to the top—or rather, they are not a fraction of them. . . . Ay, and you know this also, that the wrongs which the Greeks suffered from the Spartans or from us, they suffered at all events at the hands of true-born sons of Greece, and they might have been regarded as the acts of a legitimate son, born to great possessions, who should be guilty of some fault or error in the management of his estate: so far he would deserve blame and reproach, yet it could not be said that it was not one of the blood, not the lawful heir who was acting thus. But if some slave or illegitimate bastard had wasted and squandered what he had no right to, heavens! how much more monstrous and exasperating all would have called it! Yet they have no such qualms about Philip and his present conduct, though he is not only no Greek, nor related to the Greeks, but not even a barbarian from any place that can be named with honor, but a pestilent knave from Macedonia, from where it was never yet possible to buy a decent slave.

---

entered Asia Minor with an army of some 37,000 men. About half were Macedonians, the rest Greeks and other allies. The cavalry, which would play an important role as a striking force, numbered about five thousand. Architects, engineers, historians, and scientists accompanied the army, a clear indication of Alexander's grand vision and positive expectations at the beginning of his campaign.

His first confrontation with the Persians, at the Granicus River in 334 B.C. (see Map 4.1), nearly cost him his life but resulted in a major victory. By the following spring, the entire western half of Asia Minor was in Alexander's

Bust of Alexander the Great. This bust of Alexander the Great is a Roman copy of the head of a statue, possibly by Lysippus. Alexander was partial to Lysippus' portraits, believing that the sculptor was the only one who had the ability to portray the great leader's true essence. Alexander claimed to be descended from Heracles, a Greek hero worshiped as a god, and as pharaoh of Egypt, he gained recognition as a living deity. It is reported that on the base of one of his statues, now lost, in which Alexander was shown gazing at Zeus, were the words "I place the earth under my sway; you, O Zeus, keep Olympus."

hands, and the Ionian Greek cities of southwestern Asia Minor had been "liberated" from the Persian oppressor. Not all of them wished to be liberated, and many regarded Alexander simply as their new master.

Meanwhile, the Persian king, Darius III, mobilized his forces to stop Alexander's army. Although the Persian troops outnumbered Alexander's, the Battle of Issus was fought on a narrow field that canceled the advantage of superior numbers and resulted in another Macedonian success. (The Persian cause was not helped when Darius made a spectacular exit from the battlefield before it was even clear who would be victorious.) After his victory at Issus in 333 B.C., Alexander laid siege to the port cities of Tyre and Gaza to prevent Persian control of the sea. Egypt surrendered without a fight, and by the winter of 332 B.C., Syria, Palestine, and Egypt were under Alexander's domination. He took the traditional title of pharaoh of Egypt and was hailed as the "son of Amon," to the Greeks the equivalent of being called the son of Zeus. Alexander also built the first of a series of

Alexander and Darius at the Battle of Issus. This late-second or early-first-century B.C. mosaic from the floor of a Roman villa at Pompeii is thought to be a copy of a panel painting by Philoxenos of Eretria about 310 B.C. The mosaic depicts the battle between Alexander and Darius III, king of Persia, at Issus in 333 B.C. Alexander is seen at left on horseback, recklessly leading his troops into battle. Darius is shown in his chariot, already turning around to flee from the enemy.

cities named after him (Alexandria) as the Greek administrative capital of Egypt. It became (and remains today) one of the most important cities in the Mediterranean world.

In the meantime, Darius indicated his willingness to make a peace settlement, offering to cede all land west of the Euphrates River to Alexander. Alexander refused and renewed the offensive. He moved now into the territory of the ancient Mesopotamian kingdoms and fought a decisive battle with the Persians at Gaugamela in the summer of 331 B.C. At Gaugamela, Alexander's men were clearly outnumbered by the Persian forces, which had established the battle site on a broad, open plain where their war chariots could maneuver to best advantage. Alexander was able to break through the center of the Persian line with his heavy cavalry, followed by the infantry. The battle turned into a rout, although Darius managed to escape. After his victory, Alexander entered Babylon and then proceeded to the Persian capitals at Susa and Persepolis, where he acquired the Persian treasuries and took possession of vast quantities of gold and silver.

By 330 B.C., Alexander was again on the march. After Darius was killed by one of his own men, Alexander took the title and office of the Great King of the Persians. But he was not content to rest with the spoils of the Persian Empire. Over the next three years, he moved east and northeast, as far as modern Pakistan. By the summer of 327 B.C., he had entered India, which at that time was divided into a number of warring states. In 326 B.C., Alexander and his armies arrived in the plains of northwestern India. At the Battle of the Hydaspes River, Alexander won a bru-

tally fought battle (see the box on p. 89). When Alexander made clear his determination to march east to conquer more of India, his soldiers, weary of campaigning year after year, mutinied and refused to go further. Alexander surrendered to their demands and agreed to return, leading his troops through southern Persia across the Gedrosian Desert, where they suffered heavy losses from appalling desert conditions. Alexander and the remnant of his army went to Susa and then Babylon, where he planned more campaigns. But in June 323 B.C., weakened from wounds, fever, and probably excessive alcohol, he died at the young age of thirty-two.

Alexander's Ideals   Alexander is one of the most puzzling great figures in history. Historians relying on the same sources give vastly different pictures of him. Some portray him as an idealistic visionary and others as a ruthless Machiavellian. How did Alexander view himself? We know that he sought to imitate Achilles, the warrior-hero of Homer's *Iliad*. Alexander kept a copy of the *Iliad*—and a dagger—under his pillow. He also claimed to be descended from Heracles, the Greek hero who came to be worshiped as a god. No doubt Alexander aspired to divine honors; as pharaoh of Egypt, he became a living god according to Egyptian tradition and at one point even sent instructions to the Greek cities to "vote him a god."

Some historians have argued that Alexander believed in an ideal of universal humanity. As evidence they cite the fact that he urged his soldiers to marry native women, and at Susa in 324 B.C. he celebrated the marriages of ten thousand of them en masse to local women. Alexander himself married easterners—Stateira, daughter of Darius, and Roxane, daughter of a Bactrian baron. Was Alexander pursuing a lofty ideal, or was he simply looking for a realistic way to unify his newly won domains? Early on in his conquests, he adopted aspects of Persian rule. He called himself the Great King and asked his subjects to bow before him in the Persian fashion. He wore Persian dress, used Persians as administrators, and trained native youths in Macedonian military methods. His fellow Macedonians objected to these trappings of eastern despotism and the equal treatment he accorded Persians. Some even went so far as to attempt his assassination. But Alexander must have felt a need to fuse the Macedonians, Greeks, and Persians into a ruling class that would enable him to control such an extensive empire. One is left with the impression that he aspired to autocratic monarchy rather than a lofty vision of the unity of humankind.

Alexander's Legacy   Regardless of his ideals, motives, or views about himself, one fact stands out: Alexander created a new age, the Hellenistic era. The word *Hellenistic* is derived from a Greek word meaning "to imitate Greeks." It is an appropriate way to describe an age that saw the exten-

CHRONOLOGY	Macedonia and the Conquests of Alexander
Reign of Philip II	359–336 B.C.
Battle of Chaeronea; Philip II conquers Greece	338 B.C.
Reign of Alexander the Great	336–323 B.C.
Alexander invades Asia; Battle of Granicus River	334 B.C.
Battle of Issus	333 B.C.
Battle of Gaugamela	331 B.C.
Fall of Persepolis, the Persian capital	330 B.C.
Alexander enters India	327 B.C.
Battle of Hydaspes River	326 B.C.
Death of Alexander	323 B.C.

sion of the Greek language and ideas to the non-Greek world of the ancient Near East. Alexander's destruction of the Persian monarchy had extended Greco-Macedonian rule over an enormous area. It created opportunities for Greek engineers, intellectuals, merchants, soldiers, and administrators. While the Greeks on the mainland might remain committed to the ideals of their city-states, those

MAP 4.1   **The Conquests of Alexander the Great.** In just twelve years, Alexander the Great conquered vast territories. Dominating lands from west of the Nile to east of the Indus, he brought the Persian Empire, Egypt, and much of the Middle East under his control and laid the foundations for the Hellenistic world.
❓ Approximately how far did he and his troops travel during those twelve years? 🔊 **View an animated version of this map or related maps at** http://history.wadsworth.com/spielvogel06/

ALEXANDER MEETS AN INDIAN KING

N HIS CAMPAIGNS in India, Alexander fought a number of difficult battles. At the Battle of the Hydaspes River, he faced a strong opponent in the Indian king Porus. After defeating Porus, Alexander treated him with respect, according to Arrian, Alexander's ancient biographer.

Arrian, *The Campaigns of Alexander*

Throughout the action Porus had proved himself a man indeed, not only as a commander but as a soldier of the truest courage. When he saw his cavalry cut to pieces, most of his infantry dead, and his elephants killed or roaming riderless and bewildered about the field, his behavior was very different from that of the Persian King Darius: unlike Darius, he did not lead the scramble to save his own skin, but so long as a single unit of his men held together, he fought bravely on. It was only when he was himself wounded that he turned the elephant on which he rode and began to withdraw. . . . Alexander, anxious to save the life of this great and gallant soldier, sent . . . [to him] an Indian named Meroes, a man he had been told had long been Porus' friend. Porus listened to Meroes' message, stopped his elephant, and dismounted; he was much distressed by

thirst, so when he had revived himself by drinking, he told Meroes to conduct him with all speed to Alexander.

Alexander, informed of his approach, rode out to meet him. . . . When they met, he reined in his horse and looked at his adversary with admiration: he was a magnificent figure of a man, over seven feet high and of great personal beauty; his bearing had lost none of its pride; his air was of one brave man meeting another, of a king in the presence of a king, with whom he had fought honorably for his kingdom.

Alexander was the first to speak. "What," he said, "do you wish that I should do with you?" "Treat me as a king ought," Porus is said to have replied. "For my part," said Alexander, pleased by his answer, "your request shall be granted. But is there not something you would wish for yourself? Ask it." "Everything," said Porus, "is contained in this one request."

The dignity of these words gave Alexander even more pleasure, and he restored to Porus his sovereignty over his subjects, adding to his realm other territory of even greater extent. Thus he did indeed use a brave man as a king ought, and from that time forward found him in every way a loyal friend.

who followed Alexander and his successors participated in a new political unity based on the principle of monarchy. Alexander had transformed his army from a Macedonian force into an international one, owing loyalty only to himself. His successors used force to establish military monarchies that dominated the Hellenistic world after his death. Autocratic power, based on military strength and pretensions of divine rule, became a regular feature of those Hellenistic monarchies and was part of Alexander's political legacy to the Hellenistic world. His vision of empire no doubt inspired the Romans, who were, of course, the real heirs of Alexander's legacy.

But Alexander also left a cultural legacy. As a result of his conquests, Greek language, art, architecture, and literature spread throughout the Near East. The urban centers of the Hellenistic age, many founded by Alexander and his successors, became springboards for the diffusion of Greek culture. Alexander had established a number of cities and military colonies named Alexandria to guard strategic points and supervise wide areas. Most of the settlers were Greek mercenaries. It has been estimated that in the course of his campaigns, Alexander summoned some 60,000 to 65,000 additional mercenaries from Greece, at least 36,000 of whom took up residence in the garrisons and new cities. While the Greeks spread their culture in the east, they were also inevitably influenced by eastern ways. Thus Alexander's legacy became one of the hallmarks of the Hellenistic world: the clash and fusion of different cultures.

The World of the Hellenistic Kingdoms

The united empire that Alexander created by his conquests distingrated after his death. All too soon, Macedonian military leaders were engaged in a struggle for power. By 301 B.C., any hope of unity was dead.

Hellenistic Monarchies

Eventually, four Hellenistic kingdoms emerged as the successors to Alexander: Macedonia under the Antigonid dynasty, Syria and the east under the Seleucids, the Attalid kingdom of Pergamum, and Egypt under the Ptolemies (see Map 4.2).

Antigonid Kingdom of Macedonia   In Macedonia, the struggles for power led to the extermination of Alexander the Great's dynasty. Not until 276 B.C. did Antigonus Gonatus, the grandson of one of Alexander's generals, succeed in establishing the Antigonid dynasty as rulers of Macedonia. The Antigonids viewed control of Greece as essential to their power but did not see outright conquest as necessary. Macedonia was, of course, also important to the Greeks. As one ancient commentator noted, "It is in the interest of the Greeks that the Macedonian dominion should be humbled for long, but by no means that it should be destroyed. For in that case . . . [the Macedonians] would very

MAP 4.2 **The World of the Hellenistic Kingdoms.** Alexander died unexpectedly at the age of thirty-two and did not designate a successor. Upon his death, his generals struggled for power, eventually establishing four monarchies that spread Hellenistic culture and fostered trade and economic development. **?** Which kingdom encompassed most of the old Persian Empire?

View an animated version of this map or related maps at http://history.wadsworth.com/spielvogel06/

soon experience the lawless violence of the Thracians and Gauls, as they had on more than one occasion."[2] But the Greeks, like the Macedonians, eventually fell subject to Roman power.

The Seleucid Kingdom Another Hellenistic monarchy was founded by the general Seleucus, who established the Seleucid dynasty of Syria. This was the largest of the Hellenistic kingdoms and controlled much of the old Persian Empire from Turkey in the west to India in the east, although the Seleucids found it increasingly difficult to maintain control of the eastern territories. In fact, an Indian ruler named Chandragupta Maurya (324–301 B.C.) created a new Indian state, the Mauryan Empire, and drove out the Seleucid forces. His grandson Asoka (269–232 B.C.) extended the empire to include most of India and is considered the greatest ruler in India's history. Asoka, a pious Buddhist, sought to convert the remaining Greek communities in northwestern India to his religion and even sent Buddhist missionaries to Greek rulers.

The Mauryan Empire Under Asoka

The Seleucid rulers maintained relations with the Mauryan Empire. Trade was fostered, especially in such luxuries as spices and jewels. Seleucus also sent Greek and Macedonian ambassadors to the Mauryan court. Best known of these was Megasthenes, whose report on the people of India remained one of the West's best sources of information on India until the Middle Ages.

Kingdom of Pergamum A third Hellenistic kingdom came into being by freeing itself from the Seleucids. This was the kingdom of Pergamum in western Asia Minor under the Attalid dynasty. It was Pergamum that brought the Romans into the area by seeking their aid first against the Antigonids and then against the Seleucids. This led to the Roman defeat of Antiochus III, probably the strongest of the Seleucid monarchs, in 191 B.C. The Seleucids declined thereafter until their small remaining territory was made a Roman province in 63 B.C. Seventy years before that, the last of the Attalid dynasty had bequeathed his kingdom to Rome in his will.

Ptolemaic Kingdom of Egypt The fourth Hellenistic monarchy was Egypt, which had come under the control of Ptolemy, another Macedonian general. Named governor of Egypt after Alexander's death, Ptolemy had established himself as king by 305 B.C., creating the Ptolemaic dynasty of pharaohs. Hellenistic Egypt lasted longer than all the other Hellenistic monarchies; it was not until the reign of Cleopatra VII, who allied herself with the wrong side in the Roman civil wars (see Chapter 5), that Egypt fell to the Romans in 30 B.C.

The Threat from the Celts

The Celts, also known as the Gauls, were a people who had occupied large areas of Europe north of the Alps during the Early Iron Age (c. 800–500 B.C.), especially the region to the south and west of the Rhine River, west of the Alps, and north of the Pyrenees (a region known as Gaul).

At the end of the fifth century B.C., possibly as the result of overpopulation, Celtic peoples began to migrate south and east. One group sacked the city of Rome in 390 B.C. (see Chapter 5). After the death of Alexander the Great, other groups of Celts began to threaten the Hellenistic world. Celts attacked Macedonia early in the third century B.C., as one ancient writer reported: "When the defeated Macedonians had fixed themselves within the walls of their cities, the victorious Brennus ravaged the fields of the whole of Macedonia with no one to oppose him."[3] Brennus also led a group of thirty thousand Celts into Greece itself and caused considerable damage before being defeated in 278 B.C.

Other groups of Celts later attacked Asia Minor, where Attalus I bested them in 230 B.C. After his victory, Attalus gained control of much of Asia Minor and declared himself king of Pergamum. Their attacks led the Celts, or Gauls, to be feared everywhere in the Hellenistic world.

Political and Military Institutions

The Hellenistic monarchies created a semblance of stability for several centuries, even though Hellenistic kings refused to accept the new status quo and periodically engaged in wars to alter it. At the same time, an underlying strain always existed between the new Greco-Macedonian ruling class and the native populations. Together these factors created a certain degree of tension that was never truly ended until the vibrant Roman state to the west stepped in and imposed a new order.

The Hellenistic kingdoms shared a common political system that represented a break with their Greek past. To the Greeks, monarchy was an institution for barbarians, associated in their minds with people like the Persians. Although they retained democratic forms of government in their cities, the Greeks of the Hellenistic world were forced to accept monarchy as a new fact of political life.

Although Alexander the Great had apparently planned to fuse Greeks and easterners, Hellenistic monarchs relied primarily on Greeks and Macedonians to form the new ruling class. It has been estimated that in the Seleucid king-

© Giraudon/Art Resource, NY

A Gaul and His Wife: Monument to the Victory of a Hellenistic King. This statue of a Gaulish chieftain and his wife is a Roman copy of a bronze original that was part of a larger monument erected around 230–220 B.C. to commemorate the victory of Attalus I of Pergamum over the Gauls, a victory that gave Pergamum control over much of Asia Minor. In this scene, the defeated Gaulish leader plunges a sword into his chest just after he has killed his wife to prevent her from being sold into slavery.

dom, for example, only 2.5 percent of the people in authority were non-Greek, and most of them were commanders of local military units. Those who did advance to important administrative posts had learned Greek (all government business was transacted in Greek) and had become Hellenized in a cultural sense. The policy of excluding non-Greeks from leadership positions was not due to the incompetence of the natives but to the determination of the Greek ruling class to maintain its privileged position. It was the Greco-Macedonian ruling class that provided the only unity in the Hellenistic world.

Since the Hellenistic monarchs created and maintained their kingdoms by military force, warfare continued to be an integral part of the Hellenistic world. The phalanx— heavily armed infantry with long spears (lengthened by this time to 18 feet)—and the cavalry still formed the core of

© Scala/Art Resource, NY

Greek War Elephants. Some of the armies in the Hellenistic world made use of elephants obtained from North Africa and India. Pictured on this Italian plate is a Greek war elephant that was brought to the Mediterranean by one of Alexander's successors. The battle fortress on the back of the elephant was a Greek innovation.

the Hellenistic forces. Hellenistic warfare also saw some innovations. Most noticeable were the elephants, "the tanks of ancient warfare," which were especially prominent in the army of the Seleucids, who procured theirs from India, and the Ptolemies, who obtained them from North Africa. But even more important, since armies quickly learned tricks that neutralized the elephants, was the development of new siege machinery, especially the catapult and siege towers. In classical times, cities with good walls were virtually impregnable; Alexander and later Hellenistic rulers could capture cities by using their new equipment.

Hellenistic Cities

Cities played an especially important role in the Hellenistic kingdoms. Throughout his conquests, Alexander had founded a series of new cities and military settlements, and Hellenistic kings did likewise. The new population centers varied considerably in size and importance. Military settlements were meant to maintain order and might consist of only a few hundred men heavily dependent on the king. But there were also new independent cities with thousands of inhabitants. Alexandria in Egypt was the largest city in the Mediterranean region by the first century B.C. Seleucus was especially active in founding new cities, according to one ancient writer: "The other kings have exulted in destroying existing cities; he, on the other hand, arranged to build cities which did not yet exist. He established so many . . . that they were enough to carry the names of towns in Macedonia as well as the names of those in his family. . . . One can go to Phoenicia to see his cities; one can go to Syria and see even more."[4]

Hellenistic rulers encouraged this massive spread of Greek colonists to the Near East because of their intrinsic value to the new monarchies. Greeks (and Macedonians) provided not only a recruiting ground for the army but also a pool of civilian administrators and workers who would contribute to economic development. Even architects, engineers, dramatists, and actors were in demand in the new Greek cities. Many Greeks and Macedonians were quick to see the advantages of moving to the new urban centers and gladly sought their fortunes in the Near East. Greeks of all backgrounds joined the exodus until around 250 B.C., when the outpouring began to slow significantly.

Within the Hellenistic cities, the culture was primarily Greek. The political institutions of the cities were modeled after those of the Greek *polis*. Greeks of the Classical Period would easily have recognized the councils, magistracies, assemblies, and codes of law. The physical layout of the new cities was likewise modeled on those of the Greek homeland. Using the traditional rectilinear grid, cities were laid out with temples, altars, and stone theaters.

Many of the new urban centers were completely dominated by Greeks, while the native populations remained cut off from all civic institutions. The Greeks commissioned purely Greek sculpture, read literature of the Classical Period, and had separate law courts for themselves. Complaints from resentful natives have been recorded. An Egyptian camel driver, for example, complained bitterly that he was not paid regularly because he did "not know how to behave like a Greek." Not only was it difficult for easterners to enter the ranks of the ruling class, but those who did so had to become thoroughly Hellenized. This often required alienation from one's own culture.

The Greeks' belief in their own cultural superiority provided an easy rationalization for their political dominance of the eastern cities. But Greek control of the new cities was also necessary because the kings frequently used the cities as instruments of government, enabling them to rule considerable territory without an extensive bureaucracy. At the same time, for security reasons, the Greeks needed the support of the kings. After all, the Hellenistic cities were islands of Greek culture in a sea of non-Greeks. The relationship between rulers and cities, therefore, was a symbiotic one that bore serious consequences for the cities.

In their political system, religious practices, and architecture, the Greeks tried to re-create the *poleis* of their homeland in their new cities. But it was no longer possible to do so. The new cities were not autonomous entities and soon found themselves dependent on the power of the Hellenistic monarchies. Although the kings did not rule the cities directly, they restricted the cities' freedom in other ways. City administrators knew they could not conduct an independent foreign policy and did not try to do so. The kings also demanded tribute, which could be a heavy burden.

The Greek cities of the era were the chief agents for the spread of Hellenistic culture in the Near East, as far, in fact, as modern Afghanistan and India. These Greek cities were also remarkably vibrant despite their subordination to the Hellenistic monarchies and persisted in being a focal point for the loyalty of their citizens. Their continuing vitality is perhaps most evident on the Greek mainland, where the Greek cities formed two important leagues, the Aetolian League in central Greece and the Achaean League in the Peloponnesus.

※ Economic Trends

Agriculture was still of primary importance to both the native populations and the new Greek cities of the Hellenistic world. The Greek cities continued their old agrarian patterns. A well-defined body of citizens owned land and worked it with the assistance of slaves. But their farms were isolated units in a vast area of land ultimately owned by the king or assigned to large estate owners and worked by native peasants dwelling in villages. Overall, then, neither agricultural patterns nor methods of production underwent significant changes.

Few new products or manufacturing methods were introduced in the Hellenistic period, but the centers of manufacturing shifted significantly. Industry spread from Greece to the east—especially to Asia Minor, Rhodes, and Egypt. New textile centers were set up at Pergamum, and glass and silver crafts were developed in Syria. Leading all cities in manufacturing was Alexandria in Egypt, which became the center for the production of parchment, textiles, linens, oil, metalwork, and glass.

Commerce expanded considerably in the Hellenistic era. Indeed, trading contacts linked much of the Hellenistic world. The decline in the number of political barriers encouraged more commercial traffic. Although Hellenistic monarchs still fought wars, the conquests of Alexander and the policies of his successors made possible greater trade between east and west. Two major trade routes connected the east with the Mediterranean. The central route was the major one and led by sea from India to the Persian Gulf, up the Tigris River to Seleucia on the Tigris, which replaced Babylon as the center for waterborne traffic from the Persian Gulf and overland caravan routes as well. Overland routes from Seleucia then led to Antioch and Ephesus. A southern route wound its way from India by sea but went around Arabia and up the Red Sea to Petra or later Berenice. Caravan routes then led overland to Coptos on the Nile, thence to Alexandria and the Mediterranean.

An incredible variety of products was traded: gold and silver from Spain; iron from northern Armenia; salt from Asia Minor; timber from Macedonia; purple dye from Tyre; ebony, gems, ivory, and spices from India; frankincense (used on altars) from Arabia; slaves from Thrace, Syria, and Asia Minor; fine wines from Syria and western Asia Minor; olive oil from Athens; and numerous exquisite foodstuffs, such as the famous prunes of Damascus. The greatest trade, however, was in the basic staple of life—grain. The great exporting areas were Egypt, Sicily, and the Black Sea region, while Rhodes and Delos served as the major depots for the international grain trade.

Hellenistic Society

One of the noticeable features of social life in the Hellenistic world was the emergence of new opportunities for women—at least for upper-class women. No doubt this was related to the changes in Hellenistic society itself, since the subordination of the cities to the kings altered the way men related to their *polis* and to each other. Some historians maintain that the visible role of Hellenistic queens may also have contributed to a new model for upper-class women.

※ New Opportunities for Upper-Class Women

The creation of the Hellenistic monarchies, which represented a considerable departure from the world of the city-state, gave new scope to the role played by the monarchs' wives, the Hellenistic queens. In Macedonia, a pattern of alliances between mothers and sons provided openings for women to take an active role in politics, especially in political intrigue. In Egypt, opportunities for royal women were even greater after the Ptolemaic rulers adopted the Egyptian custom of kings marrying their own sisters. Of the first eight Ptolemaic rulers, four wed their sisters. Ptolemy II and his sister-wife Arsinoë II were both worshiped as gods in their lifetimes. Arsinoë played an energetic role in government and was involved in the expansion of the Egyptian navy. She was also the first Egyptian queen whose portrait appeared on coins with her husband. Hellenistic queens also showed an intense interest in culture. They wrote poems, collected art, and corresponded with intellectuals.

The most notable gains for upper-class women came in the economic area. Documents show increasing numbers of women involved in managing slaves, selling property, and making loans. Even then, legal contracts in which women were involved had to include their official male guardians, although in numerous instances these men no longer played an important role but were listed only to satisfy legal requirements. In Sparta, women were allowed to own land and manage their own economic affairs. As many of their husbands were absent or had died in war, many Spartan women became wealthy; females owned 40 percent of the privately held land in Sparta.

Spartan women, however, were an exception, especially on the Greek mainland. Women in Athens, for example, still remained highly restricted and supervised. Although a few philosophers welcomed female participation in men's affairs, many philosophers rejected equality between men and women and asserted that the traditional roles of wives and mothers were most satisfying for women. In her treatise "On Chastity," Phintys wrote that "serving as generals, public officials, and statesmen is appropriate

Portrait of Queen Arsinoë II. Arsinoë II, sister and wife of King Ptolemy II, played an active role in Egyptian political affairs. This statue from 250 B.C. depicts the queen in the traditional style of a pharaoh.

(rotated text on right of image) Metropolitan Museum of Art, New York, Rogers Fund, 1920, (20.2.21) Photograph © 1986 The Metropolitan Museum of Art

for men," but "keeping house, remaining within, and taking care of husbands belongs to women."[5]

But the opinions of philosophers did not prevent upper-class women from making gains in areas other than the economic sphere (see the box on p. 95). New possibilities for females arose when women in some areas of the Hellenistic world were allowed to pursue education in the fields of literature, music, and even athletics. Education, then, provided new opportunities for women: female poets appeared again in the third century B.C., and there are instances of women involved in both scholarly and artistic pursuits.

Some wealthy aristocratic women even became politically active in the running of their cities. In the second century B.C., a number of cities passed decrees honoring women for their service to the community. Cyme, in Asia Minor, for example, paid homage to Archippe for her enormous financial contributions. In return, some women were given political rights and in a few instances were allowed to hold office as city magistrates. But often economic motives were attached to this generosity. When Phile of Priene was made a magistrate of her city, it was probably with the understanding that she would donate funds for public works. Once in office, she did build an aqueduct and a reservoir for the community.

Improvements in the position of females were largely restricted to upper-class women. A harsher reality existed for a large group of women condemned to the practice of prostitution. Inscriptional evidence indicates that small families were common in the Hellenistic world; boys were preferred, and rarely was more than one daughter raised. Unwanted girl babies were often exposed to the elements and left to die. Some of these infants were gathered up by eager entrepreneurs and raised to be slave prostitutes. Only the most beautiful and luckiest prostitutes came to be the companions (the *hetairai*) of upper-class men.

The Role of Slavery

The Hellenistic world witnessed the migration of large numbers of people from one area to another. Greeks and Macedonians went into the Hellenistic kingdoms of the east as administrators, mercenaries, engineers, scholars, artists, teachers, and merchants. Moreover, significantly large numbers of non-Greeks moved around for economic and military purposes. But the largest number of uprooted people were slaves. Slavery was viewed as a normal part of life in the Hellenistic world and in antiquity in general.

Slaves were obtained from four chief sources: the children of slaves; children who were sold by their parents or abandoned to perish; persons kidnapped by pirates; and perhaps the largest source of all, prisoners of war. Delos, a major trading center, could handle ten thousand slaves a day in its markets. Although slaves came from everywhere, Thracians and Syrians were the most numerous. Slaves varied in price; Macedonians, Thracians, and Italians drew the highest prices.

Slaves were put to work in numerous ways in the Hellenistic world. States employed slaves as servants for government officials and in government-run industries such as weaving. Most slaves were used in domestic service, farming, and mines, but the situation could vary from state to state. Egypt had no slave class in the countryside, nor was there much domestic slavery outside Alexandria. But the Egyptians did use slave labor in state-run textile factories and made especially brutal use of them in mining operations (see the box on p. 96). Women were also sold as slaves to be concubines for Greek and Macedonian soldiers and civilians.

The effects of slavery could also be important. The employment of large numbers of slaves in the Hellenistic kingdoms contributed to the Hellenizing process. Slaves

A New Autonomy for Women

HERE WERE noticeable gains for upper-class women in Hellenistic society. But even in the lives of ordinary women, a new assertiveness came to the fore despite the continuing domination of society by men. The first selection is taken from the letter of a wife to her husband, complaining about his failure to return home. In the second selection, a father complains that his daughter has abandoned him, contrary to Egyptian law providing that children who have been properly raised should support their parents.

Letter from Isias to Hephaistion, 168 B.C.

If you are well and other things are going right, it would accord with the prayer that I make continually to the gods. I myself and the child and all the household are in good health and think of you always. When I received your letter from Horos, in which you announce that you are in detention in the Serapeum at Memphis, for the news that you are well I straightway thanked the gods, but about your not coming home, when all the others who had been secluded there have come, I am ill-pleased, because after having piloted myself and your child through such bad times and been driven to every extremity owing to the price of wheat, I thought that now at least, with you at home, I should enjoy some respite, whereas you have not even thought of coming home nor given any regard to our circumstances, remembering how I was in want of everything while you were still here, not to mention this long lapse of time and these critical days, during which you have sent us nothing.

As, moreover, Horos who delivered the letter has brought news of your having been released from detention, I am thoroughly ill-pleased. Notwithstanding, as your mother also is annoyed, for her sake as well as for mine please return to the city, if nothing more pressing holds you back. You will do me a favor by taking care of your bodily health. Farewell.

Letter from Ktesikles to King Ptolemy, 220 B.C.

I am wronged by Dionysios and by Nike my daughter. For though I raised her, my own daughter, and educated her and brought her to maturity, when I was stricken with bodily ill-health and was losing my eyesight, she was not minded to furnish me with any of the necessities of life. When I sought to obtain justice from her in Alexandria, she begged my pardon, and in the eighteenth year she swore me a written royal oath to give me each month twenty drachmas, which she was to earn by her own bodily labor. . . . But now corrupted by Dionysios, who is a comic actor, she does not do for me anything of what was in the written oath, despising my weakness and ill-health. I beg you, therefore, O King, not to allow me to be wronged by my daughter and by Dionysios the actor who corrupted her, but to order Diophanes the strategus [provincial administrator] to summon them and hear us out; and if I am speaking the truth, let Diophanes deal with her corrupter as seems good to him and compel my daughter Nike to do justice to me. If this is done I shall no longer be wronged but by fleeing to you, O King, I shall obtain justice.

---

working in homes, farms, or factories had opportunities to absorb Greek ways. This is especially evident in the case of the slave-wives of Hellenistic soldiers.

The Transformation of Education

In the Hellenistic world, education underwent a significant transformation. In the classical period of Greek history, education had been left largely to private enterprise. Greek cities now began to supervise education in new ways. The Greek **gymnasium,** which had been primarily an athletic institution, evolved into a secondary school. The curriculum centered on music, physical exercise, and literature, especially the poetry of Homer. Wealthy individuals often provided the money for the schools and also specified how it should be spent. An inscription from the city of Teos in Asia Minor specified that Polythroos "gave 34,000 drachmas . . . for there to be appointed each year . . . three grammar-masters to teach the boys and the girls; . . . for two gymnastics-masters to be appointed, . . . for a lyre—or harp—player to be appointed . . . [to] teach music and lyre—or harp—playing to the children."[6]

The school in Teos was unusual, however, in that education was ordinarily for upper-class male children. An official known as the *gymnasiarch* served as the head of a gymnasium. This was a civic position of considerable prestige. He was not paid and was expected to provide money for sacrifices, competitions, entertainment, and even school repairs. Many cities passed decrees awarding praise and a "gold crown" to the gymnasiarch for his "munificence toward the people." The educational year culminated with various musical, academic, and athletic contests in which students competed for the honor of having their names inscribed on a victory column.

Hellenistic kings also served as patrons of gymnasia, recognizing their importance in training youths who might serve later as administrators of the state. The institution of the gymnasium played a significant role in the diffusion of Greek culture throughout the Hellenistic world. Whether an upper-class Greek youth lived on the Greek mainland, in Alexandria, or in another city in the east, he could imbibe Greek culture and maintain that sense of superiority that characterized the Greek overlords of the Hellenistic kingdoms.

TREATMENT OF SLAVES IN THE EGYPTIAN GOLD MINES

*S*LAVERY WAS a common practice throughout antiquity. In both Classical Greece and the Hellenistic world, the worst-treated slaves were those who worked in the mines. The Egyptians were especially notorious for their treatment of slaves in the gold mines in Nubia, described in this account by Diodorus of Sicily, who lived in the first century B.C. His account was based on the now lost work of the second-century writer Agatharchides.

Diodorus of Sicily, *Library of History*

And those who have been condemned in this way—and they are a great multitude and are all bound in chains—work at their task unceasingly both by day and throughout the entire night, enjoying no respite and being carefully cut off from any means of escape; since guards of foreign soldiers who speak a language different from theirs stand watch over them, so that not a man, either by conversation or by some contact of a friendly nature, is able to corrupt one of his keepers. . . . And the entire operations are in charge of a skilled worker who distinguishes the stone and points it out to the laborers; and of those who are assigned to this unfortunate task the physically strongest break the quartz-rock with iron hammers, applying no skill to the task but only force, and cutting tunnels through the stone, not in a straight line but wherever the seam of gleaming rock may lead. Now these men, working in darkness as they do because of the bending and winding of the passages, carry lamps bound on their foreheads; and since much of the time they change the position of their bodies to follow the particular character of the stone they throw the blocks, as

they cut them out, on the ground, and at this task they labor without ceasing beneath the sternness and blows of an overseer.

The boys there who have not yet come to maturity, entering through the tunnels into the galleries formed by the removal of the rock, laboriously gather up the rock as it is cast down piece by piece and carry it out into the open to the place outside the entrance. Then those who are above thirty years of age take this quarried stone from them and with iron pestles pound a specified amount of it in stone mortars, until they have worked it down to a smaller size. Thereupon the women and older men receive from them the rock of this size and cast it into mills of which a number stand there in a row, and taking their places in groups of two or three at the spoke or handle of each mill they grind it until they have worked down the amount given them to the consistency of the finest flour. And since no opportunity is afforded any of them to care for his body and they have no garment to cover their shame, no man can look upon the unfortunate wretches without feeling pity for them because of the exceeding hardships they suffer. For no leniency or respite of any kind is given to any man who is sick, or maimed or aged, or in the case of a woman for her weakness, but all without exception are compelled by blows to persevere in their labors, until through ill-treatment they die in the midst of their tortures. Consequently the poor unfortunates believe, because their punishment is so excessively severe, that the future will always be more terrible than the present and therefore look forward to death as more to be desired than life.

Culture in the Hellenistic World

Although the Hellenistic kingdoms encompassed vast areas and many diverse peoples, the Greeks provided a sense of unity as a result of the diffusion of Greek culture throughout the Hellenistic world. The Hellenistic era was a period of considerable cultural accomplishment in many fields—literature, art, science, medicine, and philosophy. Although these achievements occurred throughout the Hellenistic world, certain centers, especially the great Hellenistic cities of Alexandria and Pergamum, stood out. In both cities, cultural developments were encouraged by the rulers themselves. Rich Hellenistic kings had considerable resources with which to patronize culture.

The Ptolemies in Egypt made Alexandria an especially important cultural center. The library became the largest in ancient times, with over half a million scrolls. The museum (literally, "temple of the Muses") created a favorable environment for scholarly research. Alexandria became home to poets, writers, philosophers, and scien-

tists—scholars of all kinds. The library encouraged the systematic study of language and literature. As a result of patronage from the Attalid dynasty, Pergamum, the greatest city in Asia Minor, also became a leading cultural center that attracted both scholars and artists. Its library was second only to that of Alexandria.

New Directions in Literature

The Hellenistic Age produced an enormous quantity of literature, most of which has not survived. Hellenistic monarchs, who held literary talent in high esteem, subsidized writers on a grand scale. The Ptolemaic rulers of Egypt were particularly lavish. The combination of their largess and the famous library drew a host of scholars and authors to Alexandria, including a circle of poets. Theocritus (c. 315–250 B.C.), originally a native of the island of Sicily, wrote "little poems" or idylls dealing with erotic themes, lovers' complaints, and above all, pastoral themes express-

THE PASTORAL IDYLL OF THEOCRITUS

LITTLE IS KNOWN of the poet Theocritus (c. 315–250 B.C.). Born in Syracuse on the island of Sicily, he also lived in Miletus, Cos, and Alexandria. He is best known as the creator of pastoral idylls that portray his great love of nature. This selection is from the famous *Seventh Idyll* (called the "queen of pastorals"), which describes a delightful day on the island of Cos.

Theocritus, *The Seventh Idyll*

This I sang, and Lykidas laughed
again pleasantly, and gave me his stick
in fellowship of the Muses,
and turned left, taking the road
to Pyxa, but Eukritos
and handsome Amyntas and I
turned off at Phrasidamos's
and happily laid ourselves down
on beds of sweet grass and vine-leaves,
freshly picked. Overhead, many elms
and poplars rustled, and nearby
the sacred waters splashed down
from the Nymphs' cave. Brown cicadas
shrilled from the shady branches,
and far off the tree-frog whined
in the heavy underbrush.

Lark and finches sang, doves crooned,
and bees hummed about the spring.
Everything smelled of rich summer
and rich fruits. Pears lay at our feet,
apples in plenty rolled beside us,
and branches loaded down with plums
bent to the ground. And we broke
the four-year seals on the wine-jars.
Nymphs of Kastalia that live
on the slopes of Parnassos, tell me,
was it such a cup old Chiron
offered Herakles in Pholos'
rocky cave? Was it a drink like this
set Polyphemos dancing,
that mighty shepherd who grazed
his flocks beside the Anapos
and pelted ships with mountains—
such nectar as you mixed for us,
you Nymphs, that day by the altar
of Demeter of the Harvest?
May I plant the great winnowing-fan
another time in her grain-heaps,
while she stands and smiles at us
with wheat-sheaves and poppies in her hand.

ing his love of nature and his appreciation of nature's beauty (see the box above).

In the Hellenistic era, Athens remained the theatrical center of the Greek world. While little remained of tragedy, a new kind of comedy developed that completely rejected political themes and sought only to entertain and amuse. The Athenian playwright Menander (c. 342–291 B.C.) was perhaps the best representative of New Comedy. Plots were simple: typically, a hero falls in love with a not-really-so-bad prostitute who turns out eventually to be the long-lost daughter of a rich neighbor. The hero marries her, and they live happily ever after.

The Hellenistic period saw a great outpouring of historical and biographical literature. The chief historian of the Hellenistic Age was Polybius (c. 203–c. 120 B.C.), a Greek who lived for some years in Rome. He is regarded by many historians as second only to Thucydides among Greek historians. His major work consisted of forty books narrating the history of the "inhabited Mediterranean world" from 221 to 146 B.C. Only the first five books are extant, although long extracts from the other books survive. His history focuses on the growth of Rome from a city-state to a vast empire. It is apparent that Polybius understood the significance of the Romans' achievement. He followed Thucydides in seeking rational motives for his-

torical events. He also approached his sources critically and used firsthand accounts.

Hellenistic Art

In addition to being patrons of literary talent, the Hellenistic monarchs were eager to spend their money to beautify and adorn the cities in their states. The founding of new cities and the rebuilding of old ones provided numerous opportunities for Greek architects and sculptors. The structures of the Greek homeland—gymnasia, baths, theaters, and temples—lined the streets of these cities. Most noticeable in the construction of temples was the use of the more ornate Corinthian order (see Chapter 3), which became especially popular during the Hellenistic era.

Sculptors were patronized by Hellenistic kings and rich citizens. Thousands of statues, many paid for by their subjects, were erected in towns and cities all over the Hellenistic world. Hellenistic sculptors traveled widely, attracted by the material rewards offered by wealthy patrons. While maintaining the technical skill of the Classical Period, Hellenistic sculptors moved away from the idealism of fifth-century classicism to a more emotional and realistic art, seen in numerous statues of old women, drunks, and

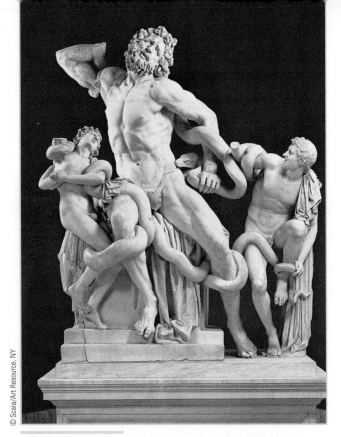

Laocoön and His Sons. Three sculptors from Rhodes created this famous piece. This version is probably a Roman copy of the original. The scene illustrates an episode from the Trojan War when the gods sent serpents into Troy to kill the Trojan priest Laocoön and his sons. The intense struggles of the figures are reflected in the pained expressions on their faces.

Old Market Woman. Hellenistic sculptors no longer tried to capture ideal beauty in their sculpture, a quest that characterized Greek classicism, but moved toward a more emotional and realistic art. This statue of an old market woman is typical of this new trend in art. She is seen carrying chickens and a basket of fruit. Old and haggard, mired in poverty, she struggles to just go on living.

little children at play. They also placed a new emphasis on the female nude.

Alexander's incursion into the western part of India also resulted in some Greek cultural influences there, especially during the Hellenistic era. During the first century B.C., Indian sculptors began to create statues of the Buddha. Especially evident in the Buddhist statues done in Gandhara, which is today part of Pakistan, was the impact of Greek statues.

⟫ A Golden Age of Science and Medicine

The Hellenistic era witnessed a more conscious separation of science from philosophy. In Classical Greece, what we would call the physical and life sciences had been divisions of philosophical inquiry. Nevertheless, the Greeks, by the time of Aristotle, had already established an important principle of scientific investigation, empirical research, or systematic observation, as the basis for generalization. In the Hellenistic Age, the sciences tended to be studied in their own right.

One of the traditional areas of Greek science was astronomy, and two Alexandrian scholars continued this exploration. Aristarchus of Samos (c. 310–230 B.C.) developed a *heliocentric* view of the universe, contending that the sun and the fixed stars remain stationary while the earth

rotates around the sun in a circular orbit. He also argued that the earth rotates around its own axis. This view was not widely accepted, and most scholars clung to the earlier *geocentric* view of the Greeks, which held that the earth was at the center of the universe. Another astronomer, Eratosthenes (c. 275–194 B.C.), determined that the earth was round and calculated the earth's circumference at 24,675 miles, an estimate that was within 200 miles of the actual figure.

A third Alexandrian scholar was Euclid, who lived around 300 B.C. He established a school in Alexandria but is primarily known for his work titled *Elements*. This was a systematic organization of the fundamental elements of geometry as they had already been worked out; it became the standard textbook of plane geometry and was used up to modern times.

Archimedes   The most famous of the scientists of the Hellenistic period, Archimedes (287–212 B.C.) came from the western Mediterranean region. Archimedes was especially

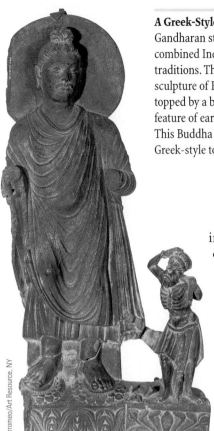

© Borromeo/Art Resource, NY

A Greek-Style Buddha. The Buddhist Gandharan style in the first century B.C. combined Indian and Hellenistic artistic traditions. This is evident in this stone sculpture of Buddha. Note the wavy hair topped by a bun tied with a ribbon, also a feature of earlier statues of Greek deities. This Buddha is also seen wearing a Greek-style toga.

important for his work on the geometry of spheres and cylinders, for establishing the value of the mathematical constant pi, and for creating the science of hydrostatics. Archimedes was also a practical inventor. He may have devised the so-called Archimedean screw used to pump water out of mines and to lift irrigation water, as well as a compound pulley for transporting heavy weights. During the Roman siege of his native city of Syracuse, he constructed a number of devices to thwart the attackers. According to Plutarch's account, the Romans became so frightened "that if they did but see a little rope or a piece of wood from the wall, instantly crying out, that there it was again, Archimedes was about to let fly some engine at them, they turned their backs and fled."[7] Archimedes' accomplishments inspired a wealth of semilegendary stories. Supposedly, he discovered specific gravity by observing the water he displaced in his bath and became so excited by his realization that he jumped out of the water and ran home naked, shouting, "Eureka!" ("I have found it!"). He is said to have emphasized the importance of levers by proclaiming to the king of Syracuse: "Give me a lever and a place to stand on, and I will move the earth." The king was so impressed that he encouraged Archimedes to lower his sights and build defensive weapons instead.

Medicine The scientific foundations of medicine also made considerable strides in the Hellenistic period. This represents a continuation from the fifth century when Hippocrates, a contemporary of Socrates, is credited with having been the "first to separate medicine from philosophy" by stressing natural explanations and natural cures for disease. Herophilus and Erasistratus, both well-known physicians, were active in Alexandria in the first half of the third century B.C. Both were interested in anatomy and used dissection and vivisection (the dissection of living bodies)

to expand their knowledge, or so the Roman author Celsus claimed:

> Moreover, as pains, and also various kinds of diseases, arise in the more internal parts, they hold that no one can apply remedies for these who is ignorant about the parts themselves; hence it becomes necessary to lay open the bodies of the dead and to scrutinize their viscera and intestines. They hold that Herophilus and Erasistratus did this in the best way by far, when they laid open men while alive—criminals received out of prison from the kings—and while these were still breathing, observed parts which beforehand nature had concealed, their position, color, shape, size, arrangement, hardness, softness, smoothness, relation, processes and depressions of each, and whether any part is inserted into or is received into another.[8]

Herophilus added significantly to the understanding of the brain, eye, liver, and the reproductive and nervous systems. Erasistratus made discoveries in the process of digestion.

It would be misleading to think of medicine in the Hellenistic world only in terms of scientific advances. Alongside these developments, a wide range of alternative methods of healing continued to exist. These included magical practices, such as the use of amulets to cast off evil spirits, herbal remedies, and the healing powers of deities, especially those of Asclepius, the god of healing (see the box on p. 100).

Philosophy: New Schools of Thought

While Alexandria and Pergamum became the renowned cultural centers of the Hellenistic world, Athens remained the prime center for philosophy. After Alexander the Great, the home of Socrates, Plato, and Aristotle continued to attract the most illustrious philosophers from the Greek world who chose to establish their schools there. New schools of philosophical thought—the Epicureans and Stoics—reinforced Athens's reputation as a philosophical center.

Epicureanism Epicurus (341–270 B.C.), the founder of **Epicureanism,** established a school in Athens near the end of the fourth century B.C. Epicurus' famous belief in a doctrine of "pleasure" began with his view of the world. Although he did not deny the existence of the gods, he did not believe they played any active role in the world. The universe ran on its own. This left human beings free to follow self-interest as a basic motivating force. Happiness was the goal of life, and the means to achieve it was the pursuit of pleasure, the only true good. But the pursuit of pleasure was not meant in a physical, hedonistic sense:

> When, therefore, we maintain that pleasure is the end, we do not mean the pleasures of profligates and those that consist in sensuality, as is supposed by some who are either ignorant or disagree with us or do not understand, but freedom from pain in the body and from trouble in the mind. For it is not continuous drinkings and revelings, nor the satisfaction of lusts, nor the enjoyment of fish and other luxuries of the wealthy table, which produce a pleasant life, but sober reasoning, searching out the motives for all choice and avoidance, and banishing mere opinions, to which are due the greatest disturbance of the spirit.

MIRACULOUS CURES

*A*LTHOUGH ALL GODS and goddesses were believed to have healing powers, special curative powers were attributed to Asclepius, the god of healing. A cult of supernatural healing came to be associated with him. Dreams that people experienced when they slept in a sanctuary dedicated to Asclepius supposedly had curative powers, as these texts demonstrate.

Texts on the Miraculous Cures at Epidaurus

A man with the fingers of his hand paralyzed except for one came as a suppliant to the god, and when he saw the tablets in the sanctuary he would not believe the cures and was rather contemptuous of the inscriptions, but when he went to sleep he saw a vision: he thought that as he was playing dice below the sanctuary and was about to throw the dice, the god appeared, sprang on his hand and stretched out his fingers, and when the god moved away, the man thought he bent his hand and stretched out the fingers one by one.

When he had straightened them all out, the god asked him whether he still did not believe the inscriptions on the tablets in the sanctuary, and the man said he did. The god said: "Since previously you would not believe them, although they are not incredible, in future let [your name] be 'Incredulous!'" When day came he went away cured.

Ambrosia from Athens, blind in one eye. She came as a suppliant to the god, and as she walked about the sanctuary she ridiculed some of the cures as being incredible and impossible, that persons who were lame and blind should be restored to health merely by seeing a dream. But when she went to sleep she saw a vision: she thought the god was standing next to her and saying that he would restore her to health, but she must dedicate in the sanctuary as a reward a silver pig, as a memorial of her stupidity. Having said this he split open the diseased eye and poured in a medicine. When day came she went away cured.

Pleasure was not satisfying one's desire in an active, gluttonous fashion but rather freedom from emotional turmoil, freedom from worry, the freedom that came from a mind at rest. To achieve this passive pleasure, one had to free oneself from public activity: "We must release ourselves from the prison of affairs and politics." They were too strenuous to give peace of mind. But this was not a renunciation of all social life, for to Epicurus, a life could be complete only when it was centered on the basic ideal of friendship: "Of all the things which wisdom acquires to produce the blessedness of the complete life, far the greatest is the possession of friendship."[9] Epicurus' own life in Athens was an embodiment of his teachings. He and his friends created their own private community where they could pursue their ideal of true happiness.

Stoicism   Epicureanism was eventually overshadowed by another school of thought known as **Stoicism,** which became the most popular philosophy of the Hellenistic world and persisted in the Roman Empire as well. It was the product of a teacher named Zeno (335–263 B.C.), who came to Athens and began to teach in a public colonnade known as the Painted Portico (the *Stoa Poikile*—hence the name Stoicism). Like Epicureanism, Stoicism was concerned with how individuals find happiness. But Stoics took a radically different approach. To them, happiness, the supreme good, could be found only in virtue, which meant essentially living in harmony with divine will: "And this very thing constitutes the virtue of the happy man and the smooth current of life, when all actions promote the harmony of the spirit dwelling in the individual man with the will of him who orders the universe."[10] One achieved happiness by choosing to follow divine will through the free exercise of one's own will. To the Stoics, divine will was the

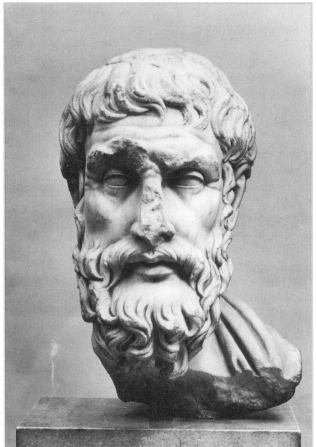

Portrait of Epicurus.   Epicurus was the founder of the Epicurean school of philosophy, which became very popular during the Hellenistic period. He maintained an "atomic" theory of the universe—that the only things that exist are atoms moving through the void—and an ethical theory based on the pursuit of pleasure.

same as the will of nature, since nature was simply a manifestation or expression of the gods. "Living according to nature," therefore, meant following divine will or the natural laws that the gods established to run the universe.

Virtuous living, then, was living in accordance with the laws of nature or submitting to divine will (see the box above). This led to the acceptance of whatever one received in life, since divine will for us was by its very nature good. By accepting divine law, people mastered themselves and gained inner peace. Life's problems could not disturb such individuals, and they could bear whatever life offered (hence our word *stoic*).

Unlike Epicureans, Stoics did not believe in the need to separate oneself from the world and politics. Public service was regarded as noble. The real Stoic was a good citizen and could even be a good government official. Because Stoics believed that a divine principle was present throughout the universe, each human being also contained a divine spark. This led to a belief in the oneness of humanity. The world constituted a single society of equal human beings. Although not equal in the outer world, the divine spark in each meant that all were free to follow divine will (what was best for each individual). All persons, then, even slaves, though unfree in body, were equal at the level of the soul.

Epicureanism and especially Stoicism appealed to large numbers of people in the Hellenistic world. Both of these philosophies focused primarily on the problem of human happiness. Their popularity would suggest a fundamental change in the character of the Greek lifestyle. In the Classical Greek world, the happiness of individuals and the meaning of life were closely associated with the life of the *polis*. One found fulfillment within the community. In the Hellenistic kingdoms, although the *polis* continued to exist, the sense that one could find satisfaction and fulfillment through life in the *polis* had weakened. Not only did individuals seek new philosophies that offered personal happiness, but in the cosmopolitan world of the Hellenistic states, with their mixtures of peoples, a new openness to thoughts of universality could also emerge. For some people, Stoicism embodied this larger sense of community.

The appeal of new philosophies in the Hellenistic era can also be explained by the apparent decline in certain aspects of traditional religion.

Religion in the Hellenistic World

When the Greeks spread throughout the Near East, they took their gods with them. Hellenistic cities increased the number of public festivals and celebrated them with great magnificence. But as time went on, there was a noticeable decline in the vitality of the traditional Greek Olympian religion. The civic cults based on the traditional gods no longer seemed sufficient to satisfy people's emotional needs.

This left Greeks receptive to the numerous religious cults of the eastern world. The Greeks were always tolerant of other existing religious institutions. Hence in the Hellenistic cities of the Near East, the traditional civic cults of their own gods and foreign cults existed side by side. Alexandria had cults of the traditional Greek gods, Egyptian deities such as Isis and Horus, the Babylonian Astarte, and the Syrian Atargatis.

But for many people, the search for personal meaning remained unfulfilled. Among educated Greeks, the philosophies of Epicureanism and especially Stoicism offered help. Another source of solace came in the form of **mystery religions.**

Mystery Religions

Mystery cults, with their secret initiations and promises of individual salvation, were not new to the Greek world. But the Greeks of the Hellenistic era were also strongly influenced by eastern mystery cults, such as those of Egypt, which offered a distinct advantage over the Greek mystery religions. The latter had usually been connected to specific locations (such as Eleusis), which meant that a would-be initiate had to undertake a pilgrimage in order to participate in the rites. In contrast, the eastern mystery religions were readily available since temples to their gods and goddesses were located throughout the Greek cities of the east.

All of the mystery religions were based on the same fundamental premises. Individuals could pursue a path to salvation and achieve eternal life by being initiated into a union with a savior god or goddess who had died and risen again. The ritual of initiation, by which the seeker identified with the god or goddess, was no doubt a highly emotional experience.

The Egyptian cult of Isis was one of the most popular of the mystery religions. The cult of Isis was very ancient but became truly universal in Hellenistic times. Isis was the goddess of women, marriage, and children, as one of her hymns states: "I am she whom women call goddess. I ordained that women should be loved by men: I brought wife and husband together, and invented the marriage contract. I ordained that women should bear children."[11] Isis was also portrayed as the giver of civilization who had brought laws and letters to all humankind. The cult of Isis offered a precious commodity to its initiates—the promise of eternal life. In many ways, the mystery religions of the Hellenistic era helped pave the way for Christianity.

The Jews in the Hellenistic World

In observing the similarities among their gods and goddesses, Greeks and easterners tended to assume they were the same beings with different names, giving rise to a process of **syncretism.** But a special position was occupied in the Hellenistic world by the Jews, whose monotheistic religion was exclusive and did not permit this kind of fusion of spiritual beings.

The Jewish province of Judaea was ruled by the Ptolemies until it fell under the control of the Seleucids by 200 B.C. In the reign of the Seleucid king Antiochus IV (175–163 B.C.), conflict erupted in Judaea. Hellenistic monarchs were generally tolerant of all religions, but problems with Rome prompted Antiochus to try to impose more cultural and religious unity in Judaea. When he sent troops to Jerusalem and seized the Temple, he sparked a Jewish uprising led by Judas Maccabaeus (164 B.C.). The rebels succeeded in recapturing the Temple, a joyous event that has been celebrated every year since in the Jewish holiday of Hanukkah (Hebrew for "rededication"). Although the conflict in Judaea continued, the Seleucids ultimately made concessions and allowed the Jews considerable freedom.

The Cult of Isis. The cult of Isis was one of the most popular mystery religions in the Hellenistic world. This fresco from Herculaneum in Italy depicts a religious ceremony in front of the temple of Isis. At the top a priest holds a golden vessel, while below him another priest leads the worshipers with a staff. A third priest fans the flames at the altar.

But since the Diaspora (see Chapter 2), large numbers of Jews no longer lived in Judaea. There was a large Jewish population in Egypt, particularly in Alexandria, as well as Jewish settlements throughout the cities of Asia Minor and Syria. In each city, Jews generally set up a synagogue and formed a private association for worship as other foreigners did. But some city authorities also allowed the Jews to form a political corporation that gave them greater rights than other resident aliens. Most important, they gained the privilege to live by their own laws and their own judicial system. The Jews were not really interested in citizenship in the cities in which they resided because full citizenship meant worship of the city's gods, anathema to Jews who believed only in Yahweh.

TIMELINE

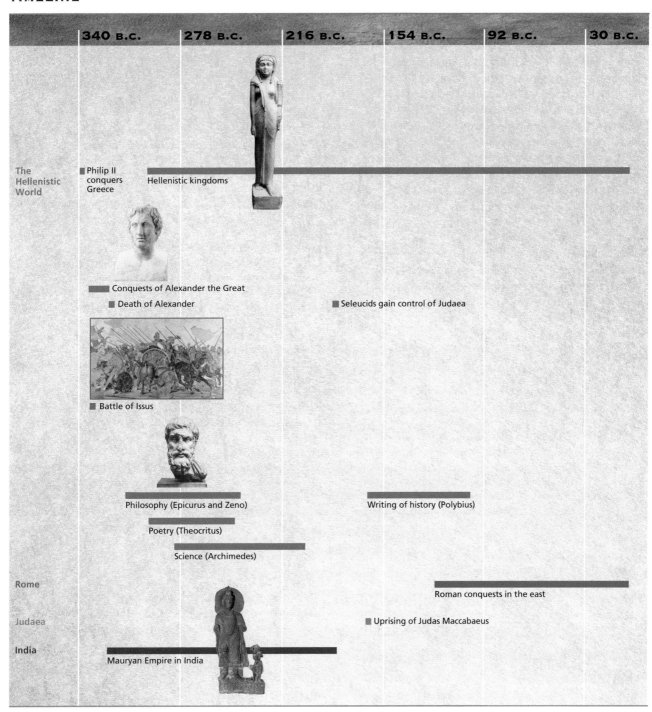

CONCLUSION

*A*LTHOUGH HISTORIANS USED TO VIEW the Hellenistic era as a period of stagnation after the brilliant Greek civilization of the fifth century B.C., our survey of the Hellenistic world has shown the weakness of that position. The Hellenistic period was, in its own way, a vibrant one. New cities arose and flourished. New philosophical ideas captured the minds of many people. Significant achievements occurred in art, literature, and science. Greek culture spread throughout the Near East and made an impact wherever it was carried. In some areas of the Hellenistic world, queens played an active role in political life, and many upper-class women found new avenues for expressing themselves.

But serious problems remained. Hellenistic kings continued to engage in inconclusive wars. The gulf between rich and poor was indeed great. Much of the formal culture was the special preserve of the Greek conquerors, whose attitude of superiority kept them largely separated from the native masses of the Hellenistic kingdoms. Although the Hellenistic world achieved a degree of political stability, signs of decline were beginning to multiply by the late third century B.C. Some of the more farsighted denizens of the Hellenistic world may have realized the danger represented by the growing power of Rome, which would ultimately inherit Alexander's empire. We must now try to understand what made the Romans such successful conquerors.

NOTES

1. Quoted in Sarah B. Pomeroy et al., *Ancient Greece: A Political, Social, and Cultural History* (Oxford, 1999), p. 390.
2. Polybius, *The Histories,* trans. W. R. Paton (Cambridge, Mass., 1960), 18.37.8–10.
3. Quoted in Graham Shipley, *The Greek World After Alexander, 323–30 B.C.* (London, 2000), p. 53.
4. Quoted in ibid., p. 304.
5. Maureen B. Fant and Mary R. Lefkowitz, *Women's Life in Greece and Rome: A Source Book in Translation* (Baltimore, 1992), no. 208.
6. Roger S. Bagnall and Peter Derow, *Greek Historical Documents: The Hellenistic Period* (Chico, Calif., 1981), p. 113.
7. Plutarch, *Life of Marcellus,* trans. John Dryden (New York, n.d.), p. 378.
8. Celsus, *De Medicina,* trans. W. G. Spencer (Cambridge, Mass., 1935), Prooemium 23–24.
9. *Epicurus: The Extant Remains,* trans. Cyril Bailey (Oxford, 1926), pp. 89–90, 115, 101.
10. Diogenes Laertius, *Life of Zeno,* vol. 2, trans. R. D. Hicks (London, 1925), p. 195.
11. Quoted in W. W. Tarn, *Hellenistic Civilization* (London, 1930), p. 324.

SUGGESTIONS FOR FURTHER READING

For a general introduction to the Hellenistic era, see **J. Boardman, J. Griffin, and O. Murray, eds.,** *The Oxford History of the Classical World* (Oxford, 1986), pp. 315–385. The best general surveys are **F. W. Walbank,** *The Hellenistic World* (Cambridge, Mass., 1993), and **G. Shipley,** *The Greek World After Alexander, 323–30 B.C.* (New York, 2000). Other studies include **W. W. Tarn and G. T. Griffith,** *Hellenistic Civilization,* 3d ed. (London, 1952); **M. Grant,** *From Alexander to Cleopatra: The Hellenistic World* (London, 1982); and **P. Green,** *Alexander to Actium: The Historic Evolution of the Hellenistic Age* (Berkeley, Calif., 1990).

For a good introduction to the early history of Macedonia, see **E. N. Borza,** *In the Shadow of Olympus: The Emergence of Macedon* (Princeton, N.J., 1990), and **R. M. Errington,** *A History of Macedonia* (Berkeley, Calif., 1990). Philip II is covered well in **G. L. Cawkwell,** *Philip of Macedon* (London, 1978). There are considerable differences of opinion on Alexander the Great. Good biographies include **R. L. Fox,** *Alexander the Great* (London, 1973); **P. Cartledge,** *Alexander the Great* (New York, 2004); **N. G. L. Hammond,** *The Genius of Alexander the Great* (Chapel Hill, N.C., 1997); and **P. Green,** *Alexander of Macedon* (Berkeley, Calif., 1991).

Studies on the various Hellenistic monarchies include **N. G. L. Hammond and F. W. Walbank,** *A History of Macedonia,* vol. 3, *336–167 B.C.* (Oxford, 1988); **S. Sherwin-White and A. Kuhrt,** *From Samarkand to Sardis: A New Approach to the Seleucid Empire* (Berkeley, Calif., 1993); **N. Lewis,** *Greeks in Ptolemaic Egypt* (Oxford, 1986); and **R. E. Allen,** *The Attalid Kingdom* (Oxford, 1983).

On the Celts, see **B. Cunliffe,** *The Ancient Celts* (London, 1997), and the beautifully illustrated brief study by **J. Davies,** *The Celts* (London, 2000).

A good survey of Hellenistic cities can be found in **A. H. M. Jones,** *The Greek City from Alexander to Justinian* (Oxford, 1940). Alexandria is covered in **P. M. Fraser,** *Ptolemaic Alexandria* (Oxford, 1972). On economic and social trends, see **M. I. Finley,** *The Ancient Economy,* 2d ed. (London, 1985), and the classic and still indispensable **M. I. Rostovtzeff,** *Social and Economic History of the Hellenistic World,* 3 vols., 2d ed. (Oxford, 1953).

Hellenistic women are examined in two works by **S. B. Pomeroy,** *Goddesses, Whores, Wives, and Slaves: Women in Classical Antiquity* (New York, 1975), pp. 120–148, and *Women in Hellenistic Egypt* (New York, 1984). Slavery is examined in **W. L. Westermann,** *The Slave-Systems of Greek and Roman Antiquity* (Philadelphia, 1955). The classic work on education is **H. I. Marrou,** *A History of Education in Antiquity* (London, 1956).

For a general introduction to Hellenistic culture, see **J. Onians,** *Art and Thought in the Hellenistic Age* (London, 1979). On art, see **J. J. Pollitt,** *Art in the Hellenistic Age* (New York, 1986). The best general survey of Hellenistic philosophy is **A. A. Long,** *Hellenistic Philosophy: Stoics, Epicureans, Skeptics,* 2d ed. (London, 1986). A superb work on Hellenistic science is **G. E. R. Lloyd,** *Greek Science After Aristotle* (London, 1973).

On various facets of Hellenistic religion, see **L. Martin,** *Hellenistic Religions: An Introduction* (New York, 1987), and **R. E. Witt,** *Isis in the Graeco-Roman World* (London, 1971).

On the entry of Rome into the Hellenistic world, see the basic work by **E. S. Gruen,** *The Hellenistic World and the Coming of Rome,* 2 vols. (Berkeley, Calif., 1984).

History Now™

Enter *HistoryNow* using the access card that is available for *Western Civilization*. *HistoryNow* will assist you in understanding the content in this chapter with lesson plans generated for your needs. In addition, you can read the following documents, and many more, online:

Plutarch, Life of Alexander

Aristotle, excerpt from *Nicomachean Ethics*

Aristotle, *Metaphysics,* Chapter 12

INFOTRAC SEARCH TERMS

For additional reading, go to InfoTrac College Edition, your online research library at http://infotrac.thomsonlearning.com

Key Term Search

Greek history

Alexander the Great

Archimedes

WESTERN CIVILIZATION RESOURCES

 Visit the *Western Civilization* Companion Web site for resources specific to this book:

http://history.wadsworth.com/spielvogel06/

For a variety of tools to help you succeed in this course, visit the Western Civilization Resource Center at

http://history.wadsworth.com/western/

Included are quizzes; images; documents; interactive simulations; maps and timelines; movie explorations; and a wealth of other sources.

THE ROMAN REPUBLIC

Horatius defending the bridge as envisioned by Charles Le Brun, a seventeenth-century French painter

© Dulwich Picture Gallery, London, UK/Bridgeman Art Library

$\mathcal{E}$ARLY ROMAN HISTORY is filled with legendary tales of the heroes who made Rome great. One of the best known is the story of Horatius at the bridge. Threatened by attack from the neighboring Etruscans, Roman farmers abandoned their fields and moved into the city, where they would be protected by the walls. One weak point in the Roman defenses, however, was a wooden bridge over the Tiber River. Horatius was on guard at the bridge when a sudden assault by the Etruscans caused many Roman troops to throw down their weapons and flee. Horatius urged them to make a stand at the bridge to protect Rome; when they hesitated, as a last resort he told them to destroy the bridge behind him while he held the Etruscans back. Astonished at the sight of a single defender, the confused Etruscans threw their spears at Horatius, who caught them on his shield and barred the way. By the time the Etruscans had regrouped and were about to overwhelm the lone defender, the Roman soldiers brought down the bridge. When Horatius heard the bridge crash into the river behind him, he dived fully armed into the water and swam safely to the other side through a hail of arrows. Rome had been saved by the courageous act of a Roman who knew his duty and was determined to carry it out. Courage, duty, determination—these qualities would also serve the many Romans who believed that it was their mission to rule nations and peoples.

In the first millennium B.C., a group of Latin-speaking people established a small community on the plain of Latium on the Italian peninsula. This community, called Rome, was one of numerous Latin-speaking communities in Latium, and the Latin speakers, in turn, constituted only some of the many peoples in Italy. Roman history is basically the story of the Romans' conquest of the plain of Latium, then Italy, and finally the entire Mediterranean world. Why were the Romans able to do this? The Romans made the right decisions at the right time; in other words, the Romans had political wisdom.

The Romans were also practical. Unlike the Greeks, who reserved their citizenship for small, select groups, the Romans often offered citizenship to the peoples they conquered, thus laying the basis for a strong, integrated empire. The Romans also did not hesitate to borrow ideas and culture from the Greeks. Roman strength lay in government, law, and engineering. The Romans knew how to govern people, establish legal structures, and construct the roads that took them to the ends of the known world. Throughout their empire, they carried their law, their political institutions, their engineering skills, and their Latin language. And even after the Romans were gone, those same gifts continued to play an important role in the continuing saga of Western civilization.

The Emergence of Rome

Not much is known about the prehistoric peoples who lived in Italy. We do know that Indo-European peoples moved into Italy during the second half of the second millennium B.C. By the first millennium B.C., other peoples had also settled in Italy, the two most notable being the Greeks and the Etruscans. Before examining these peoples, however, we need to consider the influence geography had on the historical development of the peoples on the Italian peninsula.

Geography of the Italian Peninsula

Geography had a major impact on Roman history. Italy is a narrow peninsula extending about 750 miles from north to south but averaging only about 120 miles across (see Map 5.1). The Apennine Mountains traverse the peninsula from north to south, forming a ridge down the middle that divides west from east. Nevertheless, Italy has some fairly large fertile plains ideal for farming. Most important were the Po valley in the north, probably the most fertile agricultural area; the plain of Latium, on which Rome was located; and Campania to the south of Latium. To the east of the Italian peninsula is the Adriatic Sea, and to the west,

the Tyrrhenian Sea and the large islands of Corsica and Sardinia. Sicily lies just west of the toe of the boot-shaped peninsula.

Although the Apennines bisect Italy, they are less rugged than the mountain ranges of Greece and so did not divide the peninsula into many small isolated communities. Italy also possessed considerably more productive farmland than Greece, enabling it to support a large population. Rome's location was favorable from a geographical point of view. Located 18 miles inland on the Tiber River, Rome had access to the sea but was far enough inland to be safe from pirates. Built on seven hills, it was easily defended, and because it was situated where the Tiber could be readily forded, Rome became a natural crossing point for north-south traffic in western Italy. All in all, Rome had a good central location in Italy from which to expand.

Moreover, the Italian peninsula juts into the Mediterranean Sea, making it an important crossroads between the western and eastern Mediterranean. Once Rome had unified Italy, involvement in Mediterranean affairs was natural. And after the Romans had conquered their Mediterranean empire, Italy's central location made their task of governing that empire considerably easier.

The Greeks

The Greeks arrived on the Italian peninsula in large numbers during the age of Greek colonization (750–550 B.C.; see Chapter 3). Initially, the Greeks settled in southern Italy. They founded Cumae in the Bay of Naples, Naples itself, and Tarentum and then crept around the coast and up the peninsula as far as Brindisi. They also occupied the eastern two-thirds of Sicily. In establishing their colonies, the Greeks planned permanent communities, secured the coastal plains for agriculture, and built walled cities with harbors to carry on trade. Ultimately, the Greeks had considerable influence on Rome. They cultivated the olive and the vine, passed on their alphabetic system of writing, and provided artistic and cultural models through their sculpture, architecture, and literature. Indeed, many historians view Roman culture as a continuation of Greek culture. While Greek influence initially touched Rome indirectly through the Etruscans, the Roman conquest of southern Italy and Sicily brought them into direct contact with the Greeks.

The Etruscans

The initial development of Rome was influenced most by a people known as the Etruscans, who had settled north of Rome in Etruria. They were a city-dwelling people who established their towns in commanding positions and fortified them with walls. Numerous inscriptions in tombs show that the Etruscans adopted alphabetic writing from the Greeks before 600 B.C.

The origins of the Etruscans are not clear, but after 650 B.C., they expanded in Italy and became the dominant

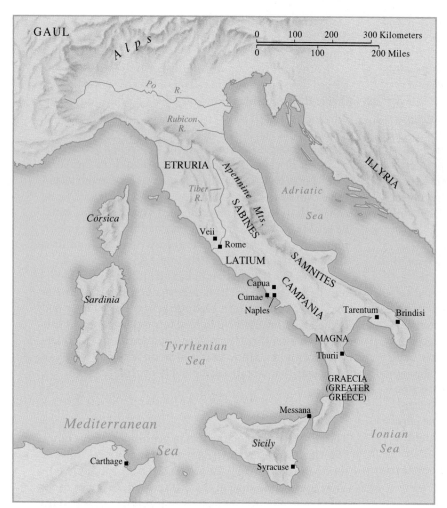

MAP 5.1 **Ancient Italy.** Ancient Italy was home to several groups. Both the Etruscans in the north and the Greeks in the south had a major influence on the development of Rome. ❓ Once Rome conquered the Etruscans, Sabines, Samnites, and other local groups, what aspects of the Italian peninsula helped make it defensible against outside enemies? 🌐 **View an animated version of this map or related maps at** http://history.wadsworth .com/spielvogel06/

cultural and economic force in a number of areas. To the north, they moved into north-central Italy. To the south, according to Roman tradition and archaeological evidence, they controlled Rome and possibly all of Latium. From Latium they moved south into Campania, founded a settlement at Capua, and came into direct contact with Greek colonists in southern Italy. In the sixth century B.C., the Etruscans were at the height of their power. But by 480 B.C., their power had begun to decline, and by 400 B.C., they were again limited to Etruria itself. Later they were invaded by the Gauls and then conquered by the Romans. But by then the Etruscans had already made an impact. By transforming villages into towns and cities, they brought urbanization to northern and central Italy (the Greeks brought urbanization to southern Italy). Rome was, of course, the Etruscans' most famous creation.

The City of Rome

🍃 Early Rome

According to Roman legend, Rome was founded by the twin brothers Romulus and Remus in 753 B.C. Of course, the Romans invented this story to provide a noble ancestry for their city. Archaeologists have found, however, that by the eighth century there was a settlement consisting of huts on the tops of Rome's hills. The early Romans, basically a pastoral people, spoke Latin, which, like Greek, belongs to the Indo-European family of languages (see Table 1.2 in Chapter 1). The Roman historical tradition also maintained that early Rome (753–509 B.C.) had been under the control of seven kings and that two of the last three had been Etruscans. Some historians believe that the king list may have some historical accuracy. What is certain is that Rome did fall under the influence of

Etruscan Tomb Mural. Like the Egyptians, the Etruscans filled their tombs with furniture, bowls, and other objects of daily life, as well as murals showing diversions experienced in life and awaiting the dead in the afterlife. Shown in this mural found in an Etruscan tomb at Tarquinia are servants and musicians at a banquet. This mural was painted in the first half of the fifth century B.C.

the Etruscans for about one hundred years during the period of the kings.

By the beginning of the sixth century, under Etruscan influence, Rome began to emerge as a city. The Etruscans were responsible for an outstanding building program. They constructed the first roadbed of the chief street through Rome—the Sacred Way—before 575 B.C. and oversaw the development of temples, markets, shops, streets, and houses. By 509 B.C., supposedly when the monarchy was overthrown, a new Rome had emerged, essentially a product of the fusion of Etruscan and native Roman elements. After Rome had expanded over its seven hills and the valleys in between, the Servian Wall was built in the fourth century B.C. to surround the city.

The Etruscans had an impact on Roman civilization in numerous ways, both large and small. The Romans adopted Etruscan dress—the toga and short cloak. The insignia of the Etruscan kings became the insignia of Roman magistrates. Most impressive was the *fasces,* an ax surrounded by a bundle of rods used as a symbol for the power to scourge and execute, hence to rule. The Romans were also indebted to the Etruscans for the alphabet. The Latin alphabet was a modification of the Etruscan one derived from the Greeks.

The Romans traditionally associated the end of both monarchy and Etruscan domination with the rape of Lucretia, a Roman noblewoman of great virtue. Raped by a son of the king, Lucretia informed her father, husband, and their friends what had happened and then committed suicide "rather than be an example of unchastity to other wives," as an ancient Roman historian put it. Lucretia became the model Roman woman: a faithful wife and a pure and courageous woman who chose death rather than be seen as lacking in virtue. In revenge, the Roman nobles drove the king and his family from Rome and established a republican form of government, which ushered in the era of the Republic. According to the Romans of the late Republic, all this occurred in 509 B.C. Though interesting, the story has little historical foundation. It is more likely that the overthrow of the monarchy was accomplished by

Lictors with *Fasces*. Pictured are lictors bearing the *fasces,* an ax surrounded by a bundle of rods tied with a red thong, an insignia borrowed from the Etruscan kings. The *fasces* was a symbol of the power to rule, and the consuls, the chief executives of the Roman Republic, were always preceded by twelve lictors bearing the *fasces.*

nobles who experienced a loss of power because of the shift from cavalry to heavy-armed infantry during the reign of Servius Tullius, the next-to-last king. The overthrow was not a patriotic uprising but an attempt by Roman nobles to maintain their position of power. Some scholars have even argued that the continuation of Etruscan influence at Rome into the fifth century necessitates dating the beginning of the Roman Republic to around 475 B.C., but most historians remain committed to a date close to the traditional 509 B.C.

The Roman Republic (c. 509–264 B.C.)

The transition from monarchy to republican government was not easy. Rome felt threatened by enemies from every direction and in meeting these threats embarked on a course of military expansion that led to the conquest of the entire Italian peninsula. During this period of expansion in Italy, the Roman Republic developed political institutions that were in many ways determined by the social divisions that existed within the community.

The Roman State

In politics and law, as in conquest, the Romans took a practical approach and fashioned political institutions in response to problems as they arose. Hence it is important to remember that the political institutions we will discuss evolved over a period of centuries.

Political Institutions The Romans had a clear concept of executive authority, embodied in their word *imperium,* or "the right to command." Invested with *imperium,* the chief magistrates of the Roman state exercised a supreme power that was circumscribed only by extraneous means—officials held office for a limited term and could be tried for offenses committed in office once their term ended. While political institutions changed, the concept of *imperium* did not, and it is the one factor that gives Roman constitutional history continuity and unity.

The chief executive officers of the Roman Republic who possessed *imperium* were the consuls and praetors. After the monarchy was overthrown, two **consuls,** chosen annually, administered the government and led the Roman army into battle. In 366 B.C., a new office, that of the **praetor,** was created. The praetor also possessed *imperium* and could govern Rome when the consuls were away from the city and could also lead armies. The praetor's primary function, however, was the execution of justice. He was in charge of the civil law as it applied to Roman citizens. In 242 B.C., reflecting Rome's growth, another praetor was added to judge cases in which one or both parties were noncitizens.

As Rome expanded into the Mediterranean, additional praetors were established to govern the newly conquered provinces (two in 227, two more in 197 B.C.). But as the number of provinces continued to grow, the Romans devised a new system in which ex-consuls and ex-praetors who had served their one-year terms were given the title of *proconsul* and *propraetor,* respectively, and sent out as provincial governors. This demonstrates once again the Romans' practical solution to an immediate problem. It was reasonable to assume that officials with governmental experience would make good provincial administrators, although this was not always true in practice due to the opportunities for financial corruption in the provinces.

Periodically, the Republic also created an extraordinary executive. In an emergency, the consuls would resign, and a **dictator** with unlimited power would be chosen to run the state. This office was supposed to last only for the duration of the emergency, the usual limit being six months. The Roman state also had administrative officials with specialized duties. **Quaestors** assisted consuls and praetors in the administration of financial affairs. **Aediles** supervised the public games and watched over the grain supply of the city, a major problem for a rapidly growing urban community that came to rely on imported grain to feed its population. **Censors** were chosen every five years with the chief responsibility of making an assessment of the population on the basis of age and property for purposes of taxes, military service, and officeholding.

The Roman **senate** came to hold an especially important position in the Republic. The senate or council of elders was a select group of about three hundred men who served for life. The senate was not a legislative body and could only advise the magistrates. This advice of the senate was not taken lightly, however, and by the third century B.C. had virtually the force of law. No doubt the prestige of the senate's members furthered this development. But it also helped that the senate met continuously, while the chief magistrates changed annually and the popular assemblies operated slowly and met only periodically.

The Roman Republic possessed a number of popular assemblies. By far the most important was the **centuriate assembly,** essentially the Roman army functioning in its political role. Organized by classes based on wealth, it was structured in such a way that the wealthiest citizens always had a majority. The centuriate assembly elected the chief magistrates and passed laws. It is important to remember, however, that the Romans passed few statutory laws and simply left much governance to magisterial authority. As a result of the struggle between the orders, another assembly, the council of the plebs, came into being in 471 B.C.

The government of the Roman Republic, then, consisted of three major elements. Two consuls and later other elected officials served as magistrates and ran the state. An assembly of adult males (the centuriate assembly), controlled by the wealthiest citizens, elected these officials, while the senate, a small group of large landowners, advised them. Thus the Roman state was an aristocratic republic controlled by a relatively small group of privileged people.

Social Organization The family was the basis of Roman society. At its head was the *paterfamilias,* who theoretically had unlimited power over his family. With the *paterfamilias* at the head, the family resembled a kind of miniature state within the state. When a father died, his sons became heads of their own families. Families were often grouped into social units known as *gentes* or clans, descended from the same ancestor and bearing the same family name.

Closely associated with clan and family was the practice of clientage. Clients constituted a dependent class, people who did not have the means to protect themselves or their families without the assistance of a patron. The patron, usually a wealthy member of the upper classes, gave protection and especially legal assistance to his clients. In return, clients provided their patrons with certain services, such as field labor, military assistance, and, especially important in the Republic, votes in the assemblies.

The most noticeable element in the social organization of early Rome was the division between two groups—the **patricians** and the **plebeians.** The word *patrician* is derived from *patres*—the fathers—as the members of the Roman senate were called. The patrician class in Rome consisted of families descended from the original senators appointed during the period of the kings. Their initial prominence was probably due to their wealth as great landowners. Thus the patricians constituted an aristocratic governing class. Only they could be consuls, other magistrates, and senators. Through their patronage of large numbers of dependent clients, they could control the centuriate assembly and many other facets of Roman life.

The plebeians constituted the considerably larger group of "independent, unprivileged, poorer and vulnerable men" as well as nonpatrician large landowners, less wealthy landholders, artisans, merchants, and small farmers. Although they were citizens, they did not possess the same rights as the patricians and at the beginning of the fifth century B.C. began a struggle to rectify that situation. The plebeians who led the struggle for plebeian rights were large landowners who were equal in wealth to many patricians and therefore considered themselves equally qualified to enjoy the same privileges.

The Struggle of the Orders   Two major problems that existed in the fifth century probably fueled the struggle between the patricians and the plebeians. Both patricians and plebeians could vote, but only the patricians could be elected to governmental offices. Both had the right to make legal contracts and marriages, but intermarriage between patricians and plebeians was forbidden. The wealthy plebeians wanted political equality with the patricians, namely, the right to hold office, and social equality in the form of the right of intermarriage.

The first success for the plebeians came in 494 B.C., when they withdrew physically from the state. The patricians, realizing that they could not defend Rome by themselves, were forced to compromise. Two new officials known as **tribunes of the plebs** were instituted (later the number was raised to five and then ten). These tribunes were given the power to protect plebeians against arrest by patrician magistrates. Moreover, after a new popular assembly for plebeians only, called the **council of the plebs,** was created in 471 B.C., the tribunes became responsible for convoking and placing proposals before it. If adopted, these measures became *plebiscita* ("it is the opinion of the plebs"), but they were binding only on the plebeians, not on the patricians. Nevertheless, the plebeian council gave the plebeians considerable political leverage.

First secession of the plebeians; creation of tribunes of the plebs	494 B.C.
Creation of the council of the plebs	471 B.C.
Publication of the Twelve Tables of Law	450 B.C.
Canuleian law: Right of plebeians to marry patricians	445 B.C.
Licinian-Sextian laws: One consul may be a plebeian	367 B.C.
Both consuls may be plebeians; one must be	342 B.C.
Hortensian law: Laws passed by plebeian assembly are binding on all Romans	287 B.C.

The next step for the plebeians involved the law. The plebeians came to realize that if they were to increase their power, they needed knowledge of the law and the legal and governmental procedures carefully guarded by the patricians. Due to plebeian pressure, a special commission of ten officials known as the *decemviri* ("ten men") was created with the task of regularizing and publishing the laws. This action resulted in the publication in 450 B.C. of the Twelve Tables of Law, which included the legal procedures for going to court; provisions on family, women, and divorce; regulations concerning private property; rules governing relationships and injuries to others; and a provision prohibiting intermarriage between patricians and plebeians (see the box on p. 112). This publication of the laws produced further agitation from the plebeians between 450 and 445 since they could now see how disadvantaged they were. In particular, they demanded the right of intermarriage and admission to the chief magistracies, especially the consulship. In 445 B.C., the Canuleian law allowed patricians and plebeians to intermarry. Once this was permitted, the division between the two groups became less important, and the solidarity of the patrician class against plebeian gains began to falter. But it was not until 367 B.C. that the consulship was opened to plebeians. The Licinian-Sextian laws stipulated that one consul could now be a plebeian. From 366 to 361 B.C., however, only two plebeians were elected to the consulship, and from 361 to 340, only three, a clear indication that only the most prominent plebeian families could obtain the office. In 342 B.C., another law stipulated that both consuls could be plebeians but at least one had to be plebeian.

The chief landmark in Roman constitutional history—and the climax of the struggle between the orders—came in 287 B.C. with the Hortensian law. Henceforth all *plebiscita* passed by the plebeian assembly had the force of law and were binding on the entire community, both plebeians and patricians. Moreover, unlike the laws passed by the centuriate assembly, these *plebiscita* did not need the approval of the senate.

THE TWELVE TABLES

*T*HE TWELVE TABLES represents the first formal codification of Roman laws and customs. The code was inscribed on bronze plaques, which were eventually destroyed. These selections are taken from reconstructions of the code preserved in the works of later writers.

Selections from the Twelve Tables

Table III: Execution; Law of Debt

When a debt has been acknowledged, or judgment about the matter has been pronounced in court, thirty days must be the legitimate time of grace. After that, the debtor may be arrested by laying on of hands. Bring him into court. If he does not satisfy the judgment, or no one in court offers himself as surety in his behalf, the creditor may take the defaulter with him. He may bind him either in stocks or in fetters. . . .

Unless they make a settlement, debtors shall be held in bond for sixty days. During that time they shall be brought before the praetor's court in the meeting place on three successive market days, and the amount for which they are judged liable shall be announced; on the third market day they shall suffer capital punishment or be delivered up for sale abroad, across the Tiber.

Table IV: Rights of Head of Family

Quickly kill . . . a dreadfully deformed child.

If a father three times surrenders a son for sale, the son shall be free from the father.

A child born ten months after the father's death will not be admitted into legal inheritance.

Table V: Guardianship; Succession

Females shall remain in guardianship even when they have attained their majority.

If a man is raving mad, rightful authority over his person and chattels shall belong to his agnates [nearest male relatives] or to his clansmen.

A spendthrift is forbidden to exercise administration over his own goods. . . . A person who, being insane or a spendthrift, is prohibited from administering his own goods shall be under trusteeship of agnates.

Table VII: Rights Concerning Land

Branches of a tree may be lopped off all round to a height of more than 15 feet. . . . Should a tree on a neighbor's farm be bent crooked by a wind and lean over your farm, action may be taken for removal of that tree.

It is permitted to gather up fruit falling down on another man's farm.

Table VIII: Torts or Delicts

If any person has sung or composed against another person a song such as was causing slander or insult to another, he shall be clubbed to death.

If a person has maimed another's limb, let there be retaliation in kind unless he makes agreement for settlement with him.

Any person who destroys by burning any building or heap of corn deposited alongside a house shall be bound, scourged, and put to death by burning at the stake, provided that he has committed the said misdeed with malice aforethought, but if he shall have committed it by accident, that is, by negligence, it is ordained that he repair the damage, or, if he be too poor to be competent for such punishment, he shall receive a lighter chastisement.

Table IX: Public Law

The penalty shall be capital punishment for a judge or arbiter legally appointed who has been found guilty of receiving a bribe for giving a decision.

Table XI: Supplementary Laws

Intermarriage shall not take place between plebeians and patricians.

The struggle between the orders, then, had a significant impact on the development of the Roman constitution. Plebeians could hold the highest offices of state, they could intermarry with the patricians, and they could help pass laws binding on the entire Roman community. Although the struggle had been long, the Romans had handled it by compromise, not violent revolution. Theoretically, by 287 B.C. all Roman citizens were equal under the law, and all could strive for political office. But in reality, as a result of the right of intermarriage, a select number of wealthy patrician and plebeian families formed a new senatorial aristocracy called the *nobiles,* which came to dominate the political offices. The Roman Republic had not become a democracy.

The Roman Conquest of Italy

At the beginning of the Republic, Rome was surrounded by enemies, including the Etruscans to the north and the Sabines, Volscians, and Aequi to the east and south. The Latin communities on the plain of Latium posed an even more immediate threat. After the expulsion of the Etruscan kings, a league of Latin allies formed and challenged Roman leadership in Latium. But in 493 B.C., the Romans established an alliance with the Latin communities, which provided for a common defense of Latium.

Rome was under constant pressure from its neighbors for the next hundred years. If we are to believe Livy, one of the chief ancient sources for the history of the early

CINCINNATUS SAVES ROME: A ROMAN MORALITY TALE

$\mathcal{T}$HERE IS PERHAPS no better account of how the virtues of duty and simplicity enabled good Roman citizens to prevail during the travails of the fifth century B.C. than Livy's account of Cincinnatus. He was chosen dictator, supposedly in 457 B.C., to defend Rome against the attacks of the Aequi. The position of dictator was a temporary expedient used only in emergencies; the consuls would resign, and a leader with unlimited power would be appointed for a limited period (usually six months). In this account, Cincinnatus did his duty, defeated the Aequi, and returned to his simple farm in just fifteen days.

Livy, *The Early History of Rome*

The city was thrown into a state of turmoil, and the general alarm was as great as if Rome herself were surrounded. Nautius was sent for, but it was quickly decided that he was not the man to inspire full confidence; the situation evidently called for a dictator, and, with no dissenting voice, Lucius Quinctius Cincinnatus was named for the post.

Now I would solicit the particular attention of those numerous people who imagine that money is everything in this world, and that rank and ability are inseparable from wealth: let them observe that Cincinnatus, the one man in whom Rome reposed all her hope of survival, was at that moment working a little three-acre farm . . . west of the Tiber, just opposite the spot where the shipyards are today. A mission from the city found him at work on his land—digging a ditch, maybe, or plowing. Greetings were exchanged, and he was asked—with a prayer for divine blessing on himself and his country—to put on his toga and hear the Senate's instructions. This naturally surprised him, and, asking if all were well, he told his wife Racilia to run to their cottage and fetch his toga. The toga was brought, and wiping the grimy sweat from his hands and face he put it on; at once the envoys from the city saluted him, with congratulations, as Dictator, invited him to enter Rome, and informed him of the terrible danger of Municius' army. A state vessel was waiting for him on the river, and on the city bank he was welcomed by his three sons who had come to meet him, then by other kinsmen and friends, and finally by nearly the whole body of senators. Closely attended by all these people and preceded by his lictors he was then escorted to his residence through streets lined with great crowds of common folk, who, be it said, were by no means so pleased to see the new Dictator, as they thought his power excessive and dreaded the way in which he was likely to use it.

[Cincinnatus proceeds to raise an army, march out, and defeat the Aequi.]

In Rome the Senate was convened by Quintus Fabius the City Prefect, and a decree was passed inviting Cincinnatus to enter in triumph with his troops. The chariot he rode in was preceded by the enemy commanders and the military standards, and followed by his army loaded with its spoils. . . . Cincinnatus finally resigned after holding office for fifteen days, having originally accepted it for a period of six months.

Roman Republic, Rome was engaged in almost continuous warfare with its neighbors.

In his account of these years, Livy provided a detailed narrative of Roman efforts. Many of Livy's stories were legendary in character and indeed were modeled on events in Greek history. But Livy, writing in the first century B.C., used these stories to teach Romans the moral values and virtues that had made Rome great. These included tenacity, duty, courage, and especially discipline (see the box above). Indeed, Livy recounted stories of military leaders who executed their own sons for leaving their place in battle, a serious offense since the success of the hoplite infantry depended on maintaining a precise order. These stories had little basis in fact, but like the story of George Washington and the cherry tree in American history, they provided mythic images to reinforce Roman patriotism.

In 340 B.C., Rome had to deal with a revolt of the Latin states in Latium, which had come to resent Rome's increasing domination of their alliance. The Romans crushed the revolt and established complete supremacy in Latium. Between 343 and 290 B.C., the Romans waged a fierce struggle with the Samnites, a hill people from the central Apennines, some of whom had settled in Campania, south of Rome. The conquest of the Samnites gave Rome considerable control over a large part of Italy and also brought it into direct contact with the Greek communities of southern Italy. Soon the Romans were involved in hostilities with some of these Greek cities. The Greek communities were primarily commercial cities and had no standing armies. They were accustomed to hiring mercenaries to fight their battles for them. Consequently, they bought the aid of King Pyrrhus of Epirus (approximately modern-day Epirus in Greece), who crossed the Adriatic with twenty thousand troops and defeated the Romans twice. In both battles, however, Pyrrhus experienced heavy losses, leading him to comment that one more victory would ruin him (hence our phrase "Pyrrhic victory"). After a diversion to Sicily, Pyrrhus came back for one more battle with the Romans and this time was decisively defeated. By 267 B.C., the Romans completed their conquest of southern Italy. After crushing the remaining Etruscan states to the north, Rome had conquered all of Italy, except the extreme north, by 264 B.C.

To rule Italy, the Romans devised the Roman confederation. Under this system, Rome allowed some peoples—especially the Latins—to have full Roman citizenship. Most of the remaining communities were made allies. They remained free to run their own local affairs but were required to provide soldiers for Rome. Moreover, the Romans made it clear that loyal allies could improve their status and even aspire to becoming Roman citizens. Thus the Romans had found a way to give conquered states a stake in Rome's success.

In the course of their expansion throughout Italy, the Romans had pursued consistent policies that help explain their success. The Romans excelled in making the correct diplomatic decisions; they were superb diplomats. While firm and even cruel when necessary—rebellions were crushed without mercy—they were also shrewd in extending their citizenship and allowing autonomy in domestic affairs. Their conquest of Italy could hardly be said to be the result of a direct policy of expansion. Much of it was opportunistic. The Romans did not hesitate to act once they felt their security threatened. And surrounded by potential enemies, Rome in a sense never felt secure. The Romans were not only good soldiers but also persistent ones. The loss of an army or a fleet did not cause them to quit but spurred them on to build new armies and new fleets. Finally, the Romans had a practical sense of strategy. As they conquered, they settled Romans and Latins in new communities outside Latium. By 264 B.C., the Romans had established colonies—fortified towns—at all strategic locations. By building roads to these settlements and connecting them, the Romans assured themselves of an impressive military and communications network that enabled them to rule effectively and efficiently. By insisting on military service from the allies in the Roman confederation, Rome essentially mobilized the entire military manpower of all Italy for its wars.

Roman Roads in Italy. The Romans built a remarkable system of roads. After laying a foundation with gravel, which allowed for drainage, the Roman builders placed flagstones, closely fitted together. Unlike other peoples who built similar kinds of roads, the Romans did not follow the contours of the land but made their roads as straight as possible to facilitate communications and transportation, especially for military purposes. Seen here is a view of the Via Appia (Appian Way), built in 312 B.C. under the leadership of the censor and consul Appius Claudius (Roman roads were often named after the great Roman families who encouraged their construction). The Via Appia (shown on the map) was meant to make it easy for Roman armies to march from Rome to the newly conquered city of Capua, a distance of 152 miles.

The Roman Conquest of the Mediterranean (264–133 B.C.)

After their conquest of the Italian peninsula, the Romans found themselves face to face with a formidable Mediterranean power—Carthage. Founded around 800 B.C. by Phoenicians from Tyre, Carthage was located in a favorable position for commanding Mediterranean trade routes and had become an important commercial center (see Map 5.2).

In the sixth century B.C., Carthage was governed by two judges, who were elected annually. They were usually men of wealth from prominent families. Separately elected generals led the military forces, which consisted primarily of mercenaries recruited from different parts of the western Mediterranean. There was also a senate composed of several hundred prominent men chosen for life. Ordinary citizens had little power, although a group of 104 judges examined the activities of officials and generals and prevented anyone from either group from establishing a tyranny.

Carthage gradually became a military strong state. By the third century B.C., its empire included the coast of North Africa, southern Spain, Sardinia, Corsica, and western Sicily. With its monopoly of western Mediterranean trade, Carthage was the largest and richest state in the area. The presence of Carthaginians in Sicily made the Romans apprehensive about Carthaginian encroachment on the Italian coast. In 264 B.C., mutual suspicions drove the two powers into a lengthy struggle for control of the western Mediterranean.

The Struggle with Carthage

The First Punic War (264–241 B.C.)—the Latin word for Phoenician was *Punicus*—began when the Romans decided to intervene in a struggle between two Sicilian cities and sent an army to Sicily. The Carthaginians, who considered Sicily within their own sphere of influence, regarded this as just cause for war. In going to war, both sides determined on the conquest of Sicily. The Romans realized that the war would be long and drawn out if they could not supplement land operations with a navy and promptly developed a substantial fleet. The Carthaginians, however, had difficulty finding mercenaries to continue the fight. After a long struggle in which both sides lost battles in North Africa and Sicily, a Roman fleet defeated the Carthaginian navy off Drepana, Sicily, in 242 B.C. The cities of western Sicily that had been controlled by Carthage

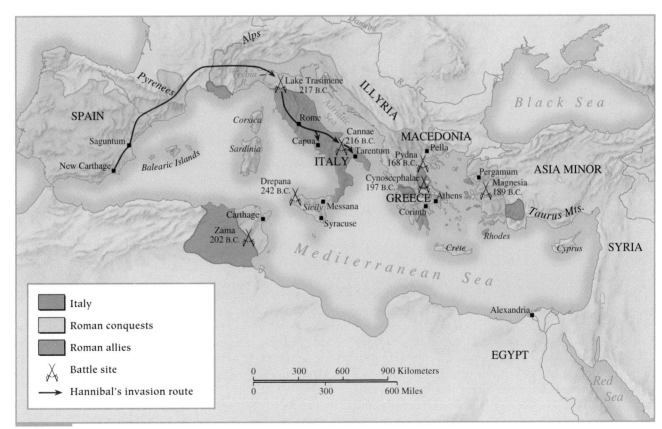

MAP 5.2 Roman Conquests in the Mediterranean, 264–133 B.C. Beginning with the Punic Wars, Rome expanded its holdings, first in the western Mediterranean at the expense of Carthage and later in Greece and western Asia Minor. ❓ What aspects of Mediterranean geography, combined with the territorial holdings and aspirations of Rome and the Carthaginians, made the Punic Wars more likely?

View an animated version of this map or related maps at http://history.wadsworth.com/spielvogel06/

capitulated. Carthage sued for peace, and the war ended in 241 B.C. Carthage gave up all rights to Sicily and had to pay an indemnity. Three years later, Rome took advantage of Carthage's problems with its mercenaries to seize the islands of Sardinia and Corsica. This act so angered the Carthaginians that, according to one story, their leading general, Hamilcar Barca, made his nine-year-old son swear that he would hate Rome ever after. The son's name was Hannibal.

Hannibal and the Second Punic War Between the wars, Carthage made an unexpected recovery under the leadership of the general who had been briefly successful in Sicily in the First Punic War, Hamilcar Barca. Hamilcar extended Carthage's domains in Spain to compensate for the territory lost to Rome. A major goal in creating the Spanish empire was to get manpower for Carthage. The Spanish natives made great soldiers, being physically strong and possessing excellent swords. Hamilcar and his successors proceeded to build up a formidable land army in the event of a second war with Rome because they realized that Carthage's success depended on defeating Rome on land. In 221 B.C., Hamilcar's son Hannibal, now twenty-five, took over direction of Carthaginian policy. Within three years, Rome and Carthage were again at war.

Carthage and Rome had agreed to divide Spain into respective spheres of influence. Although Saguntum was located in the Carthaginian sphere, Rome made an alliance with the city and encouraged its inhabitants in anti-Carthaginian activities. Thoroughly provoked by the Roman action, Hannibal attacked Saguntum, and the Romans declared war on Carthage in 218 B.C. This time the Carthaginian strategy aimed at bringing the war home to the Romans and defeating them in their own backyard. In an amazing march, Hannibal crossed the Alps with an army of thirty to forty thousand men and six thousand horses and elephants and advanced into northern Italy. After defeating the Romans at the Trebia River, he added thousands of Gauls to his army and proceeded into central Italy. At Lake Trasimene in Etruria, he again defeated the Romans. In desperation, the Romans elected as consul Quintus Fabius Maximus, who became known as the "Delayer" because of his tactics of following and delaying Hannibal's army without risking a pitched battle. Hannibal hoped to destroy the Roman confederation and win Italian cities away from Rome. The policy failed; virtually all remained loyal to Rome.

In 216 B.C., the Romans decided to meet Hannibal head on. It was a serious mistake. At Cannae, Hannibal's forces devastated a Roman army, killing as many as forty thousand soldiers. At last, some of the southern Italian cities rebelled against Roman rule and went over to Han-

Roman Legionaries. The Roman legionaries, famed for their courage and tenacity, made possible Roman domination of the Mediterranean Sea. At the time of the Punic Wars, the Roman legionaries wore chain-mail armor and plumed helmets and carried oval shields, as seen in this portrait of two legionaries on the altar of Domitius Ahenobarbus. Heavy javelins and swords were their major weapons. This equipment remained standard until the time of Julius Caesar.

nibal. Rome seemed on the brink of disaster but refused to give up and raised yet another army.

Rome gradually recovered. Although Hannibal remained free to roam in Italy, he had neither the men nor the equipment to lay siege to the major cities, including Rome itself. The Romans began to reconquer some of the rebellious Italian cities. More important, the Romans pursued a Spanish strategy that aimed at undermining the Carthaginian empire in Spain. Publius Cornelius Scipio, later known as Scipio Africanus the Elder, was given command of the Roman forces in Spain even though he was too young to hold the position legally. But he was a brilliant general who learned from Hannibal's tactics and by 206 B.C. had pushed the Carthaginians out of Spain.

THE DESTRUCTION OF CARTHAGE

HE ROMANS USED a technical breach of Carthage's peace treaty with Rome as a pretext to undertake a third and final war with Carthage (149–146 B.C.). Although Carthage posed no real threat to Rome's security, the Romans still remembered the traumatic experiences of the Second Punic War when Hannibal had ravaged much of their homeland. The hard-liners gained the upper hand in the senate and called for the complete destruction of Carthage. The city was razed, the survivors were sold into slavery, and the land was made a province of Rome. In this passage, the historian Appian of Alexandria describes the final destruction of Carthage by the Romans under the command of Scipio Aemilianus.

Appian, *Roman History*

Then came new scenes of horror. The fire spread and carried everything down, and the soldiers did not wait to destroy the buildings little by little, but pulled them all down together. So the crashing grew louder, and many fell with the stones into the midst dead. Others were seen still living, especially old men, women, and young children who had hidden in the inmost nooks of the houses, some of them wounded, some more or less burned, and uttering horrible cries. Still others, thrust out and falling from such a height with the stones, timbers, and fire, were torn asunder into all kinds of horrible shapes, crushed and mangled. Nor was this the end of their miseries, for the street cleaners, who were removing the rubbish with axes, mattocks, and boat-hooks, and making the roads passable, tossed with these instruments the dead and the living together into holes in the ground, sweeping them along like sticks and stones or turning them over with their iron tools, and man was used for filling up a ditch. Some were thrown in head foremost, while their legs, sticking out of the ground, writhed a long time. Others fell with their feet downward and their heads above the ground. Horses ran over them, crushing their faces and skulls, not purposely on the part of the riders, but in their headlong haste. Nor did the street cleaners either do these things on purpose; but the press of war, the glory of approaching victory, the rush of the soldiery, the confused noise of heralds and trumpeters all round, the tribunes and centurions changing guard and marching the cohorts here and there—all together made everybody frantic and heedless of the spectacle before their eyes.

Six days and nights were consumed in this kind of turmoil, the soldiers being changed so that they might not be worn out with toil, slaughter, lack of sleep, and these horrid sights. . . .

Scipio, beholding this city, which had flourished 700 years from its foundation and had ruled over so many lands, islands, and seas, as rich in arms and fleets, elephants, and money as the mightiest empires, but far surpassing them in hardihood and high spirit . . . now come to its end in total destruction—Scipio, beholding this spectacle, is said to have shed tears and publicly lamented the fortune of the enemy. After meditating by himself a long time and reflecting on the inevitable fall of cities, nations, and empires, as well as of individuals, upon the fate of Troy, that once proud city, upon the fate of the Assyrian, the Median, and afterwards of the great Persian empire, and, most recently of all, of the splendid empire of Macedon, either voluntarily or otherwise the words of the poet [Homer, *Iliad*] escaped his lips:

> The day shall come in which our sacred Troy
> And Priam, and the people over whom
> Spear-bearing Priam rules, shall perish all.

Being asked by Polybius in familiar conversation (for Polybius had been his tutor) what he meant by using these words, Polybius says that he did not hesitate frankly to name his own country, for whose fate he feared when he considered the mutability of human affairs. And Polybius wrote this down just as he heard it.

The Romans then took the war directly to Carthage. Late in 204 B.C., Scipio led a Roman army from Sicily into North Africa and forced the Carthaginians to recall Hannibal from Italy. At the Battle of Zama in 202 B.C., Scipio decisively defeated Hannibal and the Carthaginian forces, and the war was over. Eventually, Hannibal left Carthage and went to help Antiochus, the ruler of the Seleucid kingdom, in his struggle with Rome. After Antiochus made peace with the Romans, Hannibal fled to Bithynia, near the Black Sea. Pursued by the Romans, Hannibal killed himself after saying, "Let us free Rome of her dread of one old man."

By the peace treaty signed in 201 by the Carthaginians and Romans, Carthage lost Spain, agreed to pay an indemnity, and promised not to go to war without Rome's permission. Spain, like Sicily, Corsica, and Sardinia earlier, was made into a Roman province. Rome had become the dominant power in the western Mediterranean.

The Destruction of Carthage But some Romans wanted even more. A number of prominent Romans, especially the conservative politician Cato, advocated the complete destruction of Carthage. Cato ended every speech he made to the senate with the words, "And I think Carthage must be destroyed." When the Carthaginians technically broke their peace treaty with Rome by going to war against one of Rome's North African allies who had been encroaching on Carthage's home territory, the Romans declared war. Led by Scipio Aemilianus Africanus the Younger, Roman forces undertook their third and last war with Carthage (149–146 B.C.). This time, Carthage was no match for the Romans, who seized this opportunity to carry out the final destruction of Carthage (see the box above). The territory of Carthage was made a province called Africa.

First Punic War	264–241 B.C.
Rome seizes Corsica and Sardinia	238 B.C.
Second Punic War	218–201 B.C.
Battle of Cannae	216 B.C.
Scipio completes seizure of Spain	206 B.C.
Battle of Zama	202 B.C.
Third Punic War	149–146 B.C.
Incorporation of Macedonia as a Roman province	148 B.C.
Destruction of Carthage	146 B.C.
Roman acquisition of Pergamum	133 B.C.

The Eastern Mediterranean

During the Punic Wars, Rome had become acutely aware of the Hellenistic states of the eastern Mediterranean when the king of Macedonia made an alliance with Hannibal after the Roman defeat at Cannae. But Rome was preoccupied with the Carthaginians, and it was not until after the defeat of Carthage that Rome became involved in the world of Hellenistic politics as an advocate for the freedom of the Greek states. This support of the Greeks brought the Romans into conflict with both Macedonia and the kingdom of the Seleucids. Roman military victories and diplomatic negotiations rearranged the territorial boundaries of the Hellenistic kingdoms and brought the Greek states their freedom in 196 B.C. For fifty years, the Romans tried to be a power broker in the affairs of the Greeks without direct control of their lands. When the effort failed, the Romans changed their policy.

Macedonia was made a Roman province in 148 B.C., and when some of the Greek states rose in revolt against Rome's restrictive policies, Rome acted decisively. The city of Corinth, leader of the revolt, was destroyed in 146 B.C. to teach the Greeks a lesson, and Greece was placed under the control of the Roman governor of Macedonia. Thirteen years later, in 133 B.C., the king of Pergamum deeded his kingdom to Rome, giving Rome its first province in Asia. Rome was now master of the Mediterranean Sea.

The Nature of Roman Imperialism

Rome's empire was built in three stages: the conquest of Italy, the conflict with Carthage and expansion into the western Mediterranean, and the involvement with and domination of the Hellenistic kingdoms in the eastern Mediterranean. The Romans did not have a master plan for the creation of an empire. Much of their expansion was opportunistic; once involved in a situation that threatened their security, the Romans did not hesitate to act. And the more they expanded, the more threats to their security appeared on the horizon, involving them in yet more con-

flicts. Indeed, the Romans liked to portray themselves as declaring war only for defensive reasons or to protect allies. That is only part of the story, however. It is likely, as some historians have recently suggested, that at some point a group of Roman aristocratic leaders emerged who favored expansion both for the glory it offered and for the economic benefits it provided. Certainly by the second century B.C., aristocratic senators perceived new opportunities for lucrative foreign commands, enormous spoils of war, and an abundant supply of slave labor for their growing landed estates. By that same time, as the destruction of Corinth and Carthage indicates, Roman imperialism had become more arrogant and brutal as well. Rome's foreign success also had enormous repercussions for the internal development of the Roman Republic.

Society and Culture in the Roman Republic

One of the most noticeable aspects of Roman society and culture is the impact of the Greeks. The Romans had experienced Greek influence early on through the Greek cities in southern Italy. By the end of the third century B.C., however, Greek civilization played an ever-increasing role in Roman culture. Greek ambassadors, merchants, and artists traveled to Rome and spread Greek thought and practices. After their conquest of the Hellenistic kingdoms, Roman military commanders shipped Greek manuscripts and art back to Rome. Multitudes of educated Greek slaves were used in Roman households. Greek models affected virtually every area of Roman life, from literature and philosophy to religion and education. Wealthy Romans hired Greek tutors and sent their sons to Athens to study. As the Roman poet Horace said, "Captive Greece took captive her rude conqueror." Greek thought captivated the less sophisticated Roman minds, and the Romans became willing transmitters of Greek culture—not, however, without some resistance from Romans who had nothing but contempt for Greek politics and feared the end of old Roman values. Even those who favored Greek culture, such as Scipio Aemilianus, blamed the Greeks for Rome's new vices, including luxury and homosexual practices.

Roman Religion

Every aspect of Roman society was permeated with religion. The official state religion focused on the worship of a pantheon of gods and goddesses, including Juno, the patron goddess of women; Minerva, the goddess of craftspeople; Mars, the god of war; and Jupiter Optimus Maximus ("best and greatest"), who became the patron deity of Rome and assumed a central place in the religious life of the city. As Rome developed and came into contact with other peoples and gods, the community simply adopted new deities. Hence the Greek Hermes became the Roman Mercury, and the Greek Demeter, Ceres. Eventually, a com-

THE VESTAL VIRGINS

☉HE VESTAL VIRGINS guarded the fire on the state hearth in the temple of Vesta (goddess of the hearth) in Rome. To the Romans, the extinguishing of the fire was a warning of the destruction of the city. It was also a sign that a Vestal Virgin had lost her virginity, an act that was punished harshly, as is explained in this selection from the historian Dionysius of Halicarnassus, a Greek who lived in Rome and published his *Roman Antiquities* near the end of the first century B.C.

⚐ Dionysius of Halicarnassus, *Roman Antiquities*

Originally there were four virgins who served the goddess Vesta. They were chosen by the king in accordance with the regulations which Numa established. Because of the numerous sacred duties which they perform, their number was increased to six, and six it has remained up to our own time. The virgins live in the sanctuary of the goddess, and no one can be prevented from entering there in the day if he so wishes, but it is forbidden for any man to stay there at night.

The priestesses remain pure and unmarried for 30 years, offering sacrifices, and performing other religious rituals in accordance with the law. They learn these rituals in the first ten years, and for the second ten years they perform them, and during the remaining ten years they must teach them to their successors. When the 30 years have been completed, nothing prohibits those who want to from putting aside their headbands and other insignia of their service and getting married. But only a few have done that, and their lives for their remaining years were neither enviable nor very happy. Therefore, taking what has happened to those unhappy few as a warning, the rest of the virgins remain in service to the goddess until their deaths, at which time another virgin is appointed by the priests to take the place of the one who has died.

They receive many splendid honors from the city, and therefore they do not want children or marriage. And anyway, there are heavy penalties for misbehavior. Misdeeds are investigated and punished by priests according to the law. They whip those who have committed some lesser offense, but those who have lost their virginity are sentenced to a shameful and pitiful death. While they are still alive they are carried in a funeral procession. Their friends and relatives join the procession and mourn for them as though for someone deceased. They are taken as far as the Colline gate, and interred (alive) in an underground cell which has been built within the walls of the gate. They are dressed in funeral clothes but they receive no monument or funeral offering or any of the other rites which are customary at funerals.

There are said to be many clues which indicate that a priestess who is performing a holy ritual is no longer a virgin, but the principal clue is that the fire goes out, something which the Romans fear more than all catastrophes, since they believe that whatever was the cause of the fire going out, it warns of the destruction of the city. They reintroduce the fire with many rituals of atonement.

---

plete amalgamation of Greek and Roman religion occurred, giving the Romans and the Greeks essentially the same "Greco-Roman" religion. The Romans were generally tolerant of new religious cults and only occasionally outlawed them.

The Importance of Ritual Roman religion focused on the worship of the gods for a very practical reason—human beings were thought to be totally dependent on them. The exact performance of ritual was crucial to establishing a right relationship with the gods. What was true for individuals was also valid for the state: it also had to observe correct ritual in order to receive its reward. Accurate performance of ritual was consequently important, and the Romans established a college of priests or *pontiffs* to carry out that responsibility. Initially three in number, by the first century B.C., they had increased to sixteen. At the head of the pontiffs was the *pontifex maximus* (chief pontiff), a powerful figure who controlled the state religion. First Julius Caesar and later all emperors until A.D. 381 held this position. The pontifex maximus also chose six girls between the ages of six and ten to serve as Vestal Virgins (see the box above).

The pontiffs were in charge of what the Romans called the divine law, maintaining the right relationship between the state and the gods. The pontiffs performed all public religious acts and supervised magistrates in the correct ritual for public political acts. If the rituals were performed correctly, the Romans would obtain the "peace of the gods." The Romans' success in creating an empire was no doubt taken as confirmation of divine favor. As Cicero, the first-century B.C. politician and writer, claimed, "We have overcome all the nations of the world, because we have realized that the world is directed and governed by the gods."[1]

The Use of Omens In addition to the college of pontiffs, a college of *augurs* existed whose responsibility was to interpret the signs (*auspices*) or warnings—such as unusual changes in the weather or the migratory pattern of birds—that the gods gave to men. Before every important act of state, a magistrate with *imperium* took the auspices to make sure the gods approved. The Romans attributed great importance to this—if the omens were unfavorable, the act was invalid or the planned action was not auspicious. As Cicero later commented, the augurs had "the highest and most important authority in the State" because "no act of

Temple of Portunus. The Romans considered the proper worship of the gods an important key to success. Typical of Roman religious architecture was the small urban temple located in the midst of a crowded commercial center. Pictured here is a rectangular temple built in Rome in the late second or early first century B.C. and dedicated to Portunus, the god of harbors. The temple was located in the cattle market close to the Tiber River.

any magistrate at home or in the field can have any validity for any person without their authority."[2] Auspices were taken by observing the flights of birds, lightning and other natural phenomena, and the behavior of certain animals.

Household Cults Just as the state had an official cult, so did families. Because the family was regarded as a small state within the state, it had its own household cults, which included Janus, the spirit of the doorway; Vesta, the goddess of the hearth; and the Penates, the spirits of the storehouse. Here, too, proper ritual was important, and it was the responsibility of the *paterfamilias* as head of the family to ensure that the religious obligations were properly fulfilled.

One of the most important ceremonies involved purification. In his manual *On Agriculture,* Marcus Cato the Elder spelled out the proper ritual for purification of a landed estate. The ceremony included these words, addressed to Mars, the god of vegetation as well as war:

> Father Mars, I beg and entreat you to be of good will and favorable to me and to our house and household, for which purpose I have ordered the swine-sheep-bull procession to be led around my land and fields and farm. And [I beg] that you will check, thrust back, and avert diseases seen and unseen, crop failure and crop destruction, sudden losses and storms,

and that you will permit the annual crops, the grain crops, the vineyards, and tree and vine slips to grow and turn out well. And [that you] keep safe the shepherds and the flocks and give good health and strength to me and to our house and household: with these purposes in view . . . receive the honor of this suckling swine-sheep-bull sacrifice.[3]

Proper observance of the ritual was so crucial that any error necessitated a repetition of the entire ritual.

Religious Festivals Religious festivals were an important part of Roman religious practice. There were two kinds: public festivals ordained and paid for by the state and private festivals celebrated by individuals and families. By the mid-second century B.C., six public festivals were celebrated annually, each lasting several days.

The practice of holding games also grew out of religious festivals. The games were inaugurated in honor of Jupiter Optimus Maximus but had become annual events by 366 B.C. In the late Republic, both the number of games and the number of days they lasted were increased. Consequently, state funds became inadequate for the magnificence expected, and the aediles, who were in charge of the games and hoped to use their office as a stepping-stone to higher political offices, paid additional expenses out of their own pocket. Originally, the games consisted of chariot racing in the Circus Maximus; later, animal hunts and theatrical performances were added. In the empire, gladiatorial contests would become the primary focus (see Chapter 6).

Education: The Importance of Rhetoric

The Romans did not possess a system of public education. In the early Republic, the family provided training in the various skills needed by a Roman citizen. Boys were expected to master the basic elements of farming, develop the physical skills needed to be good soldiers, learn the traditions of the state through the legends of heroic Roman ancestors, and become acquainted with public affairs. Girls were supposed to learn the skills needed to be good wives and mothers. Every upper-class Roman boy or girl was expected to learn to read.

Through contact with the Greek world, Roman education took on new ideals in the third and second centuries B.C. The wealthy classes wanted their children exposed to Greek studies and were especially attracted to the training in **rhetoric** and philosophy that would prepare their sons for a successful public career. For upper-class males, rhetoric—the art of persuasive speaking—was an especially important part of their education. To pursue a public career, they needed to learn good speaking skills that would enable them to win elections and lawsuits in the court. By winning lawsuits, a person could make a name for himself and build political support.

Since knowledge of Greek was a crucial ingredient in education, schools taught by professional teachers emerged to supply this need. Those who could afford to might provide Greek tutors for their children, but less well endowed

Schoolmaster and Pupils. In the third and second centuries B.C., wealthy Romans sought to prepare their sons for successful public careers with a thorough education in rhetoric and philosophy. Pictured here is a Roman teacher with his two pupils, who are reading from papyrus scrolls.

families could turn to private schools where most of the instructors were educated slaves or freedmen, usually of Greek origin. After several years of primary instruction, whose aim was simply to teach the basics of reading, writing, and arithmetic, the pupil went to a secondary school run by a *grammaticus,* or grammarian. These schools had a standard curriculum based on the liberal arts: literature, dialectic (logic), arithmetic, geometry, astronomy, and music. The core of the liberal arts and the curriculum, however, was Greek literature. As a result, by the second and first centuries B.C., educated Romans had become increasingly bilingual.

The Growth of Slavery

Slavery was a common institution throughout the ancient world, but no people possessed more slaves or relied so much on slave labor as the Romans eventually did. Before the third century B.C., a small Roman farmer might possess one or two slaves who would help farm his few acres and perform domestic chores. These slaves would most likely be from Italy and be regarded as part of the family household. Only the very rich would have large numbers of slaves.

The Roman conquest of the Mediterranean brought a drastic change in the use of slaves. Large numbers of foreign slaves were brought back to Italy. During the Republic, then, the chief source of slaves was from capture in war, followed by piracy. Of course, the children of slaves also became slaves. While some Roman generals brought back slaves to be sold to benefit the public treasury, ambitious generals of the first century, such as Pompey and Caesar, made personal fortunes by treating slaves captured by their armies as private property.

Slaves were used in many ways in Roman society. The rich, of course, owned the most and the best. In the late Republic, it became a badge of prestige to be attended by many slaves. Greeks were in much demand as tutors, musi-

cians, doctors, and artists. Roman businesses would employ them as shop assistants or craftspeople. Slaves were also used as farm laborers; the large landed estates known as *latifundia* were worked by huge gangs of slaves living in pitiful conditions. Cato the Elder argued that it was cheaper to work slaves to death and then replace them than to treat them well. Many slaves of all nationalities were used as menial household workers, such as cooks, valets, waiters, cleaners, and gardeners. Contractors used slave labor to build roads, aqueducts, and other public facilities. The total number of slaves is difficult to judge—estimates range from one-fourth to one-half the number of free people.

It is also difficult to generalize about the treatment of Roman slaves. There are numerous instances of humane treatment by masters and situations where slaves even protected their owners from danger out of gratitude and esteem. But slaves were also subject to severe punishments, torture, abuse, and hard labor that drove some to run away or even revolt against their owners. The Republic had stringent laws against aiding a runaway slave. The murder of a master by a slave usually meant the execution of all the other household slaves. Near the end of the second century B.C., large-scale slave revolts occurred in Sicily, where enormous gangs of slaves were subjected to horrible working conditions on large landed estates. Slaves were branded, beaten, fed inadequately, worked in chains, and housed at night in underground prisons. It took three years (135–132 B.C.) to crush a revolt of seventy thousand slaves, and the great revolt on Sicily (104–101 B.C.) involved most of the island and took a Roman army of seventeen thousand men to suppress. The most famous revolt on the Italian peninsula occurred in 73 B.C. Led by a Thracian gladiator named Spartacus, the revolt broke out in southern Italy and involved seventy thousand slaves. Spartacus managed to defeat several Roman armies before he was finally trapped and killed in southern Italy in 71 B.C. Six thousand of his followers were crucified, the traditional form of execution for slaves.

CATO THE ELDER ON WOMEN

DURING THE Second Punic War, the Romans enacted the Oppian law, which limited the amount of gold women could possess and restricted their dress. In 195 B.C., an attempt was made to repeal the law, and women demonstrated in the streets on behalf of the effort. According to the Roman historian Livy, the conservative Roman official Cato the Elder spoke against repeal and against the women favoring it. His words reflect a traditional male Roman attitude toward women.

Livy, *The History of Rome*

"If each of us, citizens, had determined to assert his rights and dignity as a husband with respect to his own spouse, we should have less trouble with the sex as a whole; as it is, our liberty, destroyed at home by female violence, even here in the Forum is crushed and trodden underfoot, and because we have not kept them individually under control, we dread them collectively. . . . But from no class is there not the greatest danger if you permit them meetings and gatherings and secret consultations. . . .

"Our ancestors permitted no woman to conduct even personal business without a guardian to intervene in her behalf; they wished them to be under the control of fathers, brothers, husbands; we (Heaven help us!) allow them now even to interfere in public affairs, yes, and to visit the Forum and our informal and formal sessions. What else are they doing now on the streets and at the corners except urging the bill of the tribunes and voting for the repeal of the law? Give loose rein to their uncontrollable nature and to this untamed creature and expect that they will themselves set no bounds to their license. Unless you act, this is the least of the things enjoined upon women by custom or law and to which they submit with a feeling of injustice. It is complete liberty or rather, if we wish to speak the truth, complete license that they desire.

"If they win in this, what will they not attempt? Review all the laws with which your forefathers restrained their license and made them subject to their husbands; even with all these bonds you can scarcely control them. What of this? If you suffer them to seize these bonds one by one and wrench themselves free and finally to be placed on a parity with their husbands, do you think you will be able to endure them? The moment they begin to be your equals, they will be your superiors. . . .

"Now they publicly address other women's husbands, and, what is more serious, they beg for a law and votes, and from various men they get what they ask. In matters affecting yourself, your property, your children, you, Sir, can be importuned; once the law has ceased to set a limit to your wife's expenditures you will never set it yourself. Do not think, citizens, that the situation which existed before the law was passed will ever return."

The Roman Family

At the heart of the Roman social structure stood the family, headed by the *paterfamilias*—the dominant male. The household also included the wife, sons with their wives and children, unmarried daughters, and slaves. As we have seen, a family was virtually a small state within the state, and the power of the *paterfamilias* paralleled that of the state magistrates over citizens. He held absolute authority over his children; he could sell them or have them put to death. Like the Greeks, Roman males believed that the weakness of the female sex necessitated male guardians (see the box above). The *paterfamilias* exercised that authority; on his death, sons or the nearest male relatives assumed the role of guardians. By the late Republic, however, although the rights of male guardians remained legally in effect, many upper-class women found numerous ways to circumvent the power of their guardians.

Marriage   Fathers arranged the marriages of daughters, although there are instances of mothers and daughters influencing the choice. In the Republic, women married *cum manu*, "with legal control" passing from father to husband. By the mid-first century B.C., the dominant practice had changed to *sine manu*, "without legal control," which meant that married daughters officially remained within the father's legal power. Since the fathers of most married women were dead, not being in the "legal control" of a husband made possible independent property rights that forceful women could translate into considerable power within the household and outside it. Traditionally, Roman marriages were intended to be for life, but divorce was introduced in the third century and became relatively easy to obtain since either party could initiate it and no one needed to prove the breakdown of the marriage. Divorce became especially prevalent in the first century B.C.—a period of political turmoil—when marriages were used to cement political alliances.

Some parents in upper-class families provided education for their daughters. Some girls had private tutors, and others may have gone to primary schools. But at the age when boys were entering secondary schools, girls were pushed into marriage. The legal minimum age was twelve; fourteen was a more common age in practice. Although some Roman doctors warned that early pregnancies could be dangerous to young girls, early marriages persisted due to the desire to benefit from dowries as soon as possible and the reality of early mortality. A good example is Tullia, Cicero's beloved daughter. She was married at sixteen, widowed at twenty-two, remarried one year later, divorced at twenty-eight, remarried at twenty-nine, and divorced at thirty-three. She died at thirty-four, not unusual for females in Roman society.

A Roman Lady. Roman women, especially those of the upper class, had comparatively more freedom than women in Classical Athens despite the persistent male belief that women required guardianship. This mural decoration was found in the remains of a villa destroyed by the eruption of Mount Vesuvius.

Upper-Class Women In contrast to upper-class Athenian women, Roman upper-class women were not segregated from males in the home. Wives were appreciated as enjoyable company and were at the center of household social life. Women talked to visitors and were free to shop, visit friends, and go to games, temples, and theaters. Nevertheless, they were not allowed to participate in public life, although there are examples of women exerting considerable political influence through their husbands. In fact, while upper-class men served the government abroad or in the military, they depended on their wives and mothers to manage their estates and protect their political interests.

The Evolution of Roman Law

One of Rome's chief gifts to the Mediterranean world of its day and to succeeding generations of Western civilization was its development of law. After the Twelve Tables of 450 B.C., there was no complete codification of Roman law until that of the Byzantine emperor Justinian in the sixth century A.D. (see Chapter 7). The Twelve Tables, though inappropriate for later times, were never officially abrogated and were still memorized by schoolboys in the first century B.C. Civil law (*ius civile*) derived from the Twelve Tables proved inadequate for later Roman needs, however, and gave way to corrections and additions by the praetors. On taking office, a praetor issued an edict listing his guidelines

for dealing with different kinds of legal cases. The praetors were knowledgeable in law, but they also relied on Roman jurists—amateur law experts—for advice in preparing their edicts. The interpretations of the jurists, often embodied in the edicts of the praetors, created a body of legal principles.

In 242 B.C., the Romans appointed a second praetor who was responsible for examining suits between a Roman and a non-Roman as well as between two non-Romans. The Romans found that although some of their rules of law could be used in these cases, special rules were often needed. These rules gave rise to a body of law known as the *ius gentium*—the law of nations—defined by the Romans as "that part of the law which we apply both to ourselves and to foreigners." But the influence of Greek philosophy, primarily Stoicism, led Romans in the late Republic to develop the idea of *ius naturale*—natural law—or universal divine law derived from right reason. The Romans came to view their law of nations as derived from or identical to this natural law, thus giving Roman jurists a philosophical justification for systematizing Roman law according to basic principles.

The Development of Literature and Art

The Romans produced little literature before the third century B.C., and the Latin literature that emerged in that century was strongly influenced by Greek models. The demand for plays at public festivals eventually led to a growing number of native playwrights. The best known were Plautus and Terence.

Plautus Plautus (c. 254–184 B.C.) used plots from Greek New Comedy (see Chapter 4) for his own plays (see the box on p. 124). The actors wore Greek costumes and Greek masks and portrayed the same stock characters: dirty old men, clever slaves, prostitutes, and young men in love, whose pains are recounted in this brief excerpt:

> Not the throes of all mankind
> Equal my distracted mind.
> I strain and I toss
> On a passionate cross:
> Love's goad makes me reel,
> I whirl on Love's wheel,
> In a swoon of despair
> Hurried here, hurried there—
> Torn asunder, I am blind
> With a cloud upon my mind.[4]

While indebted to the Greeks, Plautus managed to infuse his plays with his own earthy Latin quality, incorporating elements that appealed to the Romans: drunkenness, gluttony, and womanizing. Plautus wrote for the masses and became a very popular playwright in Rome.

Terence A second playwright of distinction was Terence (185–159 B.C.), who was born in Carthage and brought to

ROMAN COMEDY

THIS EXCERPT IS a scene from one of the plays of Plautus. While Plautus made use of Greek New Comedy, his devious plots and earthiness were original. His farcical humor and buffoonery made his plays exceedingly popular, especially with the masses. This excerpt is from *Miles Gloriosus* ("The Swaggering Soldier"). This opening scene features a pompous general and a parasitical bootlicker. Plautus loved to create fantastic names for his characters. Pyrgopolynices means "Often victorious over fortresses," and Artotrogus means "Bread eater."

Plautus, *The Swaggering Soldier*

PYRGOPOLYNICES: My shield, there—have it burnished brighter than the bright splendor of the sun on any summer's day. Next time I have occasion to use it in the press of battle, it must flash defiance into the eyes of the opposing foe. My sword, too, I see, is pining for attention; poor chap, he's quite disheartened and cast down, hanging idly at my side so long; he's simply itching to get at an enemy and carve him into little pieces. . . . Where's Artotrogus?

ARTOTROGUS: Here, at his master's heels, close to his hero, his brave, his blessed, his royal, his doughty warrior—whose valor Mars himself could hardly challenge or outshine.

PYRGOPOLYNICES [*reminiscent*]: Ay—what of the man whose life I saved on the Curculionean field, where the enemy was led by Bumbomachides Clytomestoridysarchides, a grandson of Neptune?

ARTOTROGUS: I remember it well. I remember his golden armor, and how you scattered his legions with a puff of breath, like a wind sweeping up leaves or lifting the thatch from a roof.

PYRGOPOLYNICES: [*modestly*]: It was nothing much, after all.

ARTOTROGUS: Oh, to be sure, nothing to the many more famous deeds you did—[*aside*] or never did. [*He comes down, leaving the captain attending to his men.*] If anyone ever saw a bigger liar or more conceited braggart than this one, he can have me for keeps. . . . The only thing to be said for him is, his cook makes a marvelous olive salad. . . .

PYRGOPOLYNICES [*missing him*]: Where have you got to, Artotrogus?

ARTOTROGUS [*obsequiously*]: Here I am, sir. I was thinking about that elephant in India, and how you broke his ulna with a single blow of your fist.

PYRGOPOLYNICES: His ulna, was it?

ARTOTROGUS: His femur, I should have said.

PYRGOPOLYNICES: It was only a light blow, too.

ARTOTROGUS: By Jove, yes, if you had really hit him, your arm would have smashed through the animal's hide, bones, and guts.

PYRGOPOLYNICES [*modestly*]: I'd rather not talk about it, really.

Rome as a slave by a Roman senator who freed him. Terence died at an early age after he had written six plays. He also used plots from Greek New Comedy, but his plays contained less slapstick than those of Plautus. Terence was more concerned with the subtle portrayal of character and the artistry of his language. His refined Latin style appealed more to a cultivated audience than to the masses. In the prologue to *The Brothers*, he stated, "The author . . . takes it as a high compliment if he can win the approval of men who themselves find favor with you all and with the general public, men whose services in war, in peace, and in your private affairs, are given at the right moment, without ostentation, to be available for each one of you."[5] Terence wrote for Rome's aristocracy.

Latin Prose Latin prose developed later than poetry and playwriting and was often the product of Rome's ruling elite. These upper classes were interested in history as a means of exalting their ideals and in oratory because it could be an important instrument for effective statecraft. Hence their emphasis in writing prose was on creating works of a practical value. This is a prominent feature of the oldest existing work of Latin prose, Cato the Elder's treatise *On Agriculture*. In effect, this was a technical manual reminiscent of the practical handbooks produced in the Hellenistic world.

Despite their attraction to the Greek world, Romans were generally repelled by much of Greek philosophy with the exception of Stoicism. The latter's emphasis on virtuous conduct and performance of duty (see Chapter 4) fit well with Roman ideals and the practical bent of the Roman character. Panaetius of Rhodes (c. 180–111 B.C.), whose works helped introduce Stoicism to the Romans, was especially popular.

Roman Art The Romans were also dependent on the Greeks for artistic inspiration. During the third and second centuries B.C., they adopted many features of the Hellenistic style of art (see Chapter 4). The Romans excelled in architecture, a highly practical art. In addition to their justly famous highways, they built sturdy bridges and aqueducts that made use of the arch. They also developed the technique of using concrete in construction projects, which enabled them to erect giant amphitheaters, public baths, and the high-rise tenement buildings that housed Rome's exploding population in the late second and first centuries B.C.

The Romans developed a taste for Greek statues, which they placed not only in public buildings but in their homes as well. When demand outstripped the supply of original works, reproductions of Greek statues became fashionable. The Romans' own portrait sculpture was characterized

Roman Theater: Rehearsal of a Greek Play. This mosaic found at Pompeii shows Roman actors preparing to present a Greek play. The seated figure is the chorus master, who observes two actors dancing to the music of a pipe.

by an intense realism that included even unpleasant physical details.

Values and Attitudes

The Romans were by nature a conservative people. They were very concerned about maintaining the *mos maiorum,* the customs or traditions of their ancestors. The Romans emphasized parental authority and, above all, their obligations to the state. The highest virtue was *pietas*—the dutiful execution of one's obligations to one's fellow citizens, to the gods, and to the state.

By the second century B.C., however, the creation of an empire had begun to weaken the old values. The Romans began to place greater stress on affluence, status, and material possessions. There was also more emphasis on individualism and less on collective well-being, on the old public spirit that had served Rome so well. Romans who worried about the decline of the old values blamed it on different causes. Some felt that after the destruction of Carthage, the Romans no longer had any strong enemies to challenge them. Others believed that the Romans had simply been overwhelmed by the affluence created by the new empire. And finally, there were those who blamed everything on the Greeks for importing ideas and practices baneful to the Romans.

Of course, Romans responded differently to the changes brought by the creation of an empire. Two examples from the second century demonstrate this well. Marcus Cato the Elder (234–149 B.C.) was a Roman praetor, consul, and member of the ruling class who became censor in 184. Cato scorned the "Greeklings"—people who fol-

lowed Greek ways and read Greek philosophy and literature. He even introduced a decree to force all Greek philosophers to leave Rome. He wrote to his son:

> I shall speak about those Greek fellows in their proper place, son Marcus, and point out the results of my inquiries at Athens, and convince you what benefit comes from dipping into their literature, and not making a close study of it. They are a quite worthless people, and an intractable one, and you must consider my words prophetic. When that race gives us its literature it will corrupt all things.[6]

But Cato was not stupid. He not only learned Greek himself but also allowed his own son to study in Athens. He knew only too well that, like it or not, Greek was becoming a necessity for Roman political life.

Scipio Aemilianus (185–129 B.C.) was a member of a patrician family and a brilliant general who easily achieved the top offices of the Roman state. Scipio was also concerned about the traditional Roman values, but he was much more inclined to accept Rome's growing urbanization as it became the center of the Mediterranean world and was consequently more open to the Greeks as well. He was an admirer of Greek philosophy and literature. He created a group of intellectuals dedicated to Greek thought, which included Polybius, Terence, and Panaetius. While desirous of maintaining old Roman virtues, Scipio was well aware that the acquisition of an empire had created a new world with new demands and values.

The Decline and Fall of the Roman Republic (133–31 B.C.)

By the mid-second century B.C., Roman domination of the Mediterranean Sea was well established. Yet the process of building an empire had weakened and threatened the internal stability of Rome. This internal instability characterizes the period of Roman history from 133 until 31 B.C., when the armies of Octavian defeated Mark Antony and stood supreme over the Roman world. By that time, the constitution of the Roman Republic was in shambles (see the box on p. 126).

Background: Social, Economic, and Political Problems

By the second century B.C., the senate had become the effective governing body of the Roman state. It had achieved this position through its own initiative—not through law, but by custom. As always, it comprised some three hundred men drawn primarily from the landed aristocracy who remained senators for life and held the chief magistracies of the Republic. During the wars of the third and second centuries, the senate came to exercise enormous power. It directed the wars and took control of both foreign and domestic policy, including financial affairs. The advice of the senate to the consuls had come to have the force of law.

THE DECLINE OF THE ROMAN REPUBLIC

*A*LTHOUGH ROME STOOD supreme over the Mediterranean world, by 133 B.C. the internal structure of the Republic had begun to disintegrate. During the next hundred years, the Republic was afflicted with mob violence, assassinations, civil wars, and unscrupulous politicians who seized every opportunity to advance their own interests. The Roman historian Sallust (86–35 B.C.), who lived through many of these crises, reflected on the causes of Rome's problems. In this selection, he discusses the moral decline that set in after the destruction of Carthage in 146 B.C.

Sallust, *The War with Catiline*

Good morals were cultivated at home and in the field; [in the early Republic] there was the greatest harmony and little or no avarice; justice and honesty prevailed among them, thanks not so much to laws as to nature. Quarrels, discord, and strife were reserved for their enemies; citizen vied with citizen only for the prize of merit. They were lavish in their offerings to the gods, frugal in the home, loyal to their friends. By practicing these two qualities, boldness in warfare and justice when peace came, they watched over themselves and their country. In proof of these statements, I present this convincing evidence: firstly, in time of war punishment was more often inflicted for attacking the enemy contrary to orders, or for withdrawing too tardily when recalled from the field, than for venturing to abandon the standards or to give ground under stress; and secondly, in time of peace they ruled by kindness rather than by fear, and when wronged preferred forgiveness to vengeance.

But when our country had grown great through toil and the practice of justice, when great kings had been vanquished in war, savage tribes and mighty people subdued by force of arms, when Carthage, the rival of Rome's sway, had perished root and branch, and all seas and lands were open, then Fortune began to grow cruel and to bring confusion into all our affairs. Those who had found it easy to bear hardships and dangers, anxiety and adversity, found leisure and wealth, desirable under other circumstances, a burden and a curse. Hence the lust for power first, then for money, grew upon them; these were, I may say, the root of all evils. For avarice destroyed honor, integrity, and all other noble qualities; taught in their place insolence, cruelty, to neglect the gods, to set a price on everything. Ambition drove many men to become false; to have one thought locked in the breast, another ready on the tongue; to value friendships and enmities not on their merits but by the standard of self-interest, and to show a good front rather than a good heart. At first these vices grew slowly; from time to time they were punished; finally, when the disease had spread like a deadly plague, the state was changed and a government second to none in justice and excellence became cruel and intolerable.

Moreover, the magistracies and senate were increasingly controlled by a relatively select circle of wealthy and powerful families—both patrician and plebeian—called the *nobiles* ("nobles"). The *nobiles* were essentially the men whose families were elected to the more important political offices of the Republic. In the hundred years from 233 to 133 B.C., 80 percent of the consuls came from twenty-six families; 50 percent came from only ten families. Hence the *nobiles* constituted a governing oligarchy that managed, through landed wealth, patronage, and intimidation, to maintain its hold over the magistracies and senate and thus guide the destiny of Rome while running the state in its own interests. When a new man—a *novus homo*—did win a consulship, he and his descendants became members of this select oligarchy.

Division of the Aristocrats   By the end of the second century B.C., two types of aristocratic leaders, called the *optimates* ("the best men") and the *populares* ("favoring the people"), became prominent. These were not political parties or even individual cliques but leaders who followed two different approaches to politics. *Optimates* and *populares* were terms of political rhetoric that were used by individuals within the aristocracy against fellow aristocratic rivals to distinguish one set of tactics from another. The *optimates* tended to be the *nobiles* who controlled the senate and wished to maintain their oligarchical privileges, while the *populares* were usually other ambitious aristocrats who used the people's assemblies, especially the council of the plebs, as instruments to break the domination of the *optimates*. The conflicts between these aristocratic leaders and their supporters engulfed the first century B.C. in political turmoil.

Role of the Equestrians   Another social group in Rome also became entangled in this political turmoil—the *equites* or **equestrians,** a name derived from the fact that they had once formed Rome's cavalry. Many equestrians had become extremely wealthy through a variety of means, often related to the creation of the empire. Some, for example, were private contractors who derived their wealth from government contracts for the collection of taxes, the outfitting of armies, and the construction of fleets and public works. In 218 B.C., the senate enacted a law that forbade senators to bid for state contracts or engage in commerce. The law effectively barred the equestrians from high office, since to serve in the senate they would have to give up their livelihoods. By the end of the second century B.C., the equestrians were seeking real political power commensurate with their financial stake in the empire. They would play an important role in the political turmoil that brought an end to the Republic.

The Land Problem Of course, equestrians and aristocrats together formed only a tiny minority of the Roman people. The backbone of the Roman state and army had traditionally been the small farmers who tilled their little plots of land and made up the chief source of recruits for the army. But economic changes that began in the period of the Punic Wars increasingly undermined the position of that group. This occurred for several reasons. Their lands had been severely damaged during the Second Punic War when Hannibal invaded Italy. Moreover, in order to win the wars, Rome had to increase the term of military service from two to six years. The Roman army was never meant to serve in distant wars but was called out for the "war season," after which the soldiers returned to their farms. Now when the soldiers returned home after many years of service abroad, they found their farms so deteriorated that they chose to sell out instead of remaining on the land. By this time, capitalistic agriculture was also increasing rapidly. Landed aristocrats had been able to develop large estates (*latifundia*) by taking over state-owned land and by buying out small peasant owners. These large estates relied on slave and tenant labor and frequently concentrated on cash crops, such as grapes for wine, olives, and sheep for wool, which small farmers could not afford to do. Thus the rise of *latifundia* contributed to the decline in the number of small citizen farmers. Since the latter group traditionally formed the basis of the Roman army—Romans conscripted only people with a financial stake in the community—the number of men available for military service declined. Many of the newly landless families stayed in the countryside, finding agricultural work as best they could. Some of them, however, drifted to the cities, especially Rome, forming a large class of day laborers who possessed no property. This new class of urban proletariat formed a highly unstable mass with the potential for much trouble in depressed times. Thus Rome's economic, social, and political problems were serious and needed attention. In 133 B.C., a member of the aristocracy proposed a solution that infuriated his fellow aristocrats.

The Reforms of Tiberius and Gaius Gracchus

Tiberius Gracchus (163–133 B.C.) was a member of the *nobiles* who ruled Rome. Although concerned with the immediate problem of a shortage of military recruits, Tiberius believed that the underlying cause of Rome's problems was the decline of the small farmers. Tiberius was not a revolutionary, and his proposals for reform, drafted with the help of several prominent senators, were essentially conservative; he was looking backward to what had constituted the foundation of Rome's greatness.

Tiberius Gracchus was elected one of the tribunes of the plebs for 133 B.C. Without consulting the senate, where he knew his rivals would oppose his proposal, Tiberius took his legislation directly to the council of the plebs, which passed his land reform bill. It authorized the government to reclaim public land held by large landowners and to distribute it to landless Romans. Many senators, themselves large landowners whose estates included large tracts of public land, were furious, and a group of them took the law into their own hands and assassinated Tiberius.

The efforts of Tiberius Gracchus were continued by his brother Gaius (153–121 B.C.), elected tribune for both 123 and 122 B.C. Gaius broadened his reform program to appeal to more people disenchanted with the current senatorial leadership. Gaius, too, pushed for the rapid distribution of land to displaced farmers. To win the support of the *equites,* he replaced the senators on the jury courts that tried provincial governors accused of extortion with members of the equestrian order and opened the new province of Asia to equestrian tax collectors. Thus Gaius gave the *equites* two instruments of public power: control over the jury courts that often tried provincial governors and control over provincial taxation. Fellow senators, hostile to Gaius' reforms and fearful of his growing popularity, made use of a constitutional innovation, a "final decree of the senate," which encouraged the consuls to "do everything possible to prevent any misfortune befalling the Republic." As a result, Gaius and many of his followers were killed in 121 B.C. The attempts of the Gracchus brothers to bring reforms by using the tribuneship and council of the plebs had opened the door to more instability and further violence and marked the beginning of the breakdown of the republican form of government.

Marius and the New Roman Army

In the closing years of the second century B.C., a series of military disasters gave rise to a fresh outburst of popular anger against the old leaders of the senate and resulted in the rise of Marius (157–86 B.C.).

Marius came to prominence during the war in North Africa against Jugurtha and the Numidians. The senate had badly bungled the war effort. Marius had served as legate to the senate-appointed commanding general Metellus but quarreled with his superior, returned to Rome, and ran for the consulship with "Win the War" as his campaign slogan. Despite being a *novus homo* from the equestrian order, Marius won and became a consul for 107 B.C. The council of the plebs then voted to give Marius command of the army in Africa, a definite encroachment on the senate's right to conduct wars. Generals no longer needed to be loyal to the senate.

Marius brought the Jugurthine War to a successful conclusion and was then called on to defeat the Celtic tribes (or Gauls, as the Romans called them), who had annihilated a Roman army and threatened an invasion of Italy. Marius was made consul for five years, from 104 to 100 B.C., raised a new army, and decisively defeated the Celts, leaving him in a position of personal ascendancy in Rome.

In raising a new army, Marius initiated military reforms that proved to have drastic consequences. The Roman army had traditionally been a conscript army of small landholders. Marius recruited volunteers from both the urban and the rural proletariat who possessed no property. These volunteers swore an oath of loyalty to the general, not the senate, and thus inaugurated a professional-type army that might no longer be subject to the state. Moreover, to recruit these men, a general would promise them land, so generals had to play politics to get legislation passed that would provide the land for their veterans. Marius left a powerful legacy. He had created a new system of military recruitment that placed much power in the hands of the individual generals. Roman republican politics was entering a new and potentially dangerous stage.

The Role of Sulla

After almost a decade of relative quiet, the Roman Republic was threatened with another crisis—the Italian or Social War (90–88 B.C.). This war resulted from Rome's unwillingness to deal constructively with the complaints of its Italian allies. These allies had fought loyally on Rome's side but felt they had not shared sufficiently in the lands and bonuses given to Roman veterans. In 90 B.C., the Italians rebelled and formed their own confederation. Two years of bitter fighting left Italy devastated and took an enormous number of lives. The Romans managed to end the rebellion but only by granting full rights of Roman citizenship to all free Italians. "Rome was now Italy, and Italy Rome."[7] This influx of new voters into the popular assemblies drastically altered the voting power structure in favor of the *populares,* who had earlier favored enfranchisement of the Italians.

During this war, a new figure came into prominence— Lucius Cornelius Sulla (138–78 B.C.), a member of the *nobiles.* Sulla had been made consul for 88 B.C. and been given command by the senate of the war against Mithridates, the king of Pontus in Asia Minor, who had rebelled against Roman power. However, Marius, who had retired from Roman politics, now returned to the scene. The council of the plebs, contradicting the senate's wishes, transferred command of the war against Mithridates to Marius. Considering this action illegal, Sulla marched on Rome with his army. Marius fled, and Sulla reestablished his command. After Sulla left again for the east, Marius joined forces with the consul Cinna, marched on Rome, seized control of the government, outlawed Sulla, and killed many of Sulla's supporters. Civil war had become a fact of life in Roman politics.

Marius soon died, but Cinna continued to use his forces to remain as consul. His control, however, really depended on the fortunes of Sulla and his army. After defeating Mithridates in the east, Sulla returned to Rome, crushed the armies opposing him in Italy, and seized Rome itself in 82 B.C. He forced the senate to grant him the title of dictator to "reconstitute the Republic." After conducting a reign of terror to wipe out all opposition, Sulla revised the constitution to restore power to the senate. He eliminated most of the powers of the popular assemblies and the tribunes of the plebs and restored the senators to the jury courts. He also enlarged the senate by adding men of the equestrian order. In 79 B.C., believing that he had restored the traditional Republic governed by a powerful senate, he resigned his office of dictator, retired, and soon died, leaving a power vacuum. But his real legacy was quite different from what he had intended. His example of how an army could be used to seize power would prove most attractive to ambitious men.

The Death of the Republic

For the next fifty years, Roman history would be characterized by two important features: the jostling for power by a number of powerful individuals and the civil wars generated by their conflicts.

The Rise of Pompey　Not long after Sulla's attempts to revive senatorial power, the senate made two extraordinary military appointments that raised to prominence two very strong personalities—Crassus (c. 112–53 B.C.) and Pompey (106–48 B.C.). Crassus had fought for Sulla and had also become extremely rich—it was said that he "owned most of Rome." In 73 B.C., the senate gave Crassus a military command against the slave rebellion led by Spartacus, which he successfully completed. Pompey had also fought for Sulla and was given an important military command in Spain in 77 B.C. When he returned six years later, he was hailed as a military hero.

Despite their jealousy of one another, Pompey and Crassus joined forces and were elected consuls for 70 B.C.

Pompey. A popular and powerful figure of the late Republic, Pompey was a successful general who joined with Caesar and Crassus in a coalition known as the First Triumvirate in order to secure his reorganization of the east and to obtain lands for his veterans. He later opposed Caesar during the civil war of 49–45 B.C. Pictured is a marble copy of an earlier sculpted head of Pompey; in keeping with Roman artistic practices, the portrait is quite realistic.

Although both men had been supporters of Sulla, they undid his work. They restored the power of the tribunes and helped put *equites* back on the jury courts, thereby reviving the *populares* as a path to political power.

With their power reestablished by this action, friendly plebeian tribunes now proposed legislation that gave two important military commands to Pompey. In 67 B.C., he cleared the Mediterranean Sea of the pirates who were harassing Roman commerce. After this success, he was put in charge of the campaign against Mithridates, who thought he could take advantage of Rome's internal troubles to pursue his plans of conquest. Pompey defeated Mithridates and reorganized the east, winning immense success and prestige as well as enormous wealth. When he returned to Rome, he disbanded his army, expecting that the senate would automatically ratify his eastern settlement and give land to his veterans. But new forces and new personalities had risen to prominence during his absence, and his requests encountered complications.

The Role of Cicero Marcus Tullius Cicero (106–43 B.C.) was one of these new personalities. A *novus homo* from the equestrian order and the first of his family to achieve the consulship, Cicero made a name for himself as a lawyer, using his outstanding oratorical skills to defend people accused of crimes and to prosecute others, including a corrupt provincial governor. He became consul in 63 B.C. and upheld the interests of the senate. While consul, he added to his reputation by acting forcefully to suppress a political conspiracy led by a desperate and bankrupt aristocrat named Catiline. Cicero was one of the few prominent politicians who attempted to analyze the problems of the Republic systematically. He believed in a "concord of the orders," meaning the cooperation of the equestrians and senators. In effect, Cicero harked back to the days of collective rule, a time when political leaders were motivated to work together for the good of the Roman state. But collective rule was no longer meaningful to ambitious men seeking personal power. Cicero himself had few military skills and could not command an army. He realized that the senate needed the support of a powerful general if the concord of the orders was to be made a reality. In 62 B.C., he saw Pompey as that man. But a large element in the senate felt that Pompey had become too powerful, and they now refused to grant his wishes after his return from the east. This same element in the senate treated Julius Caesar in a similar fashion when he returned from Spain. That turned out to be a big mistake.

The Struggle Between Pompey and Caesar Julius Caesar (100–44 B.C.) had been a spokesman for the *populares* from the beginning of his political career, an alliance that ran in the family—Marius was his uncle by marriage. Caesar pursued political power by appealing to many of the same groups who had supported Marius. After serving as aedile and praetor, he sought a military command and was sent to Spain. He returned from Spain in 60 B.C. and requested a special dispensation so that he could both celebrate a tri-

Cicero. The great orator Marcus Tullius Cicero, whose writings provide much information about politics and upper-class life, rose to the highest offices in the Republic due to his oratorical skills. He was a supporter of the senate and wished to establish a "concord of the orders," cooperative rule by the equestrians and the senators. This realistic portrait, typical of Republican Rome, gives a sense of Cicero's rigid character.

umph with his troops and run for the consulship, which would place him in the highest rank within the senate. Rival senators blocked his request. Consequently, Caesar joined with two fellow senators, Crassus and Pompey, who were also being stymied by the senate. Historians call their coalition the First Triumvirate. Though others had made political deals before, the combined wealth and power of these three men was enormous, enabling them to dominate the political scene. Caesar was elected consul for 59 B.C. and used the popular assemblies to achieve the basic aims of the triumvirs: Pompey received his eastern settlement and lands for his veterans; equestrian allies of Crassus were given a reduction on tax contracts for which they had overbid; and Caesar was granted a special military command in Gaul (modern France, Belgium, and parts of the Netherlands) for five years.

Caesar did so well in Gaul that Crassus and Pompey realized anew the value of military command. They became consuls again for 55 B.C. and garnered more benefits for the coalition: Caesar was given a five-year extension in Gaul; Crassus, a command in Syria; and Pompey, one in Spain. When Crassus was killed in battle in 53 B.C., his death left two powerful men with armies in direct competition. Caesar had used his time in Gaul to gain fame and military experience. He had waged numerous campaigns, costing the lives, it has been estimated, of almost two million men, women, and children. But his wars had also enabled him to amass enough booty and slaves to pay off all of the debts

Caesar. Conqueror of Gaul and member of the First Triumvirate, Julius Caesar is perhaps the best-known figure of the late Republic. Caesar became dictator of Rome in 47 B.C. and after his victories in the civil war was made dictator for life. Some members of the senate who resented his power assassinated him in 44 B.C. Pictured is a marble copy of a bust of Caesar.

© Scala/Art Resource, NY

he had accumulated in gaining political offices. Moreover, he now had an army of seasoned veterans who were loyal to him. No doubt most senators would have preferred both Pompey and Caesar to lay down their commands and give up their armies. Since both refused, the leading senators fastened on Pompey as the less harmful to their cause and voted for Caesar to lay down his command and return as a private citizen to Rome. Such a step was intolerable to Caesar, as it would leave him totally vulnerable to his enemies. He chose to keep his army and moved into Italy by crossing the Rubicon, the river that formed the southern boundary of his province, on January 10, 49 B.C. (The phrase "crossing the Rubicon" is still used today to mean being unable to turn back.)

Pompey and his followers fled to Greece, where they raised a new army. Meanwhile it took Caesar until the end of 49 to raise a fleet and ship his troops to Greece. The next spring, at the Battle of Pharsalus, Caesar's veterans carried the day against Pompey's forces. The defeated Pompey fled to Egypt, where the king was one of his foreign clients, but one of the king's advisers had Pompey killed. The war continued, however, since some of the senators on his side, including Cato the Younger, had recruited new troops. After victories in North Africa and Spain, Caesar returned triumphant to Rome in 45 B.C.

No doubt Caesar realized that the old order of unfettered political competition could not be saved. He was unwilling to take the title of king, which was intensely disliked by the Roman upper classes, but he had no intention of giving up his control. Caesar had officially been made dictator in 47 B.C., and in 44 B.C. he was made dictator for life. He continued to hold elections for offices but saw to it that his supporters chose the people he recommended. As Rome's new ruler, he quickly instituted a number of ambitious reforms. He increased the senate to nine hundred members by filling it with many of his followers. He granted citizenship to a number of people in the provinces who had provided assistance to him. By establishing colonies of Roman citizens in North Africa,

Gaul, and Spain, he initiated a process of Romanization in those areas. He tried to reorganize the administrative structures of cities in Italy in order to create some sense of rational order in their government.

Caesar was a generous victor and pardoned many of the republican leaders who had opposed him, allowing them to return to Rome. He also replaced the Roman calendar with the Egyptian solar year of 365 days (this so-called Julian calendar, with later changes made in 1582, became the basis of our modern calendar). He planned much more in the way of building projects and military adventures in the east but was not able to carry them out. In 44 B.C., a group of leading senators who resented his domination assassinated him, believing that the old republican system would now return (see the box on p. 131). In truth, however, they had set the stage for another civil war that delivered the death blow to the Republic.

The Final Struggle: Octavian Versus Antony   A new struggle for power soon ensued. Caesar's heir and adopted son, his grandnephew Octavian, though only nineteen, took command of some of Caesar's legions. After forcing the senate to name him consul, he joined forces with Mark Antony, Caesar's ally and assistant, and Marcus Lepidus, who had been commander of Caesar's cavalry. Together, the three formed the Second Triumvirate, which was legally empowered to rule Rome. Their first act was to restore Sulla's policy of proscription, as described by the ancient historian Appian:

> As soon as they were on their own, the three drew up a list of those who were to die. They put on the list, both then and later, those of whom they were suspicious because of their ability, as well as their personal enemies, trading with each other for the lives of their own relations and friends. They decreed death and confiscation of property for about 300 senators and 2,000 equestrians, among them their own brothers and uncles, as well as senior officers serving under them who had had cause to offend them or their own colleagues.[8]

In addition to proscribing their enemies at home (Cicero was one of those killed), the three commanders pursued Caesar's assassins, who had in the meantime raised an army, and defeated them at Philippi in Macedonia. Lepidus was soon shunted aside, and Octavian and Antony then divided the Roman world between them—Octavian taking the west and Antony the east. To seal their bargain, Antony married Octavia, Octavian's sister.

THE ASSASSINATION OF JULIUS CAESAR

*W*HEN IT BECAME apparent that Julius Caesar had no intention of restoring the Republic as they conceived it, about sixty senators, many of them his friends or pardoned enemies, formed a conspiracy to assassinate the dictator. It was led by Gaius Cassius and Marcus Brutus, who naively imagined that this act would restore the traditional Republic. The conspirators set the Ides of March (March 15) of 44 B.C. as the date for the assassination. Caesar was in the midst of preparations for a campaign in the eastern part of the empire. Although warned about a plot against his life, he chose to disregard it. This account of Caesar's death is taken from his biography by the Greek writer Plutarch.

Plutarch, *Life of Caesar*

Fate, however, is to all appearance more unavoidable than unexpected. For many strange prodigies and apparitions are said to have been observed shortly before this event. . . . One finds it also related by many that a soothsayer bade him [Caesar] prepare for some great danger on the Ides of March. When this day was come, Caesar, as he went to the senate, met this soothsayer, and said to him mockingly, "The Ides of March are come," who answered him calmly, "Yes, they are come, but they are not past. . . ."

All these things might happen by chance. But the place which was destined for the scene of this murder, in which the senate met that day, was the same in which Pompey's statue stood, and was one of the edifices which Pompey had raised and dedicated with his theater to the use of the public, plainly showing that there was something of a supernatural influence which guided the action and ordered it to that particular place. Cassius, just before the act, is said to have looked toward Pompey's statue, and silently implored his assistance. . . . When Caesar entered, the senate stood up to show their respect to him, and of Brutus' confederates, some came about his chair and stood behind it, others met him, pretending to add their petitions to those of Tillius Cimber, in behalf of his brother, who was in exile; and they followed him with their joint applications till he came to his seat. When he sat down, he refused to comply with their requests, and upon their urging him further began to reproach them severely for their demand, when Tillius, laying hold of his robe with both his hands, pulled it down from his neck, which was the signal for the assault. Casca gave him the first cut in the neck, which was not mortal nor dangerous, as coming from one who at the beginning of such a bold action was probably very much disturbed; Caesar immediately turned about, and laid his hand upon the dagger and kept hold of it. And both of them at the same time cried out, he that received the blow, in Latin, "Vile Casca, what does this mean?" and he that gave it, in Greek to his brother, "Brother, help!" Upon this first onset, those who were not privy to the design were astonished, and their horror and amazement at what they saw were so great that they dared not fly nor assist Caesar, nor so much as speak a word. But those who came prepared for the business enclosed him on every side, with their naked daggers in their hands. Which way soever he turned he met with blows, and saw their swords leveled at his face and eyes, and was encompassed like a wild beast in the toils on every side. For it had been agreed they should each of them make a thrust at him, and flesh themselves with his blood: for which reason Brutus also gave him one stab in the groin. Some say that he fought and resisted all the rest, shifting his body to avoid the blows, and calling out for help, but that when he saw Brutus' sword drawn, he covered his face with his robe and submitted, letting himself fall, whether it were by chance or that he was pushed in that direction by his murderers, at the foot of the pedestal on which Pompey's statue stood, and which was thus wetted with his blood. So that Pompey himself seemed to have presided, as it were, over the revenge done upon his adversary, who lay here at his feet, and breathed out his soul through his multitude of wounds, for they say he received three-and-twenty. And the conspirators themselves were many of them wounded by each other while they all leveled their blows at the same person.

But the empire of the Romans, large as it was, was still too small for two masters, and Octavian and Antony eventually came into conflict. Antony abandoned Octavia and allied himself with the Egyptian queen Cleopatra VII, with whom, like Caesar before him, he fell deeply in love. Octavian began a propaganda campaign, accusing Antony of catering to Cleopatra and giving away Roman territory to this "whore of the east." Finally, at the Battle of Actium in Greece in 31 B.C., Octavian's forces smashed the army and navy of Antony and Cleopatra. Both fled to Egypt, where, according to the Roman historian Florus, they committed suicide a year later:

Antony was the first to commit suicide, by the sword. Cleopatra threw herself at Octavian's feet, and tried her best to attract his gaze: in vain, for his self-control was impervious to her beauty. It was not her life she was after, for that had already been granted, but a portion of her kingdom. When she realized this was hopeless and that she had been earmarked to feature in Octavian's triumph in Rome, she took advantage of her guard's carelessness to get herself into the mausoleum, as the royal tomb is called. Once there, she put on the royal robes which she was accustomed to wear, and lay down in a richly perfumed coffin beside her Antony. Then she applied poisonous snakes to her veins and passed into death as though into a sleep.[9]

The Decline and Fall of the Roman Republic

Reforms of Tiberius Gracchus	133 B.C.
Reforms of Gaius Gracchus	123–122 B.C.
Jugurthine War	111–105 B.C.
Marius: First consulship	107 B.C.
Marius: Consecutive consulships	104–100 B.C.
Italian or Social War	90–88 B.C.
Sulla's march on Rome	88 B.C.
Sulla as dictator	82–79 B.C.
Pompey's command in Spain	77–71 B.C.
Campaign of Crassus against Spartacus	73–71 B.C.
Consulship of Crassus and Pompey	70 B.C.
First Triumvirate (Caesar, Pompey, Crassus)	60 B.C.
Caesar in Gaul	59–49 B.C.
Crassus and Pompey as consuls	55 B.C.
Crassus killed by Parthians	53 B.C.
Caesar crosses the Rubicon	49 B.C.
Battle of Pharsalus; Pompey killed in Egypt	48 B.C.
End of civil war	47–44 B.C.
Caesar as dictator	45 B.C.
Second Triumvirate (Octavian, Antony, Marcus Lepidus); Cicero killed	43 B.C.
Caesar's assassins defeated at Philippi	42 B.C.
Octavian defeats Antony at Actium	31 B.C.

Octavian, at the age of thirty-two, stood supreme over the Roman world (see Map 5.3). The civil wars had ended. And so had the Republic.

Literature in the Late Republic

The last century of the Roman Republic had witnessed the completion of the union of Greek and Roman culture in a truly Greco-Roman civilization. Greek was now the language not just of Greece but of the entire Hellenistic world of the eastern Mediterranean, which Rome had conquered, and educated, upper-class Romans spoke it fluently. The influence of Greece would continue to be felt in the development of Latin literature.

In the last century of the Republic, the Romans began to produce a new poetry, less dependent on epic themes and more inclined to personal expression. Latin poets now took to using various Greek forms to express their own feelings about people, social and political life, and love. The finest example is the work of Catullus (c. 87–54 B.C.), the best lyric poet Rome produced and one of the greatest in world literature.

Catullus Like most of the great Roman writers of the first century B.C., Catullus was not from Rome. He grew up in northern Italy but came to Rome, where he joined a group of carefree, youthful aristocrats. He became a master at adapting and refining Greek forms of poetry to express emotions. He wrote a variety of poems on, among other themes, political figures, social customs, the use of language, the death of his brother, and the travails of love. Catullus became infatuated with Clodia, the promiscuous sister of a tribune and wife of a provincial governor, and addressed a number of poems to her (he called her Lesbia), describing his passionate love and hatred for her (Clodia had many other lovers besides Catullus):

> You used to say that you wished to know only Catullus,
>   Lesbia, and wouldn't take even Jove before me!
> I didn't regard you just as my mistress then: I cherished you
>   as a father does his sons or his daughters' husbands.
> Now that I know you, I burn for you even more fiercely,
>   though I regard you as almost utterly worthless.
> How can that be, you ask? It's because such cruelty forces
>   lust to assume the shrunken place of affection.[10]

The ability of Catullus to express in simple fashion his intense feelings and curiosity about himself and his world had a noticeable impact on later Latin poets.

Lucretius Another important poet of the late Republic was Lucretius (c. 94–55 B.C.), who followed an old Greek tradition of expounding philosophy in the form of poetry. Although Stoicism was the Greek school of philosophy that the Romans found most congenial, the philosophy of Epicurus also enjoyed a period of intense popularity between 60 and 40 B.C. Lucretius' lengthy poem *On the Nature of the Universe* played a role in furthering that philosophy. In this work, Lucretius attempted to set out poetically Epicurus' idea that the world and all its creatures had been created by an accidental combination of atoms and not by the operation of divine forces. Two themes are repeated: divine forces have no effect on us, and death is of no real consequence because the soul, like the body, is material and after death also dissolves into atoms. Lucretius was especially adept at using vivid imagery. Describing the movement of atoms in the void, he wrote:

> Consider the rays of the sun that are always stealing
> Into the shade of a house to pour their light.
> There in the void you'll notice many and sundry
> Dust flecks that mingle among the rays themselves,
> Stirring up in a sort of ceaseless strife
> Skirmishes, wars, realigning their squadrons, never
> Stopping for breath, assailed by alliance, secession;
> From this you can project how atoms are
> Constantly tossed along the gulf of space.[11]

If the gods and death are of no significance, how then are we to lead our lives? Lucretius' Epicurean argument that a simple life free of political worries was the highest good ran counter to Roman ideals but had an obvious appeal to Romans sick of the civil discord of the first century B.C.

MAP 5.3 **Roman Dominions in the Late Republic, 31 B.C.** Rome expanded its empire not only in response to military threats on its borders but also for increased access to economic resources and markets, in addition to the vanity of conquest itself. For comparison, look back at Map 5.2. **?** In what areas did the Romans gain the greatest amount of territory, and how? 🌐 **View an animated version of this map or related maps at** http://history.wadsworth.com/spielvogel06/

Cicero The development of Roman prose was greatly aided by the practice of oratory. Romans had great respect for oratory, for the ability to persuade people in public debate led to success in politics. Oratory was brought to perfection in a literary fashion by Cicero, the best exemplar of the literary and intellectual interests of the elite of the late Republic and, indeed, the greatest prose writer of that period. For Cicero, oratory was not simply skillful speaking. An orator was a statesman, a man who achieved his highest goal by pursuing an active life in public affairs.

Later, when the turmoil of the late Republic forced him into semiretirement politically, Cicero turned his attention to writing philosophical treatises. He performed a valuable service for Roman society by popularizing and making understandable the works of Greek philosophers. In his philosophical works, Cicero, more than anyone else, transmitted the classical intellectual heritage to the Western world. Cicero's original contributions to Western thought

came in the field of politics. His works *On the Laws* and *On the Republic* provided fresh insights into political thought, including the need for a mixed constitution: "A moderate and well-balanced form of government which is a combination of the three simple good forms (monarchy, aristocracy, and democracy) is preferable even to monarchy."[12] His emphasis on the need to pursue an active life to benefit and improve humankind would greatly influence the later Italian Renaissance.

Sallust Rome's upper classes continued to have a strong interest in history. The best-known historian of the late Republic is Sallust (86–35 B.C.), who established an approach to historical studies that influenced later Roman historians. Sallust, who served as governor of the province of Africa, was on Caesar's side in the civil war and after Caesar's death went into retirement and turned to the writing of history. His two extant works are *War with Jugurtha,* which discusses the Roman war with the African king from 111 to 105 B.C., and *War with Catiline,* an account of the conspiracy of the disaffected aristocrat Catiline, whom Cicero had opposed during his consulship in 63 B.C.

Sallust modeled his style after that of the Greek historian Thucydides, whose historical work experienced a sudden wave of popularity in the 50s and 40s B.C. Sallust's works expressed his belief that the most important causative factor in Roman history was the moral degeneration of Roman society, which he attributed to the lack of a strong enemy after Carthage and the corrupting influence of the Greeks (see the box on p. 126).

Caesar   Brief mention should also be made of the historical writing of Julius Caesar. Most famous is his *Commentaries on the Gallic War,* an account of his conquest of Gaul between 58 and 51 B.C. The work was published in 51 B.C., at a time when Caesar was afraid that his political enemies would take advantage of his absence from Rome.

Although the *Commentaries* served a partisan purpose by defending his actions in Gaul, Caesar presented his material in straightforward, concise prose. He referred to himself in the third person and, as the following passage indicates, was not averse to extolling his own bravery:

> Caesar saw that the situation was critical, and there was no reserve to throw in. He snatched a shield from a soldier in the rear—he had not brought one himself—and moved to the front line; he called upon the centurions by name, encouraged the men to advance, and directed them to open their lines out to give freer play to their swords. His coming inspired the men with hope and gave them new heart. Even in a desperate situation each man was anxious to do his utmost when his general was looking on, and the enemy's onset was somewhat slowed down.[13]

Caesar's work reminds us that some of the best prose of the late Republic was written by politicians who were concerned with enhancing their own position in a world of civil conflict.

CONCLUSION

$\mathscr{I}$N THE EIGHTH AND SEVENTH CENTURIES B.C., the pastoral community of Rome emerged as a true city. Between 509 and 264 B.C., the expansion of this city led to the union of almost all of Italy under Rome's control. Even more dramatically, between 264 and 133 B.C., Rome expanded to the west and east and became master of the Mediterranean Sea.

After 133 B.C., however, Rome's republican institutions proved inadequate for the task of ruling an empire. In the breakdown that ensued, ambitious individuals saw opportunities for power unparalleled in Roman history and succumbed to the temptations. After a series of bloody civil wars, peace was finally achieved when Octavian defeated Antony and Cleopatra. Octavian's real task was to create a new system of government that seemed to preserve the Republic while establishing the basis for a new order that would rule the empire in an orderly fashion. Octavian proved equal to the task of establishing a Roman imperial state.

NOTES

1. Quoted in Chester Starr, *Past and Future in Ancient History* (Lanham, Md., 1987), pp. 38–39.
2. Cicero, *Laws,* trans. C. W. Keyes (Cambridge, Mass., 1966), 2.12.31.
3. Cato the Censor, *On Farming,* trans. Ernest Brehaut (New York, 1933), 141.

4. Quoted in J. Wright Duff, *A Literary History of Rome* (London, 1960), pp. 136–137.
5. Terence, *The Comedies,* trans. Betty Radice (Harmondsworth, England, 1976), p. 339.
6. Pliny, *Natural History,* trans. W. H. S. Jones (Cambridge, Mass., 1963), 29.7.
7. Mary Beard and Michael Crawford, *Rome in the Late Republic* (London, 1985), p. 3.
8. Appian, *Roman History: The Civil Wars,* trans. H. White (Cambridge, Mass., 1961), 4.2.149–151.
9. Florus, *Epitome of Roman History,* trans. E. S. Forster (Cambridge, Mass., 1960), 2.22.327.
10. *The Poems of Catullus,* trans. Charles Martin (Baltimore, 1990), p. 109.
11. Lucretius, *On the Nature of Things,* trans. Anthony M. Esolen (Baltimore, 1995), 2.115–123.
12. Quoted in Anthony Everitt, *Cicero* (New York, 2001), p. 181.
13. Julius Caesar, *The Gallic War and Other Writings,* trans. Moses Hadas (New York, 1957), 2.25.

SUGGESTIONS FOR FURTHER READING

For a general account of the Roman Republic, see **J. Boardman, J. Griffin, and O. Murray, eds.,** *The Oxford History of the Roman World* (Oxford, 1991). A standard one-volume reference is **M. Cary and H. H. Scullard,** *A History of Rome down to the Reign of Constantine,* 3d ed. (New York, 1975). Good surveys of Roman history include **M. H. Crawford,** *The Roman Republic,* 2d ed. (Cambridge, Mass., 1993); **H. H. Scullard,** *History of the Roman World, 753–146 B.C.,* 4th ed. (London, 1978) and *From the Gracchi to Nero,* 5th ed. (London, 1982); **M. Le Glay, J.-L. Voisin, and Y. Le Bohec,** *A History of Rome,* trans. **A. Nevill,** 2d ed. (Oxford, 2000); **M. T. Boatwright, D. J. Gargola, and R. J. A. Talbert,** *The Romans: From Village to Empire* (New York, 2004); and **A. Kamm,** *The Romans* (London, 1995). For beautifully illustrated surveys, see **J. F. Drinkwater and A. Drummond,** *The World of the Romans* (New York, 1993), and **G. Woolf,**

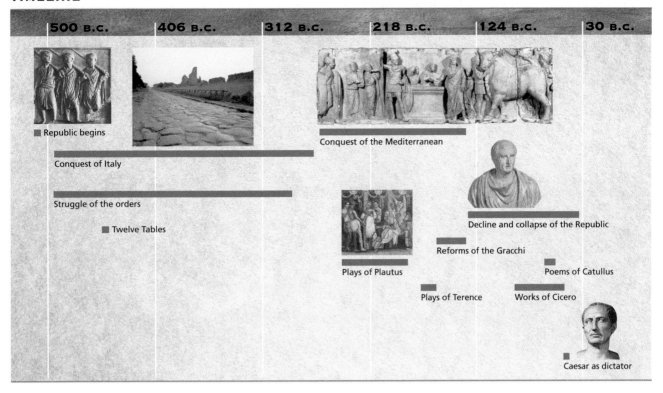

500 B.C. 406 B.C. 312 B.C. 218 B.C. 124 B.C. 30 B.C.

Republic begins

Conquest of Italy

Struggle of the orders

Twelve Tables

Conquest of the Mediterranean

Decline and collapse of the Republic

Reforms of the Gracchi

Plays of Plautus

Poems of Catullus

Plays of Terence   Works of Cicero

Caesar as dictator

ed., *Cambridge Illustrated History of the Roman World* (Cambridge, 2003). The history of early Rome is well covered in **T. J. Cornell**, *The Beginnings of Rome: Italy and Rome from the Bronze Age to the Punic Wars (c. 1000–264 B.C.)* (London, 1995). A good work on the Etruscans is **M. Pallottino**, *The Etruscans,* rev. ed. (Bloomington, Ind., 1975).

Aspects of the Roman political structure can be studied in **R. E. Mitchell**, *Patricians and Plebeians: The Origin of the Roman State* (Ithaca, N.Y., 1990). Changes in Rome's economic life can be examined in **A. H. M. Jones**, *The Roman Economy* (Oxford, 1974). On the Roman social structure, see **G. Alföldy**, *The Social History of Rome* (London, 1985).

A general account of Rome's expansion in the Mediterranean is provided by **R. M. Errington**, *The Dawn of Empire: Rome's Rise to World Power* (Ithaca, N.Y., 1971). On the conquest of Italy, see **J.-M. David**, *The Roman Conquest of Italy,* trans. **A. Nevill** (Oxford, 1996). On Rome's struggle with Carthage, see **N. Bagnall**, *The Punic Wars* (Oxford, 2002), and **A. Goldsworthy**, *The Punic Wars* (New York, 2001). Especially important works on Roman expansion and imperialism include **W. V. Harris**, *War and Imperialism in Republican Rome* (Oxford, 1979), and **E. Badian**, *Roman Imperialism in the Late Republic* (Oxford, 1968). On Roman expansion in the eastern Mediterranean, see **A. N. Sherwin-White**, *Roman Foreign Policy in the Greek East* (London, 1984). On Roman military forces, see **A. Goldsworthy**, *The Complete Roman Army* (London, 2003).

Roman religion can be examined in **J. Liebeschuetz**, *Continuity and Change in Roman Religion* (Oxford, 1979), and **H. H. Scullard**, *Festivals and Ceremonies of the Roman Republic* (Ithaca, N.Y., 1981). A general study of daily life in Rome is available in **F. Dupont**, *Daily Life in Ancient Rome* (Oxford, 1994). On the Roman family, see **S. Dixon**, *The Roman Family* (Baltimore, 1992). Roman women are examined in **J. Balsdon**, *Roman Women,* rev. ed. (London, 1974); **S. B. Pomeroy**, *Goddesses, Whores, Wives, and Slaves: Women in Classical Antiquity* (New York, 1975), pp. 149–189; **R. Baumann**, *Women and Politics in Ancient Rome* (New York, 1995); and **S. Dixon**, *The Roman Mother* (Norman, Okla., 1988). On slavery and its consequences, see **K. R. Bradley**, *Slavery and Rebellion in the Roman World, 140–70 B.C.* (Bloomington, Ind., 1989). For a brief and readable survey of Latin literature, see **R. M. Ogilvie**, *Roman Literature and Society* (Harmondsworth, England, 1980). On Roman art and architecture, see **R. Ling**, *Roman Painting* (New York, 1991); **D. E. Kleiner**, *Roman Sculpture* (New Haven, Conn., 1992); and **M. Wheeler**, *Roman Art and Architecture* (London, 1964).

An excellent account of basic problems in the history of the late Republic can be found in **M. Beard and M. H. Crawford**, *Rome in the Late Republic* (London, 1985). Also valuable are **D. Shotter**, *The Fall of the Roman Republic* (London, 1994); **C. Nicolet**, *The World of the Citizen in Republican Rome* (London, 1980); and **E. Hildinger**, *Swords Against the Senate: The Rise of the Roman Army and the Fall of the Republic* (Cambridge, Mass., 2002). Numerous biographies provide many details on the politics of the period. Especially worthwhile are **A. H. Bernstein**, *Tiberius Sempronius Gracchus: Tradition and Apostasy* (Ithaca, N.Y., 1978); **D. Stockton**, *The Gracchi* (Oxford, 1979); **C. Meier**, *Caesar* (London, 1995); **R. Seager**, *Pompey: A Political Biography* (Berkeley, Calif., 1980); **A. Ward**, *Marcus Crassus and the Late Roman Republic* (Columbia, Mo., 1977); and **A. Everitt**, *Cicero* (New York, 2001).

History Now™

Enter *HistoryNow* using the access card that is available for *Western Civilization*. *HistoryNow* will assist you in understanding the content in this chapter with lesson plans generated for your needs. In addition, you can read the following documents, and many more, online:

Terence, *Phormio*

Plutarch, Life of Caesar

Cicero, Oration in Defense of Aulus Licinius Archias

Cicero, Tusculan Disputations

INFOTRAC SEARCH TERMS

For additional reading, go to InfoTrac College Edition, your online research library at http://infotrac.thomsonlearning.com

Subject Guide Search	*Key Term Search*
Roman mythology	Rome history
Roman law	Roman Republic

WESTERN CIVILIZATION RESOURCES

Visit the *Western Civilization* Companion Web site for resources specific to this book:

http://history.wadsworth.com/spielvogel06/

For a variety of tools to help you succeed in this course, visit the Western Civilization Resource Center at

http://history.wadsworth.com/western/

Included are quizzes; images; documents; interactive simulations; maps and timelines; movie explorations; and a wealth of other sources.

THE ROMAN EMPIRE

CHAPTER OUTLINE AND FOCUS QUESTIONS

The Age of Augustus (31 B.C.–A.D. 14)

● In his efforts to solve the problems Rome had faced during the late Republic, what changes did Augustus make in Rome's political, military, and social institutions?

The Early Empire (14–180)

● What were the chief features of the Roman Empire at its height during the second century?

Roman Culture and Society in the Early Empire

● What were the chief intellectual, artistic, and social developments in the Early Empire?

Transformation of the Roman World: Crises in the Third Century

● What problems did the Roman Empire face during the third century?

Transformation of the Roman World: The Rise of Christianity

● What characteristics of Christianity enabled it to grow and ultimately to triumph?

CRITICAL THINKING

● What did one historian mean when he said that the Romans became Christians and the Christians became Romans?

Entry of Hadrian (with outstretched arms) into Rome

WITH THE VICTORIES OF OCTAVIAN, peace finally settled on the Roman world. Although civil conflict still erupted occasionally, the new imperial state constructed by Octavian experienced a period of remarkable stability for the next two hundred years. The Romans imposed their peace on the largest empire established in antiquity. Indeed, Rome's writers proclaimed that "by heaven's will my Rome shall be capital of the world."[1] Rome's writers were not quite accurate, but few Romans were aware of the Han Empire, which flourished at the same time (202 B.C.–A.D. 221) and extended from Central Asia to the Pacific. Although there was little contact between them, the Han and Roman empires had remarkable similarities: they lasted for centuries, they had remarkable success in establishing centralized control, and they maintained their law and political institutions, their technical skills, and their languages throughout the empire.

To the Romans, their divine mission was clearly to rule nations and peoples. Hadrian, one of the emperors of the second century A.D., was but one of many Roman rulers who believed in Rome's mission. He was a strong

137

The Han Chinese Empire

and intelligent ruler who took his responsibilities quite seriously. Between 121 and 132, he visited all of the provinces in the empire. According to his Roman biographer, Aelius Spartianus, "Hardly any emperor ever traveled with such speed over so much territory." When he arrived in a province, Hadrian dealt firsthand with any problems and bestowed many favors on the local population. He also worked to establish the boundaries of the provinces and provide for their defense. New fortifications, such as the 80-mile-long Hadrian's Wall across northern Britain, were built to defend the borders. Hadrian insisted on rigid discipline for frontier armies and demanded that the soldiers be kept in training "just as if war were imminent." He also tried to lead by personal example; according to his biographer, he spent time with the troops and "cheerfully ate out of doors such camp food as bacon, cheese, and vinegar." Moreover, he "would walk as much as twenty miles fully armed."

By the third century A.D., however, Rome's ability to rule nations and people began to weaken as the Roman Empire began to experience renewed civil war, economic chaos, and invasions. In the meantime, the growth of Christianity, one of the remarkable success stories of Western civilization, led to the emergence of a new and vibrant institution.

The Age of Augustus (31 B.C.–A.D. 14)

In 27 B.C., Octavian proclaimed the "restoration of the Republic." He understood that only traditional republican forms would satisfy the senatorial aristocracy. At the same time, Octavian was aware that the Republic could not be fully restored and managed to arrive at a compromise that worked, at least during his lifetime. In 27 B.C., the senate awarded him the title of Augustus—"the revered one." He preferred the title *princeps*, meaning chief citizen or first among equals. The system of rule that Augustus established is sometimes called the **principate,** conveying the idea of a constitutional monarch as coruler with the senate. But while Augustus worked to maintain this appearance, in reality, power was heavily weighted in favor of the *princeps*.

Augustus. Octavian, Caesar's adopted son, emerged victorious from the civil conflict that rocked the Republic after Caesar's assassination. The senate awarded him the title Augustus. This marble statue from Prima Porta, an idealized portrait, is based on Greek rather than Roman models. The statue was meant to be a propaganda piece, depicting a youthful general addressing his troops. At the bottom stands Cupid, the son of Venus, goddess of love, meant to be a reminder that the Julians, Caesar's family, claimed descent from Venus, thus emphasizing the ruler's divine background.

The New Order

In the new constitutional order that Augustus created, the basic governmental structure consisted of the *princeps* (Augustus) and an aristocratic senate. Augustus retained the senate as the chief deliberative body of the Roman state. Its decrees, screened in advance by the *princeps,* now had the effect of law. The title of *princeps*—first citizen of the state—carried no power in itself, but each year until 23 B.C., Augustus held the office of consul, which gave him *imperium,* or the right to command (see Chapter 5). When Augustus gave up the consulship in 23 B.C., he was granted

THE ACHIEVEMENTS OF AUGUSTUS

THIS EXCERPT IS TAKEN from a text written by Augustus and inscribed on a bronze tablet at Rome. Copies of the text in stone were displayed in many provincial capitals. Called "the most famous ancient inscription," the *Res Gestae* of Augustus summarizes his accomplishments in three major areas: his offices, his private expenditures on behalf of the state, and his exploits in war and peace. Though factual in approach, it is a highly subjective account.

Augustus, *Res Gestae*

Below is a copy of the accomplishments of the deified Augustus by which he brought the whole world under the empire of the Roman people, and of the moneys expended by him on the state and the Roman people, as inscribed on two bronze pillars set up in Rome.

1. At the age of nineteen, on my own initiative and at my own expense, I raised an army by means of which I liberated the Republic, which was oppressed by the tyranny of a faction [Mark Antony and his supporters]. . . .

2. Those who assassinated my father [Julius Caesar, his adoptive father] I drove into exile, avenging their crime by due process of law; and afterwards when they waged war against the state, I conquered them twice on the battlefield.

3. I waged many wars throughout the whole world by land and by sea, both civil and foreign, and when victorious I spared all citizens who sought pardon. . . .

5. The dictatorship offered to me . . . by the people and the senate, both in my absence and in my presence, I refused to accept. . . .

17. Four times I came to the assistance of the treasury with my own money, transferring to those in charge of the treasury 150,000,000 sesterces. And in the consulship of Marcus Lepidus and Lucius Arruntius I transferred out of my own patrimony 170,000,000 sesterces to the soldiers' bonus fund, which was established on my advice for the purpose of providing bonuses for soldiers who had completed twenty or more years of service. . . .

20. . . . I repaired the conduits of the aqueducts which were falling into ruin in many places because of age. . . .

22. I gave a gladiatorial show three times in my own name, and five times in the names of my sons or grandsons; at these shows about 10,000 fought. . . .

25. I brought peace to the sea by suppressing the pirates. In that war I turned over to their masters for punishment nearly 30,000 slaves who had run away from their owners and taken up arms against the state. . . .

26. I extended the frontiers of all the provinces of the Roman people on whose boundaries were peoples not subject to our empire. . . .

27. I added Egypt to the empire of the Roman people. . . .

28. I established colonies of soldiers in Africa, Sicily, Macedonia, in both Spanish provinces, in Achaea, Asia, Syria, Narbonese Gaul, and Pisidia. Italy, moreover, has twenty-eight colonies established by me, which in my lifetime have grown to be famous and populous. . . .

35. When I held my thirteenth consulship, the senate, the equestrian order, and the entire Roman people gave me the title of "father of the country" and decreed that this title should be inscribed in the vestibule of my house, in the Julian senate house, and in the Augustan Forum on the pedestal of the chariot which was set up in my honor by decree of the senate. At the time I wrote this document I was in my seventy-sixth year.

---

maius imperium—greater *imperium* than all others. The consulship was now unnecessary. Moreover, very probably in 23 B.C., Augustus was given the power of a tribune without actually holding the office itself; this power enabled him to propose laws and veto any item of public business. Although officials continued to be elected, Augustus' authority ensured that his candidates for office usually won. This situation caused participation in elections to decline. Consequently, the popular assemblies, shorn of any real role in elections and increasingly overshadowed by the senate's decrees, gradually declined in importance.

Augustus proved highly popular. As the Roman historian Tacitus commented, "Indeed, he attracted everybody's goodwill by the enjoyable gift of peace. . . . Opposition did not exist."[2] The ending of the civil wars had greatly bolstered Augustus' popularity (see the box above). At the same time, his continuing control of the army, while making possible the Roman peace, was a crucial source of his power.

The Army

The peace of the Roman Empire depended on the army, and so did the security of the *princeps*. Though primarily responsible for guarding the frontiers of the empire, the army was also used to maintain domestic order within the provinces. Moreover, the army played an important social role. It was an agent of upward mobility for both officers and recruits and provided impetus for Romanization wherever the legions were stationed. The colonies of veterans established by Augustus throughout the empire proved especially valuable in Romanizing the provinces.

Augustus maintained a standing army of twenty-eight legions. Since each legion at full strength numbered 5,400 soldiers, the Roman Empire had an army of about 150,000 men, certainly not large either by modern standards or in terms of the size of the empire itself (the population of the empire was probably close to fifty million). Roman legionaries served twenty years and were recruited only from the citizenry and, under Augustus, largely from Italy. Augustus also maintained a large contingent of auxiliary forces enlisted from the subject peoples. They served as both light-armed troops and cavalry and were commanded by Roman officers as well as tribal leaders. During the principate of Augustus, the **auxiliaries** numbered around 130,000. They were recruited only from noncitizens, served for twenty-four years, and along with their families received citizenship after their terms of service.

The Praetorian Guard Augustus was responsible for establishing the **praetorian guard.** These "nine cohorts of elite troops," roughly nine thousand men, had the important task of guarding the person of the *princeps*. They were recruited from Roman citizens in Italy and served for sixteen years. Eventually, the praetorian guard would play an important role in making and deposing emperors.

The role of the *princeps* as military commander gave rise to a title by which this ruler eventually came to be known. When victorious, a military commander was acclaimed by his troops as *imperator*. Augustus was so acclaimed on a number of occasions. *Imperator* is our word

emperor. Although such a title was applied to Augustus and his successors, Augustus still preferred to use the title *princeps*. Not until the reign of Vespasian (69–79) did *emperor* become the common title for the Roman ruler.

Roman Provinces and Frontiers

Augustus inaugurated a new system for governing the provinces. Under the Republic, the senate had appointed the provincial governors. Now certain provinces were allotted to the *princeps*, who assigned deputies known as *legates* to govern them. These legates were from the senatorial class and held office as long as the emperor chose. The remaining provinces were designated as senatorial provinces. They continued to be ruled by proconsuls and propraetors as governors who were appointed annually by lot for one year and reported directly to the senate. Although a dual system of provincial administration seemed to have been created, in reality the greater proconsular *imperium* that had been granted to Augustus gave him the power to overrule the senatorial governors and thus to establish a unified imperial policy. Because all provincial governors, whether of imperial or senatorial provinces, now received regular salaries, there was less need for the kind of extortion that had characterized provincial administration in the late Republic. In general, although there were still abuses, especially in the area of tax collection, provincial administration under Augustus was more efficient than under the Republic, and provincials were better protected against abuses of power.

Since a governor had relatively few administrative officials to assist him, effective government of the provinces necessitated considerable cooperation from local authorities. By supporting the power of local elites—the upper classes—in return for their cooperation, Roman policy encouraged a substantial degree of self-government and local autonomy in the cities. By fostering municipal life, Rome essentially made cities and city-states the basic units of imperial administration. City councils of leading citizens made for stable local government, and leading city officials were rewarded for their administrative services with Roman citizenship.

Frontier Policy Augustus' frontier policy was not wholly defensive, as it is sometimes portrayed. He was not immune to the glories of military conquest and in fact added more territory to the Roman Empire than any other single Roman. In the east, instead of creating new provinces, Augustus encouraged the establishment of client kingdoms, a policy that enabled him to minimize the Roman military presence in the east so that he could use his forces elsewhere. After the final pacification of Spain in 19 B.C., the *princeps* expended his greatest mil-

The Praetorian Guard. Augustus was responsible for setting up the praetorian guard as an imperial bodyguard of elite troops. Pictured in this second-century relief are members of the praetorian guard. Their body armor was like that of the legionaries, although the cohort serving in the palace wore togas.

itary efforts along the northern frontiers of the Roman Empire. He conquered the central and maritime Alps and then expanded Roman control of the Balkan peninsula up to the Danube River.

The extension of Roman power to the Danube now opened the door for Augustus' major military project—expansion into Germany. After 15 B.C., Roman forces advanced across the Rhine and by 9 B.C. had reached the Elbe River in eastern Germany. In A.D. 6, the Romans began another advance between the Elbe and the Danube but encountered a series of difficulties, including the great catastrophe of A.D. 9 when three Roman legions under Varus were massacred in the Teutoburg Forest by a coalition of German tribes led by Arminius, a German tribal leader who had served in the Roman auxiliary forces and had even received Roman citizenship. Roman historians blamed Varus for the disaster: "He [Varus] entertained the notion that the Germans were a people who were men only in voice and limbs. . . . With this purpose in mind, he entered the heart of Germany as though he were going among a people enjoying the blessings of peace."[3] The defeat severely dampened Augustus' enthusiasm for continued expansion in central Europe. Thereafter, the Romans were content to use the Rhine as the frontier between the Roman province of Gaul and the German tribes to the east. In fact, Augustus' difficulties had convinced him that "the empire should not be extended beyond its present frontiers."[4] His defeats in Germany taught Augustus that Rome's power was limited. They also left him devastated; for months he would beat his head against a door and shout, "Varus, give me back my legions!"

Augustan Society

Society in the Early Roman Empire was characterized by a system of social stratification, inherited from the Republic, in which Roman citizens were divided into three basic classes: the senatorial, equestrian, and lower classes.

The Social Order   Augustus had accepted the senatorial order as a ruling class for the empire. Senators filled the chief magistracies of the Roman government, held the most important military posts, and governed the provinces. One needed to possess property worth 1 million sesterces (an unskilled laborer in Rome received 3 sesterces a day; a Roman legionary, 900 sesterces a year in pay) to belong to the senatorial order. When Augustus took charge, the senate had over a thousand members. Augustus revised the senatorial list and reduced its size to six hundred but also added new men from wealthy families throughout Italy. Overall, Augustus was successful in winning the support of the senatorial class for his new order.

The equestrian order was expanded under Augustus and given a share of power in the new imperial state. The order was open to all Roman citizens of good standing who possessed property valued at 400,000 sesterces. They could now hold military and governmental offices, but the positions open to them were less important than those held by

the senatorial order. At the end of his career, an equestrian might be rewarded by membership in the senatorial order.

Citizens not of the senatorial or equestrian orders belonged to the lower classes, who obviously constituted the overwhelming majority of the free citizens. The diminution of the power of the Roman assemblies ended whatever political power they may have possessed earlier in the Republic. Many of these people were provided with free grain and public spectacles to keep them from creating disturbances. Nevertheless, by gaining wealth and serving as lower officers in the Roman legions, it was sometimes possible for them to advance to the equestrian order.

Augustus' Reforms   Augustus was very concerned about certain aspects of Rome's social health. He believed that the civil strife of the first century B.C. had sapped the strength of public religion, which he considered the cornerstone of a strong state. Therefore, he restored traditional priesthoods that had fallen into disuse in the late Republic, rebuilt many ruined temples and shrines, and constructed new ones to honor the Roman gods.

Augustus also instituted a new religious cult that would serve to strengthen the empire. Since the Roman state was intimately tied to Roman religion, an imperial cult served as a unifying instrument for the Roman world. Augustus did not claim to be a god, but he did permit the construction of temples to his deified adoptive father, Julius Caesar. Augustus also permitted the building of temples to Augustus and Roma, the personification of the Roman state. The worship of Augustus and Roma became the foundation of the imperial cult. Its development was furthered when Augustus was acclaimed as a god upon his death.

Augustus' belief that Roman morals had been corrupted during the late Republic led him to initiate social legislation to arrest the decline. He thought that increased luxury had undermined traditional Roman frugality and simplicity and caused a decline in morals, evidenced by easy divorce, a falling birthrate among the upper classes, and lax behavior manifested in hedonistic parties and the love affairs of prominent Romans with fashionable women and elegant boys.

Through his new social legislation, Augustus hoped to restore respectability to the upper classes and reverse the declining birthrate as well. Expenditures for feasts were limited, and other laws made adultery a criminal offense. In fact, Augustus exiled his own daughter Julia for adultery—a rather hypocritical act in view of Augustus' numerous sexual affairs. Augustus also revised the tax laws to penalize bachelors, widowers, and married persons who had fewer than three children.

A Golden Age of Latin Literature

The high point of Latin literature was reached in the time of Augustus. The literary accomplishments of the Augustan Age were such that the period has been called the golden age of Latin literature.

Virgil The most distinguished poet of the Augustan Age was Virgil (70–19 B.C.). The son of a small landholder in northern Italy, he welcomed the rule of Augustus and wrote his greatest work in the emperor's honor. Virgil's masterpiece was *The Aeneid,* an epic poem clearly meant to rival the work of Homer. The connection between Troy and Rome is made explicitly. Aeneas, the son of Anchises of Troy, survives the destruction of Troy and eventually settles in Latium; thus Roman civilization is linked to Greek history. The character of Aeneas is portrayed in terms that remind us of the ideal Roman—his virtues are duty, piety, and faithfulness. Virgil's overall purpose was to show that Aeneas had fulfilled his mission to establish the Romans in Italy and thereby start Rome on its divine mission to rule the world:

> Let others fashion from bronze more lifelike, breathing images—
> For so they shall—and evoke living faces from marble;
> Others excel as orators, others track with their instruments
> The planets circling in heaven and predict when stars will appear.
> But, Romans, never forget that government is your medium!
> Be this your art:—to practice men in the habit of peace,
> Generosity to the conquered, and firmness against aggressors.[5]

As Virgil expressed it, ruling was Rome's gift.

Horace Another prominent Augustan poet was Horace (65–8 B.C.), a friend of Virgil. Horace was a very sophisticated writer whose overriding concern seems to have been to point out to his contemporaries the "follies and vices of his age." In the *Satires,* a medley of poems on a variety of subjects, Horace is revealed as a detached observer of human weaknesses. He directed his attacks against movements, not living people, and took on such subjects as sexual immorality, greed, and job dissatisfaction ("How does it happen, Maecenas, that no man alone is content with his lot?"[6]). Horace mostly laughs at the weaknesses of humankind and calls for forbearance: "Supposing my friend has got liquored and wetted my couch. . . . Is he for such a lapse to be deemed less dear as a friend, or because when hungry he snatched up before me a chicken from my side of the dish?"[7] In his final work, the *Epistles,* Horace used another Greek form—the imaginary letter in verse—to provide a portrait of his friends and society and the things he held most dear: a simple life, good friends, and his beloved countryside.

Ovid Ovid (43 B.C.–A.D. 18) was the last of the great poets of the golden age. He belonged to a privileged group of Roman youths who liked to ridicule old Roman values. In keeping with the spirit of this group, Ovid wrote a frivolous series of love poems known as the *Amores.* Intended to entertain and shock, they achieved their goal. Ovid's most popular work was the *Metamorphoses,* a series of fifteen complex mythological tales involving transformations of shapes, such as the change of chaos into order. A storehouse of mythological information, the *Metamorphoses* inspired many Western painters, sculptors, and writers, including Shakespeare.

Another of Ovid's works was *The Art of Love.* This was essentially a takeoff on didactic poems. Whereas authors of earlier didactic poems had written guides to farming, hunting, or some such subject, Ovid's work was a handbook on the seduction of women (see the box on p. 143). *The Art of Love* appeared to applaud the loose sexual morals of the Roman upper classes at a time when Augustus was trying to clean up the mores of upper-class Rome. The *princeps* was not pleased. Ovid chose to ignore the wishes of Augustus and paid a price for it. In A.D. 8, Ovid was implicated in a sexual scandal, possibly involving the emperor's daughter Julia. He was banished to a small town on the coast of the Black Sea and died in exile.

Livy The most famous Latin prose work of the golden age was written by the historian Livy (59 B.C.–A.D. 17). Livy's masterpiece was a history of Rome from the foundation of the city to 9 B.C., written in 142 books. Only 35 of the books have survived, although we do possess brief summaries of the whole work from other authors. Livy perceived history in terms of moral lessons. He stated in the preface:

> The study of history is the best medicine for a sick mind; for in history you have a record of the infinite variety of human experience plainly set out for all to see; and in that record you can find for yourself and your country both examples and warnings: fine things to take as models, base things, rotten through and through, to avoid.[8]

For Livy, human character was the determining factor in history.

Livy's history celebrated Rome's greatness. He built scene upon scene that not only revealed the character of the chief figures but also demonstrated the virtues that had made Rome great. Of course, he had serious weaknesses as a historian. He was not always concerned about the factual accuracy of his stories and was not overly critical of his sources. But he did tell a good tale, and his work remained the standard history of Rome for centuries.

The Augustan Age was a lengthy one. Augustus died in A.D. 14 after dominating the Roman world for forty-five years. He had created a new order while placating the old by restoring and maintaining traditional values, a fitting combination for a leader whose favorite maxim was "Make haste slowly." By the time of his death, his new order was so well established that few Romans agitated for an alternative. Indeed, as the Roman historian Tacitus pointed out, "Actium had been won before the younger men were born. Even most of the older generation had come into a world of civil wars. Practically no one had ever seen truly Republican government. . . . Political equality was a thing of the past; all eyes watched for imperial commands."[9] The Republic was now only a memory and, given its last century of warfare, an unpleasant one at that. The new order was here to stay.

*O*VID HAS BEEN CALLED the last great poet of the Augustan golden age of literature. One of his most famous works was *The Art of Love,* a guidebook for the seduction of women. Unfortunately for Ovid, the work appeared at a time when Augustus was anxious to improve the morals of the Roman upper class. Augustus considered the poem offensive, and Ovid soon found himself in exile.

Ovid, *The Art of Love*

Now I'll teach you how to captivate and hold the woman of your choice. This is the most important part of all my lessons. Lovers of every land, lend an attentive ear to my discourse; let goodwill warm your hearts, for I am going to fulfill the promises I made you.

First of all, be quite sure that there isn't a woman who cannot be won, and make up your mind that you will win her. Only you must prepare the ground. Sooner would the birds cease their song in the springtime, or the grasshopper be silent in the summer, . . . than a woman resist the tender wooing of a youthful lover. . . .

Now the first thing you have to do is to get on good terms with the fair one's maid. She can make things easy for you. Find out whether she is fully in her mistress's confidence, and if she knows all about her secret dissipations. Leave no stone unturned to win her over. Once you have her on your side, the rest is easy. . . .

In the first place, it's best to send her a letter, just to pave the way. In it you should tell her how you dote on her; pay her pretty compliments and say all the nice things lovers always say. . . . And promise, promise, promise. Promises will cost you nothing. Everyone's a millionaire where promises are concerned. . . .

If she refuses your letter and sends it back unread, don't give up; hope for the best and try again. . . .

Don't let your hair stick up in tufts on your head; see that your hair and your beard are decently trimmed. See also that your nails are clean and nicely filed; don't have any hair growing out of your nostrils; take care that your breath is sweet, and don't go about reeking like a billy-goat. . . .

When you find yourself at a feast where the wine is flowing freely, and where a woman shares the same couch with you, pray to that god whose mysteries are celebrated during the night, that the wine may not overcloud your brain. 'Tis then you may easily hold converse with your mistress in hidden words whereof she will easily divine the meaning. . . .

By subtle flatteries you may be able to steal into her heart, even as the river insensibly overflows the banks which fringe it. Never cease to sing the praises of her face, her hair, her taper fingers and her dainty foot. . . .

Tears, too, are a mighty useful resource in the matter of love. They would melt a diamond. Make a point, therefore, of letting your mistress see your face all wet with tears. Howbeit, if you can't manage to squeeze out any tears— and they won't always flow just when you want them to— put your finger in your eyes.

The Early Empire (14–180)

There was no serious opposition to Augustus' choice of successor, his stepson Tiberius. By designating a family member as *princeps,* Augustus established the Julio-Claudian dynasty; the next four rulers were related either to his own family or to that of his wife, Livia.

The Julio-Claudians (14–68)

The Julio-Claudian rulers varied greatly in ability. Tiberius (14–37) was a competent general and an able administrator who tried initially to involve the senate in government. Caligula (37–41) was a grandnephew of Tiberius and great-grandson of Augustus. He exhibited tyrannical behavior and was excessively erratic. Claudius (41–54) had been mistreated by his family because of a physical disability due to partial paralysis, but he was intelligent, well educated, and competent. He was followed by Nero (54–68), who was only sixteen when he came to power. Nero's interest in the arts caused him to neglect affairs of state, especially the military, and that proved to be his undoing.

Several major tendencies emerged during the reigns of the four Julio-Claudians. In general, more and more of the responsibilities that Augustus had given to the senate tended to be taken over by the emperors. Moreover, an imperial bureaucracy was instituted under Claudius. He rationalized the central government by developing bureaucratic departments with talented freedmen as their chiefs. This practice further undermined the authority of the senators, who had previously shared in these responsibilities.

As the Julio-Claudian successors of Augustus began to behave openly like real rulers rather than "first citizens of the state," the opportunity for arbitrary and corrupt acts increased. Caligula, who became mentally unbalanced, wanted to be hailed as a god and neglected affairs of state while indulging his passions. Nero freely eliminated people he wanted out of the way, including his own mother, whom he had murdered. Without troops, the senators proved unable to oppose these excesses. Only the praetorian guard established by Augustus seemed capable of interfering with these rulers but did so in a manner that did not bode well for future stability. Caligula proved so capricious that the officers of the praetorian guard hatched a plot and assassinated him before he had ruled for four complete years. Afterward, they chose Claudius, uncle of Caligula, as the next emperor and forced the senate to confirm their act, thereby demonstrating the power of the military units stationed around Rome.

THE FATE OF CREMONA IN THE YEAR OF THE FOUR EMPERORS

*A*FTER THE DEATH of Nero in A.D. 68, a power struggle ensued that resulted in a year of confusion with four different emperors, each the leader of a field army. Galba replaced Nero and was succeeded by Otho, who was then defeated by Vitellius. Finally, Vespasian established a new dynasty. Some of the Italian cities suffered greatly in these struggles between Roman legions loyal to their commanders. This excerpt is from Tacitus' account of the destruction of Cremona by the forces that had declared for Vespasian.

Tacitus, *The Histories*

Forty thousand armed men forced their way into the city.... Neither rank nor years saved the victims from an indiscriminate orgy in which rape alternated with murder and murder with rape. Graybeards and frail old women, who had no value as loot, were dragged off to raise a laugh. But any full-grown girl or good-looking lad who crossed their path was pulled this way and that in a violent tug-of-war between the would-be captors, and finally drove them to destroy each other. A single looter trailing a hoard of money or temple-offerings of massive gold was often cut to pieces by others who were stronger. Some few turned up their noses at the obvious finds and inflicted flogging and torture on the owners in order to rummage after hidden valuables and dig for buried treasure. In their hands they held firebrands, which, once they had got their spoil away, they wantonly flung into the empty houses and rifled temples. It is not surprising that, in an army of varied tongues and conventions, including Romans, allies and foreigners [auxiliaries], there was a diversity of wild desires, differing conceptions of what was lawful, and nothing barred. Cremona lasted them four days. While all its buildings, sacred and secular, collapsed in flames, only the temple of Melitis [goddess of pestilential vapors] outside the walls remained standing, defended by its position or the power of the divinity.

The downfall of the Julio-Claudian dynasty came during the reign of Nero. His early reign had been quite successful. The young emperor worked hard and with the assistance of his childhood tutor, the philosopher Seneca, gave the empire a sound government. But Nero soon tired of his duties and began to pursue other interests, including singing, acting, horse racing, and sexual activities. After Seneca resigned his position in disgust in 62, Nero's rule deteriorated. His obsession with singing and acting in public was greeted with contempt by the senatorial class. At the same time, he aroused animosity by executing a number of prominent figures, including a popular general, on a charge of treason. His actions finally led to a conspiracy, not by the praetorian guard, but by the Roman legions themselves. In 68, Galba, governor of one of the Spanish provinces, rose in revolt and secured the principate for himself. Nero, abandoned by his guards, chose to commit suicide by stabbing himself in the throat after uttering his final words, "What an artist the world is losing in me."

The Flavians (69–96)

Galba, however, was not readily accepted by the other provincial armies, which led to civil wars in 69, known as the year of the four emperors (see the box above). Finally, Vespasian, commander of the legions in the east, established himself as sole ruler and his family as a new dynasty known as the Flavians. The significance of the year 69 was summed up precisely by Tacitus when he stated that "a well-hidden secret of the principate had been revealed: it was possible, it seemed, for an emperor to be chosen outside Rome"[10]—chosen, of course, by members of the Roman army.

The accession of Vespasian to the imperial power *needed military backing* demonstrated that it was no longer necessary to be descended from an ancient aristocratic family to be emperor. In fact, the family of Vespasian (69–79) was from the equestrian order. Once in control, he managed to reestablish the economy on a sound basis after the extravagances of Nero and the destruction wrought by the civil wars of 69. More important, Vespasian had no compunctions whatever about establishing the principle of dynastic succession for the principate. He was followed by his sons Titus (79–81) and Domitian (81–96). The Flavians, especially Domitian, dropped the pretense of the word *princeps* and began to use the title of *imperator,* emperor, freely. The emperor was rapidly becoming an absolute monarch.

The Five "Good Emperors" (96–180)

Many historians see the **Pax Romana** (the Roman peace) and the prosperity it engendered as the chief benefits of Roman rule during the first and second centuries A.D. These benefits were especially noticeable during the reigns of the five so-called **good emperors.** These rulers treated the ruling classes with respect, cooperated with the senate, ended arbitrary executions, maintained peace in the empire, and supported domestic policies generally beneficial to the empire. Though absolute monarchs, they were known for their tolerance and diplomacy.

The first of the five good emperors was Nerva (96–98), chosen by the senate after the assassination of Domitian. By chance, Nerva and his next three successors had no sons and had to resort to adoption to obtain heirs. According to one Roman historian, "Nerva, therefore, finding himself held in such contempt by reason of his old age, ascended the Capital and said in a loud voice: 'May good success

Julio-Claudian Dynasty	
Augustus	31 B.C.–A.D. 14
Tiberius	14–37
Caligula	37–41
Claudius	41–54
Nero	54–68
Flavian Dynasty	
Vespasian	69–79
Titus	79–81
Domitian	81–96
Five Good Emperors	
Nerva	96–98
Trajan	98–117
Hadrian	117–138
Antoninus Pius	138–161
Marcus Aurelius	161–180

attend the Roman senate and people and myself: I hereby adopt Marcus Ulpius Nerva Trajan."[11] Trajan (98–117) was a capable man who was also acceptable to the army, an increasingly important requirement. He had been born in Spain to an old Roman family and was the first emperor born outside Italy.

Trajan was succeeded by his second cousin Hadrian (117–138), who spent years inspecting the provinces and restoring the military forces to good order. Hadrian adopted as his successor Antoninus Pius (138–161), who achieved a reputation as the most beneficent of the five good emperors. It was said of him that "one should behave in all things like a pupil of Antoninus: his energy on behalf of what was done in accord with reason, his equability everywhere, his serene expression, his sweetness, his disdain of glory, his ambition to grasp affairs."[12] Unlike Hadrian, who traveled extensively in the provinces, Antonius Pius stayed in Rome and made even greater use of the senate. He in turn adopted Marcus Aurelius (161–180), who has been viewed as a philosopher-king of the sort Plato envisioned (see Chapter 3). Highly influenced by Stoicism, Marcus Aurelius wrote his *Meditations,* reflecting the ideal of Stoic duty as a religious concept.

Under the five good emperors, the powers of the emperor continued to expand at the expense of the senate. Increasingly, imperial officials appointed and directed by the emperor took over the running of the government. The five good emperors also extended the scope of imperial administration to areas previously untouched by the imperial government. Trajan established a program that provided state funds to assist poor parents in raising and educating their children. He was not motivated simply by benevolence, since he believed that such assistance would materially aid in creating a larger pool of young men in Italy eligible for military service.

The five good emperors were widely praised by their subjects for their extensive building programs. Trajan and Hadrian were especially active in constructing public works—aqueducts, bridges, roads, and harbor facilities—throughout the provinces and in Rome. Trajan built a new forum in Rome to provide a setting for his celebrated victory column. Hadrian's Pantheon, a temple of "all the gods," is one of the grandest ancient buildings surviving in Rome.

The Roman Empire at Its Height: Frontiers and Provinces

At its height in the second century, the Roman Empire (see Map 6.1) covered about 3.5 million square miles and had a population, like that of Han China, estimated at more than fifty million. While the emperors and the imperial administration provided a degree of unity, considerable leeway was given to local customs, and the privileges of Roman citizenship were extended to many people throughout the empire. In A.D. 212, the emperor Caracalla completed the process by giving Roman citizenship to every free inhabitant of the empire. Latin was the language of the western part of the empire, while Greek was used in the east. Although Roman culture spread to all parts of the empire, there were limits to Romanization since local languages persisted and many of the empire's residents spoke neither Latin nor Greek.

Roman Frontiers   With the exception of Claudius' annexation of Britain, the first-century successors of Augustus had largely followed his advice to curb expansion and remain within the natural frontiers of the empire—the ocean to the west, the rivers in the north, and the desert in the east and south. Two areas prompted special concern. The Rhine-Danube frontier in the north became the most heavily fortified border area because of the threat from restless barbarian tribes. In the east, the Romans used a system of client states to serve as a buffer against the troublesome Parthians.

Although Trajan broke with Augustus' policy of defensive imperialism by extending Roman rule into Dacia (modern Romania), Mesopotamia, and the Sinai peninsula, his conquests represent the high-water mark of Roman expansion. His successors recognized that the empire was overextended and pursued a policy of retrenchment. Hadrian withdrew Roman forces from much of Mesopotamia. Although he retained Dacia and Arabia, he went on the defensive in his frontier policy, reinforcing the fortifications along a line connecting the Rhine and Danube Rivers and building a defensive wall 80 miles long across northern Britain. By the end of the second century, the vulnerability of the empire had become apparent. Frontiers were stabilized, and the Roman forces were established in permanent bases behind the frontiers. But when one frontier was attacked, troops had to be drawn from other

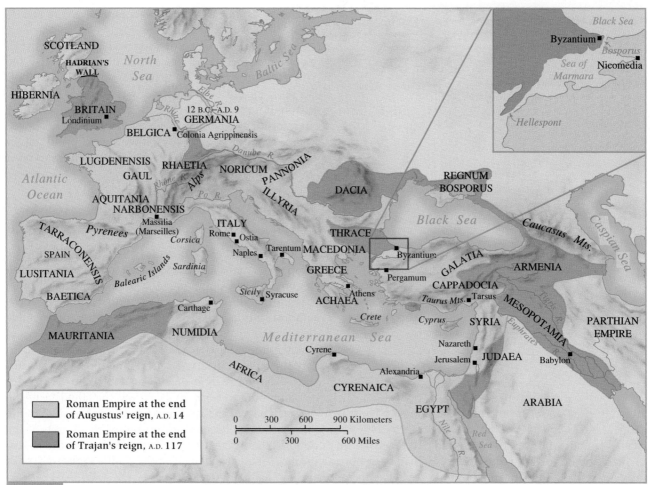

MAP 6.1 **The Roman Empire from Augustus to Trajan (14–117).** Augustus and later emperors continued the expansion of the Roman Empire, adding more resources but also increasing the tasks of administration and keeping the peace. Compare this map with Map 5.3. ❓ Which territories were conquered by Augustus, and which were added by the end of Trajan's reign? 🌐 **View an animated version of this map or related maps at** http://history.wadsworth.com/spielvogel06/

frontiers, leaving them vulnerable. The empire lacked a real strategic reserve, and its weakness would become ever more apparent.

Role of the Army   The Roman army was the primary instrument for the defense of the Roman frontiers. In A.D. 14, it numbered twenty-five legions but had increased to thirty by the time of Trajan. The auxiliaries were increased correspondingly, making a Roman army of about 400,000 by the end of the second century. Since legionaries had to be Roman citizens, most recruits in Augustus' time were from Italy. But in the course of the first century, the Italians' reluctance to serve in the military led to the recruitment of citizens from the provinces. By A.D. 100, only one in five of the legionaries was Italian.

In addition to defense and protection, the Roman army also served as an important instrument for Romanizing the provinces. Roman military camps became centers for the spread of the Latin language and Roman institutions and ways of thought and conduct. The presence of large num-

bers of troops and their dependent women and slaves encouraged the development of trade and local production to meet the army's need for supplies. Urban centers developed around army bases or nearby colonies. Many cities along the Rhine had their roots in legionary bases or auxiliary forts. The city of Cologne, for example, grew out of the military colony the Romans called Colonia Agrippinensis.

Importance of Cities   The administration and cultural life of the Roman Empire depended greatly on cities and towns. A provincial governor's staff was not large, so it was left to local city officials to act as Roman agents in carrying out many government functions, especially those related to taxes. Most towns and cities were not large by modern standards. The largest was Rome, but there were also some large cities in the east: Alexandria in Egypt numbered over 300,000 inhabitants, Ephesus in Asia Minor had 200,000, and Antioch in Syria had around 150,000. In the west, cities were usually small, with only a few thousand inhabitants. Cities were important in the spread of things Roman. They

Rome in Germany. The Roman army helped bring Roman culture and institutions to the provinces. Local production and trade grew up around the military camps to meet the soldiers' needs, and cities often developed from the bases themselves or from colonies located nearby. Pictured are the remains of the Porta Nigra, or gateway to the Roman city of Augusta Treverorum (modern Trier). In the Early Empire, Trier became the headquarters of the imperial procurator of Belgica and the two Germanies. Its close location to Roman military camps along the Rhine enabled it to flourish as one of the most significant cities in the western Roman Empire.

were also uniform in physical appearance, with similar temples, markets, amphitheaters, and other public buildings.

Magistrates and town councillors chosen from the ranks of the wealthy upper classes directed municipal administration. These municipal offices were unsalaried but were nevertheless desired by wealthy citizens because the offices conferred prestige and power at the local level as well as Roman citizenship. Roman municipal policy effectively tied the upper classes to Roman rule and ensured that these classes would retain control over the rest of the population.

The process of Romanization in the provinces was reflected in significant changes in the governing classes of the empire. In the course of the first century, there was a noticeable decline in the number of senators from Italian families. By the end of the second century, Italian senators made up less than half the total. Increasingly, the Roman senate was being recruited from wealthy provincial equestrian families. The provinces also provided many of the legionaries for the Roman army and, beginning with Trajan, supplied many of the emperors.

Prosperity in the Early Empire

The Early Empire was a period of considerable prosperity. Internal peace resulted in unprecedented levels of trade (see Map 6.2). Merchants from all over the empire came to the chief Italian ports of Puteoli on the Bay of Naples and Ostia at the mouth of the Tiber. Trade extended beyond the Roman boundaries and included even goods from China. Chinese merchants traveled across Central Asia, forming part of the Silk Road, which became a regular overland route between west and east. By the first century A.D., Chinese goods, including silk and lacquerware, were being sent into the eastern part of the Roman Empire, in southwestern Asia, where they were traded for woolen textiles, glass, and precious stones. Moreover, the importation of large quantities of grain to feed the populace of Rome and an incredible quantity of luxury items for the wealthy upper classes in the west led to a steady drain of gold and silver coins from Italy and the west to the eastern part of the empire.

The Shipping of Grain. Trade was an important ingredient in the prosperity of the Early Empire. This tomb painting from Ostia, the port of Rome at the mouth of the Tiber River, shows workers loading grain onto the *Isis Giminiana,* a small merchant vessel, for shipment upriver to Rome. The captain of the ship stands by the rudder. Next to him is Abascantus, the ship's owner.

MAP 6.2 **Trade Routes and Products in the Roman Empire, c. 200.** Although still primarily an agrarian economy, the Roman Empire provided the single currency and stable conditions necessary for an expansion of trade in various commodities and products. An extensive system of roads and shipping routes also facilitated trade. ❓ What truth is there to the statement "All roads lead to Rome"?

View an animated version of this map or related maps at http://history.wadsworth.com/spielvogel06/

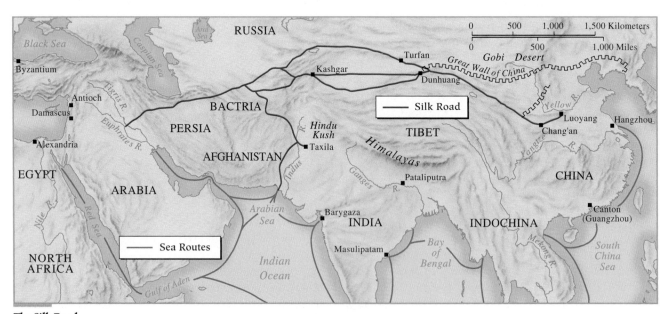

The Silk Road

The Daily Life of an Upper-Class Roman

HERE WAS AN enormous gulf between rich and poor in Roman society. The upper classes lived lives of great leisure and luxury in their villas and on their vast estates. Pliny the Younger (c. 62–c. 113) was an upper-class Roman who rose to the position of governor of Bithynia in Asia Minor. In this excerpt from one of his letters, Pliny describes a typical day vacationing at one of his Italian villas. Although Pliny owned four villas in Italy, we should note that he did not belong to the ranks of the really rich in Roman society.

Pliny, Letter to Fuscus Salinator

You want to know how I plan the summer days I spend in Tuscany. I wake when I like, usually about sunrise, often earlier but rarely later. My shutters stay closed, for in the stillness and darkness I feel myself surprisingly detached from any distractions and left to myself in freedom. . . . If I have anything on hand I work it out in my head, choosing and correcting the wording, and the amount I achieve depends on the ease or difficulty with which my thoughts can be marshaled and kept in my head. Then I call my secretary, the shutters are opened, and I dictate what I have put into shape; he goes out, is recalled, and again dismissed. Three or four hours after I first wake (but I don't keep to fixed times) I betake myself according to the weather either to the terrace or the covered arcade, work

out the rest of my subject, and dictate it. I go for a drive, and spend the time in the same way as when walking or lying down; my powers of concentration do not flag and are in fact refreshed by the change. After a short sleep and another walk I read a Greek or Latin speech aloud and with emphasis, not so much for the sake of my voice as my digestion, though of course both are strengthened by this. Then I have another walk, am oiled, take exercise, and have a bath. If I am dining alone with my wife or with a few friends, a book is read aloud during the meal and afterward we listen to a comedy or some music; then I walk again with the members of my household, some of whom are educated. Thus the evening is prolonged with varied conversations, and even when the days are at their longest, comes to a satisfying end.

Sometimes I vary this routine, for, if I have spent a long time on my couch or taking a walk, after my siesta and reading I go out on horseback instead of a carriage so as to be quicker and take less time. Part of the day is given up to friends who visit me from neighboring towns and sometimes come to my aid with a welcome interruption when I am tired. Occasionally I go hunting, but not without my notebooks so that I shall have something to bring home even if I catch nothing. I also give some time to my tenants (they think it should be more) and the boorishness of their complaints gives fresh zest to our literary interests and the more civilized pursuits of town.

Increased trade helped stimulate manufacturing. The cities of the east still produced the items made in Hellenistic times (see Chapter 4). The first two centuries of the empire also witnessed the high point of industrial development in Italy. Some industries became concentrated in certain areas, such as bronze work in Capua and pottery in Arretium in Etruria. Other industries, such as brickmaking, were pursued in rural areas on large landed estates. Much industrial production remained small-scale and was done by individual artisans, usually freedmen or slaves. In the course of the first century, Italian centers of industry experienced increasing competition from the provinces. Pottery produced in Gaul, for example, began to outsell Italian pottery from Arretium.

Despite the prosperity from trade and commerce, agriculture remained the chief occupation of most people and the underlying basis of Roman prosperity. While the large landed estates, the *latifundia,* still dominated agriculture, especially in southern and central Italy, small peasant farms persisted, particularly in Etruria and the Po valley. Although large estates concentrating on sheep and cattle raising used slave labor, the lands of some *latifundia* were worked by free tenant farmers called *coloni*. The *colonus* was essentially a sharecropper who paid rent in labor, produce, or sometimes cash.

In considering the prosperity of the Roman world, it is important to remember the enormous gulf between rich and poor underlying it (see the box above). The development of towns and cities, so important to the creation of any civilization, is based to a large degree on the agricultural surpluses of the countryside. In ancient times, the margin of surplus produced by each farmer was relatively small. Therefore, the upper classes and urban populations had to be supported by the labor of a large number of agricultural producers who never found it easy to produce much more than enough for themselves. In lean years, when there were no surpluses, the townspeople often took what they wanted, leaving little for the peasants.

Roman Culture and Society in the Early Empire

Although the cultural and social developments of the Early Empire were similar to those of the last century of the Republic, there were also significant changes as a result of the new imperial order.

The Silver Age of Latin Literature

In the history of Latin literature, the century and a half after Augustus is often labeled the "silver age" to indicate that the literary efforts of the period, while good, were not equal to the high standards of the Augustan "golden age." The popularity of rhetorical training encouraged the use of clever literary expressions, often at the expense of original and meaningful content. A good example of this trend can be found in the works of Seneca.

Seneca   Educated in Rome, Seneca (c. 4 B.C.–A.D. 65) became strongly attached to the philosophy of Stoicism (see Chapter 4). After serving as tutor to Nero, he helped run the government during the first five years of Nero's reign. Seneca began to withdraw from politics after Nero took a more active role in government. In 65, he was charged with involvement in a conspiracy against Nero and committed suicide at Nero's command.

In letters written to a young friend, Seneca expressed the basic tenets of Stoicism: living according to nature, accepting events dispassionately as part of the divine plan, and a universal love for all humanity. Thus "the first thing philosophy promises us is the feeling of fellowship, of belonging to mankind and being members of a community. . . . Philosophy calls for simple living, not for doing penance, and the simple way of life need not be a crude one."[13] Viewed in retrospect, Seneca displays some glaring inconsistencies. While preaching the virtues of simplicity, he amassed a fortune and was ruthless at times in protecting it. His letters show humanity, benevolence, and fortitude, but his sentiments are often undermined by an attempt to be clever with words.

The silver age also produced a work called the *Satyricon,* described by some literary historians as the first picaresque novel in Western literature. It was written by Petronius (d. 66), probably a former governor of Bithynia who had joined Nero's inner circle. The *Satyricon* is a humorous satire on the excesses of the Roman social scene. Basically, it is the story of a young man and his two male companions who engage in a series of madcap escapades and homosexual antics. The longest surviving episode contains a description of an elaborate and vulgar dinner party given by Trimalchio, a freedman who had become a millionaire through an inheritance from his former master. In Trimalchio, Petronius gave a hilarious, satirical portrait of Rome's new rich.

Tacitus   The greatest historian of the silver age was Tacitus (c. 56–120). His main works included the *Annals* and the *Histories,* which presented a narrative account of Roman history from the reign of Tiberius through the assassination of Domitian in 96. Tacitus believed that history had a moral purpose: "It seems to me a historian's foremost duty to ensure that merit is recorded, and to confront evil deeds and words with the fear of posterity's denunciations."[14] As a member of the senatorial class, Tacitus was disgusted with the abuses of power perpetrated by the emperors and was determined that the "evil deeds" of wicked men would not be forgotten. Many historians believe he went too far in projecting the evils of his own day back into his account of the past. Tacitus' work *Germania* is especially important as a source of information about the early Germans. But it too is colored by his attempt to show the Germans as noble savages in contrast to the decadent Roman upper classes.

Juvenal   By the second century A.D., though still influenced by the familiar Greek models, Latin authors were increasingly imitating the great Latin writers of earlier ages. This was evident in the work of Juvenal, the best poet of the silver age. Juvenal (c. 55–c. 128) wrote five books of satires in which he pilloried the manners and vices of his generation. He attacked the affectations of Roman women, the abuse of slaves, the excesses of emperors, the eastern and Greek immigrants, his own poverty, and the inequities of Roman society. For example: "They demand that the teacher shall mold these tender minds. . . . 'See to it,' you're told, and when the school year's ended, you'll get as much as a jockey makes from a single race."[15] But Juvenal was not a reformer. Though he attacked many vices, he offered no basic critique of his society.

Art in the Early Empire

The Romans contributed little that was original to painting and sculpture. Much work was done by Greek artists and craftspeople who adhered to the Roman desire for realism and attention to details. Wall paintings and frescoes in the houses of the rich realistically depicted landscapes, portraits, and scenes from mythological stories.

In architecture, the Romans continued to imitate Greek styles and made use of colonnades, rectangular structures, and post-and-lintel construction. But the Romans were innovative in their own way. They made considerable use of curvilinear forms: the arch, vault, and dome. The Romans were the first people in antiquity to use concrete on a massive scale. By combining concrete and curvilinear forms, they were able to construct massive buildings—public baths, such as those of Caracalla, and amphitheaters, the most famous of which was the Colosseum in Rome. These large buildings were made possible by Roman engineering skills. These same skills were put to use in constructing roads (the Romans built a network of 50,000 miles of roads throughout their empire), aqueducts (in Rome, almost a dozen aqueducts kept the population supplied with water), and bridges.

Imperial Rome

At the center of the colossal Roman Empire was the ancient city of Rome (see Map 6.3). Truly a capital city, Rome had the largest population of any city in the empire. It is estimated that its population was close to one million by the time of Augustus. For anyone with ambitions, Rome was the place to be. A magnet to many people, Rome was extremely

The Pantheon. Shown here is the Pantheon, one of Rome's greatest buildings. Constructed of brick, six kinds of concrete, and marble, it was a stunning example of the Romans' engineering skills. The outside porch of the Pantheon contained eighteen Corinthian granite columns, but it was the inside of the temple that amazed onlookers. The interior is a large circular space topped by a huge dome. A hole in the center of the roof was the only source of light. The dome, built up layer by layer, was made of concrete, weighing 5,000 tons. The walls holding the dome are almost 20 feet thick.

cosmopolitan. Nationalities from all over the empire resided there, with entire neighborhoods inhabited by specific groups, such as Greeks and Syrians.

Rome was no doubt an overcrowded and noisy city. Because of the congestion, cart and wagon traffic was banned from the streets during the day. The noise from the resulting vehicular movement at night often made sleep difficult. Evening pedestrian travel was dangerous. Although Augustus had organized a police force, lone travelers might be assaulted, robbed, or soaked by filth thrown out of the upper-story windows of Rome's massive apartment buildings.

An enormous gulf existed between rich and poor in the city of Rome. While the rich had comfortable villas, the poor lived in apartment blocks called *insulae*, which might be six stories high. Constructed of concrete, they were often poorly built and prone to collapse. The use of wooden beams in the floors and movable stoves, torches, candles, and lamps for heat and light made the danger of fire constant. Once started, fires were extremely difficult to put out. The famous conflagration of 64, which Nero was unjustly accused of starting, devastated a good part of the city.

Roman Aqueduct. The engineering skills of the Romans enabled them to build massive constructions, including aqueducts such as this one in southern France, known as the Pont du Gard. The Pont du Gard is a three-story bridge built of blocks of stone without cement, at the top of which was a channel that carried water. Nîmes received its water from a source 30 miles away. Since gravity kept the water flowing, channels holding the water had to have a gradual decline from the source of water to its final destination. The Pont du Gard, which crosses the Gardon River outside Nîmes, was built to the exact height needed to maintain the flow of water into the city.

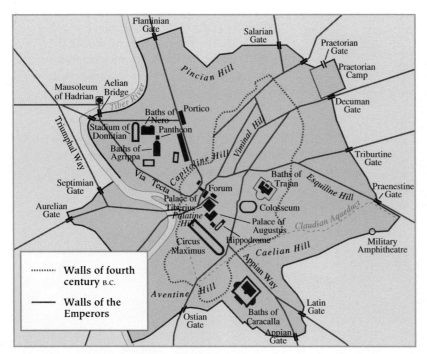

MAP 6.3 **Imperial Rome.** A large, overcrowded, and dirty city, Rome was the political, economic, social, and cultural hub of the Roman Empire. Squalid and desperate living conditions for the poor contrasted dramatically with the city's magnificent architectural works. ❓ How did roads from outside enter Rome, and what could possibly explain this? 🌐 **View an animated version of this map or related maps at** http://history .wadsworth .com/spielvogel06/

Besides the hazards of collapse and fire, living conditions were miserable. High rents forced entire families into one room. In the absence of plumbing and central heating, conditions were so uncomfortable that poorer Romans spent most of their time outdoors in the streets.

Fortunately for these people, Rome boasted public buildings unequaled anywhere in the empire. Its temples, forums, markets, baths, theaters, triumphal arches, governmental buildings, and amphitheaters gave parts of the city an appearance of grandeur and magnificence (see the box on p. 153).

Though the center of a great empire, Rome was also a great parasite. Beginning with Augustus, the emperors accepted responsibility for providing food for the urban populace, with about 200,000 people receiving free grain. Rome needed about six million sacks of grain a year and imported large quantities from its African and Egyptian provinces to meet these requirements. But even the free grain did not change the grim condition of the poor. Early in the second century A.D., a Roman doctor claimed that rickets was common among the city's children.

In addition to food, entertainment was also provided on a grand scale for the inhabitants of Rome. The poet Juvenal said of the Roman masses: "Nowadays, with no vote to sell, their motto is 'Couldn't care less.' Time was when their vote elected generals, heads of state, commanders of legions: but now they've pulled in their horns, there's only two things that concern them: Bread and Circuses."[16] The emperor and other state officials provided public spectacles as part of the great festivals—most of them religious in origin—celebrated by the state. More than one hundred days a year were given over to these public holidays. The festivals included three major types of entertainment. At the Circus Maximus, horse and chariot races attracted

hundreds of thousands, while dramatic and other performances were held in theaters. But the most famous of all the public spectacles were the gladiatorial shows.

The Gladiatorial Shows

The gladiatorial shows were an integral part of Roman society. They took place in amphitheaters; the first permanent one was constructed at Rome in 29 B.C. Perhaps the most famous was the Flavian amphitheater, called the Colosseum, constructed at Rome under Vespasian and his son Titus to seat fifty thousand spectators. Amphitheaters were constructed throughout the empire. They varied in size, with capacities ranging from a few thousand to tens of thousands. Considerable resources and ingenuity went into building them, especially in the arrangements for moving wild beasts efficiently into the arena. In most cities and towns, amphitheaters came to be the biggest buildings, rivaled only by the circuses for races and the public baths. As we shall see repeatedly in the course of Western civilization, where a society invests its money gives an idea of its priorities. Since the amphitheater was the primary location for the gladiatorial games, it is fair to say that public slaughter was an important part of Roman culture.

Programs of gladiatorial games lasted from dawn to dusk. Their main features were contests to the death between trained fighters. Most gladiators were slaves or condemned criminals, although some free men, lured by the hope of popularity and patronage by wealthy fans, participated voluntarily. They were trained for combat in special gladiatorial schools.

Gladiatorial games included other forms of entertainment as well. Criminals of all ages and both sexes were sent into the arena without weapons to face certain death from

THE PUBLIC BATHS OF THE ROMAN EMPIRE

THE PUBLIC BATHS in Rome and other cities played an important role in urban life. Introduced to Rome in the second century B.C. as a result of Greek influence, the number of public baths grew at a rapid pace in the Early Empire as the emperors contributed funds for their construction. The public baths were especially noisy near the end of the afternoon when Romans stopped in after work to use the baths before dinner. The following description is by Lucian, a traveling lecturer who lived in the second century. This selection is taken from *Hippias, or the Bath*.

Lucian, *Hippias, or the Bath*

The building suits the magnitude of the site, accords well with the accepted idea of such an establishment, and shows regard for the principles of lighting. The entrance is high, with a flight of broad steps of which the tread is greater than the pitch, to make them easy to ascend. On entering, one is received into a public hall of good size, with ample accommodations for servants and attendants. On the left are the lounging rooms, also of just the right sort for a bath, attractive, brightly lighted retreats. Then, besides them, a hall larger than need be for the purposes of a bath, but necessary for the reception of richer persons. Next, capacious locker rooms to undress in, on each side, with a very

high and brilliantly lighted hall between them, in which are three swimming pools of cold water. . . .

On leaving this hall, you come into another which is slightly warmed instead of meeting you at once with fierce heat; it is oblong, and has an apse on each side. Next to it, on the right, is a very bright hall, nicely fitted up for massage. . . . Then near this is another hall, the most beautiful in the world, in which one can stand or sit with comfort, linger without danger, and stroll about with profit. It also is radiant with Phrygian marble clear to the roof. Next comes the hot corridor, faced with Numidian marble. The hall beyond it is very beautiful, full of abundant light and aglow with color like that of purple hangings. It contains three hot tubs.

When you have bathed you need not go back through the same rooms, but can go directly to the cold room through a slightly warmed chamber. Everywhere there is copious illumination and full indoor daylight. . . . Why should I go on to tell you of the exercising floor and the cloak rooms? . . . Moreover, it is beautiful with all other marks of thoughtfulness—with two toilets, many exits, and two devices for telling time, a water clock that makes a bellowing sound and a sundial.

Interior of the Colosseum of Rome. The Colosseum was a large amphitheater constructed under the emperor Vespasian and his son Titus. Such amphitheaters, in which gladiatorial contests were held, were built throughout the empire. They varied in size, but the one at Rome was the largest. The Colosseum was named after the Colossus of Nero, a large statue of the first-century A.D. emperor that stood nearby. Although scene to many bloody gladiatorial spectacles, the arena of the Colosseum was also flooded for a spectacular naval battle when the emperor Titus held the first games there.

The Gladiatorial Games. Although some gladiators were free men enticed by the possibility of rewards, most were condemned criminals, slaves, or prisoners of war who were trained in special schools. A great gladiator could win his freedom through the games. This mosaic from the fourth century A.D. depicts different aspects of gladiatorial fighting and clearly shows the bloody nature of the contests.

wild animals who would tear them to pieces. Numerous kinds of animal contests were also held: wild beasts against each other, such as bears against buffalo; staged hunts with men shooting safely from behind iron bars; and gladiators in the arena with bulls, tigers, and lions. Reportedly, five thousand beasts were killed in one day of games when the emperor Titus inaugurated the Colosseum in A.D. 80. Enormous resources were invested in capturing and shipping wild animals for slaughter, and whole species were hunted to extinction in parts of the empire.

These bloodthirsty spectacles were extremely popular with the Roman people. Tacitus reported, "Few indeed are to be found who talk of any other subjects in their homes, and whenever we enter a classroom, what else is the conversation of the youths."[17] But the gladiatorial games served a purpose beyond mere entertainment. Like the other forms of public entertainment, the games fulfilled both a political and a social function. Certainly, the games served to divert the idle masses from political unrest. It was said of the emperor Trajan that he understood that although the distribution of grain and money satisfied the individual, spectacles were necessary for the "contentment of the masses."

Disaster in Southern Italy

Gladiatorial spectacles were contrived by humans, but the Roman Empire also experienced some horrific natural spectacles. One of the greatest was the eruption of Mount Vesuvius on August 24, 79. Although known to be a volcano, Vesuvius was thought to be extinct, its hillsides green with flourishing vineyards. Its eruption threw up thousands of tons of lava and ash. Toxic fumes killed many people, and the nearby city of Pompeii was quickly buried under volcanic ash. To the west, Herculaneum and other communities around the Bay of Naples were submerged beneath

a mud flow (see the box on p. 155). Not for another 1,700 years were systematic excavations begun on the buried towns. The examination of their preserved remains have enabled archaeologists to reconstruct the everyday life and art of these Roman towns. Their discovery in the eighteenth century was an important force in stimulating both scholarly and public interest in classical antiquity and helped give rise to the Neoclassical style of that century.

The Art of Medicine

Although early Romans had no professional physicians, they did possess an art of medicine. Early Roman medicine was essentially herbal. The *paterfamilias* would prepare various remedies to heal wounds and cure illnesses. Knowledge of the healing properties of plants was passed down from generation to generation. This traditional approach to medicine continued in the Early Empire. Of course, numerous recipes for nonillnesses, such as remedies to prevent baldness, were also passed on. One such formula consisted of wine, saffron, pepper, vinegar, *laserpicium* (the queen of Roman medicinal plants, now extinct), and rat dung.

As in other areas of Roman life, Greek influence was also felt in medicine. At the end of the third century B.C., scientific medicine entered the Roman world through professional practitioners from the Hellenistic world. Doctors became fashionable in Rome, although prejudice against them was never completely abandoned. Many were Greek slaves who belonged to the households of large aristocratic families. The first public doctors in Rome were attached to the Roman army. Military practices were then extended to imperial officials and their families in the provinces and included the establishment of public hospitals. Gladiatorial schools had their own resident doctors as well. In fact, one of the most famous physicians, the Greek Galen (129–199), emerged from the ranks of gladiatorial doctors

THE ERUPTION OF MOUNT VESUVIUS

PLINY THE YOUNGER, whose description of his villa we read in the box on p. 149, also wrote a letter to the Roman historian Tacitus describing the death of his uncle, Pliny the Elder, as a result of the eruption of Mount Vesuvius. Pliny the Elder was the commander of a fleet at Misenum. When the eruption occurred, his curiosity led him to take a detachment of his fleet to the scene. He landed at Stabiae, where he died from the toxic fumes.

Pliny, Letter to Cornelius Tacitus

Thank you for asking me to send you a description of my uncle's death so that you can leave an accurate account of it for posterity. . . . It is true that he perished in a catastrophe which destroyed the loveliest regions of the earth, a fate shared by whole cities and their people, and one so memorable that it is likely to make his name live for ever. . . .

My uncle was stationed at Misenum, in active command of the fleet. On 24 August, in the early afternoon, my mother drew his attention to a cloud of unusual size and appearance. . . . He called for his shoes and climbed up to a place which would give him the best view of the phenomenon. It was not clear at that distance from which mountain the cloud was rising (it was afterwards known to be Vesuvius); its general appearance can best be expressed as being like an umbrella pine, for it rose to a great height on a sort of trunk and then split off into branches, I imagine because it was thrust upwards by the first blast and then left unsupported as the pressure subsided, or else it was borne down by its own weight so that it spread out and gradually dispersed. In places it looked white, elsewhere blotched and dirty, according to the amount of soil and ashes it carried with it. My uncle's scholarly acumen saw at once that it was important enough for a closer inspection, and he ordered a boat to be made ready. . . .

[Unable to go further by sea, he lands at Stabiae.]

Meanwhile on Mount Vesuvius broad sheets of fire and leaping flames blazed at several points, their bright glare emphasized by the darkness of night. My uncle tried to allay the fears of his companions by repeatedly declaring that these were nothing but bonfires left by the peasants in their terror, or else empty houses on fire in the districts they had abandoned. . . .

They debated whether to stay indoors or take their chance in the open, for the buildings were now shaking with violent shocks, and seemed to be swaying to and fro as if they were torn from their foundations. Outside on the other hand, there was the danger of falling pumice-stones, even though these were light and porous; however, after comparing the risks they chose the latter. In my uncle's case one reason outweighed the other, but for the others it was a choice of fears. As a protection against falling objects they put pillows on their heads tied down with cloths.

Elsewhere there was daylight by this time, but they were still in darkness, blacker and denser than any ordinary night, which they relieved by lighting torches and various kinds of lamp. My uncle decided to go down to the shore and investigate on the spot the possibility of any escape by sea, but he found the waves still wild and dangerous. A sheet was spread on the ground for him to lie down, and he repeatedly asked for cold water to drink. Then the flames and smell of sulphur which gave warning of the approaching fire drove the others to take flight and roused him to stand up. He stood leaning on two slaves and then suddenly collapsed, I imagine because the dense fumes choked his breathing by blocking his windpipe which was constitutionally weak and narrow and often inflamed. When daylight returned on the 26th—two days after the last day he had seen—his body was found intact and uninjured, still fully clothed and looking more like sleep than death.

to become court physician to the emperor Marcus Aurelius. Roman scientific medicine also witnessed the development of numerous specialists. For example, Alcon, the famous surgeon of the Flavian age, specialized in bone diseases and hernia operations.

Roman Law in the Early Empire

The Early Empire experienced great progress in the study and codification of law. The second and early third centuries A.D. witnessed the "classical age of Roman law," a period in which a number of great jurists classified and compiled basic legal principles that have proved valuable to the Western world. Most jurists emphasized the emperor as the source of law: "What has pleased the emperor has the force of law."

In the "classical age of Roman law," the identification of the law of nations with natural law led to a concept of natural rights. According to the jurist Ulpian (d. 228), natural rights implied that all men are born equal and should therefore be equal before the law. In practice, however, the principle was not applied.

The Romans did, however, establish standards of justice, applicable to all people, that included principles that we would immediately recognize. A person was considered innocent until proved otherwise. People accused of wrongdoing were allowed to defend themselves before a judge. A judge was expected to weigh evidence carefully before arriving at a decision. These principles lived on in Western civilization long after the fall of the Roman Empire.

Principles of motion Law we still have today

THE ROMAN FEAR OF SLAVES

THE LOWEST STRATUM of the Roman population consisted of slaves. They were used extensively in households and the court, as craftspeople in industrial enterprises, as business managers, and in numerous other ways. Although some historians have argued that slaves were treated more humanely during the Early Empire, these selections by the Roman historian Tacitus and the Roman statesman Pliny indicate that slaves still rebelled against their masters because of mistreatment. Many masters continued to live in fear of their slaves, as witnessed by the saying "as many enemies as you have slaves."

Tacitus, *The Annals of Imperial Rome*

The City Prefect, Lucius Pedanius Secundus, was murdered by one of his slaves [in A.D. 61]. Either Pedanius had refused to free the murderer after agreeing to a price, or the slave, in a homosexual infatuation, found competition from his master intolerable. After the murder, ancient custom required that every slave residing under the same roof must be executed. But a crowd gathered, eager to save so many innocent lives; and rioting began. The senate-house was besieged. Inside, there was feeling against excessive severity, but the majority opposed any change. Among the latter was Gaius Cassius Longinus, who when his turn came spoke as follows. . . .

"An ex-consul has been deliberately murdered by a slave in his own home. None of his fellow-slaves prevented or betrayed the murderer, though the senatorial decree threatening the whole household with execution still stands. Exempt them from the penalty if you like. But then, if the City Prefect was not important enough to be immune, who will be? Who will have enough slaves to protect him if Pedanius' 400 were too few? Who can rely on his household's help if even fear for their own lives does not make them shield us?" [The sentence of death was carried out.]

Pliny, Letter to Acilius

This horrible affair demands more publicity than a letter—Larcius Macedo, a senator and ex-praetor, has fallen a victim to his own slaves. Admittedly he was a cruel and overbearing master, too ready to forget that his father had been a slave, or perhaps too keenly conscious of it. He was taking a bath in his house at Formiae when suddenly he found himself surrounded; one slave seized him by the throat while the others struck his face and hit him in the chest and stomach and—shocking to say—in his private parts. When they thought he was dead they threw him on to the hot pavement, to make sure he was not still alive. Whether unconscious or feigning to be so, he lay there motionless, thus making them believe that he was quite dead. Only then was he carried out, as if he had fainted with the heat, and received by his slaves who had remained faithful, while his concubines ran up, screaming fanatically. Roused by their cries and revived by the cooler air he opened his eyes and made some movement to show that he was alive, it being now safe to do so. The guilty slaves fled, but most of them have been arrested and a search is being made for the others. Macedo was brought back to life with difficulty, but only for a few days; at least he died with the satisfaction of having revenged himself, for he lived to see the same punishment meted out as for murder. There you see the dangers, outrages, and insults to which we are exposed. No master can feel safe because he is kind and considerate; for it is their brutality, not their reasoning capacity, which leads slaves to murder masters.

Slaves and Their Masters

The number of slaves had increased dramatically in the Roman Republic as the empire was expanded through warfare. Consequently, slaves were highly visible in the Early Empire. The residences of the rich were filled with slaves. Possessing a large number of slaves was a status symbol; a single household might include dozens of slaves, serving as hairdressers, footmen, messengers, accountants, secretaries, carpenters, plumbers, librarians, goldsmiths, and doctors as well as ordinary domestic servants. The reliance on slaves, especially as skilled craftspeople, undoubtedly created unemployment among the free population. Some slaves worked at high-status jobs as architects and managers of businesses, while some imperial slaves held positions in the government bureaucracy. Slaves were also used on landed estates.

But the number of slaves probably peaked in the Early Empire. The defensive imperial policies pursued after Augustus led to a decline in the supply of slaves from foreign conquest. Manumission also contributed to the decline in the number of slaves. It had been customary in Rome for "good masters" to free their slaves, especially well-educated ones or good workers. Although freedmen became Roman citizens, they were not given full rights of citizenship. They could vote but not run for office.

Many authors have commented on the supposed advance in humanitarian attitudes toward slaves in the Early Empire, especially in the second century. They argue that the philosophy of Stoicism, with its emphasis on the universality of humanity, had an influence in this direction. Seneca stressed the need for kindness to slaves. Very likely, however, the practical Romans were as much, if not more, concerned about the usefulness of their slaves than about any humanitarian attitudes. New laws in the second century moralized more than they actually improved the condition of slaves. Hadrian, for example, forbade the sale of slaves for immoral or gladiatorial purposes. Such laws had little impact, however, on how masters actually treated their slaves. Despite the changes, there were still instances of slaves murdering their owners, and Romans continued to live in unspoken fear of their slaves (see the box above).

The Upper-Class Roman Family

By the second century A.D., significant changes were occurring in the Roman family. The foundations of the authority of the *paterfamilias* over his family, which had already begun to weaken in the late Republic, were further undermined. The *paterfamilias* no longer had absolute authority over his children; he could no longer sell his children into slavery or have them put to death. Moreover, the husband's absolute authority over his wife also disappeared, a process that had begun in the late Republic. In the Early Empire, the idea of male guardianship continued to weaken significantly, and by the late second century, it had become a mere formality.

[margin note: decay of paterfamilias]

Upper-class Roman women in the Early Empire had considerable freedom and independence. They had acquired the right to own, inherit, and dispose of property. Upper-class women could attend races, the theater, and events in the amphitheater, although in the latter two places they were forced to sit in separate female sections. Moreover, ladies of rank were still accompanied by maids and companions when they went out. Some women operated businesses, such as shipping firms. Women still could not participate in politics, but the Early Empire saw a number of important women who influenced politics through their husbands, including Livia, the wife of Augustus; Agrippina, the mother of Nero; and Plotina, the wife of Trajan.

At the end of the first century and beginning of the second, there was a noticeable decline in the number of children among the upper classes, a trend that had already begun in the late Republic. Especially evident was an increase in childless marriages. Despite imperial laws aimed at increasing the number of children, the low birthrate persisted. Not only did **infanticide** continue to be practiced, but upper-class Romans also used contraception and abortion to limit their families. There were numerous techniques for contraception. Though highly touted, amulets, magical formulas, and potions to induce temporary sterility proved ineffective, as did the rhythm method, since Roman medical writers believed that a woman was most fertile just when menstruation was ending. A more dependable practice involved the use of oils, ointments, and soft wool to obstruct the opening of the uterus. Contraceptive techniques for males were also advocated. An early version of a condom involved using the bladder of a goat, but it was prohibitively expensive. Although the medical sources do not mention it, the Romans may also have used the ubiquitous coitus interruptus. Abortion was practiced, using drugs or surgical instruments. Ovid chastises Corinna: "Ah, women, why will you thrust and pierce with the instrument, and give dire poisons to your children yet unborn?"[18]

Women also faced great dangers in childbirth. The birth of a child occurred at home with the assistance of a midwife and a few female relatives. Fathers-to-be and other males were not present. Although exact numbers are not available, we do know that many upper-class women between the ages of sixteen and thirty-five died in childbirth. Prominent women who died in childbirth or soon after due to complications include Cicero's daughter Tullia and Caesar's daughter Julia.

Transformation of the Roman World: Crises in the Third Century

During the reign of Marcus Aurelius, the last of the five good emperors, a number of natural catastrophes struck Rome. Floods of the Tiber, famine, and plague brought back from the east by the army led to considerable loss of population and a shortage of military manpower. To many Romans, these natural disasters seemed to portend an ominous future for Rome. New problems arose soon after the death of Marcus Aurelius.

Political and Military Woes

Unlike the first four good emperors, who chose capable successors by adopting competent men as their sons, Marcus Aurelius allowed his own son, Commodus (180–192), to become emperor. A cruel man, Commodus was a poor choice, and his assassination led to a brief renewal of civil war until Septimius Severus (193–211), who was born in North Africa and spoke Latin with an accent, used his legions to seize power. On his deathbed, Septimius Severus advised his sons, "Live in harmony, make the soldiers rich, and don't give a damn for anything else." His advice set the tone for the new dynasty he established. The Severan rulers (193–235) began to create a military monarchy. The army was expanded, soldiers' pay was increased, and military officers were appointed to important government positions. A new stability seemed at hand, but the increased power of the military led new military leaders to aspire to become emperor, and the military monarchy of the Severan rulers degenerated into military anarchy.

For the next fifty years (235–284), the empire was mired in the chaos of continual civil war. Contenders for the imperial throne found that bribing soldiers was an effective way to become emperor. In these five decades, there were twenty-two emperors, only two of whom did not meet a violent end. At the same time, the empire was beset by a series of invasions, no doubt encouraged by the internal turmoil. In the east, the Sassanid Persians made inroads into Roman territory. A fitting symbol of Rome's crisis was the capture of the Roman emperor, Valerian (253–260), by the Persians and his death in captivity, an event unprecedented in Roman history. Valerian's body was displayed in the chief towns of Persia. Germanic tribes also poured into the empire. The Goths overran the Balkans and moved into Greece and Asia Minor. The Franks advanced into Gaul and Spain. Not until the reign of Aurelian (270–275) were most of the boundaries restored. Although he abandoned the Danubian province of Dacia, Aurelian reconquered Gaul and reestablished order in the east and along the Danube. He also built a new defensive wall

Septimius Severus and His Family. This portrait painted on wood about A.D. 200, found in Egypt, is the only existing painted likeness of a Roman emperor. The emperor is portrayed with gray hair and beard in memory of Marcus Aurelius. To legitimize his authority, Septimius Severus had himself adopted into the Antonine dynasty, calling himself the son of Marcus Aurelius. The emperor stands next to his wife with their two sons in front of them. The face of his son Geta has been blotted out, no doubt by order of the other son standing next to him, Caracalla, who had his brother killed when he succeeded to the throne.

around Rome to defend the city against invaders. Grateful citizens hailed him as "restorer of the world."

As civil wars and invasions wore down the central government, provinces began to break away from the empire. A military commander named Postumus seized control of Gaul and then gained the support of Britain and Spain. He defended his "Gallic empire" until he was killed by his own soldiers in 269. In the east, Zenobia, the wife of the ruler of Syria, seized power after his death and then in 270 extended her control over Egypt and much of Asia Minor. In 272, Emperor Aurelian ended this threat to imperial power by defeating Zenobia and her forces in Syria.

Economic and Social Crises

Invasions, civil wars, and a recurrence of the plague came close to causing an economic collapse of the Roman Empire in the third century. The population declined drastically, possibly by as much as one-third. There was a significant decline in trade and small industry. The manpower shortage created by the plague affected both military recruiting and the economy. Farm production deteriorated as fields were ravaged by barbarians and even more often by the defending Roman armies. Many farmers complained that Roman commanders and their soldiers were confiscating produce and livestock. Provincial governors seemed powerless to stop these depredations, and some even joined in the frenzy.

The monetary system began to show signs of collapse as a result of debased coinage and the onset of serious inflation. Gold coins disappeared from circulation, and silver coins were diluted. The standard coin, the denarius, was now worth less than half of its first-century value. After further decline, it was replaced by new coins of even less value. Goods began to replace money as a medium of exchange.

Armies were needed more than ever, but financial strains made it difficult to enlist and pay the necessary soldiers. Short of cash, the imperial government paid its soldiers with produce, causing bitter resentment. Whereas in the second century the Roman army had been recruited among the inhabitants of frontier provinces, by the mid-third century, the state had to rely on hiring barbarians to fight under Roman commanders. These soldiers had no understanding of Roman traditions and no real attachment to either the empire or the emperors. By the end of the third century, a new form of political structure would emerge (see Chapter 7).

Transformation of the Roman World: The Rise of Christianity

The advent of Christianity marks a fundamental break with the dominant values of the Greco-Roman world. Christian views of God, human beings, and the world were quite different from those of the Greeks and Romans. Nevertheless, to understand the rise of Christianity, we must first examine both the religious environment of the Roman world and the Jewish background from which Christianity emerged.

The Religious World of the Roman Empire

Augustus had taken a number of steps to revive the Roman state religion, which had declined during the turmoil of the late Republic. The official state religion focused on the worship of a pantheon of Greco-Roman gods and goddesses, including Jupiter, Juno, Minerva, and Mars. Observance of proper ritual by state priests theoretically brought the Romans into proper relationship with the gods and guaranteed security, peace, and prosperity. The polytheistic Romans were extremely tolerant of other religions. The Romans allowed the worship of native gods and goddesses throughout their provinces and even adopted some of the local gods. In addition, the imperial cult of Roma and Augustus was developed to bolster support for the emperors. After Augustus, dead emperors deified by the Roman senate were included in the official imperial cult.

The desire for a more emotional spiritual experience led many people to the mystery religions of the Hellenistic east, which flooded into the western Roman world during the Early Empire. The mystery religions offered secret teachings that supposedly brought special benefits. They promised their followers advantages unavailable through Roman religion: an entry into a higher world of reality and the promise of a future life superior to the present one. They also featured elaborate rituals with deep emotional appeal. By participating in their ceremonies and performing their rites, an adherent could achieve communion with spiritual beings and undergo purification that opened the door to life after death.

Although many mystery cults vied for attention in the Roman world, perhaps the most important was Mithraism. Mithra was the chief agent of Ahuramazda, the supreme god of light in Persian Zoroastrianism (see Chapter 2). In the Roman world, Mithra came to be identified with the sun god and was known by his Roman title of the Unconquered Sun. Mithraism had spread rapidly in Rome and the western provinces by the second century A.D. and was especially favored by soldiers, who viewed Mithra as their patron deity. It was a religion for men only and featured an initiation ceremony in which devotees were baptized in the blood of a sacrificed bull. Mithraists paid homage to the sun on the first day of the week (Sunday), commemorated the sun's birthday around December 25, and celebrated ceremonial meals.

The Jewish Background

Christianity emerged out of Judaism, and so it is to the Jewish political-religious world that we must turn to find the beginnings of Christianity. In Hellenistic times, the Jewish people had enjoyed considerable independence under their Seleucid rulers (see Chapter 4). Roman involvement with the Jews began in 63 B.C., and by A.D. 6, Judaea had been made a province and placed under the direction of a Roman procurator. But unrest continued, augmented by divisions among the Jews themselves. The Sadducees favored a rigid adherence to Hebrew law, rejected the possibility of personal immortality, and favored cooperation with the Romans. The Pharisees adhered strictly to Jewish ritual and, although they wanted Judaea to be free from Roman control, did not advocate violent means to achieve this goal. The Essenes were a Jewish sect that lived in a religious community near the Dead Sea. As revealed in the Dead Sea Scrolls, a collection of documents first discovered in 1947, the Essenes, like many other Jews, awaited a Messiah who would save Israel from oppression, usher in the kingdom of God, and establish a paradise on earth. A fourth group, the Zealots, were militant extremists who advocated the violent overthrow of Roman rule. A Jewish revolt in A.D. 66 was crushed by the Romans four years later. The Jewish Temple in Jerusalem was destroyed, and Roman power once more stood supreme in Judaea.

The Origins of Christianity

Jesus of Nazareth (c. 6 B.C.–A.D. 30) was a Palestinian Jew who grew up in Galilee, an important center of the militant Zealots. He began his itinerant public preaching as a young adult amid the confusion and conflict in Judaea. Jesus' message was basically simple. He reassured his fellow Jews that he did not plan to undermine their traditional religion: "Do not think that I have come to abolish the Law or the Prophets; I have not come to abolish them but to fulfill them."[19] According to Jesus, what was important was not strict adherence to the letter of the law and attention to rules and prohibitions but the transformation of the inner person: "So in everything, do to others what you would have them do to you, for this sums up the Law and the Prophets."[20] God's command was simply to love God and one another: "Love the Lord your God with all your heart and with all your soul and with all your mind and with all your strength. The second is this: Love your neighbor as yourself."[21] In the Sermon on the Mount (see the box on p. 160), Jesus presented the ethical concepts—humility, charity, and brotherly love—that would form the basis for the value system of medieval Western civilization. As we have seen, these were not the values of classical Greco-Roman civilization.

Although some Jews welcomed Jesus as the Messiah who would save Israel from oppression and establish God's kingdom on earth, Jesus spoke of a heavenly kingdom, not an earthly one: "My kingdom is not of this world."[22] Consequently, he disappointed the radicals. At the same time, conservative religious leaders believed Jesus was another false Messiah who was undermining respect for traditional Jewish religion. To the Roman authorities of Palestine and their local allies, the Nazarene was a potential revolutionary who might transform Jewish expectations of a messianic kingdom into a revolt against Rome. Therefore, Jesus found himself denounced on many sides and was given

Christian Ideals: The Sermon on the Mount

HRISTIANITY WAS SIMPLY one of many religions competing for attention in the Roman Empire during the first and second centuries. The rise of Christianity marked a fundamental break with the value system of the upper-class elites who dominated the world of classical antiquity. As these excerpts from the Sermon on the Mount in the Gospel of Matthew illustrate, Christians emphasized humility, charity, brotherly love, and a belief in the inner being and a spiritual kingdom superior to this material world. These values and principles were not those of classical Greco-Roman civilization as exemplified in the words and deeds of its leaders.

The Gospel According to Matthew

Now when he saw the crowds, he went up on a mountainside and sat down. His disciples came to him, and he began to teach them saying:

> Blessed are the poor in spirit: for theirs is the kingdom of heaven.
> Blessed are those who mourn: for they will be comforted.
> Blessed are the meek: for they will inherit the earth.
> Blessed are those who hunger and thirst for righteousness: for they will be filled.
> Blessed are the merciful: for they will be shown mercy.
> Blessed are the pure in heart: for they will see God.
> Blessed are the peacemakers: for they will be called sons of God.
> Blessed are those who are persecuted because of righteousness: for theirs is the kingdom of heaven. . . .

You have heard that it was said, "Eye for eye, and tooth for tooth." But I tell you, Do not resist an evil person. If someone strikes you on the right cheek, turn to him the other also. . . .

You have heard that it was said, "Love your neighbor, and hate your enemy." But I tell you, Love your enemies and pray for those who persecute you. . . .

Do not store up for yourselves treasures on earth, where moth and rust destroy, and where thieves break in and steal. But store up for yourselves treasures in heaven, where moth and rust do not destroy, and where thieves do not break in and steal. For where your treasure is, there your heart will be also. . . .

No one can serve two masters. Either he will hate the one and love the other, or he will be devoted to the one and despise the other. You cannot serve both God and Money.

Therefore I tell you, do not worry about your life, what you will eat or drink; or about your body, what you will wear. Is not life more important than food, and the body more important than clothes? Look at the birds of the air; they do not sow or reap to store away in barns, and yet your heavenly Father feeds them. Are you not much more valuable than they? . . . So do not worry, saying, What shall we eat? or What shall we drink? or What shall we wear? For the pagans run after all these things, and your heavenly Father knows that you need them. But seek first his kingdom and his righteousness, and all these things will be given to you as well.

---

over to the Roman authorities. The procurator Pontius Pilate ordered his crucifixion. But that did not solve the problem. A few loyal disciples of Jesus spread the story, common to mystery cults (see Chapter 4), that he had overcome death, been resurrected, and then ascended into heaven. The belief in Jesus' resurrection became an important tenet of Christian doctrine. Jesus was now hailed by his followers as the "anointed one" (*Christ* in Greek), the Messiah who would return and usher in the kingdom of God on earth.

The Importance of Paul   Christianity began, then, as a religious movement within Judaism and was viewed that way by Roman authorities for many decades. Although tradition holds that one of Jesus' disciples, Peter, founded the Christian church at Rome, the most important figure in early Christianity after Jesus was Paul of Tarsus (c. 5–c. 67). Paul reached out to non-Jews and transformed Christianity from a Jewish sect into a broader religious movement.

Called the "second founder of Christianity," Paul was a Jewish Roman citizen who had been strongly influenced by Hellenistic Greek culture. He believed that the message

of Jesus should be preached not only to Jews but to Gentiles (non-Jews) as well. Paul was responsible for founding Christian communities throughout Asia Minor and along the shores of the Aegean.

It was Paul who provided a universal foundation for the spread of Jesus' ideas. He taught that Jesus was, in effect, a savior-God, the son of God, who had come to earth to save all humans, who were basically sinners as a result of Adam's original sin of disobedience against God. By his death, Jesus had atoned for the sins of all humans and made it possible for all men and women to experience a new beginning with the potential for individual salvation. By accepting Jesus as their savior, they, too, could be saved.

The Spread of Christianity   At first, Christianity spread slowly. Although the teachings of early Christianity were mostly disseminated by the preaching of convinced Christians, written materials also appeared. Paul had written a series of letters, or epistles, outlining Christian beliefs for different Christian communities. Some of Jesus' disciples may also have preserved some of the sayings of the master in writing and would have passed on personal memo-

Jesus and His Apostles. Pictured is a fourth-century fresco from a Roman catacomb depicting Jesus and his apostles. Catacombs were underground cemeteries where early Christians buried their dead. Christian tradition holds that in times of imperial repression, Christians withdrew to the catacombs to pray and hide.

ries that became the basis of the written *gospels*—the "good news" concerning Jesus—which attempted to give a record of Jesus' life and teachings and formed the core of the New Testament. Although Jerusalem was the first center of Christianity, its destruction by the Romans in A.D. 70 left individual Christian churches with considerable independence. By 100, Christian churches had been established in most of the major cities of the east and in some places in the western part of the empire. Many early Christians came from the ranks of Hellenized Jews and the Greek-speaking populations of the east. But in the second and third centuries, an increasing number of followers were Latin-speaking people. A Latin translation of the Greek New Testament that appeared soon after 200 aided this process.

Early Christian Communities   Early Christian groups met in private homes in the evening to share a common meal called an *agape* or love feast and to celebrate what became known as the sacrament of the **Eucharist** or Lord's Supper—the communal celebration of Jesus' Last Supper:

> While they were eating, Jesus took bread, gave thanks and broke it, and gave it to the disciples, saying, Take and eat; this is my body. Then he took the cup, gave thanks, and offered it to them, saying, Drink from it, all of you. This is my blood of the covenant, which is poured out for many for the forgiveness of sins.[23]

Early Christian communities were loosely organized, with both men and women playing significant roles. Some women held important positions, often as preachers. Local churches were under the leadership of boards of elders (*presbyters*), but by the beginning of the second century, officials known as *bishops* came to exercise considerable authority over the presbyters. These bishops based their superior position on apostolic succession—as the successors to Jesus' original twelve apostles (disciples), they were living representatives of Jesus' power. As Ignatius of Antioch wrote in 107, "It is clear that we must regard a bishop as the Lord Himself. . . . Your clergy . . . are attuned to their

bishop like the strings of a harp, and the result is a hymn of praise to Jesus Christ from minds that are in unison."[24] Bishops were men, a clear indication that by the second century A.D., most Christian communities were following the views of Paul that Christian women should be subject to Christian men.

Although some of the fundamental values of Christianity differed markedly from those of the Greco-Roman world, the Romans initially did not pay much attention to the Christians, whom they regarded at first as simply another sect of Judaism. The structure of the Roman Empire itself aided the growth of Christianity. Christian missionaries, including some of Jesus' original twelve apostles, used Roman roads to travel throughout the empire spreading their "good news."

The Changing Roman View of Christianity   As the popular appeal of Christianity grew, the Roman attitude toward it began to change. As we have seen, the Romans were tolerant of other religions except when they threatened public order or public morals. Many Romans came to view Christians as harmful to the order of the Roman state. These views were often based on misperceptions. The celebration of the Lord's Supper, for example, led to rumors that Christians practiced horrible crimes, such as the ritualistic murder of children. Although we know these rumors are untrue, some Romans believed them and used them to incite people against the Christians during times of crisis. Moreover, because Christians held their meetings in secret and seemed to be connected to Christian groups in distant areas, the government could view them as potentially dangerous to the state.

Some Romans felt that Christians were overly exclusive and hence harmful to the community and public order. The Christians did not recognize other gods and therefore abstained from public festivals honoring the popular deities. Finally, Christians refused to participate in the worship of the state gods and the imperial cult. Since the

Romans regarded these as important to the state, the Christians' refusal undermined the security of the state and hence constituted an act of treason, punishable by death. It was also proof of atheism (disbelief in the gods) and subject to punishment on those grounds. But to the Christians, who believed there was only one real God, the worship of state gods and the emperors was idolatry and would endanger their own salvation.

Roman persecution of Christians in the first and second centuries was never systematic but sporadic and local. Persecution began during the reign of Nero. After the fire that destroyed much of Rome, the emperor used the Christians as scapegoats, accusing them of arson and hatred of the human race and subjecting them to cruel deaths in Rome. In the second century, Christians were often ignored as harmless. By the end of the reigns of the five good emperors, Christians still represented a small minority, but one of considerable strength. That strength lay in their conviction of the rightness of their path, a conviction that had been reinforced by the willingness of the first Christians to become martyrs for their faith.

The Growth of Christianity

The sporadic persecution of Christians by the Romans in the first and second centuries had done nothing to stop the growth of Christianity. It had, in fact, served to strengthen Christianity as an institution in the second and third centuries by causing it to shed the loose structure of the first century and move toward a more centralized organization of its various church communities. Crucial to this change was the emerging role of the bishops. Though still chosen by the community, bishops began to assume more control, with the bishop serving as leader and the presbyters emerging as clergy subject to the bishop's authority. By the third century, bishops were nominated by the clergy, simply approved by the congregation, and then officially ordained into office. The Christian church was creating a well-defined hierarchical structure in which the bishops and clergy were salaried officers separate from the laity or regular church members.

The Appeal of Christianity Christianity grew slowly in the first century, took root in the second, and had spread widely by the third. Why was Christianity able to attract so many followers? Historians are not really sure but have offered several answers. Certainly, the Christian message had much to offer the Roman world. The promise of salvation, made possible by Jesus' death and resurrection, had immense appeal in a world full of suffering and injustice. Christianity seemed to imbue life with a meaning and purpose beyond the simple material things of everyday reality. Second, Christianity was not entirely unfamiliar. It could be viewed as simply another eastern mystery religion, offering immortality as the result of the sacrificial death of a savior-god. At the same time, it offered advantages that the other mystery religions lacked. Jesus had been a human fig-

ure, not a mythological one, such as Isis or Mithra. Moreover, Christianity had universal appeal. Unlike Mithraism, it was not restricted to men. Furthermore, it did not require a difficult or expensive initiation rite as other mystery religions did. Initiation was accomplished simply by baptism—a purification by water—by which one entered into direct communion with Jesus. In addition, Christianity gave new meaning to life and offered what the Roman state religions could not—a personal relationship with God and a link to higher worlds.

Finally, Christianity fulfilled the human need to belong. Christians formed communities bound to one another in which people could express their love by helping each other and offering assistance to the poor, sick, widows, and orphans. Christianity satisfied the need to belong in a way that the huge, impersonal, and remote Roman Empire could never do.

Christianity proved attractive to all classes. The promise of eternal life was for all—rich, poor, aristocrats, slaves, men, and women. As Paul stated in his Epistle to the Colossians: "And [you] have put on the new self, which is being renewed in knowledge in the image of its Creator. Here there is no Greek nor Jew, circumcised or uncircumcised, barbarian, Scythian, slave or free, but Christ is all, and is in all."[25] Although it did not call for revolution or social upheaval, Christianity emphasized a sense of spiritual equality for all people.

Many women found that Christianity offered them new roles and new forms of companionship with other women. Christian women fostered the new religion in their own homes and preached their convictions to other people in their towns and villages. Many also died for their faith. Perpetua (d. 203) was an aristocratic woman who converted to Christianity. Her pagan family begged her to renounce her new faith, but she refused. Arrested by the Roman authorities, she chose instead to die for her faith and was one of a group of Christians who were slaughtered by wild beasts in the arena at Carthage on March 7, 203.

Persecution As the Christian church became more organized, two emperors in the third century responded with more systematic persecutions. The emperor Decius (249–251) blamed the Christians for the disasters befalling the Roman Empire in the terrible third century: it was they who had failed to acknowledge the state gods and consequently brought on the gods' retribution against the Romans. Moreover, as the administrative organization of the church grew, Christianity appeared to Decius even more like a state within a state that was undermining the empire. Accordingly, he initiated the first systematic persecution of Christians. All citizens were required to appear before their local magistrates and offer sacrifices to the Roman gods. Christians of course refused to do so. Decius' scheme, however, failed to work. Local officials did not cooperate, and Decius' reign was also not that long. The last great persecution was by Diocletian at the beginning of the fourth century, but by then it was too late. Christianity had become too strong to be eradicated by force.

	100 B.C.	0	100 A.D.	200 A.D.	300 A.D.

Rome

Age of Augustus

The Julio-Claudian rulers

Five good emperors

■ Roman citizenship to all free inhabitants of empire

Jesus of Nazareth

The Pantheon

Severan rulers

■ Aurelian pacifies empire

Augustan poets (Virgil, Horace)

Silver age of Latin literature

China

Han Chinese Empire

CONCLUSION

𝒯HE ROMAN REPUBLIC had created one of the largest empires in antiquity, but its republican institutions had proved inadequate for the task of ruling an empire. After a series of bloody civil wars, Augustus created a new order that began the Roman Empire, which experienced a lengthy period of peace and prosperity between 14 and 180. During this Pax Romana, trade flourished and the provinces were governed efficiently. In addition, within their empire, the Romans developed a remarkable series of achievements that were bequeathed to the future.

These achievements were fundamental to the development of Western civilization. The Romance languages of today (French, Italian, Spanish, Portuguese, and Romanian) are based on Latin. Western practices of impartial justice and trial by jury owe much to Roman law. As great builders, the Romans left monuments to their skills throughout Europe, some of which, including aqueducts and roads, are still in use today. Other monuments provided models for public buildings in the West for hundreds of years. Aspects of Roman administrative practices survived in the Western world for centuries. The Romans also preserved the intellectual heritage of the Greco-Roman world of antiquity.

By the third century, the Roman world was being buffeted by civil wars, invasions, and economic problems. At the same time, a new religion—Christianity—was spreading throughout the empire. As we shall see in the next chapter, the response to these developments slowly brought a transformation of the Roman Empire.

NOTES

1. Livy, *The Early History of Rome*, trans. Aubrey de Sélincourt (Harmondsworth, England, 1960), p. 35.
2. Tacitus, *The Annals of Imperial Rome*, trans. Michael Grant (Harmondsworth, England, 1956), p. 30.
3. Velleius Paterculus, *Compendium of Roman History*, trans. Frederick Shipley (Cambridge, Mass., 1967), 2.117.
4. Tacitus, *Annals of Imperial Rome*, p. 37.
5. Virgil, *The Aeneid*, trans. C. Day Lewis (Garden City, N.Y., 1952), p. 154.
6. Horace, *Satires*, in *The Complete Works of Horace*, trans. Lord Dunsany and Michael Oakley (London, 1961), 1.1.
7. Ibid., 1.3.
8. Livy, *Early History of Rome*, p. 18.
9. Tacitus, *Annals of Imperial Rome*, p. 31.
10. Tacitus, *The Histories*, trans. Kenneth Wallesley (Harmondsworth, England, 1964), p. 23.

11. Quoted in Martin Goodman, *The Roman World, 44 B.C.–A.D. 180* (London, 1997), p. 67.

12. Quoted in ibid., p. 72.

13. Seneca, *Letters from a Stoic,* trans. Robin Campbell (Harmondsworth, England, 1969), let. 5.

14. Tacitus, *Annals of Imperial Rome,* p. 147.

15. Juvenal, *The Sixteen Satires,* trans. Peter Green (Harmondsworth, England, 1967), satire 7, p. 171.

16. Ibid., satire 10, p. 207.

17. Tacitus, *A Dialogue on Oratory,* in *The Complete Works of Tacitus,* trans. Alfred Church and William Brodribb (New York, 1942), 29, p. 758.

18. Ovid, *The Amores,* trans. Grant Showerman (Cambridge, Mass., 1963), 2.14.26–27.

19. Matthew 5:17.

20. Matthew 7:12.

21. Mark 12:30–31.

22. John 18:36.

23. Matthew 26:26–28.

24. *Early Christian Writings* (Harmondsworth, England, 1968), pp. 76–77.

25. Colossians 3:10–11.

SUGGESTIONS FOR FURTHER READING

For a general account of the Roman Empire, see **J. Boardman, J. Griffin, and O. Murray, eds.,** *The Oxford History of the Roman World* (Oxford, 1991), and **G. Wolf, ed.,** *Cambridge Illustrated History of the Roman World* (Cambridge, 2003). Good surveys of the Early Empire include **P. Garnsey and R. P. Saller,** *The Roman Empire: Economy, Society and Culture* (London, 1987); **C. Wells,** *The Roman Empire,* 2d ed. (London, 1992); **M. Goodman,** *The Roman World, 44 B.C.–A.D. 180* (London, 1997); **J. Wacher,** *The Roman Empire* (London, 1987); and **F. Millar,** *The Roman Empire and Its Neighbours,* 2d ed. (London, 1981).

Studies of Roman emperors of the first and second centuries include **W. Eck,** *The Age of Augustus,* trans. **D. L. Schneider** (Oxford, 2003); **R. Seager,** *Tiberius* (London, 1972); **A. Barrett,** *Caligula: The Corruption of Power* (New Haven, Conn., 1998); **A. Momigliano,** *Claudius: The Emperor and His Achievement,* trans. **W. D. Hogarth** (Cambridge, 1961); **E. Champlin,** *Nero* (Cambridge, Mass., 2003); **E. Speller,** *Following Hadrian* (Oxford, 2003); and **M. Hammond,** *The Antonine Monarchy* (Rome, 1959). For brief biographies of all the Roman emperors, see **M. Grant,** *The Roman Emperors* (New York, 1985). On the wife of Augustus, see **A. A. Barrett,** *Livia: First Lady of Imperial Rome* (New Haven, Conn., 2002).

The Roman army is examined in **J. B. Campbell,** *The Emperor and the Roman Army* (Oxford, 1984). On the provinces and Roman foreign policy, see **E. N. Luttwak,** *The Grand Strategy of the Roman Empire from the First Century A.D. to the Third* (Baltimore, 1976); **B. Isaac,** *The Limits of Empire: The Roman Empire in the East* (Oxford, 1990); and **S. L. Dyson,** *The Creation of the Roman Frontier* (Princeton, N.J., 1985). On the battle in the Teutoburg Forest, see **P. S. Wells,** *The Battle That Stopped Rome: Emperor Augustus, Arminius and the Slaughter of the Legions in the Teutoburg Forest* (New York, 2003).

A good survey of Roman literature can be found in **R. M. Ogilvie,** *Roman Literature and Society* (Harmondsworth, England, 1980). More specialized studies include **R. O. Lyne,** *The Latin Love Poets from Catullus to Horace* (Oxford, 1980), and **K. Galinsky,** *Augustan Culture* (Princeton, N.J., 1996).

A survey of Roman art can be found in **D. E. Strong,** *Roman Art* (Harmondsworth, England, 1976). Architecture is covered in the standard work by **J. B. Ward-Perkins,** *Roman Imperial Architecture* (Harmondsworth, England, 1981).

Various aspects of Roman society are covered in **L. Adkins and R. A. Adkins,** *Handbook to Life in Ancient Rome* (New York, 1994). Also useful on urban life is **J. E. Stambaugh,** *The Ancient Roman City* (Baltimore, 1988). On public festivals, see **P. Veyne,** *Bread and Circuses* (London, 1992). On the gladiators, see **T. Wiedemann,** *Emperors and Gladiators* (New York, 1992). Studies on Roman women include **J. P. V. D. Balsdon,** *Roman Women: Their History and Habits* (London, 1969), and S. B. Pomeroy, *Goddesses, Whores, Wives, and Slaves: Women in Classical Antiquity* (New York, 1975), pp. 149–226. On slavery, see **K. Bradley,** *Slavery and Society at Rome* (New York, 1994).

For a general introduction to early Christianity, see **J. Court and K. Court,** *The New Testament World* (Cambridge, 1990). Useful works on early Christianity include **W. A. Meeks,** *The First Urban Christians* (New Haven, Conn., 1983); **W. H. C. Frend,** *The Rise of Christianity* (Philadelphia, 1984); and **R. MacMullen,** *Christianizing the Roman Empire* (New Haven, Conn., 1984). For a detailed analysis of Christianity in the 30s and 40s of the first century A.D., see **J. D. Crossan,** *The Birth of Christianity* (New York, 1998). On Christian women, see **D. M. Scholer, ed.,** *Women in Early Christianity* (New York, 1993), and **R. Kraemer,** *Her Share of the Blessings: Women's Religion Among the Pagans, Jews and Christians in the Graeco-Roman World* (Oxford, 1995).

History Now™

Enter *HistoryNow* using the access card that is available for *Western Civilization. HistoryNow* will assist you in understanding the content in this chapter with lesson plans generated for your needs. In addition, you can read the following documents, and many more, online:

Virgil, Book 1 of *The Aeneid*

Horace, Satire 1 of Book 1

The Gospel of Mark (New Testament)

Eusebius, Edict of Milan

Ignatius, "Letter to the Ephesians"

INFOTRAC SEARCH TERMS

For additional reading, go to InfoTrac College Edition, your online research library at http://infotrac.thomsonlearning.com

Key Term Search	*Subject Guide Search*
Roman Empire	Roman mythology
	Roman law

WESTERN CIVILIZATION RESOURCES

 Visit the *Western Civilization* Companion Web site for resources specific to this book:

http://history.wadsworth.com/spielvogel06/

For a variety of tools to help you succeed in this course, visit the Western Civilization Resource Center at

http://history.wadsworth.com/western/

Included are quizzes; images; documents; interactive simulations; maps and timelines; movie explorations; and a wealth of other sources.

LATE ANTIQUITY AND THE EMERGENCE OF THE MEDIEVAL WORLD

CHAPTER OUTLINE AND FOCUS QUESTIONS

The Late Roman Empire

● What reforms did Diocletian and Constantine institute, and to what extent were the reforms successful?

The Germanic Kingdoms

● What changes did the Germanic peoples make to the political, economic, and social conditions of the Western Roman Empire?

Development of the Christian Church

● What were the chief characteristics of Benedictine monasticism, and what role did monks play in both the conversion of Europe to Christianity and the intellectual life of the Germanic kingdoms?

The Byzantine Empire

● How did the Byzantine Empire that had emerged by the eighth century differ from the empire of Justinian and from the Germanic kingdoms in the west?

The Rise of Islam

● What was the basic message of Islam, and why was it able to expand so successfully?

CRITICAL THINKING

● In what ways were the Byzantine and Islamic civilizations different from the civilization developing in western Europe? In what ways were they similar?

A fourteenth-century French manuscript illustration of the baptism of Clovis

© Giraudon/Bridgeman Art Library

BY THE THIRD CENTURY, the Roman Empire was experiencing a number of problems as well as witnessing the growth of a new religion—Christianity. To restore the empire, the emperors Diocletian and Constantine initiated a number of reforms that created the so-called Late Empire. Constantine also converted to Christianity, starting a process that gave the Late Empire a new state religion.

After Constantine, the Late Roman Empire survived, but it was increasingly faced in the west by the incursions of Germanic tribes. By the second half of the fifth century, new political arrangements were taking shape that brought the collapse of the old imperial structure in the west and the emergence of a series of German kingdoms in western Europe that would form the basis of a new civilization. In these kingdoms, the Christian church also played a role as it drew these Germanic tribes to its faith.

The conversion to Christianity of the pagan leaders of German tribes was sometimes dramatic, at least as reported by the sixth-century historian Gregory of Tours. Clovis, leader of the Franks, married Clotilde, daughter of the king of the Burgundians. She was a Christian, but Clovis refused her pleas to become a Christian, telling her, "Your god can do nothing." But during a battle with the Alemanni, when Clovis's army was close to utter destruction, "he saw the danger; his heart was stirred; and he raised his eyes to heaven, saying, 'Jesus Christ, I beseech the glory of your aid. If you shall grant me victory over these enemies, I will believe in you and be baptized in your name.'" When he had uttered these words, the Alemanni began to flee. Clovis kept his vow and became a Christian.

While the Germanic kingdoms were putting down roots in the west, the eastern part of the old Roman Empire, increasingly Greek in culture, continued as the Byzantine Empire. Serving as a buffer between Europe and the peoples to the east, the Byzantine or Eastern Roman Empire also preserved the intellectual and legal accomplishments of Greek and Roman antiquity. At the same time, a new culture centered on Islam emerged in the east; it spread through large parts of the old Roman Empire, preserved much of Greek culture, and created its own flourishing civilization. This chapter, then, concerns the transformation of the Roman world in late antiquity, the heirs of the Roman Empire, and the new world—the medieval world—they began to create.

The Late Roman Empire

At the end of the third century and the beginning of the fourth, the Roman Empire gained a new lease on life through the efforts of two strong emperors, Diocletian and Constantine, who restored order and stability. The empire was virtually transformed into a new state, the Late Roman Empire, which included a new governmental structure, a rigid economic and social system, and a new state religion—Christianity.

The Reforms of Diocletian and Constantine

Diocletian had risen through the ranks to become a prominent military leader. After the murder of the emperor Numerian by his praetorian prefect, Diocletian executed the prefect and was then hailed as emperor by his soldiers. Diocletian's own rise to power led him to see the need for a new system for ruling the Roman Empire.

Political Reforms   Diocletian (284–305) created a new administrative system for a restructured empire. The number of provinces was increased to almost one hundred by creating smaller districts superintended by more officials. The provinces were in turn grouped into twelve dioceses, each headed by an official called a vicar. The twelve dioceses were grouped into four prefectures (see Map 7.1), and the entire Roman Empire was divided into two parts, east and west. Each part contained two prefectures and was ruled by an "Augustus." Diocletian ruled the east, and Maximian, a strong military commander, the west. Each Augustus was assisted by a chief lieutenant or "vice-emperor"

called a "Caesar," who theoretically would eventually succeed to the position of Augustus. This new system was called the **tetrarchy** (rule by four). Diocletian had obviously come to believe that one man was incapable of ruling such an enormous empire, especially in view of the barbarian invasions of the third century. Each of the four tetrarchs—two Augusti and two Caesars—resided in a different administrative capital. Diocletian, for example, established his base at Nicomedia in Bithynia. Despite the appearance of four-man rule, however, it is important to note that Diocletian's military seniority enabled him to claim a higher status and hold the ultimate authority.

Soon after Diocletian's retirement in 305, a new struggle for power ensued. The victory of Constantine (306–337) in 312 led to his control of the entire west, although he continued to share imperial authority with Licinius, a fellow emperor. Twelve years later, in 324, Constantine's army routed Licinius' forces, and Constantine established himself as the sole ruler.

Constantine continued and even expanded the autocratic policies of Diocletian. Under these two rulers, the Roman Empire was transformed into a system where the emperor had far more personal power than Augustus, Trajan, or any of the other emperors had had during the Pax Romana. The emperor, now clothed in jewel-bedecked robes of gold and blue, was seen as a divinely sanctioned monarch whose will was law. Government officials were humble servants required to kneel before the emperor and kiss his robe. The Roman senate was stripped of any power and became merely the city council for Rome.

Diocletian and Constantine greatly strengthened and enlarged the administrative bureaucracies of the Roman Empire. Henceforth, civil and military bureaucracies were sharply separated. Each contained a hierarchy of officials who exercised control at the various levels. The emperor presided over both hierarchies and served as the only link between them. New titles of nobility—such as *illustres* ("illustrious ones") and *illustrissimi* ("most illustrious ones")—were instituted to dignify the holders of positions in the civil and military bureaucracies.

Military Reforms   Additional military reforms were also instituted. The army was enlarged to 400,000 men, including units filled with Germans. By the end of Constantine's reign, a new organization of the army had also been put in place. Military forces were divided into two kinds: garrison troops, which were located on the frontiers and intended as a first line of defense against invaders, and mobile units, which were located behind the frontier but could be quickly moved to support frontier troops when the borders were threatened. This gave the empire greater flexibility in responding to invasion.

Economic and Social Trends   The political and military reforms of Diocletian and Constantine greatly enlarged two institutions—the army and the civil service—that drained most of the public funds. Although more revenues were needed to pay for the military and the bureaucracy, the

MAP 7.1 **Divisions of the Late Roman Empire, c. 300.** Diocletian imposed order and a new economic and administrative structure on the Late Empire. He divided the Roman Empire into four regions, each ruled by either an "Augustus" or a "Caesar," although Diocletian retained supreme power.

❓ Compare this map with Map 6.1. How much territory was lost by the time of Diocletian?

🌐 **View an animated version of this map or related maps at** http://history.wadsworth.com/spielvogel06/

population was not growing, so the tax base could not be expanded. Diocletian and Constantine devised new economic and social policies to deal with these financial burdens. Like their political policies, these economic and social policies were all based on coercion and loss of individual freedom.

To fight **inflation,** in 301 Diocletian resorted to issuing an edict that established maximum wages and prices for the entire empire. It was applied mostly in the east, but despite severe penalties, like most wage and price controls, it was largely unenforceable. The decline in circulation of coins led Diocletian to collect taxes and make government payments in produce. Constantine, however, managed to introduce a new gold coin, the solidus, and new silver coins that remained in circulation during his reign.

In the third century, the city councils, which had formed one of the most important administrative units of the empire, had begun to decline. Since the *curiales* (the city councillors) were forced to pay expenses out of their own pocket when the taxes they collected were insufficient, the wealthy no longer wanted to serve in these positions. Diocletian and Constantine responded by issuing edicts that forced the rich to continue in their posts as *curiales,* virtually making the positions hereditary. Some *curiales* realized that their fortunes would be wiped out and fled the cities to escape the clutches of the imperial bureaucracy. If caught, however, they were returned to their cities like runaway slaves and forced to resume their duties.

Coercion also came to form the underlying basis for numerous occupations in the Late Roman Empire. To ensure the tax base and keep the empire going despite the shortage of labor, the emperors issued edicts that forced people to remain in their designated vocations. Hence basic jobs, such as bakers and shippers, became hereditary.

Free tenant farmers—the *coloni*—continued to decline and soon found themselves bound to the land as well. Large landowners took advantage of depressed agricultural conditions to enlarge their landed estates. Free tenant farmers, unable to survive on their own, became dependent on these large estates and soon found that landlords, in order to guarantee their supply of labor, gained government cooperation in attaching them to their estates. One imperial edict stated: "And as for *coloni* themselves, it will be proper for such as contemplate flight to be bound with chains to a servile status, so that by virtue of such condemnation to servitude they may be compelled to fulfill the duties that befit free men."[1]

In addition to facing increased restrictions on their freedom, the lower classes were burdened with enormous taxes, since the wealthiest classes in the Late Roman Empire were either exempt from paying taxes or evaded them by bribing the tax collectors. These tax pressures undermined lower-class support for the regime. A fifth-century writer reported that the Roman peasants welcomed the Visigothic invaders of southern Gaul as liberators because the enemy was more lenient to them than the tax collectors.

In general, the economic and social policies of Diocletian and Constantine were based on an unprecedented degree of control and coercion. Though temporarily successful, in the long run such authoritarian policies stifled the very vitality the Late Empire needed to revive its sagging fortunes.

Constantine's Building Program   Constantine was especially interested in building programs despite the strain they placed on the budget. Much of the construction took place in the provinces, since Rome had become merely a symbolic capital. It was no longer an imperial administrative center, as it was considered too far from the frontiers. Between 324 and 330, Constantine engaged in his biggest project, the construction of a new capital city in the east, on the site of the Greek city of Byzantium, on the shores of the Bosporus. Named the "city of Constantine," or Constantinople (modern Istanbul), it was developed for defensive reasons; it had an excellent strategic location. Calling it his "New Rome," Constantine endowed the city with a forum, large palaces, and a vast amphitheater. It was officially dedicated on May 11, 330, "by the commandment of God," and in the following years, many Christian churches were built there.

Constantine did not entirely forget Rome. Earlier he was responsible for building public baths and the triumphal Arch of Constantine, built between 312 and 315. Constantine was also the first emperor to build churches for the Christian faith in Rome, including the first basilica dedicated to Saint Peter, built on the supposed site of Saint Peter's burial. Constantine also gave grants to Christian leaders in Rome, enabling them to assume a more conspicuous role in the city. These acts by Constantine are a reminder of the new role Christianity was beginning to play in the Late Empire.

The Empire's New Religion

In the fourth century, Christianity prospered as never before, and the emperor Constantine played an important role in its status.

The Emperor Constantine. Constantine played an important role in restoring order and stability to the Roman Empire at the beginning of the fourth century. This marble head of Constantine, which is 8 feet 6 inches high, was part of an enormous 30-foot-tall seated statue of the emperor in the New Basilica in Rome. Constantine used these awe-inspiring statues throughout the empire to build support for imperial policies by reminding his subjects of his position as an absolute ruler with immense power. The casting of his eyes toward heaven also emphasized Constantine's special relationship with God.

The Conversion of Constantine   Constantine's support for Christianity supposedly began in 312, when his army was about to fight a crucial battle against the forces of Maxentius at the Milvian Bridge, which crossed the Tiber River just north of the city of Rome. According to the traditional story, before the battle, Constantine saw a vision of a Christian cross with the words, "In this sign you will conquer." Having won the battle, the story goes, Constantine was convinced of the power of the Christian God. Although he was not baptized until the end of his life, in 313 he issued the famous Edict of Milan, which officially tolerated the existence of Christianity.

After Constantine, the emperors were Christian with the exception of Julian (360–363), who tried briefly to restore the traditional Greco-Roman polytheistic religion. But he died in battle, and his reign was too short to make a difference. Under Theodosius "the Great" (378–395), Christianity was made the official religion of the Roman Empire. Once in control, Christian leaders used their influence and power to outlaw pagan religious practices. Christianity had triumphed.

Organization and Religious Disputes   By the fourth century, the Christian church had developed a system of government based on a territorial plan borrowed from Roman administration. The Christian community in each city was headed by a bishop, whose area of jurisdiction was known as a bishopric or diocese. The bishoprics of each Roman province were clustered together under the direction of an archbishop. The bishops of four great cities, Rome, Jerusalem, Alexandria, and Antioch, held positions of special power in church affairs because the churches in these cities all asserted that they had been founded by the original apostles sent out by Jesus.

One reason the church needed a more formal organization was the problem of **heresy.** As Christianity developed and spread, contradictory interpretations of important doctrines emerged. Heresy came to be viewed as a teaching different from the official "catholic" or universal beliefs of the church. In a world where people were concerned about salvation, the question of whether Jesus' nature is divine or human took on great significance. These doctrinal differences also became political issues, creating political factions that actually warred with one another. It is highly unlikely, though, that ordinary people understood what these debates meant.

The two major heresies of the fourth century were Donatism and Arianism. Donatus was a priest in North Africa who taught that the sacraments of the church, the channels by which a Christian received God's grace, were not valid if administered by an immoral priest or one who had denied his faith under persecution. Donatus' deviation from traditional teaching on the subject created so much dissension that it came to the attention of the Emperor Constantine, who convened a council of western bishops to denounce it. It was not until a century later, in 411, however, that the church declared authoritatively that the efficacy of the sacraments was not dependent on the moral state of the priest administering them as long as the priest had been properly ordained.

Arianism was a product of the followers of Arius, a priest from Alexandria in Egypt. Arius postulated that Jesus had been human and thus not truly God. Arius was opposed by Athanasius, a bishop of Alexandria, who argued that Jesus was human but also truly God. Emperor Constantine, disturbed by the controversy, called the first ecumenical council of the church, a meeting composed of representatives from the entire Christian community. The Council of Nicaea, held in 325, condemned Arianism and stated that Jesus was of "the same substance" as God: "We believe in one God the Father All-sovereign, maker of all things visible and invisible; And in one Lord Jesus Christ, the Son of God, begotten of the Father, only-begotten, that is, of the substance of the Father, God of God, Light of Light, true God of true God, begotten not made, of one substance with the Father."[2] The Council of Nicaea did not end the controversy, however; not only did Arianism persist in some parts of the Roman Empire for many years, but even more important, many of the Germanic Goths who established states in the west converted to Arian Christianity (see "The Germanic Kingdoms" later in this chapter). As a result of these fourth-century religious controversies, the Roman emperor came to play an increasingly important role in church affairs.

The End of the Western Empire

Constantine had reunited the Roman Empire and restored a semblance of order. After his death, however, the empire continued to divide into western and eastern parts as fighting erupted on a regular basis between elements of the Roman army backing the claims of rival emperors. By 395, the western and eastern parts of the empire became virtually two independent states. In the course of the fifth century, while the empire in the east remained intact under the Roman emperor in Constantinople (see "The Byzantine Empire" later in this chapter), the administrative structure of the empire in the west collapsed and was replaced by an assortment of Germanic kingdoms. The process was a gradual one, involving the movement of Germans into the empire, military failures, the struggles for power on the part of both Roman and German military leaders, and the efforts of wealthy aristocrats to support the side that seemed to offer them the greatest security.

The Germans During the first and second centuries A.D., the Romans had established the Rhine and Danube Rivers as the empire's northern boundary. The Romans called all the peoples to the north of the rivers "Germans" and regarded them as uncivilized barbarians. In fact, the Germans consisted of different groups with their own customs and identities, but these constantly changed as tribes broke up and came together in new configurations. At times they formed larger confederations under strong warrior leaders. The Germans lived by herding and farming and also traded with people living along the northern frontiers of the Roman Empire.

Although the Romans had established a series of political frontiers along the Rhine and Danube Rivers, Romans and Germans often came into contact across these boundaries. For some time, the Romans had hired Germanic tribes to fight other Germanic tribes that threatened Rome or enlisted groups of Germans to fight for Rome. In any case, until the fourth century, the empire had proved capable of absorbing these people without harm to its political structure. In the second half of the fourth century, this situation began to change.

German Migrations In the late fourth century, the Germanic tribes came under new pressure when the Huns, a fierce tribe of nomads from the steppes of Asia (see the box on p. 170), moved into the Black Sea region, possibly attracted by the riches of the empire to its south. One of the groups displaced by the Huns was the Visigoths, who in 376 asked the Roman emperor Valens (364–378) to allow them to cross the Danube and farm in the Balkans in return for providing troops for the Roman military. But the Roman military commanders mistreated them, as one ancient German historian recounted:

[They] crossed the Danube and settled Dacia Ripensis, Moesia, and Thrace by permission of the Emperor. Soon famine and want came upon them. . . . Their leaders . . . begged the Roman commanders to open a market. But to what will not the "cursed

The Huns

HE FIRST SELECTION is a description of the Huns by Ammianus Marcellinus (c. 330–c. 393), who has been called the "last great Roman historian." Ammianus wrote a history of Rome from A.D. 96 to his own day. Only the chapters that deal with the period from 354 to 378 have survived. Historians believe that his account of the Huns is largely based on stereotypes. The second selection is taken from an account by Priscus, an envoy from the Eastern Roman Empire to the court of Attila, king of the Huns from 434 to 453. His description of the Huns in 448 is quite different from that of Ammianus Marcellinus.

Ammianus Marcellinus, *The Later Roman Empire*

The Huns . . . are quite abnormally savage. From the moment of their birth they make deep gashes in their children's cheeks, so that when in due course hair appears its growth is checked by the wrinkled scars. . . . They have squat bodies, strong limbs, and thick necks, and are so prodigiously ugly and bent that they might be two-legged animals, or the figures crudely carved from stumps which are seen on the parapets of bridges. Still, their shape, however disagreeable, is human; but their way of life is so rough that they have no use for fire or seasoned food, but live on the roots of wild plants and the half-raw flesh of any sort of animal, which they warm a little by placing it between their thighs and the backs of their horses. They have no buildings to shelter them, but avoid anything of the kind; . . . not so much as a hut thatched with reeds is to be found among them. . . . They wear garments of linen or of the skins of field-mice stitched together, and there is no difference between their clothing whether they are at home or abroad. Once they have put their necks in some dingy shirt they never take it off or change it till it rots and falls to pieces from incessant wear. They have round caps of fur on their heads, and protect their hairy legs with goatskins. Their shapeless shoes . . . make it hard to walk easily. In consequence they are ill-fitted to fight on foot, and remain glued to their horses, hardy but ugly beasts, on which they sometimes sit like women to perform their everyday business. Buying or selling, eating or drinking, are all done by day or night on horseback, and they even bow forward over their beasts' narrow necks to enjoy a deep and dreamy sleep. . . .

They sometimes fight by challenging their foes to single combat, but when they join battle they advance in packs, uttering their various warcries. Being lightly equipped and very sudden in their movements they can deliberately scatter and gallop about at random, inflicting tremendous slaughter; their extreme nimbleness enables them to force a rampart or pillage an enemy's camp before one catches sight of them. . . . None of them plows or ever touches a plow-handle. They have no fixed abode, no home or law or settled manner of life, but wander like refugees with the wagons in which they live. In these their wives weave their filthy clothing, mate with their husbands, and give birth to their children, and rear them to the age of puberty.

Priscus, *An Account of the Court of Attila the Hun*

[We were invited to a banquet with Attila.] When the hour arrived we went to Attila's palace, along with the embassy from the western Romans, and stood on the threshold of the hall in the presence of Attila. The cup-bearers gave us a cup, according to the national custom, that we might pray before we sat down. Having tasted the cup, we proceeded to take our seats, all the chairs being ranged along the walls of the room on either side. Attila sat in the middle on a couch; a second couch was set behind him, and from it steps led up to his bed, which was covered with linen sheets and coverlets. . . .

[First the king and his guests pledged one another with the wine.] When this ceremony was over the cup-bearers retired and tables, large enough for three or four, or even more, to sit at, were placed next the table of Attila, so that each could take of the food on the dishes without leaving his seat. The attendant of Attila first entered with a dish full of meat, and behind him came the other attendants with bread and other dishes, which they laid on the tables. A luxurious meal, served on silver plate, had been made ready for us and the other guests, but Attila ate nothing but meat on a wooden platter. In everything else, too, he showed himself temperate; his cup was of wood, while to the guests were given goblets of gold and silver. His dress, too, was quite simple, affecting only to be clean.

---

lust for gold" compel men to assent? The generals, swayed by greed, sold them at a high price not only the flesh of sheep and oxen, but even the carcasses of dogs and unclean animals. . . . When their goods and chattels failed, the greedy traders demanded their sons in return for the necessities of life. And the parents consented even to this.[3]

Outraged at the Romans' behavior, the Visigoths revolted. In 378, Emperor Valens and an army of forty thousand soldiers confronted the Visigoths at Adrianople. The emperor was killed, and two-thirds of the Roman army was left dead on the battlefield.

The loss was not fatal, although the new emperor, Theodosius I (379–395), resettled the Visigoths and incorporated many of their soldiers into the Roman army. Some of the Visigoths even became army leaders. By the second half of the fourth century, Roman policy continued to allow Roman army units to be composed entirely of Germanic tribes, known as **federates,** or allies of Rome.

The Threat of the Germans The existence of such military groups proved dangerous to the Late Empire. This was especially evident after Alaric became the leader of the

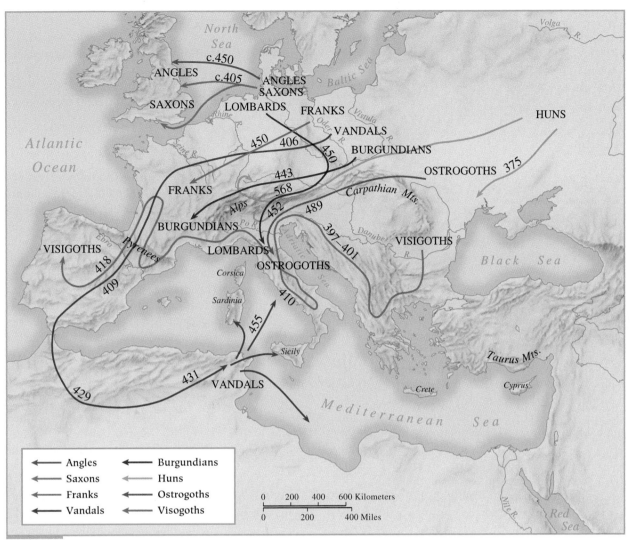

MAP 7.2 German Migration Routes. In the fifth century, German groups migrated throughout the Western Roman Empire. Pressure from Huns in the east forced some tribes west into the empire, and many tribes already in the empire experienced conflict. Some fought the empire, while others were induced to move to the empire's far regions. ❓ How far did the Vandals travel in what period of time? 🌐 **View an animated version of this map or related maps at** http://history.wadsworth.com/spielvogel06/

Visigoths. Between 395 and 401, Alaric and his soldiers moved through the Balkans and then into Italy, seeking food and cash payments from Roman officials. When the city of Rome refused his demands in 408, Alaric marched to the gates and besieged the city, causing the senate of Rome to agree to pay 5,000 pounds of gold and 30,000 pounds of silver for his withdrawal. Two years later, frustrated in his demand that the Visigoths be given part of northern Italy, Alaric and his forces sacked Rome for three days. Alaric died soon after, and his Visigothic followers left Italy, crossed the Alps, and moved into Spain and southern Gaul as Roman allies (see Map 7.2).

By this time, other Germanic tribes were also passing into the Roman Empire and settling down. At the end of 406, several groups crossed the frozen Rhine River, making their way into Gaul and then Spain. One of these groups, the Vandals, under their leader Gaiseric, crossed the Strait of Gibraltar into North Africa and seized Carthage, the capital city, in 439.

As the Germanic tribes moved into the empire and settled down, Roman forces were often withdrawn from the provinces, effectively reducing the central authority of the emperors. In Britain, for example, the emperor Honorius removed the last Roman legions in 410. As one ancient commentator remarked, "Honorius sent letters to the cities in Britain, urging them to fend for themselves."[4] With the withdrawal, the Saxons, who had arrived earlier as Roman allies, now expanded their control in Britain. Within another decade, both Spain and Gaul had also become free of imperial authority.

Role of Masters of the Soldiers By the middle of the fifth century, the western provinces of the Roman Empire had been taken over by Germanic peoples who were in the

Diocletian	284–305
Constantine	306–337
Edict of Milan	313
Construction of Constantinople	324–330
Valens	364–378
Battle of Adrianople	378
Theodosius "the Great"	378–395
Division of the empire	395
Alaric and Visigoths sack Rome	410
Roman legions abandon Britain	410
Vandals sack Rome	455
Odoacer deposes Romulus Augustulus	476

process of creating independent kingdoms. At the same time, a semblance of imperial authority remained in Rome, although the real power behind the throne tended to rest in the hands of important military officials known as Masters of the Soldiers. These military commanders controlled the government and dominated the imperial court. The three most prominent in the fifth century were Stilicho, Aetius, and Ricimer. Stilicho and Ricimer were both Germans, and although all three propped up emperors to maintain the fiction of imperial rule, they were also willing to cooperate with the Germans to maintain their power. But even the Masters of the Soldiers were never safe in the bloody world of fifth-century Roman political life. Stilicho was executed by order of Emperor Honorius. Aetius was killed by Emperor Valentinian III, who was in turn assassinated by a group of Aetius' German bodyguards, who sought to avenge their betrayed leader. Ricimer died a natural death, an unusual event in fifth-century Rome. No doubt, the constant infighting at the center of the Western Empire added to the instability of imperial rule.

By the mid-fifth century, imperial authority in the west remained operating only in Italy and small parts of Gaul. But Rome itself was not safe. In 455, after a treaty made between Rome and Gaiseric, leader of the Vandals, was broken by the Romans, Gaiseric sent a Vandal fleet to Italy and sacked the undefended city of Rome. Twenty-one years later, in 476, Odoacer, a new Master of the Soldiers, himself of German origin, deposed the Roman emperor, the boy Romulus Augustulus. To many historians, the deposition of Romulus signaled the end of the Roman Empire. Of course, this is only a symbolic date, since much of direct imperial rule had already been lost in the course of the fifth century. Even then the empire remained, as Odoacer presented himself as a German king obedient in theory to the Roman emperor Zeno in Constantinople.

By the end of the fifth century, Roman imperial authority in the west had ceased. Nevertheless, the intellectual, governmental, and cultural traditions of the Late Roman Empire continued to live in the new Germanic kingdoms.

The Germanic Kingdoms

By 500, the Western Roman Empire was being replaced politically by a series of kingdoms ruled by German kings (see Map 7.3). The pattern of settlement and the fusion of the Romans and Germans took different forms in the various Germanic kingdoms.

The Ostrogothic Kingdom of Italy

Zeno, the Roman emperor in Constantinople, was not pleased with Odoacer's actions and plotted to unseat him. In his desire to act against the German leader, Zeno brought another German tribe, the Ostrogoths, into Italy. The Ostrogoths had recovered from a defeat by the Huns in the fourth century and under their king Theodoric (493–526) had attacked Constantinople. To divert them, Emperor Zeno had invited Theodoric to act as his deputy to defeat Odoacer and bring Italy back into the empire. Theodoric accepted the challenge, marched into Italy, killed Odoacer, and then, contrary to Zeno's wishes, established himself as ruler of Italy in 493.

Theodoric's Rule   More than any other Germanic state, the Ostrogothic kingdom of Italy managed to maintain the Roman tradition of government. The Ostrogothic king, Theodoric, had received a Roman education while a hostage in Constantinople. After taking control of Italy, he was eager to create a synthesis of Ostrogothic and Roman practices (see the box on p. 173). In addition to maintaining the entire structure of imperial Roman government, he established separate systems of rule for the Ostrogoths and Romans. The Italian population lived under Roman law administered by Roman officials. The Ostrogoths were governed by their own customs and their own officials. However, while the Roman administrative system was kept intact, it was the Ostrogoths alone who controlled the army. Despite the apparent success of this "dual approach," Theodoric's system was unable to keep friction from developing between the Italian population and their Germanic overlords.

Religion proved to be a major source of trouble between Ostrogoths and Romans. The Ostrogoths had been converted earlier to Christianity, but to Arian Christianity, and consequently were viewed by western Christians and the Italians as heretics. Theodoric's rule grew ever harsher as discontent with Ostrogothic rule deepened.

End of the Ostrogothic Kingdom   After Theodoric's death in 526, it quickly became apparent that much of his success had been due to the force of his own personality. His successors soon found themselves face to face with opposition from the imperial forces of the Byzantine or Eastern Roman Empire. Under Emperor Justinian (527–565) (see "The Reign of Justinian" later in this chapter), Byzantine armies reconquered Italy between 535 and 552, devastating much of the peninsula and destroying Rome as one of the great urban centers of the Mediterranean world.

THEODORIC AND OSTROGOTHIC ITALY

*T*HE OSTROGOTHIC KING Theodoric (493–526), who had been educated in Constantinople, was determined to maintain Roman culture rather than destroy it. His attempt to preserve *civilitas,* the traditional Roman civic culture, was well expressed in the official letters written in his name by Cassiodorus, who became master of offices in 525. Theodoric's efforts were largely undone by opposition from the Roman nobility and especially by Justinian's reconquest of the Italian peninsula shortly after Theodoric's death.

Letters of Cassiodorus

King Theodoric to Colossaeus

We delight to entrust our mandates to persons of approved character. . . .

Show forth the justice of the Goths, a nation happily situated for praise, since it is theirs to unite the forethought of the Romans and the virtue of the Barbarians. Remove all ill-planted customs, and impress upon all your subordinates that we would rather that our Treasury lost a suit than that it gained one wrongfully, rather that we lost money than the taxpayer was driven to suicide.

King Theodoric to Unigis, the Sword-Bearer

We delight to live after the law of the Romans, whom we seek to defend with our arms; and we are as much interested in the maintenance of morality as we can possibly be in war. For what profit is there in having removed the turmoil of the Barbarians, unless we live according to law?

. . . Let other kings desire the glory of battles won, of cities taken, of ruins made; our purpose is, God helping us, so to rule that our subjects shall grieve that they did not earlier acquire the blessing of our dominion.

King Theodoric to All the Jews of Genoa

The true mark of *civilitas* is the observance of law. It is this which makes life in communities possible, and which separates man from the brutes. We therefore gladly accede to your request that all the privileges which the foresight of antiquity conferred upon the Jewish customs shall be renewed to you, for in truth it is our great desire that the laws of the ancients shall be kept in force to secure the reverence due to us. Everything which has been found to conduce to *civilitas* should be held fast with enduring devotion.

King Theodoric to All the Goths Settled in Picenum and Samnium

The presence of the Sovereign doubles the sweetness of his gifts, and that man is like one dead whose face is not known to his lord. Come therefore by God's assistance, come all into our presence on the eighth day before the Ides of June [June 7], there solemnly to receive our royal largesse. But let there be no excesses by the way, no plundering the harvest of the cultivators nor trampling down their meadows, since for this cause do we gladly defray the expense of our armies that *civilitas* may be kept intact by armed men.

Amalsuntha, Theodoric's Successor. After Theodoric's death in 526, his daughter Amalsuntha, acting as regent for her son Athalaric, took control of Italy. But she was murdered by relatives in 535, and Italy soon fell subject to the forces of Justinian. This ivory panel of 530 shows Amalsuntha seated on a throne. The frame probably depicts part of Theodoric's palace at Ravenna.

The Byzantine reconquest proved ephemeral, however. Another German tribe, the Lombards, invaded Italy in 568 and conquered much of northern and central Italy. Unlike the Ostrogoths, the Lombards were harsh rulers and cared little for Roman structures and traditions. The Lombards' fondness for fighting each other enabled the Byzantines to retain control of some parts of Italy, especially the area around Ravenna, which became the capital of imperial government.

The Visigothic Kingdom of Spain

The Visigothic kingdom in Spain demonstrated a number of parallels to the Ostrogothic kingdom of Italy. Both favored coexistence between the Roman and German populations, both featured a warrior caste dominating a larger

Kunsthistorisches Museum, Vienna

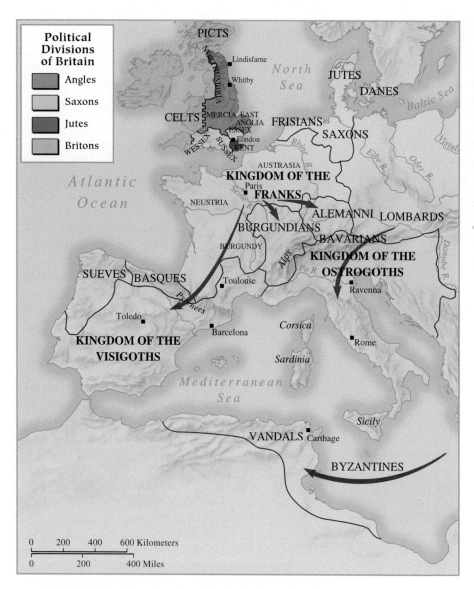

MAP 7.3 **The Germanic Kingdoms of the Old Western Empire.** The Germanic tribes filled the power vacuum caused by the demise of the Roman Empire, building states that blended elements of Germanic customs and laws with those of Roman culture, including large-scale conversions to Christianity. The Franks established the most durable of these Germanic states. **?** How did the movements of Franks during this period correspond to the borders of present-day France? **View an animated version of this map or related maps at** http://history.wadsworth.com/spielvogel06/

Political Divisions of Britain
- Angles
- Saxons
- Jutes
- Britons

native population, and both continued to maintain much of the Roman structure of government while largely excluding Romans from power. There were also noticeable differences, however. Perceiving that their Arianism was a stumbling block to good relations, the Visigothic rulers in the late sixth century converted to Latin or Catholic Christianity and ended the tension caused by this heresy. Laws preventing intermarriage were dropped, and the Visigothic and Hispano-Roman peoples began to fuse together. A new body of law common to both peoples also developed.

The kingdom possessed one fatal weakness, however—the Visigoths fought constantly over the kingship. The Visigoths had no hereditary monarchy and no established procedure for choosing new rulers. Church officials tried to help develop a sense of order, as this canon from the Fourth Council of Toledo in 633 illustrates: "No one of us shall dare to seize the kingdom; no one shall arouse sedition among the citizenry; no one shall think of killing the king. . . ." Church decrees failed to stop the feuds, however,

and assassinations remained a way of life in Visigothic Spain. In 711, Muslim invaders destroyed the Visigothic kingdom itself (see "The Rise of Islam" later in this chapter).

The Frankish Kingdom

Only one of the German states on the European continent proved long-lasting—the kingdom of the Franks. The establishment of a Frankish kingdom was the work of Clovis (c. 482–511), the leader of one group of Franks who eventually became king of them all.

The Rule of Clovis   Around 500, Clovis became a Catholic Christian. He was not the first German king to convert to Christianity, but the others had joined the Arian sect of Christianity. The Christian church in Rome, which had become known as the Roman Catholic church, regarded the Arians as heretics, people who believed in teachings that departed from the official church doctrine. Clovis found that his conversion to Catholic Christianity gained him the sup-

Bibliotheque Nationale, Paris, France

Baptism of Clovis. The conversion of Clovis to Catholic Christianity around 500 was an important factor in gaining papal support for his Frankish kingdom. In this illustration from a medieval manuscript, bishops and nobles look on while Clovis is baptized. One of the nobles holds a crown while a dove, symbol of the Holy Spirit, descends from heaven bringing sacred oil for the ceremony.

port of the Roman Catholic church, which was only too eager to obtain the friendship of a major Germanic ruler who was a Catholic Christian. The conversion of the king also paved the way for the conversion of the Frankish peoples. Finally, Clovis could pose as a defender of the orthodox Catholic faith in order to justify his expansion at the beginning of the sixth century. He defeated the Alemanni in southwest Germany and the Visigoths in southern Gaul. By 510, Clovis had established a powerful new Frankish kingdom stretching from the Pyrenees in the west to German lands in the east (modern-day France and western Germany).

Clovis was responsible, then, for establishing a Frankish kingdom under the Merovingian dynasty, a name derived from Merovech, their semilegendary ancestor. Clovis came to rely on his Frankish followers to rule in the old Roman city-states under the title of count. Often these officials were forced to share power with the Gallo-Roman Catholic bishops, producing a gradual fusion of Latin and German cultures, with the church serving to preserve the Latin culture. Clovis spent the last years of his life ensuring the survival of his dynasty by killing off relatives who were leaders of other groups of Franks.

The Successors of Clovis   After the death of Clovis, his sons divided the newly created kingdom, as was the Frankish custom. During the sixth and seventh centuries, the once-united Frankish kingdom came to be partitioned into three major areas: Neustria in northern Gaul; Austrasia, consisting of the ancient Frankish lands on both sides of the Rhine; and the former kingdom of Burgundy. All three were ruled by members of the Merovingian dynasty. Within the three territories, members of the dynasty were assisted

by powerful nobles. Frankish society possessed a ruling class that gradually intermarried with the old Gallo-Roman senatorial class to form a new nobility. These noble families took advantage of their position to strengthen their own lands and wealth at the expense of the monarchy. Within the royal household, the position of *major domus,* or mayor of the palace, the chief officer of the king's household, began to overshadow the king. Essentially, both nobles and mayors of the palace were expanding their power at the expense of the kings.

At the beginning of the eighth century, the most important political development in the Frankish kingdom was the rise of Charles Martel, who served as mayor of the palace of Austrasia beginning in 714. Charles Martel led troops that defeated the Muslims near Poitiers in 732 and by the time of his death in 741 had become virtual ruler of the three Merovingian kingdoms. Though he was not king, Charles Martel's dynamic efforts put his family on the verge of creating a new dynasty that would establish an even more powerful Frankish state (see Chapter 8).

During the sixth and seventh centuries, the Frankish kingdom witnessed a process of fusion between Gallo-Roman and Frankish cultures and peoples, a process accompanied by a significant decline in Roman standards of civilization and commercial activity. The Franks were warriors and did little to encourage either urban life or trade. Commerce declined in the interior, though seacoast towns maintained some activity. By 750, Frankish Gaul was basically an agricultural society in which the old Roman *latifundia* system of the Late Empire continued unimpeded. Institutionally, however, Germanic concepts of kingship and customary law had replaced the Roman governmental structure.

Anglo-Saxon England

The barbarian pressures on the Western Roman Empire had forced the emperors to withdraw the Roman armies and abandon Britain by the beginning of the fifth century. This opened the door to the Angles and Saxons, Germanic tribes from Denmark and northern Germany. Although these same peoples had made plundering raids for a century, the withdrawal of the Roman armies enabled them to make settlements instead. They met with resistance from the Celtic Britons, however, who still controlled the western regions of Cornwall, Wales, and Cumberland at the beginning of the seventh century (see Map 7.3). The German invaders eventually succeeded in carving out small kingdoms throughout the island, Kent in southeast England being one of them. This wave of German invaders would eventually be converted to Christianity by new groups of Christian missionaries (see "The Conversion of England" later in this chapter).

The Society of the Germanic Kingdoms

As the Germans infiltrated the Roman Empire, they were influenced by the Roman society they encountered. Consequently, the Germanic peoples of the fifth, sixth, and seventh centuries were probably quite different from the Germans that the forces of Augustus encountered in the first century A.D. Moreover, there was a meaningful fusion of Roman and German upper classes in the new kingdoms. In Merovingian Frankish lands, upper-class Gallo-Romans intermarried with Frankish nobles to produce a new ruling class. Each influenced the other. Franks constructed Roman-style villas; Gallo-Romans adopted Frankish weapons.

The crucial social bond among the Germanic peoples was the family, especially the extended or patriarchal family of husbands, wives, children, brothers, sisters, cousins, and grandparents. In addition to working the land together and passing it down to succeeding generations, the extended family provided protection, which was sorely needed in the violent atmosphere of Merovingian times.

Germanic Law   The German conception of family and kinship affected the way Germanic law treated the problem of crime and punishment. In the Roman system, as in our own, a crime such as murder was considered an offense against society or the state and was handled by a court that heard evidence and arrived at a decision. Germanic law tended to be personal. An injury by one person against another could mean a blood feud in which the family of the injured party took revenge on the kin of the wrongdoer. Feuds could lead to savage acts of revenge, such as hacking off hands or feet, gouging out eyes, or slicing off ears and noses. Since this system had a tendency to get out of control and allow mayhem to multiply, an alternative system arose that made use of a fine called *wergeld*. This was the amount paid by a wrongdoer to the family of the person who had been injured or killed. *Wergeld,* which means "money for a man," was the value of a person in monetary terms. That value varied considerably according to social status. The law of the Salic Franks, which was first written down under Roman influence at the beginning of the sixth century, stated, "If any one shall have killed a free Frank, or a barbarian living under the Salic law, and it have been proved on him, he shall be sentenced to 8,000 denars. . . . But if any one has slain a man who is in the service of the king, he shall be sentenced to 24,000 denars."[5] An offense against a noble obviously cost considerably more than one against a free person or a slave.

Under German customary law, compurgation and the ordeal were the two most commonly used procedures for determining whether an accused person was guilty and should have to pay *wergeld*. Compurgation was the swearing of an oath by the accused person, backed up by a group of "oathhelpers," numbering twelve or twenty-five, who would also swear that the accused person should be believed. The ordeal functioned in a variety of ways, all of which were based on the principle of divine intervention; divine forces (whether pagan or Christian) would not allow an innocent person to be harmed (see the box on p. 177).

The Frankish Family and Marriage   For the Franks, like other Germanic peoples of the Early Middle Ages, the extended family was at the center of social organization. The Frankish family structure was quite simple. Males were dominant and made all the important decisions. A woman obeyed her father until she married and then fell under the legal domination of her husband. A widow, however, could hold property without a male guardian. In Frankish law, the *wergeld* of a wife of childbearing age—of value because she could produce children—was considerably higher than that of a man. The Salic law stated: "If any one killed a free woman after she had begun bearing children, he shall be sentenced to 24,000 denars. . . . After she can have no more children, he who kills her shall be sentenced to 8,000 denars."[6]

Since marriage affected the extended family group, fathers or uncles could arrange marriages for the good of the family without considering their children's wishes. Most important was the engagement ceremony in which a prospective son-in-law made a payment symbolizing the purchase of paternal authority over the bride. The essential feature of the marriage itself involved placing the married couple in bed to achieve their physical union. In first marriages, it was considered important that the wife be a virgin so as to ensure that any children would be the husband's. A virgin symbolized the ability of the bloodline to continue. For this reason, adultery was viewed as pollution of the woman and her offspring, poisoning the future. Adulterous wives were severely punished (an adulterous woman could be strangled or even burned alive); adulterous husbands were not. Divorce was relatively simple and was initiated primarily by the husband. Divorced wives simply returned to their families.

For most women in the new Germanic kingdoms, their legal status reflected the material conditions of their lives. Archaeological evidence suggests that most women had life expectancies of only thirty or forty years and that about 10 to 15 percent of women died in their childbearing years, no doubt due to complications associated with childbirth. For most women, life consisted of domestic labor: providing food and clothing for the household, caring for the children, and assisting with numerous farming chores. Of all the duties of women, the most important was childbearing, because it was crucial to the maintenance of the family and its properties.

GERMANIC CUSTOMARY LAW: THE ORDEAL

N GERMANIC CUSTOMARY LAW, the ordeal came to be a means by which accused persons might clear themselves. Although the ordeal took different forms, all involved a physical trial of some sort, such as holding a red-hot iron. It was believed God would protect the innocent and allow them to come through the ordeal unharmed. The sixth-century account by Gregory of Tours describes an ordeal by hot water.

Gregory of Tours, *An Ordeal of Hot Water* (c. 580)

An Arian priest disputing with a deacon of our religion made venomous assertions against the Son of God and the Holy Ghost, as is the habit of that sect [the Arians]. But when the deacon had discoursed a long time concerning the reasonableness of our faith and the heretic, blinded by the fog of unbelief, continued to reject the truth, . . . the former said: "Why weary ourselves with long discussions? Let acts approve the truth; let a kettle be heated over the fire and someone's ring be thrown into the boiling water. Let him who shall take it from the heated liquid be approved as a follower of the truth, and afterward let the other party be converted to the knowledge of the truth. And do you also understand, O heretic, that this our party will fulfill the conditions with the aid of the Holy Ghost; you shall confess that there is no discordance, no dissimilarity in the Holy Trinity [belief that God, Jesus (son of God), and Holy Spirit (Ghost) are three manifestations of the same unique Deity]." The heretic consented to the proposition and they separated after appointing the next morning for the trial. But the fervor of faith in which the deacon had first made this suggestion began to cool through the instigation of the enemy. Rising with the dawn he bathed his arm in oil and smeared it with ointment. But nevertheless he made the round of the sacred places and called in prayer on the Lord. . . . About the third hour they met in the market place. The people came together to see the show. A fire was lighted, the kettle was placed upon it, and when it grew very hot the ring was thrown into the boiling water. The deacon invited the heretic to take it out of the water first. But he promptly refused, saying, "You who did propose this trial are the one to take it out." The deacon all of a tremble bared his arm. And when the heretic saw it besmeared with ointment he cried out: "With magic arts you have thought to protect yourself, that you have made use of these salves, but what you have done will not avail." While they were thus quarreling there came up a deacon from Ravenna named Iacinthus and inquired what the trouble was about. When he learned the truth he drew his arm out from under his robe at once and plunged his right hand into the kettle. Now the ring that had been thrown in was a little thing and very light so that it was thrown about by the water as chaff would be blown about by the wind; and searching for it a long time he found it after about an hour. Meanwhile the flame beneath the kettle blazed up mightily so that the greater heat might make it difficult for the ring to be followed by the hand; but the deacon extracted it at length and suffered no harm, protesting rather that at the bottom the kettle was cold while at the top it was just pleasantly warm. When the heretic beheld this he was greatly confused and audaciously thrust his hand into the kettle saying, "My faith will aid me." As soon as his hand had been thrust in all the flesh was boiled off the bones clear up to the elbow. And so the dispute ended.

Development of the Christian Church

By the end of the fourth century, Christianity had become the predominant religion of the Roman Empire. As the official Roman state disintegrated, the Christian church played an increasingly important role in the new civilization built on the ruins of the old Roman Empire.

The Church Fathers

Many early Christians expressed considerable hostility toward the pagan culture of the classical world. Tertullian (c. 160–c. 225), a Christian writer from Carthage, had proclaimed: "What has Jerusalem to do with Athens, the Church with the Academy, the Christian with the heretic? . . . After Jesus Christ we have no need of speculation, after the Gospel no need of research."[7] To many early Christians, the Bible contained all the knowledge anyone needed.

Others, however, thought it was not possible to separate Christian theological thought from classical traditions and education and encouraged Christians to absorb the classical heritage. As it spread in the eastern Roman world, Christianity adopted Greek as its language. The New Testament was written in Greek. Christians also turned to Greek thought for help in expressing complicated theological concepts. An especially important influence was Neoplatonism, a revival of Platonic thought that reached its high point in the third century A.D. Neoplatonists believed that one could use reason to perceive the link between the invisible spiritual world and the visible material world. Christian theologians used Neoplatonic concepts to explain doctrines on Jesus, especially the distinction between his human and divine natures. In many ways, then, Christianity served to preserve Greco-Roman culture.

The Work of Augustine The work of Saint Augustine (354–430) provides one of the best examples of how Christian theologians used pagan culture in the service of Christianity.

THE CONFESSIONS OF AUGUSTINE

AINT AUGUSTINE'S spiritual and intellectual auto-biography is a revealing self-portrait of the inner struggles of one of the intellectual giants of early Christianity. The first excerpt is taken from Book 8, in which Augustine describes how he heard a voice from heaven and was converted from his old habits. In the second excerpt, from Book 9, Augustine expresses joy and gratitude for his conversion.

Augustine, *Confessions*

From Book 8

So was I speaking and weeping in the most bitter contrition of my heart, when, lo! I heard from a neighboring house a voice as of boy or girl, I know not, chanting, and oft repeating, "Take up and read; Take up and read." Instantly, my countenance altered, I began to think most intently whether children were wont in any kind of play to sing such words: nor could I remember ever to have heard the like. So checking the torrent of my tears, I arose; interpreting it to be no other than a command from God to open the book, and read the first chapter I should find. For I had heard of Antony, that coming in during the reading of the Gospel, he received the admonition, as if what was being read was spoken to him: Go, sell all that you have, and give to the poor, and you shall have treasure in heaven, and come and follow me:

and by such oracle he was forthwith converted unto You. Eagerly then I returned to the place where Alypius was sitting; for there I had laid the volume of the Apostle [Paul] when I arose thence. I seized, opened, and in silence read that section on which my eyes first fell: Not in rioting and drunkenness, not in chambering and wantonness, not in strife and envying; but put you on the Lord Jesus Christ, and make not provision for the flesh. . . . No further would I read; nor need I: for instantly at the end of this sentence, by a light as it were of serenity infused into my heart, all the darkness of doubt vanished away.

From Book 9

O Lord I am your servant; I am your servant, and the son of your handmaid: You have broken my bonds in sunder. I will offer to You the sacrifice of praise. Let my heart and my tongue praise You; yea, let all my bones say, O Lord, who is like unto You? Let them say, and answer You me, and say unto my soul, I am your salvation. Who am I, and what am I? What evil have not been either my deeds, or if not my deeds, my words, or if not my words, my will? But You, O Lord, are good and merciful, and your right hand had respect unto the depth of my death, and from the bottom of my heart emptied that abyss of corruption.

Augustine came to be seen as one of the Latin Fathers of the Catholic church, intellectuals who wrote in Latin and profoundly influenced the development of Christian thought in the west.

Born in North Africa, Augustine was reared by his mother, an ardent Christian. He eventually became a professor of rhetoric at Milan in 384. But two years later, after experiencing a profound and moving religious experience, Augustine gave up his teaching position and went back to North Africa, where he served as bishop of Hippo from 396 until his death in 430.

Augustine's two most famous works are the *Confessions* and *The City of God*. Written in 397, the *Confessions* was a self-portrait not of Augustine's worldly activities but of the "history of a heart," an account of his own personal and spiritual experiences, written to help others with their search. Augustine describes how he struggled throughout his early life to find God until in his thirty-second year he experienced a miraculous conversion (see the box above).

The City of God, Augustine's other major work, was a profound expression of a Christian philosophy of government and history. It was written in response to a line of argument that arose soon after the sack of Rome in 410. Some pagan philosophers maintained that Rome's problems stemmed from the Roman state's recognition of Christianity and abandonment of the old, traditional gods. Augustine argued that Rome's troubles began long before

Christianity arose in the empire. In *The City of God*, Augustine theorized on the ideal relations between two kinds of societies existing throughout time—the City of God and the City of the World. Those who loved God would be loyal to the City of God, whose ultimate location was the kingdom of heaven. Earthly society would always be insecure because of human beings' imperfect nature and inclination to violate God's commandments. And yet the City of the World was still necessary, for it was the duty of rulers to curb the depraved instincts of sinful humans and maintain the peace necessary for Christians to live in the world. Hence Augustine posited that secular government and authority were necessary for the pursuit of the true Christian life on earth; in doing so, he provided a justification for secular political authority that would play an important role in medieval thought.

Augustine was also important in establishing the Christian church's views on sexual desire. Many early Christians had seen **celibacy,** or complete abstinence from sexual activity, as the surest way to holiness. Augustine, too, believed Christians should reject sex, but he maintained that many Christians were unable to do so. For them, marriage was a good alternative, but with the understanding that even in marriage, sex between a man and woman had to serve a purpose—the procreation of children. It was left to the clergy of the church to uphold the high ideal of celibacy.

Jerome and the Bible   Another Latin Father was Jerome (345–420), who pursued literary studies in Rome and became a master of Latin prose. Jerome had mixed feelings about his love for liberal studies, however, and like Augustine experienced a spiritual conversion, after which he tried to dedicate himself more fully to Jesus. He had a dream in which Jesus appeared as his judge:

> Asked who and what I was, I replied: "I am a Christian." But He who presided said: "You lie, you are a follower of Cicero, not of Christ. For where your treasure is, there will your heart be also." Instantly, I became dumb. . . . Accordingly I made oath and called upon His name, saying: "Lord, if ever again I possess worldly books [the classics], or if ever again I read such, I have denied You."

After this dream, Jerome determined to "read the books of God with a zeal greater than I had previously given to the books of men."[8]

Ultimately, Jerome found a compromise by purifying the literature of the pagan world and then using it to further the Christian faith. Jerome was the greatest scholar among the Latin Fathers, and his extensive knowledge of both Hebrew and Greek enabled him to translate the Old and New Testaments into Latin. In the process, he created the so-called Latin Vulgate, or common text, of the Scriptures that became the standard edition for the Catholic church in the Middle Ages.

The Power of the Pope

In the early centuries of Christianity, the churches in the larger cities had great influence in the administration of the church. It was only natural, then, that the bishops of those cities would also exercise considerable power. One of the far-reaching developments in the history of the Christian church was the emergence of one bishop—that of Rome—as the recognized leader of the western Christian church.

The doctrine of **Petrine supremacy,** based on the belief that the bishops of Rome occupied a preeminent position in the church, was grounded in Scripture. According to the Gospel of Matthew, when Jesus asked his disciples, "Who do you say I am?" Simon Peter answered:

> You are the Christ, the Son of the living God. Jesus replied, Blessed are you, Simon, son of Jonah, for this was not revealed by man, but by my Father in heaven. And I tell you that you are Peter, and on this rock I will build my church, and the gates of hell will not overcome it. I will give you the keys of the kingdom of heaven; whatever you bind on earth will be bound in heaven; and whatever you loose on earth will be loosed in heaven.[9]

According to church tradition, Jesus had given the keys to the kingdom of heaven to Peter, who was considered the chief apostle and the first bishop of Rome. Subsequent bishops of Rome were considered Peter's successors and later the "vicars of Christ" on earth. Though this exalted view of the bishops of Rome was by no means accepted by all early Christians, Rome's position as the traditional capital of the Roman Empire served to buttress this claim.

By the end of the fourth century, the bishops of Rome were using the title of *papa,* "father" (which became the English *pope*). Pope Leo I (440–461) was especially energetic in systematically expounding the doctrine of Petrine supremacy. He portrayed himself as the heir of Peter, whom Jesus had chosen to be head of the Christian church. But state authorities were also claiming some power over the church.

Church and State

Once the Roman emperors became Christians, they came to play a significant role in the affairs of the church. Christian emperors viewed themselves as God's representatives on earth. They not only built churches and influenced the structure of the church's organization but also became involved in church government and doctrinal controversies.

While emperors were busying themselves in church affairs, the spiritual and political vacuum left by the disintegration of the Roman state allowed bishops to play a more active role in imperial government. Increasingly, they served as advisers to Christian Roman emperors. Moreover, as imperial authority declined, bishops often played a noticeably independent political role. Ambrose (c. 339–397) of Milan was an early example of a strong and independent bishop. Through his activities and writings, Ambrose created an image of the ideal Christian bishop. Among other things, this ideal bishop would defend the independence of the church against the tendency of imperial officials to oversee church policy: "Exalt not yourself, but if you would reign the longer, be subject to God. It is written, God's to God and Caesar's to Caesar. The palace is the Emperor's, the Churches are the Bishop's."[10] When Emperor Theodosius I ordered the massacre of many citizens in Thessalonika for refusing to obey his commands, Ambrose denounced the massacre and refused to allow the emperor to take part in church ceremonies. Theodosius finally agreed to do public penance in the cathedral of Milan for his dastardly deed. Ambrose proved himself a formidable advocate of the position that spiritual authority should take precedence over temporal power, at least in spiritual matters.

The weakness of the political authorities on the Italian peninsula also contributed to the church's independence in that area. In the Germanic kingdoms, the kings controlled both churches and bishops. But in Italy, a different tradition prevailed, fed by semilegendary accounts of papal deeds. Pope Leo I, for example, supposedly caused Attila the Hun to turn away from Rome in 452. Although plague rather than papal persuasion was probably more to account for Attila's withdrawal, the pope got the credit. Popes, then, played significant political roles in Italy, which only added to their claims of power vis-à-vis the secular authorities. Pope Gelasius I (492–496) could write to the emperor at Constantinople:

> There are two powers, august Emperor, by which this world is ruled from the beginning: the consecrated authority of the bishops, and the royal power. In these matters the priests bear the heavier burden because they will render account, even for

rulers of men, at the divine judgment. Besides, most gracious son, you are aware that, although you in your office are the ruler of the human race, nevertheless you devoutly bow your head before those who are leaders in things divine and look to them for the means of your salvation.[11]

According to Gelasius, though there were two ruling powers, spiritual and temporal, with different functions, the church was ultimately the higher authority because all men, including emperors, must look to the church "for the means of . . . salvation."

Pope Gregory the Great

Although western Christians came to accept the bishop of Rome as head of the church, there was no unanimity on the extent of the powers the pope possessed as a result of his position. Nevertheless, the emergence in the sixth century of a strong pope, Gregory I, known as Gregory the Great, set the papacy and the Roman Catholic church on an energetic path that enabled the church in the seventh and eighth centuries to play an increasingly prominent role in civilizing the Germans and aiding the emergence of a distinctly new European civilization.

Pope Gregory I. Pope Gregory the Great became one of the most important popes of the Early Middle Ages. This ninth-century manuscript illustration shows Gregory dictating a work to two monks. Over Gregory's right shoulder is a dove, symbol of the Holy Spirit, which is providing divine inspiration for what he is dictating.

As pope, Gregory I (590–604) assumed direction of Rome and its surrounding territories, which had suffered enormously from the Ostrogothic-Byzantine struggle and the Lombard invasion of the sixth century. Gregory described the conditions in a sermon to the people of Rome:

> What Rome herself, once deemed the Mistress of the World, has now become, we see—wasted away with afflictions grievous and many, with the loss of citizens, the assaults of enemies, the frequent fall of ruined buildings. . . . Where is the Senate? Where is the people? The bones are all dissolved, the flesh is consumed, all the pomp of the dignities of this world is gone.[12]

Gregory took charge and made Rome and its surrounding area into an administrative unit that eventually came to be known as the Papal States. Although historians disagree about Gregory's motives in establishing papal temporal power, no doubt Gregory was probably only doing what he felt needed to be done: to provide for the defense of Rome against the Lombards, to establish a government for Rome, and to feed the people. Gregory remained loyal to the empire and continued to address the Byzantine emperor as the rightful ruler of Italy.

Gregory also pursued a policy of extending papal authority over the Christian church in the west. He intervened in ecclesiastical conflicts throughout Italy and corresponded with the Frankish rulers, urging them to reform the church in Gaul. He successfully initiated the efforts of missionaries to convert England to Christianity and was especially active in converting the pagan peoples of Germanic Europe. His primary instrument was the monastic movement.

The Monks and Their Missions

A **monk** (Latin *monachus*, meaning "someone who lives alone") was a man who sought to live a life divorced from the world, cut off from ordinary human society, in order to pursue an ideal of godliness or total dedication to the will of God. Christian **monasticism,** which developed first in Egypt, was initially based on the model of the solitary hermit who forsakes all civilized society to pursue spirituality. Saint Anthony (c. 250–350) was a prosperous Egyptian peasant who decided to follow Jesus' injunction in the Gospel of Mark: "Go your way, sell whatsoever you have, and give to the poor, and you shall have treasure in heaven: and come, take up the cross, and follow me."[13] Anthony gave his 300 acres of land to the poor and went into the desert to pursue his ideal of holiness (see the box on p. 181). Others did likewise, often to extremes. Saint Simeon the Stylite lived for three decades in a basket atop a pillar over 60 feet high. These spiritual gymnastics established a new ideal for Christianity. Whereas the early Christian model had been the martyr who died for the faith and achieved eternal life in the process, the new ideal was the monk who died to the world and achieved spiritual life through denial, asceticism, and mystical experience of God.

The Life of Saint Anthony

N THE THIRD and early fourth centuries, the lives of martyrs had provided important models for early Christianity. But in the course of the fourth century, monks who attempted to achieve spiritual perfection through asceticism, the denial of earthly life, and the struggle with demons became the new spiritual ideal for Christians. Consequently, spiritual biographies of early monks became a significant new form of Christian literature. Especially noteworthy was *The Life of Saint Anthony* by Saint Athanasius, the defender of Catholic orthodoxy against the Arians. His work had been translated into Latin before 386. This excerpt describes how Anthony fought off the temptations of Satan.

Athanasius, *The Life of Saint Anthony*

Now when the Enemy [Satan] saw that his craftiness in this matter was without profit, and that the more he brought temptation into Saint Anthony, the more strenuous the saint was in protecting himself against him with the armor of righteousness, he attacked him by means of the vigor of early manhood which is bound up in the nature of our humanity. With the goadings of passion he sued to trouble him by night, and in the daytime also he would vex him and pain him with the same to such an extent that even those who saw him knew from his appearance that he was waging war against the Adversary. But the more the Evil One brought unto him filthy and maddening thoughts, the more Saint Anthony took refuge in prayer and in abundant supplication, and amid them all he remained wholly chaste. And the Evil One was working upon him every shameful deed according to his wont, and at length he even appeared unto Saint Anthony in the form of a woman; and other things which resembled this he performed with ease, for such things are a subject for boasting to him.

But the blessed Anthony knelt down upon his knees on the ground, and prayed before Him who said, "Before you criest unto Me, I will answer you," and said, "O my Lord, this I entreat you. Let not Your love be blotted out from my mind, and behold, I am, by Your grace, innocent before You." And again the Enemy multiplied in him the thoughts of lust, until Saint Anthony became as one who was being burned up, not through the Evil One, but through his own lusts; but he girded himself about with the threat of the thought of the Judgment, and of the torture of Gehenna [Hell], and of the worm which does not die. And while meditating on the thoughts which could be directed against the Evil One, he prayed for thoughts which would be hostile to him. Thus, to the reproach and shame of the Enemy, these things could not be performed; for he who imagined that he could be God was made a mock of by a young man, and he who boasted over flesh and blood was vanquished by a man who was clothed with flesh.

These early monks, however, soon found themselves unable to live in solitude. Their feats of holiness attracted followers on a wide scale, and as the monastic ideal spread throughout the east, a new form of monasticism, based on the practice of communal life, soon became the dominant form. Monastic communities soon came to be seen as the ideal Christian society that could provide a moral example to the wider society around them.

Benedictine Monasticism   Saint Benedict of Nursia (c. 480–c. 543), who founded a monastic house for which he wrote a set of rules sometime between 520 and 530, established the fundamental form of monastic life in the western Christian church. Benedict's rules largely rejected the ascetic ideals of eastern monasticism, which had tended to emphasize such practices as fasting and self-inflicted torments (such as living atop pillars for thirty years), in favor of an ideal of moderation. In Chapter 40 of the rules, on the amount of drink a monk should imbibe, this sense of moderation becomes apparent:

> "Every man has his proper gift from God, one after this manner, another after that." And therefore it is with some misgiving that we determine the amount of food for someone else. Still, having regard for the weakness of some brothers, we believe that a hemina [a quarter liter] of wine per day will suffice for all. Let those, however, to whom God gives the gift of abstinence, know that they shall have their proper reward. But if either the circumstances of the place, the work, or the heat of summer necessitates more, let it lie in the discretion of the abbot to grant it. But let him take care in all things lest satiety or drunkenness supervene.

At the same time, moderation did not preclude a hard and disciplined existence based on the ideals of poverty, chastity, and obedience.

Benedict's rules divided each day into a series of activities with primary emphasis on prayer and manual labor. Physical work of some kind was required of all monks for several hours a day because "idleness is the enemy of the soul." At the very heart of community practice was prayer, the proper "work of God." While this included private meditation and reading, all monks gathered together seven times during the day for common prayer and chanting of psalms. A Benedictine life was a communal one; monks ate, worked, slept, and worshiped together.

Each Benedictine monastery was strictly ruled by an **abbot,** or "father" of the monastery, who had complete authority over the monks, who bent unquestioningly to the will of the abbot. Each Benedictine monastery owned lands that enabled it to be a self-sustaining community, isolated from and independent of the world surrounding it. Within

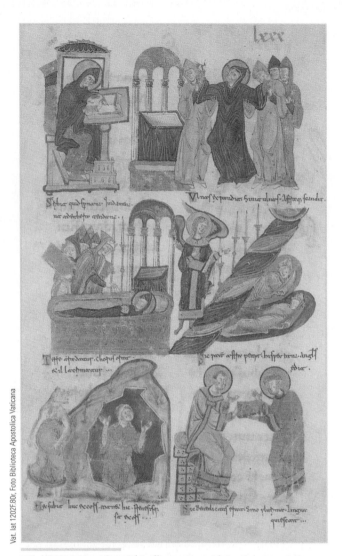

Life of Saint Benedict. This illustration with its six scenes is from an eleventh-century manuscript of Pope Gregory the Great's *Life of Saint Benedict,* written in 593 or 594. *Top left,* Benedict writes his rules; *top right,* the death of Benedict; *middle left,* his burial; *middle right* and *bottom left,* scenes of miracles attributed to Saint Benedict's intercession; *bottom right,* Gregory finishes his *Life of Saint Benedict.*

Vat. lat 1202F.80r, Foto Biblioteca Apostolica Vaticana

celibate life in the desert, however. In a number of cities in the fourth century, women organized religious communities in their own homes.

Monasticism played an indispensable role in early medieval civilization. Monks became the new heroes of Christian civilization. Their dedication to God became the highest ideal of Christian life. Moreover, the monks played an increasingly significant role in spreading Christianity to all of Europe.

Irish Monks as Missionaries   Ireland had remained a Celtic outpost beyond the reach of the Roman Empire and the Germanic invaders. The most famous of the Christian missionaries to Ireland in the fifth century was Saint Patrick (c. 390–461). Son of a Romano-British Christian, Patrick was kidnapped as a young man by Irish raiders and kept as a slave in Ireland. After his escape to Gaul, he became a monk and chose to return to Ireland to convert the Irish to Christianity. Irish tradition ascribes to Patrick the title of "founder of Irish Christianity," a testament to his apparent success.

Since Ireland had not been part of the Roman world and was fairly isolated from the European continent even after its conversion, Irish Christianity tended to develop along lines somewhat different from Roman Christianity. Whereas Catholic ecclesiastical structure had followed Roman government models, the absence of these models in Ireland engendered a different pattern of church organization. Rather than bishoprics, monasteries became the fundamental units of church organization, and abbots, the heads of the monasteries, exercised far more control over the Irish church than bishops did.

By the sixth century, Irish monasticism was a flourishing institution with its own striking characteristics. It was strongly ascetic. Monks performed strenuous fasts, prayed and meditated frequently under extreme privations, and confessed their sins on a regular basis to their superiors. In fact, Irish monasticism gave rise to the use of penitentials or manuals that provided a guide for examining one's life to see what offenses against the will of God one had committed (see the box on p. 183).

A great love of learning also characterized Irish monasticism. The Irish eagerly absorbed both Latin and Greek culture and fostered education as a major part of their monastic life. Irish monks were preserving classical Latin at the same time spoken Latin was being corrupted on the Continent into new dialects that eventually became the Romance languages, such as Italian, French, and Spanish. Irish monasteries produced extraordinary illuminated manuscripts illustrated with abstract geometric patterns.

The emphasis on asceticism led many Irish monks to go into voluntary exile. This "exile for the love of God" was not into isolation, however, but into missionary activity. Irish monks became fervid missionaries. Saint Columba (521–597) left Ireland in 565 as a "pilgrim for Christ" and founded a highly influential monastic community off the coast of Scotland on the island of Iona. From there Irish missionaries went to northern England to begin the process

the monastery, however, monks were to fulfill their vow of poverty: "Let all things be common to all, as it is written, lest anyone should say that anything is his own or arrogate it to himself."[14] By the eighth century, Benedictine monasticism had spread throughout the west.

Women, too, sought to withdraw from the world to dedicate themselves to God. Already in the third century, groups of women abandoned the cities to form communities in the deserts of Egypt and Syria. The first monastic rules for western women were produced by Caesarius of Arles for his sister in the fifth century. They strongly emphasized a rigid cloistering of female religious, known as **nuns,** to preserve them from dangers. Later in the west, in the seventh and eighth centuries, the growth of double monasteries allowed monks and nuns to reside close by and follow a common set of rules. Not all women pursued the

IRISH MONASTICISM AND THE PENITENTIAL

*I*RISH MONASTICISM became well known for its ascetic practices. Much emphasis was placed on careful examination of conscience to determine if one had committed a sin against God. To facilitate this examination, penitentials were developed that listed possible sins with appropriate penances. Penance usually meant fasting a number of days each week, taking only bread and water. Although these penitentials were eventually used throughout Christendom, they were especially important in Irish Christianity. This excerpt from the penitential of Cummean, an Irish abbot, was written about 650 and demonstrates a distinctive feature of the penitentials, an acute preoccupation with sexual sins.

The Penitential of Cummean

A bishop who commits fornication shall be degraded and shall do penance for twelve years.

A priest or a deacon who commits natural fornication, having previously taken the vow of a monk, shall do penance for seven years. He shall ask pardon every hour; he shall perform a special fast during every week except in the days between Easter and Pentecost.

He who defiles his mother shall do penance for three years, with perpetual pilgrimage.

So shall those who commit sodomy do penance every seven years.

He who merely desires in his mind to commit fornication, but is not able, shall do penance for one year, especially in the three forty-day periods.

He who is willingly polluted during sleep shall arise and sing nine psalms in order, kneeling. On the following day, he shall live on bread and water.

A cleric who commits fornication once shall do penance for one year on bread and water; if he begets a son he shall do penance for seven years as an exile; so also a virgin.

He who loves any woman, but is unaware of any evil beyond a few conversations, shall do penance for forty days.

He who is in a state of matrimony ought to be continent during the three forty-day periods and on Saturday and on Sunday, night and day, and in the two appointed week days [Wednesday and Friday], and after conception, and during the entire menstrual period.

After a birth he shall abstain, if it is a son, for thirty-three [days]; if a daughter, for sixty-six [days].

Boys talking alone and transgressing the regulations of the elders [in the monastery], shall be corrected by three special fasts.

Children who imitate acts of fornication, twenty days; if frequently, forty.

But boys of twenty years who practice masturbation together and confess [shall do penance] twenty or forty days before they take communion.

---

of converting the Angles and Saxons. Aidan of Iona, for example, founded the island monastery of Lindisfarne in the Anglo-Saxon kingdom of Northumbria. Lindisfarne in turn became a training center for monks who spread out to different parts of Anglo-Saxon England. Meanwhile, other Irish monks traveled to the European mainland. New monasteries founded by the Irish became centers of learning wherever they were located.

The Conversion of England At the same time the Irish monks were busy bringing their version of Christianity to the Anglo-Saxons of Britain, Pope Gregory the Great had set in motion his own effort to convert England to Roman Christianity. His most important agent was Augustine, a monk from Saint Andrew's monastery in Rome, who arrived in England in 597. England at that time had a number of Germanic kingdoms. Augustine went first to Kent, where he converted King Ethelbert, whereupon most of the king's subjects followed suit. Pope Gregory's conversion techniques emphasized persuasion rather than force, and as seen in this excerpt from one of his letters, he was willing to assimilate old pagan practices in order to coax the pagans into the new faith:

We wish you [Abbot Mellitus] to inform him [Augustine] that we have been giving careful thought to the affairs of the English, and have come to the conclusion that the temples of the idols among that people should on no account be destroyed. The idols are to be destroyed, but the temples themselves are to be sprinkled with holy water, altars set up in them, and relics deposited there. For if these temples are well-built, they must be purified from the worship of demons and dedicated to the service of the true God. In this way, we hope that the people, seeing that their temples are not destroyed, may abandon their error and, flocking more readily to their accustomed resorts, may come to know and adore the true God.[15]

Freed of their pagan past, temples had become churches, as one Christian commentator noted with joy: "The dwelling place of demons has become a house of God. The saving light has come to shine, where shadows covered all. Where sacrifices once took place and idols stood, angelic choirs now dance. Where God was angered once, now God is made content."[16]

Likewise, old pagan feasts were to be given new names and incorporated into the Christian calendar. No doubt Gregory was aware that early Christians had done the same. The Christian feast of Christmas, for example, was held on December 25, the day of the pagan celebration of the winter solstice.

As Roman Christianity spread northward in Britain, it encountered Irish Christianity moving southward. Soon arguments arose over the differences between Celtic and Roman Christianity, especially over matters of discipline. At the Synod of Whitby, held in the kingdom of Northumbria

The Book of Kells. Art historians use the term *Hiberno-Saxon* (Hibernia was the ancient name for Ireland) or *Insular* to refer to works produced primarily in the monasteries of the British Isles, especially Ireland. The best example of Hiberno-Saxon art is *The Book of Kells,* a richly decorated illuminated manuscript of the Christian Gospels. Kells was the name of the monastery that owned it, but the work was produced by the monks of Iona, who combined Celtic and Anglo-Saxon abstract designs with elaborate portrayals of human figures and animals. A twelfth-century priest who viewed it observed: "Look . . . keenly at it and you . . . will make out intricacies, so delicate and subtle, so exact and compact, so full of knots and links, with colors so fresh and vivid, that you might say that all this was the work of an angel, and not of a man." Shown here is a page centered on the figure of Jesus.

in 664, the king of Northumbria accepted the arguments of the representatives of Roman Christianity and decided the issue in favor of Roman practices. A gradual fusion of Celtic and Roman Christianity now ensued. Despite its newfound unity and loyalty to Rome, the English church retained some Irish features. Most important was the concentration on monastic culture with special emphasis on learning and missionary work. By 700, the English clergy had become the best trained and most learned in western Europe.

Following the Irish example, English monks journeyed to the European continent to carry on the work of conversion (see Map 7.4). Most important was Boniface (c. 675–754), who undertook the conversion of pagan Germans in Frisia, Bavaria, and Saxony. By 740, Saint Boniface, the "Apostle of the Germans," had become the most famous churchman in Europe. Fourteen years later, he was killed while trying to convert the pagan Frisians. Boniface was a brilliant example of the numerous Irish and English monks whose tireless efforts made Europe the bastion of the Roman Catholic faith.

Women and Monasticism Women, too, played an important role in the monastic missionary movement and the conversion of the Germanic kingdoms. Double monasteries, where both monks and nuns lived in separate houses but attended church services together, were found in both the English and Frankish kingdoms. The monks and nuns followed common rules under a common head— frequently an **abbess** rather than an abbot. Many of these abbesses belonged to royal houses, especially in Anglo-Saxon England. In the kingdom of Northumbria, for example, Saint Hilda founded the monastery of Whitby in 657. As abbess, she was responsible for giving learning an important role in the life of the monastery; five future bishops were educated under her tutelage (see the box on p. 185). For female intellectuals, monasteries offered opportunities for learning not found elsewhere in the society of their day.

Nuns of the seventh and eighth centuries were not always as heavily cloistered as they once had been and were therefore able to play an important role in the spread of Christianity. The great English missionary Boniface relied on nuns in England for books and money. He also asked the abbess of Wimborne to send groups of nuns to establish convents in newly converted German lands. A nun named Leoba established the first convent in Germany at Bischofsheim.

The Path of Celibacy The monastic movement enabled some women to pursue a new path to holiness. Cloisters for both men and women offered the ideal place to practice the new Christian ideal of celibacy. This newfound emphasis on abstaining from sexual relations, especially evident in the emphasis on virginity, created a new image of the human body in late antiquity. To many Greeks and Roman, the human body had been a source of beauty, joy, and enjoyment, noticeable in numerous works of art.

AN ANGLO-SAXON ABBESS: HILDA OF WHITBY

ℋILDA, ABBESS OF the monastery of Whitby, is a good example of the abbesses from royal families in Anglo-Saxon England who played important roles in English monastic institutions. Hilda was especially known for her exemplary life and high regard for learning. This account of her life is taken from Bede, considered by many the first major historian of the Middle Ages.

Bede, *The Ecclesiastical History of the English People*

In the following year, that is the year of our Lord 680, Hilda, abbess of the monastery of Whitby, a most religious servant of Christ, passed away to receive the reward of eternal life on the seventeenth of November at the age of sixty-six, after a life full of heavenly deeds. Her life fell into two equal parts, for she spent thirty-three years most nobly in secular occupations, and dedicated the remainder of her life even more nobly to our Lord in the monastic life. She was nobly born, the daughter of Hereric, nephew to King Edwin, with whom she received the Faith and sacraments of Christ through the preaching of Paulinus of blessed memory, first bishop of the Northumbrians, and she preserved this Faith inviolate until she was found worthy to see him in heaven. . . .

When she had ruled this monastery (Heruteu) for some years, constantly occupied in establishing the regular life, she further undertook to found or organize a monastery at a place known as Streaneshalch, and carried out this appointed task with great energy. She established the same regular life as in her former monastery, and taught the observance of justice, devotion, purity, and other virtues, but especially in peace and charity. After the example of the primitive Church, no one there was rich or poor, for everything was held in common, and none possessed any personal property.

So great was her prudence that not only ordinary folk, but kings and princes used to come and ask her advice in their difficulties. Those under her direction were required to make a thorough study of the Scriptures and occupy themselves in good works, in order that many might be found fitted for Holy Orders and the service of God's altar. Subsequently, five bishops were chosen from this monastery—Bosa, Hedda, Oftfor, John, and Wilfrid—all of them men of outstanding merit and holiness. . . .

Christ's servant Abbess Hilda, whom all her acquaintances called Mother because of her wonderful devotion and grace, was not only an example of holy life to members of her own community, for she also brought about the amendment and salvation of many living far distant, who heard the inspiring story of her industry and goodness. . . . When Hilda ruled this monastery for many years, it pleased the Author of our salvation to try her holy soul by a long sickness, in order that, like the Apostle, her strength might be perfected in weakness. She was attacked by a burning fever that racked her continually for six years; but during all this time she never ceased to give thanks to her Maker, or to instruct the flock committed to her both privately and publicly. For her own example taught them all to serve God rightly when in health, and to render thanks to him faithfully when in trouble or bodily weakness. In the seventh year of her illness she suffered interior pains, and her last day came. About dawn she received holy Communion, and when she had summoned all the servants of Christ in the monastery, she urged them to maintain the gospel peace among themselves and with others. And while she was still speaking, she joyfully welcomed death, and in the words of our Lord, passed from death to life.

To many Christians, the body was seen as a hindrance to a spiritual connection with God. The refusal to have sex was a victory over the desires of the flesh and thus an avenue to holiness.

In the fourth and fifth centuries, a cult of virginity also moved beyond the walls of monasteries and convents. Throughout the Mediterranean world, groups of women met together to study the importance and benefits of celibacy. In Rome, a woman named Marcella supported a group of aristocratic women who studied the ideas of celibacy and also aided Jerome, the church father, with his work on translating the Bible into Latin.

Christian Intellectual Life in the Germanic Kingdoms

Although the Christian church came to accept classical culture, it was not easy to do so in the new German kingdoms.

Nevertheless, some Christian scholars managed to keep learning alive.

Cassiodorus   Most prominent was Cassiodorus (c. 490–585), who came from an aristocratic Roman family and served as an official of the Ostrogothic king Theodoric. The conflicts that erupted after the death of Theodoric led Cassiodorus to withdraw from public life and retire to his landed estates in southern Italy, where he wrote his final work, *Divine and Human Readings*, a compendium of the literature of both Christian and pagan antiquity. Cassiodorus accepted the advice of earlier Christian intellectuals to make use of classical works while treasuring the Scriptures above all else.

Cassiodorus continued the tradition of late antiquity of classifying knowledge according to certain subjects. In assembling his compendium of authors, he followed the works of late ancient authors in placing all secular knowledge into

MAP 7.4 **The Spread of Christianity, 400–800.** The Christian church had penetrated much of the Roman Empire by the end of the fifth century. It emerged as a major base of power after the fall of the empire, and it pushed its influence into new areas through the activities of missionaries.

❓ What aspects of geography help explain the relatively late conversions of the Anglo-Saxons in Britain and the Frisians and Saxons east of the Rhine River? 🌐 **View an animated version of this map or related maps at** http://history.wadsworth.com/spielvogel06/

the categories of the seven **liberal arts,** which were divided into two major groups: the *trivium,* consisting of grammar, **rhetoric,** and dialectic or logic, and the *quadrivium,* consisting of arithmetic, geometry, astronomy, and music. The seven liberal arts would be the cornerstone of Western education for nearly twelve hundred years.

Bede The Venerable Bede (c. 672–735) was a scholar and product of Christian Anglo-Saxon England. He entered a monastery at Jarrow as a small boy and remained there most of the rest of his life. His *Ecclesiastical History of the English People,* completed in 731, was a product of the remarkable flowering of English ecclesiastical and monastic culture in the eighth century. His history of England begins with the coming of Christianity to Britain. Although Bede shared the credulity of his age in regard to stories of miracles, he had a remarkable sense of history. He used his

sources so judiciously that they remain our chief source of information about early Anglo-Saxon England (see the box on p. 185). His work was a remarkable accomplishment for a monk from a small corner of England and reflects the high degree of intellectual achievement of England in the eighth century.

The Byzantine Empire

As noted earlier, in the fourth century, a separation between the western and eastern parts of the Roman Empire began to occur. Even as the Germans moved into the western part of the empire and established various kingdoms over the course of the fifth century, the Roman Empire in the east, centered on Constantinople, solidified and prospered.

Justinian and His Court. Ravenna remained the center of the Byzantine presence in Italy for two hundred years. The Church of San Vitale at Ravenna contains some of the finest examples of sixth-century Byzantine mosaics (works of art made by assembling small colored pieces of glass or rock). This mosaic depicts the Byzantine emperor Justinian and his court dressed in their elaborate robes. Justinian is seen with soldiers, his staff, and members of the clergy.

© Scala/Art Resource, NY

The Reign of Justinian (527–565)

In the sixth century, the empire in the east came under the control of one of its most remarkable rulers, the emperor Justinian. As the nephew and heir of the previous emperor, Justinian had been well trained in imperial administration. He was determined to reestablish the Roman Empire in the entire Mediterranean world and began his attempt to reconquer the west within a year after the revolt had failed.

Justinian's army under Belisarius, probably the best general of the late Roman world, presented a formidable force. Belisarius sailed to North Africa and quickly destroyed the Vandals in two major battles. From North Africa, he led his forces onto the Italian peninsula after occupying Sicily in 535. But it was not until 552 that the Ostrogoths were finally defeated. The struggle devastated Italy, which suffered more from Justinian's reconquest than from all of the previous barbarian invasions.

Justinian has been criticized for overextending his resources and bankrupting the empire. Historians now think, however, that a devastating plague in 542 and long-term economic factors were far more damaging to the Eastern Roman Empire than Justinian's conquests. Before he died, Justinian appeared to have achieved his goals. He had restored the imperial Mediterranean world; his empire included Italy, part of Spain, North Africa, Asia Minor, Palestine, and Syria (see Map 7.5). But the conquest of the Western Empire proved fleeting. Only three years after Justinian's death, the Lombards entered Italy. Although the Eastern Empire maintained the fiction of Italy as a province, its forces were limited to southern and central Italy, Sicily, and coastal areas, such as the territory around Ravenna.

The Codification of Roman Law   Though his conquests proved short-lived, Justinian made a lasting contribution to Western civilization through his codification of Roman law. The Eastern Empire was heir to a vast quantity of materials connected to the development of Roman law. These included laws passed by the senate and assemblies, legal commentaries of jurists, decisions of praetors, and the edicts of emperors. Justinian had been well trained in imperial government and was thoroughly acquainted with Roman law. He wished to codify and simplify this mass of materials.

To accomplish his goal, Justinian authorized the jurist Trebonian to make a systematic compilation of imperial edicts. The result was the Code of Law, the first part of the *Corpus Iuris Civilis* (Body of Civil Law), completed in 529. Four years later, two other parts of the *Corpus* appeared: the *Digest,* a compendium of writings of Roman jurists, and the *Institutes,* a brief summary of the chief principles of Roman law that could be used as a textbook on Roman law. The fourth part of the *Corpus* was the *Novels,* a compilation of the most important new edicts issued during Justinian's reign.

Justinian's codification of Roman law became the basis of imperial law in the Byzantine Empire until its end in 1453. More important, however, since it was written in Latin (it was, in fact, the last product of eastern Roman culture to be written in Latin, which was soon replaced by Greek), it was also eventually used in the west and in fact became the basis of the legal system of all of continental Europe.

Intellectual Life Under Justinian   The intellectual life of the Eastern Roman Empire was highly influenced by the traditions of classical civilization. Scholars actively strived to preserve the works of the ancient Greeks while basing a great deal of their own literature on classical models. Initially, however, the most outstanding literary achievements of the Eastern Empire were historical and religious works.

The best known of the early Byzantine historians was Procopius (c. 500–c. 562), court historian during the reign

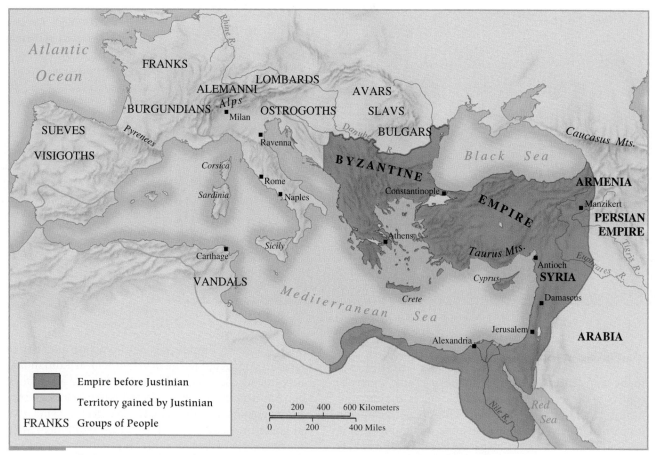

MAP 7.5 **The Byzantine Empire in the Time of Justinian.** The Byzantine emperor Justinian briefly restored much of the Mediterranean portion of the old Roman Empire. His general Belisarius quickly conquered the Vandals in North Africa but wrested Italy from the Ostrogoths only after a long and devastating struggle. ❓ Examine Map 6.1. What former Roman territories lay outside Justinian's control?

🌐 **View an animated version of this map or related maps at** http://history.wadsworth.com/spielvogel06/

of Justinian. Procopius served as secretary to the great general Belisarius and accompanied him on his wars on behalf of Justinian. Procopius' best historical work, the *Wars,* is a firsthand account of Justinian's wars of reconquest in the western Mediterranean and his wars against the Persians in the east. Deliberately modeled after the work of his hero, the Greek historian Thucydides (see Chapter 3), Procopius' narrative features vivid descriptions of battle scenes, clear judgment, and noteworthy objectivity.

Procopius also wrote a work that many historians consider mostly scandalous gossip, his infamous *Secret History.* At the beginning of this work, Procopius informed his readers that "what I shall write now follows a different plan, supplementing the previous formal chronicle with a disclosure of what really happened throughout the Roman Empire."[17] What he revealed constituted a scathing attack on Justinian and his wife Theodora for their alleged misdeeds.

The Empress Theodora Theodora was the daughter of the "keeper of bears" for the games at Constantinople, who died when she was a child. Theodora followed in her mother's footsteps by becoming an actress, which at that time was considered a lowborn activity. Often actresses also worked as prostitutes, and Theodora was no exception. At the age of twenty-five, she met Justinian, who was forty. His father, the Emperor Justin, had to change the law to allow an aristocratic senator to marry a woman who had been an actress. After his father died in 527, Justinian became emperor and Theodora empress, a remarkable achievement for a woman from the lower classes.

Justinian and Theodora were close and loving companions. She also influenced her husband in both church and state affairs. A strong-willed and intelligent woman, she proved especially valuable in 532, when the two factions of charioteer supporters in Constantinople joined forces and rioted against the emperor. The riots soon became a revolt as the rioters burned and looted the center of the city, shouting "*Nika!*" ("win"), a word normally used to cheer on their favorite charioteer teams. Justinian seemed ready to flee, but Theodora strengthened his resolve by saying, "My opinion then is that the present time, above all others, is inopportune for flight, even though it bring safety. . . . For one who has been emperor it is unendurable to be a fugitive, . . . and may I not live that day on which those who

Theodora and Attendants. This mosaic, located on the south wall of the apse of the Church of San Vitale (Justinian is on the north wall), depicts Theodora and her attendants. Her presence on the wall of this church indicates the important role she played in the Byzantine state. At the bottom of her robe is a scene of the three Wise Men, an indication that Theodora was special enough to have belonged in the company of the three kings who visited the newborn Jesus.

meet me shall not address me as mistress."[18] Justinian resolved to fight. Many of the protesters were killed, and the so-called Nika Revolt was ended.

The Emperor's Building Program　After riots destroyed much of Constantinople, Justinian rebuilt the city and gave it the appearance it would keep for almost a thousand years (see Map 7.6). Earlier, Emperor Theodosius II (408–450) had constructed an enormous defensive wall to protect the city on its land side. The city was dominated by an immense palace complex, a huge arena known as the Hippodrome, and hundreds of churches. No residential district was particularly fashionable; palaces, tenements, and slums ranged alongside one another. Justinian added many new

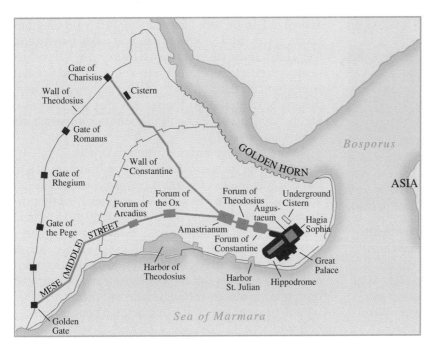

MAP 7.6　Constantinople. Constantinople was the largest European city, and until the twelfth century, it was the nexus of trade between east and west. Emperor Justinian oversaw a massive building program that produced important architectural monuments such as Hagia Sophia. **?** What natural and human-built aspects of the city helped protect it from invasion?　**View an animated version of this map or related maps at** http://history .wadsworth.com/spielvogel06/

buildings. His public works projects included roads, bridges, walls, public baths, law courts, and colossal underground reservoirs to hold the city's water supply. He also built hospitals, schools, monasteries, and churches. Churches were his special passion, and in Constantinople alone he built or rebuilt thirty-four of them. His greatest achievement was the famous Hagia Sophia, the Church of the Holy Wisdom.

Completed in 537, Hagia Sophia was designed by a Greek architect who departed radically from the simple, flat-roofed basilica of Western architecture. The center of Hagia Sophia consisted of four huge piers crowned by an enormous dome, which seemed to be floating in space. This effect was emphasized by Procopius, the court historian, who, at Justinian's request, wrote a treatise on the emperor's building projects: "From the lightness of the building, it does not appear to rest upon a solid foundation, but to cover the place beneath as though it were suspended from heaven by the fabled golden chain." In part, this impression was created by putting forty-two windows around the base

of the dome, which allowed an incredible play of light within the cathedral. Light served to remind the worshipers of God; as Procopius commented:

> Whoever enters there to worship perceives at once that it is not by any human strength or skill, but by the favor of God that this work has been perfected; his mind rises sublime to commune with God, feeling that He cannot be far off, but must especially love to dwell in the place which He has chosen; and this takes place not only when a man sees it for the first time, but it always makes the same impression upon him, as though he had never beheld it before.[19]

As darkness is illumined by invisible light, so too it was believed the world is illumined by invisible spirit.

The royal palace complex, Hagia Sophia, and the Hippodrome were the three greatest buildings in Constantinople. This last was a huge amphitheater, constructed of brick covered by marble, holding as many as sixty thousand spectators. Although gladiator fights were held there, the main events were the chariot races; twenty-four would usually be presented in one day. The citizens of Constantinople were passionate fans of chariot racing. Successful charioteers were acclaimed as heroes and honored with public statues. Crowds in the Hippodrome also took on political significance. Being a member of the two chief factions of charioteers—the Blues or the Greens—was the only real outlet for political expression. Even emperors had to be aware of their demands and attitudes: the loss of a race in the Hippodrome frequently resulted in bloody riots, and rioting could threaten the emperor's power.

Life in Constantinople With a population estimated in the hundreds of thousands, Constantinople was the largest city in Europe during the Middle Ages. It viewed itself as the center of an empire and a special Christian city.

Until the twelfth century, Constantinople was Europe's greatest commercial center. The city was the chief entrepôt for the exchange of products between west and east. Highly desired in Europe were the products of the east: silk from China, spices from Southeast Asia and India, jewelry and ivory from India (the latter used by artisans for church items), wheat and furs from southern Russia, and flax and honey from the Balkans. Many of these eastern goods were then shipped to the Mediterranean area and northern Europe. Despite the Germanic incursions, European trade did not entirely end.

Moreover, imported raw materials were used in Constantinople for local industries. During Justinian's reign, two Christian monks smuggled silkworms from China to begin a silk industry. The state had a monopoly on the production of silk cloth, and the workshops themselves were housed in Constantinople's royal palace complex. European demand for silk cloth made it the city's most lucrative product. It is interesting to note that the upper classes, including emperors and empresses, were not discouraged from making money through trade and manufacturing. Indeed, one empress even manufactured perfumes in her bedroom.

Interior of Hagia Sophia. This view of the interior of the Church of the Holy Wisdom, constructed under Justinian by Anthemius of Tralles and Isidore of Milan, gives an idea of how the windows around the base of the dome produced a special play of light within the cathedral. The pulpits and plaques bearing inscriptions from the Qur'an were introduced when the Turks converted this church to a mosque in the fifteenth century.

From Eastern Roman to Byzantine Empire

Justinian's accomplishments had been spectacular, but when he died, he left the Eastern Roman Empire with serious problems: too much distant territory to protect, an empty treasury, a smaller population after the plague, and renewed threats to the frontiers. In the first half of the seventh century, during the reign of Heraclius (610–641), the empire faced attacks from the Persians to the east and the Slavs to the north.

The empire was left exhausted by these struggles. In the midst of them, it had developed a new system of defense by creating a new administrative unit, the *theme,* which combined civilian and military offices in the hands of the same person. Thus the civil governor was also the military leader of the area. Although this innovation helped the empire survive, it also fostered an increased militarization of the empire. By the mid-seventh century, it had become apparent that a restored Mediterranean empire was simply beyond the resources of the Eastern Empire, which now increasingly turned its back on the Latin west. A renewed series of external threats in the second half of the seventh century strengthened this development.

The most serious challenge to the Eastern Empire was the rise of Islam, which unified the Arab tribes and created a powerful new force that swept through the east (see "The Rise of Islam" later in this chapter). The defeat of an eastern Roman army at Yarmuk in 636 meant the loss of the provinces of Syria and Palestine. The Arabs also moved into the old Persian Empire and conquered it. An Arab attempt to besiege Constantinople failed, in large part due to the use of Greek fire against the Arab fleets. Greek fire was a petroleum-based compound containing quicklime and sulfur. Because it would burn under water, the Byzantines created the equivalent of modern flamethrowers by using tubes to blow Greek fire onto wooden ships, with frightening effect. Arabs and eastern Roman forces now faced each other along a frontier in southern Asia Minor.

Problems also arose along the northern frontier, especially in the Balkans, where an Asiatic people known as the Bulgars had arrived earlier in the sixth century. In 679, the Bulgars defeated the eastern Roman forces and took possession of the lower Danube valley, setting up a strong Bulgarian kingdom.

By the beginning of the eighth century, the Eastern Roman Empire was greatly diminished in size, consisting only of the eastern Balkans and Asia Minor. It was now an eastern Mediterranean state. These external challenges had important internal repercussions as well. By the eighth century, the Eastern Roman Empire had been transformed into what historians call the Byzantine Empire, a civilization with its own unique character that would last until 1453

CHRONOLOGY	The Byzantine Empire
Protective walls of Theodosius II	408–450
Justinian codifies Roman law	529–533
Reconquest of Italy by the Byzantines	535–552
Completion of Hagia Sophia	537
Attacks on the empire in reign of Heraclius	610–641
Arab defeat of Byzantines at Yarmuk	636
Defeat by the Bulgars; losses in the Balkans	679

(Constantinople was built on the site of an older city named Byzantium—hence the term *Byzantine*).

The Byzantine Empire in the Eighth Century The Byzantine Empire was a Greek state. Justinian's *Corpus Iuris Civilis* had been the last official work published in Latin. Increasingly, Latin fell into disuse as Greek became not only the common language of the Byzantine Empire but its official language as well.

The Byzantine Empire was also a Christian state, built on a faith in Jesus that was shared in a profound way by almost all its citizens. An enormous amount of artistic talent was poured into the construction of churches, church ceremonies, and church decoration. Spiritual principles deeply permeated Byzantine art. The importance of religion to the Byzantines explains why theological disputes took on an exaggerated form. The most famous of these disputes, the so-called iconoclastic controversy, threatened the stability of the empire in the first half of the eighth century.

Beginning in the sixth century, the use of religious images, especially in the form of icons or pictures of sacred figures, became so widespread that charges of idolatry, the worship of images, began to be heard. The use of images or icons had been justified by the argument that icons were not worshiped but were simply used to help illiterate people understand their religion. This argument failed to stop the **iconoclasts,** as the opponents of icons were called. Beginning in 730, the Byzantine emperor Leo III (717–741) outlawed the use of icons. Strong resistance ensued, especially from monks. Leo also used the iconoclastic controversy to add to the prestige of the patriarch of Constantinople, the highest church official in the east and second in dignity only to the bishop of Rome. The Roman popes were opposed to the iconoclastic edicts, and their opposition created considerable dissension between the popes and the Byzantine emperors. Late in the eighth century, the Byzantine rulers reversed their stand on the use of images, but not before considerable damage had been

The Byzantine Empire, c. 750

done to the unity of the Christian church. Although the final separation between Roman Catholicism and Greek Orthodoxy (as the Christian church in the Byzantine Empire was called) did not occur until 1054, the iconoclastic controversy was important in moving both sides in that direction.

The emperor occupied a crucial position in the Byzantine state. Portrayed as chosen by God, the Byzantine emperor was crowned in sacred ceremonies, and his subjects were expected to prostrate themselves in his presence. His power was considered absolute and was limited in practice only by deposition or assassination. Because the emperor appointed the patriarch, he also exercised control over both church and state. The Byzantines believed that God had commanded their state to preserve the true faith—Orthodox Christianity. Emperor, clergy, and civic officials were all bound together in service to this ideal. It can be said that spiritual values truly held the Byzantine state together.

By 750, it was apparent that two of Rome's heirs, the Germanic kingdoms and the Byzantine Empire, were moving in different directions. Nevertheless, Byzantine influence on the Western world was significant. The images of a Roman imperial state that continued to haunt the west lived on in Byzantium. The legal system of the west came to owe much to Justinian's codification of Roman law. In addition, the Byzantine Empire served in part as a buffer state, protecting the west for a long time from incursions from the east. Although the Byzantine Empire would continue to influence the west until its demise in 1453, it went its own unique way. One of its bitterest enemies was the new power known as Islam.

The Rise of Islam

Like the Hebrews and the Assyrians, the Arabs were a Semitic-speaking people of the Near East with a long history. In Roman times, the Arabian peninsula came to be dominated by Bedouin nomads who moved constantly to find water and food for their animals. Although some Arabs prospered from trading activities, especially in the north, the majority of the Arabs consisted of poor Bedouins, whose tribes were known for their independence, their warlike qualities, and their dislike of urban-dwelling Arabs.

Although these early Arabs were polytheistic, there was a supreme God named Allah (Arabic for "God") who ruled over the other gods. There was no priesthood; all members of the tribe were involved in the practice of the faith. Allah was symbolized by a sacred stone, and each tribe had its own stone. All tribes, however, worshiped a massive black meteorite—the Black Stone, which had been placed in a central shrine called the *Ka'ba* in the city of Mecca.

In the fifth and sixth centuries A.D., the Arabian peninsula took on new importance. As a result of political disorder in Mesopotamia and Egypt, the usual trade routes in the region began to change. A new trade route—from the Mediterranean through Mecca to Yemen and then by ship across the Arabian Sea and the Indian Ocean—became more popular, and communities in that part of the Arabian peninsula, such as Mecca, began to prosper from this caravan trade. As a result, tensions arose between the Bedouins in the desert and the increasingly wealthy merchant classes in the towns. Into this intense world came Muhammad.

Muhammad

Born in Mecca to a merchant family, Muhammad (c. 570–632) was orphaned at the age of five. He grew up to become a caravan manager and eventually married a rich widow who was also his employer. In his middle years, he began to experience visions that he believed were inspired by Allah. Muhammad believed that although Allah had already revealed himself in part through Moses and Jesus—and thus through the Hebrew and Christian traditions—the final revelations were now being given to him. Out of these revelations, which were eventually written down, came the Qur'an or Koran, which contained the guidelines by which followers of Allah were to live. Muhammad's teachings formed the basis for the religion known as Islam, which means "submission to the will of Allah." Allah was the all-powerful being who had created the universe and everything in it. Humans must subject themselves to Allah if they wished to achieve everlasting life. His followers were called Muslims, meaning "practitioners of Islam."

After receiving the revelations, Muhammad set out to convince the people of Mecca that the revelations were true. At first, many thought he was insane, and others feared that his attacks on the corrupt society around him would upset the established social and political order. Discouraged by the failure of the Meccans to accept his message, in 622 Muhammad and some of his closest supporters left the city and moved north to the rival city of Yathrib, later renamed Medina ("city of the Prophet"). The year of the journey to Medina, known in history as the *Hegira* ("departure"), became year 1 in the official calendar of Islam.

Muhammad, who had been invited to the town by a number of prominent residents, soon began to win support from people in Medina as well as from members of Bedouin tribes in the surrounding countryside. From these groups, he formed the first Muslim community. Muslims saw no separation between political and religious authority; submission to the will of Allah meant

Arabia in the Time of Muhammad

submission to his Prophet, Muhammad. Muhammad soon became both a religious and a political leader. His political and military skills enabled him to put together a reliable military force, with which he returned to Mecca in 630, conquering the city and converting the townspeople to the new faith. From Mecca, Muhammad's ideas spread quickly across the Arabian peninsula and within a relatively short time had resulted in both the religious and the political unification of Arab society.

The Teachings of Islam

At the heart of Islam was its sacred book, the Qur'an, with its basic message that there is no God but Allah and Muhammad is his Prophet. Essentially, the Qur'an contains Muhammad's revelations of a heavenly book written down by secretaries. Consisting of 114 chapters, the Qur'an recorded the beliefs of the Muslims and served as their code of ethics and law.

Islam was a direct and simple faith, emphasizing the need to obey the will of Allah. This meant following a basic ethical code consisting of the Five Pillars of Islam: belief in Allah and Muhammad as his Prophet; standard prayer five times a day and public prayer on Friday at midday to worship Allah; observance of the holy month of Ramadan (the ninth month on the Muslim calendar) by fasting from dawn to sunset; making a pilgrimage (known as the *hajj*) to Mecca in one's lifetime, if possible (see the box on p. 194); and giving alms to the poor and unfortunate. The faithful who observed the law were guaranteed a place in an eternal paradise.

Islam was not just a set of religious beliefs but a way of life as well. After the death of Muhammad, Muslim scholars drew up a law code, called the *Shari'a*, to provide believers with a set of prescriptions to regulate their daily lives. Much of the *Shari'a* was drawn from the Qur'an. Believers'

behavior was subject to strict guidelines. In addition to the Five Pillars, Muslims were forbidden to gamble, to eat pork, to drink alcoholic beverages, and to engage in dishonest behavior. Sexual practices were also strict. Marriages were to be arranged by parents, and contacts between unmarried men and women were discouraged. In accordance with Bedouin custom, males were permitted to have more than one wife, but Muhammad attempted to limit the practice by restricting the number of wives to four.

The Spread of Islam

The death of Muhammad presented his followers with a dilemma. Although Muhammad had not claimed to be divine, Muslims saw no separation between religious and political authority. Submission to the will of Allah was the same thing as submission to his Prophet, Muhammad. According to the Qur'an: "Whoever obeys the messenger obeys Allah." But Muhammad had never named a successor, and although he had several daughters, he left no sons. In a male-oriented society, who would lead the community of the faithful? Shortly after Muhammad's death, a number of his closest followers selected Abu Bakr, a wealthy merchant who was Muhammad's father-in-law, as **caliph**, or temporal leader, of the Islamic community.

Muhammad and the early caliphs who succeeded him took up the Arab tribal custom of the *razzia* or raid in the struggle against their enemies. Some have called this activity a *jihad*, which they misleadingly interpret as a holy war. **Jihad** actually means "striving in the way of the Lord" to achieve personal betterment, although it can also mean fair, defensive fighting to preserve one's life and one's faith. Arab conquests were not carried out to convert others, since conversion to Islam was purely voluntary. Those who did not convert were required only to submit to Muslim rule and pay taxes.

Muslims Celebrate the End of Ramadan.
Ramadan is the holy month of Islam during which all Muslims must fast from dawn to sunset. Observance of this holy month is regarded as one of the Five Pillars of the faith. Muhammad instituted the fast during his stay at Medina. It was designed to replace the single Jewish Day of Atonement. This Persian miniature depicts Muslims on horseback celebrating the end of Ramadan.

THE QUR'AN: THE PILGRIMAGE

HE QUR'AN IS the sacred book of the Muslims, comparable to the Bible in Christianity. This selection from Chapter 22, titled "Pilgrimage," discusses the importance of making a pilgrimage to Mecca, one of the Five Pillars of Islam. The pilgrim's final destination was the Ka'ba at Mecca, containing the Black Stone.

Qur'an, Chapter 22: "Pilgrimage"

Exhort all men to make the pilgrimage. They will come to you on foot and on the backs of swift camels from every distant quarter; they will come to avail themselves of many a benefit, and to pronounce on the appointed days the name of God over the cattle which He has given them for food. Eat of their flesh, and feed the poor and the unfortunate.

Then let the pilgrims tidy themselves, make their vows, and circle the Ancient House. Such is God's commandment. He that reveres the sacred rites of God shall fare better in the sight of his Lord.

The flesh of cattle is lawful for you, except for that which has been specified before. Guard yourselves against the filth of idols; and avoid the utterance of falsehoods.

Dedicate yourselves to God, and serve none besides Him. The man who serves other deities besides God is like him who falls from heaven and is snatched by the birds or carried away by the wind to some far-off region. Even such is he.

He that reveres the offerings made to God shows the piety of his heart. Your cattle are useful to you in many ways until the time of their slaughter. Then they are offered for sacrifice at the Ancient House.

For every community We have ordained a ritual, that they may pronounce the name of God over the cattle which He has given them for food. Your God is one God; to Him surrender yourselves. Give good news to the humble, whose hearts are filled with awe at the mention of God; who endure adversity with fortitude, attend to their prayers, and give in alms from what We gave them.

We have made the camels a part of God's rites. They are of much use to you. Pronounce over them the name of God as you draw them up in line and slaughter them; and when they have fallen to the ground eat of their flesh and feed the uncomplaining beggar and the demanding supplicant. Thus have We subjected them to your service, so that you may give thanks.

Their flesh and blood does not reach God; it is your piety that reaches Him. Thus has He subjected them to your service, so that you may give glory to God for guiding you.

Give good news to the righteous. God will ward off evil from true believers. God does not love the treacherous and the thankless.

Once the Arabs had become unified under Abu Bakr, they began to direct the energy they had once expended against each other outward against neighboring peoples. The Byzantines and the Persians were the first to feel the strength of the newly united Arabs. At Yarmuk in 636, the Muslims defeated the Byzantine army, and by 640, they had taken possession of the province of Syria (see Map 7.7). To the east, the Arabs defeated Persian forces in 637 and then went on to conquer the entire Persian Empire by 650. In the meantime, Egypt and other areas of northern Africa had been added to the new Muslim empire. Led by a series of brilliant generals, the Arabs had put together a large and highly motivated army, whose valor was enhanced by the belief that Muslim warriors were guaranteed a place in paradise if they died in battle.

Early caliphs, ruling from Medina, organized their newly conquered territories into taxpaying provinces. By the mid-seventh century, problems arose again over the succession to the Prophet until Ali, Muhammad's son-in-law, was assassinated and the general Muawiya, the governor of Syria and one of Ali's chief rivals, became caliph in 661. Muawiya was known for one outstanding virtue: he used force only when necessary. As he said, "I never use my sword when my whip will do, nor my whip when my tongue will do."[20] Muawiya moved quickly to make the caliphate hereditary in his own family, thus establishing the Umayyad dynasty. As one of their first actions, the Umayyads moved the capital of the Muslim empire from Medina to Damascus in Syria. This internal dissension over the caliphate created a split in Islam between the Shi'ites, or those who accepted only the descendants of Ali, Muhammad's son-in-law, as the true rulers, and the Sunnites, who claimed that the descendants of the Umayyads were the true caliphs. This seventh-century split in Islam has lasted until the present day.

Internal dissension did not stop the expansion of Islam, however. At the beginning of the eighth century, new attacks were made at both the western and eastern ends of the Mediterranean. After sweeping across North Africa, the Muslims crossed the Strait of Gibraltar and moved into Spain around 710. The Visigothic kingdom collapsed, and by 725, most of Spain had become a Muslim state with its center at Córdoba. In 732, a Muslim army, making a foray into southern France, was defeated at the Battle of Tours near Poitiers. Muslim expansion in Europe came to a halt.

Meanwhile, in 717, another Muslim force had launched a naval attack on Constantinople with the hope of destroying the Byzantine Empire. In the spring of 718, the Byzantines destroyed the Muslim fleet and saved the Byzantine Empire and indirectly Christian Europe, since the fall of Constantinople would no doubt have opened the door to Muslim invasion of eastern Europe. The Byzantine Empire and Islam now established an uneasy frontier in southern Asia Minor.

The Arab advance had finally come to an end, but not before the southern and eastern Mediterranean parts of the old Roman Empire had been conquered. Islam had truly become heir to much of the old Roman Empire. The Umayyad dynasty at Damascus now ruled an enormous empire. While expansion had conveyed untold wealth and new ethnic groups into the fold of Islam, it also brought contact with Byzantine and Persian civilization. As a result, the new Arab empire would be influenced by Greek culture as well as the older civilizations of the ancient Near East. The children of the conquerors would be educated in new ways and produce a brilliant culture that would eventually influence western Europe intellectually.

CHRONOLOGY   **The Rise of Islam**

Birth of Muhammad	c. 570
Muhammad's flight from Mecca (*Hegira*)	622
Death of Muhammad	632
Defeat of Byzantines at Yarmuk	636
Defeat of Persians	637–650
Seizure of Byzantine provinces of Syria and Egypt	640–642
Invasion of Spain	c. 710
Arab failure to capture Constantinople	717–718
Defeat of Muslims near Poitiers	732

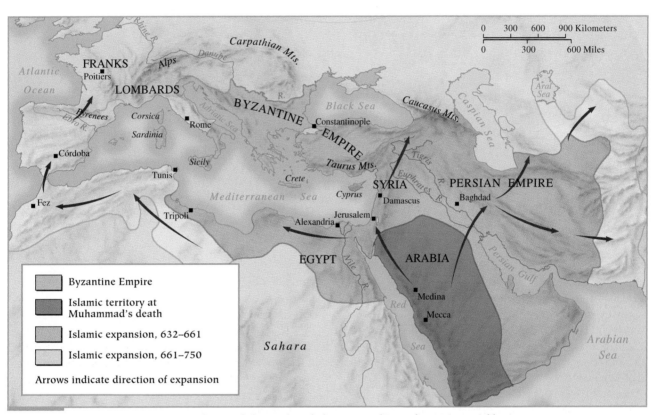

MAP 7.7 The Expansion of Islam. Muhammad, the prophet of Islam, engaged in warfare against neighboring tribes. Militaristic expansion continued with great zeal under the Prophet's successors. Islamic rule spread rapidly in the decades after Muhammad's death, stopped finally by the Byzantine Empire and the Franks. [?] Why was the continuance of the Byzantine Empire a key factor in stopping the spread of Islam into Europe?

View an animated version of this map or related maps at http://history.wadsworth.com/spielvogel06/

CONCLUSION

THE PERIOD FROM the mid-third century to the mid-eighth century was both chaotic and creative. During late antiquity, the Roman world of the Mediterranean was gradually transformed. Three new entities fell heir to Roman civilization: the Germanic kingdoms of western Europe, the Byzantine Empire, and the world of Islam.

In the west, Roman elements combined with German and Celtic influences; in the east, Greek and eastern elements of late antiquity were of more consequence. Although the Germanic kingdoms of the west and the Byzantine civilization of the east came to share a common bond in Christianity, it proved incapable of keeping them in harmony politically as the two civilizations continued to move apart. Christianity, however, remained a dominant influence in both civilizations and in the west was especially important as a civilizing agent that brought pagan peoples into the new European civilization that was slowly being born. The rise of Islam, Rome's third heir, resulted in the loss of the southern and eastern Mediterranean portions of the old Roman Empire to a religious power that was neither Roman nor Christian. The new Islamic empire forced Europe proper back on itself, and slowly, a new civilization emerged that became the heart of what we know as Western civilization.

NOTES

1. Naphtali Lewis and Meyers Reinhold, eds., *Roman Civilization,* vol. 2 (New York, 1955), p. 191.
2. "The Creed of Nicaea," in Henry Bettenson, ed., *Documents of the Christian Church* (London, 1963), p. 35.
3. Charles C. Mierow, trans., *The Gothic History of Jordanes* (Princeton, N.J., 1915), pp. 88–89.
4. Quoted in Averil Cameron, *The Mediterranean World in Late Antiquity* (London, 1993), p. 37.
5. Ernest F. Henderson, *Selected Historical Documents of the Middle Ages* (London, 1892), p. 182.
6. Ibid., p. 181.
7. Tertullian, "The Prescriptions Against the Heretics," in *The Library of Christian Classics,* vol. 5, *Early Latin Theology,* ed. and trans. S. L. Greenslade (Philadelphia, 1956), p. 36.
8. Anne Fremantle, ed., *A Treasury of Early Christianity* (New York, 1953), p. 91.
9. Matthew 16:15–19.
10. R. C. Petry, ed., *A History of Christianity: Readings in the History of Early and Medieval Christianity* (Englewood Cliffs, N.J., 1962), p. 70.
11. Brian Pullan, ed., *Sources for the History of Medieval Europe* (Oxford, 1966), p. 46.

TIMELINE

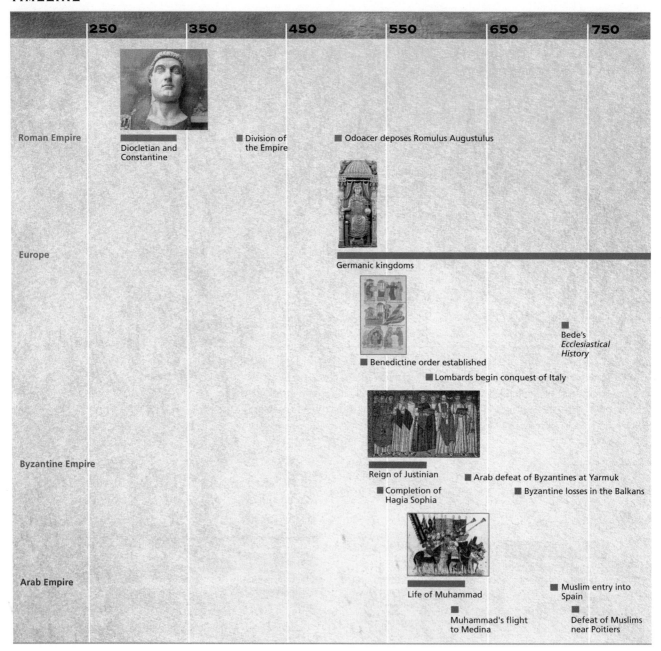

	250	350	450	550	650	750

Roman Empire
Diocletian and Constantine
■ Division of the Empire
■ Odoacer deposes Romulus Augustulus

Europe
Germanic kingdoms
■ Benedictine order established
■ Lombards begin conquest of Italy
■ Bede's *Ecclesiastical History*

Byzantine Empire
Reign of Justinian
■ Completion of Hagia Sophia
■ Arab defeat of Byzantines at Yarmuk
■ Byzantine losses in the Balkans

Arab Empire
Life of Muhammad
■ Muhammad's flight to Medina
■ Muslim entry into Spain
■ Defeat of Muslims near Poitiers

12. Quoted in Sidney Painter and Brian Tierney, *Western Europe in the Middle Ages, 300–1475* (New York, 1983), p. 106.

13. Mark 10:21.

14. Norman F. Cantor, ed., *The Medieval World, 300–1300* (New York, 1963), pp. 104, 101, 108, 103.

15. Bede, *A History of the English Church and People,* trans. Leo Sherley-Price (Harmondsworth, England, 1968), pp. 86–87.

16. Quoted in Peter Brown, *The Rise of Western Christendom: Triumph and Adversity,* A.D. *200–1000* (Oxford, 1997), p. 98.

17. Procopius, *Secret History,* trans. Richard Atwater (Ann Arbor, Mich., 1963), p. 3.

18. H. B. Dewing, trans., *Procopius,* vol. 1 (Cambridge, Mass., 1914), p. 48.

19. Procopius, *Buildings of Justinian* (London, 1897), pp. 9, 6–7, 11.

20. Quoted in Arthur Goldschmidt Jr., *A Concise History of the Middle East,* 4th ed. (Boulder, Colo., 1991), p. 56.

SUGGESTIONS FOR FURTHER READING

For good introductions to late antiquity, see **P. Brown, *The World of Late Antiquity,* A.D. *150–750*** (New York, 1989); **J. Moorhead, *The Roman Empire Divided, 400–700*** (London, 2001); **A. Cameron, *The Mediterranean World in Late Antiquity,* A.D. *395–600*** (London, 1993); and **R. Collins, *Early Medieval Europe, 300–1000*** (New York, 1991). There is an excellent collection of essays and encyclopedic entries in **G. W. Bowersock, P. Brown, and O. Grabar, *Late Antiquity: A Guide to the Postclassical World*** (Cambridge, Mass., 1999).

On the Late Roman Empire, see **A. Cameron, *The Later Roman Empire*** (Cambridge, Mass., 1993). On the fourth century, see **M. Grant, *Constantine the Great: The Man and His Times*** (New York, 1993), and **T. D. Barnes, *The New Empire of Diocletian and Constantine*** (Cambridge, Mass., 1982). Studies analyzing the aristocratic circles, the barbarian invasions, and the military problem include **E. A. Thompson, *Romans and Barbarians*** (Madison, Wis., 1982); **A. Ferrill, *The Fall of the Roman Empire: The Military Explanation*** (London, 1986); and **J. M. O'Flynn, *Generalissimos of the Western Roman Empire*** (Edmonton, Canada, 1983).

For surveys of the German tribes and their migrations, see **L. Musset, *The German Invasions*** (University Park, Pa., 1975); **T. S. Burns, *A History of the Ostrogoths*** (Bloomington, Ind., 1984); **F. P. Heather, *Goths and Romans*** (Oxford, 1991); **E. James, *The Franks*** (Oxford, 1988); **H. Wolfram, *The Goths, trans.* T. J. Dunlop** (Berkeley, Calif., 1988); and **I. N. Wood, *Merovingian Kingdoms*** (London, 1994). On the relationship between the Romans and the Germans, see **T. S. Burns, *Rome and the Barbarians, 100* B.C.–A.D. *400*** (Baltimore, 2003).

For a superb introduction to early Christianity, see **P. Brown, *The Rise of Western Christendom: Triumph and Adversity,* A.D. *200–1000,* 2d ed.** (Oxford, 2002). On Saints Augustine and Jerome, see **H. Chadwick, *Augustine*** (Oxford, 1986), and **J. N. D. Kelly, *Saint Jerome*** (London, 1975). For a good account of early monasticism, see **C. H. Lawrence, *Medieval Monasticism,* 2d ed.** (London, 1989). On Saint Benedict, see **O. Chadwick, *The Making of the Benedictine Ideal*** (London, 1981). For women in monastic life, see **S. F. Wemple, *Women in Frankish Society: Marriage and the Cloister, 500–900*** (Philadelphia, 1981). On women in general, see **G. Clark, *Women in Late Antiquity: Pagan and Christian Life-Styles*** (Oxford, 1993).

A brief survey of the development of the papacy can be found in **G. Barraclough, *The Medieval Papacy*** (New York, 1968). **J. Richards, *The Popes and the Papacy in the Early Middle Ages, 476–752*** (Boston, 1979), is a more detailed study of the early papacy. On Pope Gregory the Great, see **C. Straw, *Gregory the Great: Perfection in Imperfection*** (Berkeley, Calif., 1988). On Irish monasticism, see **L. M. Bitel, *Isle of the Saints: Monastic Settlement and Christian Community in Early Ireland*** (Ithaca, N.Y., 1990).

Brief but good introductions to Byzantine history can be found in **J. Haldon, *Byzantium: A History*** (Charleston, S.C., 2000), and **W. Treadgold, *A Concise History of Byzantium*** (London, 2001). The best single political history is **G. Ostrogorsky, *A History of the Byzantine State,* 2d ed.** (New Brunswick, N.J., 1968). For a comprehensive survey of the Byzantine Empire, see **W. Treadgold, *A History of the Byzantine State and Society*** (Stanford, Calif., 1997). See also **C. Mango, ed., *The Oxford History of Byzantium*** (Oxford, 2002). On Justinian, see **J. Moorhead, *Justinian*** (London, 1995), and **J. A. S. Evans, *The Age of Justinian*** (New York, 1996). On Constantinople, see **D. T. Rice, *Constantinople: From Byzantium to Istanbul*** (New York, 1965). The role of the Christian church is discussed in **J. Hussey, *The Orthodox Church in the Byzantine Empire*** (Oxford, 1986).

Good brief surveys of the Islamic Middle East include **A. Goldschmidt Jr., *A Concise History of the Middle East,* 7th ed.** (Boulder, Colo., 2001), and **S. N. Fisher and W. Ochsenwald, *The Middle East: A History*** (New York, 2003). On the rise of Islam, see **F. E. Peters, *Muhammad and the Origins of Islam*** (Albany, N.Y., 1994); **M. Lings, *Muhammad: His Life Based on the Earliest Sources*** (New York, 1983); **K. Armstrong, *Muhammad: A Biography of the Prophet*** (New York, 1992); and **F. Donner, *The Early Islamic Conquests*** (Princeton, N.J., 1980).

History Now™

Enter *HistoryNow* using the access card that is available for *Western Civilization. HistoryNow* will assist you in understanding the content in this chapter with lesson plans generated for your needs. In addition, you can read the following documents, and many more, online:

Saint Paul's First Epistle to the Corinthians

Pliny the Younger, Letter 97

Plotinus, excerpts from the first book of the Six Enneads

INFOTRAC SEARCH TERMS

 For additional reading, go to InfoTrac College Edition, your online research library at http://infotrac.thomsonlearning.com

Key Term Search	*Subject Guide Search*
early Christianity	Byzantium
Augustine	

WESTERN CIVILIZATION RESOURCES

Visit the *Western Civilization* Companion Web site for resources specific to this book:

> http://history.wadsworth.com/spielvogel06/

For a variety of tools to help you succeed in this course, visit the Western Civilization Resource Center at

> http://history.wadsworth.com/western/

Included are quizzes; images; documents; interactive simulations; maps and timelines; movie explorations; and a wealth of other sources.

EUROPEAN CIVILIZATION
IN THE EARLY MIDDLE AGES,
750–1000

CHAPTER OUTLINE AND FOCUS QUESTIONS

Europeans and the Environment
● What were the main features of the physical environment of the Early Middle Ages?

The World of the Carolingians
● In what ways did the political, intellectual, and daily life in the Carolingian Empire represent a fusion of Gallo-Roman, Germanic, and Christian practices?

Disintegration of the Carolingian Empire
● What impact did the Vikings have on the history and culture of medieval Europe?

The Emerging World of Lords and Vassals
● What was fief-holding, and how was it related to manorialism?

The Zenith of Byzantine Civilization
● What were the chief developments in the Byzantine Empire between 750 and 1000?

The Slavic Peoples of Central and Eastern Europe
● What patterns of development occurred in central and eastern Europe as a result of the Slavic peoples?

The Expansion of Islam
● What were the chief developments in the Islamic world between 750 and 1000?

CRITICAL THINKING
● Why can it be said that the Islamic civilization was superior to the civilization of western Europe in the ninth and tenth centuries?

A medieval French manuscript illustration of the coronation of Charlemagne by Pope Leo III

© Scala/Art Resource, NY

IN 800, CHARLEMAGNE, the king of the Franks, journeyed to Rome to help Pope Leo III, who was barely clinging to power in the face of rebellious Romans. On Christmas Day, Charlemagne and his family, attended by Romans, Franks, and visitors from the Byzantine Empire, crowded into Saint Peter's Basilica to hear Mass. Quite unexpectedly, according to a Frankish writer, "as the king rose from praying before the tomb of the blessed apostle Peter, Pope Leo placed a golden crown on his head." In keeping with ancient tradition, the people in the church shouted, "Long life and victory to Charles Augustus, crowned by God the great and pacific Emperor of the Romans." Seemingly, the Roman Empire in the west had been reborn, and Charles had become the first western emperor since 476. But this "Roman emperor" was actually a German king, and he had been crowned by the head of the western Christian church. In truth, the coronation of Charlemagne was a sign not of the rebirth of the Roman Empire but of the emergence of a new European civilization.

By the year of Charlemagne's coronation, the contours of this new European civilization were beginning to emerge in western Europe. Increasingly,

Europe would become the focus and center of Western civilization. Building on a fusion of Germanic, Greco-Roman, and Christian elements, the medieval European world first became visible in the Carolingian Empire of Charlemagne. The agrarian foundations of the eighth and ninth centuries proved inadequate to maintain a large monarchical system, however, and a new political and military order based on the decentralization of political power subsequently evolved to become an integral part of the political world of the Middle Ages.

European civilization began on a shaky and uncertain foundation, however. In the ninth century, Vikings, Magyars, and Muslims posed threats that could easily have stifled the new society. But the Vikings and Magyars were assimilated, and recovery slowly began to set in. By 1000, European civilization was ready to embark on a period of dazzling vitality and expansion.

Europeans and the Environment

The number of people in early medieval Europe is a matter of considerable uncertainty. In all probability, the population of the eighth century had still not recovered from the losses caused by the plagues of the sixth and seventh centuries. Historians generally believe that in the Early Middle Ages, Europe was a sparsely populated landscape dotted with villages and clusters of villages of farmers and warriors. Although rivers, such as the Loire, Seine, Rhine, Elbe, and Oder, served as major arteries of communication, villages were still separated from one another by forests, swamps, and mountain ridges. Forests, which provided building and heating materials as well as game, covered the European landscape. In fact, it has been estimated that less than 10 percent of the land was cultivated, a figure so small that some economic historians believe that Europe had difficulty feeding even its modest population. Thus hunting and fishing were necessary to supplement the European diet.

Farming

The cultivation of new land proved especially difficult in the Early Middle Ages. Given the crude implements of the time, it was not easy to clear forests and prepare the ground for planting. Moreover, German tribes had for centuries considered trees sacred and resisted cutting them down to make room for farms. Even conversion to Christianity did not entirely change these attitudes. In addition, the heavy soils of northern Europe were not easily plowed. Agricultural methods also worked against significant crop yields. Land was allowed to lie fallow (unplanted) every other year to regain its fertility, but even so it produced low yields. Evidence indicates that Frankish estates yielded incredibly low ratios of two measures of grain to one measure of seed.

The Climate

Climatic patterns show that European weather began to improve around 700 after several centuries of wetter and colder conditions. Nevertheless, natural disasters were always a threat, especially since the low yields meant that little surplus could be saved for bad times. Drought or too much rain could mean meager harvests, famine, and dietary deficiencies that made people susceptible to a wide range of diseases. This was a period of low life expectancy. One study of Hungarian graves found that of every five skeletons, one was a child below the age of one, and two were children between one and fourteen; more than one in five was a woman below the age of twenty. Overall, then, the picture of early medieval Europe is of a relatively small population subsisting on the basis of a limited agricultural economy and leading, in most cases, a precarious existence.

The World of the Carolingians

By the eighth century, the Merovingian dynasty was losing its control of the Frankish lands. Charles Martel, the Carolingian mayor of the palace of Austrasia, became the virtual ruler of these territories. When Charles Martel died in 741, his son, Pepin, deposed the Merovingians and assumed the kingship of the Frankish state for himself and his family. Pepin's actions, which were approved by the pope, created a new form of Frankish kingship. Pepin (751–768) was crowned king and formally anointed by a representative of the pope with holy oil in imitation of an Old Testament practice. The anointing not only symbolized that the kings had been entrusted with a sacred office but also provides yet another example of how a Germanic institution fused with a Christian practice in the Early Middle Ages.

Charlemagne and the Carolingian Empire (768–814)

Pepin's death in 768 brought to the throne of the Frankish kingdom his son, a dynamic and powerful ruler known to history as Charles the Great or Charlemagne (*Carolus magnus* in Latin—hence our word *Carolingian*). Charlemagne was a determined and decisive man, intelligent and inquisitive. A fierce warrior, he was also a wise patron of learning and a resolute statesman (see the box on p. 200). He greatly expanded the territory of the Carolingian Empire during his lengthy rule.

Expansion of the Carolingian Empire   In the tradition of the Germanic kings, Charlemagne was a determined warrior who undertook fifty-four military campaigns. Even though the Frankish army was relatively small—only eight thousand men gathered each spring for campaigning—supplying it and transporting it to distant areas could still present serious problems. The Frankish army comprised mostly infantry, with some cavalry armed with swords and spears.

THE ACHIEVEMENTS OF CHARLEMAGNE

EINHARD, THE BIOGRAPHER of Charlemagne, was born in the valley of the Main River in Germany about 775. Raised and educated in the monastery of Fulda, an important center of learning, he arrived at the court of Charlemagne in 791 or 792. Although he did not achieve high office under Charlemagne, he served as private secretary to Louis the Pious, Charlemagne's son and successor. Einhard's *Life of Charlemagne,* written between 817 and 830, was modeled on Suetonius' *Lives of the Caesars,* especially his biography of Augustus. In this selection, Einhard discusses some of Charlemagne's acccomplishments.

Einhard, *Life of Charlemagne*

Such are the wars, most skillfully planned and successfully fought, which this most powerful king waged during the forty-seven years of his reign. He so largely increased the Frank kingdom, which was already great and strong when he received it at his father's hands, that more than double its former territory was added to it. . . . He subdued all the wild and barbarous tribes dwelling in Germany between the Rhine and the Vistula, the Ocean and the Danube, all of which speak very much the same language, but differ widely from one another in customs and dress. . . .

He added to the glory of his reign by gaining the good will of several kings and nations; so close, indeed, was the alliance that he contracted with Alfonso, King of Galicia and Asturias, that the latter, when sending letters or ambassadors to Charles, invariably styled himself his man. . . . The Emperors of Constantinople [the Byzantine emperors] sought friendship and alliance with Charles by several embassies; and even when the Greeks [the Byzantines] suspected him of designing to take the empire from them, because of his assumption of the title Emperor, they made a close alliance with him, that he might have no cause of offense. In fact, the power of the Franks was always viewed with a jealous eye, whence the Greek proverb, "Have the Frank for your friend, but not for your neighbor."

This King, who showed himself so great in extending his empire and subduing foreign nations, and was con-

stantly occupied with plans to that end, undertook also very many works calculated to adorn and benefit his kingdom, and brought several of them to completion. Among these, the most deserving of mention are the basilica of the Holy Mother of God at Aix-la-Chapelle, built in the most admirable manner, and a bridge over the Rhine River at Mainz, half a mile long, the breadth of the river at this point. . . . Above all, sacred buildings were the object of his care throughout his whole kingdom; and whenever he found them falling to ruin from age, he commanded the priests and fathers who had charge of them to repair them, and made sure by commissioners that his instructions were obeyed. . . . Thus did Charles defend and increase as well as beautify his kingdom. . . .

He cherished with the greatest fervor and devotion the principles of the Christian religion, which had been instilled into him from infancy. Hence it was that he built the beautiful church at Aix-la-Chapelle, which he adorned with gold and silver and lamps, and with rails and doors of solid brass. He had the columns and marbles for this structure brought from Rome and Ravenna, for he could not find such as were suitable elsewhere. He was a constant worshiper at this church as long as his health permitted, going morning and evening, even after nightfall, besides attending Mass. . . .

He was very forward in caring for the poor, so much so that he not only made a point of giving in his own country and his own kingdom, but when he discovered that there were Christians living in poverty in Syria, Egypt, and Africa, at Jerusalem, Alexandria, and Carthage, he had compassion on their wants, and used to send money over the seas to them. . . . He sent great and countless gifts to the popes, and throughout his whole reign the wish that he had nearest at heart was to reestablish the ancient authority of the city of Rome under his care and by his influence, and to defend and protect the Church of St. Peter, and to beautify and enrich it out of his own store above all other churches.

Charlemagne's campaigns took him to many areas of Europe. In 773, he led his army into Italy, crushed the Lombards, and took control of the Lombard state. Although his son was crowned king of Italy, Charlemagne was its real ruler. Four years after his invasion of Italy, Charlemagne and his forces advanced into northern Spain. This campaign proved disappointing; not only did the Basques harass his army as it crossed the Pyrenees on the way home, but they also ambushed and annihilated his rear guard. Charlemagne was considerably more successful with his eastern campaigns into Germany, especially against the Saxons, who had settled between the Elbe River and the North Sea. As Einhard, Charlemagne's biographer, recounted it:

No war ever undertaken by the Frank nation was carried on with such persistence and bitterness, or cost so much labor, because the Saxons, like almost all the tribes of Germany, were a fierce people, given to the worship of devils, and hostile to our religion, and did not consider it dishonorable to transgress and violate all law, human and divine.[1]

Charlemagne's insistence that the Saxons convert to Christianity simply fueled their resistance. Not until 804, after eighteen campaigns, was Saxony finally pacified and added to the Carolingian domain.

In southeastern Germany, Charlemagne invaded the land of the Bavarians in 787 and brought them into his empire by the following year, an expansion that brought him into contact with the southern Slavs and the Avars. The

Bronze Equestrian Statue of Charlemagne. This small bronze statue is believed to represent the emperor Charles the Great, although some scholars believe it is his grandson, Charles the Bald. The figure dates from the ninth century, but the horse is a sixteenth-century restoration. The attire on the figure accords with Einhard's account of how Charlemagne dressed. The imperial crown rests on his head, and in his left hand he grasps a globe, a symbol of world power and a reminder that the power of the Roman Empire had been renewed.

latter disappeared from history after their utter devastation at the hands of Charlemagne's army. Now at its height, Charlemagne's empire covered much of western and central Europe (see Map 8.1); not until the time of Napoleon in the nineteenth century would an empire of this size be seen again in Europe.

Governing the Empire   Charlemagne continued the efforts of his father in organizing the Carolingian kingdom. Because there was no system of public taxation, Charlemagne was dependent on the royal estates for the resources he needed to govern his empire. Food and goods derived from these lands provided support for the king, his household staff, and officials. To keep the nobles in his service, Charlemagne granted part of the royal lands as lifetime holdings to nobles who assisted him.

Besides the household staff, the administration of the empire depended on counts, who were the king's chief representatives in local areas, although in dangerous border districts officials known as margraves (literally, *mark graf*, count of the border district) were used. Counts were members of the nobility who had already existed under the Merovingians. They had come to control public services in their own lands and thus acted as judges, military leaders, and agents of the king. Gradually, as the rule of the Merovingian kings weakened, many counts had simply attached the royal lands and services performed on behalf of the king to their own family possessions.

In an effort to gain greater control over his kingdom, Charlemagne attempted to limit the power of the counts. They were required to serve outside their own family lands and were moved about periodically rather than being permitted to remain in a county for life. By making the offices appointive, Charlemagne tried to prevent the counts' children from automatically inheriting their offices. Moreover, as another check on the counts, Charlemagne instituted the *missi dominici* ("messengers of the lord king"), two men, one lay lord and one church official, who were sent out to local districts to ensure that the counts were executing the king's wishes. The counts also had assistants, but they were members of their households, not part of a bureaucratic office.

The last point is an important reminder that we should not think of Carolingian government in the modern sense of government offices run by officials committed to an impersonal ideal of state service. The Carolingian system was glaringly inefficient. Great distances had to be covered on horseback, making it impossible for Charlemagne and his household staff to exercise much supervision over local affairs. What held the system together was personal loyalty to a single ruler who was strong enough to ensure loyalty by force when necessary.

Charlemagne also realized that the Catholic church could provide valuable assistance in governing his kingdom. By the late seventh century, the system of ecclesiastical government within the Christian church that had been created in the Late Roman Empire had largely disintegrated. Many church offices were not filled or were held by grossly unqualified relatives of the royal family. Both Pepin and his son Charlemagne took up the cause of church

MAP 8.1 The Carolingian Empire. Charlemagne inherited the Carolingian Empire from his father, Pepin. He expanded his territories in several directions, creating an empire that would not be rivaled in size until the conquests of Napoleon in the early nineteenth century. ❓ How might Charlemagne's holdings in northern Italy have influenced his relationship with the pope?

🌐 **View an animated version of this map or related maps at** http://history.wadsworth.com/spielvogel06/

reform by creating new bishoprics and archbishoprics, restoring old ones, and seeing to it that the clergy accepted the orders of their superiors and executed their duties.

Charlemagne as Emperor As Charlemagne's power grew, so did his prestige as the most powerful Christian ruler; one monk even wrote of his empire as the "kingdom of Europe." Charlemagne acquired a new title—emperor of the Romans—in 800, but substantial controversy surrounds this event, and it can only be understood within the context of the relationship between the papacy and the Frankish monarchs.

Already during the reign of Pepin, a growing alliance had emerged between the kingdom of the Franks and the papacy. The popes welcomed this support, and in the course of the second half of the eighth century, they severed more and more of their ties with the Byzantine Empire

and drew closer to the Frankish kingdom. Charlemagne encouraged this development. In 799, after a rebellion against his authority, Pope Leo III (795–816) managed to escape from Rome and flee to safety at Charlemagne's court. Charlemagne offered assistance, and when he went to Rome in November 800 to settle affairs, he was received by the pope like an emperor. On Christmas Day in 800, after Mass, Pope Leo placed a crown on Charlemagne's head and proclaimed him emperor of the Romans.

The significance of this imperial coronation has been much debated by historians. We are not even sure whether the pope or Charlemagne initiated the idea or whether Charlemagne was pleased or displeased. His biographer Einhard claimed that "at first [he] had such an aversion that he declared that he would not have set foot in the Church the day that [it was] conferred, although it was a great feast-day, if he could have foreseen the design of the Pope."[2]

The Coronation of Charlemagne. After a rebellion in 799 forced Pope Leo III to seek refuge at Charlemagne's court, Charlemagne went to Rome to settle the affair. There, on Christmas Day in 800, he was crowned emperor of the Romans by the pope. This manuscript illustration shows Leo III placing a crown on Charlemagne's head.

For the most part, the revival of classical studies and the efforts to preserve Latin culture took place in the monasteries, many of which had been established by the Irish and English missionaries of the seventh and eighth centuries (see Chapter 7). By the ninth century, the work required of Benedictine monks was the copying of manuscripts. Monasteries established **scriptoria,** or writing rooms, where monks copied not only the works of early Christianity, such as the Bible and the treatises of the church fathers, but also the works of Latin classical authors.

Following the example of the Irish and English monks, their Carolingian counterparts developed new ways of producing books. Their texts were written on pages made of parchment or sheepskin rather than papyrus and then bound in covers decorated with jewels and precious metals. The use of parchment made books very expensive; an entire herd of sheep could be required to make a Bible. (Papyrus was no longer available because Egypt was in Muslim hands, and the west could no longer afford to import it.) Carolingian monastic scribes also developed a new writing style called the Carolingian minuscule (see the illustration on p. 208). This was really hand printing rather than cursive writing and was far easier to read than the Merovingian script.

The production of manuscripts, some of which were illustrated, in Carolingian monastic scriptoria was a crucial factor in the preservation of the ancient legacy. About eight thousand manuscripts survive from Carolingian times. Virtually 90 percent of the ancient Roman works that we have today exist because they were copied by Carolingian monks.

Charlemagne personally promoted learning by establishing a palace school and encouraging scholars from all over Europe to come to the Carolingian court. These included men of letters from Italy, Spain, Germany, and Ireland. Best known was Alcuin, called by Einhard the "greatest scholar of that day." He was from the famous school at York that was a product of the great revival of learning in the Anglo-Saxon kingdom of Northumbria. From 782 to 796, while serving at Charlemagne's court as an adviser on ecclesiastical affairs, Alcuin also provided the leadership for the palace school. He concentrated on teaching classical Latin and adopted Cassiodorus' sevenfold division of knowledge known as the liberal arts (see Chapter 7), which became the basis for all later medieval education. All in all, the Carolingian Renaissance played a crucial role in keeping the classical heritage alive as well as maintaining the intellectual life of the Catholic church.

But Charlemagne also perceived the usefulness of the imperial title; after all, he was now on a level of equality with the Byzantine emperor, a status he did not reject. Moreover, the papacy now had a defender of great stature, although later popes in the Middle Ages would become involved in fierce struggles with emperors over who possessed the higher power.

In any case, Charlemagne's coronation as Roman emperor certainly demonstrated the strength, even after three hundred years, of the concept of an enduring Roman Empire. More important, it symbolized the fusion of the Roman, Christian, and Germanic elements that constituted the foundation of European civilization. A Germanic king had been crowned emperor of the Romans by the spiritual leader of western Christendom. A new civilization had emerged.

The Carolingian Intellectual Renewal

Charlemagne had a strong desire to revive learning in his kingdom, an attitude that stemmed from his own intellectual curiosity as well as the need to provide educated clergy for the church and literate officials for the government. His efforts led to a revival of learning and culture that some historians have labeled a Carolingian Renaissance, or "rebirth" of learning.

Monks as Copyists. The copying of manuscripts was a major task of monastic establishments in the Middle Ages. This work took place in a scriptorium or writing room. This medieval manuscript illustration from the early eleventh century shows two German monks at work in the scriptorium of a monastery in Echternach. To copy a whole book was considered a work of special spiritual merit. Copying the Bible was especially important because it was considered a sacred object.

© Dr. Ludwig Reichert Verlag, Wiesbaden

Life in the Carolingian World

In daily life as well as intellectual life, the Europe of the Carolingian era witnessed a fusion of Roman, Germanic, and Christian practices. The last in particular seem to have exercised an ever-increasing influence.

The Family and Marriage By Carolingian times, the Catholic church had begun to make a significant impact on Frankish family life and marital and sexual attitudes. Marriages in Frankish society were arranged by fathers or uncles to meet the needs of the extended family. Although wives were expected to be faithful to their husbands, Frankish aristocrats often kept concubines, either slave girls or free women from their estates. Even the "most Christian king" Charlemagne had a number of concubines.

To limit such sexual license, the church increasingly emphasized its role in marriage and attempted to Christianize it. Although marriage was a civil arrangement, priests tried to add their blessings and strengthen the concept of a special marriage ceremony. Moreover, the church tried to serve as the caretaker of marriage by stipulating that a girl over fifteen must give her consent to her guardian's choice of a husband or her marriage would not be valid in the eyes of the church.

To stabilize marriages, the church also began to emphasize **monogamy** and permanence. A Frankish church council in 789 stipulated that marriage was an "indissoluble sacrament" and condemned the practice of concubinage and easy divorce; during the reign of Emperor Louis the Pious (814–840), the church finally established the right to prohibit divorce. Now a man who married was expected to remain with his wife "even though she were sterile, deformed, old, dirty, drunken, a frequenter of bad company, lascivious, vain, greedy, unfaithful, quarrelsome, abusive . . . for when that man was free, he freely engaged himself."[3] This was not easily accepted, since monogamy and indissoluble marriages were viewed as obstacles to the well-established practice of concubinage. Not until the thirteenth century was divorce largely stamped out among both the common people and the nobility.

The acceptance and spread of the Catholic church's views on the indissolubility of marriage encouraged the development of the **nuclear family** at the expense of the extended family. Although the kin was still an influential social and political force, the conjugal unit came to be seen as the basic unit of society. The new practice of young couples establishing their own households had a significant impact on women (see the box on p. 205). In the extended family, the eldest woman controlled all the other female members; in the nuclear family, the wife was still dominated by her husband, but at least she now had control of her own household and children.

Christianity and Sexuality The early church fathers had stressed that celibacy and complete abstinence from sexual activity constituted an ideal state superior to marriage. Subsequently, the early church gradually developed a case for clerical celibacy, although it proved impossible to enforce in the Early Middle Ages.

The early fathers had also emphasized, however, that not all people had the self-discipline to remain celibate. It was thus permissible to marry, as Paul had indicated in his first epistle to the Corinthians: "It is good for a man not to touch a woman. Nevertheless, to avoid fornication, let every man have his own wife, and let every woman have her own husband. . . . I say therefore to the unmarried and widows, It is good for them if they abide even as I. But if they cannot contain, let them marry: for it is better to marry than to burn [with passion]."[4] The church thus viewed marriage as the lesser of two evils; it was a concession to human weakness and fulfilled the need for companionship, sex, and children. Although marriage was the subject of much debate in the early medieval church, it was generally agreed that marriage gave the right to indulge in sexual intercourse. Sex, then, was permissible

ADVICE FROM A CAROLINGIAN MOTHER

HE WIFE OF a Carolingian aristocrat bore numerous responsibilities. She was entrusted with the management of the household and even the administration of extensive landed estates while her husband was absent in the royal service or on a military campaign. A wife was also expected to bear larger numbers of children and to supervise their upbringing. This selection by Dhouda, wife of Bernard, marquis of Septimania (in southern France), is taken from a manual she wrote to instruct her son on his duties to his new lord, King Charles the Bald (840–877).

Dhouda, *Handbook for William*

Direction on your comportment toward your lord.

You have Charles as your lord; you have him as lord because, as I believe, God and your father, Bernard, have chosen him for you to serve at the beginning of your career, in the flower of your youth. Remember that he comes from a great and noble lineage on both sides of his family. Serve him not only so that you please him in obvious ways, but also as one clearheaded in matters of both body and soul. Be steadfastly and completely loyal to him in all things. . . .

This is why, my son, I urge you to keep this loyalty as long as you live, in your body and in your mind. For the advancement that it brings you will be of great value both to you and to those who in turn serve you. May the madness of treachery never, not once, make you offer an angry insult. May it never give rise in your heart to the idea of being disloyal to your lord. There is harsh and shameful talk about men who act in this fashion. I do not think that such will befall you or those who fight alongside you because such an attitude has never shown itself among your ancestors. It has not been seen among them, it is not seen now, and it will not be seen in the future.

Be truthful to your lord, my son William, child of their lineage. Be vigilant, energetic, and offer him ready assistance as I have said here. In every matter of importance to royal power take care to show yourself a man of good judgment—in your own thoughts and in public—to the extent that God gives you strength. Read the sayings and the lives of the holy Fathers who have gone before us. You will there discover how you may serve your lord and be faithful to him in all things. When you understand this, devote yourself to the faithful execution of your lord's commands. Look around as well and observe those who fight for him loyally and constantly. Learn from them how you may serve him. Then, informed by their example, with the help and support of God, you will easily reach the celestial goal I have mentioned above. And may your heavenly Lord God be generous and benevolent toward you. May he keep you safe, be your kind leader and your protector. May he deign to assist you in all your actions and be your constant defender.

---

within marriage, but only so long as it was used for the purpose of procreation, or the begetting of children, not for pleasure.

Because the church developed the tradition that sexual relations between man and wife were legitimate only if engaged in for procreation, it condemned all forms of contraception. The church also strongly condemned abortion, although its prohibition failed to stop the practice. Various herbal potions, whose formulas appear in writings from Roman and Byzantine doctors, were available to prevent conception or cause abortion. The Catholic church accepted only one way to limit children: abstinence from intercourse, either periodic or total.

The church's condemnation of sexual activity outside marriage also included homosexuality. Neither Roman religion nor Roman law had recognized any real difference between homosexual and heterosexual eroticism, and the Roman Empire had taken no legal measures against the practice of homosexuality between adults. Later, in the Byzantine Empire, Emperor Justinian in 538 condemned homosexuality, emphasizing that such practices brought down the wrath of God ("we have provoked Him to anger") and endangered the welfare of the state:

> For because of such crimes, there are famines, earthquakes, and pestilences; wherefore we admonish men to abstain from the aforesaid unlawful acts, that they may not lose their souls. . . .

> We order the most illustrious prefect of the capital to arrest those who persist in the aforesaid lawless and impious acts after they have been warned by us, and to inflict on them the extreme punishments, so that the city and the state may not come to harm by reason of such wicked deeds.[5]

Justinian recommended that the guilty parties be punished by castration. Although the church in the Early Middle Ages similarly condemned homosexuality, it also pursued a flexible policy in its treatment of homosexuals. In the Early Middle Ages, homosexuals were treated less harshly than married couples who practiced contraception.

New Attitudes Toward Children   The Catholic church also had an impact on another aspect of family life—children. The ancient Romans had limited their family size through infanticide, primarily the exposure of unwanted children, which was accepted in classical society. Romans then paid much attention to the children chosen to survive, as is especially evident in the education of upper-class children. In the emerging early medieval world, barbarian practices of child rearing became influential. As we saw in Chapter 7, the Germanic law codes listed *wergelds*, whose size represented a crude evaluation of a person's importance. According to a Visigothic code of the mid-seventh century, for example, male children were valued at 60 solidi. At the age of twenty, when they had become warriors, the *wergeld* increased fivefold to 300 solidi, where it remained until the adult male reached fifty, after which it again declined. The value of females was only half that of males, although it also jumped tremendously (to 250 solidi) for women between the ages of fifteen and forty because of their importance as bearers of children.

Although the Christian church condemned infanticide, it was not able to eliminate the practice, especially among the poor and among victims of seduction who did not want to keep their illegitimate offspring. Nevertheless, priests tried to discourage such practices by urging people to abandon unwanted children in churches. Often such children were taken in by monasteries and convents and raised to be monks and nuns. Following the example of Jesus' love for children, monks and nuns tended to respect and preserve the virtues of childhood. As children grew older, however, it was thought necessary to use strict discipline to control what was considered the natural inclination of children to sin, especially by disobeying their elders.

Travel and Hospitality   Monasteries served another important function in the early medieval world as providers of hospitality. Both monasteries and aristocratic households were expected to provide a place to stay for weary travelers, who were ever at risk from thieves or violence of many kinds. Indeed, Burgundian law stipulated that "anyone who refused to offer a visitor shelter and warmth shall pay a fine of three solidi."[6] Hospitality, then, was a sacred duty, and

MS Hunter 252, f.70. Courtesy of the Librarian, Glasgow University Library

Travelers Arriving at an Inn. Inns provided refuge for the many pilgrims, merchants, and others who traveled Europe's dangerous roads in the Middle Ages. In this illustration, a group of merchants has stopped at an inn, which like most medieval inns provided basic necessities but not individual beds. Medieval people generally slept in the nude.

monasteries were especially active in providing it. It was customary for monasteries to have two guest houses, one for the rich and another for the poor. The plan for the monastery of Saint Gall, for example, provided pilgrims and paupers with a house containing benches, two dormitories, and outbuildings. For travelers of high rank, there was a separate guest house with two heated rooms, servants' bedrooms, and stables for horses. One could not always be sure of hospitality in the Early Middle Ages, however. The famous English missionary to Germany, Saint Boniface, reported that female pilgrims to Rome had been forced to become prostitutes in every town along their route in order to obtain their sustenance and reach their goal. The church responded by forbidding females to go on such pilgrimages.

Diet   For both rich and poor, the main staple of the Carolingian diet was bread. The aristocratic classes, as well as the monks, consumed it in large quantities. Ovens at the monastery of Saint Gall were able to bake a thousand loaves of bread. Sometimes a gruel made of barley and oats was substituted for bread in the peasant diet.

The upper classes in Carolingian society enjoyed a much more varied diet than the peasants. Pork was the major meat. Domestic pigs, allowed to run wild in the forests to find their own food, were collected and slaughtered in the fall, then smoked and salted to be eaten during the winter months. Because Carolingian aristocrats were especially fond of roasted meat, hunting wild game became one of their favorite activities. They ate little beef or mutton, however, because cattle were kept as dairy cows and oxen to draw plows, and sheep were raised for wool.

Dairy products became prevalent in the Carolingian diet. Milk, which spoiled rapidly, was made into cheese and butter. Chickens were raised for their eggs. Vegetables also formed a crucial part of the diet of both rich and poor. These included legumes, such as beans, peas, and lentils, and roots, such as garlic, onions, and carrots.

The Carolingian diet, especially of the upper classes, was also heavily dependent on honey and spices. Honey was used as a sweetener, both for foods and for many drinks, including wine and ale. Spices included domestic varieties that were grown in home gardens, such as thyme, sage, and chives, and more exotic—and outrageously expensive—varieties imported from the East, such as pepper, cumin, cloves, and cinnamon. Aristocrats were especially fond of spicy dishes, not just for their taste but as a sign of prestige and wealth; spices were also believed to aid the digestion.

Both gluttony and drunkenness were vices shared by many people in Carolingian society. Monastic rations were greatly enlarged in the eighth century to include a daily allotment of 3.7 pounds of bread (nuns were permitted 3 pounds), 1½ quarts of wine or ale, 2 or 3 ounces of cheese, and 8 ounces of vegetables (4 ounces for nuns). These rations provided a total of 6,000 calories a day, and since only heavy and fatty foods—bread, milk, and cheese—were considered nourishing, we begin to understand why some

MEDICAL PRACTICES IN THE EARLY MIDDLE AGES

A NUMBER OF medical manuscripts written in Old English have survived from Anglo-Saxon England. Although most of the medical texts date from the tenth to twelfth centuries, scholars believe that they include copies of earlier works and contain older influences as well. As the following selections from three of these treatises illustrate, herbs were the basic materials of the Anglo-Saxon physicians (or *leeches,* as they were called), and treatments consequently focused almost entirely on botanical remedies. The identity of many of the plants used remains unknown.

The Anglo-Saxon Herbal

 Cress (Nasturtium)

1. In case a man's hair falls out, take juice of the plant which one names nasturtium and by another name cress, put it on the nose, the hair shall grow.
2. This plant is not sown but it is produced of itself in springs and in brooks; also it is written that in some lands it will grow against walls.
3. For a sore head, that is for scurf [dandruff] and for itch, take the seed of this same plant and goose grease, pound together, it draws from off the head the whiteness of the scurf.
4. For soreness of the body [indigestion], take this same plant nasturtium and pennyroyal, soak them in water and give to drink; the soreness and the evil departs.

The Leechbook of Bald

Here are wound salves for all wounds and drinks and cleansings of every sort, whether internally or externally.

Waybroad beaten and mixed with old lard, the fresh is of no use. Again, a wound salve: take waybroad seed, crush it small, shed it on the wound and soon it will be better.

For a burn, if a man be burned with fire only, take woodruff and lily and brooklime; boil in butter and smear therewith. If a man be burned with a liquid, let him take elm rind and roots of the lily, boil them in milk, smear thereon three times a day. For sunburn, boil in butter tender ivy twigs and smear thereon.

The Peri-Didaxeon

 For a Broken Head

For a broken or wounded head which is caused by the humors of the head. Take betony and pound it and lay it on the wound and it will relieve all the pain.

 For Sleep

Thus must one do for the man who cannot sleep; take wormwood and rub it into wine or warm water and let the man drink it and soon it will be better with him.

 For Sore Hands

This leechcraft is good for sore hands and for sore fingers which is called chilblains. Take white frankincense and silver cinders and brimstone and mingle together, then take oil and add it into this mixture, then warm the hands and smear them with the mixture thus made. Wrap up the hands in a linen cloth.

Carolingians were known for their potbellies. Malnutrition, however, remained a widespread problem for common people in this period.

Everyone in Carolingian society, including abbots and monks, drank heavily and often to excess. Taverns became a regular feature of life and were found everywhere: in marketplaces, at pilgrimage centers, and on royal, episcopal, and monastic estates. Drinking contests were not unusual; one penitential stated: "Does drunken bravado encourage you to attempt to out-drink your friends? If so, thirty days' fast."

The aristocrats and monks favored wine above all other beverages, and much care was lavished on its production, especially by monasteries. Although ale was considered inferior in some quarters, it was especially popular in the northern and eastern parts of the Carolingian world. Water was also drunk as a beverage, but much care had to be taken to obtain pure sources from wells or clear streams. Monasteries were particularly active in going to the sources of water and building conduits to bring it to the cloister or kitchen fountains.

Water was also used for bathing. Although standards of personal hygiene were not high, medieval people did not ignore cleanliness. A royal palace, such as Charlemagne's, possessed both hot and cold baths. Carolingian aristocrats changed clothes and bathed at least once a week, on Saturdays. The Saturday bath was also a regular practice in many Carolingian monasteries. To monks, bathing more than once a week seemed an unnecessary luxury; to aristocrats, it often seemed desirable.

Health Medical practice in Carolingian times stressed the use of medicinal herbs (see the box above) and bleeding. Although the latter was practiced regularly, moderation was frequently recommended. Some advised carefulness as well: "Who dares to undertake a bleeding should see to it that his hand does not tremble."

Physicians were also available when people faced serious illnesses. Many were clerics, and monasteries trained their own. Monastic libraries kept medical manuscripts copied from ancient works and grew herbs to provide stocks of medicinal plants. Carolingian medical manuscripts contained scientific descriptions of illnesses, recipes for medical potions, and even gynecological advice, although monks in particular expended little effort on female medical needs. Some manuals even included instructions for operations, especially for soldiers injured in battle. Some sources clearly demonstrate that there were accurate techniques for amputating gangrenous limbs:

> If you must cut off an unhealthy limb from a healthy body, then do not cut to the limit of the healthy flesh, but cut further into the whole and quick flesh, so that a better and quicker cure may be obtained. When you set fire on the man [i.e., cauterize], take leaves of tender leek and grated salt, overlay the places so that the heat of the fire be more quickly drawn away.[7]

Although scholars are not sure whether anesthesia was used for such operations, medieval manuals recommended poppy, mandrake, and henbane for their narcotic properties.

Physicians of the Early Middle Ages supplemented their medicines and natural practices with appeals for otherworldly help. Magical rites and influences were carried over from pagan times; the Germanic tribes had used magical medicine for centuries. Physicians recommended that patients wear amulets and charms around their bodies to ward off diseases:

> Procure a little bit of the dung of a wolf, preferably some which contains small bits of bone, and pack it in a tube which the patient may easily wear as an amulet.

For epilepsy take a nail of a wrecked ship, make it into a bracelet and set therein the bone of a stag's heart taken from its body whilst alive; put it on the left arm; you will be astonished at the result.[8]

But as pagans were converted to Christianity, miraculous healing through the intervention of God, Jesus, or the saints soon replaced pagan practices. Medieval chronicles abound with accounts of people healed by touching a saint's body. The use of Christian prayers, written down and used as amulets, however, reminds us that for centuries Christian and pagan medical practices survived side by side.

Disintegration of the Carolingian Empire

The Carolingian Empire began to disintegrate soon after Charlemagne's death. Charlemagne was succeeded by his son Louis the Pious (814–840). Though a decent man, Louis was not a strong ruler and was unable to control either the Frankish aristocracy or his own four sons, who fought continually. In 843, after their father's death, the three surviving brothers signed the Treaty of Verdun. This agreement divided the Carolingian Empire among them into three major sections: Charles the Bald (843–877) obtained the western Frankish lands, which formed the

Bibliotheque Nationale, Paris, France

The First Bible of Charles the Bald. Charles the Bald, who took control of the western Frankish lands, is pictured here in an illustration from his first Bible, which dates from between 843 and 851. Illustrated Bibles were one of the finest achievements of Carolingian art. Also pictured is a page from the Bible, showing the use of the Carolingian minuscule style of writing.

Bibliotheque Nationale, Paris, France

core of the eventual kingdom of France; Louis the German (843–876) took the eastern lands, which became Germany; and Lothar (840–855) received the title of emperor and a "Middle Kingdom" extending from the North Sea to the Mediterranean, including the Netherlands, the Rhineland, and northern Italy. The territories of the Middle Kingdom became a source of incessant struggle between the other two Frankish rulers and their heirs. Indeed, France and Germany would fight over the territories of this Middle Kingdom for centuries.

Although this division of the Carolingian Empire was made for political and not nationalistic reasons (dividing a kingdom among the male heirs was a traditional Frankish custom), two different cultures began to emerge. By the ninth century, inhabitants of the western Frankish area were speaking a Romance language derived from Latin that became French. Eastern Franks spoke a Germanic dialect. The later kingdoms of France and Germany did not yet exist, however. In the ninth century, the frequent struggles among the numerous heirs of the sons of Louis the Pious led to further disintegration of the Carolingian Empire. In the meantime, while powerful aristocrats acquired even more power in their own local territories at the expense of the squabbling Carolingian rulers, the process of disintegration was abetted by external attacks on different parts of the old Carolingian world.

Invasions of the Ninth and Tenth Centuries

In the ninth and tenth centuries, western Europe was beset by a wave of invasions by several non-Christian peoples—one old enemy, the Muslims, and two new ones, the Magyars and the Vikings (see Map 8.2 on p. 212). Although battered by these onslaughts, Christian Europe hung on and, with the exception of the Muslims, wound up assimilating its assailants into Christian European civilization.

Muslims and Magyars   The first great wave of Muslim expansion had ended at the beginning of the eighth century (see Chapter 7). Gradually, the Muslims built up a series of sea bases in their occupied territories in North Africa, Spain, and southern Gaul and began a new series of attacks in the Mediterranean in the ninth century. They raided the southern coasts of Europe, especially Italy, and even threatened Rome in 843. Their invasion of Sicily in 827 eventually led to a successful occupation of the island. Muslim forces also destroyed the Carolingian defenses in northern Spain and conducted forays into southern France.

The Magyars were a people from western Asia. When the Byzantine emperors encouraged them to attack the troublesome Bulgars, the latter in turn encouraged a people known as the Pechenegs to attack the Magyars instead.

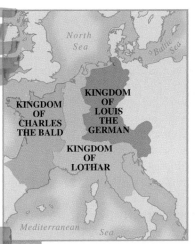

Division of the Carolingian Empire by the Treaty of Verdun, 843

Consequently, the Magyars, under severe Pecheneg pressure, had moved west into eastern and central Europe by the end of the ninth century. They established themselves on the plains of Hungary and from there made raids into western Europe. The Magyars were finally crushed at the Battle of Lechfeld in Germany in 955. At the end of the tenth century, they were converted to Christianity and settled down to establish the kingdom of Hungary.

The Vikings   By far the most devastating and far-reaching attacks of the time came from the Northmen or Norsemen of Scandinavia, also known to us as the Vikings. The Vikings were a Germanic people based in Scandinavia and constitute, in a sense, the final wave of Germanic migration. Why they moved is not very clear to historians. One common explanation focuses on overpopulation, although recent research indicates that this may have been true only in western Norway. Other reasons have included the Vikings' great love of adventure and their search for wealth and new avenues of trade.

Two features of Viking society help explain what the Vikings accomplished. First of all, they were warriors. Second, they were superb shipbuilders and sailors. Their ships were the best of the period. Long and narrow with beautifully carved arched prows, the Viking dragon ships carried about fifty men. They had banks of oars as well as a single great sail. Their shallow draft enabled them to sail up European rivers and attack places at some distance inland. Although Viking raids in the eighth century tended to be small-scale and sporadic, they became more regular and more devastating in the ninth (see the box on p. 210). Vikings sacked villages and towns, destroyed churches, and easily defeated small local armies. Viking attacks frightened people and led many a clergyman to exhort his parishioners to change their behavior to appease God's anger, as in this sermon by an English archbishop in 1014:

Things have not gone well now for a long time at home or abroad, but there has been devastation and persecution in every district again and again, and the English have been for a long time now completely defeated and too greatly disheartened through God's anger; and the pirates [Vikings] so strong with God's consent that often in battle one puts to flight ten, and sometimes less, sometimes more, all because of our sins. . . . We pay them continually and they humiliate us daily; they ravage and they burn, plunder, and rob and carry on board; and lo, what else is there in all these events except God's anger clear and visible over this people?[9]

Because there were different groups of Scandinavians, Viking expansion varied a great deal. Norwegian Vikings moved into Ireland and western England; Danes attacked eastern England, Frisia, and the Rhineland and navigated

THE VIKINGS INVADE ENGLAND

NEAR THE END of the ninth century, a number of monks in England began to compile a series of chronicles, or yearly records of events. Although there are several chronicles, they have come to be known as the *Anglo-Saxon Chronicle*. Although much of the chronicle focuses on politics, there are also numerous accounts of events of immediate concern to the monks, such as the death of a bishop or inclement weather conditions. This selection from the *Anglo-Saxon Chronicle* focuses on the Danish Viking invasions of England. These selections, taken from the accounts for the years 994, 997, 998, 999, and 1003, show how regular and devastating the Viking invasions were.

Anglo-Saxon Chronicle

994. Olaf and Swein came to London, on the Nativity of St. Mary, with ninety-four ships, fighting constantly the city, and they meant, moreover, to set it on fire. But they there suffered more harm and evil than they ever believed any town-dwellers could have done them. In this God's holy mother showed her mercy to the town-dwellers and delivered them from their enemies; then they went from there, and wrought the most evil that any force had ever done, in burning, ravaging and killing, both along the sea-coast, in Essex, and in Kent, Sussex and Hampshire; finally they seized horses for themselves, and rode as widely as they would, working unspeakable evil.

997. The Danes went around Devonshire into the mouth of the Severn, and there ravaged in Cornwall, Wales and Devon. Then they put in at Watchet and did much evil by burning and slaughtering. After that, they went around Land's End again on the south side, and went into the mouth of the Tamar, continuing up until they came to Lydford, burning or killing each thing they met—they burnt down Ordulf's monastery at Tavistock, and brought with them to their ships indescribable plunder.

998. The force went eastward again into the mouth of the Frome, and went inland as widely as they pleased into Dorset. Troops were often gathered against them, but as soon as they should have come together, always, in some way, flight was ordered, and they always had the victory in the end. Another time they settled themselves on the Isle of Wight, and fed themselves from Hampshire and Sussex.

999. The force came again into the Thames, and went up along Medway to Rochester; there the Kentish troops came against them, and they came together resolutely. But alas, they moved too quickly, and fled because they had not the help they should have had—then the Danes had the power of the battlefield, seized horses, and rode as widely as they pleased. They ravaged and destroyed nearly all West Kent.

1003. Exeter was ruined, because of the Frankish peasant Hugh, whom the lady had set up as her reeve [local official]; the Danish force destroyed the town completely, and took much booty. A very great army was gathered from Wiltshire and Hampshire, and went very resolutely against the force. The ealdorman [town official] Aelfric should have led the army, but he displayed his old wiles. As soon as they were close enough to look on one another, he feigned sickness, and began retching to vomit, and said that he was taken ill; so he betrayed the people he should have led, as it is said: 'When the war-leader weakens, all the army is greatly hindered.' When Swein saw that they were not resolute, and all scattering, he led his force into Wilton, ravaged and burnt the borough, went to Salisbury, and from there went back to the sea, where he knew his wave-coursers were.

rivers to enter western Frankish lands. Swedish Vikings dominated the Baltic Sea and progressed into the Slavic areas to the east. Moving into northwestern Russia, they went down the rivers of Russia to Novgorod and Kiev and established fortified ports throughout these territories. There they made contact with the Byzantine Empire, either as traders or as invaders. They also made contact with Arab traders on the Volga River and the Sea of Azov.

Early Viking raids had been carried out largely in the summer; by the mid-ninth century, however, the Norsemen had begun to establish winter settlements in Europe from which they could make expeditions to conquer and settle new lands. By 850, groups of Norsemen had settled in Ireland, and the Danes occupied an area known as the Danelaw in northeastern England by 878. Agreeing to accept Christianity, the Danes were eventually assimilated into a larger Anglo-Saxon kingdom. Beginning in 911, the ruler of the western Frankish lands gave one band of Vikings land at the mouth of the Seine River, forming a section of France that ultimately came to be known as Normandy. This policy of settling the Vikings and converting them to Christianity was a deliberate one, since the new inhabitants served as protectors against additional Norseman attacks.

The Vikings were also daring explorers. After 860, they sailed westward in their long ships across the North Atlantic Ocean, reaching Iceland in 874. Erik the Red, a Viking exiled from Iceland, traveled even farther west and discovered Greenland in 985. The only known Viking site in North America was found in Newfoundland.

By the tenth century, Viking expansion was drawing to a close. Greater control by the monarchs of Denmark, Norway, and Sweden over their inhabitants and the increasing Christianization of both the Scandinavian kings and peoples tended to inhibit Viking expansion, but not before Viking settlements had been established through-

The Vikings Attack England. An illustration from an eleventh-century English manuscript depicts a group of armed Vikings invading England. Two ships have already reached the shore, and a few Vikings are shown walking down a long gangplank onto English soil. Also shown is a replica of a well-preserved Viking ship found at Oseberg, Norway. The Oseberg ship was one of the largest Viking ships in its day.

out many parts of Europe. Like the Magyars, the Vikings were also assimilated into European civilization. Once again, Christianity proved a decisive civilizing force in Europe. Europe and Christianity were becoming virtually synonymous.

The Viking raids and settlements also had important political repercussions. The inability of royal authorities to protect their peoples against these incursions caused local populations to turn instead to the local aristocrats to provide security for them. In the process, the landed aristocrats not only increased their strength and prestige but also assumed even more of the functions of local government that had previously belonged to the kings; over time these developments led to a new political and military order.

The Emerging World of Lords and Vassals

The renewed invasions and the disintegration of the Carolingian Empire led to the emergence of a new type of relationship between free individuals. When governments ceased to be able to defend their subjects, it became important to find some powerful lord who could offer protection in exchange for service. The contract sworn between a lord and his subordinate is the basis of a form of social organization that later generations of historians called *feudalism*. But feudalism was never a system, and many historians today prefer to avoid using the term.

Vassalage

The practice of **vassalage** was derived from Germanic society, in which warriors swore an oath of loyalty to their leader. They fought for their chief, and he in turn took care of their needs. By the eighth century, an individual who served a lord in a military capacity was known as a *vassal*.

With the breakdown of governments, powerful nobles took control of large areas of land. They needed men to fight

MAP 8.2 **Invasions of the Ninth and Tenth Centuries.** Attacks by invading Vikings, Magyars, and Muslims terrorized much of Europe in the ninth and tenth centuries, disrupting economic development and spurring the development of fief-holding. The Vikings were the biggest problem, but they eventually formed settlements, converted to Christianity, and were assimilated. **?** Why was it important for the marauding Vikings to build sound boats and develop good seafaring skills?

🌐 **View an animated version of this map or related maps at** http://history.wadsworth.com/spielvogel06/

for them, so the practice arose of giving grants of land to vassals, who would in return fight for their lord. The Frankish army had originally consisted of foot soldiers, dressed in coats of mail and armed with swords. But in the eighth century, when larger horses and the stirrup were introduced, a military change began to occur. Earlier, horsemen had been throwers of spears. Now they wore armored coats of mail (the larger horse could carry the weight) and wielded long lances that enabled them to act as battering rams (the stirrups kept the riders on their horses). For almost five hundred years, warfare in Europe would be dominated by heavily armored cavalry, or *knights,* as they came to be called.

Of course, a horse, armor, and weapons were expensive to purchase and maintain, and learning to wield these instruments skillfully from horseback took much time and practice. Consequently, lords who wanted men to fight for them had to grant each vassal a piece of land that provided

for the support of the vassal and his family. In return for the land, the vassal provided his lord with one major service, his fighting skills. Each needed the other. In the society of the Early Middle Ages, where there was little trade and wealth was based primarily on land ownership, land became the most important gift a lord could give to a vassal in return for military service.

The relationship between lord and vassal was made official by a public ceremony. To become a vassal, a man performed an act of homage to his lord, as described in this passage from a medieval treatise of law:

> The man should put his hands together as a sign of humility, and place them between the two hands of his lord as a token that he vows everything to him and promises faith to him; and the lord should receive him and promise to keep faith with him. Then the man should say: "Sir, I enter your homage and faith and become your man by mouth and hands [i.e., by taking the oath and

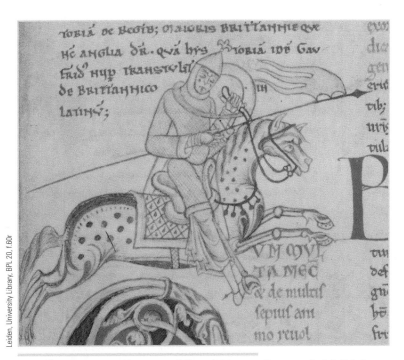

A Knight's Equipment Showing Saddle and Stirrups. In return for his fighting skills, a knight received a piece of land from his lord that provided for his economic support. Pictured here is a charging knight with his equipment. The introduction of the high saddle, stirrup, and larger horses allowed horsemen to wear heavier armor and to wield long lances, vastly improving the fighting ability of the cavalry.

placing his hands between those of the lord], and I swear and promise to keep faith and loyalty to you against all others, and to guard your rights with all my strength.[10]

As in the earlier Germanic band, loyalty to one's lord was the chief virtue.

Fief-Holding

The land granted to a vassal in return for military service came to be known as a **fief.** In time, many vassals who held such grants of land came to exercise rights of jurisdiction or political and legal authority within their fiefs. As the Carolingian world disintegrated politically under the impact of dissension within and invasions from without, an increasing number of powerful lords arose. Instead of a single government, many people were now responsible for keeping order. In some areas of France, for example, some lords—called *castellans*—constructed castles and asserted their authority to collect taxes and dispense justice to the local population. Lack of effective central control led to ever larger numbers of castles and castellans.

Fief-holding also became increasingly complicated as **subinfeudation** developed. The vassals of a king, who were themselves great lords, might also have vassals who would owe them military service in return for a grant of land from their estates. Those vassals, in turn, might likewise have vassals, who at such a level would be simple knights with barely enough land to provide their equipment. The lord-vassal relationship, then, bound together both greater and lesser landowners. Historians used to speak of a hierarchy with the king at the top, greater lords on the next level, lesser lords on the next, and simple knights at the bottom; however, this was only a model and rarely reflected reality. Such a hierarchy implies a king at the top. The reality in the tenth-century west Frankish kingdom was that the Capetian kings (see "New Political Configurations in the Tenth Century" later in this chapter) actually controlled no more land than the region around Paris. They possessed little real power over the great lords who held fiefs throughout France.

The lord-vassal relationship at all levels always constituted an honorable relationship between free men and did not imply any sense of servitude. Since kings could no longer provide security in the midst of the breakdown created by the invasions of the ninth century, the system of subinfeudation became ever more widespread. With their rights of jurisdiction, fiefs gave lords virtual possession of the rights of government.

The new practice of lordship was basically a product of the Carolingian world, but it also spread to England, Germany, central Europe, and in modified form to Italy. Fief-holding came to be characterized by a set of practices worked out in the course of the tenth century, although they became more prominent after 1000. These practices included a series of mutual obligations of lord toward vassal and vassal toward lord, but it is crucial to remember that such obligations varied considerably from place to place and even from fief to fief. As usual, practice almost always diverged from theory.

Mutual Obligations   Because the basic objective of fief-holding was to provide military support, it is no surprise to learn that the major obligation of a vassal to his lord was to perform military service. In addition to his own personal service, a great lord was also responsible for providing a group of knights for the king's army. Moreover, vassals had to furnish suit at court; this meant that a vassal was obliged to appear at his lord's court when summoned, either to give advice to the lord or to sit in judgment in a legal case, since the important vassals of a lord were peers, and only they could judge each other. Many vassals were also obliged to provide hospitality for their lord when he stayed at a vassal's castle. This obligation was especially important to medieval kings because they tended to be itinerant. Finally, vassals were responsible for aids, or financial payments, to the lord on a number of occasions, among them the knighting of the lord's eldest son, the marriage of his eldest daughter, and the ransom of the lord's person if the lord was held captive (see the box on p. 214).

Lords, Vassals, and Fiefs

HE UPHEAVALS of the Early Middle Ages produced a number of new institutions—lordship, vassalage, fiefs. The first selection records the granting of a fief by a lord to a vassal. The second is the classic statement by Bishop Fulbert of Chartres in 1020 on the mutual obligations between lord and vassal.

Record of a Grant Made by Abbot Faritius to Robert, a Knight

Abbot Faritius also granted to Robert, son of William Mauduit, the land of four hides in Weston which his father had held from the former's predecessor, to be held as a fief. And he should do this service for it, to wit: that whenever the church of Abingdon should perform its knight's service he should do the service of half a knight for the same church; that is to say, in castle ward, in military service beyond and on this side of the sea, in giving money in proportion to the knights on the capture of the king, and in the rest of the services which the other knights of the church perform.

Bishop Fulbert of Chartres

Asked to write something concerning the form of fealty, I have noted briefly for you, on the authority of the books, the things which follow. He who swears fealty to his lord ought always to have these six things in memory: what is harmless, safe, honorable, useful, easy, practicable. *Harmless,* that is to say, that he should not injure his lord in his body; *safe,* that he should not injure him by betraying his secrets or the defenses upon which he relies for safety; *honorable,* that he should not injure him in his justice or in other matters that pertain to his honor; *useful,* that he should not injure him in his possessions; *easy* and *practicable,* that that good which his lord is able to do easily he make not difficult, nor that which is practicable he make not impossible to him.

That the faithful vassal should avoid these injuries is certainly proper, but not for this alone does he deserve his holding; for it is not sufficient to abstain from evil, unless what is good is done also. It remains, therefore, that in the same six things mentioned above he should faithfully counsel and aid his lord, if he wishes to be looked upon as worthy of his benefice and to be safe concerning the fealty which he has sworn.

The lord also ought to act toward his faithful vassal reciprocally in all these things. And if he does not do this, he will be justly considered guilty of bad faith, just as the former, if he should be detected in avoiding or consenting to the avoidance of his duties, would be perfidious and perjured.

In turn, a lord had responsibilities toward his vassals. His major obligation was to protect his vassal, either by defending him militarily or by taking his side in a court of law if necessary. The lord was also responsible for the maintenance of the vassal, usually by granting him a fief.

As this system of mutual obligations between lord and vassal evolved, certain practices became common. If a lord acted improperly toward his vassal, the bond between them could be dissolved. Likewise, if a vassal failed to fulfill his vow of loyalty, he was subject to forfeiture of his fief. Upon a vassal's death, his fief theoretically reverted to the lord, since it had been granted to the vassal for use, not as a possession. In practice, however, fiefs by the tenth century tended to be hereditary. Following the principle of primogeniture, the eldest son inherited the father's fief. If a man died without heirs, the lord could reclaim the fief.

New Political Configurations in the Tenth Century

In the tenth century, Europe began to recover from the invasions of the century before. The disintegration of the Carolingian Empire and the emergence of great and powerful lords soon produced new political configurations.

The Eastern Franks In the east Frankish kingdom, the last Carolingian king died in 911, whereupon local rulers, especially the powerful dukes (the title of *duke* is derived from the Latin word *dux*, meaning "leader") of the Saxons, Swabians, Bavarians, Thuringians, and Franconians, who exercised much power in their large dukedoms, elected one of their own number, Conrad of Franconia, to serve as king of Germany (as we think of it) or of the eastern Franks (as contemporaries thought of it). But Conrad did not last long, and after his death, the German dukes chose Henry the Fowler, duke of Saxony, as the new king of Germany (919–936). The first of the Saxon dynasty of German kings, Henry was not particularly successful in creating a unified eastern Frankish kingdom, lacking the resources to impose effective rule over the entire area.

The best known of the Saxon kings of Germany was Henry's son, Otto I (936–973). He defeated the Magyars at the Battle of Lechfeld in 955 and encouraged an ongoing program of Christianization of both the Slavic and Scandinavian peoples. Even more than his father, he relied on bishops and abbots in governing his kingdom. This practice was in part a response to the tendency of the lay lords to build up their power at the expense of the king. Since the clergy were theoretically celibate, bishops and abbots could not make their offices hereditary, thus allowing the king to maintain more control over them.

Otto also intervened in Italian politics and for his efforts was crowned emperor of the Romans by the pope in 962, reviving a title that had fallen into disuse with the disintegration of Charlemagne's empire. Once again a pope had conferred the Roman imperial title on a king of the Franks, even though he was a Saxon king of the eastern Franks. Otto's creation of a new "Roman Empire" in the hands of the eastern Franks (or Germans) added a tremendous burden to the kingship of Germany. To the difficulties of governing Germany was appended the onerous task of ruling Italy as well. It proved a formidable and ultimately impossible task.

The Western Franks In the ninth and tenth centuries, the Carolingian kings had little success in controlling the great lords of the western Frankish kingdom. The counts, who were supposed to serve as the chief administrative officials, often paid little attention to the wishes of the Carolingian kings. In 987, when the Carolingian king died, the western Frankish nobles and chief prelates of the church chose Hugh Capet, count of Orléans and Paris, as the new king (987–996).

The nobles who elected Hugh Capet did not intend to establish a new royal dynasty. After all, although Hugh was officially king of the western Franks and overlord of the great nobles of the kingdom, his own family controlled only the Île-de-France, the region around Paris. Other French nobles possessed lands equal to or greater than those of the Capetians and assumed that the king would be content to live off the revenues of his personal lands and not impose any burdensome demands on the nobility. Hugh Capet did succeed in making his position hereditary, however. He asked the nobles, and they agreed, to choose his eldest son, Robert, as his anointed associate in case Hugh died on a campaign to Spain in 987. And although Hugh Capet could not know it then, the Capetian dynasty would rule the western Frankish kingdom, or France, as it eventually came to be known, for centuries. In the late tenth century, however, the territory that would become France was not a unified kingdom but a loose alliance of powerful lords who treated the king as an equal. They assisted him only when it was in their own interests to do so.

Anglo-Saxon England England's development in the ninth and tenth centuries took a course somewhat different from that of the Frankish kingdoms. The long struggle of the Anglo-Saxon kingdoms against the Viking invasions ultimately produced a unified kingdom. Alfred the Great, king of Wessex (871–899), played a crucial role. He defeated a Danish army in 879, according to an account by Asser, his adviser, who wrote a biography of the king:

> [Alfred] gained the victory through God's will. He destroyed the Vikings with great slaughter, and pursued those who fled as far as the stronghold, hacking them down; he seized everything which he found outside the stronghold—men (whom he killed

immediately), horses and cattle—and boldly made camp in front of the gate of the Viking stronghold with all his army. When he had been there for fourteen days the Vikings, thoroughly terrified by hunger, cold and fear, and in the end by despair, sought peace.[11]

Alfred eventually made peace with the Danes after strengthening his army and creating a navy.

Alfred also believed in the power of education. He invited scholars to his court and encouraged the translation of the works of such church fathers as Augustine and Gregory the Great from Latin into Anglo-Saxon (Old English), the vernacular, or the language spoken by the people. Old English was also soon used for official correspondence as well.

Alfred's successors reconquered the remaining areas occupied by the Danes and established a unified Anglo-Saxon monarchy. By the time of King Edgar (959–975), Anglo-Saxon England had a well-developed and strong monarchical government. Although the kingship was elective, only descendants of Alfred were chosen for the position. In the counties or *shires,* the administrative units into which England was divided, the king was assisted by an agent appointed and controlled by him, the shire-reeve or sheriff. An efficient chancery or writing office was responsible for issuing writs (or royal letters) conveying the king's orders to the sheriffs.

The Manorial System

The landholding class of nobles and knights comprised a military elite whose ability to function as warriors depended on having the leisure time to pursue the arts of war. Landed estates worked by a dependent peasant class provided the economic sustenance that made this way of life possible. A **manor** (see Map 8.3) was simply an agricultural estate operated by a lord and worked by peasants. Lords

CHRONOLOGY	New Political Configurations of the Tenth Century
Eastern Franks	
Conrad of Franconia	911–918
Saxon dynasty: Henry I	919–936
Otto I	936–973
Defeat of Magyars	955
Coronation as emperor	962
Western Franks	
Election of Hugh Capet as king	987
Anglo-Saxon England	
Alfred the Great, king of Wessex	871–899
Peace with the Danes	886
Reign of King Edgar	959–975

MAP 8.3 **A Typical Manor.** The manorial system created small, tightly knit communities in which peasants were economically and physically bound to their lord. Crops were rotated, with roughly one-third of the fields lying fallow at any one time, which helped replenish soil nutrients (see Chapter 9). ❓ How does the area of the lord's manor, other buildings, garden, and orchard compare to that of the peasant holdings in the village?

🌐 **View an animated version of this map or related maps at** http://history.wadsworth .com/spielvogel06/

provided protection; peasants gave up their freedom, became tied to the lord's land, and provided labor services for him.

Manorialism grew out of the unsettled circumstances of the Early Middle Ages, when small farmers often needed protection or food in a time of bad harvests. Free peasants gave up their freedom to the lords of large landed estates in return for protection and use of the lord's land. Although a large class of free peasants continued to exist, increasing numbers of them became bound to the land as serfs. Unlike slaves, **serfs** could not be bought and sold, but they were subservient to their lords in a variety of ways. Serfs were required to provide labor services, pay rents, and be subject to the lord's jurisdiction. By the ninth century, probably 60 percent of the population of western Europe had become serfs.

A serf's labor services consisted of working the lord's **demesne,** the land retained by the lord, which might consist of one-third to one-half of the cultivated lands scat-

tered throughout the manor (the rest would have been allotted to the serfs for their maintenance), as well as building barns and digging ditches. Although labor requirements varied from manor to manor and person to person, a common work obligation was three days a week.

The serfs paid rents by giving the lords a share of every product they raised. Serfs also paid the lord for the use of the manor's common pasturelands, streams, ponds, and surrounding woodlands. For example, if tenants fished in the pond or stream on a manor, they turned over part of the catch to their lord. For grazing a cow in the common pasture, a serf paid a rent in cheese produced from the cow's milk. Serfs were also obliged to pay a **tithe** (a tenth of their produce) to their local village church.

Lords also possessed a variety of legal rights over their serfs. Serfs were legally bound to the lord's land; they could not leave without his permission. Although free to marry, serfs could not marry anyone outside their manor without the lord's approval. Moreover, lords sometimes exercised

Peasants in the Manorial System. In the manorial system, peasants were required to provide labor services for their lord. This thirteenth-century illustration shows a group of English peasants harvesting grain. Overseeing their work is a bailiff, or manager, who supervised the work of the peasants.

THE MANORIAL COURT

*T*HE WAY OF LIFE of the medieval lord was made possible by the labors of the serfs on his manor. In addition to his right to collect rents, labor services, and fees from his serfs, the lord also possessed political authority over them, including the right to hold a manorial court to try tenants for crimes and infractions of the manor's rules. This selection, taken from the records of an English manorial court, lists the cases heard, the decisions of the jurors, and the subsequent penalties.

✍ Select Pleas in Manorial Courts

John Sperling complains that Richard of Newmere on the Sunday next before S. Bartholomew's day [August 24] last past with his cattle, horses, and pigs wrongfully destroyed the corn on his (John's) land to his damage to the extent of one thrave of wheat, and to his dishonor to the extent of two shillings; and of this he produces suit. And Richard comes and defends all of it. Therefore let him go to the law six handed [with three companions who will swear to his innocence]. His pledges, Simon Combe and Hugh Frith [like bail bondsmen, pledges stood surety for a person ordered to show up in court or pay a fine].

Hugh Free in mercy [fined] for his beast caught in the lord's garden. Pledges, Walter Hill and William Slipper, Fine 6d. [sixpence].

(The) twelve jurors say that Hugh Cross has right in the bank and hedge about which there was a dispute between him and William White. Therefore let him hold in peace and let William be distrained [forced to comply by seizing his property] for his many trespasses. (Afterwards he made fine for 12d.)

From the whole township of Little Ogbourne, except seven, for not coming to wash the lord's sheep, 6s. 8d. [six shillings, eight pence].

Gilbert Richard's son gives 5s. for license to marry a wife. Pledge, Seaman. Term (for payments), the Purification [February 2].

William Jordan in mercy for bad plowing on the lord's land. Pledge, Arthur. Fine, 6d.

The parson of the Church is in mercy for his cow caught in the lord's meadow. Pledges, Thomas Ymer and William Coke.

From Martin Shepherd 6d. for the wound that he gave Pekin.

Ragenhilda of Bec. gives 2s. for having married without license. Pledge, William of Primer.

Walter Hull gives 13s. 4d. for license to dwell on the land of the Prior of Harmondsworth so long as he shall live and as a condition finds pledges, to wit, William Slipper, John Bisuthe, Gilbert Bisuthe, Hugh Tree, William Johnson, John Hulle, who undertake that the said Walter shall do to the lord all the services and customs which he would do if he dwelt on the lord's land. . . .

It was presented that Robert Carter's son by night invaded the house of Peter Burgess and in felony threw stones at his door so that the said Peter raised the hue [alarm]. Therefore let the said Robert be committed to prison. Afterwards he made fine with 2s.

All the plowmen of Great Ogbourne are convicted by the oath of twelve men . . . because by reason of their default (the land) of the lord is damaged to the amount of 9s. . . . And Walter Reaper is in mercy for concealing (i.e., not giving information as to) the said bad plowing. Afterwards he made fine with the lord with 1 mark [thirteen shillings, four pence].

---

public rights or political authority on their lands. This gave the lord the right to try serfs in his own court, although only for lesser crimes (called "low justice"). In fact, the lord's manorial court provided the only law that most serfs knew (see the box above). Finally, the lord's political authority enabled him to establish monopolies on certain services that provided additional revenues. Serfs could be required to bring their grain to the lord's mill and pay a fee to have it ground into flour. Thus the rights a lord possessed on his manor gave him virtual control over both the lives and property of his serfs.

The administration of manors varied considerably. If the lord of a manor was a simple knight, he would probably live on the estate and supervise it in person. Great lords possessed many manors and relied on a steward or bailiff to run each estate. Note that manors were controlled not only by lay lords but also by monasteries and cathedral churches. Monasteries tended to be far more conscientious

about keeping accurate records of their manorial estates than lay lords, and their surveys provide some of the best sources of information on medieval village life. The relationship between manors and villages was highly variable. A single village might constitute a manor, or a large manor might encompass several villages.

In the Early Middle Ages, a vast majority of men and women, free or unfree—possibly as many as 90 percent—worked the land. This period had witnessed a precipitous decline in trade. Coins and jewelry were often hoarded, and at the local level, goods were frequently bartered because so few coins were in circulation. But trade never entirely disappeared. Even in an agrarian society, surplus products could be exchanged at local markets. More significant, however, was that both aristocrats and wealthy clerics desired merchandise not produced locally, such as spices, silk cloth, wine, gold, and silver jewelry, and it took trade to obtain these items.

Much trade in luxury goods, especially beginning in the ninth century, was with the Byzantine Empire, particularly the city of Constantinople, and the Islamic caliphs of Baghdad. Products from the west included iron, timber, furs, and slaves (many from eastern Europe, including captured Slavs, from whom the modern word *slave* is derived). Traders, often Jews, carried goods by boat on European rivers or on caravans with horses or mules. An Arab geographer of the ninth century left this account of Jewish traders from southern France:

> [They] speak Arabic, Persian, Greek, Frankish, Spanish, and Slavonic. They travel from west to east and from east to west, by land and by sea. From the west they bring eunuchs, slave-girls, boys, brocade, marten and other furs, and swords. They take ship from Frankland in the western Mediterranean sea and land at Farama, whence they take their merchandise on camel-back to Qulzum. . . . Then they sail on the eastern [Red] sea from Qulzum, and onward to India and China. From China they bring back musk, aloes, camphor, cinnamon, and other products of those parts, and return to Qulzum. Then they transport them to Farama and sail again on the western sea. Some sail with their goods to Constantinople and sell them to the Greeks, and some take them to the king of the Franks and sell them there.[12]

By 900, Italian merchants, especially the Venetians, were entering the trade picture. Overall, however, compared to the Byzantine Empire or Muslim caliphates, western Europe in the Early Middle Ages was an underdeveloped, predominantly agrarian society and could not begin to match the splendor of either of the other heirs of the Roman Empire.

The Zenith of Byzantine Civilization

In the seventh and eighth centuries, the Byzantine Empire had lost much of its territory to Slavs, Bulgars, and Muslims. By 750, the empire consisted only of Asia Minor, some lands in the Balkans, and the southern coast of Italy. Although Byzantium was beset with internal dissension and invasions in the ninth century, it was able to deal with them and not only endured but even expanded, reaching its high point in the tenth century, which some historians have called the golden age of Byzantine civilization.

During the reign of Michael III (842–867), the Byzantine Empire began to experience a revival. Iconoclasm was finally abolished in 843, and reforms were made in education, church life, the military, and the peasant economy. There was a noticeable intellectual renewal. But the Byzantine Empire under Michael was still plagued by persistent

The Byzantine Empire in 1025

problems. The Bulgars mounted new attacks, and the Arabs continued to harass the empire. Moreover, a new church problem with political repercussions erupted over differences between the pope as leader of the western Christian church and the patriarch of Constantinople as leader of the eastern (or Orthodox) Christian church. Patriarch Photius condemned the pope as a heretic for accepting a revised form of the Nicene Creed stating that the Holy Spirit proceeded from the Father and the Son instead of "the Holy Spirit, who proceeds from the Father." A council of eastern bishops followed Photius' wishes and excommunicated the pope, creating the so-called Photian schism. Although the differences were later papered over, this controversy served to further the division between the eastern and western Christian churches.

The Macedonian Dynasty

The problems that arose during Michael's reign were effectively dealt with by a new dynasty of Byzantine emperors known as the Macedonians (867–1081), who managed to hold off the external enemies, go over to the offensive, and reestablish domestic order. Supported by the church, the emperors thought of the Byzantine Empire as a continuation of the Christian Roman Empire of late antiquity. Although for diplomatic reasons they occasionally recognized the imperial title of western emperors, such as Charlemagne and Otto I, they still regarded them as little more than barbarian parvenus.

The Macedonian emperors could boast of a remarkable number of achievements in the late ninth and tenth centuries. They worked to strengthen the position of the free farmers, who felt threatened by the attempts of landed aristocrats to expand their estates at the expense of the farmers. The emperors were well aware that the free farmers made up the rank and file of the Byzantine cavalry and provided the military strength of the empire. The Macedonian emperors also fostered a burst of economic prosperity by expanding trade relations with western Europe, especially by selling silks and metalwork. Thanks to this prosperity, the city of Constantinople flourished. Foreign visitors continued to be astounded by its size, wealth, and physical surroundings. To western Europeans, it was the stuff of legends and fables (see the box on p. 219).

In the midst of this prosperity, Byzantine cultural influence expanded due to the active missionary efforts of eastern Byzantine Christians. Eastern Orthodox Christianity was spread to eastern European peoples, such as the Bulgars and Serbs. Perhaps the greatest missionary success occurred when the prince of Kiev in Russia converted to Christianity in 987.

Under the Macedonian rulers, Byzantium enjoyed a strong civil service, talented emperors, and

A Western View of the Byzantine Empire

BISHOP LIUDPRAND of Cremona undertook diplomatic missions to Constantinople on behalf of two western kings, Berengar of Italy and Otto I of Germany. This selection is taken from the bishop's description of his mission to the Byzantine emperor Constantine VII as an envoy for Berengar, king of Italy from 950 until his overthrow by Otto I of Germany in 964. Liudprand had mixed feelings about Byzantium: admiration, yet also envy and hostility because of its superior wealth.

Liudprand of Cremona, *Antapodosis*

Next to the imperial residence at Constantinople there is a palace of remarkable size and beauty which the Greeks call Magnavra . . . the name being equivalent to "fresh breeze." In order to receive some Spanish envoys, who had recently arrived, as well as myself . . . , Constantine gave orders that his palace should be got ready. . . .

Before the emperor's seat stood a tree, made of bronze gilded over, whose branches were filled with birds, also made of gilded bronze, which uttered different cries, each according to its varying species. The throne itself was so marvelously fashioned that at one moment it seemed a low structure, and at another it rose high into the air. It was of immense size and was guarded by lions, made either of bronze or of wood covered over with gold, who beat the ground with their tails and gave a dreadful roar with open mouth and quivering tongue. Leaning upon the shoulders of two eunuchs I was brought into the emperor's presence. At my approach the lions began to roar and the birds to cry out, each according to its kind; but I was neither terrified nor surprised, for I had previously made enquiry about all

these things from people who were well acquainted with them. So after I had three times made obeisance to the emperor with my face upon the ground, I lifted my head, and behold! The man whom just before I had seen sitting on a moderately elevated seat had now changed his raiment and was sitting on the level of the ceiling. How it was done I could not imagine, unless perhaps he was lifted up by some such sort of device as we use for raising the timbers of a wine press. On that occasion he did not address me personally . . . but by the intermediary of a secretary he enquired about Berengar's doings and asked after his health. I made a fitting reply and then, at a nod from the interpreter, left his presence and retired to my lodging.

It would give me some pleasure also to record here what I did then for Berengar. . . . The Spanish envoys . . . had brought handsome gifts from their masters to the emperor Constantine. I for my part had brought nothing from Berengar except a letter and that was full of lies. I was very greatly disturbed and shamed at this and I began to consider anxiously what I had better do. In my doubt and perplexity it finally occurred to me that I might offer the gifts, which on my account I had brought for the emperor, as coming from Berengar, and trick out my humble present with fine words. I therefore presented him with nine excellent curaisses, seven excellent shields with gilded bosses, two silver gilt cauldrons, some swords, spears and spits, and what was more precious to the emperor than anything, four carzimasia; that being the Greek name for young eunuchs who have had both their testicles and their penis removed. This operation is performed by traders at Verdun, who take the boys into Spain and make a huge profit.

military advances. The Byzantine civil service was staffed by well-educated, competent aristocrats from Constantinople who oversaw the collection of taxes, domestic administration, and foreign policy. At the same time, the Macedonian dynasty produced some truly outstanding emperors skilled in administration and law, including Leo VI (886–912) and Basil II (976–1025). In the tenth century, competent emperors combined with a number of talented generals to mobilize the empire's military resources and take the offensive. The Bulgars were defeated, and both the eastern and western parts of Bulgaria were annexed to the empire. The Byzantines went on to add the islands of Crete and Cyprus to the empire and defeat the Muslim forces in Syria, expanding the empire to the upper Euphrates. By the end of the reign of Basil II in 1025, the Byzantine Empire was the largest it had been since the beginning of the seventh century.

The Slavic Peoples of Central and Eastern Europe

North of Byzantium and east of the Carolingian Empire lay a spacious plain through which a number of Asiatic nomads, including the Huns, Bulgars, Avars, and Magyars, had pushed their way westward, terrorizing and plundering the settled peasant communities. Eastern Europe was ravaged by these successive waves of invaders, who found it relatively easy to create large empires that were in turn overthrown by the next invaders. Over a period of time, the invaders themselves were largely assimilated with the native Slavic peoples of the area.

The Slavic peoples were originally a single people in central Europe who through mass migrations and nomadic invasions were gradually divided into three major groups: the western, southern, and eastern Slavs (see Map 8.4).

Emperor Leo VI. Under the Macedonian dynasty, the Byzantine Empire achieved economic prosperity through expanded trade and gained new territories through military victories. This mosaic over the western door of Hagia Sophia in Constantinople depicts the Macedonian emperor Leo VI prostrating himself before Jesus. This act of humility symbolized the emperor's function as an intermediary between God and the empire.

Western Slavs

In the region east of the Germanic kingdom emerged the Polish and Bohemian kingdoms of the western Slavs. The Germans assumed responsibility for the conversion of these Slavic peoples because German emperors considered it their duty to spread Christianity to the "barbarians." Of course, it also gave them the opportunity to extend their political authority as well. German missionaries had converted the Czechs in Bohemia by the end of the ninth century, and a bishopric eventually occupied by a Czech bishop was established at Prague in the tenth century. The Slavs in Poland were not converted until the reign of Prince Mieszko (c. 960–992). In 1000, an independent Polish archbishopric was set up at Gniezno by the pope. The non-Slavic kingdom of Hungary, which emerged after the Magyars settled down after their defeat at Lechfeld in 955, was also converted to Christianity by German missionaries. Saint Stephen, king of Hungary from 997 to 1038, facilitated the acceptance of Christianity by his people. The

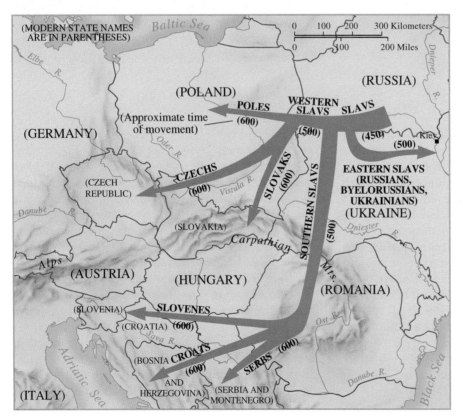

MAP 8.4 **The Migrations of the Slavs.** Originally from east-central Europe, the Slavic people broke into three groups. The western Slavs converted to Catholic Christianity, while the eastern Slavs and southern Slavs, under the influence of the Byzantine Empire, embraced the Eastern Orthodox faith. [?] What connections do these Slavic migrations have with what we today characterize as eastern Europe?

View an animated version of this map or related maps at http://history.wadsworth.com/spielvogel06/

A Muslim's Description of the Rus

ESPITE THE DIFFICULTIES that travel presented, early medieval civilization did witness some contact among the various cultures. This might occur through trade, diplomacy, or the conquest and migration of peoples. This document is a description of the Swedish Rus who eventually merged with the native Slavic peoples to form the principality of Kiev, commonly regarded as the first Russian state. This account was written by Ibn Fadlan, a Muslim diplomat sent from Baghdad in 921 to a settlement on the Volga River. His comments on the filthiness of the Rus reflect the Muslim preoccupation with cleanliness.

Ibn Fadlan, *Description of the Rus*

I saw the Rus folk when they arrived on their trading-mission and settled at the river Atul (Volga). Never had I seen people of more perfect physique. They are tall as date-palms, and reddish in color. They wear neither coat nor kaftan, but each man carried a cape which covers one half of his body, leaving one hand free. No one is ever parted from his axe, sword, and knife. Their swords are Frankish in design, broad, flat, and fluted. Each man has a number of trees, figures, and the like from the fingernails to the neck. Each woman carried on her bosom a container made of iron, silver, copper or gold—its size and substance depending on her man's wealth. . . .

They [the Rus] are the filthiest of God's creatures. They do not wash after discharging their natural functions, neither do they wash their hands after meals. They are as lousy as donkeys. They arrive from their distant river, and there they build big houses on its shores. Ten or twenty of them may live together in one house, and each of them has a couch of his own where he sits and diverts himself with the pretty slave girls whom he had brought along for sale. He will make love with one of them while a comrade looks on; sometimes they indulge in a communal orgy, and, if a customer should turn up to buy a girl, the Rus man will not let her go till he has finished with her.

They wash their hands and faces every day in incredibly filthy water. Every morning the girl brings her master a large bowl of water in which he washes his hands and face and hair, then blows his nose into it and spits into it. When he has finished the girl takes the bowl to his neighbor—who repeats the performance. Thus the bowl goes the rounds of the entire household. . . .

If one of the Rus folk falls sick they put him in a tent by himself and leave bread and water for him. They do not visit him, however, or speak to him, especially if he is a serf. Should he recover he rejoins the others; if he dies they burn him. But if he happens to be a serf they leave him for the dogs and vultures to devour. If they catch a robber they hang him to a tree until he is torn to shreds by wind and weather. . . .

Poles, Czechs, and Hungarians all accepted Catholic or western Christianity and became closely tied to the Roman Catholic church and its Latin culture.

Southern Slavs

The southern and eastern Slavic populations took a different path because of their proximity to the Byzantine Empire. The southern Slavic peoples were converted to the Eastern Orthodox Christianity of the Byzantine Empire by two Byzantine missionary brothers, Cyril and Methodius, who began their activities in 863. They created a Slavonic (Cyrillic) alphabet, translated the Bible into Slavonic, and developed Slavonic church services. Although the southern Slavic peoples accepted Christianity, a split eventually developed between the Croats, who accepted the Roman church, and the Serbs, who remained loyal to eastern Christianity.

Although the Bulgars were originally an Asiatic people who conquered much of the Balkan peninsula, they were eventually absorbed by the larger native southern Slavic population. Together, by the ninth century, they formed a largely Slavic Bulgarian kingdom. Although the conversion to Christianity of this state was complicated by the rivalry between the Roman Catholic and Eastern Orthodox churches, the Bulgarians eventually accepted the latter. By the end of the ninth century, they embraced the Slavonic church services earlier developed by Cyril and Methodius. The acceptance of Eastern Orthodoxy by the southern Slavic peoples, the Serbs and Bulgarians, meant that their cultural life was also linked to the Byzantine state.

Eastern Slavs

The eastern Slavic peoples, from whom the modern Russians, White Russians (Byelorussians), and Ukrainians are descended, had settled in the territory of present-day Ukraine and European Russia. There, beginning in the late eighth century, they began to contend with Viking invaders. Swedish Vikings, known to the eastern Slavs as Varangians, moved down the extensive network of rivers into the lands of the eastern Slavs in search of booty and new trade routes. After establishing trading links with the Byzantine state, the Varangians built trading settlements, became involved in the civil wars among the Slavic peoples, and eventually came to dominate the native peoples, just as their fellow Vikings were doing in parts of western Europe. According to the traditional version of the story, the semilegendary Rurik secured his ruling dynasty in the Slavic settlement of Novgorod in 862. Rurik and his fellow Vikings were called the Rus, from which the name that eventually became attached to the state they founded, Russia, is derived (see the box above). Although much about Rurik is unclear, it is certain that his follower Oleg (c. 873–913) took up residence in Kiev and created the Rus state, a union of eastern Slavic territories known as the principality of Kiev. Oleg's successors extended their control over the eastern Slavs and expanded the territory of Kiev until it encompassed the lands between the Baltic and Black Seas and the Danube and Volga Rivers. By marrying Slavic wives, the Viking ruling class was gradually assimilated into the Slavic population, a process confirmed by their assumption of Slavic names.

The growth of the principality of Kiev attracted religious missionaries, especially from the Byzantine Empire. One Rus ruler, Vladimir (c. 980–1015), married the Byzantine emperor's sister and officially accepted Christianity for himself and his people in 987. His primary motive was probably not spiritual. By all accounts, Vladimir was a cruel and vicious man who believed an established church would be helpful in developing an organized state. From the end of the tenth century on, Byzantine Christianity became the model for Russian religious life, just as Byzantine imperial ideals came to influence the outward forms of Russian political life.

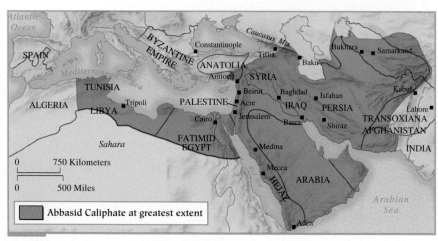

The Abbasid Caliphate at the Height of Its Power

The Expansion of Islam

The Umayyad dynasty of caliphs had established Damascus as the center of an Islamic empire created by Arab expansion in the seventh and eighth centuries. But Umayyad rule created resentment, and the Umayyad's corrupt behavior also helped bring about their end. One caliph, for example, supposedly swam in a pool of wine and drank enough of it to lower the wine level considerably. Finally, in 750, Abu al-Abbas, a descendant of the uncle of Muhammad, brought an end to the Umayyad dynasty and established the Abbasid dynasty, which lasted until 1258.

The Abbasid Dynasty

The Abbasid rulers brought much change to the world of Islam. They tried to break down the distinctions between Arab and non-Arab Muslims. All Muslims, regardless of their ethnic background, could now hold both civil and military offices. This helped open Islamic life to the influences of the conquered civilizations. Many Arabs now began to intermarry with their conquered peoples.

In 762, the Abbasids built a new capital city, Baghdad, on the Tigris River far to the east of Damascus. The new capital was well placed. It took advantage of river traffic to the Persian Gulf and at the same time was located on the caravan route from the Mediterranean to Central Asia. The move eastward allowed Persian influence to come to the fore, encouraging a new cultural orientation. Under the Abbasids, judges, merchants, and government officials, rather than warriors, were viewed as the ideal citizens.

The new Abbasid dynasty experienced a period of splendid rule well into the ninth century. Best known of the caliphs of the time was Harun al-Rashid (786–809), whose reign is often described as the golden age of the Abbasid caliphate. His son al-Ma'mun (813–833) was a great patron of learning. He founded an astronomical observatory and created a foundation for translating classical Greek works. This was also a period of growing economic prosperity. The Arabs had conquered many of the richest provinces of the old Roman Empire, and they now controlled the trade routes to the east. Baghdad became the center of an enormous trade empire that extended into Europe, Asia, and Africa, greatly adding to the wealth of the Islamic world.

Despite the prosperity, all was not quite well in the empire of the Abbasids. There was much fighting over the succession to the caliphate. When Harun al-Rashid died, his two sons fought to succeed him in a struggle that almost destroyed the city of Baghdad. As the tenth-century Muslim historian al-Mas'udi wrote: "Mansions were destroyed, most remarkable monuments obliterated; prices soared. . . . Brother turned his sword against brother, son against father, as some fought for Amin, others for Ma'mun. Houses and palaces fueled the flames; property was put to the sack."[13]

Vast wealth also gave rise to financial corruption. By awarding important positions to court favorites, the Abbasid caliphs began to undermine the foundations of their own power and soon became figureheads. Provincial rulers broke away from the control of the caliphs and established their own independent dynasties. Even earlier, in the eighth century, a separate caliphate had already been established in Spain when Abd al-Rahman of the Umayyad dynasty had fled there. In 756, he seized control of southern Spain and then expanded his power into the center of the peninsula. He took the title of *emir*, or commander, and set up the emirate of al-Andalus (the Arabic name for Spain) with its center at Córdoba. In 929, Abd al-Rahman III (912–961) proclaimed himself caliph. The rulers of al-Andalus developed a unique society in which all religions were tolerated. The court also supported writers and artists, creating a brilliant and flourishing culture.

The fragmentation of the Islamic empire accelerated in the tenth century. The Fatimid family established a caliphate in Egypt in 973, and an independent dynasty also operated in North Africa. Despite the political disunity of the Islamic world, however, there was an underlying Islamic civilization based on two common bonds, the Qur'an and the Arabic language.

Islamic Civilization

From the beginning of their empire, Muslim Arabs had demonstrated a willingness to absorb the culture of their conquered territories. The Arabs were truly heirs to the remaining Greco-Roman culture of the Roman Empire. Just as readily, they assimilated Byzantine and Persian culture. In the eighth and ninth centuries, numerous Greek, Syrian, and Persian scientific and philosophical works were translated into Arabic. As the chief language in the southern Mediterranean and the Near East and the required language of Muslims, Arabic became a truly international tongue.

The Muslims created a brilliant urban culture at a time when western Europe was predominantly a rural world of farming villages. This can be seen in such new cities as Baghdad and Cairo, but also in Córdoba, the capital of the Umayyad caliphate in Spain. With a population of possibly 100,000, Córdoba was Europe's largest city after Constantinople. It had seventy public libraries, and the number of manuscripts in the caliph's private library reached 400,000. One caliph, al-Hakem (961–976), collected books from different parts of the world and then had them translated into Arabic and Latin. These included works on geography that later proved valuable to Western sailors and merchants. Schools were also established, and the Great Mosque of Córdoba became a center for scholars from all over the Islamic world. Large numbers of women served as teachers and librarians in Córdoba.

Islamic cities had a distinctive physical appearance due to their common use of certain architectural features, such as the pointed arch and traceried windows, and specific kinds of buildings. The latter included palaces and public buildings with fountains and secluded courtyards, mosques for worship, public baths, and bazaars or marketplaces. Muslims embellished their buildings with a unique decorative art that avoided representation of living things because of their religion's prohibition of the making of graven images. Islamic cities other than Córdoba were also distinguished by their numerous libraries. Baghdad had more than thirty libraries, and the library in Cairo contained 1.1 million manuscripts.

During the first few centuries of the Arab empire, it was the Islamic world that saved and spread the scientific

Mosque at Córdoba. The first Great Mosque of Córdoba was built by Abd al-Rahman, founder of the Umayyad dynasty of Spain, in the eighth century. The mosque was later enlarged in the tenth century. Shown here is the interior of the sanctuary, with its two levels of arches. Although the Umayyad caliphs of Damascus were overthrown and replaced by the Abbasid dynasty in the eighth century, the independent Umayyad dynasty in Spain lasted until the eleventh century.

© Photodisc Green/Getty Images

and philosophical works of ancient civilizations. At a time when the ancient Greek philosophers were largely unknown in Europe, key works by Plato and Aristotle were translated into Arabic. They were put in a library called the House of Wisdom in Baghdad, where they were read and studied by Muslim scholars. The library also contained texts on mathematics brought from India. The preservation of ancient texts was aided by the use of paper. The making of paper was introduced from China in the eighth century, and by the end of that century, paper factories had been established in Baghdad. Booksellers and libraries soon followed. European universities later benefited from this scholarship when these works were translated from Arabic into Latin.

Although Islamic scholars are rightly praised for preserving much of classical knowledge for the West, they also made considerable advances of their own. Nowhere is this more evident than in their contributions to mathematics and the natural sciences. The list of achievements in mathematics and astronomy alone is impressive. The Muslims adopted and passed on the numerical system of India, including the use of the zero. In Europe, it became known as the Arabic system. Al-Khwarizmi, a ninth-century Persian mathematician, created the discipline of algebra. Muslim astronomers studied the positions of the stars from the observatory established by al-Ma'mun at Baghdad. They were aware that the earth was round and named many stars. They also perfected the astrolabe, an instrument used by sailors to determine their location by observing the positions of heavenly bodies. It was the astrolabe that later made it possible for Europeans to sail to the Americas.

Muslim scholars also made many new discoveries in chemistry and developed medicine as a field of scientific study. Especially renowned was Ibn Sina (known as Avicenna in the West, 980–1037), who wrote a medical encyclopedia that, among other things, stressed the contagious nature of certain diseases and showed how they could be spread by contaminated water supplies. After its translation into Latin, Avicenna's work became a basic medical textbook for medieval European university students. Avicenna was but one of many Muslim scholars whose work was translated into Latin and contributed to the development of intellectual life in Europe in the twelfth and thirteenth centuries.

TIMELINE

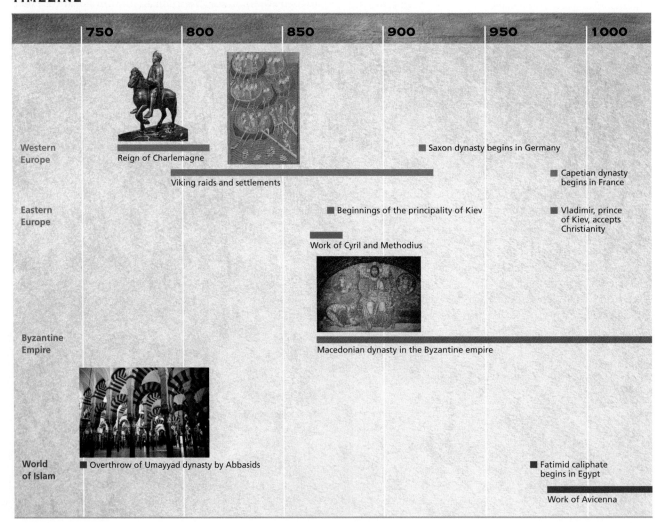

	750	800	850	900	950	1000

Western Europe
Reign of Charlemagne
Viking raids and settlements
■ Saxon dynasty begins in Germany
■ Capetian dynasty begins in France

Eastern Europe
■ Beginnings of the principality of Kiev
■ Vladimir, prince of Kiev, accepts Christianity
Work of Cyril and Methodius

Byzantine Empire
Macedonian dynasty in the Byzantine empire

World of Islam
■ Overthrow of Umayyad dynasty by Abbasids
■ Fatimid caliphate begins in Egypt
Work of Avicenna

CONCLUSION

𝒜FTER THE TURMOIL OF the disintegration of the Roman Empire and the establishment of the Germanic states, a new European civilization began to emerge slowly in the Early Middle Ages. The coronation of Charlemagne, descendant of a Germanic tribe converted to Christianity, as Roman emperor in 800 symbolized the fusion of the three chief components of the new European civilization: the German tribes, the classical tradition, and Christianity. In the long run, the creation of a western empire fostered the idea of a distinct European identity and marked a shift of power from the south to the north. Italy and the Mediterranean had been the center of the Roman Empire. The lands north of the Alps now became the political center of Europe.

With the disintegration of the Carolingian Empire, new forms of political institutions in which lords exercised legal, administrative, and military power began to develop in Europe. The practice of fief-holding transferred public power into many private hands and seemed to provide the security sorely lacking in a time of weak central government and new invasions by Muslims, Magyars, and Vikings. While Europe struggled, the Byzantine and Islamic worlds continued to prosper and flourish, the brilliance of their urban cultures standing in marked contrast to the underdeveloped rural world of Europe. By 1000, however, that rural world had not only recovered but was beginning to expand in ways undreamed of by previous generations. Europe stood poised for a giant leap.

NOTES

1. Einhard, *The Life of Charlemagne,* trans. Samuel Turner (Ann Arbor, Mich., 1960), p. 30.
2. Ibid., p. 57.
3. Quoted in Pierre Riché, *Daily Life in the World of Charlemagne,* trans. Jo Ann McNamara (Philadelphia, 1978), p. 56.
4. 1 Corinthians 7:1–2, 8–9.
5. Quoted in Derrick Bailey, *Homosexuality and the Western Christian Tradition* (London, 1955), p. 73.
6. Quoted in Paul Veyne, ed., *A History of Private Life,* vol. 1, *From Pagan Rome to Byzantium,* trans. Arthur Goldhammer (Cambridge, Mass., 1987), p. 440.
7. Stanley Rubin, *Medieval English Medicine* (New York, 1974), p. 136.
8. Quoted in Brian Inglis, *A History of Medicine* (New York, 1965), p. 51.
9. Quoted in Simon Keynes, "The Vikings in England, c. 790–1016," in Peter Sawyer, ed., *The Oxford Illustrated History of the Vikings* (Oxford, 1997), p. 81.
10. Quoted in Oliver Thatcher and Edgar McNeal, *A Source Book for Medieval History* (New York, 1905), p. 363.
11. Simon Keynes and Michael Lapidge, *Alfred the Great: Asser's "Life of King Alfred" and Other Contemporary Sources* (Harmondsworth, England, 1983), pp. 84–85.
12. Quoted in Bernard Lewis, *The Arabs in History* (London, 1958), p. 90.
13. al-Mas'udi, *The Meadows of Gold: The Abbasids,* ed. Paul Lunde and Caroline Stone (London, 1989), p. 151.

SUGGESTIONS FOR FURTHER READING

Good general histories of the entire medieval period can be found in **S. Painter and B. Tierney,** *Western Europe in the Middle Ages, 300– 1475* (New York, 1983); **E. Peters,** *Europe and the Middle Ages,* 2d ed. (Englewood Cliffs, N.J., 1989); **D. Nicholas,** *The Evolution of the Medieval World: Society, Government, and Thought in Europe, 312– 1500* (London, 1993); and **G. Holmes, ed.,** *The Oxford Illustrated History of Medieval Europe* (Oxford, 1988). For a good general survey of the social history of the Middle Ages, see **C. B. Bouchard,** *Life and Society in the West: Antiquity and the Middle Ages* (San Diego, Calif., 1988). For excellent reference works on medieval history, see **N. F. Cantor,** *The Encyclopedia of the Middle Ages* (New York, 1999), and **J. R. Strayer, ed.,** *Dictionary of the Middle Ages,* 13 vols. (New York, 1982–1989). For a brief history of the period covered in this chapter, see **R. Collins,** *Early Medieval Europe, 300–1000* (New York, 1991). See also the brief works by **B. Rosenwein,** *A Short History of the Middle Ages* (Orchard Park, N.Y., 2002), and **C. W. Hollister and J. Bennett,** *Medieval Europe: A Short History,* 9th ed. (New York, 2001). For a good collection of essays, see **R. McKitterick, ed.,** *Early Middle Ages: Europe, 400–1000* (Oxford, 2001).

Surveys of Carolingian Europe include **D. Bullough,** *The Age of Charlemagne* (New York, 1966); **P. Riché,** *The Carolingians: A Family Who Forged Europe* (Philadelphia, 1993); **L. Halphen,** *Charlemagne and the Carolingian Empire* (New York, 1977); and **R. McKitterick,** *The Frankish Kingdoms Under the Carolingians, 751–987* (London, 1983). On Charlemagne, see **H. R. Loyn and J. Percival,** *The Reign of Charlemagne* (New York, 1976), and the popular biography by **R. Winston,** *Charlemagne: From the Hammer to the Cross* (Indianapolis, Ind., 1954). On Carolingian culture, see *The Carolingians and the Written Word* (Cambridge, 1989), *Carolingian Culture: Emulation and Innovation* (New York, 1994), and the collection of essays titled *The Frankish Kings and Culture in the Early Middle Ages* (Brookfield, Vt., 1995), all by **R. McKitterick.**

Various aspects of social life in the Carolingian world are examined in **P. Riché,** *Daily Life in the World of Charlemagne,* trans. **J. A. McNamara** (Philadelphia, 1978); **M. Rouche,** "The Early Middle Ages in the West," in **P. Veyne, ed.,** *A History of Private Life* (Cambridge, Mass., 1987), vol. 1, pp. 411–549; **C. B. Bouchard,** *Life and Society in the West: Antiquity and the Middle Ages* (San Diego, Calif., 1988), ch. 5; and **S. F. Wemple,** *Women in Frankish Society: Marriage and the Cloister* (Philadelphia, 1981). On children, see **S. Shamar,** *Childhood in the Middle Ages,* trans. **C. Galai** (London, 1992), and **J. Boswell,** *The Kindness of Strangers* (New York, 1988). On attitudes toward sexuality in the early Christian church, see the important works by **P. Brown,** *The Body and Society* (New York, 1988), and **E. Pagels,** *Adam, Eve, and the Serpent* (New York, 1988).

The Vikings are examined in **P. Sawyer,** *Kings and Vikings* (London, 1982); **F. D. Logan,** *The Vikings in History,* 2d ed. (London, 1991); **G. Jones,** *A History of the Vikings,* rev. ed. (Oxford, 2001); and **P. Sawyer, ed.,** *The Oxford Illustrated History of the Vikings* (New York, 1997).

Two introductory works on fief-holding are **J. R. Strayer,** *Feudalism* (Princeton, N.J., 1985), and the classic work by **M. Bloch,** *Feudal Society,* trans. **L. A. Manyon** (London, 1961). For an important revisionist view, see **S. Reynolds,** *Fiefs and Vassals* (Oxford, 1994). Works on the new political configurations that emerged in the tenth century are cited in Chapter 9.

For the economic history of the Early Middle Ages, see **G. Duby,** *The Early Growth of the European Economy: Warriors and Peasants from the Seventh to the Twelfth Century* (Ithaca, N.Y., 1974). On the manorial court, see **Z. Razi and R. Smith, eds.,** *Medieval Society and the Manor Court* (New York, 1996).

Byzantine civilization in this period is examined in **R. Jenkins,** *Byzantium: The Imperial Centuries, 610–1071* (New York, 1969), and **W. Treadgold,** *The Byzantine Revival, 780–842* (Stanford, Calif., 1988). On the Slavic peoples of central and eastern Europe, see **F. Dvornik,** *The Slavs in European History and Civilization* (New Brunswick, N.J., 1962); **A. P. Vlasto,** *The Entry of the Slavs into Christendom* (Cambridge, 1970); **Z. Vana,** *The World of the Ancient Slavs* (London, 1983); and **S. Franklin and J. Shepard,** *The Emergence of Rus, 750–1200* (New York, 1996). The world of Islam in this period is discussed in **H. Kennedy,** *The Prophet and the Age of the Caliphates: The Islamic Near East from the Sixth to the Eleventh Century* (London, 1986), and **J. Lassner,** *The Shaping of Abbasid Rule* (Princeton, N.J., 1980). For a broad view on the relations between Islam and the West, see **B. Lewis,** *Islam and the West* (Oxford, 1994).

History Now™

Enter *HistoryNow* using the access card that is available for *Western Civilization. HistoryNow* will assist you in understanding the content in this chapter with lesson plans generated for your needs. In addition, you can read the following documents, and many more, online:

Saint Benedict, Rule

Saint Finnian of Clonard, Penitential

Einhard, *Life of Charlemagne*

INFOTRAC SEARCH TERMS

 For additional reading, go to InfoTrac College Edition, your online research library at http://infotrac.thomsonlearning.com

Key Term Search	*Subject Guide Search*
Carolingian	feudal
Charlemagne	feudalism
Vikings not Minnesota	

WESTERN CIVILIZATION RESOURCES

Visit the *Western Civilization* Companion Web site for resources specific to this book:

http://history.wadsworth.com/spielvogel06/

For a variety of tools to help you succeed in this course, visit the Western Civilization Resource Center at

http://history.wadsworth.com/western/

Included are quizzes; images; documents; interactive simulations; maps and timelines; movie explorations; and a wealth of other sources.

THE RECOVERY AND GROWTH OF EUROPEAN SOCIETY IN THE HIGH MIDDLE AGES

CHAPTER OUTLINE AND FOCUS QUESTIONS

Land and People in the High Middle Ages

● What new agricultural practices arose in the High Middle Ages?

● What roles did peasants and aristocrats play in the civilization of the High Middle Ages?

The New World of Trade and Cities

● What developments contributed to the revival of trade during the High Middle Ages, and what areas were the primary beneficiaries of the revival?

● What were the major features of medieval cities?

The Intellectual and Artistic World of the High Middle Ages

● What were the major intellectual and cultural achievements of European civilization in the High Middle Ages?

CRITICAL THINKING

● What is the relationship between economic and social changes and intellectual and artistic developments in the High Middle Ages?

Town street scene in thirteenth-century England

Mary Evans Picture Library

HE NEW EUROPEAN CIVILIZATION that had emerged in the ninth and tenth centuries began to come into its own in the eleventh and twelfth centuries as Europeans established new patterns that reached their zenith in the thirteenth century. The High Middle Ages (1000–1300) was a period of recovery and growth for Western civilization, characterized by a greater sense of security and a burst of energy and enthusiasm. New agricultural practices that increased the food supply helped give rise to a commercial and urban revival that, accompanied by a rising population, created new dynamic elements in a formerly static society.

Townspeople themselves were often great enthusiasts for their new way of life. In the twelfth century, William Fitz-Stephen spoke of London as one of the noble cities of the world: "It is happy in the healthiness of its air, in the Christian religion, in the strength of its defences, the nature of its site, the honor of its citizens, the modesty of its women; pleasant in sports; fruitful of noble men." To Fitz-Stephen, London offered myriad opportunities and pleasures. Fairs and markets were held regularly, and "practically anything that man may need is brought daily not only into special places but even into the open squares." Any man, according to Fitz-Stephen, "if he is healthy and not a good-for-nothing, may earn his living expenses and esteem according to his station." Then, too, there are the happy inhabitants of the city: Where else has one "ever met such a wonderful show of people this side or the other side of the sea?" Sporting events and leisure activities are available in every season of the year: "In Easter holidays they fight battles on water." In summer, "the youths are exercised in leaping, dancing, shooting, wrestling, casting the stone; the maidens dance as long as they can well see." In winter, "when the great fen, or moor, which waters the walls of the city on the north side, is frozen, many young men play upon the ice; some, striding as wide as they may, do slide swiftly." To Fitz-Stephen, "every convenience for human pleasure is known to be at hand" in London. One would hardly know from his cheerful description that medieval cities faced over-crowded conditions, terrible smells from rotting garbage and raw sewage, and the constant challenge of epidemics and fires.

By the twelfth and thirteenth centuries, both the urban centers and the urban population of Europe were experiencing a dramatic expansion. New forms of cultural and intellectual expression also arose in this new urban world. Although European society in the High Middle Ages remained overwhelmingly agricultural, the growth of trade and cities along with the development of a money economy and new commercial practices and institutions constituted a veritable commercial revolution that affected most of Europe.

Land and People in the High Middle Ages

The period from 1000 to 1300 witnessed an improvement in climate as a small but nevertheless significant rise in temperature made for longer and better growing seasons. At the same time, the European population experienced a dramatic increase, virtually doubling between 1000 and 1300, from 38 million to 74 million people. As Table 9.1 indicates, the rate of growth tended to vary from region to region. This rise in population was physically evident in the growth of agricultural villages, towns, and cities and the increase in arable land.

What accounted for this dramatic increase in population? Obviously, fertility rates increased sufficiently to gradually outstrip the relatively high mortality rates of medieval society, which were especially acute in infancy and the childhood years. Traditionally, historians have cited two factors to explain the population increase: increased security stemming from more settled and peaceful conditions after the invasions of the Early Middle Ages had stopped and a dramatic increase in agricultural production capable of sustaining a larger population.

TABLE 9.1 Population Estimates (in millions), 1000 and 1340

Area	1000	1340
Mediterranean		
Greece and Balkans	5	6
Italy	5	10
Iberia	7	9
Total	17	25
Western and Central Europe		
France and Low Countries	6	19
British Isles	2	5
Germany and Scandinavia	4	11.5
Total	12	35.5
Eastern Europe		
Russia	6	8
Poland	2	3
Hungary	1.5	2
Total	9.5	13
Grand Total	38.5	73.5

SOURCE: J. C. Russell, *The Control of Late Ancient and Medieval Population* (Philadelphia: American Philosophical Society, 1985), p. 36. Demographic specialists admit that these are merely estimates. Some figures, especially those for eastern Europe, could be radically revised by new research.

The New Agriculture

During the High Middle Ages, significant changes occurred in the way Europeans farmed. Although the warmer climate played an underlying role by improving growing conditions, another important factor in increasing the production of food was the expansion of cultivated or arable land. This was done primarily by clearing forested areas for cultivation. Millions of acres of forests were also cut down to provide timber for fuel, houses, mills, bridges, fortresses, ships, and charcoal for the iron industry (see the box on p. 229). Eager for land, peasants cut down trees, drained swamps, and in the Netherlands even began to reclaim land from the sea. By the thirteenth century, the total acreage available for farming in Europe was greater than at any time before or since.

Technological Changes Technological changes also furthered the expansion of agriculture. Many of them depended on the use of iron, which was mined in various areas of Europe and traded to places where it was not found. Iron was in demand to make swords and armor as well as scythes, axheads, new types of farming implements such as hoes, and saws, hammers, and nails for building purposes. It was crucial to the development of the heavy, wheeled plow, the *carruca*, which made an enormous impact on medieval agriculture north of the Alps.

The plow of the Mediterranean and Near Eastern worlds had been the *aratum*, a nonwheeled, light scratch plow made mostly of wood that was sufficient to break the top layer of the light soils of those areas. It could be pulled by a single donkey, ox, or horse. But such a light plow was

THE ELIMINATION OF MEDIEVAL FORESTS

*O*NE OF THE INTERESTING environmental changes of the Middle Ages was the elimination of millions of acres of forest to create new areas of arable land and to meet the demand for timber. Timber was used as fuel and to build houses, mills of all kinds, bridges, fortresses, and ships. Incredible quantities of wood were burned to make charcoal for the iron forges. The clearing of the forests caused the price of wood to skyrocket by the thirteenth century. This document from 1140 illustrates the process. Suger, the abbot of Saint-Denis, needed 35-foot beams for the construction of a new church. His master carpenters told him that there were no longer any trees big enough in the area around Paris and that he would have to go far afield to find such tall trees. This selection recounts his efforts.

Suger's Search for Wooden Beams

On a certain night, when I had returned from celebrating Matins [a prayer service], I began to think in bed that I myself should go through all the forests of these parts. . . . Quickly disposing of all duties and hurrying up in the early morning, we hastened with our carpenters, and with the measurements of the beams, to the forest called Iveline. When we traversed our possession in the Valley of Chevreuse we summoned . . . the keepers of our own forests as well as men who know about the other woods, and questioned them under oath whether we would find there, no matter with how much trouble, any timbers of that measure. At this they smiled, or rather would have laughed at us if they had dared; they wondered whether we were quite ignorant of the fact that nothing of the kind could be found in the entire region, especially since Milon, the Castellan of Chevreuse, . . . had left nothing unimpaired or untouched that could be used for palisades and bulwarks while he was long subjected to wars both by our Lord the King and Amaury de Montfort. We however—scorning whatever they might say—began, with the courage of our faith as it were, to search through the woods; and toward the first hour we found one timber adequate to the measure. Why say more? By the ninth hour or sooner, we had, through the thickets, the depths of the forest and the dense, thorny tangles, marked down twelve timbers (for so many were necessary) to the astonishment of all.

totally ineffective in the heavy clay soils north of the Alps. The *carruca*, a heavy, wheeled plow with an iron plowshare, came into widespread use by the tenth century. It could turn over heavy soils and allow them to drain. Because of its weight, a team of oxen was needed to pull it. Oxen were slow, however. Two new inventions for the horse made greater productivity possible. In the tenth century, a new horse collar was developed that distributed the weight around the shoulders and chest rather than the throat and could be used to hitch up a series of horses, enabling them to pull the new heavy plow faster and cultivate more land. The use of horseshoes, iron shoes nailed to a horse's hooves, produced greater traction and better protection against the rocky and heavy clay soils of northern Europe.

The use of the heavy, wheeled plow also led to cooperative agricultural villages. Because iron was expensive, a heavy, wheeled plow had to be purchased by the entire community. An individual family could not afford a team of animals, so villagers shared their beasts. Moreover, the plow's size and weight made it hard to maneuver, so land was cultivated in long strips to minimize the amount of turning that would have to be done.

Besides using horsepower, the High Middle Ages harnessed the power of water and wind to do jobs formerly done by human or animal power. Although the watermill

The Heavy, Wheeled Plow. The heavy, wheeled plow was an important invention that enabled peasants to turn over the heavy clay soil of northern Europe. This sixteenth-century illumination shows the heavy, wheeled plow pulled by draft horses with collars.

had been invented as early as the second century B.C., it did not come into widespread use until the High Middle Ages. Located along streams, watermills were used to grind grain into flour. Often dams were constructed to increase the waterpower. The development of the cam enabled millwrights to mechanize entire industries; waterpower was used in certain phases of cloth production and to run triphammers for the working of metals.

Where rivers were unavailable or not easily dammed, Europeans developed windmills to yoke the power of the wind. By the end of the twelfth century, these were beginning to dot the European landscape. The watermill and windmill were the most important devices for the harnessing of power before the invention of the steam engine in the eighteenth century.

The Three-Field System The shift from a two-field to a three-field system of crop rotation also contributed to the increase in agricultural production. In the Early Middle Ages, it was common to plant half of one's fields while allowing the other half to lie fallow to regain its fertility. Now estates were divided into three parts. One field was planted in the fall with grains such as rye and wheat, while spring-sown grains, such as oats and barley, and legumes, such as peas, beans, or lentils, were planted in the second field. The third was allowed to lie fallow. By rotating their use, only one-third, rather than one-half, of the land lay fallow at any time. The rotation of crops also prevented the soil from being exhausted so quickly, especially since legumes improve soil fertility because their roots fix nitrogen in the soil. Grain yields increased as well. The three-field system was not adopted everywhere, however. It was not used in Mediterranean lands, and even in northern Europe the two-field and three-field systems existed side by side for centuries.

By the thirteenth century, the growing demand for agricultural produce in the towns and cities led to higher food prices. This led lords to try to grow more food for profit. One way to do so was to lease their demesne land to their serfs. Labor services were then transformed into money payments or fixed rents, thereby converting many serfs into free peasants. Although many peasants still remained economically dependent on their lords, they were no longer legally tied to the land. Lords, in turn, became collectors of rents rather than operators of a manor with political and legal privileges. The political and legal powers formerly exercised by lords were increasingly reclaimed by the monarchical states.

Peasant Activities. The seasons of the year largely determined the life of the European peasant. The kind of work that peasants did was dictated by the month and the season. This French calendar of 1460 shows a number of medieval farming activities, including sowing seeds, harvesting crops, pruning plants, shearing sheep, threshing, pressing grapes, and taking care of animals.

The Life of the Peasantry

Peasant activities were largely determined by the seasons of the year. Each season brought a new round of tasks appropriate for the time, although some periods were considerably more hectic than others, especially summer and fall. The basic staple of the peasant diet was bread, so an adequate harvest of grains was crucial to survival in the winter months. A new cycle began in October when peasants prepared the ground for the planting of winter crops. In November came the slaughter of excess livestock because there was usually insufficient fodder to keep animals all winter. The meat would be salted to preserve it for winter use. In February and March, the land was plowed for spring crops—oats, barley, peas, beans, and lentils. Early summer was a comparatively relaxed time, although there was still weeding and sheepshearing to be done. In every season, the serfs worked not only their own land but also the lord's demesne. They also tended the gardens adjacent to their dwellings where they grew the vegetables and fruits that made up part of their diet.

Holidays and the Village Church But peasants did not face a life of constant labor thanks to the feast days or holidays of the Catholic church, which commemorated the great events of the Christian faith or the lives of Christian saints or holy persons. The three great feasts of the Catholic church were Christmas (celebrating the birth of Jesus), Easter (celebrating the resurrection of Jesus), and Pentecost (celebrating the descent of the Holy Spirit on Jesus' disciples fifty days after his resurrection). Numerous other feasts dedicated to saints or the Virgin Mary, the mother of Jesus, were also celebrated, making a total of over fifty holidays.

Religious feast days, Sunday Mass, baptisms, marriages, and funerals all brought peasants into contact with the village church, a crucial part of manorial life. In the village church, the peasant was baptized as an infant, confirmed in the faith, sometimes married, and given the sacrament of Holy Communion as well as the last rites of the church before death. The village priest instructed the peasants in the basic elements of Christianity so that they might attain the Christian's ultimate goal—salvation. But village priests were often barely literate peasants themselves, and it is hard to know how much church doctrine the peasants actually understood. Very likely, they regarded God as an all-powerful force who needed to be appeased by prayer to bring good harvests.

The Peasant Household   Peasant dwellings were very simple. In timber-rich areas, peasant cottages had wood frames filled in with wattling (a lattice of laths) and plastered with a "daub" of clay, straw, animal hair, and dung. Roofs were often thatched with reeds or straw. In timber-poor areas, peasants built their houses out of stone. The houses of poorer peasants consisted of a single room, but others had at least two rooms—a main room for cooking, eating, and other activities and another room for sleeping. There was little privacy in a medieval household. A hearth in the main room was used for heating and cooking, but since there were few or no windows and no chimney, the smoke from fires in the hearth went out a hole in the roof or gable.

Family and the Role of Women   Surveys of monastic manors reveal that the typical peasant household consisted of a husband and wife with two or three children. Infant mortality rates were high. Peasant women occupied both an important and a difficult position in manorial society. They were expected to carry and bear children, do the spinning and weaving that provided the household's clothes, tend the family's vegetable garden, and provide the meals. A woman's ability to manage the household might determine whether her family would starve or survive in difficult times. At the same time, peasant women often worked with men in the fields, especially at harvest time.

The Peasant Diet   Though simple, a peasant's daily diet was potentially nutritious when food was available. The basic staple of the peasant diet, and the medieval diet in general, was bread. While women made the dough for the bread, the loaves were usually baked in community ovens, which were a monopoly of the lord of the manor. Peasant bread was made of the cheaper grains (rye, barley, millet, and oats), rather than expensive wheat. It was dark and had

a very heavy, hard texture. Bread was supplemented by legumes (peas and beans) from the household gardens, bacon from the family pig, cheese from cow's or goat's milk, and where available, wild game and fish from hunting and fishing. Manorial lords tended to regulate fishing, however, and were especially reluctant to allow peasants to hunt for fear that insufficient game would remain for the nobility. Woodlands also provided nuts, berries, and a foraging area for pigs. Fruits, such as apples, pears, and cherries, were also available. Chickens provided eggs and occasionally meat. Peasants usually ate fresh meat only on the great feast days, such as Christmas, Easter, and Pentecost.

Grains were important not only for bread but also for making ale. In many northern European countries, ale was the most common drink of the poor. If records are accurate, enormous quantities of ale were consumed. A monastery in the twelfth century recorded a daily allotment of three gallons a day to each monk, far above the weekend consumption of many present-day college students. Peasants in the field undoubtedly consumed even more. This high consumption of alcohol might explain the large number of fights and accidents recorded in medieval court records.

The Aristocracy of the High Middle Ages

In the High Middle Ages, European society was dominated by a group of men whose primary preoccupation was warfare. King Alfred of England had said that a "well-peopled land" must have "men of prayer, men of war, and men of work," and medieval ideals held to a tripartite division of society into these three basic groups. The "men of war" were the **aristocracy** who came to form a distinct social group, albeit one with considerable variation in wealth among its members. Nevertheless, they, along with their wives and children, shared a common ethos and a distinctive lifestyle.

The Significance of the Aristocracy   King Alfred's "men of war" were the lords and vassals of medieval society. The lords were the kings, dukes, counts, barons, and viscounts (and even bishops and archbishops) who held extensive lands and considerable political power. They formed an aristocracy or nobility that consisted of people who held real political, economic, and social power. Nobles relied for military help on knights, mounted warriors who fought for them in return for weapons and daily sustenance. Knights were by no means the social equals of nobles; many knights in fact possessed little more than peasants. But in the course of the twelfth and thirteenth centuries, knights improved their social status and joined the ranks of the nobility. In the process, *noble* and *knight* came to mean much the same thing, and warfare likewise tended to become a distinguishing characteristic of the nobleman. The great lords and knights came to form a common caste. Although social divisions based on extremes of wealth and landholdings persisted, they were all warriors united by the institution of knighthood.

The Men of War Medieval theory maintained that the warlike qualities of the nobility were justified by their role as defenders of society. Knights, however, were also notorious for fighting each other. The Catholic church intervened, and though it could not stop the incessant bloodletting, it did at least try to limit it by instituting the "Peace of God." Beginning in the eleventh century, the church encouraged knights to take an oath to respect churches and pilgrimage centers and to refrain from attacking noncombatants, such as clergy, poor people, merchants, and women. It was, of course, permissible to continue killing each other. At the same time, the church initiated the "Truce of God," which forbade fighting on Sundays and the primary feast days.

In addition to trying to diminish fighting, the church also worked to redirect the nobility's warlike energy into different channels, such as the Crusades against the Muslims (see Chapter 10), and was quite willing to justify violence when used against peace-breakers and especially against non-Christians. Hence being a warrior on behalf of God easily vindicated the nobles' love of war and in fact justified their high social status as the defenders of Christian society. The church furthered this process by steeping knighthood in Christian symbols. A knight formally received his arms in a religious ceremony, and weapons were blessed by a priest for Christian service. Throughout the Middle Ages, a constant tension existed between the ideals of a religion founded on the ideal of peace and the ethos of a nobility based on the love of war.

Castles The growth of the European nobility in the High Middle Ages was made visible by an increasing number of castles scattered across the landscape. Although castle architecture varied considerably, castles did possess two common features: they were permanent residences for the noble family, its retainers, and servants, and they were defensible fortifications. For defensive purposes, castles were surrounded by open areas and large stone walls. At the heart of the castle was the keep, a large, multistoried building that housed kitchens, stables, storerooms, a great hall for visitors, dining, and administrative business, and numerous rooms for sleeping and living. The growing wealth of the High Middle Ages made it possible for the European nobility to build more secure castles with thicker walls and more elaborately decorated interiors. As castles became more sturdily built, they proved to be more easily defended and harder to seize by force.

Aristocratic Women Although women could legally hold and inherit property, most women remained under the control of men—their fathers until they married and their husbands after they married. Nevertheless, aristocratic women had numerous opportunities to play important roles. Because the lord was often away at war, on a Crusade, or at court, the lady of the castle had to manage the estate, a considerable responsibility in view of the fact that households, even of lesser aristocrats, could include large numbers of officials and servants. Supervising financial accounts, both for the household and for the landed estate,

© Giraudon/Art Resource, NY

Castle and Aristocrats. This illustration is from the *Très Riches Heures* (Very Sumptuous Hours) of Jean, duke of Berry. The three Limbourg brothers created this Book of Hours, which was a book containing prayers to be recited at different times each day. This scene depicts the château at Dourdan, France, and its surrounding lands. In the foreground, elaborately dressed aristocratic men and women are seen amusing themselves.

alone required considerable financial knowledge. The lady of the castle was also often responsible for overseeing the food supply and maintaining all other supplies for the smooth operation of the household.

Childhood ended early for the daughters of aristocrats. Since aristocratic girls were married in their teens (usually at the age of fifteen or sixteen) and were expected by their husbands to assume their responsibilities immediately, the training of girls in a large body of practical knowledge could never start too early. Sent at a young age to the castles of other nobles to be brought up, girls were trained as ladies-in-waiting. The lady of the castle taught them how to sew and weave and instructed them in all the skills needed for running an estate. They also learned how to read and write, dance, sing, and play musical instruments.

WOMEN IN MEDIEVAL THOUGHT

W HETHER A NUN or the wife of an aristocrat, townsman, or peasant, a woman in the Middle Ages was considered inferior to a man and subject to a man's authority. Although there are a number of examples of strong women who ignored such attitudes, church teachings also reinforced these notions. The first selection from Gratian, the twelfth-century jurist who wrote the first systematic work on canon law, supports this view. The second selection was written in the 1390s by a wealthy fifty-year-old Parisian who wanted to instruct his fifteen-year-old bride on how to be a good wife.

Gratian, *Decretum*

Women should be subject to their men. The natural order for mankind is that women should serve men and children their parents, for it is just that the lesser serve the greater.

The image of God is in man and it is one. Women were drawn from man, who has God's jurisdiction as if he were God's vicar, because he has the image of one God. Therefore woman is not made in God's image.

Woman's authority is nil; let her in all things be subject to the rule of man. . . . And neither can she teach, nor be a witness, nor give a guarantee, nor sit in judgment.

Adam was beguiled by Eve, not she by him. It is right that he whom woman led into wrongdoing should have her under his direction, so that he may not fail a second time through female levity.

A Merchant of Paris, *On Marriage*

I entreat you to keep his linen clean, for this is up to you. Because the care of outside affairs is men's work, a husband must look after these things, and go and come, run here and there in rain, wind, snow, and hail—sometimes wet, sometimes dry, sometimes sweating, other times shivering, badly fed, badly housed, badly shod, badly bedded—and nothing harms him because he is cheered by the anticipation of the care his wife will take of him on his return—of the pleasures, joys, and comforts she will provide, or have provided for him in her presence: to have his shoes off before a good fire, to have his feet washed, to have clean shoes and hose, to be well fed, provided with good drink, well served, well honored, well bedded in white sheets and white nightcaps, well covered with good furs, and comforted with other joys and amusements, intimacies, affections, and secrets about which I am silent. And on the next day fresh linen and garments. . . .

Also keep peace with him. Remember the country proverb that says there are three things that drive a good man from his home: a house with a bad roof, a smoking chimney, and a quarrelsome woman. I beg you, in order to preserve your husband's love and good will, be loving, amiable, and sweet with him. . . . Thus protect and shield your husband from all troubles, give him all the comfort you can think of, wait on him, and have him waited on in your home. . . . If you do what is said here, he will always have his affection and his heart turned toward you and your service, and he will forsake all other homes, all other women, all other help, and all other households.

Although women were expected to be subservient to their husbands (see the box above), there were many strong women who advised and sometimes even dominated their husbands. Perhaps the most famous was Eleanor of Aquitaine (c. 1122–1204), heiress to the duchy of Aquitaine in southwestern France. Married first to King Louis VII of France (1137–1180), Eleanor even accompanied her husband on a Crusade, but her failure to bear sons led Louis to have their marriage annulled. Eleanor then married Henry, count of Anjou, who became King Henry II of England (1154–1189) and duke of Normandy. She bore him both sons and daughters and took an active role in politics, even assisting her sons in rebelling against Henry in 1173–1174. Imprisoned by her husband for her activities, after Henry's death she again assumed an active political life, providing both military and political support for her sons.

Blanche of Castile (1188–1252) was another powerful medieval queen. She became regent while her son Louis IX was a boy and ruled France with a powerful hand during much of the 1220s and 1230s. She repelled the attempt of some rebellious French nobles to seize her son, the young king, and defeated Henry III of England when he tried to incite an uprising in France in order to reconquer Normandy. Blanche's political sense was so astute that even when Louis IX came of age, he continued to rely on her as his chief adviser. One medieval chronicler gave her the highest compliment he could think of: "she ruled as a man."

The Way of the Warrior At the age of seven or eight, aristocratic boys were sent either to a clerical school to pursue a religious career or to another nobleman's castle, where they prepared for the life of a noble. Their chief lessons were military; they learned how to joust, hunt, ride, and handle weapons properly. Occasionally, aristocrats' sons might also learn the basic fundamentals of reading and writing. After his apprenticeship in knighthood, at about the age of twenty-one, a young man formally entered the adult world in the ceremony of "knighting." A sponsor girded a sword on the young candidate and struck him on the cheek or neck with an open hand (or later touched him three times on the shoulder with the blade of a sword), possibly signifying the passing of the sponsor's military valor to the new knight.

In the eleventh and twelfth centuries, under the influence of the church, an ideal of civilized behavior called **chivalry** gradually evolved among the nobility. Chivalry represented a code of ethics that knights were supposed to uphold. In addition to their oath to defend the church and the defenseless, knightly honor also demanded that unarmed knights should not be attacked. Chivalry also implied that knights should fight only for glory, but this account of a group of English knights by a medieval writer reveals another motive for battle: "The whole city was plundered to the last farthing, and then they proceeded to rob all the churches throughout the city, . . . and seizing gold and silver, cloth of all colors, women's ornaments, gold rings, goblets, and precious stones. . . . They all returned to their own lords rich men."[1] Apparently, not all chivalric ideals were taken seriously.

After his formal initiation into the world of warriors, a young man returned home to find himself once again subject to his parents' authority. Young men were discouraged from marrying until their fathers died, at which time they could marry and become lords of the castle. Trained to be warriors but with no adult responsibilities, young knights naturally gravitated toward military activities and often furthered the private warfare endemic to the noble class.

The Role of Tournaments In the twelfth century, tournaments began to appear as an alternative to the socially destructive fighting that the church was trying to curb. Initially, tournaments consisted of the "melee," in which warriors on horseback fought with blunted weapons in free-for-all combat. The goal was to take prisoners who would then be ransomed, making success in tournaments a path to considerable gain. Within an eight-month span, the English knight William Marshall made a tour of the tournament circuit, defeated 203 knights, and made so much money that he had to hire two clerks to take care of it.

By the late twelfth century, the melee was preceded by the joust, or individual combat between two knights. Gradually, jousts became the main part of the tournament. No matter how much the church condemned tournaments, knights themselves continued to see them as an excellent way to train for war. As one knight explained: "A knight cannot distinguish himself in that [war] if he has not trained for it in tourneys. He must have seen his blood flow, heard his teeth crack under fist blows, felt his opponent's

The Tournament. The tournament arose as a socially acceptable alternative to the private warfare that plagued the nobility in the Middle Ages. This fifteenth-century Flemish illustration shows a joust between two heavily armored knights. Shown watching are King Richard II in the middle and other onlookers at the right.

weight bear down upon him as he lay on the ground and, after being twenty times unhorsed, have risen twenty times to fight."[2]

Marriage Patterns of the Aristocracy

Aristocratic marriages were expected to establish alliances with other families, bring new wealth, and provide heirs to carry on the family line. Parents therefore supervised the choice of spouses for their children. One of the most noticeable features of aristocratic marriages was the usually wide discrepancy in the ages of the marital partners.

Marriage. Marriage festivities for members of the aristocracy were usually quite elaborate. As seen in this illustration of the marriage of Renaud de Montaubon and Clarisse, daughter of the ruler of Gascogne, after the festivities, the wedding party would accompany the new couple to their bedroom to prepare them for the physical consummation of their marriage. Only after physical union was a medieval marriage considered valid.

AN ITALIAN BANKER DISCUSSES TRADING BETWEEN EUROPE AND CHINA

*W*ORKING ON BEHALF of a banking guild in Florence, Francesco Balducci Pegolotti journeyed to England and Cyprus. As a result of his contacts with many Italian merchants, he acquired considerable information about long-distance trade between Europe and China. In this account, written in 1340, he provides advice for Italian merchants.

Francesco Balducci Pegolotti, *An Account of Traders Between Europe and China*

In the first place, you must let your beard grow long and not shave. And at Tana [modern Rostov] you should furnish yourself with a guide. And you must not try to save money in the matter of guides by taking a bad one instead of a good one. For the additional wages of the good one will not cost you so much as you will save by having him. And besides the guide it will be well to take at least two good menservants who are acquainted with the Turkish tongue. . . .

The road you travel from Tana to China is perfectly safe, whether by day or night, according to what the merchants say who have used it. Only if the merchant, in going or coming, should die upon the road, everything belonging to him will become the possession of the lord in the country in which he dies. . . . And in like manner if he dies in China. . . .

China is a province which contains a multitude of cities and towns. Among others there is one in particular, that is to say the capital city, to which many merchants are attracted, and in which there is a vast amount of trade; this city is called Khanbaliq [modern Beijing]. And the said city has a circuit of one hundred miles, and is all full of people and houses and of dwellers in the said city. . . .

Whatever silver the merchants may carry with them as far as China, the emperor of China will take from them and put into his treasury. And to merchants who thus bring silver they give that paper money of theirs in exchange . . . and with this money you can readily buy silk and all other merchandise that you have a desire to buy. And all the people of the country are bound to receive it. And yet you shall not pay a higher price for your goods because your money is of paper.

Daughters of the nobles married at fifteen or sixteen, but their husbands might be in their thirties or even forties, since men did not marry until they came into their inheritances.

By the twelfth century, the efforts of the church since Carolingian times to end divorce (see Chapter 8) had borne much fruit. As a sacrament, marriage was intended to last for a lifetime and could not be dissolved. In certain cases, however, the church accepted the right of married persons to separate by granting them an annulment or official recognition that their marriage had not been valid in the first place. If it could be established that the couple had not consented to the marriage, that one or the other suffered from a sexual incapacity that prevented the consummation of the marriage, or that the couple were related by blood (more closely than sixth or, after 1215, third cousins), the church would approve an annulment of their marriage, and the partners would be free to marry again.

The New World of Trade and Cities

Medieval Europe was an overwhelmingly agrarian society with most people living in small villages. In the eleventh and twelfth centuries, however, new elements were introduced that began to transform the economic foundation of Western civilization: a revival of trade, considerable expansion in the circulation of money, a restoration of specialized craftspeople and artisans, and the growth and development of towns. These changes were made possible by the new agricultural practices and subsequent increase in food production, which freed some European families from the need to produce their own food. Merchants and craftspeople could now buy their necessities.

The Revival of Trade

The revival of commercial activity was a gradual process. During the chaotic conditions of the Early Middle Ages, large-scale trade had declined in western Europe except for Byzantine contacts with Italy and the Jewish traders who moved back and forth between the Muslim and Christian worlds. By the end of the tenth century, however, people with both the skills and the products for commercial activity were emerging in Europe.

Cities in Italy assumed a leading role in the revival of trade (see Map 9.1). By the end of the eighth century, Venice, on the northeastern coast, had emerged as a town with close trading ties to the Byzantine Empire. Venice developed a trading fleet and by the end of the tenth century had become the chief western trading center for Byzantine and Islamic commerce. Venice sent wine, grain, and timber to Constantinople in exchange for silk cloth, which was then peddled to other communities. Other coastal communities in western Italy, such as Genoa and Pisa, also opened new trade routes. By 1100, Italian merchants began to benefit from the Crusades and were able to establish new trading centers in eastern ports. There the merchants obtained silks, sugar, and spices, which they subsequently carried back to Italy and the West.

In the High Middle Ages, Italian merchants became even more daring in their trade activities. They established trading posts in Cairo, Damascus, and a number of Black Sea ports, where they acquired goods brought by Muslim merchants from India, China, and Southeast Asia. A few Italian merchants even journeyed to India and China in search of trade (see the box above).

While the northern Italian cities were busy trading in the Mediterranean, the towns of Flanders were doing

MAP 9.1 **Medieval Trade Routes.** Italian cities and Flanders were the centers of gradually expanding trade in Europe. They fostered the exchange of goods from the Byzantine Empire and the Far East with those of various regions of Europe. The diminishing threats of violence over time greatly helped trade. ❓ Look at Map 6.2. In what areas had trade expanded, and how can you account for this? 🌐 **View an animated version of this map or related maps at** http://history.wadsworth.com/spielvogel06/

likewise in northern Europe. Flanders, the area along the coast of present-day Belgium and northern France, was known for the production of a much desired high-quality woolen cloth. Flanders's location made it a logical entrepôt for the traders of northern Europe. Merchants from England, Scandinavia, France, and Germany converged there to trade their wares for woolen cloth. Flanders prospered in the eleventh and twelfth centuries, and such Flemish towns as Bruges and Ghent became centers for the trade and manufacture of woolen cloth.

By the twelfth century, it was almost inevitable that a regular exchange of goods would develop between Flanders and Italy. To encourage this trade, the counts of Champagne in northern France devised a series of six fairs held

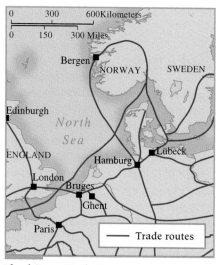

Flanders as a Trade Center

annually in the chief towns of their territory. They guaranteed the safety of visiting merchants, supervised the trading activities, and of course collected a sales tax on all goods exchanged at the fairs. The fairs of Champagne became the largest commercial marketplace in western Europe where the goods of northern Europe could be exchanged for the goods of southern Europe and the East. Northern merchants brought the furs, woolen cloth, tin, hemp, and honey of northern Europe and exchanged them for the cloth and swords of northern Italy and the silks, sugar, and spices of the East. The prosperity of the Champagne fairs caused lords everywhere to follow their example and establish trading fairs.

As trade increased, both gold and silver came to be in demand at fairs and trading markets of all kinds. Slowly, a money economy began to emerge. New trading companies as well as banking firms were set up to manage the exchange and sale of goods. All of these new practices were part of the rise of **commercial capitalism,** an economic system in which people invested in trade and goods in order to make profits.

The Growth of Cities

The revival of trade led to a revival of cities. Merchants needed places where they could live and build warehouses to store their goods. Towns had greatly declined in the Early Middle Ages, especially in Europe north of the Alps. Old Roman cities continued to exist but had dwindled in size and population. With the revival of trade, merchants began to settle in these old cities, followed by craftworkers or artisans, people who had developed skills on manors or elsewhere and now perceived the opportunity to ply their trade producing objects that could be sold by the merchants. In the course of the eleventh and twelfth centuries, the old Roman cities came alive with new residents. By 1100, the old areas of these cities had been repopulated; soon the population outgrew the walls, necessitating the construction of new city walls outside the old.

In the Mediterranean world, cities had survived in a more visible fashion. Spain's Islamic cities had a flourishing urban life, and southern Italy still possessed such thriving cities as Bari, Salerno, Naples, and Amalfi. Although greatly reduced in size, Rome, the old capital of the Roman world, had survived as the center of papal administration. In northern Italy, Venice had already emerged as a town by the end of the eighth century because of its commercial connections to the Byzantine Empire.

Founding of New Cities and Towns Beginning in the late tenth century, many new cities or towns were founded, particularly in northern Europe. Usually, a group of artisans and merchants established a settlement near some fortified stronghold, such as a castle or monastery. Castles were particularly favored because they were usually located along major routes of transportation or at the intersection of two trade routes; the lord of the castle also offered protection. If the settlement prospered and expanded, walls were built to protect it. The original meaning of the English *borough* or *burgh* and the German *Burg* as a fortress or walled enclosure is still evident in the names of many cities, such as Edinburgh and Hamburg. The merchants and artisans of these boroughs and burghs came to be called burghers or **bourgeoisie.**

Fortified Town of Carcassonne. The expansion of commerce and industry led to an ongoing growth of towns and cities in the High Middle Ages. As seen in this picture of the French town of Carcassonne, medieval towns were surrounded by walls (here, double walls) strengthened by defensive towers and punctuated by gates. As is evident here, medieval urban skylines were dominated by towers of all kinds.

Most towns were closely tied to their surrounding territories because they were dependent on the countryside for their food supplies. In addition, they were often part of the territory belonging to a lord and were subject to his jurisdiction. Although lords wanted to treat towns and townspeople as they would their vassals and serfs, cities had totally different needs and a different perspective. Townspeople needed mobility to trade. Consequently, the merchants and artisans of the towns constituted a revolutionary group who needed their own unique laws to meet their requirements. Since the townspeople were profiting from the growth of trade and sale of their products, they were willing to pay for the right to make their own laws and govern themselves. In many instances, lords and kings saw the potential for vast new sources of revenues and were willing to grant (or more accurately, sell) to the townspeople the liberties they were beginning to demand.

The Rights of Townspeople

By 1100, townspeople were obtaining charters of liberties from their territorial lords that granted them the privileges they wanted, including the right to bequeath goods and sell property, freedom from military obligation to the lord, written urban law that guaranteed their freedom, and the right for serfs to become free after residing a year and a day in the town. The last provision made it possible for a runaway serf who could avoid capture to become a free person in a city. Almost all new urban communities gained these elementary liberties, but only some towns obtained the right to govern themselves by choosing their own officials and administering their own courts of law. Where townspeople experienced difficulty in obtaining privileges, they often swore an oath, forming an association called a **commune,** and resorted to force against their lay or ecclesiastical lords.

Communes made their first appearance in Italy, where urban communities existed even in the Early Middle Ages. In northern Italy, in the regions called Tuscany and Lombardy, towns were governed by their bishops, but the nobles whose lands surrounded the towns took an active interest in them. Bishops were usually supported by the emperors, who used them as their chief administrators. In the eleventh century, city residents rebelled against the rule of the bishops, swore communal associations with the bishops' noble vassals, and overthrew the authority of the bishops by force. The alliance between town residents and rural nobles was overwhelming, and in the course of the eleventh and twelfth centuries, bishops were shorn of their authority. Communes took over the rights of government and created new offices, such as consuls and city councils, for self-rule. Pisa, Milan, Arezzo, and Genoa all attained self-government by the end of the eleventh century.

Although communes were also sworn in northern Europe, especially in France and Flanders, townspeople did not have the support of rural nobles. Revolts against lay lords were usually brutally suppressed; those against bishops, as in Laon at the beginning of the twelfth century (see the box on p. 239), were more frequently successful. When they succeeded, communes received the right to choose their own officials, hold their own courts, and run their own cities. Unlike the towns in Italy, however, where the decline of the emperor's authority ensured that the northern Italian cities could function as self-governing republics, towns in France and England did not become independent city-states but remained ultimately subject to royal authority.

Medieval cities, then, possessed varying degrees of self-government, depending on the amount of control retained over them by the lord or king in whose territory they were located. Nevertheless, all towns, regardless of the degree of outside control, evolved institutions of government for running the affairs of the community.

City Governments

Medieval cities defined citizenship narrowly and accorded it only to males who had been born in the city or who had lived there for some time. In many cities, citizens elected members of a city council that bore primary responsibility for running the affairs of the city. City councilors (known as *consuls* in Italy and southern France) not only enacted legislation but also served as judges and city magistrates. The electoral process was carefully engineered to ensure that only members of the wealthiest and most powerful families, who came to be called the *patricians,* were elected. They kept the reins of government in their hands despite periodic protests from lesser merchants and artisans. In the twelfth and thirteenth centuries, cities added some kind of sole executive leader, even if he was only a figurehead. Although the title varied from town to town, this executive officer was frequently called a *mayor.*

City governments kept close watch over the activities of their community. To care for the welfare and safety of the community, a government might regulate air and water pollution; provide water barrels and delegate responsibility to people in every section of the town to fight fires, which were an ever-present danger; construct warehouses to stockpile grain in the event of food emergencies; and establish and supervise the standards of weights and measures used in the various local trades and industries.

Crime was not a major problem in the towns of the High Middle Ages because the relatively small size of communities made it difficult for criminals to operate openly. Nevertheless, medieval urban governments did organize town guards to patrol the streets by night and the city walls by day. People caught committing criminal acts were quickly tried for their offenses. Serious offenses, such as murder, were punished by execution, usually by hanging. Lesser crimes were punished by fines, flogging, branding, public exposure (as in the pillory), or expulsion.

Medieval cities remained relatively small in comparison to either ancient or modern cities. A large trading city would number about five thousand inhabitants. By 1300, London was the largest city in England, with eighty thousand people or more. Otherwise, north of the Alps, only a few great commercial urban centers, such as Bruges and Ghent, had a population close to forty thousand. Italian cities tended to be larger, with Venice, Florence, Genoa, Milan, and Naples numbering almost one hundred thou-

A COMMUNAL REVOLT

HE GROWTH OF TOWNS and cities was a major aspect of economic life in the High Middle Ages. When townspeople were unable to gain basic liberties for themselves from the lord in whose territory their town was located, they sometimes swore a "commune" to gain these privileges by force. This selection by a contemporary abbot describes the violence that accompanied the formation of a commune at Laon in France in 1116. The bishop of Laon, lord of the town, had granted privileges to the townspeople in return for a large payment. Later he rescinded his grant but kept the money, thereby angering the citizens.

The Autobiography of Guibert, Abbot of Nogent-sous-Coucy

All the efforts of the prelate and nobles in these days were reserved for fleecing their inferiors. But those inferiors were no longer moved by mere anger, but goaded into a murderous lust for the death of the bishop and his accomplices and bound themselves by oath to effect their purpose. Now they say that 400 took the oath. Such a mob could not be secret and when it came to the ears of Anselm [the bishop's assistant] toward evening of the holy Sabbath, he sent word to the bishop, as he was retiring to rest, not to go out to the early morning service, knowing that if he did he must certainly be killed. But he, infatuated with excessive pride said, "Fie, surely I shall not perish at the hands of such. . . ."

The next day, that is, the fifth in Easter week, after midday, as he [the bishop] was engaged in business with Archdeacon Walter about the getting of money, behold there arose a disorderly noise throughout the city, men shouting "Commune!" and . . . citizens now entered the bishop's court with swords, battle-axes, bows and hatchets, and carrying clubs and spears, a very great company. As soon as this sudden attack was discovered, the nobles rallied from all sides to the bishop, having sworn to give him aid against such an onset, if it should occur. . . . [Despite the assistance of the nobles, the commoners were victorious.]

Next the outrageous mob attacking the bishop and howling before the walls of his palace, he with some who were aiding him fought them off by hurling of stones and shooting of arrows. For he now, as at all times, showed great spirit as a fighter, but because he had wrongly and in vain taken up another sword, by the sword he perished. Therefore, being unable to stand against the reckless assaults of the people, he put on the clothes of one of his servants and flying to the vaults of the church hid himself in a cask, shut up in which with the head fastened on by a faithful follower he thought himself safely hidden. And as they ran hither and thither demanding where, not the bishop, but the hangdog, was, they seized one of his pages, but through his faithfulness could not get what they wanted. Laying hands on another, they learned from the traitor's nod where to look for him. Entering the vaults therefore, and searching everywhere, at last they found [him]. . . .

[The bishop] therefore, sinner though he was, yet the Lord's anointed, was dragged forth from the cask by the hair, beaten with many blows and brought out into the open air in the narrow lane of the clergy's cloister before the house of the chaplain Godfrey. And as he piteously implored them, ready to take oath that he would henceforth cease to be their bishop, that he would leave the country, and as they with hardened hearts jeered at him, one named Bernard . . . lifting his battle-axe brutally dashed out the brains of that sacred, though sinner's, head, and he slipping between the hands of those who held him, was dead before he reached the ground stricken by another thwart blow under the eye-sockets and across the middle of the nose. There brought to his end, his legs were cut off and many another wound inflicted. But Thibaut seeing the ring on the finger of the erstwhile prelate and not being able to draw it off, cut off the dead man's finger and took it. And so stripped to his skin he was thrown into a corner in front of his chaplain's house. My God, who shall recount the mocking words that were thrown at him by passersby, as he lay there, and with what clods and stones and dirt his corpse was covered?

---

sand. Even the largest European city, however, seemed insignificant alongside the Byzantine capital of Constantinople or the Arab cities of Damascus, Baghdad, and Cairo. For a long time to come, Europe remained predominantly rural, but in the long run, the rise of towns and the growth of trade laid the foundation for the eventual transformation of Europe from a rural agricultural society to an urban industrial one.

Life in the Medieval City   Medieval towns were surrounded by stone walls that were expensive to build, so the space within was precious and tightly filled. This gave medieval cities their characteristic appearance of narrow, winding streets with houses crowded against each other. Streets were generally left unpaved until the thirteenth century, and buildings fronted directly on them. To gain more space, inhabitants frequently added balconies or built the second and third stories of their dwellings out over the streets. Since dwellings were crowded so closely together and candles and wood fires were used for light and heat, the danger of fire was great.

A medieval urban skyline was dominated by the towers of castles and town halls, but especially of churches, whose number could be staggering. At the beginning of the thirteenth century, London had 120 monastic and parish churches. If a city was the center of a bishop's see, a large cathedral would dominate the other buildings and be visible for miles outside the city.

The Execution of Criminals. Violence was a common feature of medieval life. Criminals, if apprehended, were punished quickly and severely, and public executions were considered a deterrent to crime. As one can surmise from this illustration, executions were also a form of entertainment.

Most of the people who lived in the cities were merchants involved in trade and artisans engaged in manufacturing of some kind. Sometimes merchants and artisans had their own sections in a city. The merchant area included warehouses, inns, and taverns. Artisan sections were usually divided along craft lines, and each craft might have its own street where its activity was pursued.

The physical environment of medieval cities was not pleasant. They were often dirty and rife with smells from animal and human waste deposited in backyard privies or on the streets (see the box on p. 241). In some places, city governments required citizens to periodically collect garbage and waste and cart it outside the town. Atmospheric pollution was also a fact of life, not only from the ubiquitous wood fires but also from the use of coal, a cheap fuel that was used industrially by lime-burners, brewers, and dyers. Burning coal emitted ill-smelling, noxious fumes and was sometimes prohibited under pain of fine.

Cities were also unable to stop water pollution, especially from the animal-slaughtering and tanning industries. Butchers dumped blood and other waste products from their butchered animals into the river, while tanners

Shops in a Medieval Town. Most urban residents were merchants involved in trade and artisans who manufactured a wide variety of products. Master craftspeople had their workshops in the ground-level rooms of their houses. In this illustration, two well-dressed burghers are touring the shopping districts of a French town. Tailors, furriers, a barber, and a grocer (from left to right) are visible at work in their shops.

POLLUTION IN A MEDIEVAL CITY

ENVIRONMENTAL POLLUTION is not new. Medieval cities and towns had their own problems with filthy living conditions. This excerpt is taken from an order sent by the king of England to the town of Boutham, a suburb of York, which was then being used by the king as headquarters in a war with the Scots. It demands rectification of the town's pitiful physical conditions.

The King's Command to Boutham

To the bailiffs of the abbot of St. Mary's, York, at Boutham. Whereas it is sufficiently evident that the pavement of the said town of Boutham is so very greatly broke up that all and singular passing and going through that town sustain immoderate damages and grievances, and in addition the air is so corrupted and infected by the pigsties situated in the king's highways and in the lanes of that town and by the swine feeding and frequently wandering about in the streets and lanes and by dung and dunghills and many other foul things placed in the streets and lanes, that great repugnance overtakes the king's ministers staying in that town and also others there dwelling and passing through, the advantage of more wholesome air is impeded; the state of men is grievously injured, and other unbearable inconveniences and many other injuries are known to proceed from such corruption, to the nuisance of the king's ministers aforesaid and of others there dwelling and passing through, and to the peril of their lives. . . . The king, being unwilling longer to tolerate such great and unbearable defects there, orders the bailiffs to cause the pavement to be suitably repaired within their liberty before All Saints next, and to cause the pigsties, aforesaid streets and lanes to be cleansed from all dung and dunghills, and to cause proclamation to be made throughout their bailiwick forbidding any one, under pain of grievous forfeiture, to cause or permit their swine to feed or wander outside his house in the king's streets or the lanes aforesaid.

---

unloaded tannic acids, dried blood, fat, hair, and the other waste products of their operations. Forcing both industries to locate downstream to avoid polluting the water used by the city upstream was only partly effective. Tanneries and slaughterhouses existed in every medieval town, so the river could rapidly become polluted from other towns' wastes.

Because of the pollution, cities were not inclined to use the rivers for drinking water but relied instead on wells. Occasionally, communities repaired the system of aqueducts or conduits left over from Roman times and sometimes even constructed new ones. Private and public baths also existed in medieval towns. Paris, for example, had thirty-two public baths for men and women. City laws did not allow lepers and people with "bad reputations" to use them, but such measures did not prevent the public baths from being known for permissiveness due to public nudity. One contemporary commented on what occurred in public bathhouses: "Shameful things. Men make a point of staying all night in the public baths and women at the break of day come in and through 'ignorance' find themselves in the men's rooms."[3] Authorities came under increasing pressure to close the baths down, and the great plague of the fourteenth century sealed their fate. The standards of medieval hygiene broke down, and late medieval and early modern European society would prove to be remarkably dirty.

Because of the limited space in medieval towns, houses were narrow, built next to one another, and usually multi-storied. In many houses, the shops or workrooms of merchants and craftspeople occupied the ground floor. Inhabitants, who might include husband and wife, children, servants, and apprentices, would live upstairs.

For most ordinary merchants and artisans, home life and work life were thus closely intertwined. Merchants and artisans taught their trades to their children and their wives and apprentices, or their children might be apprenticed to another merchant or artisan. Women, in addition to supervising the household, purchasing food and preparing meals, washing clothes, and managing the family finances, were also often expected to help their husbands in their trades. While men produced goods at home, their wives often peddled them at markets or fairs.

Some women also developed their own trades, such as brewing ale or making glass, to earn extra money. Other women worked at making hats and cloth. Widows often carried on their husband's trade. Some women in medieval towns were thus able to lead lives of considerable independence.

Industry in Medieval Cities

The revival of trade enabled cities and towns to become important centers for manufacturing a wide range of goods, such as cloth, metalwork, shoes, and leather goods. A host of crafts were carried on in houses along the narrow streets of the medieval cities. From the twelfth century on, merchants and artisans began to organize themselves into **guilds,** which came to play a leading role in the economic life of the cities.

By the thirteenth century, virtually every group of craftspeople, such as tanners, carpenters, and bakers, had their own guild, and specialized groups of merchants, such as dealers in silk, spices, wool, or banking, had their separate guilds as well. Florence alone, for example, had fifty different guilds. Some communities were so comprehensive in covering all trades that they even had guilds for prostitutes.

Craft guilds directed almost every aspect of the production process. They set standards for the articles produced, specified the actual methods of production to be used, and even fixed the price at which the finished goods could be sold. Guilds also determined the number of individuals who could enter a specific trade and the procedure they must follow to do so.

A person who wanted to learn a trade first became an apprentice to a master craftsman, usually at around the age of ten. Apprentices were not paid but did receive room and board from their masters. After five to seven years of service, during which they learned their craft, apprentices became journeymen (or journeywomen, although most were male) who then worked for wages for other masters. Journeymen aspired to become masters as well. To do so, a journeyman had to produce a "masterpiece," a finished piece in his craft that allowed the master craftsmen of the guild to judge whether the journeyman was qualified to become a master and join the guild.

Craft guilds continued to dominate manufacturing in industries where raw materials could be acquired locally and the products sold locally. But in industries that required raw materials from outside the local area to produce high-quality products for growing markets abroad, a new form of industry dependent on large concentrations of capital and unskilled labor began to emerge. It was particularly evident in the "putting-out" or domestic system used in the production of woolen cloth in both Flanders and northern Italy. An entrepreneur, whose initial capital outlay probably came from commercial activities, bought raw wool and distributed it to workers who carried out the various stages of carding, spinning, weaving, dyeing, and fulling to produce a finished piece of woolen cloth. These laborers worked in their own homes and were paid wages. As wage earners, they were dependent on their employers and the fluctuations in prices that occurred periodically in the international market for the finished goods. The entrepreneur collected the final products and sold the finished cloth, earning a profit that could then be invested in more production. Woolen industries operated by capitalist entrepreneurs in seventeen principal centers in northern Europe, mostly in Flanders, produced most of the woolen cloth used in northern Europe. An Italian chronicler at the beginning of the fourteenth century estimated that the woolen industry in Florence produced eighty thousand pieces of cloth a year and employed thirty thousand men, women, and children, usually at pitiful wages.

The Intellectual and Artistic World of the High Middle Ages

The High Middle Ages was a time of tremendous intellectual and artistic vitality. The period witnessed the growth of educational institutions, a rebirth of interest in ancient culture, a quickening of theological thought, the revival of law, the development of a vernacular literature, and a burst of activity in art and architecture. Although monks continued to play an important role in intellectual activity, increasingly the secular clergy, cities, and courts, whether of kings, princes, or high church officials, began to exert a newfound influence. Especially significant were the new cultural expressions that emerged in towns and cities.

The Rise of Universities

The university as we know it with faculty, students, and degrees was a product of the High Middle Ages. The word *university* is derived from the Latin word *universitas,* meaning a corporation or guild, and referred to either a guild of teachers or a guild of students. Medieval universities were educational guilds or corporations that produced educated and trained individuals.

The Origins of Universities   Education in the Early Middle Ages rested primarily with the clergy, especially the monks. Although monastic schools were the centers of learning from the ninth century, they were surpassed in the course of the eleventh century by the cathedral schools organized by the secular (nonmonastic) clergy. Cathedral schools, like the cities in which they were located, expanded rapidly in the eleventh century. There were twenty of them in 900, but by 1100 the number had grown to at least two hundred since every cathedral city felt compelled to establish one. The most famous were Chartres, Reims, Paris, Laon, and Soissons, all in France, which was the intellectual center of Europe by the twelfth century (see Map 9.2). Although the primary purpose of cathedral schools was to educate priests to be more literate men of God, they also attracted other individuals who desired some education but did not want to become priests. Many university administrators today carry titles, such as chancellor, provost, and dean, that were originally used for the officials of cathedral chapters.

The first European university appeared in Bologna, Italy (unless one accords this distinction to the first medical school, established earlier at Salerno, Italy). The emergence of the University of Bologna coincided with the revival of interest in Roman law, especially the rediscovery of Justinian's *Corpus Iuris Civilis* (see "The Revival of Roman Law" later in this chapter). In the twelfth century, a great teacher, such as Irnerius (1088–1125), attracted students from all over Europe. Most of them were laymen, usually older individuals who served as administrators to kings and princes and were eager to learn more about law so they could apply it in their jobs. To protect themselves, students at Bologna formed a guild or *universitas,* which was recognized by Emperor Frederick Barbarossa and given a charter in 1158. Although the faculty also organized itself as a group, the *universitas* of students at Bologna was far more influential. It obtained a promise of freedom for students from local authorities, regulated the price of lodging, and determined the curriculum, fees, and standards for their masters. Teachers were fined if they missed a class or began their lectures late. The University of Bologna remained the greatest law school in Europe throughout the Middle Ages.

In northern Europe, the University of Paris became the first recognized university. A number of teachers or mas-

MAP 9.2 **Intellectual Centers of Medieval Europe.** Products of the High Middle Ages, universities provided students with a basic liberal arts education and the opportunity to pursue further studies in law, medicine, or theology. Courses were taught in Latin, primarily by professors reading from books. There were no exams in individual courses, but students had to pass a comprehensive oral exam to gain a degree. **?** In what ways did France qualify as the intellectual capital of Europe? **View an animated version of this map or related maps at** http://history.wadsworth.com/spielvogel06/

ters who had received licenses to teach from the cathedral school of Notre-Dame in Paris began to take on extra students for a fee. By the end of the twelfth century, these masters teaching at Paris had formed a *universitas* or guild of masters. By 1200, the king of France, Philip Augustus, officially acknowledged the existence of the University of Paris. The University of Oxford in England, organized on the Paris model, first appeared in 1208. A migration of scholars from Oxford in 1209 led to the establishment of Cambridge University. In the Late Middle Ages, kings, popes, and princes vied to found new universities. By the end of the Middle Ages, there were eighty universities in Europe, most of them located in France, Italy, Germany, and England.

Teaching in the Medieval University   A student's initial studies at a medieval university centered around the traditional liberal arts curriculum.

The *trivium* consisted of grammar, rhetoric, and logic, and the *quadrivium* was comprised of arithmetic, geometry, astronomy, and music. All classes were conducted in Latin, which provided a common means of communication for students, regardless of their country of origin. Basically, medieval university instruction used the lecture method.

University Classroom. This illustration shows a university classroom in fourteenth-century Germany. As was customary in medieval classrooms, the master is reading from a text. The students vary considerably in age and in the amount of attention they are willing to give the lecturer.

The word *lecture* is derived from Latin and means "to read." Before the development of the printing press in the fifteenth century, books were expensive, and few students could afford them, so masters read from a text (such as a collection of laws if the subject were law) and then added commentaries, which came to be known as *glosses*. No exams were given after a series of lectures, but when a student applied for a degree, he (women did not attend universities in the Middle Ages) was given a comprehensive oral examination by a committee of teachers. These exams were taken after a four- or six-year period of study. The first degree a student could earn was an A.B., the *artium baccalaureus*, or bachelor of arts; later he might receive an A.M., *artium magister*, master of arts. All degrees were technically licenses to teach, although most students receiving them did not become teachers.

After completing the liberal arts curriculum, a student could go on to study law, medicine, or theology, which was the most highly regarded subject of the medieval curriculum. The study of law, medicine, or theology was a long process that could take a decade or more. A student who passed his final oral examinations was granted a doctor's degree, which officially enabled him to teach his subject. Most students who pursued advanced degrees received their master's degrees first and taught the arts curriculum while continuing to pursue their advanced degrees. Students who received degrees from medieval universities could pursue other careers besides teaching that proved to be much more lucrative. A law degree was deemed essential for those who wished to serve as advisers to kings and princes. The growing administrative bureaucracies of popes and kings also demanded a supply of clerks with a university education who could keep records and draw up official documents.

Students in the Medieval University   Students at medieval universities stemmed predominantly from the middle groups of medieval society, the families of lesser knights, merchants, and artisans. All were male; many were poor but ambitious and upwardly mobile. Many medieval students started when they were fourteen to eighteen years old and received their bachelor's or master's degrees by their early twenties. Study for a doctorate in one of the specialized schools of law, medicine, or theology entailed at least another ten years. It was not unusual for men to receive their doctorates in their late thirties or early forties.

There are obvious similarities between medieval and modern students. Then as now, many students took their studies seriously and worked hard. Then as now, alcohol, sex, and appeals for spending money were all too common. In medieval universities, handbooks provided form letters that students could use in requesting money from their fathers, guardians, or patrons. This is an example from Oxford:

> B. to his venerable master A., greeting. This is to inform you that I am studying at Oxford with the greatest of diligence, but the matter of money stands greatly in the way of my promotion, as it is now two months since I have spent the last of what

you sent me. The city is expensive and makes many demands; I have to rent lodgings, buy necessaries, and provide for many other things which I cannot now specify. Wherefore I respectfully beg your paternity that by the promptings of divine pity you may assist me, so that I may be able to complete what I have well begun.[4]

Lack of studiousness is not just a modern phenomenon, as this letter from a medieval father to his son illustrates:

> To his son G. residing at Orléans, P. of Besançon sends greetings with paternal zeal. It is written, "He also that is slothful in his work is brother to him that is a great waster." I have recently discovered that you live dissolutely and slothfully, preferring license to restraint and play to work and strumming a guitar while the others are at their studies, whence it happens that you have read but one volume of law while your more industrious companions have read several. Wherefore I have decided to exhort you herewith to repent utterly of your dissolute and careless ways, that you may no longer be called a waster and your shame may be turned to good repute.[5]

We have no idea whether the letter convinced the student to change his ways.

Medieval universities shared in the violent atmosphere of the age. Records from courts of law reveal numerous instances of disturbances at European universities. One German professor was finally dismissed for stabbing one too many of his colleagues in faculty meetings. A student in Bologna was attacked in the classroom by another student armed with a sword. Oxford regulations attempted to dampen the violence by forbidding students to bring weapons to class. Not uncommonly, town and gown struggles (gown refers to the academic robe worn by teachers and students) escalated into bloody riots between townspeople and students (see the box on p. 245).

Despite the violence, universities proved important to medieval civilization, not only for the growth of learning, which, after all, is the main task of the university, but also by providing a mechanism for training the personnel who served as teachers, administrators, lawyers, and doctors in an increasingly specialized society.

A Revival of Classical Antiquity

Another aspect of the intellectual revival of the High Middle Ages was a resurgence of interest in the works of classical antiquity—the works of the Greeks and Romans. In the twelfth century, western Europe was introduced to a large number of Greek scientific and philosophical works, including those of Galen and Hippocrates on medicine, Ptolemy on geography and astronomy, and Euclid on mathematics. Above all, the West now had available the complete works of Aristotle. During the second half of the twelfth century, all of Aristotle's scientific works were translated into Latin, which served as an international language for both speaking and writing in the West. This great influx of Aristotle's works had an overwhelming impact on the West. He came to be viewed as the "master of those who know," the man who seemed to have understood every field of knowledge.

UNIVERSITY STUDENTS AND VIOLENCE AT OXFORD

*M*EDIEVAL UNIVERSITIES shared in the violent atmosphere of their age. Town and gown quarrels often resulted in bloody conflicts, especially during the universities' formative period. This selection is taken from an anonymous description of a student riot at Oxford at the end of the thirteenth century.

A Student Riot at Oxford

They [the townsmen] seized and imprisoned all scholars on whom they could lay hands, invaded their inns [halls of residence], made havoc of their goods and trampled their books under foot. In the face of such provocation the proctors [university officials] sent their assistants about the town, forbidding the students to leave their inns. But all commands and exhortations were in vain. By nine o'clock next morning, bands of scholars were parading the streets in martial array. If the proctors failed to restrain them, the mayor was equally powerless to restrain his townsmen. The great bell of St. Martin's rang out an alarm; oxhorns were sounded in the streets; messengers were sent into the country to collect rustic allies. The clerks [students and teachers], who numbered 3,000 in all, began their attack simultaneously in various quarters. They broke open warehouses in the Spicery, the Cutlery and elsewhere. Armed with bow and arrows, swords and bucklers, slings and stones, they fell upon their opponents. Three they slew, and wounded fifty or more. One band . . . took up a position in High Street between the Churches of St. Mary and All Saints', and attacked the house of a certain Edward Hales. This Hales was a longstanding enemy of the clerks. There were no half measures with him. He seized his crossbow, and from an upper chamber sent an unerring shaft into the eye of the pugnacious rector. The death of their valiant leader caused the clerks to lose heart. They fled, closely pursued by the townsmen and country-folk. Some were struck down in the streets, and others who had taken refuge in the churches were dragged out and driven mercilessly to prison, lashed with thongs and goaded with iron spikes.

Complaints of murder, violence and robbery were lodged straightway with the king by both parties. The townsmen claimed 3,000 pounds' damage. The commissioners, however, appointed to decide the matter, condemned them to pay 200 marks, removed the bailiffs, and banished twelve of the most turbulent citizens from Oxford.

The recovery of Greek scientific and philosophical works was not a simple process, however. Little knowledge of Greek had survived in Europe. Thus it was through the Muslim world that the West recovered Aristotle and other Greek works. The translation of Greek works into Arabic had formed but one aspect of a brilliant Muslim civilization. In the twelfth century, these writings were now translated from Arabic into Latin, making them available to the West. Wherever Muslim and Christian cultures met—in the Norman kingdom of Sicily, southern Italy, and above all Spain—the work of translation was carried on by both Arabic and Jewish scholars.

The Islamic world had more to contribute intellectually to the West than translations, however. Scientific work in the ninth and tenth centuries had enabled it to forge far ahead of the Western world, and in the twelfth and thirteenth centuries, Arabic works on physics, mathematics, medicine, and optics became available to the West in Latin translations. Adelard of Bath (1090–1150) was one source of these works. Having traveled throughout the Mediterranean region, he later translated an Arabic version of Euclid's *Elements* (see Chapter 4) into Latin, as well as the mathematical works of al-Khwarizmi (see Chapter 8). Adelard also introduced to Europeans the astrolabe, an Arabic astronomical instrument that proved valuable to sailors.

When Aristotle's works arrived in the West in the second half of the twelfth century, they were accompanied by commentaries written by outstanding Arabic and Jewish philosophers. One example was Ibn-Rushd, or Averroës (1126–1198), who lived in Córdoba and composed a systematic commentary on virtually all of Aristotle's surviving works. The works of Arabic philosophers proved highly influential to Western intellectuals.

The West was also receptive to the works of Jewish scholars living in the Islamic world. Perhaps the best known is Moses ben Maimon, or Maimonides (1135–1204), who also lived in Córdoba. He was conversant with Greek and Arabic traditions and interested in the problem of reconciling faith and reason. In his *Guide for the Perplexed*, written in Arabic, Maimonides attempted to harmonize the rational and natural philosophy of Aristotle with the basic truths of Judaism. Although it was attacked by some Orthodox Jews, Western scholars in the thirteenth century paid close attention to it after its translation into Latin.

The Development of Scholasticism

Christianity's importance in medieval society probably made inevitable theology's central role in the European intellectual world. Whether in monastic or cathedral schools or the new universities, theology, the formal study of religion, reigned as "queen of the sciences."

Beginning in the eleventh century, the effort to apply reason or logical analysis to the church's basic theological doctrines had a significant impact on the study of theology. The word *scholasticism* is used to refer to the philosophical and theological system of the medieval schools. A primary preoccupation of scholasticism was the attempt to reconcile faith and reason, to demonstrate that what was accepted on faith was in harmony with what could be learned by reason. The scholastic method came to be the basic instructional mode of the universities. In essence, this method consisted of posing a question, presenting contradictory authorities on that question, and then arriving at conclusions. It was a system that demanded rigorous analytical thought. Although scholasticism reached its high point in the thirteenth century, it had its beginnings in the theological world of the eleventh and twelfth centuries, especially in the work of Abelard.

Abelard   Peter Abelard (1079–1142) studied in northern France but scorned his teachers as insignificant and took up the teaching of theology in Paris. Possessed of a colorful personality, Abelard was a very popular teacher who attracted many students. A man with a strong ego, he became known for the zest with which he entered into arguments with fellow students as well as for his affair with his student Heloise. Heloise bore a child by Abelard and secretly married him. But her uncle, who had hired Abelard as a tutor for his niece, sought revenge, as Abelard related in an account of his life titled *History of My Misfortunes:* "One night they took from me a most cruel and shameful vengeance, as I was resting and sleeping in the inner room of my lodging. . . . For they cut off those parts of my body, by which I had committed the deed which sorrowed them."[6]

Above all others, Abelard was responsible for furthering the new scholastic approach to theology. In his most famous work, *Sic et Non* (*Yes and No*), he listed passages from Scripture and the church fathers that stood in direct contradiction to one another and stressed the need to use logic or dialectical reasoning to reconcile the apparent differences systematically. He summed up his method thus: "By doubting we come to inquiry, through inquiry to the truth."

The Problem of Universals   Beginning in the twelfth century, a major controversy—the problem of universals—began to occupy many theologians. The basic issue involved the nature of reality itself: What constitutes what is real? Theologians were divided into two major schools of thought reflecting the earlier traditions of Greek thought, especially the divergent schools of Plato and Aristotle.

Following Plato, the scholastic **realists** took the position that the individual objects that we perceive with our senses, such as trees, are not real but merely manifestations of universal ideas ("treeness") that exist in the mind of God. All knowledge, then, is based on the ideas implanted in human reason by the creator. To the realists, truth can be discovered only by contemplating universals. The **nominalists** were adherents of Aristotle's ideas and believed that only individual objects are real. In their view, universal ideas and concepts were simply names (Latin *nomina*, hence *nominalism*). Truth could be discovered only by examining individual objects.

By the thirteenth century, the scholastics were confronting a new challenge—how to harmonize Christian revelation with the work of Aristotle. The great influx of Aristotle's works into the West in the High Middle Ages threw many theologians into consternation. Aristotle was so highly regarded that he was called "the philosopher," yet he had arrived at his conclusions by rational thought, not revelation, and some of his doctrines, such as the mortality of the individual soul, contradicted the teachings of the church. The most famous attempt to reconcile Aristotle and the doctrines of Christianity was that of Saint Thomas Aquinas.

Aquinas   Thomas Aquinas (1225–1274) studied theology at Cologne and Paris and taught at both Naples and Paris, and it was at the latter that he worked on his famous *Summa Theologica* (*A Summa of Theology*—a summa was a compendium of knowledge that attempted to bring together all the received learning of the preceding centuries on a given subject into a single whole). Aquinas' masterpiece was organized according to the dialectical method of the scholastics. Aquinas first posed a question, cited sources that offered opposing opinions on the question, and then resolved them by arriving at his own conclusions. In this fashion, Aquinas raised and discussed some six hundred articles or issues (see the box on p. 247).

Aquinas' reputation derives from his masterful attempt to reconcile faith and reason. He took it for granted that there were truths derived by reason and truths derived by faith. He was certain, however, that the two truths could not be in conflict with each other:

> The light of faith that is freely infused into us does not destroy the light of natural knowledge [reason] implanted in us naturally. For although the natural light of the human mind is insufficient to show us these things made manifest by faith, it is nevertheless impossible that these things which the divine principle gives us by faith are contrary to these implanted in us by nature [reason]. Indeed, were that the case, one or the other would have to be false, and since both are given to us by God, God would have to be the author of untruth, which is impossible. . . . It is impossible that those things which are of philosophy can be contrary to those things which are of faith.[7]

The natural mind, unaided by faith, could arrive at truths concerning the physical universe. Without God's help, however, unaided reason alone could not grasp spiritual truths, such as the Trinity (the belief that God, Jesus, and the Holy Spirit are three manifestations of the same unique deity) or the Incarnation (the belief that Jesus in his lifetime was God in human form).

The Revival of Roman Law

A systematic approach to knowledge was also expressed in the area of law. Of special importance was the rediscovery of the great legal work of Justinian, the *Corpus Iuris Civilis*, known to the medieval West before 1100 only at second hand. Initially, teachers of law, such as Irnerius of Bologna, were content merely to explain the meaning of Roman legal terms to their students. Gradually, they became more sophisticated so that by the mid-twelfth century, "doctors of law" had developed commentaries and

THE DIALECTICAL METHOD OF THOMAS AQUINAS

IN HIS MASTERPIECE of scholastic theology, the *Summa Theologica,* Thomas Aquinas attempted to resolve some six hundred theological issues by the dialectical method. This method consisted of posing a question, stating the objections to it, and then replying to the objections. This selection from the *Summa Theologica* focuses on Article 4 of Question 92, "The Production of the Woman."

Thomas Aquinas, *Summa Theologica*

Question 92: The Production of the Woman (in Four Articles)

We must next consider the production of the woman. Under this head there are four points of inquiry: (1) Whether the woman should have been made in that first production of things? (2) Whether the woman should have been made from man? (3) Whether of man's rib? (4) Whether the woman was made immediately by God? . . .

Fourth Article: Whether the Woman Was Formed Immediately by God?

We proceed thus to the Fourth Article:—

Objection 1. It would seem that the woman was not formed immediately by God. For no individual is produced immediately by God from another individual alike in species. But the woman was made from a man who is of the same species. Therefore she was not made immediately by God.

Objection 2. Further, Augustine says that corporeal things are governed by God through the angels. But the woman's body was formed from corporeal matter. Therefore it was made through the ministry of the angels, and not immediately by God.

Objection 3. Further, those things which preexist in creatures as to their causal virtues are produced by the power of some creature, and not immediately by God. But the woman's body was produced in its causal virtues among the first created works, as Augustine says. Therefore it was not produced immediately by God.

On the contrary, Augustine says, in the same work: *God alone, to Whom all nature owes its existence, could form or build up the woman from the man's rib.*

I answer that, as was said above, the natural generation of every species is from some determinate matter. Now the matter whence man is naturally begotten is the human semen of man or woman. Wherefore from any other matter an individual of the human species cannot naturally be generated. Now God alone, the Author of nature, can produce an effect into existence outside the ordinary course of nature. Therefore God alone could produce either a man from the slime of the earth, or a woman from the rib of a man.

Reply Objection 1. This argument is verified when an individual is begotten, by natural generation, from that which is like it in the same species.

Reply Objection 2. As Augustine says, we do not know whether the angels were employed by God in the formation of the woman; but it is certain that, as the body of man was not formed by the angels from the slime of the earth, so neither was the body of the woman formed by them from the man's rib.

Reply Objection 3. As Augustine says, The first creation of things did not demand that woman should be made thus; it made it possible for her to be thus made. Therefore the body of the woman did indeed preexist in these causal virtues, in the things first created; not as regards active potentiality, but as regards a potentiality passive in relation to the active potentiality of the Creator.

---

systematic treatises on the legal texts. Italian cities, above all Pavia and Bologna, became prominent centers for the study of Roman law. By the thirteenth century, Italian jurists were systematizing the various professional commentaries on Roman law into a single commentary known as the ordinary gloss. Study of Roman law at the universities came to consist of learning the text of the law along with this gloss.

This revival of Roman law occurred in a world dominated by a body of law quite different from that of the Romans. European law comprised a hodgepodge of Germanic law codes, feudal customs, and urban regulations. The desire to know a more orderly world, already evident in the study of theology, perhaps made it inevitable that Europeans would enthusiastically welcome the more systematic approach of Roman law.

The training of students in Roman law at medieval universities led to further application of its principles as these students became judges, lawyers, scribes, and councilors for the towns and monarchies of western Europe. By the beginning of the thirteenth century, the old system of the ordeal was being replaced by a rational, decision-making process based on the systematic collection and analysis of evidence, a clear indication of the impact of Roman law on the European legal system.

Literature in the High Middle Ages

Latin was the universal language of medieval civilization. Used in the church and schools, it enabled learned people to communicate anywhere in Europe. The intellectual revival of the High Middle Ages included an outpouring of

Latin literature. While Latin continued to be used for literary purposes, by the twelfth century much of the creative literature was being written in the **vernacular** (the local language, such as Spanish, French, English, or German). Throughout the Middle Ages, there had been a popular vernacular literature, especially manifest in the Germanic, Celtic, Old Icelandic, and Slavonic sagas. But a new market for vernacular literature appeared in the twelfth century when educated laypeople at courts and in the new urban society sought fresh avenues of entertainment.

Troubadour Poetry   Perhaps the most popular vernacular literature of the twelfth century was *troubadour poetry,* chiefly the product of nobles and knights. This poetry focused on themes of courtly love, the love of a knight for a lady, generally a married noble lady, who inspires him to become a braver knight and a better poet. A good example is found in the laments of a crusading noble Jaufré Rudel, who cherished a dream lady from afar whom he said he would always love but feared he would never meet:

> Most sad, most joyous shall I go away,
> Let me have seen her for a single day,
>   My love afar,
> I shall not see her, for her land and mine
> Are sundered, and the ways are hard to find,
> So many ways, and I shall lose my way,
>   So wills it God.
>
> Yet shall I know no other love but hers,
> And if not hers, no other love at all.
>   She has surpassed all.
> So fair she is, so noble, I would be
>   A captive with the hosts of paynimrie [the Muslims]
> In a far land, if so be upon me
>   Her eyes might fall.[8]

Although it originated in southern France, troubadour poetry also spread to northern France, Italy, and Germany.

The Heroic Epic   Another type of vernacular literature was the *chanson de geste,* or heroic epic. The earliest and finest example is the *Chanson de Roland* (*The Song of Roland*), which appeared around 1100 and was written in a dialect of French, a Romance language derived from Latin (see the box on p. 249). The *chansons de geste* were written for a male-dominated society. The chief events described in these poems, as in *The Song of Roland,* are battles and political contests. Their world is one of combat in which knights fight courageously for their kings and lords. Women play little or no role in this literary genre.

The Courtly Romance   Although *chansons de geste* were still written in the twelfth century, a different kind of long poem, the *courtly romance,* also became popular. It was composed in rhymed couplets and dwelt on romantic subjects: brave knights, virtuous ladies, evil magicians, bewitched palaces, fairies, talking animals, and strange forests. The story of King Arthur, the legendary king of the fifth-century Britons, became a popular subject for the courtly romance. The best versions of the Arthurian legends survive in the works of Chrétien de Troyes, a French writer in the second half of the twelfth century, whose courtly romances were viewed by contemporaries as the works of a master storyteller.

Romanesque Architecture: "A White Mantle of Churches"

The eleventh and twelfth centuries witnessed an explosion of building, both private and public. The construction of castles and churches absorbed most of the surplus resources of medieval society and at the same time reflected its basic preoccupations, warfare and God. The churches were by far the most conspicuous of the public buildings. As a chronicler of the eleventh century commented:

> [After the] year of the millennium, which is now about three years past, people all over the world, but especially in Italy and France, began to rebuild their churches. Although most of them were well built and in little need of alterations, Christian

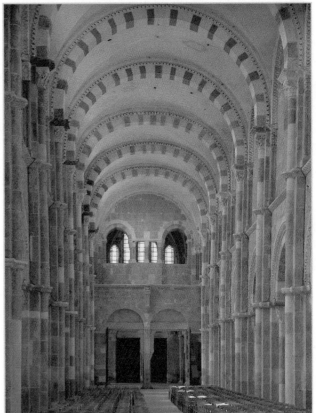

Barrel Vaulting. The eleventh and twelfth centuries witnessed an enormous amount of church construction. Utilizing the basilica shape, master builders replaced flat wooden roofs with long, round stone vaults known as barrel vaults. As this illustration of a Romanesque church in Vienne, France, indicates, the barrel vault limited the size of a church and left little room for windows.

THE SONG OF ROLAND

T̶HE SONG OF ROLAND is one of the best examples of the medieval *chanson de geste,* or heroic epic. Inspired by a historical event, it recounts the ambush of the rear guard of Charlemagne's Frankish army in the Pyrenees. It was written three hundred years after the event it supposedly describes, however, and reveals more about the eleventh century than about the age of Charlemagne. Christian Basques who ambushed Charlemagne's army have been transformed into Muslims, the Frankish soldiers into French knights. This selection describes the death of Roland, Charlemagne's nephew, who was the commander of the ill-fated rear guard.

 The Song of Roland

Now Roland feels that he is at death's door;
Out of his ears the brain is running forth.
Now for his peers he prays God call them all,
And for himself St. Gabriel's aid implores;
Then in each hand he takes, lest shame befall,
His Olifant [horn] and Durendal his sword.
Far as a quarrel flies from a cross-bow drawn,
Toward land of Spain he goes, to a wide lawn,
And climbs a mound where grows a fair tree tall,
And marble stones beneath it stand by four.

Face downward there on the green grass he falls,
And swoons away, for he is at death's door....
Now Roland feels death press upon him hard;
It's creeping down from his head to his heart.
Under a pine-tree he hastens him apart,
There stretches him face down on the green grass,
And lays beneath him his sword and Olifant.
He's turned his head to where the Paynims [Muslims] are,
And this he does for the French and for Charles,
Since fain is he that they should say, brave heart,
That he has died a conqueror at last.
He beats his breast full many a time and fast,
Gives, with his glove, his sins into God's charge.

Now Roland feels his time is at an end;
On the steep hill-side, toward Spain he's turned his head,
And with one hand he beats upon his breast;
Saying: "Mea culpa; Thy mercy, Lord, I beg
For all the sins, both the great and the less,
That e'er I did since first I drew my breath
Unto this day when I'm struck down by death."
His right-hand glove he unto God extends;
Angels from Heaven now to his side descend.

---

nations were rivaling each other to have the most beautiful edifices. One might say the world was shaking herself, throwing off her old garments, and robing herself with a white mantle of churches. Then nearly all the cathedrals, the monasteries dedicated to different saints, and even the small village chapels were reconstructed more beautifully by the faithful.[9]

Hundreds of new cathedrals and abbey and pilgrimage churches, as well as thousands of parish churches in rural villages, were built in the eleventh and twelfth centuries. This building spree reflected both the revived religious culture and the increased wealth of the period produced by agriculture, trade, and the growth of cities.

The cathedrals of the eleventh and twelfth centuries were built in a truly international style, the **Romanesque.** The construction of churches required the services of professional master builders, whose employment throughout Europe guaranteed an international unity in basic features. Prominent examples of Romanesque churches can be found in Germany, France, and Spain.

Romanesque churches were normally built in the rectangular basilica shape used in the construction of churches in the Late Roman Empire. Romanesque builders made a significant innovation by replacing the earlier flat wooden ceiling with a long, round stone vault called a barrel vault or a cross vault where two barrel vaults intersected (a vault is simply a curved roof made of masonry). The latter was

used when a transept was added to create a church plan in the shape of a cross. Although barrel and cross vaults were technically difficult to construct, they were considered aesthetically pleasing and technically proficient and had fine acoustics.

Because stone vaults were extremely heavy, Romanesque churches required massive pillars and walls to hold them up. This left little space for windows, making Romanesque churches notoriously dark on the inside. Their massive walls and pillars gave the churches a sense of solidity and almost the impression of a fortress. Indeed, massive walls and slit windows were also characteristic of the castle architecture of the period.

The Gothic Cathedral

Begun in the twelfth century and brought to perfection in the thirteenth, the **Gothic** cathedral remains one of the greatest artistic triumphs of the High Middle Ages. Soaring skyward, almost as if to reach heaven, it was a fitting symbol for medieval people's preoccupation with God.

Two fundamental innovations of the twelfth century made Gothic cathedrals possible. The combination of ribbed vaults and pointed arches replaced the barrel vault of Romanesque churches and enabled builders to make Gothic churches higher than their Romanesque counterparts.

The Gothic Cathedral. The Gothic cathedral was one of the great artistic triumphs of the High Middle Ages. Shown here is the cathedral of Notre-Dame in Paris. Begun in 1163, it was not completed until the beginning of the fourteenth century.

Interior of a Gothic Cathedral. The use of ribbed vaults and pointed arches gave the Gothic cathedral a feeling of upward movement. Moreover, due to the flying buttress, the cathedral could have thin walls with stained-glass windows that filled the interior with light. The flying buttress was a heavy pier of stone built onto the outside of the walls to bear the brunt of the weight of the church's vaulted ceiling. The flying buttresses are visible at the left in the illustration of the cathedral of Notre-Dame.

The use of pointed arches and ribbed vaults created an impression of upward movement, a sense of weightless upward thrust that implied the energy of God. Another technical innovation, the flying buttress, a heavy arched pier of stone built onto the outside of the walls, made it possible to distribute the weight of the church's vaulted ceilings outward and downward and thereby eliminate the heavy walls used in Romanesque churches to hold the weight of the massive barrel vaults. Thus Gothic cathedrals could be built with thin walls that were filled with magnificent stained-glass windows, which created a play of light inside that varied with the sun at different times of the day.

Medieval craftspeople of the twelfth and thirteenth centuries perfected the art of stained glass. Small pieces of glass were stained in glowing colors like jewels. The preoccupation with colored light in Gothic cathedrals was not accidental but was executed by people inspired by the belief that natural light was a symbol of the divine light of God. Light is invisible but enables people to see; so too is God invisible, but the existence of God allows the world of matter to be. Those impressed by the mystical significance of light were also impressed by the mystical significance of number. The proportions of Gothic cathedrals were based on mathematical ratios that their builders believed were derived from the ancient Greek school of Pythagoras and expressed the intrinsic harmony of the world as established by its creator.

The first fully Gothic church was the abbey church of Saint-Denis near Paris, inspired by Suger, the famous abbot of the monastery from 1122 to 1151, and built between 1140 and 1150. Although the Gothic style was the product of northern France, by the mid-thirteenth century French Gothic architecture had spread to England, Spain, Germany—indeed, to virtually all of Europe. This French Gothic style was seen most brilliantly in cathedrals in Paris (Notre-Dame), Reims, Amiens, and Chartres.

A Gothic cathedral was the work of an entire community. All classes contributed to its construction. Money was raised from wealthy townspeople who had profited from the new trade and industries as well as from kings and nobles. Master masons who were both architects and engineers designed the cathedrals. They drew up the plans and supervised the work of construction. Stonemasons and other craftspeople were paid a daily wage and provided the skilled labor to build the cathedrals. Indeed, these buildings were the first monumental structures of consequence built by free, salaried labor.

The building of cathedrals often became highly competitive as communities vied with one another to build the

Chartres Cathedral: Stained-Glass Window. The stained glass of Gothic cathedrals is remarkable for the beauty and variety of its colors. Stained-glass windows depicted a remarkable variety of scenes. The windows of Chartres cathedral, for example, present the saints, views of the everyday activities of ordinary men and women, and, as in this panel, scenes from the life of Jesus.

highest tower, a rivalry that sometimes ended in disaster. The cathedral of Beauvais in northern France collapsed in 1284 after reaching the height of 157 feet. Gothic cathedrals also depended on a community's faith. After all, it often took two or more generations to complete a cathedral, and the first generation of builders must have begun with the knowledge that they would not live to see the completed project. Most important, a Gothic cathedral symbolized the chief preoccupation of a medieval Christian community, its dedication to a spiritual ideal. As we have observed before, the largest buildings of an era reflect the values of its society. The Gothic cathedral, with its towers soaring toward heaven, gave witness to an age when a spiritual impulse still underlay most of existence.

CONCLUSION

*T*HE NEW EUROPEAN CIVILIZATION that had emerged in the Early Middle Ages began to flourish in the High Middle Ages. Better growing conditions, an expansion of cultivated land, and technological and agricultural changes combined to enable Europe's food supply to increase significantly after 1000. This increase helped sustain a dramatic rise in population that was physically apparent in the expansion of towns and cities.

The High Middle Ages witnessed economic and social changes that some historians believe set European civilization on a path that lasted until the eighteenth century. The revival of trade, the expansion of towns and cities, and the development of a money economy did not mean the end of a predominantly rural European society, but they did open the door to new ways to make a living and new opportunities for people to expand and enrich their lives. Eventually, they created the foundations for the development of a mostly urban industrial society.

The High Middle Ages also gave birth to a cultural revival. This cultural revival led to a rediscovery of important aspects of the classical heritage, to new centers of learning in the universities, to the use of reason to systematize the study of theology and law, to the development of a vernacular literature that appealed both to knights and to townspeople, and to a dramatic increase in the number and size of churches.

NOTES

1. Quoted in Joseph Gies and Frances Gies, *Life in a Medieval Castle* (New York, 1974), p. 175.
2. Quoted in Robert Delort, *Life in the Middle Ages,* trans. Robert Allen (New York, 1972), p. 218.
3. Quoted in Jean Gimpel, *The Medieval Machine* (Harmondsworth, England, 1976), p. 92.
4. Quoted in Charles H. Haskins, *The Rise of Universities* (Ithaca, N.Y., 1957), pp. 77–78.
5. Ibid., pp. 79–80.
6. Quoted in David Herlihy, *Medieval Culture and Society* (New York, 1968), p. 204.
7. Quoted in John H. Mundy, *Europe in the High Middle Ages, 1150–1309* (New York, 1973), pp. 474–475.
8. Helen Waddell, *The Wandering Scholars* (New York, 1961), p. 222.
9. Quoted in John W. Baldwin, *The Scholastic Culture of the Middle Ages, 1000–1300* (Lexington, Mass., 1971), p. 15.

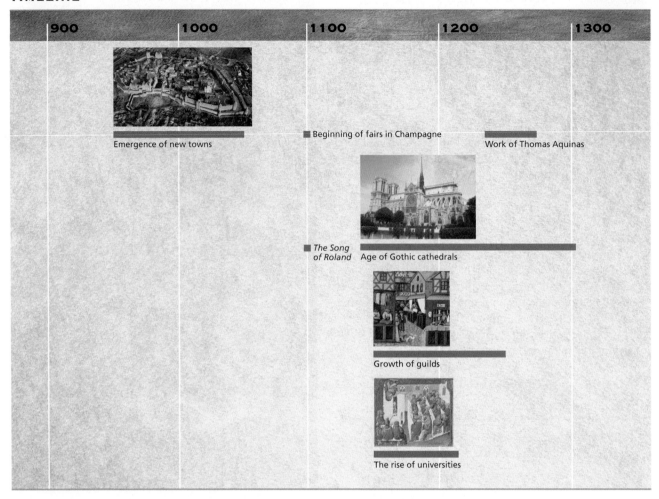

| 900 | 1000 | 1100 | 1200 | 1300 |

Emergence of new towns

■ Beginning of fairs in Champagne

Work of Thomas Aquinas

■ *The Song of Roland*   Age of Gothic cathedrals

Growth of guilds

The rise of universities

SUGGESTIONS FOR FURTHER READING

For a good introduction to this period, see **W. C. Jordan**, *Europe in the High Middle Ages* (New York, 2003); **J. H. Mundy**, *Europe in the High Middle Ages, 1150–1309*, 3d ed. (New York, 1999); **C. N. L. Brooke**, *Europe in the Central Middle Ages, 962–1154*, rev. ed. (New York, 1988); **M. Barber**, *The Two Cities: Medieval Europe, 1050–1320* (London, 1992); and **R. Bartlett**, *The Making of Europe: Conquest, Colonization, and Cultural Change, 950–1350* (Princeton, N.J., 1993). There is a good collection of essays on various facets of medieval history in **P. Linehan and J. L. Nelson, eds.**, *The Medieval World* (London, 2001). On peasant life, see **R. Fossier**, *Peasant Life in the Medieval West* (New York, 1988). Technological changes are discussed in **J. Gimpel**, *The Medieval Machine* (Harmondsworth, England, 1976), and **J. Langdon**, *Horses, Oxen, and Technological Innovation* (New York, 1986).

Works on the function and activities of the nobility in the High Middle Ages include **S. Reynolds**, *Kingdoms and Communities in Western Europe, 900–1300* (Oxford, 1984); **R. W. Barber**, *The Knight and Chivalry* (Rochester, N.Y., 1995); and the classic work by **M. Bloch**, *Feudal Society* (London, 1961). Various aspects of the social history of the nobility can be found in **G. Duby**, *The Knight, the Lady, and the Priest* (London, 1984), on noble marriages; **R. Barber and J. Barker**, *Tournaments: Jousts, Chivalry, and Pageants in the Middle Ages* (New York, 1989), on tournaments; **N. J. G. Pounds**, *The Medieval Castle in*

England and Wales: A Social and Political History (New York, 1990); and **C. B. Bouchard**, *Life and Society in the West: Antiquity and the Middle Ages* (San Diego, Calif., 1988), ch. 6. On women, see **R. T. More-wedge, ed.**, *The Role of Women in the Middle Ages* (Albany, N.Y., 1975), and **S. M. Stuard, ed.**, *Women in Medieval Society* (Philadelphia, 1976).

On the revival of trade, see **R. S. Lopez**, *The Commercial Revolution of the Middle Ages, 950–1350* (Englewood Cliffs, N.J., 1971). Urban history is covered in **D. Nicholas**, *The Growth of the Medieval City: From Late Antiquity to the Early Fourteenth Century* (New York, 1997), and the classic work of **H. Pirenne**, *Medieval Cities* (Princeton, N.J., 1969). For a good collection of essays on urban culture, see **B. Hanawalt and K. I. Reyerson, eds.**, *City and Spectacle in Medieval Europe* (Minneapolis, Minn., 1994). On women in the cities, see **B. Hanawalt, ed.**, *Women and Work in Preindustrial Europe* (Bloomington, Ind., 1986).

A general work on medieval intellectual life is **M. L. Colish**, *Medieval Foundations of the Western Intellectual Tradition, 400–1400* (New Haven, Conn., 1997). See also the classic study by **F. Artz**, *The Mind of the Middle Ages*, 3d ed. (Chicago, 1980). The development of universities is covered in **S. Ferruolo**, *The Origin of the University* (Stanford, Calif., 1985); **A. B. Cobban**, *The Medieval Universities* (London, 1975); and the brief older work by **C. H. Haskins**, *The Rise of Universities* (Ithaca, N.Y., 1957). Various aspects of the intellectual and literary developments of the High Middle Ages are examined in **J. W. Baldwin**, *The Scholastic Culture of the Middle Ages, 1000–1300* (Lexington, Mass., 1971); **J. Marenbon**, *The Philosophy of Peter Abelard* (New York, 1997); and **H. Waddell**, *The Wandering Scholars* (New York, 1961). A good biography of Thomas Aquinas is **J. Weisheipl**, *Friar Thomas d'Aquino: His Life, His Thought and Work* (New York, 1974).

For a good introduction to the art and architecture of the Middle Ages, see **A. Shaver-Crandell**, *The Middle Ages,* in the Cambridge Introduction to Art Series (Cambridge, 1982). A good introduction to Romanesque style is **A. Petzold**, *Romanesque Art* (New York, 1995). On the Gothic movement, see **M. Camille**, *Gothic Art: Glorious Visions* (New York, 1996). Good books on the construction of Gothic cathedrals are **J. Gimpel**, *The Cathedral Builders* (New York, 1961), and **A. Erlande-Brandenburg**, *Cathedrals and Castles: Building in the Middle Ages* (New York, 1995).

History ⧖ Now™

Enter *HistoryNow* using the access card that is available for *Western Civilization. HistoryNow* will assist you in understanding the content in this chapter with lesson plans generated for your needs. In addition, you can read the following documents, and many more, online:

Dante, first five cantos of the *Inferno* and Canto 33 of *Paradiso*

Giovanni Boccaccio, Introduction to the *Decameron*

Peter Abelard, *Story of My Misfortunes*

Thomas Aquinas, Part 1, Question 2, Article 3 of
    Summa Theologica

C H A P T E R

10

THE RISE OF KINGDOMS AND THE GROWTH OF CHURCH POWER

CHAPTER OUTLINE AND FOCUS QUESTIONS

The Emergence and Growth of European Kingdoms, 1000–1300

● What steps did the rulers of England and France take during the High Middle Ages to reverse the decentralizing tendencies of fief-holding?

● What were the major developments in Spain, the Holy Roman Empire, and northern and eastern Europe during the High Middle Ages?

The Recovery and Reform of the Catholic Church

● What was at issue in the Investiture Controversy, and what effect did the controversy have on the church and on Germany?

Christianity and Medieval Civilization

● What were the characteristics of the papal monarchy and the new religious orders of the High Middle Ages, and what role did women play in the religious life of the period?

The Crusades

● What were the reasons for the Crusades, and who or what benefited the most from the experience of the Crusades?

CRITICAL THINKING

● Why did centralized kingdoms develop in some parts of Europe and not in others?

A medieval monk and his abbot

akg-images/British Library

THE RECOVERY AND GROWTH of European civilization in the High Middle Ages also affected the state and the church. Both lords and vassals and the Catholic church recovered from the invasions and internal dissension of the Early Middle Ages. Although lords and vassals seemed forever mired in endless petty conflicts, some medieval kings began to exert a centralizing authority and inaugurated the process of developing new kinds of monarchical states. By the thirteenth century, European monarchs were solidifying their governmental institutions in pursuit of greater power.

The recovery of the Catholic church produced a reform movement that led to exalted claims of papal authority and subsequent conflict with state authorities. At the same time, vigorous papal leadership combined with new dimensions of religious life to make the Catholic church a forceful presence in every area of life. The role of the church in the new European civilization was quite evident in the career of a man named Samson, who became abbot, or head, of the great English abbey of Bury St. Edmonds in 1182. According to Jocelyn of Brakeland, a monk who assisted him, Abbot Samson was a devout man who wore "undergarments of horsehair and a horsehair shirt."

He loved virtue and "abhorred liars, drunkards and talkative folk." His primary concern was the spiritual well-being of his monastery, but he spent much of his time working on problems in the world beyond the abbey walls. Since the monastery had fallen into debt under his predecessors, Abbot Samson toiled tirelessly to recoup the abbey's fortunes by carefully supervising its manors. He also rounded up murderers to stand trial in St. Edmunds and provided knights for the king's army. But his actions were not always tolerant or beneficial. He was instrumental in driving the Jews from the town and was not above improving the abbey's possessions at the expense of his neighbors: "He built up the bank of the fish-pond at Babwell so high, for the service of a new mill, that by keeping back the water there is not a man, rich or poor, but has lost his garden and his orchards." The abbot's worldly cares weighed heavily on him, but he had little choice if his abbey were to flourish and fulfill its spiritual and secular functions. But he did have regrets, as he confided to Jocelyn: "If he could have returned to the circumstances he had enjoyed before he became a monk, he would never have become a monk or an abbot."

The Emergence and Growth of European Kingdoms, 1000–1300

The domination of society by the nobility reached its apex in the High Middle Ages. During this time, however, kings began the process of extending their power in more effective ways. Out of this growth in the monarchies would eventually come the European states that dominated much of later European history.

In theory, kings were regarded as the heads of their kingdoms and were expected to lead their vassals and subjects into battle. The king's power, however, was strictly limited. He had to honor the rights and privileges of his vassals, and if he failed to observe his vassals' rights, they could and did rebel. Weak kings were overthrown or, like the later Carolingians, replaced by another ruling dynasty.

However, kings did possess some sources of power that other lords did not. Kings were anointed by holy oil in ceremonies reminiscent of Old Testament precedents; thus their positions seemed sanctioned by divine favor. War and marriage alliances enabled them to increase their power, and their conquests enabled them to reward their followers with grants of land and bind powerful nobles to them. In the High Middle Ages, kings found ways to strengthen governmental institutions and consequently to extend their powers. The revival of commerce, the growth of cities, and the emergence of a money economy eventually enabled monarchs to hire soldiers and officials and to rely less on their vassals.

England in the High Middle Ages

At the beginning of the eleventh century, Anglo-Saxon England had fallen subject to Scandinavian control after a successful invasion by the Danes in 1016. King Canute (1016–1035), however, continued English institutions and laws and even supported the Catholic church. His dynastic line proved unable to maintain itself, and in 1042, the Anglo-Saxon line of kings was restored in the person of Edward the Confessor (1042–1066). After his death, the kingship was taken by Harold Godwinson, who belonged to one of England's greatest noble families.

A cousin of Edward the Confessor, William of Normandy, laid claim to the throne of England, however, and invaded England in the fall of 1066. The forces of Harold Godwinson and Duke William met at Hastings on October 14, 1066. The Saxon infantry was soundly defeated by the heavily armed Norman knights, and William was crowned king of England at Christmas in London.

William of Normandy After his conquest, William (1066–1087) treated all of England as a royal possession. Based on the Domesday Book, which William commissioned in 1086 by sending out royal officials to ascertain who owned or held land in tenancy, modern historians have estimated that the Norman royal family took possession of about one-fifth

© Michael Holford

Norman Conquest of England. The Bayeux tapestry, which consists of woolen embroidery on a linen backing, was made by English needlewomen before 1082 for Bayeux Cathedral. It depicts scenes from the Norman invasion of England. This segment shows the Norman cavalry charging the shield wall of the Saxon infantry during the Battle of Hastings.

of the land in England as the royal demesne (domain). The remaining English land was held by nobles or the church as fiefs of the king; each of these vassals was in turn responsible for supplying a quota of knights for the royal army. The great landed nobles were allowed to divide their lands among their subvassals as they wished. In 1086, however, by the Oath of Salisbury Plain, William required all subvassals to swear loyalty to him as their king and liege lord. Henceforth, all subvassals owed their primary loyalty to the king rather than to their immediate lords.

Thus the Norman conquest of England had brought a dramatic change. In Anglo-Saxon England, the king had held limited lands while great families controlled large stretches of land and acted rather independently of the king. In contrast, the Normans established a hierarchy of nobles holding land as fiefs from the king. William of Normandy had created a strong, centralized monarchy. Gradually, a process of fusion between the victorious Normans and the defeated Anglo-Saxons created a new England. Although the Norman ruling class spoke French, the intermarriage of the Norman-French with the Anglo-Saxon nobility gradually merged Anglo-Saxon and French into a new English language.

William maintained the Anglo-Saxon administrative system in which counties (shires) were divided into hundreds (groups of villages). Within each shire, the sheriff was the chief royal officer responsible for leading the military forces of the county, collecting royal tolls, and presiding over the county court. William retained the office but replaced the Anglo-Saxon sheriffs with Normans. William also more fully developed the system of taxation and royal courts begun by the Anglo-Saxon and Danish kings of the tenth and eleventh centuries.

The Norman conquest of England had repercussions in France as well. Because the new king of England was still the duke of Normandy, he was both a king (of England) and at the same time a vassal to a king (of France), but a vassal who was now far more powerful than his lord. This connection with France kept England heavily involved in Continental affairs throughout the High Middle Ages.

Henry II In the twelfth century, the power of the English monarchy was greatly enlarged during the reign of Henry II (1154–1189), the founder of the Plantagenet dynasty. The new king was particularly successful in developing administrative and legal institutions that strengthened the royal government. First of all, Henry continued the development of the **exchequer,** or permanent royal treasury. Royal officials, known as "barons of the exchequer," received taxes collected by the sheriffs while seated around a table covered by a checkered cloth that served as a counting device. (*Exchequer* is derived from the French word for chessboard.) The barons gave receipts to the sheriffs, while clerks recorded the accounts on sheets of parchment that were then rolled up. These so-called pipe rolls have served as an important source of economic and social information for historians.

Perhaps even more significant than Henry's financial reforms were his efforts to strengthen the royal courts. Henry expanded the number of criminal cases tried in the king's court and also devised ways of taking property cases from local courts to the royal courts. Henry's goals were clear: expanding the jurisdiction of royal courts extended the king's power and, of course, brought revenues into his coffers. Moreover, because the royal courts were now found throughout England, a body of **common law** (law that was common to the whole kingdom) began to replace the local law codes, which varied from place to place.

Henry was less successful at imposing royal control over the church. The king claimed the right to punish clergymen in the royal courts, but Thomas à Becket, archbishop of Canterbury and therefore the highest-ranking English cleric, claimed that only church courts could try clerics. Attempts at compromise failed, and the angry king publicly expressed the desire to be rid of Becket: "Who will free me of this priest?" he screamed. Four knights took the challenge, went to Canterbury, and murdered the archbishop in the cathedral (see the box on p. 257). Faced with public outrage, Henry was forced to allow the right of appeal from English church courts to the papal court.

King John and Magna Carta Many English nobles came to resent the ongoing growth of the king's power and rose in rebellion during the reign of Henry's son, King John (1199–1216). At Runnymede in 1215, John was forced to assent to Magna Carta, the "great charter" of feudal liberties. Much of Magna Carta was aimed at limiting government practices that affected the relations between the king and his vassals on the one hand and between the king and the church on the other (see the box on p. 258).

Magna Carta remains, above all, a feudal document. Feudal custom had always recognized that the relationship between king and vassals was based on mutual rights and obligations. Magna Carta gave written recognition to that fact and was used in subsequent years to underscore the concept that the monarch should be limited rather than absolute.

Edward I and the Emergence of Parliament In the late thirteenth century, a very talented and powerful monarch ascended the throne in the person of Edward I (1272–1307). He began the process of uniting all of the British Isles into a single kingdom. Although Wales was eventually conquered and pacified, his attempt to subdue Scotland failed. Edward managed merely to begin a lengthy conflict between England and Scotland that lasted for centuries.

Edward was successful in reestablishing monarchical rights after a period of baronial control. During his reign, the role of the English Parliament, an institution of great importance in the development of representative government, began to be defined.

Originally, the word *parliament* was applied to meetings of the king's Great Council in which the greater barons and chief prelates of the church met with the king's judges and principal advisers to deal with judicial affairs. But in need of money in 1295, Edward I invited two knights from every county and two residents (known as burgesses) from

MURDER IN THE CATHEDRAL

T HE CONFLICT BETWEEN King Henry II and Thomas à Becket, archbishop of Canterbury, was the most dramatic confrontation between church and state in English medieval history. Although Henry did not order the archbishop's murder, he certainly caused it by his reckless public words expressing his desire to be free of Becket. This excerpt is from a letter by John of Salisbury, who served as secretary to Theobald, archbishop of Canterbury, and his successor, Thomas à Becket. John was present at the murder of the archbishop in 1170.

John of Salisbury to John of Canterbury, Bishop of Poitiers

The martyr [Becket] stood in the cathedral, before Christ's altar, as we have said, ready to suffer; the hour of slaughter was at hand. When he heard that he was sought—heard the knights who had come for him shouting in the throng of clerks and monks "Where is the archbishop?"—he turned to meet them on the steps which he had almost climbed, and said with steady countenance: "Here am I! What do you want?" One of the knight-assassins flung at him in fury: "That you die now! That you should live longer is impossible." No martyr seems ever to have been more steadfast in his agony than he, . . . and thus, steadfast in speech as in spirit, he replied: "And I am prepared to die for my God, to preserve justice and my church's liberty. If you seek my head, I forbid you on behalf of God almighty and on pain of anathema to do any hurt to any other man, monk, clerk or layman, of high or low degree. Do not involve them in the punishment, for they have not been involved in the cause: on my head not on theirs be it if any of them have supported the church in its troubles. I embrace death readily, so long as peace and liberty for the Church follow from the shedding of my blood. . . ." He spoke, and saw that the assassins had drawn their swords; and bowed his head like one in prayer. His last words were "To God and St. Mary and the saints who protect and defend this church, and to the blessed Denis, I commend myself and the church's cause." No one could dwell on what followed without deep sorrow and choking tears. A son's affection forbids me to describe each blow the savage assassins struck, spurning all fear of God, forgetful of all fealty and any human feeling. They defiled the cathedral and the holy season [Christmas] with a bishop's blood and with slaughter; but that was not enough. They sliced off the crown of his head, which had been specially dedicated to God by anointing with holy oil—a fearful thing even to describe; then they used their evil swords, when he was dead, to spill his brain and cruelly scattered it, mixed with blood and bones, over the pavement. . . . Through all the agony the martyr's spirit was unconquered, his steadfastness marvelous to observe; he spoke not a word, uttered no cry, let slip no groan, raised no arm nor garment to protect himself from an assailant, but bent his head, which he had laid bare to their swords with wonderful courage, till all might be fulfilled. Motionless he held it, and when at last he fell his body lay straight; and he moved neither hand nor foot.

---

each city and town to meet with the Great Council to consent to new taxes. This was the first Parliament.

The English Parliament, then, came to be composed of two knights from every county and two burgesses from every town or city, as well as the barons and ecclesiastical lords. Eventually, the barons and church lords formed the House of Lords; the knights and burgesses, the House of Commons. The Parliaments of Edward I granted taxes, discussed politics, passed laws, and handled judicial business. Although not yet the important body it would eventually become, the English Parliament had clearly emerged as an institution by the end of the thirteenth century. The law of the realm was beginning to be determined not by the king alone but by the king in consultation with representatives of various groups that constituted the community. By the beginning of the fourteenth century, England had begun to develop a unique system of national monarchy.

The Growth of the French Kingdom

The Capetian dynasty of French kings had emerged at the end of the tenth century. Although they bore the title of king, the Capetians had little real power. They controlled as the royal domain (the lands of the king) only the lands around Paris known as the Île-de-France. As kings of France, the Capetians were formally the overlords of the great lords of France, such as the dukes of Normandy, Brittany, Burgundy, and Aquitaine. In reality, however, many of the dukes were considerably more powerful than the Capetian kings. It would take the Capetian dynasty hundreds of years to create a truly centralized monarchical authority in France.

The Conquests of Philip II The reign of King Philip II Augustus (1180–1223) was an important turning point. He perceived that the power of the French monarch would never be extended until the Plantagenets' power was defeated. After all, Henry II and his sons were not only kings of England but also rulers of the French territories of Normandy, Maine, Anjou, and Aquitaine. Accordingly, Philip II waged war against the Plantagenet rulers of England and was successful in wresting control of Normandy, Maine, Anjou, and Touraine from the English kings (see Map 10.1). Through these conquests, Philip II quadrupled the income of the French monarchy and greatly enlarged its power. To administer justice and collect royal revenues in his new territories, Philip appointed new royal officials, thus inaugurating a French royal bureaucracy.

MAGNA CARTA

AFTER THE DISMAL FAILURE of King John to reconquer Normandy from the French king, some of the English barons rebelled against their king. At Runnymede in 1215, King John agreed to seal Magna Carta, the "great charter" of liberties regulating the relationship between the king and his vassals. What made Magna Carta an important historical document was its more general clauses defining rights and liberties. These were later interpreted in broader terms to make them applicable to all the English people.

Magna Carta

John, by the Grace of God, king of England, lord of Ireland, duke of Normandy and Aquitaine, count of Anjou, to the archbishops, bishops, abbots, earls, barons, justiciars, foresters, sheriffs, reeves, servants, and all bailiffs and his faithful people greeting.

1. In the first place we have granted to God, and by this our present charter confirmed, for us and our heirs forever, that the English church shall be free, and shall hold its rights entire and its liberties uninjured. . . . We have granted moreover to all free men of our kingdom for us and our heirs forever all the liberties written below, to be had and holden by themselves and their heirs from us and our heirs.

2. If any of our earls or barons, or others holding from us in chief by military service shall have died, and when he had died his heir shall be of full age and owe relief, he shall have his inheritance by the ancient relief; that is to say, the heir or heirs of an earl for the whole barony of an earl a hundred pounds; the heir or heirs of a baron for a whole barony a hundred pounds; the heir or heirs of a knight, for a whole knight's fee, a hundred shillings at most; and who owes less let him give less according to the ancient custom of fiefs.

3. If moreover the heir of any one of such shall be under age, and shall be in wardship, when he comes of age he shall have his inheritance without relief and without a fine. . . .

12. No scutage or aid shall be imposed in our kingdom except by the common council of our kingdom, except for the ransoming of our body, for the making of our oldest son a knight, and for once marrying our oldest daughter, and for these purposes it shall be only a reasonable aid. . . .

13. And the city of London shall have all its ancient liberties and free customs, as well by land as by water. Moreover, we will and grant that all other cities and boroughs and villages and ports shall have all their liberties and free customs.

14. And for holding a common council of the kingdom concerning the assessment of an aid otherwise than in the three cases mentioned above, or concerning the assessment of a scutage we shall cause to be summoned the archbishops, bishops, abbots, earls, and greater barons by our letters under seal; and besides we shall cause to be summoned generally, by our sheriffs and bailiffs, all those who hold from us in chief, for a certain day, that is at the end of forty days at least, and for a certain place; and in all the letters of that summons, we will express the cause of the summons, and when the summons has thus been given, the business shall proceed on the appointed day, on the advice of those who shall be present, even if not all of those who were summoned have come. . . .

39. No free man shall be taken or imprisoned or dispossessed, or outlawed, or banished, or in any way destroyed, nor will we go upon him, nor send upon him, except by the legal judgment of his peers or by the law of the land. . . .

60. Moreover, all those customs and franchises mentioned above in which we have conceded in our kingdom, and which are to be fulfilled, as far as pertains to us, in respect to our men; all men of our kingdom, as well as clergy as laymen, shall observe as far as pertains to them, in respect to their men.

The Saintly Louis IX   Capetian rulers after Philip II continued to add lands to the royal domain. Although Philip had used military force, other kings used both purchase and marriage to achieve the same end. Much of the thirteenth century was dominated by Louis IX (1226–1270), one of the most celebrated of the medieval French kings. A deeply religious man, he was later canonized as a saint by the church, an unusual action regardless of the century. Louis was known for his attempts to bring justice to his people and ensure their rights. He sent out royal agents to check on the activities of royal officials after hearing complaints that they were abusing their power. Sharing in the religious sentiments of his age, Louis played a major role in two of the later Crusades (see "The Crusades" later in this chapter). Both were failures, and he met his death during an invasion of North Africa.

Philip IV and the Estates-General   One of Louis's successors, Philip IV the Fair (1285–1314), was particularly effective in strengthening the French monarchy. The machinery of government became even more specialized. French kings going back to the early Capetians had possessed a household staff for running their affairs. In effect, the division and enlargement of this household staff produced the three major branches of royal administration: a council for advice; a chamber of accounts, for finances; and the *Parlement*, or royal court. By the beginning of the fourteenth century, the Capetians had established an efficient royal bureaucracy.

MAP 10.1 **England and France in the High Middle Ages: (*left*) England and Its French Holdings; (*right*) Growth of the French State.** King Philip II Augustus of France greatly expanded the power of the Capetian royal family through his victories over the Plantagenet monarchy of England, which enabled Philip to gain control over much of north-central France. ❓ How could the presence of the English Channel have made it more difficult for England to rule its French possessions? 🖰 **View an animated version of this map or related maps at** http://history.wadsworth.com/spielvogel06/

Louis IX Departs for Tunis. The pious French king Louis IX organized the last two major Crusades of the thirteenth century. Both failed miserably. This illustration shows a robust Louis IX setting out for Tunis in 1270. In truth, the king was so weak that he had to be carried to the ship.

Philip IV also brought a French parliament into being. After he became involved in a struggle with the pope, Philip summoned representatives of the church, nobility, and towns to meet with him in 1302, thereby inaugurating the Estates-General, the first French parliament. The Estates-General came to function as an instrument to bolster the king's power because he could ask representatives of the major French social classes to change the laws or grant new taxes. By the end of the thirteenth century, France was the largest, wealthiest, and best-governed monarchical state in Europe.

Christian Reconquest: The Spanish Kingdoms

Much of Spain had been part of the Islamic world since the eighth century. Muslim Spain had flourished in the Early Middle Ages. Córdoba became a major urban center with a population exceeding 300,000 people. Agriculture prospered, and Spain became known for excellent leather, wool, silk, and paper. Beginning in the tenth century, however, the most noticeable feature of Spanish history was the weakening of Muslim power and the beginning of a Christian reconquest that lasted until the final expulsion of the Muslims at the end of the fifteenth century. The **Reconquista,** as the Spaniards called it, became over a period of time a sacred mission to many of the Christian rulers and inhabitants of the peninsula.

The Reconquest By the eleventh century, a number of small Christian kingdoms—Leon, Castile, Navarre, Aragon, and Barcelona—had become established in northern Spain. Muslim disunity and the support of French nobles, who were eager to battle the Muslim infidel, enabled these Spanish Christian states to take the offensive against the Muslims. Rodrigo Díaz de Vivar, known as El Cid, was the most famous military adventurer of the time. Unlike the Christian warriors of France, El Cid fought under either Christian or Muslim rulers. He carved out his own kingdom of Valencia in 1094 but failed to create a dynasty when it was reconquered by the Muslims after his death.

By the end of the twelfth century, the Christian reconquest of Spain had slowed considerably. The northern half had been consolidated into the Christian kingdoms of Castile, Navarre, Aragon, and Portugal, which had emerged by 1179 as a separate kingdom (see Map 10.2). The southern half of Spain remained under the control of the Muslims.

In the thirteenth century, Christian rulers took the offensive again in the reconquest of Muslim territory. Aragon and Castile had become the two strongest Spanish kingdoms, and Portugal had reached its modern boundaries. All three states made significant conquests of Muslim territory. Castile subdued most of Andalusia in the south, down to the Atlantic and the Mediterranean; at the same time, Aragon conquered Valencia. The crucial battle occurred in 1212 at Las Navas de Tolosa. Alfonso VIII of Castile (1155–1214) had amassed an army of sixty thousand men and crushed the Muslim forces, leading to Christian victories over the next forty years. By the mid-thirteenth century, the Muslims remained only in the kingdom of Granada, along the southeastern edge of the Iberian peninsula.

As the Christian armies moved down the peninsula, rulers followed a policy known as *repartimiento*. Rulers distributed houses, land, and property in the countryside to individuals who had made the conquests and new Christian colonists. The former—consisting of nobles, important churchmen, high-ranking soldiers, and royal officials—often received the best lands. The colonists, some of them ordinary foot soldiers, also received land. Muslims who were not expelled or killed and chose to stay under Christian rule were known as *mudejares*, most of whom continued to work in small industrial enterprises or as farmers.

To encourage other settlers to move into the newly conquered regions, Spanish kings issued written privileges that guaranteed rule in accordance with the law for most of the communities in their kingdoms. These privileges, or *fueros*, stipulated the punishments for crimes committed within community boundaries and the means for resolving civil disputes. They also established regulations for acquiring citizenship in the community, rules for service in the local militia, and laws protecting the rights of women and children living in the towns. Kings of the different regions of Spain freely borrowed from the *fueros* of other regions in an effort to develop attractive customs for their towns so that immigrants would be lured into establishing residency there. By the thirteenth century, kings were increasingly required to swear that they would respect

MAP 10.2 **Christian Reconquests in the Western Mediterranean.** Muslims seized most of Spain in the eighth century, near the end of the period of rapid Islamic expansion. In the eleventh century, small Christian kingdoms in the north began the *Reconquista,* finally conquering the last Moors near the end of the fifteenth century. **?** How can you explain the roughly north-to-south conquest of the Muslim lands in Spain? **View an animated version of this map or related maps at** http://history.wadsworth.com/spielvogel06/

these community customs before they were confirmed in office by assemblies of their leading citizens.

The Spanish kingdoms followed no consistent policy in the treatment of the conquered Muslim population. Muslim farmers continued to work the land but were forced to pay very high rents in Aragon. In Castile, King Alfonso X (1252–1284), who called himself the "King of Three Religions," encouraged the continued development of a cosmopolitan culture shared by Christians, Jews, and Muslims.

The Lands of the Holy Roman Empire: Germany and Italy

The Saxon kings of the tenth century had strengthened their hold over the German kingdom and revived the empire of Charlemagne. A new dynasty, known as the Salian kings, began in 1024 with the election of Conrad II (1024–1039) of Franconia (see Map 10.3). Both Conrad and his successors, Henry III (1039–1056) and Henry IV (1056–1106), managed to create a strong German monarchy and a powerful empire by leading armies into Italy.

The great lords of Germany took advantage of the early death of Henry III and the minority of Henry IV to extend their own power at the expense of the latter. The elective nature of the German monarchy posed a problem for the German kings. Although some dynasties were strong enough for their members to be elected regularly, the great lords who were the electors did at times deliberately choose otherwise. It was to their advantage to select a weak king.

To compensate for their weaknesses, German kings had come to rely on their ability to control the church and select bishops and abbots whom they could then use as royal administrators. But the struggle between church and state during the reign of Henry IV weakened the king's ability to use church officials in this way.

Involvement in Italy   The German kings also tried to bolster their power by using their position as emperors to exploit the resources of Italy. Italy seemed a likely area for intervention because it had no central political authority. While important nobles struggled to dominate northern Italy, central Italy remained under the control of the Papal States. In southern Italy, the Lombard dukes, Muslims, and Byzantines seemed to be in constant conflict.

In the latter half of the eleventh century, a group of Norman adventurers led by Robert Guiscard ("the cunning") conquered much of southern Italy. Robert's brother Roger subdued Muslim Sicily in 1091 after a thirty-year struggle. In 1130, Roger II, the son of Roger of Sicily, was crowned king of Sicily. By the end of the twelfth century, the Norman kingdom was one of the most powerful in Europe as well as one of the most fascinating. A melting pot of Christian, Jewish, and Muslim culture, the state issued its official documents in Latin, Greek, and Arabic.

The Norman kingdom in southern Italy was beyond any claims of the German kings, but the wealthy cities of northern Italy, which by the twelfth century had become virtually independent after overthrowing the rule of their bishops, were a tempting prize to the German kings, who never entirely gave up their dreams of a restored empire. No German dynasty proved more susceptible to the allure of this dream than the Hohenstaufens.

Frederick I   Both Frederick I (1152–1190) and Frederick II (1212–1250) tried to create a foundation for a new kind of empire. Frederick I, known as Barbarossa (Redbeard) to the Italians, was a powerful lord from the Swabian house of Hohenstaufen when he was

MAP 10.3 **The Lands of the Holy Roman Empire in the Twelfth Century.** The Hohenstaufen rulers Frederick I and Frederick II sought to expand the Holy Roman Empire to include all of Italy. Frederick II had only fleeting success: after his death, several independent city-states arose in northern Italy, while at home, German nobles had virtually free reign within their domains. **?** Why did the territorial conquests of the Holy Roman Empire cause alarm in the papacy? View an animated version of this map or related maps at http://history.wadsworth.com/spielvogel06/

THE DEEDS OF EMPEROR FREDERICK II

FREDERICK II, king of Germany and Sicily and would-be ruler of all Italy, was viewed even by contemporaries as one of the most unusual rulers of his time. This account of his "idiosyncrasies" is by Salimbene de Adam, a Franciscan friar whose *Chronicle* is one of the richest sources of information about medieval life in thirteenth-century Italy. He was, however, also known to be notoriously biased against Frederick II.

Salimbene de Adam, *Chronicle*

Note that Frederick almost always enjoyed having discord with the Church and fighting her on all sides, although she had nourished him, defended him, and raised him up. He held the true faith to be worthless. He was a cunning, crafty man, avaricious, lecherous, and malicious, easily given to wrath.

At times, however, Frederick was a worthy man, and when he wished to show his good, courtly side, he could be witty, charming, urbane, and industrious. He was adept at writing and singing, and was well-versed in the art of writing lyrics and songs. He was a handsome, well-formed man of medium height. I myself saw him and, at one time, loved him. For he once wrote Brother Elias, Minister General of the Friars Minor, on my behalf asking him to return me to my father. He also could speak many and various languages. In short, if he had been a good Catholic and had loved God, the Church, and his own soul, he would scarcely have had an equal as an emperor in the world. . . .

Now, it is necessary to speak of Frederick's idiosyncrasies.

His first idiosyncrasy is that he had the thumb of a certain notary cut off because he had written his name in a way different from the way the Emperor desired. . . .

His second idiosyncrasy was that he wanted to discover what language a child would use when he grew up if he had never heard anyone speak. Therefore, he placed some infants in the care of wet-nurses, commanding them to bathe and suckle the children, but by no means ever to speak to or fondle them. For he wanted to discover whether they would speak Hebrew, the first language, or Greek, Latin, Arabic, or the language of their parents. But he labored in vain, because all of the infants died. . . .

Furthermore, Frederick had many other idiosyncrasies: idle curiosity, lack of faith, perversity, tyranny, and accursedness, some of which I have written about in another chronicle. Once, for example, he sealed up a live man in a cask and kept him there until he died in order to prove that the soul totally perished with the body. . . . For Frederick was an Epicurean, and so he and the learned men of his court searched out whatever Biblical passage they could find to prove that there is no life after death. . . .

This sixth example of Frederick's idiosyncrasy and idle curiosity . . . was that he fed two men a fine meal, and he sent one to bed to sleep, the other out hunting. And that evening he had both men disemboweled in his presence, in order to determine which one had digested his food the best. The decisions by his doctors went to the man who had slept after the meal. . . .

I have heard and known many other idiosyncrasies of Frederick, but I keep quiet for the sake of brevity, and because reporting so many of the Emperor's foolish notions is tedious to me.

---

elected king. Previous German kings had focused on building a strong German kingdom, to which Italy might be added as an appendage. Frederick I, however, planned to get his chief revenues from Italy as the center of a "holy empire," as he called it—the Holy Roman Empire. But his attempt to conquer northern Italy ran into severe difficulties. The pope opposed him, fearful that the emperor wanted to incorporate Rome and the Papal States into his empire. The cities of northern Italy, which had become used to their freedom, were also not willing to be Frederick's subjects. An alliance of these northern Italian cities, with the support of the papacy, defeated the forces of the Emperor Frederick at Legnano in 1176.

Later Frederick returned to Italy and arranged a settlement with the northern Italian cities by which they retained their independence in return for an annual payment to the emperor. Frederick now had the financial base he had sought. Moreover, by marrying his son (who became Henry VI, 1190–1197) to the heiress of the Norman kingdom of southern Italy, Frederick seemed to be creating the foundation for making the Holy Roman Empire a reality and for realizing the pope's nightmare: the encirclement of Rome and the Papal States. After Frederick's death, Henry VI's control of Germany and both northern and southern Italy made him the strongest European ruler since Charlemagne. Henry's empire soon collapsed, however, for he died prematurely, leaving as his heir a son only two years old.

Frederick II The son, Frederick II, grew up to become the most brilliant of the Hohenstaufen rulers. King of Sicily in 1198, king of Germany in 1212, and crowned emperor in 1220, Frederick II was a truly remarkable man who awed his contemporaries (see the box above). Frederick was raised in Sicily, with its diverse peoples, languages, and religions. His court there brought together a brilliant array of lawyers, poets, artists, and scientists, and he himself took a deep interest in their work.

Until he was crowned emperor, Frederick spent much time in Germany; once he left in 1220, he rarely returned. He gave the German princes full control of their territories, voluntarily surrendering any real power over Germany in exchange for revenues while he pursued his main goal, the establishment of a strong centralized state in Italy dom-

The Coronation of Frederick II. Shown here is the coronation of Frederick II of Germany as Holy Roman Emperor by Pope Honorius II in Rome on November 22, 1220. The pope agreed to do so after Frederick promised to lead a Crusade to the Holy Land, a promise that he took years to fulfill. This scene is taken from a fifteenth-century French manuscript on the monarchs of Europe.

inated by his kingdom in Sicily. Frederick's major task was to gain control of northern Italy. In reaching to extend his power in Italy, he became involved in a deadly struggle with the popes, who realized that a single ruler of northern and southern Italy meant the end of papal secular power in central Italy. The northern Italian cities were also unwilling to give up their freedom. Frederick waged a bitter struggle in northern Italy, winning many battles but ultimately losing the war.

Frederick's preoccupation with the creation of an empire in Italy left Germany in confusion and chaos until 1273, when the major German princes, serving as electors, chose an insignificant German noble, Rudolf of Habsburg, as the new German king. In choosing a weak king, the princes were ensuring that the German monarchy would remain impotent and incapable of reestablishing a centralized monarchical state. The failure of the Hohenstaufens had led to a situation where his exalted majesty, the German king and Holy Roman Emperor, had no real power over either Germany or Italy. Unlike France and England, neither Germany

nor Italy created a unified national monarchy in the Middle Ages. Both became geographical designations for loose confederations of hundreds of petty independent states under the vague direction of king or emperor. In fact, neither Germany nor Italy would become united until the nineteenth century.

Following the death of Frederick II, Italy fell into political confusion. While the papacy remained in control of much of central Italy, the defeat of imperial power left the cities and towns of northern Italy independent of any other authority. Gradually, the larger ones began to emerge as strong city-states. Florence assumed the leadership of Tuscany, while Milan, under the guidance of the Visconti family, took control of the Lombard region. With its great commercial wealth, the republic of Venice dominated the northeastern part of the peninsula.

New Kingdoms in Northern and Eastern Europe

The Scandinavian countries of northern Europe had little political organization before 1000, and it was not until the second half of the tenth century and the first half of the eleventh that the three Scandinavian kingdoms—Denmark, Norway, and Sweden (see Map 10.4)—emerged with a noticeable political structure. At the same time, the three kingdoms were converted to Christianity by kings who believed that an organized church was a necessary accompaniment to an organized state. The adoption of Christianity, however, did not eliminate the warlike tendencies of the Scandinavians. Not only did the three kingdoms fight each other in the eleventh and twelfth centuries, but rival families were in regular conflict over the throne in each state. This period also witnessed the growth of a powerful noble landowning class.

To the south, in eastern Europe, Hungary, which had been a Christian state since 1000, remained relatively stable throughout the High Middle Ages, but the history of Poland and Russia was more turbulent. In the thirteenth century, eastern Europe was beset by two groups of invaders, the Teutonic Knights from the west and the Mongols from the east.

In the eleventh century, a Polish kingdom existed as a separate state but with no natural frontiers. Consequently, German settlers encroached on its territory on a regular basis, leading to considerable intermarriage between Slavs and Germans. During the thirteenth century, relations between the Germans and the Slavs of eastern Europe worsened due to the aggression of the Teutonic Knights. The Teutonic Knights had been founded near the end of the twelfth century to protect the Christian Holy Land. In the early thirteenth century, however, these Christian knights found greater opportunity to the east of Germany, where they

Settlements of the Teutonic Knights

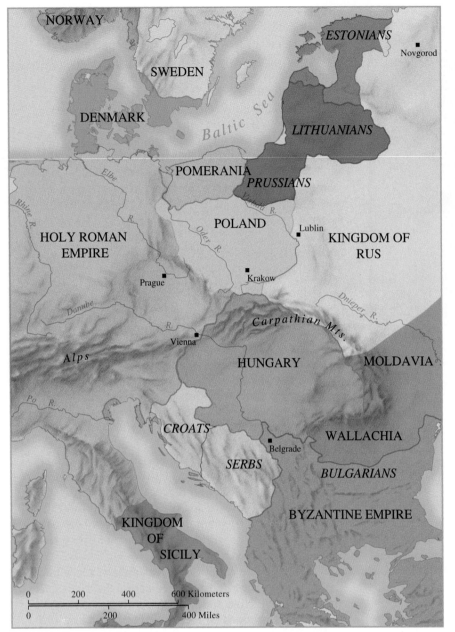

MAP 10.4 **Northern and Eastern Europe.** Acceptance of Christianity gave many northern and eastern European kingdoms greater control over their subjects. Warfare was common in the region: dynastic struggles occurred in Scandinavia, and the Teutonic Knights, based in East Prussia, attacked pagan Slavs. [?] Which areas of northern and eastern Europe had large Slavic populations? (Look back at Map 8.4.)

View an animated version of this map or related maps at http://history.wadsworth.com/spielvogel06/

Temuchin, unified the Mongol tribes and gained the title of Genghis Khan (c. 1162–1227), which means "universal ruler." From that time on, Genghis Khan created a powerful military force and devoted himself to fighting. "Man's highest joy," Genghis Khan remarked, "is in victory: to conquer one's enemies, to pursue them, to deprive them of their possessions, to make their beloved weep, to ride on their horses, and to embrace their wives and daughters."[1] Genghis Khan was succeeded by equally competent sons and grandsons.

The Mongols burst onto the scene in the thirteenth century. They advanced eastward, eventually conquering China and Korea. One of Genghis Khan's grandsons, Khubilai Khan, completed the conquest of China and established a new Chinese dynasty of rulers known as the Yuan. In 1279, Khubilai Khan moved the capital of China northward to Khanbaliq ("city of the khan"), which would later be known by the Chinese name Beijing.

The Mongols also moved westward against the Islamic empire. Persia fell by 1233, and by 1258, they had conquered Baghdad and destroyed the Abbasid caliphate. Beginning in the 1230s, the Mongols had moved into Europe. They conquered Russia, advanced into Poland and Hungary, and destroyed a force of Poles and Teutonic Knights in Silesia in 1241 (see Map 10.5). Europe then seemingly got lucky when the Mongol hordes turned back because of internal fighting; western and southern Europe escaped the wrath of the Mongols. Overall, the Mongols had little impact in Europe, although their occupation of Russia had some residual effects.

attacked the pagan Slavs. East Prussia was given to the military order in 1226, and five years later, the knights moved beyond the Vistula River, where they waged war against the Slavs for another thirty years. By the end of the thirteenth century, Prussia had become German and Christian as the pagan Slavs were forced to convert.

Central and eastern Europe had periodically been subject to invasions from fierce Asiatic nomads, such as the Huns, Avars, Bulgars, and Magyars. In the thirteenth century, the Mongols exploded onto the scene, causing far more disruption than earlier invaders.

The Mongol Empire

The Mongols rose to power in Asia with stunning speed. They were a pastoral people in the region of modern-day Mongolia organized loosely into clans and tribes, often warring with each other. This changed when one leader,

The Development of Russia

The Kievan Rus state, which had become formally Christian in 987, prospered considerably afterward, reaching its high point in the first half of the eleventh century. Kievan society was dominated by a noble class of landowners

MAP 10.5 **The Mongol Empire.** Beginning with the exploits of Genghis Khan, the Mongols used unorthodox but effective military tactics to establish an empire that stretched from Russia to China and included India and South Asia. The empire was divided into khanates. The Golden Horde, the khanate in Russia, was eventually overwhelmed by Moscow princes who went on to establish the Russian state. **?** Why would it be difficult for one khan to effectively rule the entire Mongol Empire?

View an animated version of this map or related maps at http://history.wadsworth.com/spielvogel06/

known as the **boyars.** Kievan merchants maintained regular trade with Scandinavia to the northwest and the Islamic and Byzantine worlds to the south. But destructive civil wars and new invasions by Asiatic nomads caused the principality of Kiev to disintegrate into a number of constituent parts. The sack of Kiev by North Russian princes in 1169 brought an inglorious end to the first Russian state.

The fundamental civilizing and unifying force of early Russia was the Christian church. The Russian church imitated the liturgy and organization of the Byzantine Empire, whose Eastern Orthodox priests had converted the Kievan Rus to Christianity at the end of the tenth century. The Russian church became known for its rigid religious orthodoxy. Although Christianity provided a common bond between Russian and European civilization, Russia's religious development guaranteed an even closer affinity between Russian and Byzantine civilization.

In the thirteenth century, the Mongols conquered Russia and cut it off even more from western Europe. The Mongols were not numerous enough to settle the vast Russian lands but were content to rule directly an area along the lower Volga and north of the Caspian and Black Seas to Kiev and rule indirectly elsewhere. In the latter territories, Russian princes were required to pay tribute to the Mongol overlords.

One Russian prince soon emerged as more visible and powerful than the others. Alexander Nevsky (c. 1220– 1263), prince of Novgorod, defeated a German invading army at Lake Peipus in northwestern Russia in 1242. His cooperation with the Mongols, which included denouncing his own brother and crushing native tax revolts, won him their favor. The khan, the acknowledged leader of the western part of the Mongol Empire, rewarded Alexander Nevsky with the title of grand-prince, enabling his descendants to become the princes of Moscow and eventually leaders of all Russia.

The Recovery and Reform of the Catholic Church

In the Early Middle Ages, the Catholic church had played a leading role in converting and civilizing first the Germanic invaders and later the Vikings and Magyars. Although highly successful, this had not been accomplished without challenges that undermined the spiritual life of the church itself.

The Problems of Decline

Since the eighth century, the popes of the Catholic church had reigned supreme over the affairs of the church. They had also come to exercise control over the territories in central Italy known as the Papal States; this kept popes involved in political matters, often at the expense of their spiritual obligations. At the same time, the church became increasingly entangled in the evolving lord-vassal relationships. High officials of the church, such as bishops and abbots, came to hold their offices as fiefs from nobles. As vassals, they were obliged to carry out the usual duties, including military service. Of course, lords assumed the right to choose their vassals, even when those vassals included bishops and abbots. Because lords often selected their vassals from other noble families for political reasons, these bishops and abbots were often worldly figures who cared little about their spiritual responsibilities.

The monastic ideal had also suffered during the Early Middle Ages. Benedictine monasteries had sometimes been exemplary centers of Christian living and learning, but the invasions of Vikings, Magyars, and Muslims wreaked havoc with many monastic establishments. Discipline declined, and with it the monastic reputation for learning and holiness. At the same time, a growing number of monasteries fell under the control of local lords, as did much of the church. A number of people believed that the time for reform had come.

The Cluniac Reform Movement

Reform of the Catholic church began in Burgundy in eastern France in 910 when Duke William of Aquitaine founded the abbey of Cluny. The monastery began with a renewed dedication to the highest spiritual ideals of the Benedictine rules and was fortunate in having a series of abbots in the tenth century who maintained these ideals. Cluny was deliberately kept independent from any local control. As Duke William stipulated in his original charter, "It has pleased us also to insert in this document that, from this day, those same monks there congregated shall be subject neither to our yoke, nor to that of our relatives, nor to the sway of the royal might, nor to that of any earthly power."[2] The new monastery at Cluny tried to eliminate some of the abuses that had crept into religious communities by stressing the need for work, replacing manual labor with the copying of manuscripts, and demanding more community worship and less private prayer.

The Cluniac reform movement sparked an enthusiastic response, first in France and eventually in all of western and central Europe. Hundreds of new monasteries were founded based on Cluniac ideals, and previously existing monasteries rededicated themselves by adopting the Cluniac program. The movement also began to reach beyond monasticism and into the papacy itself, which was in dire need of help.

Reform of the Papacy

By the eleventh century, a movement for change, led by a series of reforming popes, was sweeping through the Catholic church. One of the reformers' primary goals was to free the church from the interference of lords in the election of church officials. This issue was dramatically taken up by the greatest of the reform popes of the eleventh century, Gregory VII (1073–1085).

Pope Gregory VII and Reform   Elected pope in 1073, Gregory was absolutely certain that he had been chosen by God to reform the church. In pursuit of those aims, Gregory claimed that he—the pope—was God's "vicar on Earth" and that the pope's authority extended over all of Chris-

The "Gregorian Revolution": Papal Claims

N THE ELEVENTH CENTURY, a dynamic group of reformers pushed for the "freedom of the church." This came to mean not only papal control over the affairs of the church but also the elimination of lay investiture. The reformers saw the latter as the chief issue at the heart of lay control of the church. In trying to eliminate it, the reforming popes, especially Gregory VII, extended papal claims to include the right to oversee the secular authorities and, in particular, to depose rulers under certain circumstances. The following selection is from a document that was entered in the papal register in 1075. It consisted of twenty-seven assertions that probably served as headings, or a table of contents, for a collection of ecclesiastical writings that supported the pope's claims.

The Dictates of the Pope

1. That the Roman church was founded by God alone.
2. That the Roman pontiff alone can with right be called universal.
3. That he alone can depose or reinstate bishops.
4. That, in a council, his legate, even if a lower grade, is above all bishops, and can pass sentence of deposition against them.
5. That the pope may depose the absent.
6. That, among other things, we ought not to remain in the same house with those excommunicated by him. . . .
8. That he alone may use the imperial insignia.
9. That of the pope alone all princes shall kiss the feet.
10. That his name alone shall be spoken in the churches.
11. That this is the only name in the world.
12. That it may be permitted to him to depose emperors.
13. That he may be permitted to transfer bishops if need be. . . .
17. That no chapter and no book shall be considered canonical without his authority.
18. That a sentence passed by him may be retracted by no one; and that he himself, alone of all, may retract it.
19. That he himself may be judged by no one.
20. That no one shall dare to condemn one who appeals to the apostolic chair.
21. That to the latter should be referred the more important cases of every church.
22. That the Roman church has never erred; nor will it err to all eternity, the Scripture bearing witness.
23. That the Roman pontiff, if he have been canonically ordained, is undoubtedly made a saint by the merits of St. Peter. . . .
25. That he may depose and reinstate bishops without assembling a synod.
26. That he who is not at peace with the Roman church shall not be considered catholic.
27. That he may absolve subjects from their fealty to wicked men.

tendom and included the right to depose emperors if they disobeyed his wishes. Gregory sought nothing less than the elimination of **lay investiture** (both interference by nonmembers of the clergy in elections and their participation in the installation of prelates). Only in this way could the church regain its freedom, by which Gregory meant the right of the church to elect prelates and to run its own affairs. If rulers did not accept these "divine" commands, they could be deposed by the pope acting in his capacity as the vicar of Christ (see the box above). Gregory VII soon found himself in conflict with the king of Germany over these claims. (The king of Germany was also the emperor-designate since it had been accepted by this time that only kings of Germany could be emperors, but they did not officially use the title "emperor" until they were crowned by the pope.)

King Henry IV (1056–1106) of Germany was just as determined as the pope. For many years, German kings had appointed high-ranking clerics, especially bishops, as their vassals in order to use them as administrators. Without them, the king could not hope to maintain his own power vis-à-vis the powerful German nobles. In 1075, Pope Gregory issued a decree forbidding important clerics from receiving investiture from lay leaders: "We decree that no one of the clergy shall receive the investiture with a bishopric or abbey or church from the hand of an emperor or king or of any lay person."[3] Henry had no intention of obeying a decree that challenged the very heart of his administration.

The Investiture Controversy The immediate cause of the so-called Investiture Controversy was a disputed election to the bishopric of Milan in northern Italy, an important position because the bishop was also the ruler of the city. Control of the bishopric was crucial if the king wished to reestablish German power in northern Italy. Since Milan was considered second only to Rome in importance as a bishopric, papal interest in the office was also keen. Pope Gregory VII and King Henry IV backed competing candidates for the position.

To gain acceptance of his candidate, the pope threatened the king with **excommunication.** Excommunication is a censure by which a person is deprived of receiving the sacraments of the church. To counter this threat, the king called a synod or assembly of German bishops, all of whom he had appointed, and had them depose the pope.

Pope Gregory VII responded by excommunicating the king and freeing his subjects from their allegiance to him. The latter was a clever move. The German nobles were only too eager to diminish the power of a centralized monarchy because of the threat it posed to their own power, and they welcomed this opportunity to rebel against the king.

Both the nobles and the bishops of Germany agreed to hold a meeting in Germany with the pope to solve the problem, possibly by choosing a new king. Gregory set out for Germany. Henry, realizing the threat to his power, forestalled the pope by traveling to northern Italy, where he met the pope at Canossa, a castle belonging to Countess Matilda of Tuscany, an avid supporter of the papal reform program. There, in January 1077, the king admitted his transgressions and begged for forgiveness and absolution. Although he made the king wait three days, the pope was constrained by his priestly responsibility to grant absolution to a penitent sinner and lifted the ban of excommunication. This did not end the problem, however. Within three years, pope and king were again locked in combat.

The struggle continued until 1122, when a new German king and a new pope achieved a compromise called the Concordat of Worms. Under this agreement, a bishop in Germany was first elected by church officials. After election, the nominee paid homage to the king as his secular lord, who in turn invested him with the symbols of temporal office. A representative of the pope then invested the new bishop with the symbols of his spiritual office.

This struggle between church and state was an important element in the history of Europe in the High Middle Ages. In the Early Middle Ages, popes had been dependent on emperors and had allowed them to exercise considerable authority over church affairs. But a set of new ideals championed by activist reformers in the eleventh century now supported the "freedom of the church," which meant not only the freedom of the church to control its own affairs but also extreme claims of papal authority. Not only was the pope superior to all other bishops, but popes now claimed the right to depose kings under certain circumstances. Such papal claims ensured further church-state confrontations.

Christianity and Medieval Civilization

Christianity was an integral part of the fabric of medieval European society and the consciousness of Europe. Papal directives affected the actions of kings and princes alike, while Christian teaching and practices touched the economic, social, cultural, and daily lives of all Europeans.

Growth of the Papal Monarchy

The popes of the twelfth century did not abandon the reform ideals of Gregory VII, but they were less dogmatic and more inclined to consolidate their power and build a strong administrative system. By the twelfth century, the Catholic church possessed a clearly organized, hierarchical structure. The pope and **papal curia** were at the apex of the administrative structure. The curia was staffed by high church officials known as cardinals, who served as major advisers and administrators to the popes; at the pope's death, the college of cardinals, as they were collectively called, elected the new pope. Below the pope and cardinals were the archbishops, each of whom controlled a large region called an archdiocese. Each archdiocese was divided into smaller units called dioceses, each headed by a bishop. Each diocese was divided into parishes, each headed by a priest. Theoretically, the bishop chose all priests in his diocese, administered his diocese, and was responsible only to the pope.

The Pontificate of Innocent III   In the thirteenth century, the Catholic church reached the height of its political, intellectual, and secular power. The papal monarchy extended its sway over both ecclesiastical and temporal affairs, as was especially evident during the papacy of Pope Innocent III (1198–1216). At the beginning of his pontificate, in a letter to a priest, Innocent made a clear statement of his views on papal supremacy:

> As God, the creator of the universe, set two great lights in the firmament of heaven, the greater light to rule the day, and the lesser light to rule the night, so He set two great dignities in the firmament of the universal church, . . . the greater to rule the day, that is, souls, and the lesser to rule the night, that is, bodies. These dignities are the papal authority and the royal power. And just as the moon gets her light from the sun, and is inferior to the sun . . . so the royal power gets the splendor of its dignity from the papal authority.[4]

Innocent's actions were those of a man who believed that he, the pope, was the supreme judge of European affairs. He forced King Philip II Augustus of France to take back his wife and queen after Philip had coerced a group of French prelates into annulling his marriage. The pope intervened in German affairs and installed his candidate as emperor. He compelled King John of England to accept the papal choice for the position of archbishop of Canterbury. To achieve his political ends, Innocent did not hesitate to use the spiritual weapons at his command, especially the interdict. An **interdict** was imposed on a region or country rather than a person; it forbade priests there to dispense the sacraments of the church in the hope that the people, deprived of the comforts of religion, would exert pressure against their ruler. Pope Innocent's interdict was so effective that it caused King Philip Augustus to restore his wife to her rightful place as queen of France.

New Religious Orders and Spiritual Ideals

In the second half of the eleventh century and the first half of the twelfth, a wave of religious enthusiasm seized Europe, leading to a spectacular growth in the number of monasteries and the emergence of new monastic orders. Most important was the Cistercian order, founded in 1098 by a group of monks dissatisfied with the lack of strict discipline at their Benedictine monastery. Cistercian monasticism spread rapidly from southern France into the rest of Europe.

The Cistercians were strict. They ate a simple diet and possessed only a single robe apiece. All decorations were

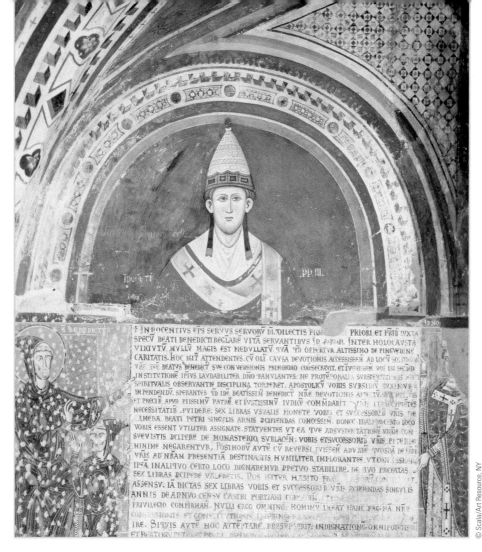

Pope Innocent III. Innocent III was an active and powerful pope during the High Middle Ages. He approved the creation of the Franciscan and Dominican religious orders and inaugurated the Fourth Crusade. He is shown here with the papal bull he issued to establish the monastery of Sacro Speco in Subiaco, Italy.

eliminated from their churches and monastic buildings. More time for prayer and manual labor was provided by shortening the number of hours spent at religious services. The Cistercians played a major role in developing a new activist spiritual model for twelfth-century Europe. A Benedictine monk often spent hours in prayer to honor God. The Cistercian ideal had a different emphasis: "Arise, soldier of Christ, arise! Get up off the ground and return to the battle from which you have fled! Fight more boldly after your flight, and triumph in glory!"[5] These were the words of Saint Bernard of Clairvaux (1090–1153), who more than any other person embodied the new spiritual ideal of Cistercian monasticism (see the box on p. 270).

Women in Religious Orders   Women were also active participants in the spiritual movements of the age. The number of women joining religious houses increased perceptibly with the spread of the new orders of the twelfth century. In the High Middle Ages, most nuns were from the ranks of the landed aristocracy. Convents were convenient for families unable or unwilling to find husbands for their daughters and for aristocratic women who did not wish to marry. Female intellectuals found them a haven for their activities. Most of the learned women of the Middle Ages, especially in Germany, were nuns. One of the most distinguished

was Hildegard of Bingen (1098–1179), who became abbess of a convent at Disibodenberg in western Germany.

Hildegard shared in the religious enthusiasm of the twelfth century. Soon after becoming abbess, she began to write an account of the mystical visions she had experienced for years. "A great flash of light from heaven pierced my brain and . . . in that instant my mind was imbued with the meaning of the sacred books," she wrote in a description typical of the world's mystical literature. Eventually she produced three books based on her visions. Hildegard gained considerable renown as a mystic and prophet, and popes, emperors, kings, dukes, and bishops eagerly sought her advice.

Hildegard of Bingen was also one of the first important female composers and a major contributor to the body of music known as Gregorian chant or plainsong. Gregorian chant was basically monophonic—a single line of unaccompanied vocal music—set to Latin texts and chanted by a group of monks or nuns during church services. Hildegard's work is especially remarkable because she succeeded at a time when music in general, and sacred music in particular, was almost exclusively the domain of men.

Living the Gospel Life   In the early thirteenth century, two religious leaders, Saint Francis and Saint Dominic, founded

A Miracle of Saint Bernard

SAINT BERNARD OF CLAIRVAUX has been called the most widely respected holy man of the twelfth century. He was an outstanding preacher, wholly dedicated to the service of God. His reputation reportedly influenced many young men to join the Cistercian order. He also inspired a myriad of stories dealing with his miracles.

A Miracle of Saint Bernard

A certain monk, departing from his monastery . . ., threw off his habit, and returned to the world at the persuasion of the Devil. And he took a certain parish living; for he was a priest. Because sin is punished with sin, the deserter from his Order lapsed into the vice of lechery. He took a concubine to live with him, as in fact is done by many, and by her he had children.

But as God is merciful and does not wish anyone to perish, it happened that many years after, the blessed abbot [Saint Bernard] was passing through the village in which the same monk was living, and went to stay at his house. The renegade monk recognized him, and received him very reverently, and waited on him devoutly . . . but as yet the abbot did not recognize him.

On the morrow, the holy man said Matins and prepared to be off. But as he could not speak to the priest, since he had got up and gone to the church for Matins, he said to the priest's son "Go, give this message to your master." Now the boy had been born dumb. He obeyed the command and feeling in himself the power of him who had

given it, he ran to his father and uttered the words of the Holy Father clearly and exactly. His father, on hearing his son's voice for the first time, wept for joy, and made him repeat the same words . . . and he asked what the abbot had done to him. "He did nothing to me," said the boy, "except to say, 'Go and say this to your father.'"

At so evident a miracle the priest repented, and hastened after the holy man and fell at his feet saying "My Lord and Father, I was your monk so-and-so, and at such-and-such a time I ran away from your monastery. I ask your Paternity to allow me to return with you to the monastery, for in your coming God has visited my heart." The saint replied unto him, "Wait for me here, and I will come back quickly when I have done my business, and I will take you with me." But the priest, fearing death (which he had not done before), answered, "Lord, I am afraid of dying before then." But the saint replied, "Know this for certain, that if you die in this condition, and in this resolve, you will find yourself a monk before God."

The saint [eventually] returned and heard that the priest had recently died and been buried. He ordered the tomb to be opened. And when they asked him what he wanted to do, he said, "I want to see if he is lying as a monk or a clerk in his tomb." "As a clerk," they said; "we buried him in his secular habit." But when they had dug up the earth, they found that he was not in the clothes in which they had buried him; but he appeared in all points, tonsure and habit, as a monk. And they all praised God.

---

two new religious orders whose members did not remain in the cloister like the monks of the contemplative orders, such as the Benedictines and Cistercians, but rather went out into the secular arena of the towns to preach the word of God. By their example, the new orders, known as mendicant ("begging") orders for their deliberate poverty, strove to provide a more personal religious experience for ordinary people.

Saint Francis of Assisi (1182–1226) was born to a wealthy Italian merchant family, but as a young man he abandoned all worldly goods and began to live and preach in poverty after a series of dramatic spiritual experiences. His simplicity, joyful nature, and love for others soon attracted a band of followers, all of whom took vows of absolute poverty, agreeing to reject all property and live by working and begging for their food. Francis drew up a simple rule for his followers that consisted merely of biblical precepts focusing on the need to preach and the importance of poverty. He sought approval for his new rule from Pope Innocent III, who confirmed the new order as the Order of Friars Minor, more commonly known as the

Saint Bernard. One of the most important religious figures of the twelfth century was Saint Bernard of Clairvaux, who advocated a militant expression of Christian ideas while favoring a more personalized understanding of the relationship between humans and God. Here Saint Bernard is shown preaching a sermon to his fellow Cistercians.

Franciscans. The Franciscans struck a responsive chord among many Europeans and became very popular. The Franciscans lived among the people, preaching repentance and aiding the poor. Their calls for a return to the simplicity and poverty of the early church, reinforced by their own example, were especially effective. The Franciscans had a female branch as well, known as the Poor Clares, which was founded by Saint Clare, an aristocratic lady of Assisi who was a great admirer of Francis.

The second new religious order of the early thirteenth century arose out of the desire to defend orthodox church teachings from heresy (see "Voices of Protest and Intolerance" later in this chapter). The Order of Preachers, popularly known as the Dominicans, was created through the efforts of a Spanish priest, Dominic de Guzmán (1170–1221). Unlike Francis, Dominic was an intellectual who was particularly appalled by the recent growth of heretical movements. He came to believe that a new religious order of men who lived lives of poverty but were learned and capable of preaching effectively would best be able to attack heresy. With the approval of Pope Innocent III, the Dominicans became an order of mendicant friars in 1215.

In addition to the friars, the thirteenth century witnessed the development of yet another kind of religious order. Known as Beguines, these were communities of women dwelling together in poverty. Devout and dedicated to prayer, they begged for their daily support or worked as laundresses in hospitals or at other menial tasks. They did not take religious vows and were free to leave the community at will. Although the Beguines originated in the Low Countries, they eventually became quite strong in the Rhineland area of Germany as well.

© Bibliotheque royale Albert Ier (Ms IV 119, fol.72 verso)

A Group of Nuns. Although still viewed by the medieval church as inferior to men, women were as susceptible to the spiritual fervor of the twelfth century as men, and female monasticism grew accordingly. This miniature shows a group of Flemish nuns listening to the preaching of an abbot, Gilles li Muisis. The nun at the far left wearing a white robe is a novice.

Popular Religion in the High Middle Ages

We have witnessed the actions of popes, bishops, and monks. But what of ordinary clergy and laypeople? What were their religious hopes and fears? What were their spiritual aspirations?

The **sacraments** of the Catholic church ensured that the church was an integral part of people's lives, from birth to death. There were (and still are) seven sacraments—the Eucharist (the Lord's Supper), baptism, marriage, penance, extreme unction, holy orders, and confirmation—administered only by the clergy. The sacraments were viewed as outward symbols of an inward grace (grace was God's freely given gift that enabled humans to be saved) and were considered imperative for a Christian's salvation. Therefore, the clergy were seen to have a key role in the attainment of salvation.

The Importance of Saints   Other church practices were also important to ordinary people. Saints, it was believed, were men and women who, through their holiness, had achieved a special position in heaven, enabling them to act as intercessors before God. The saints' ability to protect poor souls enabled them to take on great importance at the popular level. Jesus' apostles were, of course, recognized throughout Europe as saints, but there were also numerous local saints that were of special significance to the area. New cults rapidly developed, particularly in the intense religious atmosphere of the eleventh and twelfth centuries. The English introduced Saint Nicholas, the patron saint of children, who remains instantly recognizable today through his identification with Santa Claus.

Of all the saints, the Virgin Mary, the mother of Jesus, occupied the foremost position in the High Middle Ages. Mary was viewed as the most important mediator with her son Jesus, the judge of all sinners. Moreover, from the eleventh century on, a fascination with Mary as Jesus' human mother became more evident. A sign of Mary's importance was the growing number of churches all over Europe that were dedicated to her in the twelfth and thirteenth centuries, including the cathedral of Notre-Dame in Paris.

The Use of Relics   Emphasis on the role of the saints was closely tied to the use of **relics,** which also increased noticeably in the High Middle Ages. Relics were usually the bones of saints or objects intimately connected to saints that were considered worthy of veneration by the faithful. A twelfth-century English monk began his description of the abbey's relics by saying, "There is kept there a thing more precious than gold, . . . the right arm of St. Oswald. . . . This we have seen with our own eyes and have kissed, and have handled with our own hands. . . . There are kept here also part of his ribs and of the soil on which he fell."[6] The monk went on

THE RISE OF KINGDOMS AND THE GROWTH OF CHURCH POWER   271

to list additional purported relics possessed by the abbey, which included two pieces of Jesus' swaddling clothes, pieces of Jesus' manger, and parts of the five loaves of bread with which Jesus miraculously fed five thousand people. Because the holiness of the saint was considered to be inherent in his relics, these objects were believed to be capable of healing people or producing other miracles.

In the High Middle Ages, it became a regular practice of the church to attach **indulgences** to these relics. Indulgences brought a remission of time spent in **purgatory.** Purgatory was believed to be a place of punishment in which the soul of the departed could be purified before ascending to heaven. The living could ease that suffering through Masses and prayers offered on behalf of the deceased or through indulgences. Indulgences were granted for good works such as charitable contributions and viewing the relics of saints. The church specified the number of years and days of each indulgence, enabling the soul to spend less time in purgatory.

The Pilgrimage Medieval Christians believed that a pilgrimage to a holy shrine was of particular spiritual benefit. The greatest shrine but the most difficult to reach was the Holy City of Jerusalem (see Map 10.6). On the European continent, two pilgrim centers were especially popular in the High Middle Ages: Rome, which contained the relics of Saints Peter and Paul, and the town of Santiago de Compostela, supposedly the site of the tomb of the Apostle James. Local attractions, such as shrines dedicated to the Virgin Mary, also became pilgrimage centers.

Voices of Protest and Intolerance

The desire for more personal and deeper religious experience, which characterized the spiritual revival of the High Middle Ages, also led people into directions hostile to the institutional church. From the twelfth century on, **heresy,** the holding of religious doctrines different from the orthodox teachings of the church as determined by church authorities, became a serious problem for the Catholic church.

The best-known heresy of the twelfth and thirteenth centuries was Catharism. The Cathars (the word *Cathar* means "pure") were often called Albigensians after the city of Albi, one of their strongholds in southern France. They believed in a dualist system in which good and evil were separate and distinct. The things of the spirit were good because they were created by the God of light; the things of the world were evil because they were created by Satan, the prince of darkness. Humans, too, were enmeshed in **dualism.** Their souls, which were good, were trapped in material bodies, which were evil. According to the Cathars, the Catholic church, itself a materialistic institution, had nothing to do with God and was essentially evil. There was no need to follow its teachings or recognize its authority. The Cathar movement gained valuable support from important nobles in southern France and northern Italy.

The spread of heresy in southern France alarmed the church authorities. Pope Innocent III appealed to the nobles of northern France for a **Crusade** (a military campaign in defense of Christendom) against the heretics. The Crusade against the Albigensians, which began in the summer of 1209 and lasted for almost two decades, was a bloody one. Thousands of heretics (and the innocent) were slaughtered, including entire populations of some towns. In Béziers, for example, seven thousand men, women, and children were massacred when they took refuge in the local church.

Southern France was devastated, but Catharism remained, which caused the Catholic church to devise a regular method for discovering and dealing with heretics. This led to the emergence of the Holy Office, as the papal Inquisition was called, a formal court whose job it was to ferret out and try heretics.

Mass of the Holy Relics. It was customary for churches that possessed relics to hold a special Mass honoring those saints. At that time, the reliquaries would be brought out for the faithful to venerate. The large picture shows the celebration of this special Mass of the holy relics. The reliquary is shown on a table to the left. The small pictures illustrate various stages of the Mass.

MAP 10.6 **Pilgrimage Routes in the Middle Ages.** Some Christians sought spiritual solace by traveling to pilgrimage sites. Many went to local shrines honoring the Virgin Mary, but Jerusalem, Rome, and Santiago de Compostela were the most desired locations. ❓ Roughly how far would a pilgrim from Lübeck have to travel to reach Jerusalem, and how long would the journey take if he walked 20 miles per day? 🌐 **View an animated version of this map or related maps at**

http://history.wadsworth.com/spielvogel06/

Gradually, the Holy Office developed its inquisitorial procedure. Anyone could be accused of heresy, since the identity of the accuser was not revealed to the indicted heretic. If the accused heretic confessed, he or she was forced to perform public penance and was subjected to punishment, such as flogging; the heretic's property was then confiscated and divided between the secular authorities and the church. Beginning in 1252, those not confessing voluntarily were subjected to torture. Relapsed heretics—who confessed, did penance, and then reverted to heresy—were turned over to the secular authorities for execution.

To the Christians of the thirteenth century, who believed that there was only one path to salvation, heresy was a crime against God and against humanity, and force was justified to save souls from damnation. The fanaticism and fear unleashed in the struggle against heretics were also used against others, especially the best-known outgroup of Western society, the Jews.

Persecution of the Jews   The Jews constituted the only religious minority in Christian Europe that was allowed to practice a non-Christian religion. In the Early Middle Ages, Jews were actively involved in trade and crafts. Later, after being excluded from practicing most trades by the guild system, some Jews turned to moneylending as a way to survive.

Expulsion of Albigensian Heretics.   In 1209, Pope Innocent III authorized a Crusade against the heretical Albigensians. In this medieval illustration, French knights are shown expelling Albigensian heretics from the town of Caracassonne near Albi, an Albigensian stronghold in southern France.

There is little certainty about the number of Jews in Europe. England had relatively few Jews, probably 2,500 to 3,000, or one of every thousand inhabitants. Larger numbers lived in southern Italy, Spain, France, and Germany. In southern Europe, Jews served an important function as cultural and intellectual intermediaries between the Muslim and Christian worlds.

The religious enthusiasm of the High Middle Ages produced an outburst of intolerance against the supposed enemies of Christianity. Although this was evident in the Crusades against the Muslims (see "The Crusades" in the next section), Christians also took up the search for enemies at home, persecuting Jews in France and the Rhineland at the time of the first Crusades. Jews in Speyer, Worms, Mainz, and Cologne were all set upon by bands of Christian crusaders. A contemporary chronicler described how a band of English crusaders who stopped at Lisbon, Portugal, en route to the Holy Land "drove away the pagans and Jews, servants of the king, who dwelt in the city and plundered their property and possessions, and burned their houses; and they then stripped their vineyards, not leaving them so much as a grape or a cluster."[7] Even people who tried to protect the Jews were in danger. When the archbishop of Mainz provided shelter for the Jews, a mob stormed his palace and forced him to flee. Popes also came to the Jews' defense by issuing decrees ordering that Jews were not to be persecuted.

Nevertheless, in the thirteenth century, in the supercharged religious atmosphere created by the struggle with heretics, Jews were persecuted more and more (see the box on p. 275). Friars urged action against these "murderers of Christ," referring to the traditional Christian view of the Jews as being responsible for the death of Jesus, and organized public burnings of Jewish books. The Fourth Lateran Council in 1215 decreed that Jews must wear distinguishing clothing to separate themselves from Christians. The same council encouraged the development of Jewish ghettos, or walled enclosures, not to protect the Jews but to isolate them from Christians. The persecutions and the new image of the hated Jew stimulated a tradition of anti-Semitism that proved to be one of Christian Europe's most insidious contributions to the Western heritage.

By the end of the thirteenth century, European kings, who had earlier portrayed themselves as protectors of the Jews, had fleeced the Jewish communities of their money and then renounced their protection. Edward I expelled all Jews from England in 1290. The French king followed suit in 1306 but readmitted the Jews in 1315. They then left on their own accord in 1322. As the policy of expulsion spread into central Europe, most northern European Jews were forced to move into Poland as a last refuge.

Intolerance of Homosexuality   The climate of intolerance that characterized thirteenth-century attitudes toward Muslims, heretics, and Jews was also evident toward homosexuals. Although the church had condemned homosexuality in the Early Middle Ages, it had not been overly concerned with homosexual behavior, an attitude also prevalent in the secular world. By the thirteenth century, however, these tolerant attitudes had altered drastically. Some historians see this change as part of the century's climate of fear and intolerance toward any group that deviated from the standards of the majority. A favorite approach of the critics was to identify homosexuals with other detested groups. Homosexuality was portrayed as a regular practice of Muslims and such notorious heretics as the Albigensians. Between 1250 and 1300, what had been tolerated in most of Europe became a criminal act deserving of death.

The legislation against homosexuality commonly referred to it as a "sin against nature." This is precisely the argument developed by Thomas Aquinas, who formed Catholic opinion on the subject for centuries to come. In his *Summa Theologica*, Aquinas argued that because the purpose of sex was procreation, it could legitimately take place only in ways that did not exclude this possibility. Hence homosexuality was "contrary to nature" and a deviation from the natural order established by God. This argument and laws prohibiting homosexual activity on pain of severe punishment remained the norm in Europe and elsewhere in the Christian world until the twentieth century.

The Crusades

Another manifestation of the wave of religious enthusiasm that seized Europe in the High Middle Ages was the series of Crusades mounted against the Muslims. The Crusades gave the revived papacy of the High Middle Ages yet another opportunity to demonstrate its influence over European society. The Crusades were a curious mix of God and warfare, two of the chief concerns of the Middle Ages.

Background to the Crusades

Although European civilization developed in relative isolation, it had never entirely lost contact with the lands and empires of the East. At the end of the eleventh century, that contact increased, in part because developments in the Islamic and Byzantine worlds prompted the first major attempt of the new European civilization to expand beyond Europe proper.

Islam and the Seljuk Turks   By the mid-tenth century, the Islamic empire led by the Abbasid caliphate in Baghdad was disintegrating. An attempt was made in the tenth century to unify the Islamic world under the direction of a Shi'ite dynasty known as the Fatimids. Their origins lay in North Africa, but they managed to conquer Egypt and establish the new city of Cairo as their capital. In establishing a Shi'ite caliphate, they became rivals to the Sunni caliphate of Baghdad and divided the Islamic world.

Nevertheless, the Fatimid dynasty prospered and surpassed the Abbasid caliphate as the dynamic center of Islam. Benefiting from their position in the heart of the Nile

TREATMENT OF THE JEWS

HE NEW RELIGIOUS SENSIBILITIES that emerged in the High Middle Ages also had a negative side, the turning of Christians against their supposed enemies. Although the Crusades provide the most obvious example, Christians also turned on the "murderers of Christ," the Jews. As a result, Jews suffered increased persecution. These three documents show different sides of the picture. The first is Canon 68 of the decrees of the Fourth Lateran Council called by Pope Innocent III in 1215. The decree specifies the need for special dress, one of the ways Christians tried to separate Jews from their community. The second excerpt is a chronicler's account of the most deadly charge levied against the Jews—that they were guilty of the ritual murder of Christian children to obtain Christian blood for the Passover service. This charge led to the murder of many Jews. The third document, taken from a list of regulations issued by the city of Avignon, France, illustrates the contempt Christian society held for the Jews.

Canon 68

In some provinces a difference in dress distinguishes the Jews or Saracens [Muslims] from the Christians, but in certain others such a confusion has grown up that they cannot be distinguished by any difference. Thus it happens at times that through error Christians have relations with the women of Jews or Saracens, and Jews or Saracens with Christian women. Therefore, that they may not, under pretext of error of this sort, excuse themselves in the future for the excesses of such prohibited intercourse, we decree that such Jews and Saracens of both sexes in every Christian province and at all times shall be marked off in the eyes of the public from other peoples through the character of their dress. . . .

Moreover, during the last three days before Easter and especially on Good Friday, they shall not go forth in public at all, for the reason that some of them on these very days,

as we hear, do not blush to go forth better dressed and are not afraid to mock the Christians who maintain the memory of the most holy Passion by wearing signs of mourning.

An Accusation of the Ritual Murder of a Christian Child by Jews

. . . [The eight-year-old boy] Harold, who is buried in the Church of St. Peter the Apostle, at Gloucester . . . is said to have been carried away secretly by Jews, in the opinion of many, on Feb. 21, and by them hidden till March 16. On that night, on the sixth of the preceding feast, the Jews of all England coming together as if to circumcise a certain boy, pretend deceitfully that they are about to celebrate the feast [Passover] appointed by law in such case, and deceiving the citizens of Gloucester with the fraud, they tortured the lad placed before them with immense tortures. It is true no Christian was present, or saw or heard the deed, nor have we found that anything was betrayed by any Jew. But a little while after when the whole convent of monks of Gloucester and almost all the citizens of that city, and innumerable persons coming to the spectacle, saw the wounds of the dead body, scars of fire, the thorns fixed on his head, and liquid wax poured into the eyes and face, and touched it with the diligent examination of their hands, those tortures were believed or guessed to have been inflicted on him in that manner. It was clear that they had made him a glorious martyr to Christ, being slain without sin, and having bound his feet with his own girdle, threw him into the river Severn.

The Regulations of Avignon, 1243

Likewise, we declare that Jews or whores shall not dare to touch with their hands either bread or fruit put out for sale, and that if they should do this they must buy what they have touched.

---

delta, the Fatimids played a major role in the regional trade passing from the Mediterranean to the Red Sea and beyond. They were tolerant in matters of religion and created a strong army by using nonnative peoples as mercenaries. One of these peoples, the Seljuk Turks, soon posed a threat to the Fatimids themselves

The Seljuk Turks were a nomadic people from Central Asia who had been converted to Islam and flourished as military mercenaries for the Abbasid caliphate. Moving gradually into Persia and Armenia, their numbers grew until by the eleventh century they were able to take over the eastern provinces of the Abbasid empire. In 1055, a Turkish leader captured Baghdad and assumed command of the Abbasid empire with the title of **sultan** ("holder of power"). By the latter part of the eleventh century, the Seljuk Turks were exerting military pressure on Egypt and the Byzantine Empire. When the Byzantine emperor foolishly

challenged the Turks, the latter routed the Byzantine army at Manzikert in 1071. In dire straits, the Byzantines looked west for help, setting in motion the papal pleas that led to the Crusades. To understand the complexities of the situation, however, we need to look first at the Byzantine Empire.

The Byzantine Empire   The Macedonian dynasty of the tenth and eleventh centuries had restored much of the power of the Byzantine Empire; its incompetent successors, however, reversed most of the gains. After the Macedonian dynasty was extinguished in 1056, the empire was beset by internal struggles for power between ambitious military leaders and aristocratic families who attempted to buy the support of the great landowners of Anatolia by allowing them greater control over their peasants. This policy was self-destructive, however, because the peasant-warrior was the traditional backbone of the Byzantine state.

The growing division between the Catholic church of the West and the Eastern Orthodox church of the Byzantine Empire also weakened the Byzantine state. The Eastern Orthodox church was unwilling to accept the pope's claim that he was the sole head of the church. This dispute reached a climax in 1054 when Pope Leo IX and Patriarch Michael Cerularius, head of the Byzantine church, formally excommunicated each other, initiating a schism between the two great branches of Christianity that has not been healed to this day.

The Byzantine Empire faced external threats to its security as well. The greatest challenge came from the Seljuk Turks who had moved into Asia Minor—the heartland of the empire and its main source of food and manpower. After defeating the Byzantine forces at Manzikert in 1071, the Turks advanced into Anatolia, where many peasants, already disgusted by their exploitation at the hands of Byzantine landowners, readily accepted Turkish control.

A new dynasty, however, soon breathed new life into the Byzantine Empire. The Comneni, under Alexius I Comnenus (1081–1118), were victorious on the Greek Adriatic coast against the Normans, defeated the Pechenegs in the Balkans, and stopped the Turks in Anatolia. Lacking the resources to undertake additional campaigns against the Turks, Emperor Alexius I turned to the West for military assistance. The positive response to the emperor's request led to the Crusades. The Byzantine Empire lived to regret it.

✒ The Early Crusades

The Crusades were based on the idea of a holy war against the infidel or unbeliever. The wrath of Christians was directed against the Muslims, and at the end of the eleventh century, Christian Europe found itself with a glorious opportunity to attack them. The immediate impetus for the Crusades came when the Byzantine emperor, Alexius I, asked Pope Urban II (1088–1099) for help against the Seljuk Turks. The pope saw a golden opportunity to provide papal leadership for a great cause: to rally the warriors of Europe for the liberation of Jerusalem and the Holy Land from the infidel. At the Council of Clermont in southern France near the end of 1095, Urban challenged Christians to take up their weapons against the infidel and join in a holy war to recover the Holy Land (see the box on p. 277). The pope promised remission of sins: "All who die by the way, whether by land or by sea, or in battle against the pagans, shall have immediate remission of sins. This I grant them through the power of God with which I am invested."[8]

The warriors of western Europe, particularly France, formed the first crusading armies. The knights who made up this first serious crusading host were motivated by religious fervor, but there were other attractions as well. Some sought adventure and welcomed a legitimate opportunity to pursue their favorite pastime—fighting. Others saw an opportunity to gain territory, riches, status, possibly a title, and even salvation—had the pope not offered a full remission of sins for those who participated in these "armed pilgrimages"? From the perspective of the pope and European monarchs, the Crusades offered a way to rid Europe of contentious young nobles who disturbed the peace and wasted lives and energy fighting each other. And merchants in many Italian cities relished the prospect of new trading opportunities in Muslim lands.

The First Crusade   In the First Crusade, begun in 1096, three organized bands of noble warriors, most of them French, made their way to the east (see Map 10.7 on p. 279). The crusading army probably numbered several thousand cavalry and as many as ten thousand foot soldiers. After the capture of Antioch in 1098, much of the crusading host proceeded down the coast of Palestine, evading the garrisoned coastal cities, and reached Jerusalem in June 1099. After a five-week siege, the Holy City was taken amid a horrible massacre of the inhabitants, men, women, and children (see the box on p. 278).

After further conquest of Palestinian lands, the crusaders ignored the wishes of the Byzantine emperor (who foolishly believed the crusaders were working on his behalf) and organized four crusader states (Edessa, Antioch, Tripoli, and Jerusalem). Because the crusader states were surrounded by Muslim enemies, they grew increasingly dependent on the Italian commercial cities for supplies from Europe. Some Italian cities, such as Genoa, Pisa, and especially Venice, became rich and powerful in the process.

The Second Crusade   The crusader states soon foundered, and by the 1120s, the Muslims were striking back. In 1144, Edessa became the first of the four Latin states to be recaptured. Its fall led to renewed calls for another Crusade, especially from the monastic firebrand Saint Bernard of Clairvaux, who exclaimed, "Now, on account of our sins, the sacrilegious enemies of the cross have begun to show their

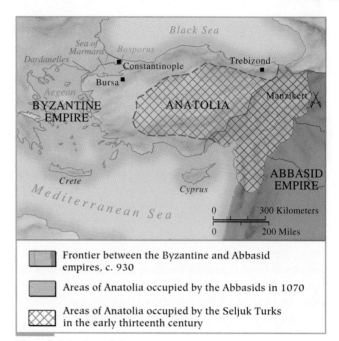

The Seljuk Turks and the Byzantines

POPE URBAN II PROCLAIMS A CRUSADE

TOWARD THE END OF the eleventh century, the Byzantine emperor Alexius I sent Pope Urban II a request for aid against the Seljuk Turks. At the Council of Clermont, Urban II appealed to a large crowd to take up weapons and recover Palestine from the Muslims. This description of Urban's appeal is taken from an account by Fulcher of Chartres.

Pope Urban II

Pope Urban II . . . addressed them [the French] in a very persuasive speech, as follows: "O race of the Franks, O people who live beyond the mountain [that is, north of the Alps], O people loved and chosen of God, as is clear from your many deeds, distinguished over all nations by the situation of your land, your catholic faith, and your regard for the holy church, we have a special message and exhortation for you. For we wish you to know what a grave matter has brought us to your country. The sad news has come from Jerusalem and Constantinople that the people of Persia, an accursed and foreign race [the Seljuk Turks], enemies of God, . . . have invaded the lands of those Christians and devastated them with the sword, rapine, and fire. Some of the Christians they have carried away as slaves, others they have put to death. The churches they have either destroyed or turned into mosques. They desecrate and overthrow the altars. They circumcise the Christians and pour the blood from the circumcision on the altars or in the baptismal fonts. Some they kill in a horrible way by cutting open the abdomen, taking out a part of the entrails and tying them to a stake; they then beat them and compel them to walk until all their entrails are drawn out and they fall to the ground. Some they use as targets for their arrows. They compel some to stretch out their necks and then they try to see whether they can cut off their heads with one strike of the sword. It is better to say nothing of their horrible treatment of the women. They have taken from the Greek empire a tract of land so large that it takes more than two months to walk through it. Whose duty is to avenge this and recover that land, if not yours? For to you more than to any other nations the Lord has given the military spirit, courage, agile bodies, and the bravery to strike down those who resist you. Let your minds be stirred to bravery by the deeds of your forefathers, and by the efficiency and greatness of Karl the Great [Charlemagne], . . . and of the other kings who have destroyed Turkish kingdoms, and established Christianity in their lands. You should be moved especially by the holy grave of our Lord and Savior which is now held by unclean peoples, and by the holy places which are treated with dishonor and irreverently befouled with their uncleanness. . . .

"O bravest of knights, descendants of unconquered ancestors, do not be weaker than they, but remember their courage. . . . Set out on the road to the holy sepulchre, take the land from that wicked people, and make it your own. . . . Jerusalem is the best of all lands, more fruitful than all others. . . . This land our Savior made illustrious by his birth, beautiful with his life, and sacred with his suffering. . . . This royal city is now held captive by her enemies, and made pagan by those who know not God. She asks and longs to be liberated and does not cease to beg you to come to her aid. . . . Set out on this journey and you will obtain the remission of your sins and be sure of the incorruptible glory of the kingdom of heaven."

When Pope Urban had said this and much more of the same sort, all who were present were moved to cry out with one accord, "It is the will of God, it is the will of God." When the pope heard this he raised his eyes to heaven and gave thanks to God, and commanding silence with a gesture of his hand, he said: "My dear brethren, today there is fulfilled in you that which the Lord says in the Gospel, 'Where two or three are gathered together in my name, there am I in the midst.' For unless the Lord God had been in your minds you would not all have said the same thing. . . . So I say unto you, God, who put those words into your hearts, has caused you to utter them. Therefore let these words be your battle cry, because God caused you to speak them. Whenever you meet the enemy in battle, you shall all cry out, 'It is the will of God, it is the will of God. . . .' Whoever therefore shall determine to make this journey and shall make a vow to God and shall offer himself as a living sacrifice, holy, acceptable to God, shall wear a cross on his brow or on his breast. And when he returns after having fulfilled his vow he shall wear the cross on his back."

faces. . . . What are you doing, you servants of the cross? Will you throw to the dogs that which is most holy? Will you cast pearls before swine?"[9] Bernard aimed his message at knights and even managed to enlist two powerful rulers, King Louis VII of France and Emperor Conrad III of Germany. Their Second Crusade, however, proved to be a total failure.

The Third Crusade   The Third Crusade was a reaction to the fall of the Holy City of Jerusalem in 1187 to the Muslim forces under Saladin. Now all of Christendom was ablaze with calls for a new Crusade in the Middle East.

Three major monarchs agreed to lead new crusading forces in person: Emperor Frederick Barbarossa of Germany (1152–1190), King Richard I the Lionhearted of England (1189–1199), and Philip II Augustus, king of France (1180–1223). Some of the crusaders finally arrived in the Middle East by 1189 only to encounter problems. Frederick Barbarossa drowned while swimming in a local river, and his army quickly fell apart. The English and French arrived by sea and met with success against the coastal cities, where they had the support of their fleets, but when they moved inland, they failed miserably. Eventually, after Philip went home, Richard negotiated a settlement whereby

THE SIEGE OF JERUSALEM: CHRISTIAN AND MUSLIM PERSPECTIVES

*D*URING THE FIRST CRUSADE, Christian knights laid siege to Jerusalem in June 1099. The first excerpt is taken from an account by Fulcher of Chartres, who accompanied the crusaders to the Holy Land. The second selection is by a Muslim writer, Ibn al-Athir, whose account of the First Crusade can be found in his history of the Muslim world.

Fulcher of Chartres, *Chronicle of the First Crusade*

Then the Franks entered the city magnificently at the noonday hour on Friday, the day of the week when Christ redeemed the whole world on the cross. With trumpets sounding and with everything in an uproar, exclaiming: "Help, God!" they vigorously pushed into the city, and straightway raised the banner on the top of the wall. All the heathen, completely terrified, changed their boldness to swift flight through the narrow streets of the quarters. The more quickly they fled, the more quickly they put to flight.

Count Raymond and his men, who were bravely assailing the city in another section, did not perceive this until they saw the Saracens [Muslims] jumping from the top of the wall. Seeing this, they joyfully ran to the city as quickly as they could, and helped the others pursue and kill the wicked enemy.

Then some, both Arabs and Ethiopians, fled into the Tower of David; others shut themselves in the Temple of the Lord and of Solomon, where in the halls a very great attack was made on them. Nowhere was there a place where the Saracens could escape swordsmen.

On the top of Solomon's Temple, to which they had climbed in fleeing, many were shot to death with arrows and cast down headlong from the roof. Within this Temple, about ten thousand were beheaded. If you had been there,

your feet would have been stained up to the ankles with the blood of the slain. What more shall I tell? Not one of them was allowed to live. They did not spare the women and children.

Account of Ibn al-Athir

In fact Jerusalem was taken from the north on the morning of Friday 22 Sha'ban 492 / 15 July 1099. The population was put to the sword by the Franks, who pillaged the area for a week. A band of Muslims barricaded themselves into the Oratory of David and fought on for several days. They were granted their lives in return for surrendering. The Franks honored their word, and the group left by night for Ascalon. In the Masjid al-Aqsa the Franks slaughtered more than 70,000 people, among them a large number of Imams and Muslim scholars, devout and ascetic men who had left their homelands to live lives of pious seclusion in the Holy Place. The Franks stripped the Dome of the Rock of more than forty silver candelabra, each of them weighing 3,600 drams, and a great silver lamp weighing forty-four Syrian pounds, as well as a hundred and fifty smaller candelabra and more than twenty gold ones, and a great deal more booty. Refugees from Syria reached Baghdad in Ramadan, among them the qadi Abu sa'd al-Harawi. They told the Caliph's ministers a story that wrung their hearts and brought tears to their eyes. On Friday they went to the Cathedral Mosque and begged for help, weeping so that their hearers wept with them as they described the sufferings of the Muslims in that Holy City: the men killed, the women and children taken prisoner, the homes pillaged. Because of the terrible hardships they had suffered, they were allowed to break the fast.

Saladin agreed to allow Christian pilgrims free access to Jerusalem.

The Crusades of the Thirteenth Century

After the death of Saladin in 1193, Pope Innocent III initiated the Fourth Crusade. On its way to the Holy Land, the crusading army became involved in a dispute over the succession to the Byzantine throne. The Venetian leaders of the Fourth Crusade saw an opportunity to neutralize their greatest commercial competitor, the Byzantine Empire. Diverted to Constantinople, the crusaders sacked the great capital city in 1204 and created a new Latin Empire of Constantinople. Not until 1261 did a Byzantine army recapture Constantinople. The Byzantine Empire had been saved, but it was no longer a great Mediterranean power. The restored empire now comprised only the city of Constantinople and its surrounding territory as well as some lands in Asia Minor. Though reduced in size, the empire limped along for another 190 years until its weakened condition finally enabled the Ottoman Turks to conquer it in 1453.

Despite the failures, the crusading ideal was not yet completely lost. In Germany in 1212, a youth known as Nicholas of Cologne announced that God had inspired him to lead a Children's Crusade to the Holy Land. Thousands of young people joined Nicholas and made their way down the Rhine and across the Alps to Italy, where the pope told them to go home. Most tried to do so. The next Crusade of adult warriors was hardly more successful. The Fifth Crusade (1219–1221) attempted to recover the Holy Land by way of the powerful Muslim state of Egypt. The Crusade achieved some early successes, but its ultimate failure marked an end to papal leadership of the western crusaders.

The Sixth Crusade, which was led by the German emperor Frederick II, took place without papal support because the emperor had been excommunicated by the pope for starting late. In 1228, Frederick marched into Jerusalem and accepted the crown as king of Jerusalem after he had made an agreement with the sultan of Egypt. The Holy City had been taken without a fight and without papal support. Once Frederick left, however, the city fell once

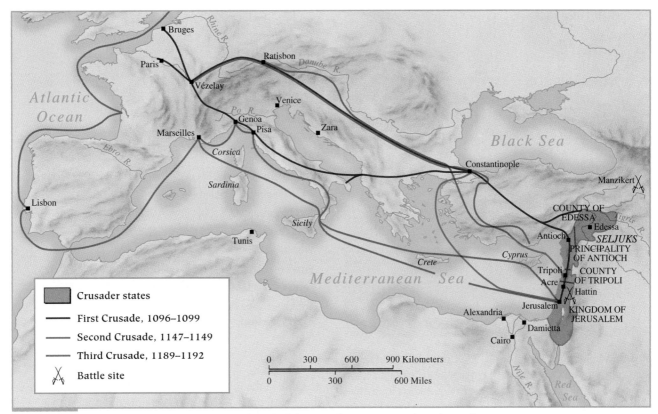

MAP 10.7 The Early Crusades. Pope Urban II launched the Crusades to recapture the Holy Land from the "enemies of God," a call met with great enthusiasm in Europe. The fighters of the First Crusade massacred the inhabitants of Jerusalem and established the Crusader States. **?** In the Third Crusade, which countries sent crusaders by land and which by sea, and why would they choose these methods of travel? **View an animated version of this map or related maps at** http://history.wadsworth.com/spielvogel06/

again, this time to a group of Turks allied with the sultan of Egypt. The last two major Crusades, poorly organized by the pious king of France, Louis IX, were complete failures. Soon the remaining Christian possessions in the Middle East were retaken. Acre, the last foothold of the crusaders, surrendered in 1291. All in all, the Crusades had failed to accomplish their primary goal of holding the Holy Land for the Christian West.

Effects of the Crusades

Whether the Crusades had much effect on European civilization is debatable. The crusaders made little long-term impact on the Middle East, where the only visible remnants of their conquests were their castles. There may have been some broadening of perspective that comes from the exchange between two cultures, but the interaction of Christian Europe with the Muslim world was actually both more intense and more meaningful in Spain and Sicily than in the Holy Land.

Did the Crusades help stabilize European society by removing large numbers of young warriors who would have fought each other in Europe? Some historians think so and believe that Western monarchs established their control more easily as a result. There is no doubt that the

Richard the Lionhearted Executing Muslims at Acre. The Third Crusade was organized in response to the capture of the kingdom of Jerusalem by the Sunni Muslims under the leadership of Saladin. Though Saladin forbade the massacre of Christians, his Christian foes were more harsh. Here Richard the Lionhearted (at right with crown) watches the execution of 2,700 Muslims at Acre.

Siege and Capture of Constantinople. This thirteenth-century miniature is a depiction of the siege and capture of Constantinople during the Fourth Crusade in 1204. At the right, soldiers use a catapult to shower the city with stones while knights use a tower to attack the walls. In the stained-glass windows above the battle are scenes from the Passion of Christ, a deliberate and ironic reminder that the purpose of the Crusades was to capture the Holy City of Jerusalem.

Crusades did contribute to the economic growth of the Italian port cities, especially Genoa, Pisa, and Venice. But it is important to remember that the growing wealth and population of twelfth-century Europe had made the Crusades

CHRONOLOGY — The Crusades

Pope Urban II's call for a Crusade at Clermont	1095
First Crusade	1096–1099
Fall of Edessa	1144
Second Crusade	1147–1149
Saladin's conquest of Jerusalem	1187
Third Crusade	1189–1192
Fourth Crusade—sack of Constantinople	1204
Latin Empire of Constantinople	1204–1261
Children's Crusade	1212
Fifth Crusade	1219–1221
Frederick II occupies Jerusalem (Sixth Crusade)	1228
First Crusade of Louis IX (Seventh Crusade)	1248–1254
Second Crusade of Louis IX (Eighth Crusade)	1270
Surrender of Acre and end of Christian presence in the Holy Land	1291

possible in the first place. The Crusades may have enhanced the revival of trade, but they certainly did not cause it. Even without the Crusades, Italian merchants would have pursued new trade contacts with the Eastern world.

The Crusades prompted evil side effects that would haunt European society for generations. The first widespread attacks on the Jews began with the Crusades. As some Christians argued, to undertake holy wars against infidel Muslims while the "murderers of Christ" ran free at home was unthinkable. The massacre of Jews became a regular feature of medieval European life.

CONCLUSION

*T*HE PERIOD FROM 1000 to 1300 was a dynamic one in the development of Western civilization. The nobles, whose warlike attitudes were rationalized by labeling themselves as the defenders of Christian society, continued to dominate the medieval world politically, economically, and socially. But kings gradually began to expand their powers. Although the popes sometimes treated rulers as if they were the popes' servants, by the thirteenth century, monarchs themselves were developing the machinery of government that would enable them to challenge exalted claims of papal power and become the centers of political authority in Europe. Although they could not know it then, the actions of these medieval monarchs laid the foundation for the European kingdoms that in one form or another have dominated the European political scene ever since.

The Catholic church shared in the challenge of new growth by reforming itself and striking out on a path toward greater papal power, both within the church and over European society. The High Middle Ages witnessed a spiritual renewal that led to numerous and even divergent paths: revived papal leadership, the development of centralized administrative machinery that buttressed papal authority, and new dimensions to the religious life of the clergy and laity. At the same time, this spiritual renewal also gave rise to the crusading "holy warrior" who killed for God.\

The religious enthusiasm of the twelfth century continued well into the thirteenth as new orders of friars gave witness to spiritual growth and passion, but underneath the calm exterior lay seeds of discontent and change. Dissent from church teaching and practices grew, leading to a climate of fear and intolerance as the church responded with inquisitorial procedures to

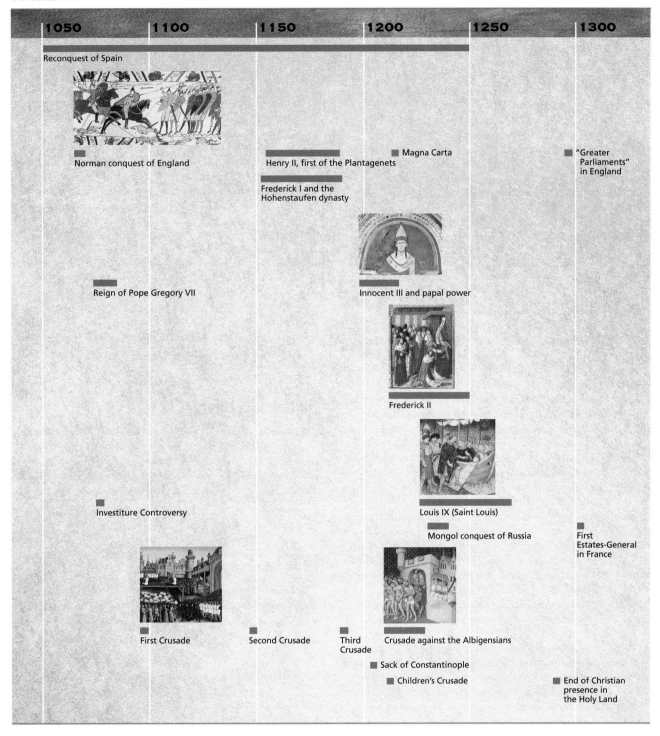

1050   1100   1150   1200   1250   1300

Reconquest of Spain

Norman conquest of England

■ Magna Carta

Henry II, first of the Plantagenets

"Greater Parliaments" in England

Frederick I and the Hohenstaufen dynasty

Reign of Pope Gregory VII

Innocent III and papal power

Frederick II

Investiture Controversy

Louis IX (Saint Louis)

Mongol conquest of Russia

First Estates-General in France

First Crusade

Second Crusade

Third Crusade

Crusade against the Albigensians

■ Sack of Constantinople

■ Children's Crusade

■ End of Christian presence in the Holy Land

enforce conformity to its teachings. At the same time, papal claims of supremacy over secular authorities were increasingly challenged by the rising power of monarchical authorities, who, thanks to the growth of cities, the revival of trade, and the emergence of a money economy, were now able to hire soldiers and officials to carry out their wishes.

The High Middle Ages of the eleventh, twelfth, and thirteenth centuries had been a period of great innovation, evident in significant economic, social, political, religious, intellectual, and cultural changes. And yet by the end of the thirteenth century, certain tensions had begun to creep into European society. As we shall see in the next chapter, these tensions soon became a torrent of troubles.

NOTES

1. Quoted in John K. Fairbank, Edwin O. Reischauer, and Albert M. Craig, *East Asia: Tradition and Transformation* (Boston, 1973), p. 164.

2. Ernest F. Henderson, ed., *Selected Historical Documents of the Middle Ages* (London, 1892), p. 332.

3. Ibid., p. 365.

4. Oliver J. Thatcher and Edgar H. McNeal, eds., *A Source Book for Medieval History* (New York, 1905), p. 208.

5. Quoted in R. H. C. Davis, *A History of Medieval Europe from Constantine to Saint Louis,* 2d ed. (New York, 1988), p. 252.

6. Quoted in Rosalind Brooke and Christopher N. L. Brooke, *Popular Religion in the Middle Ages* (London, 1984), p. 19.

7. Henry T. Riley, ed., *Memorials of London and London Life in the Thirteenth, Fourteenth, and Fifteenth Centuries* (London, 1868), vol. 2, pp. 148–149.

8. Thatcher and McNeal, *Source Book for Medieval History,* p. 517.

9. Quoted in Hans E. Mayer, *The Crusades,* trans. John Gillingham (New York, 1972), pp. 99–100.

SUGGESTIONS FOR FURTHER READING

There are numerous works on the different medieval states. On England, see **R. Frame, *The Political Development of the British Isles, 1100–1400*** (Oxford, 1990), and **M. T. Clanchy, *England and Its Rulers, 1066–1272*** (New York, 1983). On France, see **J. Dunbabin, *France in the Making, 843–1180*** (Oxford, 1985), and **E. M. Hallam, *Capetian France, 987–1328*** (London, 1980), a well-done general account. On Spain, see **B. F. Reilly, *The Medieval Spains*** (Cambridge, 1993), and **M. R. Menocal, *The Ornament of the World*** (Boston, 2002). On Germany, see **A. Haverkamp, *Medieval Germany*** (Oxford, 1988); **H. Fuhrmann, *Germany in the High Middle Ages, c. 1050–1250*** (Cambridge, 1986), an excellent account; and **B. Arnold, *Princes and Territories in Medieval Germany*** (Cambridge, 1991). On Italy, see **P. Jones, *The Italian City-State: From Commune to Signoria*** (Oxford, 1997). On eastern Europe and Scandinavia, see **N. Davies, *God's Playground: A History of Poland*** (Oxford, 1981); **T. K. Derry, *A History of Scandinavia*** (London, 1979); **J. Fennell, *The Crisis of Medieval Russia, 1200–1304*** (New York, 1983); and the books listed for Chapter 8.

For specialized studies in the political history of the thirteenth century, see **D. Abulafia, *Frederick II: A Medieval Emperor*** (London, 1987); **M. W. Labarge, *St. Louis: The Life of Louis IX of France*** (London, 1968); and **C. J. Halperin, *Russia and the Golden Horde: The Mongol Impact on Medieval Russian History*** (Bloomington, Ind., 1987).

For a good survey of religion in medieval Europe, see **B. Hamilton, *Religion in the Medieval West*** (London, 1986). On Europe during the time of the Investiture Controversy, see **U.-R. Blumenthal, *The Investiture Controversy*** (Philadelphia, 1988). For a general survey of church life, see **R. W. Southern, *Western Society and the Church in the Middle Ages,*** rev. ed. (New York, 1990).

On the papacy in the High Middle Ages, see the general surveys by **C. Morris, *The Papal Monarchy*** (Oxford, 1989), and **I. S. Robinson, *The Papacy*** (Cambridge, 1990). The papacy of Innocent III is covered in **J. E. Sayers, *Innocent III, Leader of Europe, 1198–1216*** (New York, 1994).

Good works on monasticism include **B. Bolton, *The Medieval Reformation*** (London, 1983), and **C. H. Lawrence, *Medieval Monasticism*** (London, 1984), a good general account. On the Cistercians, see **L. J. Lekai, *The Cistercians*** (Kent, Ohio, 1977). On the impact of the Franciscans and Dominicans, see **C. H. Lawrence, *The Friars: The Impact of the Early Mendicant Movement on Western Society*** (New York, 1994). On Saint Francis, see **A. House, *Francis of Assisi:***

A Revolutionary Life (London, 2001). **S. Flanagan, *Hildegard of Bingen,*** 2d ed. (London, 1998), is a good account of the twelfth-century mystic. For a good introduction to popular religion in the eleventh and twelfth centuries, see **R. Brooke and C. N. L. Brooke, *Popular Religion in the Middle Ages*** (London, 1984). The image of women in the secular and religious realms is discussed in **P. S. Gold, *The Lady and the Virgin: Image, Attitude, and Experience in Twelfth-Century France*** (Chicago, 1985).

On dissent and heresy, see **M. Lambert, *Medieval Heresy,*** 2d ed. (New York, 1992), and **J. Strayer, *The Albigensian Crusades,*** 2d ed. (New York, 1992). On the Inquisition, see **B. Hamilton, *The Medieval Inquisition*** (New York, 1981). The persecution of Jews in the thirteenth century can be examined in **J. Cohen, *The Friars and the Jews*** (Oxford, 1985). The basic study on intolerance and homosexuality is **J. Boswell, *Christianity, Social Tolerance, and Homosexuality*** (Chicago, 1980).

Two good general surveys of the Crusades are **H. E. Mayer, *The Crusades,*** 2d ed. (New York, 1988), and **J. Riley-Smith, *The Crusades: A Short History*** (New Haven, Conn., 1987). Also see **J. Riley-Smith, ed., *The Oxford Illustrated History of the Crusades*** (New York, 1995), and **A. Konstam, *Historical Atlas of the Crusades*** (New York, 2002). For works on the Byzantine and Islamic empires, see the reading suggestions at the end of Chapter 8 and **M. Angold, *The Byzantine Empire, 1025–1204*** (London, 1984). The disastrous Fourth Crusade is examined in **J. Godfrey, *1204: The Unholy Crusade*** (Oxford, 1980). On the later Crusades, see **N. Housley, *The Later Crusades, 1274–1580*** (New York, 1992).

History Now™

Enter *HistoryNow* using the access card that is available for *Western Civilization. HistoryNow* will assist you in understanding the content in this chapter with lesson plans generated for your needs. In addition, you can read the following documents, and many more, online:

> *Song of Roland*
>
> John of Salisbury, Book 5 of *Policraticus*

INFOTRAC SEARCH TERMS

 For additional reading, go to InfoTrac College Edition, your online research library at http://infotrac.thomsonlearning.com

Key Term Search	Subject Guide Search
medieval Germany	Crusades
medieval England	
Saint Francis	

WESTERN CIVILIZATION RESOURCES

Visit the *Western Civilization* Companion Web site for resources specific to this book:

> http://history.wadsworth.com/spielvogel06/

For a variety of tools to help you succeed in this course, visit the **Western Civilization Resource Center** at

> http://history.wadsworth.com/western/

Included are quizzes; images; documents; interactive simulations; maps and timelines; movie explorations; and a wealth of other sources.

THE LATER MIDDLE AGES: CRISIS AND DISINTEGRATION IN THE FOURTEENTH CENTURY

CHAPTER OUTLINE AND FOCUS QUESTIONS

A Time of Troubles: Black Death and Social Crisis

● What was the Black Death, and what was its impact on European society?

War and Political Instability

● What major problems did European states face in the fourteenth century?

The Decline of the Church

● How and why did the authority and prestige of the papacy decline in the fourteenth century?

The Cultural World of the Fourteenth Century

● What were the major developments in art and literature in the fourteenth century?

Society in an Age of Adversity

● How did the adversities of the fourteenth century affect urban life and medical practices?

CRITICAL THINKING

● To what extent were climate and disease the key factors in producing economic, social, and political changes in the fourteenth century?

Mass burial of plague victims

© The Granger Collection, New York

AS A RESULT OF THEIR CONQUESTS in the thirteenth and fourteenth centuries, the Mongols created a vast empire stretching from Russia in the west to China in the east. Mongol rule brought stability to the Eurasian trade routes; increased trade brought prosperity but also avenues for the spread of flea-infested rats that carried bubonic plague to both East Asia and Europe. The mid-fourteenth century witnessed one of the most destructive natural disasters in history—the Black Death. One contemporary observer named Henry Knighton, a canon of Saint Mary of the Meadow Abbey in Leicester, England, was simply overwhelmed by the magnitude of the catastrophe. Knighton began his account of the great plague with these words: "In this year [1348] and in the following one there was a general mortality of people throughout the whole world." Few were left untouched; the plague struck even isolated monasteries: "At Montpellier, there remained out of a hundred and forty friars only seven." Animals, too, were devastated: "During this same year, there was a great mortality of sheep everywhere in the kingdom; in one place and in one pasture, more than five thousand sheep died and became so putrefied that neither beast nor bird wanted to touch them."

Knighton was also stunned by the economic and social consequences of the Black Death. Prices dropped: "And the price of everything was cheap, because of the fear of death; there were very few who took any care for their wealth, or for anything else." Meanwhile laborers were scarce, so their wages increased: "In the following autumn, one could not hire a reaper at a lower wage than eight pence with food, or a mower at less than twelve pence with food. Because of this, much grain rotted in the fields for lack of harvesting." So many people died that some towns were deserted and some villages disappeared altogether: "Many small villages and hamlets were completely deserted; there was not one house left in them, but all those who had lived in them were dead." Some people thought the end of the world was at hand.

Plague was not the only disaster in the fourteenth century. Signs of disintegration were everywhere: famine, economic depression, war, social upheaval, a rise in crime and violence, and a decline in the power of the universal Catholic church. Periods of disintegration, however, are often fertile ground for change and new developments. Out of the dissolution of medieval civilization came a rebirth of culture that many historians have labeled the Renaissance.

A Time of Troubles: Black Death and Social Crisis

Well into the thirteenth century, Europe had experienced good harvests and an expanding population. By the end of the century, however, a period of disastrous changes had begun.

Famine and Population

Toward the end of the thirteenth century, noticeable changes in weather patterns were occurring as Europe entered a period that has been called a "little ice age." A small drop in overall temperatures resulted in shortened growing seasons and disastrous weather conditions, including heavy storms and constant rain. Between 1315 and 1317, heavy rains in northern Europe destroyed harvests and caused serious food shortages, resulting in extreme hunger and starvation. The great famine expanded to other parts of Europe in an all-too-familiar pattern, as is evident in this scene described by a contemporary chronicler:

> We saw a large number of both sexes, not only from nearby places but from as much as five leagues away, barefooted and maybe even, except for women, in a completely nude state, together with their priests coming in procession at the Church of the Holy Martyrs, their bones bulging out, devoutly carrying bodies of saints and other relics to be adorned hoping to get relief.[1]

Some historians estimate that famine killed 10 percent of the European population in the first half of the fourteenth century.

Europe had experienced a great increase in population in the High Middle Ages. By 1300, however, indications are that Europe had reached the upper limit of its population, not in an absolute sense, but in the number of people who could be supported by existing agricultural production and technology. Virtually all productive land was being farmed, including many marginal lands that needed intensive cultivation and proved easily susceptible to changing weather patterns.

We know that there was also a movement from overpopulated rural areas to urban locations. Eighteen percent of the people in the village of Broughton in England, for example, migrated between 1288 and 1340. There is no certainty that these migrants found better economic opportunities in urban areas. We might in fact conclude the opposite, based on the reports of increasing numbers of poor people in the cities. In 1330, for example, one chronicler estimated that of the 100,000 inhabitants of Florence, 17,000 were paupers. Moreover, evidence suggests that because of the increase in population, individual peasant holdings by 1300 were shrinking in size to an acreage that could no longer support a peasant family. Europe seemed to have reached an upper limit to population growth, and the number of poor appeared to have increased noticeably.

Some historians have pointed out that famine may have led to chronic malnutrition, which in turn contributed to increased infant mortality, lower birthrates, and higher susceptibility to disease because malnourished people are less able to resist infection. This, they argue, helps explain the high mortality of the great plague known as the Black Death.

The Black Death

The **Black Death** of the mid-fourteenth century was the most devastating natural disaster in European history, ravaging Europe and causing economic, social, political, and cultural upheaval. Contemporary chroniclers lamented that parents abandoned their children; one related the words: "Oh father, why have you abandoned me? . . . Mother, where have you gone?"[2] People were horrified by an evil force they could not understand and by the subsequent breakdown of all normal human relations.

Bubonic plague, the most common and most important form of plague in the time of the Black Death, was spread by black rats infested with fleas who were host to the deadly bacterium *Yersinia pestis*. Symptoms of bubonic plague included high fever, aching joints, swelling of the lymph nodes, and dark blotches caused by bleeding beneath the skin. Bubonic plague was actually the least toxic form of plague but nevertheless killed 50 to 60 percent of its victims. In pneumonic plague, the bacterial infection spread to the lungs, resulting in severe coughing, bloody sputum, and the relatively easy spread of the bacillus from human to human by coughing.

Spread of the Plague   The Black Death was the first major epidemic disease to strike Europe since the seventh century, an absence that helps explain medieval Europe's remarkable population growth. This great plague originated in Asia. After disappearing from Europe and the Middle East in the Middle Ages, bubonic plague continued to haunt areas of southwestern China, especially isolated rural territories. The arrival of Mongol troops in this area in the mid-thirteenth century became the means for the spread of the plague as flea-infested rats carrying the bacteria accompanied the Mongols into central and northwestern China and Central Asia. From there, trading caravans brought the plague to Caffa on the Black Sea in 1346.

The plague reached Europe in October 1347, when Genoese merchants brought it from Caffa to the island of Sicily off the coast of southern Italy. It spread quickly, reaching southern Italy and southern France and Spain by the end of 1347 (see Map 11.1). Usually, the diffusion of the Black Death followed commercial trade routes. In 1348, the plague spread through France and the Low Countries and into Germany. By the end of that year, it had moved to

England, ravaging it in 1349. By the end of 1349, it had expanded to northern Europe and Scandinavia. Eastern Europe and Russia were affected by 1351, although mortality rates were never as high in eastern Europe as they were in western and central Europe.

Mortality figures for the Black Death were incredibly high. Italy was hit especially hard. As the commercial center of the Mediterranean, Italy possessed scores of ports where the plague could be introduced. Italy's crowded cities, whether large, such as Florence, Genoa, and Venice, with populations near 100,000, or small, such as Orvieto and Pistoia, suffered losses of 50 to 60 percent (see the box on p. 287). France and England were also particularly devastated. In northern France, farming villages suffered mortality rates of 30 percent, while cities such as Rouen were more severely affected and experienced losses as high as 40 percent. In England and Germany, entire villages simply disappeared. In Germany, of approximately 170,000

	December 1347
	June 1348
	December 1348
	June 1349
	December 1349
	June 1350
	December 1350
	Area partially or totally spared

MAP 11.1 **Spread of the Black Death.** The plague entered Europe in Sicily in 1347 and within three years had killed between one-quarter and one-half of the population. Outbreaks continued into the early eighteenth century, and it took Europe two hundred years to return to the population level it had before the Black Death. ❓ Is there a general pattern between distance from Sicily and the elapsed time before a region was infected with the plague? 🌐 **View an animated version of this map or related maps at** http://history.wadsworth.com/spielvogel06/

Mass Burial of Plague Victims. The Black Death had spread to northern Europe by the end of 1348. Shown here is a mass burial of victims of the plague in Tournai, located in modern Belgium. As is evident in the illustration, at this stage of the plague, there was still time to make coffins for the victims' burial. Later, as the plague intensified, the dead were thrown into open pits.

inhabited locations, only 130,000 were left by the end of the fourteenth century.

It has been estimated that the European population declined by 25 to 50 percent between 1347 and 1351. If we accept the recent scholarly assessment of a European population of 75 million in the early fourteenth century, this means a death toll of 19 to 38 million people in four years. And the plague did not end in 1351. There were major outbreaks again in 1361–1362 and 1369 and then recurrences every five or six to ten or twelve years, depending on climatic and ecological conditions, until the end of the fifteenth century. The European population thus did not begin to recover until around 1500 and took several generations after that to reattain thirteenth-century levels.

Life and Death: Reactions to the Plague   Natural disasters of the magnitude of the great plague produce extreme psychological reactions. Knowing they could be dead in a matter of days, people began living for the moment; some threw themselves with abandon into sexual and alcoholic orgies. The fourteenth-century Italian writer Giovanni Boccaccio gave a classic description of this kind of reaction to the plague in Florence in the preface to his famous *Decameron*:

> [Some people] held that plenty of drinking and enjoyment, singing and free living and the gratification of the appetite in every possible way, letting the devil take the hindmost, was the best preventative . . . ; and as far as they could, they suited the action to the word. Day and night they went from one tavern to another drinking and carousing unrestrainedly. At the least inkling of something that suited them, they ran wild in other people's houses, and there was no one to prevent them, for everyone had abandoned all responsibility for his belongings as well as for himself, considering his days numbered.[3]

Wealthy and powerful people fled to their country estates, as Boccaccio recounted: "Still others . . . maintained that no remedy against plagues was better than to leave them miles behind. Men and women without number . . . , caring for nobody but themselves, abandoned the city, their houses and estates, their own flesh and blood even, and their effects, in search of a country place."[4]

The attempt to explain the Black Death and mitigate its harshness led to extreme sorts of behavior. To many people, the plague had either been sent by God as a punishment for humans' sins or been caused by the devil. Some resorted to extreme asceticism to cleanse themselves of sin and gain God's forgiveness. Such were the flagellants, whose movement became popular in 1348, especially in Germany. Groups of flagellants, both men and women, wandered from town to town, flogging themselves with whips to win the forgiveness of God, whom they believed had sent the plague to punish humans for their sinful ways. One contemporary chronicler described a flagellant procession:

> The penitents went about, coming first out of Germany. They were men who did public penance and scourged themselves with whips of hard knotted leather with little iron spikes. Some made themselves bleed very badly between the shoulder blades and some foolish women had cloths ready to catch the blood and smear it on their eyes, saying it was miraculous blood. While they were doing penance, they sang very mournful songs about the nativity and the passion of Our Lord. The object of this penance was to put a stop to the mortality, for in that time . . . at least a third of all the people in the world died.[5]

The Flagellants. Reactions to the plague were extreme at times. Believing that asceticism could atone for humanity's sins and win God's forgiveness, flagellants wandered from town to town flogging themselves and each other with whips, as in this illustration.

THE BLACK DEATH

HE BLACK DEATH was the most terrifying natural calamity of the Middle Ages. This contemporary description of the great plague in Florence is taken from the preface to the *Decameron* by the fourteenth-century Italian writer Giovanni Boccaccio.

Giovanni Boccaccio, *Decameron*

In the year of Our Lord 1348 the deadly plague broke out in the great city of Florence, most beautiful of Italian cities. Whether through the operation of the heavenly bodies or because of our own iniquities which the just wrath of God sought to correct, the plague had arisen in the East some years before, causing the death of countless human beings. It spread without stop from one place to another, until, unfortunately, it swept over the West. Neither knowledge nor human foresight availed against it, though the city was cleansed of much filth by chosen officers in charge and sick persons were forbidden to enter it, while advice was broadcast for the preservation of health. Nor did humble supplications serve. Not once but many times they were ordained in the form of processions and other ways for the propitiation of God by the faithful, but, in spite of everything, toward the spring of the year the plague began to show its ravages. . . .

It did not manifest itself as in the East, where if a man bled at the nose he had certain warning of inevitable death. At the onset of the disease both men and women were afflicted by a sort of swelling in the groin or under the armpits which sometimes attained the size of a common apple or egg. Some of these swellings were larger and some smaller, and were commonly called boils. From these two starting points the boils began in a little while to spread and appear generally all over the body. Afterwards, the manifestation of the disease changed into black or livid spots on the arms, thighs, and the whole person. In many these blotches were large and far apart, in others small and closely clus-

tered. Like the boils, which had been and continued to be a certain indication of coming death, these blotches had the same meaning for everyone on whom they appeared.

Neither the advice of physicians nor the virtue of any medicine seemed to help or avail in the cure of these diseases. Indeed, . . . not only did few recover, but on the contrary almost everyone died within three days of the appearance of the signs—some sooner, some later. . . . The virulence of the plague was all the greater in that it was communicated by the sick to the well by contact, not unlike fire when dry or fatty things are brought near it. But the evil was still worse. Not only did conversation and familiarity with the diseased spread the malady and even cause death, but the mere touch of the clothes or any other object the sick had touched or used, seemed to spread the pestilence. . . .

More wretched still were the circumstances of the common people and, for a great part, of the middle class, for, confined to their homes either by hope of safety or by poverty, and restricted to their own sections, they fell sick daily by thousands. There, devoid of help or care, they died almost without redemption. A great many breathed their last in the public streets, day and night; a large number perished in their homes, and it was only by the stench of their decaying bodies that they proclaimed their death to their neighbors. Everywhere the city was teeming with corpses. . . .

So many bodies were brought to the churches every day that the consecrated ground did not suffice to hold them, particularly according to the ancient custom of giving each corpse its individual place. Huge trenches were dug in the crowded churchyards and the new dead were piled in them, layer upon layer, like merchandise in the hold of a ship. A little earth covered the corpses of each row, and the procedure continued until the trench was filled to the top.

The flagellants attracted attention and created mass hysteria wherever they went. The Catholic church, however, became alarmed when flagellant groups began to kill Jews and attack clergy who opposed them. Some groups also developed a millenarian aspect, placing their emphasis on the coming end of the world, the return of Jesus, and the establishment of a thousand-year kingdom under his governance. Pope Clement VI condemned the flagellants in October 1349 and urged the public authorities to crush them. By the end of 1350, most of the flagellant movement had been destroyed.

An outbreak of virulent anti-Semitism also accompanied the Black Death. Jews were accused of causing the plague by poisoning town wells. Although Jews were persecuted in Spain, the worst organized massacres, or **pogroms,** against this helpless minority were carried out

in Germany; more than sixty major Jewish communities in Germany had been exterminated by 1351 (see the box on p. 288). Many Jews fled eastward to Russia and especially to Poland, where the king offered them protection. Eastern Europe became home to large Jewish communities.

The prevalence of death because of the plague and its recurrences affected people in profound ways. Some survivors apparently came to treat life as something cheap and passing. Violence and violent death appeared to be more common after the plague than before. Postplague Europe also demonstrated a morbid preoccupation with death. In their sermons, priests reminded parishioners that each night's sleep might be their last. Tombstones were decorated with macabre scenes of naked corpses in various stages of decomposition with snakes entwined in their bones and their innards filled with worms.

A MEDIEVAL HOLOCAUST: THE CREMATION OF THE STRASBOURG JEWS

IN THEIR ATTEMPT to explain the widespread horrors of the Black Death, medieval Christian communities looked for scapegoats. As at the time of the Crusades, the Jews were blamed for poisoning wells and thereby spreading the plague. This selection by a contemporary chronicler, written in 1349, gives an account of how Christians in the town of Strasbourg in the Holy Roman Empire dealt with their Jewish community. It is apparent that financial gain was also an important motive in killing the Jews.

Jacob von Königshofen, "The Cremation of the Strasbourg Jews"

In the year 1349 there occurred the greatest epidemic that ever happened. Death went from one end of the earth to the other. . . . And from what this epidemic came, all wise teachers and physicians could only say that it was God's will. . . . This epidemic also came to Strasbourg in the summer of the above-mentioned year, and it is estimated that about sixteen thousand people died.

In the matter of this plague the Jews throughout the world were reviled and accused in all lands of having caused it through the poison which they are said to have put into the water and the wells—that is what they were accused of—and for this reason the Jews were burnt all the way from the Mediterranean into Germany. . . .

[The account then goes on to discuss the situation of the Jews in the city of Strasbourg.]

On Saturday . . . they burnt the Jews on a wooden platform in their cemetery. There were about two thousand people of them. Those who wanted to baptise themselves were spared. [About one thousand accepted baptism.] Many small children were taken out of the fire and baptized against the will of their fathers and mothers. And everything that was owed to the Jews was canceled, and the Jews had to surrender all pledges and notes that they had taken for debts. The council, however, took the cash that the Jews possessed and divided it among the working-men proportionately. The money was indeed the thing that killed the Jews. If they had been poor and if the lords had not been in debt to them, they would not have been burnt. . . .

Thus were the Jews burnt at Strasbourg, and in the same year in all the cities of the Rhine, whether Free Cities or Imperial Cities or cities belonging to the lords. In some towns they burnt the Jews after a trial, in others, without a trial. In some cities the Jews themselves set fire to their houses and cremated themselves.

It was decided in Strasbourg that no Jew should enter the city for 100 years, but before 20 years had passed, the council and magistrates agreed that they ought to admit the Jews again into the city for 20 years. And so the Jews came back again to Strasbourg in the year 1368 after the birth of our Lord.

Economic Dislocation and Social Upheaval

The population collapse of the fourteenth century had dire economic and social consequences. Economic dislocation was accompanied by social upheaval. Between 1000 and 1300, Europe had been relatively stable. The division of society into the three estates of clergy (those who pray), nobility (those who fight), and laborers (those who work) had already begun to disintegrate in the thirteenth century, however. In the fourteenth century, a series of urban and rural revolts rocked European society.

Noble Landlords and Peasants   Both peasants and noble landlords were affected by the demographic crisis of the fourteenth century. Most noticeably, Europe experienced a serious labor shortage that caused a dramatic rise in the price of labor. At Cuxham manor in England, for example, a farm laborer who had received two shillings a week in 1347 was paid seven in 1349 and almost eleven by 1350. At the same time, the decline in population depressed or held stable the demand for agricultural produce, resulting in stable or falling prices for output (although in England prices remained high until the 1380s). The chronicler Henry Knighton observed: "And the price of everything was cheap. . . . A man could buy a horse for half a mark [six shillings], which before was worth forty shillings."[6] Because landlords were having to pay more for labor at the same time that their rents or incomes were declining, they began to experience considerable adversity and lower standards of living. In England, aristocratic incomes dropped more than 20 percent between 1347 and 1353.

Aristocrats responded to adversity by seeking to lower the wage rate. The English Parliament passed the Statute of Laborers (1351), which attempted to limit wages to pre-plague levels and forbid the mobility of peasants as well. Although such laws proved largely unworkable, they did keep wages from rising as high as they might have in a free market. Overall, the position of landlords continued to deteriorate during the late fourteenth and early fifteenth centuries. At the same time, the position of peasants improved, though not uniformly throughout Europe.

The decline in the number of peasants after the Black Death accelerated the process of converting labor services to rents, freeing peasants from the obligations of servile tenure and weakening the system of manorialism. But there were limits to how much the peasants could advance. They faced the same economic hurdles as the lords, while the latter attempted to impose wage restrictions, reinstate old forms of labor service, and create new obligations. New governmental taxes also hurt. Peasant complaints became widespread and soon gave rise to rural revolts.

Peasant Revolt in France   In 1358, a peasant revolt, known as the *Jacquerie,* broke out in northern France. The destruction of normal order by the Black Death and the subsequent economic dislocation were important factors in causing the revolt, but the ravages created by the Hundred Years' War also affected the French peasantry (see "War and Political Instability" later in this chapter). Both the French and English forces followed a deliberate policy of laying waste to peasants' lands while bands of mercenaries lived off the land by taking peasants' produce as well.

Peasant anger was also exacerbated by growing class tensions. Landed nobles were eager to hold on to their politically privileged position and felt increasingly threatened in the new postplague world of higher wages and lower prices. Many aristocrats looked on peasants with utter contempt. A French tale told to upper-class audiences contained this remarkable passage:

> Tell me, Lord, if you please, by what right or title does a villein [peasant] eat beef? . . . Should they eat fish? Rather let them eat thistles and briars, thorns and straw and hay on Sunday and peapods on weekdays. They should keep watch without sleep and have trouble always; that is how villeins should live. Yet each day they are full and drunk on the best wines, and in fine clothes. The great expenditures of villeins come as a high cost, for it is this that destroys and ruins the world. It is they who spoil the common welfare. From the villein comes all unhappiness. Should they eat meat? Rather should they chew grass on the heath with the horned cattle and go naked on all fours.[7]

The peasants reciprocated this contempt for their so-called social superiors.

The outburst of peasant anger led to savage confrontations. Castles were burned and nobles murdered (see the box on p. 290). Such atrocities did not go unanswered, however. The *Jacquerie* soon failed as the privileged classes closed ranks, savagely massacred the rebels, and ended the revolt.

An English Peasant Revolt   The English Peasants' Revolt of 1381 was the most prominent of all. It was a product not of desperation but of rising expectations. After the Black Death, the condition of the English peasants had improved as they enjoyed greater freedom and higher wages or lower rents. Aristocratic landlords had fought back with legislation to depress wages and attempted to reimpose old feudal dues. The most immediate cause of the revolt, however, was the monarchy's attempt to raise revenues by imposing a poll tax or a flat charge on each adult member of the population. Peasants in eastern England, the wealthiest part of the country, refused to pay the tax and expelled the collectors forcibly from their villages.

This action sparked a widespread rebellion of both peasants and townspeople led by a well-to-do peasant called Wat Tyler and a preacher named John Ball. The latter preached an effective message against the noble class, as recounted by the French chronicler Jean Froissart:

> Good people, things cannot go right in England and never will, until goods are held in common and there are no more villeins and gentlefolk, but we are all one and the same. In what way are those whom we call lords greater masters than ourselves?

Peasant Rebellion. The fourteenth century witnessed a number of revolts of the peasantry against noble landowners. Although the revolts often met with initial success, they were soon crushed. This fifteenth-century illustration shows nobles during the French *Jacquerie* of 1358 massacring the rebels in the town of Meaux, in northern France.

Bibliotheque Nationale, Paris, France

A REVOLT OF FRENCH PEASANTS

*I*N 1358, FRENCH PEASANTS rose up in a revolt known as the *Jacquerie*. The relationship between aristocrats and peasants had degenerated as a result of the social upheavals and privations caused by the Black Death and the Hundred Years' War. This excerpt from the chronicle of an aristocrat paints a horrifying picture of the barbarities that occurred during the revolt.

Jean Froissart, *Chronicles*

There were very strange and terrible happenings in several parts of the kingdom of France.... They began when some of the men from the country towns came together in the Beauvais region. They had no leaders and at first they numbered scarcely 100. One of them got up and said that the nobility of France, knights and squires, were disgracing and betraying the realm, and that it would be a good thing if they were all destroyed. At this they all shouted: "He's right! He's right! Shame on any man who saves the nobility from being wiped out!"

They banded together and went off, without further deliberation and unarmed except for pikes and knives, to the house of a knight who lived nearby. They broke in and killed the knight, with his lady and his children, big and small, and set fire to the house. Next they went to another castle and did much worse; for, having seized the knight and bound him securely to a post, several of them violated his wife and daughter before his eyes. Then they killed the wife, who was pregnant, and the daughter and all the other children, and finally put the knight to death with great cruelty and burned and razed the castle.

They did similar things in a number of castles and big houses, and their ranks swelled until there were a good 6,000 of them. Wherever they went their numbers grew, for all the men of the same sort joined them. The knights and squires fled before them with their families. They took their wives and daughters many miles away to put them in safety, leaving their houses open with their possessions inside. And those evil men, who had come together without leaders or arms, pillaged and burned everything and violated and killed all the ladies and girls without mercy, like mad dogs. Their barbarous acts were worse than anything that ever took place between Christians and Saracens [Muslims]. Never did men commit such vile deeds. They were such that no living creature ought to see, or even imagine or think of, and the men who committed the most were admired and had the highest places among them. I could never bring myself to write down the horrible and shameful things which they did to the ladies. But, among other brutal excesses, they killed a knight, put him on a spit, and turned him at the fire and roasted him before the lady and her children. After about a dozen of them had violated the lady, they tried to force her and the children to eat the knight's flesh before putting them cruelly to death.

How have they deserved it? Why do they hold us in bondage? If we all spring from a single father and mother, Adam and Eve, how can they claim or prove that they are lords more than us, except by making us produce and grow the wealth which they spend?[8]

The revolt was initially successful as the rebels burned down the manor houses of aristocrats, lawyers, and government officials and murdered several important officials, including the archbishop of Canterbury. After the peasants marched on London, the young King Richard II, age fifteen, promised to accept the rebels' demands if they returned to their homes. They accepted the king's word and dispersed, but the king reneged and with the assistance of the aristocrats arrested hundreds of the rebels. The poll tax was eliminated, however, and in the end most of the rebels were pardoned.

Revolts in the Cities Revolts also erupted in the cities. Commercial and industrial activity suffered almost immediately from the Black Death. An oversupply of goods and an immediate drop in demand led to a decline in trade after 1350. Some industries suffered greatly. Florence's woolen industry, one of the giants, produced 70,000 to 80,000 pieces of cloth in 1338; in 1378, it was yielding only 24,000 pieces. Bourgeois merchants and manufacturers responded to the decline in trade and production by attempting to restrict competition and resist the demands of the lower classes.

In urban areas, where capitalist industrialists paid low wages and managed to prevent workers from forming organizations to help themselves, industrial revolts broke out throughout Europe. Ghent experienced one in 1381, Rouen in 1382. Most famous, however, was the revolt of the *ciompi* in Florence in 1378. The *ciompi* were wool workers in Florence's most prominent industry. In the 1370s, not only was the woolen industry depressed, but the wool workers saw their real wages decline when the coinage in which they were paid was debased. Their revolt won them some concessions from the municipal government, including the right to form guilds and be represented in the government. But their newly won rights were short-lived; authorities ended *ciompi* participation in the government by 1382.

Although the peasant and urban revolts sometimes resulted in short-term gains for the participants, it is also true that the uprisings were quickly crushed and their gains lost. Accustomed to ruling, the established classes easily combined and quashed dissent. Nevertheless, the rural and urban revolts of the fourteenth century ushered in an age of social conflict that characterized much of later European history.

War and Political Instability

Famine, plague, economic turmoil, social upheaval, and violence were not the only problems of the fourteenth century. War and political instability must also be added to the list. Of all the struggles that ensued in the fourteenth century, the Hundred Years' War was the most famous and the most violent.

Causes of the Hundred Years' War

In 1259, the English king, Henry III, had relinquished his claims to all the French territories previously held by the English monarchy except for one relatively small possession known as the duchy of Gascony. As duke of Gascony, the English king pledged loyalty as a vassal to the French king. But this territory gave rise to numerous disputes between the kings of England and France. By the thirteenth century, the Capetian monarchs had greatly increased their power over their more important vassals, the great lords of France. Royal officials interfered regularly in the affairs of the vassals' fiefs, especially in matters of justice. Although this policy irritated all the vassals, it especially annoyed the king of England, who considered himself the peer of the French king.

A dispute over the right of succession to the French throne also complicated the struggle between the French and the English. In the fourteenth century, the Capetian dynasty failed to produce a male heir for the first time in almost four hundred years. In 1328, the last son of King Philip IV died without a male heir. The closest male relative in line to the throne was King Edward III of England (1327–1377), whose mother was Isabella, the daughter of Philip IV. Known for her strong personality (she was nicknamed the "she-wolf of France"), Isabella, with the assistance of her lover, led a revolt against her husband, King Edward II, overthrew him, and ruled England until her teenage son, Edward III, took sole control of the throne in 1330. As the son of the daughter of King Philip IV, King Edward III of England had a claim to the French throne, but the French nobles argued that the inheritance of the monarchy could not pass through the female line and chose a cousin of the Capetians, Philip, duke of Valois, as King Philip VI (1328–1350).

The immediate cause of the war between France and England was yet another quarrel over Gascony. In 1337, when Edward III, the king of England and duke of Gascony, refused to do homage to Philip VI for Gascony, the French king seized the duchy. Edward responded by declaring war on Philip, the "so-called king of France." There is no doubt that the personalities of the two monarchs also had much

to do with the outbreak of the Hundred Years' War. Both Edward and Philip loved luxury and shared a desire for the glory and prestige that came from military engagements. Both were only too willing to use their respective nation's resources to satisfy their own desires. Moreover, for many nobles, the promise of plunder and territorial gain was an incentive to follow the disruptive path of their rulers.

Conduct and Course of the War

The Hundred Years' War began in a burst of knightly enthusiasm. Trained to be warriors, knights viewed the clash of battle as the ultimate opportunity to demonstrate their fighting abilities. But this struggle would change the nature of warfare, for as it dragged on, the outcomes of battles were increasingly determined not by knights but by peasant foot soldiers. The French army of 1337, with its heavily armed noble cavalry, resembled its twelfth- and thirteenth-century forebears. The noble cavalrymen considered themselves the fighting elite and looked with contempt on the foot soldiers and crossbowmen, their social inferiors.

The English army, however, had evolved differently and had included peasants as paid foot soldiers since at least Anglo-Saxon times. Armed with pikes, many of these foot soldiers had also adopted the longbow, invented by the Welsh. The longbow had a more rapid speed of fire than the more powerful crossbow. Although the English made use of heavily armed cavalry, they relied even more on large numbers of foot soldiers.

Early Phases of the War Edward III's early campaigns in France achieved little. When Edward renewed his efforts in 1346 with an invasion of Normandy, Philip responded by raising a large force to crush the English army and met Edward's forces at Crécy, just south of Flanders. The larger French army followed no battle plan but simply attacked the English lines in a disorderly fashion. The arrows of the English archers devastated the French cavalry. As Jean

Philip III
king of France (1270–1285)

Philip IV
(1285–1314)

Charles of Valois
(d. 1325)

Louis X
(1314–1316)

Philip V
(1316–1322)

Charles IV
(1322–1328)

Isabella = Edward II
king of England
(1307–1327)

Philip VI
king of France
(1328–1350)

John I
(1316)

(daughters)

(daughters)

Edward III
king of England
(1327–1377)

John II
king of France
(1350–1364)

Battle of Crécy. This fifteenth-century manuscript illustration depicts the Battle of Crécy, the first of several military disasters suffered by the French in the Hundred Years' War, and shows why the English preferred the longbow to the crossbow. At the left, the French crossbowmen stop shooting and prime their weapons by cranking the handle, while English archers continue to shoot their longbows (a skilled archer could launch ten arrows a minute).

Froissart described it, "The English continued to shoot [their longbows] into the thickest part of the crowd, wasting none of their arrows. They impaled or wounded horses and riders, who fell to the ground in great distress, unable to get up again [because of their heavy armor] without the help of several men."[9] It was a stunning victory for the English. Edward followed up by capturing the French port of Calais to serve as a staging ground for future invasions.

The Battle of Crécy was not decisive, however. The English simply did not possess the resources to subjugate all of France. Truces, small-scale hostilities, and some major operations were combined in an orgy of seemingly incessant struggle. The English campaigns were waged by Edward III and his son Edward, the prince of Wales, known as the Black Prince. The Black Prince's campaigns in France were devastating (see the box on p. 293). Avoiding pitched battles, his forces deliberately ravaged the land, burning crops and entire unfortified villages and towns and stealing anything of value. For the English, such campaigns were profitable; for the French people, they meant hunger, deprivation, and death. When the army of the Black Prince was finally forced to do battle, the French, under their king, John II (1350–1364), were once again defeated. This time even the king was captured. This Battle of Poitiers (1356) ended the first phase of the Hundred Years' War. Under the Peace of Brétigny (1359), the French agreed to pay a large ransom for King John, the English territories in Gascony were enlarged, and Edward renounced his claims to the throne of France in return for John's promise to give up control over English lands in France. This first phase of the war made it clear that despite their victories, the English were not really strong enough to subdue all of France and make Edward III's claim to the French monarchy a reality.

Monarchs, however, could be slow learners. The Treaty of Brétigny was never really enforced. In the next phase of the war, in the capable hands of John's son Charles V (1364–1380), the French recovered what they had previously lost. The English returned to plundering the French countryside and avoiding pitched battles. That pleased Charles, who did not want to engage in set battles, preferring to use armed bands to reduce the English fortresses systematically. By 1374, the French had recovered their lost lands, although France itself continued to be plagued by "free companies" of mercenaries who, no longer paid by the English, simply lived off the land by plunder and ransom. Nevertheless, for the time being, the war seemed over, especially when a twenty-year truce was negotiated in 1396.

Renewal of the War   In 1415, however, the English king, Henry V (1413–1422), renewed the war at a time when the French were enduring civil war as the dukes of Burgundy and Orléans competed to control the weak French king, Charles VI. In the summer of 1413, Paris exploded with bloody encounters. Taking advantage of the chaos, Henry V invaded France in 1415. At the Battle of Agincourt (1415), the French suffered a disastrous defeat, and fifteen hundred French nobles died when the heavy, armor-plated French knights attempted to attack across a field turned to mud by heavy rain. Altogether, French losses were six thousand dead; the English lost only three hundred men.

Henry went on to reconquer Normandy and forge an alliance with the duke of Burgundy, which led Charles VI to agree to the Treaty of Troyes in 1420. By this treaty, Henry V was married to Catherine, daughter of Charles VI, and recognized as the heir to the French throne. By 1420, the English were masters of northern France (see Map 11.2).

The seemingly hopeless French cause fell into the hands of Charles the dauphin (heir to the throne), the son of Charles VI, who, despite being disinherited by the Treaty of Troyes, still considered himself the real heir to the French throne. The dauphin governed the southern two-thirds of French lands from Bourges. Charles was weak and timid and was unable to rally the French against the English, who in 1428 had turned south and were besieging the city of Orléans to gain access to the valley of the Loire. The French monarch was saved, quite unexpectedly, by a French peasant woman.

THE HUNDRED YEARS' WAR

*I*N HIS ACCOUNT OF the Hundred Years' War, the fourteenth-century French chronicler Jean Froissart described the sack of the fortified French town of Limoges by the Black Prince, Edward, the prince of Wales. It provides a vivid example of how noncombatants fared during the war.

Jean Froissart, *Chronicles*

For about a month, certainly not longer, the Prince of Wales remained before Limoges. During that time he allowed no assaults or skirmishes, but pushed on steadily with the mining. The knights inside and the townspeople, who knew what was going on, started a countermine in the hope of killing the English miners, but it was a failure. When the Prince's miners who, as they dug, were continually shoring up their tunnel, had completed their work, they said to the Prince: "My lord, whenever you like now we can bring a big piece of wall down into the moat, so that you can get into the city quite easily and safely."

The Prince was very pleased to hear this. "Excellent," he said. "At six o'clock tomorrow morning, show me what you can do."

When they knew it was the right time for it, the miners started a fire in their mine. In the morning, just as the Prince had specified, a great section of the wall collapsed, filling the moat at the place where it fell. For the English, who were armed and ready waiting, it was a welcome sight.

Those on foot could enter as they liked, and did so. They rushed to the gate, cut through the bars holding it and knocked it down. They did the same with the barriers outside, meeting with no resistance. It was all done so quickly that the people in the town were taken unawares. Then the Prince, the Duke of Lancaster, the Earl of Cambridge, Sir Guichard d'Angle, with all the others and their men burst into the city, followed by pillagers on foot, all in a mood to wreak havoc and do murder, killing indiscriminately, for those were their orders. There were pitiful scenes. Men, women, and children flung themselves on their knees before the Prince, crying: "Have mercy on us, gentle sir!" But he was so inflamed with anger that he would not listen. Neither man nor woman was heeded, but all who could be found were put to the sword, including many who were in no way to blame. I do not understand how they could have failed to take pity on people who were too unimportant to have committed treason. Yet they paid for it, and paid more dearly than the leaders who had committed it.

There is no man so hard-hearted that, if he had been in Limoges on that day, and had remembered God, he would not have wept bitterly at the fearful slaughter which took place. More than 3,000 persons, men, women, and children, were dragged out to have their throats cut. May God receive their souls, for they were true martyrs.

Joan of Arc Joan of Arc was born in 1412 to well-to-do peasants from the village of Domrémy in Champagne. Deeply religious, Joan experienced visions and came to believe that her favorite saints had commanded her to free France and have the dauphin crowned as king. In February 1429, Joan made her way to the dauphin's court, where her sincerity and simplicity persuaded Charles to allow her to accompany a French army to Orléans. Apparently inspired by the faith of the peasant girl, the French armies found new confidence in themselves and liberated Orléans, changing the course of the war. Within a few weeks, the entire Loire valley had been freed of the English. In July 1429, fulfilling Joan's other task, the dauphin was crowned king of France and became Charles VII (1422–1461). In accomplishing the two commands of her angelic voices, Joan had brought the war to a decisive turning point.

Joan, however, did not live to see the war concluded. She was captured by the Burgundian allies of the English in 1430. Wishing to eliminate the "Maid of Orléans" for obvious political reasons, the English turned Joan over to the Inquisition

Joan of Arc. Pictured here in a suit of armor, Joan of Arc is holding aloft a banner that shows Jesus and two angels. This portrait dates from the late fifteenth century; there are no known portraits of Joan made from life.

France in the Mid-Fourteenth Century

— Boundary of kingdom of France, 1360

⋯⋯ Lands held by Edward III of England on accession, 1327

→ Route taken by Edward III, 1346–1347

→ Route taken by Edward, Black Prince, 1355–1357

⚔ Site and date of important battle

▮ Lands ceded to Edward III of England

▮ Domain of king of France, 1360

▯ Lands held by relatives of the king of France

▮ Other territories held by the king of France

France in the Early Fifteenth Century

— Boundary of kingdom of France, 1429

⋯⋯ Boundary of lands left to England, 1377

— Route taken by Henry V, 1415–1416

— Route taken by Joan of Arc, 1429–1431

⚔ Site and date of important battle

▮ Lands held by Henry VI of England, 1429

▮ Lands held by Charles VII of France

▮ Lands held by the duke of Burgundy

▮ Burgundian lands recognizing Henry VI

MAP 11.2 The Hundred Years' War. This long, exhausting struggle began in 1337 and dragged on until 1453. The English initially gained substantial French territory, but in the later phases of the war, France turned the tide, eventually expelling the English from all Continental lands except the port of Calais. ❓ What gains had the English made by 1429, and how do they correlate to proximity to England and the ocean? 🖱 **View an animated version of this map or related maps at** http://history.wadsworth.com/spielvogel06/

on charges of witchcraft. In the fifteenth century, spiritual visions were thought to be inspired by either God or the devil. Because Joan dressed in men's clothing, it was easy for her enemies to believe that she was in league with the "prince of darkness." She was condemned to death as a heretic and burned at the stake in 1431, at the age of nineteen. To the end, as the flames rose up around her, she declared that her voices came from God and had not deceived her. Twenty-five years later, a church court exonerated her of these charges. To a contemporary French writer, Christine de Pizan, she became a feminist heroine (see the box on p. 295). In 1920, she was made a saint of the Roman Catholic church.

End of the War Joan of Arc's accomplishments proved decisive. Although the war dragged on for another two decades, defeats of English armies in Normandy and Aquitaine led to French victory. Important to the French success was the use of the cannon, a new weapon made possible by the invention of gunpowder. The Chinese had invented gunpowder in the eleventh century and devised a simple cannon by the thirteenth century. The Mongols greatly improved this technology, developing more accurate cannons and cannonballs; both spread to the Middle East by the thirteenth century and to Europe by the fourteenth.

A Feminist Heroine: Christine de Pizan on Joan of Arc

CHRISTINE DE PIZAN, France's "first woman of letters," was witness to the rescue of France from the hands of the English by the efforts of Joan of Arc and was also present at the coronation of Charles VII as king of France. Christine believed that a turning point had arrived in French history and that Joan—a woman—had been responsible for France's salvation. She wrote a poem to honor this great occasion. The following stanzas are taken from her poem.

Christine de Pizan, *The Poem of Joan of Arc*, July 31, 1429

The year of fourteen twenty-nine
The sun came out to shine again.
It brings the season new and good,
Which we had not directly seen
Too long a time, while many passed
Their lives in sorrow; I am one.
But now, no longer do I grieve
Because I see what pleases me. . . .

And you, the King of France, King Charles,
The seventh of that noble name,
Who fought a mighty war before
Good fortune came at all to you:
Do, now, observe your dignity
Exalted by the Maid, who bent
Your enemies beneath your flag
In record time (that's something new!)

And people thought that it would be
Impossible indeed for you
To ever have your country back,
For it was nearly lost; but now,
It's clearly yours; no matter who
Has done you wrong, it's yours once more,
And through the clever Maid who did
Her part therein—thanks be to God! . . .

When I reflect upon your state,
The youthful maiden that you are,
To whom God gives the force and strength
To be the champion and the one
To suckle France upon her milk
Of peace, the sweetest nourishment,
To overthrow the rebel host:
The wonder passes Nature's work!

That is, if God, through Joshua
Performed so many miracles
In conquering those places where

So many met defeat—a man
Of strength was Joshua. But she's
A woman—simple shepherdess—
More brave than ever man at Rome!
An easy thing for God to do!

But as for us, we've never heard
About a marvel quite so great
For all the heroes who have lived
In history can't measure up
In bravery against the Maid,
Who strives to rout our enemies.

It's God does that, who's guiding her
Whose courage passes that of men . . .
By miracle has she appeared,
Divine commandment sent her here.
God's angel led her in before
The king, to bring her help to him.
There's no illusion in her case
Because it's been indeed borne out
In council (in conclusion, then,
A thing is proved by its effect). . . .

What honor for the female sex!
God's love for it appears quite clear,
Because the kingdom laid to waste
By all those wretched people now
Stands safe, a woman rescued it
(A hundred thousand men could not
Do that) and killed the hostile foe!
A thing beyond belief before! . . .

While ridding France of enemies,
Retaking town and castle both.
No force was ever quite so great,
If hundreds or if thousands strong!
Among our men so brave and apt
She's captain over all; such strength
No Hector or Achilles had.
All this God does, who's guiding her. . . .

The English will be crushed through her,
And never will they rise again
For God who wills it hears the voice
Of guiltless folk they tried to harm!
The blood of those they've killed, who'll walk
No more, cries out. God wants an end
To this; instead He has resolved
To chastise them as evil men.

CHRONOLOGY	The Hundred Years' War
Outbreak of hostilities	1337
Battle of Crécy	1346
Battle of Poitiers	1356
Peace of Brétigny	1359
Death of Edward III	1377
Twenty-year truce declared	1396
Henry V (1413–1422) renews the war	1415
Battle of Agincourt	1415
Treaty of Troyes	1420
French recovery under Joan of Arc	1429–1431
End of the war	1453

The death of England's best commanders and the instability of the English government under King Henry VI (1421–1471) also contributed to England's defeat. By 1453, the only part of France that was left in England's hands was the coastal town of Calais, which remained English for another century.

Political Instability

The fourteenth century was a period of adversity for the internal political stability of European governments. Although government bureaucracies grew ever larger, at the same time the question of who should control the bureaucracies led to internal conflict and instability. Like the lord-serf relationship, the lord-vassal relationship based on land and military service was being replaced by a contract based on money. Especially after the Black Death, money payments called **scutage** were increasingly substituted for military service. Monarchs welcomed this development because they could now hire professional soldiers, who tended to be more reliable anyway. As lord-vassal relationships became less personal and less important, new relationships based on political advantage began to be formed, creating new avenues for political influence—and for corruption as well. Especially noticeable as the landed aristocrats suffered declining rents and social uncertainties with the new relationships was the formation of factions of nobles who looked for opportunities to advance their power and wealth at the expense of other noble factions and of their monarchs. Other nobles went to the royal courts, offering to serve the kings.

The kings had their own problems, however. By the mid-fifteenth century, reigning monarchs in many European countries were not the direct descendents of the rulers of 1300. The founders of these new dynasties had to struggle for position as factions of nobles vied to gain material advantages for themselves. As the fifteenth century began, there were two claimants to the throne of France, two aristocratic factions fighting for control of England, and three German princes struggling to be recognized as Holy Roman Emperor.

Fourteenth-century monarchs of old dynasties and new faced financial problems as well. The shift to using mercenary soldiers left monarchs perennially short of cash. Traditional revenues, especially rents from property, increasingly proved insufficient to meet their needs. Monarchs attempted to generate new sources of revenues, especially through taxes, which often meant going through parliaments. This opened the door for parliamentary bodies to gain more power by asking for favors first. Although unsuccessful in most cases, the parliaments simply added another element of uncertainty and confusion to fourteenth-century politics. Turning now to a survey of western and central European states (eastern Europe will be examined in Chapter 12), we can see how these disruptive factors worked.

The Growth of England's Political Institutions

The fifty-year reign of Edward III (1327–1377) was important for the evolution of English political institutions in the fourteenth century. Parliament increased in prominence and developed its basic structure and functions during Edward's reign. Due to his constant need for money to fight the Hundred Years' War, Edward came to rely on Parliament to levy new taxes. In return for regular grants, Edward made several concessions, including a commitment to levy no direct tax without Parliament's consent and to allow Parliament to examine the government accounts to ensure that the money was being spent properly. By the end of Edward's reign, Parliament had become an important component of the English governmental system.

During this same period, Parliament began to assume the organizational structure it has retained to this day. The Great Council of barons became the House of Lords and evolved into a body composed of the chief bishops and abbots of the realm and aristocratic peers whose position in Parliament was hereditary. The representatives of the shires and boroughs, who were considered less important than the lay and ecclesiastical lords, held collective meetings and soon came to be regarded as the House of Commons. Together, the House of Lords and House of Commons constituted Parliament. Although the House of Commons did little beyond approving measures proposed by the Lords, during Edward's reign the Commons did begin the practice of drawing up petitions, which, if accepted by the king, became law.

After Edward III's death, England began to experience the internal instability of aristocratic factionalism that was racking other European countries. The early years of the reign of Edward's grandson, Richard II (1377–1399), began inauspiciously with the peasant revolt that ended only when the king made concessions. Richard's reign was troubled by competing groups of nobles who sought to pursue their own interests. One faction, led by Henry of Lancaster, defeated the king's forces and then deposed and killed him. Henry of Lancaster became King Henry IV (1399–1413). In the fifteenth century, factional conflict would lead to a devastating series of civil wars known as the War of the Roses.

The Problems of the French Kings

At the beginning of the fourteenth century, France was the most prosperous monarchy in Europe. By the end of the century, much of its wealth had been dissipated, and rival factions of aristocrats had made effective monarchical rule virtually impossible.

The French monarchical state had always had an underlying inherent weakness that proved its undoing in difficult times. Although Capetian monarchs had found ways to enlarge their royal domain and extend their control by developing a large and effective bureaucracy, the various territories that made up France still maintained their own princes, customs, and laws. The parliamentary institutions of France provide a good example of France's basic lack of unity. The French parliament, known as the Estates-General and composed of representatives of the clergy, the nobility, and the **Third Estate** (everyone else), usually represented only the north of France, not the entire kingdom. The southern provinces had their own estates, and local estates existed in other parts of France. Unlike the English Parliament, which was evolving into a crucial part of the English government, the French Estates-General was simply one of many such institutions.

When Philip VI (1328–1350) became involved in the Hundred Years' War with England, he found it necessary to devise new sources of revenue, including a tax on salt known as the *gabelle* and a hearth tax eventually called the *taille*. These taxes weighed heavily on the French peasantry and middle class. Consequently, when additional taxes were needed to pay for the ransom of King John II after his capture at the Battle of Poitiers, the middle-class inhabitants of the towns tried to use the Estates-General to reform the French government and tax structure.

At the meeting of the Estates-General in 1357, under the leadership of the Parisian provost Étienne Marcel, representatives of the Third Estate granted taxes in exchange for a promise from King John's son, the dauphin Charles, not to tax without the Estates-General's permission and to allow the Estates-General to meet on a regular basis and participate in important political decisions. After Marcel's movement was crushed in 1358, this attempt to make the Estates-General a functioning part of the French government collapsed. The dauphin became King Charles V (1364–1380) and went on to recover much of the land lost to the English. His military successes underscored his efforts to reestablish strong monarchical powers. He undermined the role of the Estates-General by getting it to grant him taxes with no fixed time limit. Charles's death in 1380 soon led to a new time of troubles for the French monarchy, however.

The insanity of Charles VI (1380–1422), which first became apparent in 1392, opened the door to rival factions of French nobles aspiring to power and wealth. The dukes of Burgundy and Orléans competed to control Charles and the French monarchy. Their struggles created chaos for the French government and the French people. Many nobles supported the Orléanist faction, while Paris and other towns favored the Burgundians. By the beginning of the fifteenth century, France seemed hopelessly mired in a civil war. When the English renewed the Hundred Years' War in 1415, the Burgundians supported the English cause and the English monarch's claim to the throne of France.

The German Monarchy

England and France had developed strong national monarchies in the High Middle Ages. By the end of the fourteenth century, they seemed in danger of disintegrating due to dynastic problems and the pressures generated by the Hundred Years' War. In contrast, the Holy Roman Empire, whose core consisted of the lands of Germany, had already begun to fall apart in the High Middle Ages. Northern Italy, which the German emperors had tried to include in their medieval empire, had been free from any real imperial control since the end of the Hohenstaufen dynasty in the thirteenth century. In Germany itself, the failure of the Hohenstaufens ended any chance of centralized monarchical authority, and Germany became a land of hundreds of virtually independent states. These varied in size and power and included princely states, such as the duchies of Bavaria and Saxony; free imperial city-states (self-governing cities directly under the control of the Holy Roman Emperor rather than a German territorial prince), such as Nuremberg; modest territories of petty imperial knights; and ecclesiastical states, such as the archbishopric of Cologne, in which an ecclesiastical official, such as a bishop, archbishop, or abbot, served in a dual capacity as an administrative official of the Catholic church and as secular lord over the territories of the state. Although all of the rulers of these different states had some obligations to the German king and Holy Roman Emperor, more and more they acted independently.

The Holy Roman Empire in the Fourteenth Century

Electoral Nature of the German Monarchy   Because of its unique pattern of development in the High Middle Ages, the German monarchy had become established on an elective rather than a hereditary basis. This principle of election was standardized in 1356 by the Golden Bull issued by Emperor Charles IV (1346–1378). This document stated that four lay princes (the count palatine of the Rhine, the duke of Saxony, the margrave of Brandenburg, and the king of Bohemia) and three ecclesiastical rulers (the archbishops of Mainz, Trier, and Cologne) would serve as electors with the legal power to elect the "king of the Romans and future emperor, to be ruler of the world and of the

Christian people."[10] "King of the Romans" was the official title of the German king; after his imperial coronation, he would also have the title of emperor.

In the fourteenth century, the electoral principle further ensured that kings of Germany were generally weak. Their ability to exercise effective power depended on the extent of their own family possessions. At the beginning of the fifteenth century, three emperors claimed the throne. Although the dispute was quickly settled, Germany entered the fifteenth century in a condition that verged on anarchy. Princes fought princes and leagues of cities. The emperors were virtually powerless to control any of them.

The States of Italy

By the fourteenth century, Italy, too, had failed to develop a centralized monarchical state. Papal opposition to the rule of the Hohenstaufen emperors in northern Italy had virtually guaranteed that. Moreover, southern Italy was divided into the kingdom of Naples, ruled by the French house of Anjou, and Sicily, whose kings came from the Spanish house of Aragon. The center of the peninsula remained under the rather shaky control of the papacy. Lack of centralized authority had enabled numerous city-states in northern Italy to remain independent of any political authority.

In fourteenth-century Italy, two general tendencies can be discerned: the replacement of republican governments by tyrants and the expansion of the larger city-states at the expense of the less powerful ones. Nearly all the cities of northern Italy began their existence as free communes with republican governments. But in the fourteenth century, intense internal strife led city-states to resort to temporary expedients, allowing rule by one man with dictatorial powers. Limited rule, however, soon became long-term despotism as tyrants proved willing to use force to maintain themselves in power. Eventually, such tyrants tried to legitimize their power by purchasing titles from the emperor (still nominally ruler of northern Italy as Holy Roman Emperor). In this fashion, the Visconti became the dukes of Milan and the d'Este, the dukes of Ferrara.

The other change of great significance was the development of larger, regional states as the larger states expanded at the expense of the smaller ones. To fight their battles, city-states came to rely on mercenary soldiers, whose leaders, called *condottieri,* sold the services of their bands to the highest bidder. These mercenaries wreaked havoc on the countryside, living by blackmail and looting when they were not actively engaged in battles. Many were foreigners who flocked to Italy during the periods of truce of the Hundred Years' War. By the end of the fourteenth century, three major states came to dominate northern Italy: the despotic state of Milan and the republican states of Florence and Venice.

Duchy of Milan   In the fertile Po valley, where the chief trade routes from Italian coastal cities to the Alpine passes crossed, Milan was one of the richest city-states in Italy.

Mercenaries as Looters. Mercenary soldiers, like medieval armies in general, were notorious for causing havoc by looting when they were not engaged in battle. This mid-fourteenth-century manuscript illustration shows soldiers ransacking a house in Paris.

British Library, London

Politically, it was also one of the most agitated until the Visconti family established itself as the hereditary despots of Milan in 1322. Giangaleazzo Visconti, who ruled from 1385 to 1402, transformed this despotism into a hereditary duchy by purchasing the title of duke from the emperor in 1395. Under Giangaleazzo's direction, the duchy of Milan extended its power over all of Lombardy and even threatened to conquer much of northern Italy until the duke's untimely death before the gates of Florence in 1402.

Republic of Florence Florence, like the other Italian towns, was initially a free commune dominated by a patrician class of nobles known as the *grandi*. But the rapid expansion of Florence's economy made possible the development of a wealthy merchant-industrialist class known as the *popolo grasso*—literally the "fat people." In 1293, the *popolo grasso* assumed a dominant role in government by establishing a new constitution known as the Ordinances of Justice. It provided for a republican government controlled by the seven major guilds of the city, which represented the interests of the wealthier classes. Executive power was vested in the hands of a council of elected priors (the *signoria*) and a standard-bearer of justice called the *gonfaloniere,* assisted by a number of councils with advisory and overlapping powers. Near the mid-fourteenth century, revolutionary activity by the *popolo minuto,* the small shopkeepers and artisans, won them a share in the government. Even greater expansion occurred briefly when the *ciompi,* or industrial wool workers, were allowed to be represented in the government after their revolt in 1378. Only four years later, however, a counterrevolution brought the "fat people" back into virtual control of the government. After 1382, the Florentine government was controlled by a small merchant oligarchy that manipulated the supposedly republican government. By that time, Florence had also been successful in a series of wars against its neighbors. It had conquered most of Tuscany and established itself as a major territorial state in northern Italy.

Republic of Venice The other major northern Italian state was the republic of Venice, which had grown rich from commercial activity throughout the eastern Mediterranean and into northern Europe. A large number of merchant families became extremely wealthy. In the constitution of 1297, these patricians took control of the republic. In this year, the Great Council, the source of all political power, was closed to all but the members of about two hundred families. Since all other magistrates of the city were chosen either from or by this council, these families now formed a hereditary patriciate that completely dominated the city. Although the doge (or duke) had been the executive head of the

The States of Italy in the Fourteenth Century

republic since the Early Middle Ages, by 1300 he had become largely a figurehead. Actual power was vested in the hands of the Great Council and the legislative body known as the Senate, while an extraordinary body known as the Council of Ten, first formed in 1310, came to be the real executive power of the state. Venetian government was respected by contemporaries for its stability. A sixteenth- century Italian historian noted that Venice had "the best government of any city not only in our own times but also in the classical world."[11]

In the fourteenth century, Venice also embarked on a policy of expansion. By the end of the century, it had created a commercial empire by establishing colonies and trading posts in the eastern Mediterranean and Black Sea as well as continuing its commercial monopolies in the Byzantine Empire. At the same time, Venice began to conquer the territory adjoining it in northern Italy.

The Decline of the Church

The papacy of the Roman Catholic church reached the height of its power in the thirteenth century. Theories of papal supremacy included a doctrine of "fullness of power" as the spiritual head of Christendom and claims to universal temporal authority over all secular rulers. But papal claims of temporal supremacy were increasingly out of step with the growing secular monarchies of Europe and ultimately brought the papacy into a conflict with the territorial states that it was unable to win.

⚜ Boniface VIII and the Conflict with the State

The struggle between the papacy and the secular monarchies began during the pontificate of Pope Boniface VIII (1294–1303). One major issue appeared to be at stake between the pope and King Philip IV (1285–1314) of France. In his desire to acquire new revenues, Philip claimed the right to tax the French clergy. Boniface VIII responded that the clergy of any state could not pay taxes to their secular ruler without the pope's consent. Underlying this issue, however, was a basic conflict between the claims of the papacy to universal authority over both church and state, which necessitated complete control over the clergy, and the claims of the king that all subjects, including the clergy, were under the jurisdiction of the crown and subject to the king's authority on matters of taxation and justice. In short, the fundamental issue was the universal sovereignty of the papacy versus the royal sovereignty of the monarch.

Boniface VIII asserted his position in a series of papal bulls or letters, the most important of which was *Unam Sanctam,* issued in 1302. It was the strongest statement ever made by a pope on the supremacy of the spiritual authority over the temporal authority (see the box on p. 301).

When it became apparent that the pope had decided to act on his principles by excommunicating Philip IV, the latter sent a small contingent of French forces to capture Boniface and bring him back to France for trial. The pope was captured in Anagni, although Italian nobles from the surrounding countryside soon rescued him. The shock of this experience, however, soon led to the pope's death. Philip's strong-arm tactics had produced a clear victory for the national monarchy over the papacy, and no later pope has dared renew the extravagant claims of Boniface VIII.

To ensure his position and avoid any future papal threat, Philip IV brought enough pressure to bear on the college of cardinals to achieve the election of a Frenchman as pope in 1305, Clement V (1305–1314). Using the excuse of turbulence in the city of Rome, the new pope took up residence in Avignon on the east bank of the Rhône River. Although Avignon was located in the Holy Roman Empire and was not a French possession, it lay just across the river from the territory of King Philip IV. Clement may have intended to return to Rome, but he and his successors remained in Avignon for the next seventy-two years, thereby creating yet another crisis for the church.

⚜ The Papacy at Avignon (1305–1377)

The residency of the popes in Avignon for most of the fourteenth century led to a decline in papal prestige and growing antipapal sentiment. The city of Rome was the traditional capital of the universal church. The pope was the bishop of Rome, and his position was based on being the successor to the Apostle Peter, traditionally considered the first bishop of Rome. It was unseemly that the head of the Catholic church should reside elsewhere. In the 1330s, the popes began to construct a stately palace in Avignon, a clear indication that they intended to stay for some time.

Other factors also led to a decline in papal prestige during the Avignonese residency. It was widely believed that the popes at Avignon were captives of the French monarchy. Although questionable, since Avignon did not belong to the French monarchy, it was easy to believe in view of Avignon's proximity to French lands. Moreover, during the seventy-two years of the Avignonese papacy, of the 134 new cardinals created by the popes, 113 were French.

The papal residency at Avignon was also an important turning point in the church's attempt to adapt itself to the changing economic and political conditions of Europe.

Pope Boniface VIII. The conflict between church and state in the Middle Ages reached its height in the struggle between Pope Boniface VIII and Philip IV of France. This fourteenth-century miniature depicts Boniface VIII presiding over a gathering of cardinals.

Boniface VIII's Defense of Papal Supremacy

*O*NE OF THE MOST REMARKABLE documents of the fourteenth century was the exaggerated statement of papal supremacy issued by Pope Boniface VIII in 1302 in the heat of his conflict with the French king Philip IV. Ironically, this strongest statement ever made of papal supremacy was issued at a time when the rising power of the secular monarchies made it increasingly difficult for the premises to be accepted.

Pope Boniface VIII, *Unam Sanctam*

We are compelled, our faith urging us, to believe and to hold—and we do firmly believe and simply confess—that there is one holy catholic and apostolic church, outside of which there is neither salvation nor remission of sins. . . . In this church there is one Lord, one faith and one baptism. . . . Therefore, of this one and only church there is one body and one head . . . Christ, namely, and the vicar of Christ, St. Peter, and the successor of Peter. For the Lord himself said to Peter, feed my sheep. . . .

We are told by the word of the gospel that in this His fold there are two swords—a spiritual, namely, and a temporal. . . . Both swords, the spiritual and the material, therefore, are in the power of the church; the one, indeed, to be wielded for the church, the other by the church; the one by the hand of the priest, the other by the hand of kings and knights, but at the will and sufferance of the priest. One sword, moreover, ought to be under the other, and the temporal authority to be subjected to the spiritual. . . .

Therefore if the earthly power err it shall be judged by the spiritual power; but if the lesser spiritual power err, by the greater. But if the greatest, it can be judged by God alone, not by man, the apostle bearing witness. A spiritual man judges all things, but he himself is judged by no one. This authority, moreover, even though it is given to man and exercised through man, is not human but rather divine, being given by divine lips to Peter and founded on a rock for him and his successors through Christ himself whom he has confessed; the Lord himself saying to Peter: "Whatsoever you shall bind, etc." Whoever, therefore, resists this power thus ordained by God, resists the ordination of God. . . .

Indeed, we declare, announce and define, that it is altogether necessary to salvation for every human creature to be subject to the Roman pontiff.

Like the growing monarchical states, the popes centralized their administration by developing a specialized bureaucracy. In fact, the papal bureaucracy in the fourteenth century under the leadership of the pope and college of cardinals became the most sophisticated administrative system in the medieval world.

At the same time, the popes attempted to find new sources of revenue to compensate for their loss of income from the Papal States and began to impose new taxes on the clergy. Furthermore, the splendor in which the pope and cardinals were living in Avignon led to a highly vocal criticism of both clergy and papacy in the fourteenth century. Avignon had become a powerful symbol of abuses within the church, and many people began to call for the pope's return to Rome.

One of the most prominent calls came from Catherine of Siena (c. 1347–1380), whose saintly demeanor and claims of visions from God led the city of Florence to send her on a mission to Pope Gregory XI (1370–1378) in Avignon. She told the pope, "Because God has given you authority and because you have accepted it, you ought to use your virtue and power; if you do not wish to use it, it

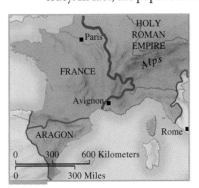

Avignon

might be better for you to resign what you have accepted; it would give more honor to God and health to your soul."[12]

The Great Schism

Catherine of Siena's admonition seemed to be heeded in 1377, when at long last Pope Gregory XI, perceiving the disastrous decline in papal prestige, returned to Rome. He died soon afterward, however, in the spring of 1378. When the college of cardinals met in conclave to elect a new pope, the citizens of Rome, fearful that the French majority would choose another Frenchman who would return the papacy to Avignon, threatened that the cardinals would not leave Rome alive unless a Roman or at least an Italian were elected pope. Indeed, the guards of the conclave warned the cardinals that they "ran the risk of being torn in pieces" if they did not choose an Italian. Wisely, the terrified cardinals duly elected the Italian archbishop of Bari, who was subsequently crowned as Pope Urban VI (1378–1389) on Easter Sunday. Following his election, Urban VI made clear his plans to reform the papal curia and even to swamp the college of cardinals with enough new Italian cardinals to eliminate the French majority. After many of the cardinals (the French ones) withdrew from Rome in late summer and were finally free of the Roman mob, they issued a manifesto, saying that they had been coerced by the mob and that Urban's election was therefore null and void. The dissenting cardinals thereupon chose one of their number, a Frenchman, who took the title of Clement VII and promptly returned to Avignon. Since Urban remained in Rome, there were now two popes, initiating what has been called the **Great Schism** of the church.

Europe's loyalties soon became divided: France, Spain, Scotland, and southern Italy supported Clement, while England, Germany, Scandinavia, and most of Italy supported Urban. These divisions generally followed political lines and reflected the bitter division between the English and the French in the Hundred Years' War. Because the French supported the Avignonese pope, so did their allies; their enemies, particularly England and its allies, supported the Roman pope. The need for political support caused both popes to subordinate their policies to the policies of these states.

The Great Schism lasted for nearly forty years and had a baleful effect on the Catholic church and Christendom in general. The schism greatly aggravated the financial abuses that had developed within the church during the Avignonese papacy. Two papal administrative systems (with only one-half the accustomed revenues) worked to increase taxation. At the same time, the schism badly damaged the faith of Christian believers. The pope was widely believed to be the leader of Christendom and, as Boniface VIII had pointed out, held the keys to the kingdom of heaven. Since each line of popes denounced the other as the Antichrist, such a spectacle could not help but undermine the institution that had become the very foundation of the church.

New Thoughts on Church and State and the Rise of Conciliarism

As dissatisfaction with the papacy grew, so did the calls for a revolutionary approach to solving the church's institutional problems. One of the most systematic was provided by Marsiglio of Padua (c. 1270–1342), rector of the University of Paris and author of a remarkable book, *Defender of the Peace.*

Marsiglio denied that the temporal authority was subject to the spiritual authority, as popes from Innocent III to Boniface VIII had maintained. Instead, he argued that the church was only one element of society and must confine itself solely to spiritual functions. Furthermore, Marsiglio argued, the church was a community of the faithful in which all authority is ultimately derived from the entire community. The clergy hold no special authority from God but serve only to administer the affairs of the church on behalf of all Christians. Final authority in spiritual matters must reside not with the pope but with a general church council representing all members.

The Conciliar Movement   The Great Schism led large numbers of churchmen to take up this theory, known as **conciliarism,** in the belief that only a general council of the church could end the schism and bring reform to the church in its "head and members." The only serious issue left to be decided was who should call the council. Church law held that only a pope could convene a council. Profes-

CHRONOLOGY The Decline of the Church	
Pope Boniface VIII	1294–1303
Unam Sanctam	1302
Papacy at Avignon	1305–1377
Pope Gregory XI returns to Rome	1377
Great Schism begins	1378
Pope Urban VI	1378–1389
Failure of Council of Pisa to end schism; election of Alexander V	1409
Council of Constance	1414–1418
End of schism; election of Martin V	1417

sors of theology argued, however, that since the competing popes would not do so, either members of the church hierarchy or even secular princes, especially the Holy Roman Emperor, could convene a council to settle all relevant issues.

In desperation, a group of cardinals from both camps finally convened a general council on their own. This Council of Pisa, which met in 1409, deposed the two popes and elected a new one, Alexander V. The council's action proved disastrous when the two deposed popes refused to step down. There were now three popes, and the church seemed more hopelessly divided than ever.

Leadership in convening a new council now passed to the Holy Roman Emperor, Sigismund. As a result of his efforts, a new ecumenical church council met at Constance from 1414 to 1418. Ending the schism proved a surprisingly easy task: after the three competing popes either resigned or were deposed, a new conclave elected Cardinal Oddone Colonna, a member of a prominent Roman family, as Pope Martin V (1417–1431). The Great Schism had finally been ended.

Popular Religion in an Age of Adversity

The concern of popes and leading clerics with finances and power during the struggles of Boniface VIII, the Avignonese papacy, and the Great Schism could not help but lead to a decline in prestige and respect for the institutional church, especially the papacy. At the same time, in the fourteenth century, the Black Death and its recurrences made an important impact on the religious life of ordinary Christians by heightening their preoccupation with death and salvation. The church often failed to provide sufficient spiritual comfort as many parish priests fled from the plague.

Christians responded in different ways to the adversities of the fourteenth century. First of all, there was a tendency to stress the performance of good works, including acts of charity, as a means of ensuring salvation. Bequests to hospitals and other charitable foundations increased. Family chapels were established, served by priests whose primary responsibility was to say Mass for the good of the souls of deceased family members. These chapels became even more significant as the importance of purgatory rose.

Purgatory was defined by the church as the place where souls went after death to be purged of punishment for sins committed in life. In effect, the soul was purified in purgatory before it ascended into heaven. It was believed that like indulgences, prayers and private Masses for the dead could shorten the amount of time souls spent in purgatory.

All of these developments were part of a larger trend—a new emphasis in late medieval Christianity on a mechanical path to salvation. Chalking up good deeds to ensure salvation was done in numerous ways but was nowhere more evident than in the growing emphasis on indulgences. We should also note that pilgrimages, which became increasingly popular, and charitable contributions were good works that could be accomplished without the involvement of clerics, a reflection of the loss of faith in the institutional church and its clergy and another noticeable feature of popular religious life. At the same time, interest in Christianity itself did not decline. Indeed, people sought to play a more active role in their own salvation. This is particularly evident in the popularity of mysticism and lay piety in the fourteenth century.

Mysticism and Lay Piety   The mysticism of the fourteenth century was certainly not new, for Christians throughout the Middle Ages had claimed to have had mystical experiences. Simply defined, **mysticism** is the immediate experience of oneness with God. It is this experience that characterized the teaching of Meister Eckhart (1260–1327), who sparked a mystical movement in western Germany. Eckhart was a well-educated Dominican theologian who wrote learned Latin works on theology, but he was also a popular preacher whose message on the union of the soul with God was typical of mysticism. According to Eckhart, such a union was attainable by all who pursued it wholeheartedly.

Eckhart's movement spread from Germany into the Low Countries, where it took on a new form, called the **Modern Devotion,** founded by Gerard Groote (1340–1384). After a religious conversion, Groote entered a monastery for several years of contemplation before reentering the world. His messages were typical of a practical mysticism. To achieve true spiritual communion with God, people must imitate Jesus and lead lives dedicated to serving the needs of their fellow human beings. Groote emphasized a simple inner piety and morality based on Scripture and an avoidance of the complexities of theology.

Eventually, Groote attracted a group of followers who came to be known as the Brothers of the Common Life. From this small beginning, a movement developed that spread through the Netherlands and back into Germany. Houses of the Brothers, as well as separate houses for women (Sisters of the Common Life), were founded in one city after another. The Sisters and Brothers of the Common Life did not constitute regular religious orders. They were laypeople who took no formal monastic vows but were nevertheless regulated by quasi-monastic rules that they imposed on their own communities. They also established schools throughout Germany and the Netherlands in which they stressed their message of imitating the life of Jesus by serving others. The Brothers and Sisters of the Common Life attest to the vitality of spiritual life among lay Christians in the fourteenth century.

Unique Female Mystical Experiences   A number of female mystics had their own unique spiritual experiences. For them, fasting and receiving the Eucharist (the communion wafer that supposedly contains the body of Jesus) became the mainstay of their religious practices. Catherine of Siena, for example, gave up eating any solid food at the age of twenty-three and thereafter lived only on cold water and herbs that she sucked and then spat out. Her primary nourishment, however, came from the Eucharist. She wrote: "The immaculate lamb [Christ] is food, table, and servant. . . . And we who eat at that table become like the food [that is, Christ], acting not for our own utility but for the honor of God and the salvation of neighbor."[13] For Catherine and a number of other female mystics, reception of the Eucharist was their primary instrument in achieving a mystical union with God.

Changes in Theology

The fourteenth century presented challenges not only to the institutional church but also to its theological framework, especially evidenced in the questioning of the grand synthesis attempted by Thomas Aquinas. In the thirteenth century, Aquinas's grand synthesis of faith and reason was not widely accepted outside his own Dominican order. At the same time, differences with Aquinas were kept within a framework of commonly accepted scholastic thought. In the fourteenth century, however, the philosopher William of Occam (1285–1329) posed a severe challenge to the scholastic achievements of the High Middle Ages.

Occam posited a radical interpretation of nominalism. He asserted that all universals or general concepts were simply names and that only individual objects perceived by the senses were real. Although the mind was capable of analyzing individual objects, it could not establish any truths about the nature of external, higher reality. Reason could not be used to substantiate spiritual truths. It could not, for example, prove the statement "God exists." For William of Occam as a Christian believer, this did not mean that God did not exist, however. It simply indicated that the truths of religion were not demonstrable by reason but could only be known by an act of faith. The acceptance of Occam's nominalist philosophy at the University of Paris brought an element of uncertainty to late medieval theology by seriously weakening the synthesis of faith and reason that had characterized the theological thought of the High Middle Ages. Nevertheless, Occam's emphasis on using reason to analyze the observable phenomena of the world had an important impact on the development of physical science by creating support for rational and scientific analysis. Some late medieval theologians came to accept the compatibility of rational analysis of the material world with mystical acceptance of spiritual truths.

The Cultural World of the Fourteenth Century

The cultural life of the fourteenth century was also characterized by ferment. In literature, several writers used their vernacular languages to produce notable works. In art, the Black Death and other problems of the century left their mark as many artists turned to morbid themes, but the period also produced Giotto, whose paintings expressed a new realism that would be developed further by the artists of the next century.

The Development of Vernacular Literature

Although Latin remained the language of the church liturgy and the official documents of both church and state throughout Europe, the fourteenth century witnessed the rapid growth of vernacular literature, especially in Italy. The development of an Italian vernacular literature was mostly the result of the efforts of three writers in the fourteenth century: Dante, Petrarch, and Boccaccio. Their use of the Tuscan dialect common in Florence and its surrounding countryside ensured that it would prevail as the basis of the modern Italian language.

Dante   Dante Alighieri (1265–1321) came from an old Florentine noble family that had fallen on hard times. Although he had held high political office in republican Florence, factional conflict led to his exile from the city in 1302. Until the end of his life, Dante hoped to return to his beloved Florence, but his wish remained unfulfilled.

Dante's masterpiece in the Italian vernacular was the *Divine Comedy,* written between 1313 and 1321. Cast in a typical medieval framework, the *Divine Comedy* is basically the story of the soul's progression to salvation, a fundamental medieval preoccupation. The lengthy poem was divided into three major sections corresponding to the realms of the afterworld: hell, purgatory, and heaven or paradise. In the "Inferno" (see the box on p. 305), Dante is led by his guide, the classical author Virgil, who is a symbol of human reason. But Virgil (or reason) can lead the poet only so far on his journey. At the end of "Purgatory," Beatrice (the true love of Dante's life), who represents revelation—which alone can explain the mysteries of heaven—becomes his guide into "Paradise." Here Beatrice presents Dante to Saint Bernard, a symbol of mystical contemplation. The saint turns Dante over to the Virgin Mary, since grace is necessary to achieve the final step of entering the presence of God, where one beholds "the love that moves the sun and the other stars."[14]

Petrarch   Like Dante, Francesco Petrarca, known as Petrarch (1304–1374), was a Florentine who spent much of his life outside his native city. Petrarch's role in the revival of the classics made him a seminal figure in the literary Italian Renaissance (see Chapter 12). His primary contribution to the development of the Italian vernacular was made in his sonnets. He is considered one of the greatest European lyric poets. His sonnets were inspired by his love for a married lady named Laura, whom he had met in 1327. While honoring an idealized female figure was a long-standing medieval tradition, Laura was very human and not just an ideal. She was a real woman with whom Petrarch was involved for a long time. He poured forth his lamentations in sonnet after sonnet:

> I am as tired of thinking as my thought
> Is never tired to find itself in you,
> And of not yet leaving this life that brought
> Me the too heavy weight of signs and rue;
>
> And because to describe your hair and face
> And the fair eyes of which I always speak,
> Language and sound have not become too weak
> And day and night your name they still embrace.
>
> And tired because my feet do not yet fail
> After following you in every part,
> Wasting so many steps without avail,
>
> From whence derive the paper and the ink
> That I have filled with you; if I should sink,
> It is the fault of Love, not of my art.[15]

In analyzing every aspect of the unrequited lover's feelings, Petrarch appeared less concerned to sing his lady's praise than to immortalize his own thoughts. This interest in his own personality reveals a sense of individuality stronger than in any previous medieval literature.

Boccaccio   Although he too wrote poetry, Giovanni Boccaccio (1313–1375) is known primarily for his prose. Another Florentine, he also used the Tuscan dialect. While working for the Bardi banking house in Naples, he fell in love with a noble lady whom he called his Fiammetta, his Little Flame. Under her inspiration, Boccaccio began to write prose romances. His best-known work, the *Decameron,* however, was not written until after he had returned to Florence. The *Decameron* is set at the time of the Black Death. Ten young people flee to a villa outside Florence to escape the plague and decide to while away the time by telling stories. Although the stories are not new and still reflect the acceptance of basic Christian values, Boccaccio does present the society of his time from a secular point of view. It is the seducer of women, not the knight or philosopher or pious monk, who is the real hero. Perhaps, as some historians have argued, the *Decameron* reflects the immediate easygoing, cynical postplague values. Boccaccio's later work certainly became gloomier and more pessimistic; as he grew older, he even rejected his earlier work as irrelevant. He commented in a 1373 letter, "I am certainly not pleased that you have allowed the illustrious women in your house to read my trifles. . . . You know how much in them is less than decent and opposed to modesty, how much stimulation to wanton lust, how many things that drive to lust even those most fortified against it."[16]

Chaucer   Another leading vernacular author was Geoffrey Chaucer (c. 1340–1400), who brought a new level of sophistication to the English vernacular language in his

DANTE'S VISION OF HELL

THE *DIVINE COMEDY* of Dante Alighieri is regarded as one of the greatest literary works of all time. Many consider it the supreme summary of medieval thought. It combines allegory with a remarkable amount of contemporary history. Indeed, forty-three of the seventy-nine people consigned to hell in the "Inferno" were Florentines. This excerpt is taken from canto 18 of the "Inferno," in which Dante and Virgil visit the eighth circle of hell, which is divided into ten trenches containing the souls of people who had committed malicious frauds on their fellow human beings.

Dante, "Inferno," *Divine Comedy*

We had already come to where the walk
crosses the second bank, from which it lifts
another arch, spanning from rock to rock.

Here we heard people whine in the next chasm,
and knock and thump themselves with open palms,
and blubber through their snouts as if in a spasm.

Steaming from that pit, a vapor rose
over the banks, crusting them with a slime
that sickened my eyes and hammered at my nose.

That chasm sinks so deep we could not sight
its bottom anywhere until we climbed
along the rock arch to its greatest height.

Once there, I peered down; and I saw long lines
of people in a river of excrement
that seemed the overflow of the world's latrines.

I saw among the felons of that pit
one wraith who might or might not have been tonsured—
one could not tell, he was so smeared with shit.

He bellowed: "You there, why do you stare at me
more than at all the others in this stew?"
And I to him: "Because if memory

serves me, I knew you when your hair was dry.
You are Alessio Interminelli da Lucca.
That's why I pick you from this filthy fry."

And he then, beating himself on his clown's head:
"Down to this have the flatteries I sold
the living sunk me here among the dead."

And my Guide prompted then: "Lean forward a bit
and look beyond him, there—do you see that one
scratching herself with dungy nails, the strumpet

who fidgets to her feet, then to a crouch?
It is the whore Thäis who told her lover
when he sent to ask her, 'Do you thank me much?'

'Much? Nay, past all believing!' And with this
Let us turn from the sight of this abyss."

---

famous *Canterbury Tales.* His beauty of expression and clear, forceful language were important in transforming his East Midland dialect into the chief ancestor of the modern English language. *The Canterbury Tales* is a collection of stories told by a group of twenty-nine pilgrims journeying from the London suburb of Southwark to the tomb of Saint Thomas à Becket at Canterbury. This format gave Chaucer the chance to portray an entire range of English society, both high- and low-born. Among others, he presented the Knight, the Yeoman, the Prioress, the Monk, the Merchant, the Student, the Lawyer, the Carpenter, the Cook, the Doctor, the Plowman, and, of course, "A Good Wife was there from beside the city of Bath—a little deaf, which was a pity." The stories these pilgrims told to while away the time on the journey were just as varied as the storytellers themselves: knightly romances, fairy tales, saints' lives, sophisticated satires, and crude anecdotes.

Chaucer also used some of his characters to criticize the corruption of the church in the late medieval period. His portrayal of the Friar leaves no doubt of Chaucer's disdain for the corrupt practices of clerics. Of the Friar, he says:

He knew the taverns well in every town.
The barmaids and innkeepers pleased his mind
Better than beggars and lepers and their kind.[17]

And yet Chaucer was still a pious Christian, never doubting basic Christian doctrines and remaining optimistic that the church could be reformed.

Christine de Pizan   One of the extraordinary vernacular writers of the age was Christine de Pizan (c. 1364–1430). Because of her father's position at the court of Charles V of France, she received a good education. Her husband died when she was only twenty-five (they had been married for ten years), leaving her with little income and three small children and her mother to support. Christine took the unusual step of becoming a writer in order to earn her living. Her poems were soon in demand, and by 1400 she had achieved financial security.

Christine de Pizan is best known, however, for her French prose works written in defense of women. In *The Book of the City of Ladies,* written in 1404, she denounced the many male writers who had argued that women needed to be controlled by men because women by their very nature were prone to evil, unable to learn, and easily swayed. With the help of Reason, Righteousness, and Justice, who appear to her in a vision, Christine refutes these antifeminist attacks. Women, she argues, are not evil by nature, and they could learn as well as men if they were permitted to attend the same schools: "Should I also tell you whether a woman's nature is clever and quick enough to

The Vision of Christine de Pizan. Christine de Pizan is one of the extraordinary vernacular writers of the late fourteenth and early fifteenth centuries. She is pictured here in a cover illustration from her *Book of the City of Ladies,* which depicts Reason, Righteousness, and Justice appearing to Christine in a dream.

learn speculative sciences as well as to discover them, and likewise the manual arts. I assure you that women are equally well-suited and skilled to carry them out and to put them to sophisticated use once they have learned them."[18] Much of the book includes a detailed discussion of women from the past and present who have distinguished themselves as leaders, warriors, wives, mothers, and martyrs for their religious faith. She ends by encouraging women to defend themselves against the attacks of men, who are incapable of understanding them.

Art and the Black Death

The fourteenth century produced an artistic outburst in new directions as well as a large body of morbid work influenced by the Black Death and the recurrences of the plague. The city of Florence witnessed the first dramatic break with medieval tradition in the work of Giotto (1266–1337), often considered a forerunner of Italian Renaissance painting. Born into a peasant family, Giotto acquired his painting skills in a workshop in Florence. Although he worked throughout Italy, his most famous works were done in Padua and Florence. Coming out of the formal Byzantine school, Giotto transcended it with a new kind of realism, a desire to imitate nature that Renaissance artists later identified as the basic component of classical art. Giotto's figures were solid and rounded; placed realistically in relationship to each other and their background, they conveyed three-dimensional depth. The expressive faces and physically realistic bodies gave his sacred figures human qualities with which spectators could identify. Although Giotto had no direct successors, Florentine painting in the early fifteenth century pursued even more dramatically the new direction his work represents.

Giotto, *Lamentation*. The work of Giotto marked the first clear innovation in fourteenth-century painting, making him a forerunner of the early Renaissance. This fresco was part of a series done on the walls of the Arena chapel in Padua begun in 1305. Giotto painted thirty-eight scenes on three levels: the lives of Mary, the mother of Jesus, and her parents (top panel); the life and work of Jesus (middle panel); and his passion, crucifixion, and resurrection (bottom panel). Shown here from the bottom panel is the *Lamentation.* A group of Jesus' followers, including his mother and Mary Magdalene, mourn over the body of Jesus before it is placed in its tomb. The solidity of Giotto's human figures gives them a three-dimensional sense. He also captured the grief and despair felt by the mourners.

The Black Death made a visible impact on art. For one thing, it wiped out entire guilds of artists. At the same time, survivors, including the newly rich who patronized artists, were no longer so optimistic. Some were more guilty about enjoying life and more concerned about gaining salvation. Postplague art began to concentrate on pain and death. A fairly large number of artistic works came to exhibit a morbid concern with death, depicting coffins, decomposing bodies, and grim figures of Death, sometimes in the form of a witch flying through the air swinging a large scythe.

Society in an Age of Adversity

In the midst of disaster, the fourteenth century proved creative in its own way. New inventions made an impact on daily life at the same time that the effects of plague were felt in many areas of medieval urban life.

Changes in Urban Life

One immediate by-product of the Black Death was greater regulation of urban activities. Authorities tried to keep cities cleaner by enacting new ordinances against waste products in the streets. Viewed as unhealthy places, bathhouses were closed down, leading to a noticeable decline in personal cleanliness. Efforts at regulation also affected the practice of female prostitution.

Medieval society had tolerated prostitution as a lesser evil: it was better for males to frequent prostitutes than to seduce virgins or married women. Since many males in medieval towns married late, the demand for prostitutes was high and was met by a regular supply, derived no doubt from the need of many poor girls and women to survive. The recession of the fourteenth century probably increased the supply of prostitutes, while the new hedonism prevalent after the Black Death also increased demand. As a result, cities intensified their regulation of prostitution.

By organizing brothels, city authorities could supervise as well as tax prostitutes. Officials granted charters to citizens who were allowed to set up brothels, provided they were located only in certain areas of town. Prostitutes were also expected to wear special items of clothing—such as red hats—to distinguish them from other women.

Family Life and Sex Roles in Late Medieval Cities The basic unit of the late medieval town was the nuclear family of husband, wife, and children. Especially in wealthier families, there might also be servants, apprentices, and other relatives, including widowed mothers and the husband's illegitimate children.

Before the Black Death, late marriages were common for urban couples. It was not unusual for husbands to be in their late thirties or forties and wives in their early twenties. The expense of setting up a household probably necessitated the delay in marriage. But the situation changed dramatically after the plague, reflecting new economic

opportunities for the survivors and a new reluctance to postpone living in the presence of so much death.

The economic difficulties of the fourteenth century also had a tendency to strengthen the development of sex roles and to set new limits on employment opportunities for women. Based on the authority of Aristotle, Thomas Aquinas and other scholastic theologians had advanced the belief that according to the natural order, men were active and domineering while women were passive and submissive. As more and more lawyers, doctors, and priests, who had been trained in universities where these notions were taught, entered society, these ideas about the different natures of men and women became widely accepted. This was evident in legal systems, many of which limited the legal capacity of women (see the box on p. 308). Increasingly, women were expected to give up any active functions in society and remain subject to direction from males. A fourteenth-century Parisian provost commented that among glass cutters, "no master's widow who keeps working at his craft after her husband's death may take on apprentices, for the men of the craft do not believe that a woman can master it well enough to teach a child to master it, for the craft is a very delicate one."[19] Although this statement suggests that some women were, in fact, running businesses, it also reveals that they were viewed as incapable of undertaking all of men's activities. Europeans in the fourteenth century imposed a division of labor roles between men and women that persisted until the Industrial Revolution.

Medieval Children Parents in the High and Later Middle Ages invested considerable resources and affection in rearing their children. The dramatic increase in specialized roles that accompanied the spread of commerce and the growth of cities demanded a commitment to educating children in the marketable skills needed for the new occupations. Philip of Navarre noted in the twelfth century that boys ought to be taught a trade "as soon as possible. Those who early become and long remain apprentices ought to be the best masters."[20] Some cities provided schools to educate the young. A chronicler in Florence related that between eight and ten thousand boys and girls between the ages of six and twelve attended the city's grammar schools, a figure that probably represented half of all school-aged children. Although grammar school completed education for girls, around eleven hundred boys went on to six secondary schools that prepared them for business careers, while another six hundred studied Latin and logic in four other schools that readied them for university training and a career in medicine, law, or the church. In the High Middle Ages, then, urban communities demonstrated a commitment to the training of the young.

As a result of the devastating effects of the plague and its recurrences, these same communities became concerned about investing in the survival and health of children. Although a number of hospitals existed in both Florence and Rome in the fourteenth century, it was not until the 1420s and 1430s that hospitals were established that catered

The Legal Rights of Women

DURING THE HIGH AND Later Middle Ages, as women were increasingly viewed as weak beings who were unable to play independent roles, legal systems also began to limit the rights of women. These excerpts are taken from a variety of legal opinions in France, England, and a number of Italian cities.

⚛ Excerpts from Legal Opinions

FRANCE, 1270: No married woman can go to court . . . unless someone has abused or beaten her, in which case she may go to court without her husband. If she is a tradeswoman, she can sue and defend herself in matters connected with her business, but not otherwise.

ENGLAND [probably fifteenth century]: Every Feme Covert [married woman] is a sort of infant. . . . It is seldom, almost never that a married woman can have any action to use her wit only in her own name: her husband is her stern, her prime mover, without whom she cannot do much at home, and less abroad. . . . It is a miracle that a wife should commit any suit without her husband.

ENGLAND [probably fifteenth century]: The very goods which a man gives to his wife, are still his own, her chain, her bracelets, her apparel, are all the goodman's goods. . . . A wife however gallant she be, glitters but in the riches of her husband, as the moon has no light but it is the sun's. . . . For thus it is, if before marriage the woman was possessed of horses . . . , sheep, corn, wool, money, plate and jewels, all manner of movable substance is presently . . . the husband's to sell, keep or bequeath if she die.

PESARO, ITALY [exact date unknown]: No wife can make a contract without the consent of her husband.

FLORENCE, ITALY, 1415: A married woman with children cannot draw up a last will in her own right, nor dispose of her dowry among the living to the detriment of husband and children.

LUCCA, ITALY [exact date unknown]: No married woman . . . can seal or give away [anything] unless she has the agreement of her husband and nearest [male] relative.

---

only to the needs of foundlings, supporting them until boys could be taught a trade and girls could marry.

⚛ New Directions in Medicine

The medical community comprised a number of functionaries. At the top of the medical hierarchy were the physicians, usually clergymen, who received their education in the universities, where they studied ancient authorities, such as Hippocrates and Galen. As a result, physicians were highly trained in theory but had little or no clinical practice. By the fourteenth century, they were educated in six chief medical schools—Salerno, Montpellier, Bologna, Oxford, Padua, and Paris. Paris was regarded as the most prestigious.

The preplague medicine of university-trained physicians was theoretically grounded in the classical Greek theory of the "four humors," each connected to a particular organ: blood (from the heart), phlegm (from the brain), yellow bile (from the liver), and black bile (from the spleen). The four humors corresponded in turn to the four elemental qualities of the universe, earth (black bile), air (blood), fire (yellow bile), and water (phlegm), making a human being a microcosm of the cosmos. Good health resulted from a perfect balance of the four humors; sickness meant that the humors were out of balance. The task of the medieval physician was to restore proper order by a number of cures, such as rest, diet, herbal medicines, or bloodletting.

Beneath the physicians in the hierarchy of the medical profession stood the surgeons, whose activities included performing operations, setting broken bones, and bleeding patients. Their knowledge was based largely on practical experience. Below surgeons were midwives, who delivered babies, and barber-surgeons, who were less trained than surgeons and performed menial tasks such as bloodletting and setting simple bone fractures. Barber-surgeons supplemented their income by shaving and cutting hair and pulling teeth. Apothecaries also constituted part of the medical establishment. They filled herbal prescriptions recommended by physicians and also prescribed drugs on their own authority.

All of these medical practitioners proved unable to deal with the plague. When King Philip VI of France requested the opinion of the medical faculty of the University of Paris on the plague, their advice proved worthless. This failure to understand the Black Death, however, produced a crisis in medieval medicine that resulted in some new approaches to health care.

One result was the rise of surgeons to greater prominence because of their practical knowledge. Surgeons were now recruited by universities, which placed them on an equal level with physicians and introduced a greater emphasis on practical anatomy into the university curriculum. Connected to this was a burgeoning of medical textbooks, often written in the vernacular and stressing practical, how-to approaches to medical and surgical problems.

Medieval Children at Play. Like children in all ages, medieval children joined with other children in playing a variety of games. Play, as we know, is important to the development of children as it helps them cultivate their physical and mental abilities. In the Middle Ages, a number of writers on children saw play as a basic symbol of childhood itself. In this series of illustrations from a medieval manuscript in the Bodleian Library in Oxford, we see children riding hobbyhorses (undoubtedly popular in a society dependent on horses), shooting arrows at a target, and engaged in throwing snowballs.

A Medical Textbook. This illustration is taken from a fourteenth-century surgical textbook that stressed a how-to approach to surgical problems. *Top left,* a surgeon shows how to remove an arrow from a patient; *top right,* how to open a patient's chest; *bottom left,* how to deal with an injury to the intestines; *bottom right,* how to diagnose an abscess.

Finally, as a result of the plague, cities, especially in Italy, gave increased attention to public health and sanitation. Public health laws were instituted, and municipal boards of health came into being. The primary concern of the latter was to prevent plague, but gradually they came to control almost every aspect of health and sanitation. Boards of public health, consisting of medical practitioners and public officials, were empowered to enforce sanitary conditions, report on and attempt to isolate epidemics by quarantine (rarely successful), and regulate the activities of doctors.

Inventions and New Patterns

Despite its problems, the fourteenth century witnessed a continuation of the technological innovations that had characterized the High Middle Ages.

The Clock   The most extraordinary of these inventions, and one that made a visible impact on European cities, was the clock. The mechanical clock was invented at the end of the thirteenth century but not perfected until the fourteenth. The time-telling clock was actually a by-product of a larger astronomical clock. The best-designed one was constructed by Giovanni di Dondi in the mid-fourteenth century. Dondi's clock contained the signs of the zodiac but also struck on the hour. Since clocks were expensive, they were usually installed only in the towers of churches or municipal buildings. The first clock striking equal hours was in a church in Milan; in 1335, a chronicler described it as "a wonderful clock, with a very large clapper which strikes a bell twenty-four times according to the twenty-four hours of the day and night and thus at the first hour of the night gives one sound, at the second two strikes . . . and so distinguishes one hour from another, which is of greatest use to men of every degree."[21]

Clocks introduced a wholly new conception of time into the lives of Europeans; they revolutionized how people thought about and used time. Throughout most of the Middle Ages, time was determined by natural rhythms (daybreak and nightfall) or church bells that were rung at more or less regular three-hour intervals, corresponding to the ecclesiastical offices of the church. Clocks made it possible to plan one's day and organize one's activities around the regular striking of bells. This brought a new regularity into the life of workers and merchants, defining urban existence and enabling merchants and bankers to see the value of time in a new way.

Eyeglasses and Paper   Like clocks, eyeglasses were introduced in the thirteenth century but not refined until the fourteenth. Even then they were not particularly effective by modern standards and were still extremely expensive. The high cost of parchment forced people to write in extremely small script; eyeglasses made it more readable. At the same time, a significant change in writing materials occurred in the fourteenth century when parchment was supplemented by much cheaper paper made from cotton rags. Although it was more subject to insect and water damage than parchment, medieval paper was actually superior to modern papers made of high-acid wood pulp.

Gunpowder and Cannons   Invented earlier by the Chinese, gunpowder also made its appearance in the West in the fourteenth century. The use of gunpowder eventually brought drastic changes to European warfare. Its primary use was in cannons, although early cannons were prone to blow up, making them as dangerous to the people firing them as to the enemy. Even as late as 1460, an attack on a castle using the "Lion," an enormous Flemish cannon, proved disastrous for the Scottish king James II when the "Lion" blew up, killing the king and a number of his retainers. Continued improvement in the construction of cannons, however, soon made them extremely valuable in reducing both castles and city walls. Gunpowder made castles, city walls, and armored knights obsolete.

CONCLUSION

*I*N THE ELEVENTH, twelfth, and thirteenth centuries, European civilization developed many of its fundamental features. Territorial states, parliaments, capitalist trade and industry, banks, cities, and vernacular literatures were all products of that fertile period. During the same time, the Catholic church under the direction of the papacy reached its apogee. Fourteenth-century European society, however, was challenged by an overwhelming number of crises. Devastating plague, declining trade and industry, bank failures, peasant revolts pitting lower classes against the upper classes, seemingly constant warfare, aristocratic factional conflict that undermined political stability, the absence of the popes from Rome, and even the spectacle of two popes condemning each other as the Antichrist all seemed to overpower Europeans in this "calamitous century." Not surprisingly, much of the art of the period depicted the Four Horsemen of the Apocalypse described in the New Testament book of Revelation: Death, Famine, Pestilence, and War. No doubt, to some people, the last days of the world appeared to be at hand.

The new European society, however, proved remarkably resilient. Periods of crisis are usually paralleled by the emergence of new ideas and new practices. Intellectuals of the period saw themselves as standing on the threshold of a new age or a rebirth of the best features of classical civilization. It is their perspective that led historians to speak of a Renaissance in the fifteenth century.

1300	1325	1350	1375	1400	1425	1450

Hundred Years' War   (truce 1396–1415)

Golden Bull in Germany   Battle of Agincourt

Popes at Avignon   The Great Schism

Black Death in Europe

Joan of Arc inspires the French

Work of Giotto

Peasant revolts in France   Peasant revolt in England

Dante, *Divine Comedy*

Giovanni di Dondi's clock

Chaucer, *The Canterbury Tales*

NOTES

1. Quoted in H. S. Lucas, "The Great European Famine of 1315, 1316, and 1317," *Speculum* 5 (1930): 359.

2. Quoted in David Herlihy, *The Black Death and the Transformation of the West,* ed. Samuel K. Cohn Jr. (Cambridge, Mass., 1997), p. 9.

3. Giovanni Boccaccio, *Decameron,* trans. Frances Winwar (New York, 1955), p. xxv.

4. Ibid., p. xxvi.

5. Jean Froissart, *Chronicles,* ed. and trans. Geoffrey Brereton (Harmondsworth, England, 1968), p. 111.

6. Quoted in James B. Ross and Mary M. McLaughlin, *The Portable Medieval Reader* (New York, 1949), pp. 218–219.

7. Quoted in Barbara W. Tuchman, *A Distant Mirror* (New York, 1978), p. 175.

8. Froissart, *Chronicles,* p. 212.

9. Ibid., p. 89.

10. Oliver J. Thatcher and Edgar H. McNeal, eds., *A Source Book for Medieval History* (New York, 1905), p. 288.

11. Quoted in D. S. Chambers, *The Imperial Age of Venice, 1380–1580* (London, 1970), p. 30.

12. Quoted in Robert Coogan, *Babylon on the Rhône: A Translation of Letters by Dante, Petrarch, and Catherine of Siena* (Washington, D.C., 1983), p. 115.

13. Quoted in Caroline Walker Bynum, *Holy Feast and Holy Fast: The Religious Significance of Food to Medieval Women* (Berkeley, Calif., 1987), p. 180.

14. Dante Alighieri, *Divine Comedy,* trans. Dorothy Sayers (New York, 1962), "Paradise," canto 33, line 145.

15. Petrarch, *Sonnets and Songs,* trans. Anna Maria Armi (New York, 1968), no. 74, p. 127.

16. Quoted in Millard Meiss, *Painting in Florence and Siena After the Black Death* (Princeton, N.J., 1951), p. 161.

17. Geoffrey Chaucer, *The Canterbury Tales,* in *The Portable Chaucer,* ed. Theodore Morrison (New York, 1949), p. 67.

18. Christine de Pizan, *The Book of the City of Ladies,* trans. E. Jeffrey Richards (New York, 1982), pp. 83–84.

19. Quoted in Susan Mosher Stuard, "The Dominion of Gender, or How Women Fared in the High Middle Ages," in Renate Bridenthal, Claudia Koonz, and Susan Stuard, eds., *Becoming Visible: Women in European History,* 3d ed. (Boston, 1998), p. 147.

20. Quoted in David Herlihy, "Medieval Children," in Bede K. Lackner and Kenneth R. Philp, eds., *Essays on Medieval Civilization* (Austin, Texas, 1978), p. 121.

21. Quoted in Jean Gimpel, The Medieval Machine (New York, 1976), p. 168.

SUGGESTIONS FOR FURTHER READING

For a general introduction to the fourteenth century, see **D. P. Waley,** *Later Medieval Europe,* 2d ed. (London, 1985); **G. Holmes,** *Europe: Hierarchy and Revolt, 1320–1450* (New York, 1975); and the well-written popular history by **B. Tuchman,** *A Distant Mirror* (New York, 1978).

On famine in the early fourteenth century, see **W. C. Jordan,** *The Great Famine: Northern Europe in the Early Fourteenth Century* (Princeton, N.J., 1996). On the Black Death, see **P. Ziegler,** *The Black Death* (New York, 1969), and **D. Herlihy,** *The Black Death and the Transformation of the West,* ed. S. K. Cohn Jr. (Cambridge, Mass., 1997).

Good accounts of the Hundred Years' War include **A. Curry,** *The Hundred Years' War* (New York, 1993), and **R. H. Neillands,** *The Hundred Years' War* (New York, 1990). For a detailed history, see **J. Sumption,** *The Hundred Years' War,* 2 vols. (Philadelphia, 1992–1999). On Joan of Arc, see **M. Warner,** *Joan of Arc: The Image of Female Heroism* (New York, 1981). On the political history of the period, see **B. Guenée,** *States and Rulers in Later Medieval Europe,* trans. J. Vale (Oxford, 1985). Works on individual countries include **P. S. Lewis,** *Later Medieval France: The Polity* (London, 1968); **A. R. Myers,** *England in the Late Middle Ages* (Harmondsworth, England, 1952); and **F. R. H. Du Boulay,** *Germany in the Later Middle Ages* (London, 1983). On the Italian political scene, see **J. Larner,** *Italy in the Age of Dante and Petrarch, 1216–1380* (London, 1980).

A good general study of the church in the fourteenth century can be found in **F. P. Oakley,** *The Western Church in the Later Middle Ages* (Ithaca, N.Y., 1980). See also **J. H. Lynch,** *The Medieval Church: A Brief History* (New York, 1992). On the Avignonese papacy, see **Y. Renouard,** *The Avignon Papacy, 1305–1403* (London, 1970). On the role of food in the spiritual practices of medieval women, see **C. W. Bynum,** *Holy Feast and Holy Fast: The Religious Significance of Food to Medieval Women* (Berkeley, Calif., 1987). On late medieval religious practices, see **R. N. Swanson,** *Religion and Devotion in Europe, c. 1215–1515* (Cambridge, 1995).

A classic work on the life and thought of the Later Middle Ages is **J. Huizinga,** *The Autumn of the Middle Ages,* trans. R. J. Payton and U. Mammitzsch (Chicago, 1996). On the impact of the plague on culture, see the brilliant study by **M. Meiss,** *Painting in Florence and Siena After the Black Death* (New York, 1964). On Dante, see **J. Freccero,** *Dante and the Poetics of Conversion* (Cambridge, Mass., 1986). On Chaucer, see **G. Kane,** *Chaucer* (New York, 1984). The best work on Christine de Pizan is by **C. C. Willard,** *Christine de Pizan: Her Life and Works* (New York, 1984).

A wealth of material on everyday life is provided in the second volume of *A History of Private Life,* edited by **G. Duby,** *Revelations of the Medieval World* (Cambridge, Mass., 1988). On women in the Later Middle Ages, see **S. Shahar,** *The Fourth Estate: A History of Women in the Middle Ages,* trans. C. Galai (London, 1983), and **D. Herlihy,** *Women, Family, and Society: Historical Essays, 1978–1991* (Providence, R.I., 1995). On childhood, see **N. Orme,** *Medieval Children* (New Haven, Conn., 2001). The subject of medieval prostitution is examined in **L. L. Otis,** *Prostitution in Medieval Society* (Chicago, 1984). Poor people are discussed in **M. Mollat,** *The Poor in the Middle Ages* (New Haven, Conn., 1986). For a general introduction to the changes in medicine, see **T. McKeown,** *The Role of Medicine* (Princeton, N.J., 1979). The importance of inventions is discussed in **J. Gimpel,** *The Medieval Machine* (New York, 1976). Another valuable discussion of medieval technology can be found in **J. Le Goff,** *Time, Work, and Culture in the Middle Ages* (Chicago, 1980).

History Now™

Enter *HistoryNow* using the access card that is available for *Western Civilization. HistoryNow* will assist you in understanding the content in this chapter with lesson plans generated for your needs. In addition, you can read the following documents, and many more, online:

> Jean Froissart, The Battle of Crécy, The Burghers of Calais, and The Battle of Poitiers

INFOTRAC SEARCH TERMS

 For additional reading, go to InfoTrac College Edition, your online research library at http://infotrac.thomsonlearning.com

Key Term Search	*Subject Guide Search*
Black Death	Middle Ages
Edward III	
Hundred Years' War	

WESTERN CIVILIZATION RESOURCES

Visit the *Western Civilization* Companion Web site for resources specific to this book:

> http://history.wadsworth.com/spielvogel06/

For a variety of tools to help you succeed in this course, visit the Western Civilization Resource Center at

> http://history.wadsworth.com/western/

Included are quizzes; images; documents; interactive simulations; maps and timelines; movie explorations; and a wealth of other sources.

RECOVERY AND REBIRTH:
THE AGE OF THE RENAISSANCE

CHAPTER OUTLINE AND FOCUS QUESTIONS

Meaning and Characteristics of the Italian Renaissance

● What characteristics distinguish the Renaissance from the Middle Ages?

The Making of Renaissance Society

● What major social changes occurred in the Renaissance?

The Italian States in the Renaissance

● How did Machiavelli's works reflect the political realities of Renaissance Italy?

The Intellectual Renaissance in Italy

● What were the chief characteristics of humanism?

The Artistic Renaissance

● What were the chief characteristics of Renaissance art?

The European State in the Renaissance

● Why do historians sometimes refer to the monarchies of the late fifteenth century as "new monarchies" or "Renaissance states"?

The Church in the Renaissance

● What were the policies of the Renaissance popes, and what impact did those policies have on the Catholic church?

CRITICAL THINKING

● How did Renaissance art and the humanist movement reflect the political, economic, and social developments of the period?

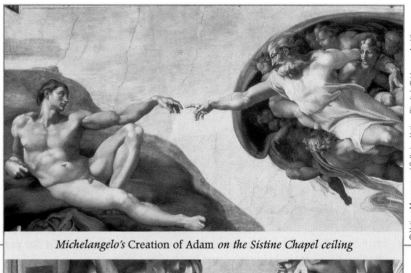

Michelangelo's Creation of Adam *on the Sistine Chapel ceiling*

© Vatican Museums and Galleries, Vatican City, Italy/Bridgeman Art Library

WERE THE FOURTEENTH and fifteenth centuries a continuation of the Middle Ages or the beginning of a new era? Both positions can be defended. Although the disintegrative patterns of the fourteenth century continued into the fifteenth, at the same time there were elements of recovery that made the fifteenth century a period of significant political, economic, artistic, and intellectual change. The humanists or intellectuals of the age called their period (from the mid-fourteenth to the mid-sixteenth century) an age of rebirth, believing that they had restored arts and letters to new glory after they had been "neglected" or "dead" for centuries. The humanists also saw their age as one of accomplished individuals who dominated the landscape of their time. Michelangelo, the great Italian artist of the early sixteenth century, and Pope Julius II, the "warrior pope," were two such titans. The artist's temperament and the pope's temper led to many lengthy and often loud quarrels between the two. The pope had hired Michelangelo to paint the ceiling of the Sistine Chapel in Rome, a difficult task for a man long accustomed to being a sculptor. Michelangelo undertook the project but refused for a long time to allow anyone, including the pope, to see his work. Julius grew anxious, pestering Michelangelo on a regular basis about when the ceiling would be finished. Exasperated by the pope's requests, Michelangelo once replied, according to Giorgio Vasari, his contemporary biographer, that the ceiling would be completed "when it satisfies me as an artist." The pope responded, "And we want you to satisfy us and finish it soon," and then threatened that if Michelangelo did not "finish the ceiling quickly," the pope would "have him thrown down from the scaffolding." Fearing the pope's anger, Michelangelo "lost no time in doing all that was wanted" and quickly completed the ceiling, one of the great masterpieces in the history of Western art.

The humanists' view of their age as a rebirth of the classical civilization of the Greeks and Romans ultimately led historians to use the French word *Renaissance* to identify this age. Although recent historians have emphasized the many elements of continuity between the Middle Ages and the Renaissance, the latter age was also distinguished by its own unique characteristics.

Meaning and Characteristics of the Italian Renaissance

Renaissance means "rebirth." Many people who lived in Italy between 1350 and 1550 believed that they had witnessed a rebirth of antiquity or Greco-Roman civilization, marking a new age. To them, the thousand or so years between the end of the Roman Empire and their own era was a middle period (the "Middle Ages"), characterized by darkness because of its lack of classical culture. Historians of the nineteenth century later used similar terminology to describe this period in Italy. The Swiss historian and art critic Jacob Burckhardt created the modern concept of the **Renaissance** in his celebrated book *The Civilization of the Renaissance in Italy,* published in 1860. He portrayed Italy in the fourteenth and fifteenth centuries as the birthplace of the modern world (the Italians were "the firstborn among the sons of modern Europe") and saw the revival of antiquity, the "perfecting of the individual," and secularism ("worldliness of the Italians") as its distinguishing features. Burckhardt exaggerated the individuality and secularism of the Renaissance and failed to recognize the depths of its religious sentiment; nevertheless, he established the framework for all modern interpretations of the period. Although contemporary scholars do not believe that the Renaissance represents a sudden or dramatic cultural break with the Middle Ages, as Burckhardt argued— there was, after all, much continuity in economic, political, and social life—the Renaissance can still be viewed as a distinct period of European history that manifested itself first in Italy and then spread to the rest of Europe.

Renaissance Italy was largely an urban society. As a result of its commercial preeminence and political evolution, northern Italy by the mid-fourteenth century was mostly a land of independent cities that dominated the country districts around them. These city-states became the centers of Italian political, economic, and social life. Within this new urban society, a secular spirit emerged as increasing wealth created new possibilities for the enjoyment of worldly things (see the box on p. 315).

Above all, the Renaissance was an age of recovery from the calamitous fourteenth century, the slow process of recuperating from the effects of the Black Death, political disorder, and economic recession. This recovery was accompanied by a rediscovery of the culture of classical antiquity. Increasingly aware of their own historical past, Italian intellectuals became intensely interested in the Greco-Roman culture of the ancient Mediterranean world. This revival of classical antiquity (the Middle Ages had in fact preserved much of ancient Latin culture) affected activities as diverse as politics and art and led to new attempts to reconcile the pagan philosophy of the Greco-Roman world with Christian thought, as well as new ways of viewing human beings.

A revived emphasis on individual ability became characteristic of the Italian Renaissance. As the fifteenth-century Florentine architect Leon Battista Alberti expressed it, "Men can do all things if they will."[1] A high regard for human dignity and worth and a realization of individual potentiality created a new social ideal of the well-rounded personality or universal person (*l'uomo universale*) who was capable of achievements in many areas of life.

These general features of the Italian Renaissance were not characteristic of all Italians but were primarily the preserve of the wealthy upper classes, who constituted a small percentage of the total population. The achievements of the Italian Renaissance were the product of an elite, rather than a mass, movement. Nevertheless, indirectly it did have some impact on ordinary people, especially in the cities, where so many of the intellectual and artistic accomplishments of the period were most visible.

The Making of Renaissance Society

After the severe economic reversals and social upheavals of the fourteenth century, the European economy gradually recovered as the volume of manufacturing and trade increased.

Economic Recovery

By the fourteenth century, Italian merchants were carrying on a flourishing commerce throughout the Mediterranean and had also expanded their lines of trade north along the Atlantic seaboard. The great galleys of the Venetian Flanders Fleet maintained a direct sea route from Venice to England and the Netherlands, where Italian merchants came into contact with the increasingly powerful Hanseatic League of merchants. Hard hit by the plague, the Italians lost their commercial preeminence while the Hanseatic League continued to prosper.

A RENAISSANCE BANQUET

*A*S IN GREEK AND ROMAN SOCIETY, the Renaissance banquet was an occasion for good food, interesting conversation, music, and dancing. In Renaissance society, it was also a symbol of status and an opportunity to impress people with the power and wealth of one's family. Banquets were held to celebrate public and religious festivals, official visits, anniversaries, and weddings. The following menu lists the foods served at a grand banquet given by Pope Pius V in the sixteenth century.

A Sixteenth-Century Banquet

First Course
Cold Delicacies from the Sideboard
Pieces of marzipan and marzipan balls
Neapolitan spice cakes
Malaga wine and Pisan biscuits
Fresh grapes
Prosciutto cooked in wine, served with capers
and grape pulp
Salted pork tongues cooked in wine, sliced
Spit-roasted songbirds, cold, with their
tongues sliced over them
Sweet mustard

Second Course
Hot Foods from the Kitchen, Roasts
Fried veal sweetbreads and liver
Spit-roasted skylarks with lemon sauce
Spit-roasted quails with sliced eggplants
Stuffed spit-roasted pigeons with capers
sprinkled over them
Spit-roasted rabbits, with sauce and crushed pine nuts
Partridges larded and spit-roasted, served with lemon
Heavily seasoned poultry with lemon slices
Slices of veal, spit-roasted, with a sauce made
from the juices
Leg of goat, spit-roasted, with a sauce made
from the juices
Soup of almond paste, with the flesh of three
pigeons to each serving

Third Course
Hot Foods from the Kitchen, Boiled Meats and Stews
Stuffed fat geese, boiled Lombard style and covered
with sliced almonds
Stuffed breast of veal, boiled, garnished with flowers
Very young calf, boiled, garnished with parsley
Almonds in garlic sauce
Turkish-style rice with milk, sprinkled with cinnamon
Stewed pigeons with mortadella sausage and
whole onions
Cabbage soup with sausages
Poultry pie, two chickens to each pie
Fricasseed breast of goat dressed with fried onions
Pies filled with custard cream
Boiled calves' feet with cheese and egg

Fourth Course
Delicacies from the Sideboard
Bean tarts
Quince pastries
Pear tarts, the pears wrapped in marzipan
Parmesan cheese and Riviera cheese
Fresh almonds on vine leaves
Chestnuts roasted over the coals and served
with salt and pepper
Milk curds
Ring-shaped cakes
Wafers made from ground grain

Expansion of Trade As early as the thirteenth century, a number of North German coastal towns had formed a commercial and military association known as the Hansa, or Hanseatic League. By 1500, more than eighty cities belonged to the League, which had established settlements and commercial bases in many cities in England and northern Europe, including the chief towns of Denmark, Norway, and Sweden. For almost two hundred years, the Hansa had a monopoly on northern European trade in timber, fish, grain, metals, honey, and wines. Its southern outlet in Flanders, the port city of Bruges, became the economic crossroads of Europe in the fourteenth century, serving as the meeting place between Hanseatic merchants and the Flanders Fleet of Venice. In the fifteenth century, however, silting of the port caused Bruges to enter a slow decline. So did the Hanseatic League, increasingly unable to compete with the developing larger territorial states.

Overall, trade recovered dramatically from the economic contraction of the fourteenth century. The Italians and especially the Venetians, despite new restrictive pressures on their eastern Mediterranean trade from the Ottoman Turks (see "The Ottoman Turks and the End of the Byzantine Empire" later in this chapter), continued to maintain a wealthy commercial empire. Not until the sixteenth century, when transatlantic discoveries gave new importance to the states along the ocean, did the petty Italian city-states begin to suffer from the competitive advantages of the ever-growing and more powerful national territorial states.

Industries Old and New The economic depression of the fourteenth century also affected patterns of manufacturing. The woolen industries of Flanders and the northern Italian cities had been particularly devastated. By the beginning of the fifteenth century, however, the Florentine

Harbor Scene at Hamburg. Hamburg was a founding member of the Hanseatic League. This illustration from a fifteenth-century treatise on the laws of Hamburg shows a busy port with ships of all sizes. At the left, a crane is used to unload barrels. In the building at the right, customs officials collect their dues. Merchants and townspeople are shown talking at dockside.

branches in Venice, Milan, Rome, Avignon, Bruges, London, and Lyons. Moreover, the family had controlling interests in industrial enterprises for wool, silk, and the mining of alum, used in the dyeing of textiles. Except for a brief interruption, the Medici were also the principal bankers for the papacy, a position that produced big profits and influence at the papal court. Despite its great success in the early and middle part of the fifteenth century, the Medici bank suffered a rather sudden decline at the end of the century due to poor leadership and a series of bad loans, especially uncollectible loans to rulers. In 1494, when the French expelled the Medici from Florence and confiscated their property, the Medici financial edifice collapsed.

woolen industry had begun to recover. At the same time, the Italian cities began to develop and expand luxury industries, especially silk, glassware, and handworked items in metal and precious stones.

Other new industries, especially printing, mining, and metallurgy, began to rival the textile industry in importance in the fifteenth century. New machinery and techniques for digging deeper mines and for separating metals from ore and purifying them were developed. When rulers began to transfer their titles to underground minerals to financiers as collateral for loans, these **entrepreneurs** quickly developed large mining operations to produce copper, iron, and silver. Especially valuable were the rich mineral deposits in central Europe, Hungary, the Tyrol, Bohemia, and Saxony. Expanding iron production and new skills in metalworking in turn contributed to the development of firearms that were more effective than the crude weapons of the fourteenth century.

Banking and the Medici The city of Florence regained its preeminence in banking in the fifteenth century, due primarily to the Medici family. The Medici had expanded from cloth production into commerce, real estate, and banking. In its best days (in the fifteenth century), the House of Medici was the greatest bank in Europe, with

Social Changes in the Renaissance

The Renaissance inherited its social structure from the Middle Ages. Society remained fundamentally divided into three **estates**: the First Estate, the clergy, whose preeminence was grounded in the belief that people should be guided to spiritual ends; the Second Estate, the nobility, whose privileges were based on the principle that the nobles provided security and justice for society; and the Third Estate, which consisted of the peasants and inhabitants of the towns and cities. This social order experienced certain adaptations in the Renaissance, which we can see by examining the Second and Third Estates (the clergy will be examined in Chapter 13).

The Nobility Throughout much of Europe, the landholding nobles faced declining real incomes during the greater part of the fourteenth and fifteenth centuries, while the expense of maintaining noble status was rising. Nevertheless, members of the old nobility survived, and new blood infused its ranks. A reconstruction of the aristocracy was well under way by 1500.

As a result, the nobles, old and new, who constituted between 2 and 3 percent of the population in most countries, managed to dominate society as they had done in the

Middle Ages, serving as military officers and holding important political posts as well as advising the king. Increasingly in the sixteenth century, members of the aristocracy pursued education as the means to maintain their role in government.

By 1500, certain ideals came to be expected of the aristocrat. These were best expressed in *The Book of the Courtier* by the Italian Baldassare Castiglione (1478–1529). First published in 1528, Castiglione's work soon became popular throughout Europe and remained a fundamental handbook for European aristocrats for centuries. In it, Castiglione described the three basic attributes of the perfect courtier. First, nobles should possess fundamental native endowments, such as impeccable character, grace, talents, and noble birth. The perfect courtier must also cultivate certain achievements. Primarily, he should participate in military and bodily exercises, because the principal profession of a courtier was bearing arms. But unlike the medieval knight, who had been required only to have military skill, the Renaissance courtier was also expected to have a classical education and to adorn his life with the arts by playing a musical instrument, drawing, and painting. In Castiglione's hands, the Renaissance ideal of the well-developed personality became a social ideal of the aristocracy. Finally, the aristocrat was expected to follow a certain standard of conduct. Nobles were to make a good impression; while being modest, they should not hide their accomplishments but show them with grace.

What was the purpose of these courtly standards? Castiglione wrote:

> I think that the aim of the perfect Courtier, which we have not spoken of up to now, is so to win for himself, by means of the accomplishments ascribed to him by these gentlemen, the favor and mind of the prince whom he serves that he may be able to tell him, and always will tell him, the truth about everything he needs to know, without fear or risk of displeasing him; and that when he sees the mind of his prince inclined to a wrong action, he may dare to oppose him . . . so as to dissuade him of every evil intent and bring him to the path of virtue.[2]

The aim of the perfect noble, then, was to serve his prince in an effective and honest way. Nobles would adhere to these principles for hundreds of years while they continued to dominate European life socially and politically.

Peasants and Townspeople   Peasants made up the overwhelming mass of the Third Estate and continued to constitute 85 to 90 percent of the European population, except in the highly urbanized areas of northern Italy and Flanders. The most noticeable trend produced by the economic crisis of the fourteenth century was the decline of the manorial system and the continuing elimination of serfdom. This process had already begun in the twelfth century when the introduction of a money economy made possible the conversion of servile labor dues into rents paid in money, although they also continued to be paid in kind or labor. The contraction of the peasantry after the Black Death simply accelerated this process, since lords found it convenient to deal with the peasants by granting freedom and accepting rents. The lords' lands were then tilled by hired workers or rented out. By the end of the fifteenth century, serfdom was declining in western Europe, and more and more peasants were becoming legally free.

The remainder of the Third Estate centered around the inhabitants of towns and cities, originally the merchants and artisans who formed the bourgeoisie. The Renaissance town or city of the fifteenth century actually possessed a multitude of townspeople widely separated socially and economically.

At the top of urban society were the patricians, whose wealth from capitalistic enterprises in trade, industry, and banking enabled them to dominate their urban communities economically, socially, and politically. Below them were the petty burghers—the shopkeepers, artisans, guildmasters, and guild members, who were largely concerned with providing goods and services for local consumption. Below these two groups were the propertyless workers earning pitiful wages and the unemployed, living squalid and miserable lives; these people constituted 30 to 40 percent of the population living in cities. In many places in Europe in the late fourteenth and fifteenth centuries, urban poverty increased dramatically. One rich merchant of Florence wrote:

> Those that are lazy and indolent in a way that does harm to the city, and who can offer no just reason for their condition, should either be forced to work or expelled from the Commune. The city would thus rid itself of that most harmful part of the poorest class. . . . If the lowest order of society earn enough food to keep them going from day to day, then they have enough.[3]

But even this large group was not at the bottom of the social scale; beneath them were the slaves, especially in the Italian cities.

Slavery in the Renaissance   Agricultural slavery existed in the Early Middle Ages but had declined for economic reasons and been replaced by serfdom by the ninth century. Although some domestic slaves remained, slavery in European society had largely disappeared by the eleventh century. It reappeared first in Spain, where both Christians and Muslims used captured prisoners as slaves during the lengthy *Reconquista*. In the second half of the fourteenth century, the shortage of workers after the Black Death led Italians to introduce slavery on a fairly large scale. In 1363, for example, the government of Florence authorized the unlimited importation of foreign slaves.

In the Italian cities, slaves were used as skilled workers, making handcrafted goods for their masters, or as household workers. Girls served as nursemaids and boys as playmates. Fiammetta Adimari wrote to her husband in 1469: "I must remind you that when Alfonso is weaned we ought to get a little slave-girl to look after him, or else one of the black boys to keep him company."[4] In Florence, wealthy merchants might possess two or three slaves. Often men of the household took slaves as concubines, which sometimes led to the birth of illegitimate children. In 1392, the wealthy merchant Francesco Datini fathered an illegitimate daughter by Lucia, his twenty-year-old slave. His wife, Margherita, who was unable to bear any children, reluctantly agreed to raise the girl as their own daughter. Many illegitimate children were not as fortunate.

Slaves for the Italian market were obtained primarily from the eastern Mediterranean and the Black Sea region and included Tartars, Russians, Albanians, and Dalmatians. There were also slaves from Africa, either Moors or Ethiopians, and Muslims from Spain. Because of the lucrative nature of the slave trade, Italian merchants became involved in the transportation of slaves. Between 1414 and 1423, ten thousand slaves were sold on the Venetian market. Most slaves were females, many of them young girls.

By the end of the fifteenth century, slavery had declined dramatically in the Italian cities. Many slaves had been freed by their owners for humanitarian reasons, and the major source of slaves dried up as the Black Sea slave markets were closed to Italian traders after the Turks conquered the Byzantine Empire. Although some other sources remained, prices rose dramatically, further cutting demand. Moreover, a general feeling had arisen that slaves—the "domestic enemy," as they were called—were dangerous and not worth the effort. By the sixteenth century, slaves were in evidence only at princely courts, where they were kept as curiosities; this was especially true of black slaves.

In the fifteenth century, the Portuguese had imported increasing numbers of African slaves for southern European markets. It has been estimated that between 1444 and 1505, some 140,000 slaves were shipped from Africa. The presence of blacks in European society was not entirely new. Saint Maurice, a Christian martyr of the fourth century, was portrayed by medieval artists as a black knight and became the center of a popular cult in the twelfth and thirteenth centuries. The number of blacks in Europe was small, however, until their importation as slaves.

The Family in Renaissance Italy

The family played an important role in Renaissance Italy. Family meant, first of all, the extended household of parents, children, and servants (if the family was wealthy) and could also include grandparents, widowed mothers, and even unmarried sisters. Families that were related and bore the same surname often lived near each other and might dominate an entire urban district. Old family names—Strozzi, Rucellai, Medici—conferred great status and prestige. The family bond was a source of great security in a dangerous and violent world, and its importance helps explain the vendetta in the Italian Renaissance. A crime committed by one family member fell on the entire family, ensuring that retaliation by the offended family would be a bloody affair involving large numbers of people.

Marriage To maintain the family, careful attention was given to marriages arranged by parents, often to strengthen business or family ties. Details were worked out well in advance, sometimes when children were only two or three, and reinforced by a legally binding marriage contract (see the box on p. 319). The important aspect of the contract was the size of the dowry, money presented by the wife's family to the husband upon marriage. The dowry could involve large sums and was expected of all families. The size of the dowry was an indication of whether the bride was moving upward or downward in society. With a large dowry, a daughter could marry a man of higher social status, thereby enabling her family to move up in society; if the daughter married a man of lower social status, however, her dowry would be smaller because the reputation of her family would raise the status of the husband's family.

Wedding Banquet. Parents arranged marriages in Renaissance Italy to strengthen business or family ties. A legally binding marriage contract was considered a necessary part of the marital arrangements. So was a wedding feast. This painting by Botticelli shows the wedding banquet in Florence that celebrated the marriage of Nastagio degli Onesti and the daughter of Paulo Traversaro.

MARRIAGE NEGOTIATIONS

MARRIAGES WERE so important in maintaining families in Renaissance Italy that much energy was put into arranging them. Parents made the choices for their children, most often for considerations that had little to do with the modern notion of love. This selection is taken from the letters of a Florentine matron of the illustrious Strozzi family to her son Filippo in Naples. The family's considerations were complicated by the fact that the son was in exile.

Alessandra Strozzi to Her Son Filippo in Naples

[April 20, 1464] . . . Concerning the matter of a wife [for you], it appears to me that if Francesco di Messer Tanagli wishes to give his daughter, that it would be a fine marriage. . . . Now I will speak with Marco [Parenti, Alessandra's son-in-law], to see if there are other prospects that would be better, and if there are none, then we will learn if he wishes to give her [in marriage]. . . . Francesco Tanagli has a good reputation, and he has held office, not the highest, but still he has been in office. You may ask: "Why should he give her to someone in exile?" There are three reasons. First, there aren't many young men of good family who have both virtue and property. Second, she has only a small dowry, 1,000 florins, which is the dowry of an artisan [although not a small sum, either—senior officials in the government bureaucracy earned 300 florins a year]. . . . Third, I believe that he will give her away, because he has a large family and he will need help to settle them. . . .

[July 26, 1465] . . . Francesco is a good friend of Marco and he trusts him. On S. Jacopo's day, he spoke to him discreetly and persuasively, saying that for several months he had heard that we were interested in the girl and . . . that when we had made up our minds, she will come to us willingly. [He said that] you were a worthy man, and that his family had always made good marriages, but that he had only a small dowry to give her, and so he would prefer to send her out of Florence to someone of worth, rather than to give her to someone here, from among those who were available, with little money. . . . We have information that she is affable and competent. She is responsible for a large family (there are twelve children, six boys and six girls), and the mother is always pregnant and isn't very competent. . . .

[August 31, 1465] . . . I have recently received some very favorable information [about the Tanagli girl] from two individuals. . . . They are in agreement that whoever gets her will be content. . . . Concerning her beauty, they told me what I had already seen, that she is attractive and well-proportioned. Her face is long, but I couldn't look directly into her face, since she appeared to be aware that I was examining her . . . and so she turned away from me like the wind. . . . She reads quite well . . . and she can dance and sing. . . .

So yesterday I sent for Marco and told him what I had learned. And we talked about the matter for a while, and decided that he should say something to the father and give him a little hope, but not so much that we couldn't withdraw, and find out from him the amount of the dowry. . . . May God help us to choose what will contribute to our tranquility and to the consolation of us all.

[September 13, 1465] . . . Marco came to me and said that he had met with Francesco Tanagli, who had spoken very coldly, so that I understand that he had changed his mind. . . .

[Filippo Strozzi eventually married Fiametta di Donato Adimari in 1466.]

The father-husband was the center of the Italian family. He gave it his name, was responsible for it in all legal matters, managed all finances (his wife had no share in his wealth), and made the crucial decisions that determined his children's lives. A father's authority over his children was absolute until he died or formally freed his children. In Renaissance Italy, children did not become adults on reaching a certain age; adulthood came only when the father went before a judge and formally emancipated them. The age of emancipation varied from early teens to late twenties.

Children The wife managed the household, a position that gave women a certain degree of autonomy in their daily lives. Most wives, however, also knew that their primary function was to bear children. Upper-class wives were frequently pregnant; Alessandra Strozzi of Florence, for example, who had been married at the age of sixteen, bore eight children in ten years. Poor women did not conceive at the same rate because they nursed their own babies. Wealthy women gave their infants out to wet nurses, which enabled them to become pregnant more quickly after the birth of a child.

For women in the Renaissance, childbirth was a fearful occasion. Not only was it painful, but it could be deadly; as many as 10 percent of mothers died in childbirth. In his memoirs, the Florentine merchant Gregorio Dati recalled that three of his four wives had died in childbirth. His third wife, after bearing eleven children in fifteen years, "died in childbirth after lengthy suffering, which she bore with remarkable strength and patience."[5] Nor did the tragedies end with childbirth. Surviving mothers often faced the death of their children. In Florence in the fifteenth century, for example, almost 50 percent of the children born to merchant families died before the age of twenty. Given these mortality rates, many upper-class families sought to have as many children as possible to ensure that there would be a surviving male heir to the family fortune.

This concern is evident in the Florentine humanist Leon Battista Alberti's treatise *On the Family,* where one of the characters remarks, "How many families do we see today in decadence and ruin! . . . Of all these families not only the magnificence and greatness but the very men, not only the men but the very names are shrunk away and gone. Their memory . . . is wiped out and obliterated."[6]

Sexual Norms Considering that marriages were arranged, marital relationships ran the gamut from deep emotional attachments to purely formal ties. The lack of emotional attachment from arranged marriages did encourage extramarital relationships, especially among groups whose lifestyle offered special temptations. Although sexual license for males was the norm for princes and their courts, women were supposed to follow different guidelines. The first wife of Duke Filippo Maria Visconti of Milan had an affair with the court musician and was executed for it.

The great age difference between husbands and wives in Italian Renaissance marriage patterns also heightened the need for sexual outlets outside marriage. In Florence in 1427–1428, the average difference was thirteen years. Though females married between the ages of sixteen and eighteen, factors of environment, wealth, and demographic trends favored relatively late ages for the first marriages of males, who were usually in their thirties or even early forties. The existence of large numbers of young, unmarried males encouraged extramarital sex as well as prostitution. Prostitution was viewed as a necessary vice; since it could not be eliminated, it should be regulated. In Florence in 1415, the city fathers established communal brothels:

> Desiring to eliminate a worse evil by means of a lesser one, the lord priors . . . have decreed that the priors . . . may authorize the establishment of two public brothels in the city of Florence, in addition to the one which already exists. . . . [They are to be located] in suitable places or in places where the exercise of such scandalous activity can best be concealed, for the honor of the city and of those who live in the neighborhood in which these prostitutes must stay to hire their bodies for lucre.[7]

A prostitute in Florence was required to wear a traditional garb of "gloves on her hands and a bell on her head."

The Italian States in the Renaissance

By the fifteenth century, five major powers dominated the Italian peninsula: Milan, Venice, Florence, the Papal States, and Naples (see Map 12.1).

The Five Major States

Northern Italy was divided between the duchy of Milan and the republic of Venice. After the death of the last Visconti ruler of Milan in 1447, Francesco Sforza, one of the leading *condottieri* of the time (see Chapter 11), turned on his

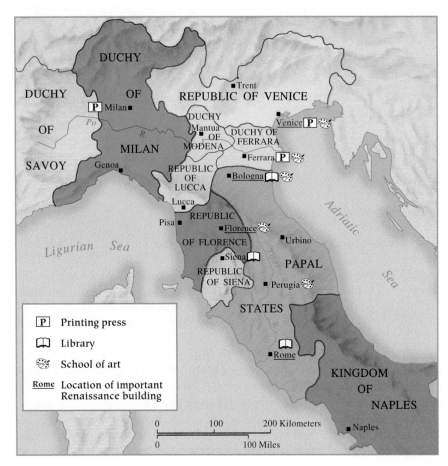

MAP 12.1 **Renaissance Italy.** Italy in the late fourteenth century was a land of five major states and numerous independent city-states. Increased prosperity and a supportive intellectual climate helped create the atmosphere for the middle and upper classes to "rediscover" Greco-Roman culture. Modern diplomacy was also a product of Renaissance Italy **?** Could the presence of several other powers within easy marching distance make a ruler recognize the importance of diplomacy?

View an animated version of this map or related maps at http://history .wadsworth.com/spielvogel06/

Milanese employers, conquered the city, and became its new duke. Both the Visconti and the Sforza rulers worked to create a highly centralized territorial state. They were especially successful in devising systems of taxation that generated enormous revenues for the government. The maritime republic of Venice remained an extremely stable political entity governed by a small oligarchy of merchant-aristocrats. Its commercial empire brought in enormous revenues and gave it the status of an international power. At the end of the fourteenth century, Venice embarked on the conquest of a territorial state in northern Italy to protect its food supply and its overland trade routes. Although expansion on the mainland made sense to the Venetians, it frightened Milan and Florence, which worked to curb what they perceived as the expansionary designs of the Venetians.

Republic of Florence   The republic of Florence dominated the region of Tuscany. By the beginning of the fifteenth century, Florence was governed by a small merchant oligarchy that manipulated the apparently republican government. In 1434, Cosimo de' Medici took control of this oligarchy. Although the wealthy Medici family maintained republican forms of government for appearance's sake, it ran the government from behind the scenes. Through lavish patronage and careful courting of political allies, Cosimo (1434–1464), and later his grandson Lorenzo the Magnificent (1469–1492), were successful in dominating the city at a time when Florence was the center of the cultural Renaissance.

Papal States   The Papal States lay in central Italy. Nominally under the political control of the popes, papal residence in Avignon and the Great Schism had enabled individual cities and territories, such as Urbino, Bologna, and Ferrara, to become independent of papal authority. The Renaissance popes of the fifteenth century directed much of their energy toward reestablishing their control over the Papal States (see "The Renaissance Papacy" later in this chapter).

Kingdom of Naples   The kingdom of Naples, which encompassed most of southern Italy and usually the island of Sicily, was fought over by the French and the Aragonese until the latter established their domination in the mid-fifteenth century. Throughout the Renaissance, the kingdom of Naples remained a backward monarchy with a population consisting largely of poverty-stricken peasants dominated by unruly nobles. It shared little in the cultural glories of the Renaissance.

Independent City-States

Besides the five major states, there were a number of independent city-states under the control of powerful ruling families that became brilliant centers of Renaissance culture in the fifteenth century. These included Mantua, under the enlightened rule of the Gonzaga lords; Ferrara, governed by the flamboyant d'Este family; and perhaps the most famous, Urbino, ruled by the Montefeltro dynasty.

Urbino   Federigo da Montefeltro, who ruled Urbino from 1444 to 1482, received a classical education typical of the famous humanist school in Mantua run by Vittorino da Feltre. He had also learned the skills of fighting, since the Montefeltro family compensated for the poverty of Urbino by hiring themselves out as *condottiere*. Federigo was not only a good ruler but also a rather unusual *condottiere* by

Piero della Francesca, *Duke and Duchess of Urbino*. Federigo da Montefeltro and his wife, Battista Sforza, ruled the small central Italian principality of Urbino. These profile portraits by Piero della Francesca gave a realistic rendering of the two figures. Visible in the background are the hills and valleys of Urbino.

THE LETTERS OF ISABELLA D'ESTE

*M*ANY ITALIAN AND EUROPEAN rulers at the beginning of the sixteenth century regarded Isabella d'Este as an important political figure. These excerpts from her letters reveal Isabella's political skills and her fierce determination. After her husband was taken prisoner by the Venetians in 1509, she refused to accept the condition for his release—namely, that her son Federico be kept as a hostage by the Venetians or the Holy Roman Emperor. She wrote to both the emperor and her husband, refusing to do as they asked.

Letter of Isabella d'Este to the Imperial Envoy

As to the demand for our dearest first-born son Federico, besides being a cruel and almost inhuman thing for any one who knows the meaning of a mother's love, there are many reasons which render it difficult and impossible. Although we are quite sure that his person would be well cared for and protected by His Majesty [the Holy Roman Emperor], how could we wish him to run the risk of this long and difficult journey, considering the child's tender and delicate age? And you must know what comfort and solace, in his father's present unhappy condition, we find in the presence of this dear son, the hope and joy of all our people and subjects. To deprive us of him, would be to deprive us of life itself, and of all we count good and precious. If you take Federico away you might as well take away our life and state. . . . Once for all, we will suffer any loss rather than part from our son, and this you may take to be our deliberate and unchanging resolution.

Letter of Isabella d'Este to Her Husband, Who Had Ordered Her to Send the Boy to Venice

If in this matter Your Excellency were to despise me and deprive me of your love and grace, I would rather endure such harsh treatment, I would rather lose our State, than deprive us of our children. I am hoping that in time your own prudence and kindness will make you understand that I have acted more lovingly toward you than you have to yourself.

Have patience! You can be sure that I think continuously of your liberation and when the time comes I will not fail you, as I have not relaxed my efforts. As witness I cite the Pope, the Emperor, the King of France, and all the other reigning heads and potentates of Christendom. Yes, and the infidels as well [she had written to the Turkish sultan for help]. If it were *really* the only means of setting you free, I would not only send Federico but all the other children as well. I will do everything imaginable. Some day I hope I can make you understand. . . .

Pardon me if this letter is badly written and worse composed, but I do not know if I am dead or alive.

Isabella, who desires the best for Your Excellency, written with her own hand

[Isabella's husband was not pleased with her response and exclaimed angrily: "That whore of my wife is the cause of it all. Send me into battle alone, do what you like with me. I have lost in one blow my state, my honor and my freedom. If she does not obey, I'll cut her vocal cords."]

---

fifteenth-century standards. Although not a brilliant general, he was reliable and honest. He did not break his promises, even when urged to do so by a papal legate. At the same time, Duke Federigo was one of the greatest patrons of Renaissance culture. Under his direction, Urbino became a well-known cultural and intellectual center. Though a despot, Federigo was also benevolent. It was said of him that he could walk safely through the streets of Urbino unaccompanied by a bodyguard, a feat few Renaissance rulers dared to emulate.

The Role of Women A noticeable feature of these smaller Renaissance courts was the important role played by women. Battista Sforza, niece of the ruler of Milan, was the wife of Federigo da Montefeltro. The duke called his wife "the delight of both my public and my private hours." An intelligent woman, she was well versed in both Greek and Latin and did much to foster art and letters in Urbino. As a prominent *condottiere*, Federigo was frequently absent, and like the wives of medieval lords, Battista Sforza was respected for governing the state "with firmness and good sense."

Perhaps the most famous of the Renaissance ruling women was Isabella d'Este (1474–1539), daughter of the duke of Ferrara, who married Francesco Gonzaga, marquis of Mantua. Their court was another important center of art and learning in the Renaissance. Educated at the brilliant court of Ferrara, Isabella was known for her intelligence and political wisdom. Called the "first lady of the world," she attracted artists and intellectuals to the Mantuan court and was responsible for amassing one of the finest libraries in all of Italy. Her numerous letters to friends, family, princes, and artists all over Europe disclose her political acumen as well as a good sense of humor (see the box above). Both before and after the death of her husband, she effectively ruled Mantua and won a reputation as a clever negotiator.

Warfare in Italy

The fragmented world of the Italian territorial states gave rise to a political practice that was later used on a larger scale by competing European states. This was the concept of a balance of power, designed to prevent the aggrandizement of any one state at the expense of the others. This system was especially evident after 1454 when the Italian states signed the Peace of Lodi, which ended almost a half-century of war and inaugurated a relatively peaceful forty-year era in Italy. An alliance system (Milan, Florence, and Naples versus Venice and the papacy) was then created that led to a workable balance of power within Italy. It failed, however, to establish lasting cooperation among the major powers or a common foreign policy.

The growth of powerful monarchical states (see "The European State in the Renaissance" later in this chapter) led to trouble for the Italians. Italy soon became a battlefield for the great power struggle between the French and Spanish monarchies. Italian wealth and splendor would probably have been inviting to its northern neighbors under any circumstances, but it was actually the breakdown of the Italian balance of power that encouraged the invasions and began the Italian wars. Feeling isolated, Ludovico Sforza, the duke of Milan, foolishly invited the French to intervene in Italian politics. The French king Charles VIII (1483–1498) was eager to do so, and in 1494, with an army of thirty thousand men, he advanced through Italy and occupied the kingdom of Naples. Other Italian states turned to the Spanish for help, and Ferdinand of Aragon indicated his willingness to intervene. For the next fifteen years, the French and Spanish competed to dominate Italy. After 1510, the war was continued by a new generation of rulers, Francis I of France and Charles I of Spain (see Chapter 13). This war was part of a long struggle for power throughout Europe between the Valois and Habsburg dynasties. Italy was only a pawn for the two great powers, a convenient arena for fighting battles. The terrible sack of Rome in 1527 by the armies of the Spanish king Charles I brought a temporary end to the Italian wars. Thereafter, the Spaniards dominated Italy.

Although some Italians had developed a sense of national consciousness and differentiated between Italians and "barbarians" (all foreigners), few Italians conceived of creating an alliance or confederation of states that could repel foreign invaders. Italians remained fiercely loyal to their own petty states, making invasion a fact of life in Italian history for all too long. Italy would not achieve unification and nationhood until 1870.

The Birth of Modern Diplomacy

The modern diplomatic system was a product of the Italian Renaissance. There were ambassadors in the Middle Ages, but they were used only on a temporary basis. Moreover, an ambassador, regardless of whose subject he was, regarded himself as the servant of all Christendom, not just of his particular employer. As a treatise on diplomacy stated, "An ambassador is sacred because he acts for the general welfare." Since he was the servant of all Christendom, "the business of an ambassador is peace."[8]

This concept of an ambassador changed during the Italian Renaissance because of the political situation in Italy. A large number of states existed, many so small that their security was easily threatened by their neighbors. To survive, the Italian states began to send resident diplomatic agents to each other to ferret out useful information. During the Italian wars, the practice of resident diplomats spread to the rest of Europe, and in the course of the sixteenth and seventeenth centuries, Europeans developed the diplomatic machinery still in use today, such as the rights of ambassadors in host countries and the proper procedures for conducting diplomatic business.

With the use of permanent resident agents or ambassadors, the conception of the purpose of the ambassador also changed. A Venetian diplomat attempted to define the function of an ambassador in a treatise written at the end of the fifteenth century. He wrote, "The first duty of an ambassador is exactly the same as that of any other servant of a government, that is, to do, say, advise, and think whatever may best serve the preservation and aggrandizement of his own state."[9] An ambassador was now simply an agent of the territorial state that sent him, not the larger body of Christendom. He could use any methods that were beneficial to the political interests of his own state. We are at the beginning of modern politics when the interests of the state supersede all other considerations.

Machiavelli and the New Statecraft

No one gave better expression to the Renaissance preoccupation with political power than Niccolò Machiavelli (1469–1527). He entered the service of the Florentine republic in 1498, four years after the Medici family had been expelled from the city. As a secretary to the Florentine Council of Ten, he made numerous diplomatic missions, including trips to France and Germany, and saw the workings of statecraft at first hand. Since Italy had been invaded in 1494, Machiavelli was active during a period of Italian tribulation and devastation. In 1512, French defeat and Spanish victory led to the reestablishment of Medici power in Florence. Staunch republicans, including Machiavelli, were sent into exile. Forced to give up politics, the great love of his life, Machiavelli now reflected on political power and

Niccolò Machiavelli. In *The Prince,* Machiavelli gave concrete expression to the Renaissance preoccupation with political power. This slender volume remains one of the most famous and most widely read Western treatises on politics. Machiavelli is seen here in a portrait by Santi di Tito.

wrote books, including *The Prince* (1513), one of the most famous treatises on political power in the Western world.

The Prince   Machiavelli's ideas on politics stemmed from two major sources, his preoccupation with Italy's political problems and his knowledge of ancient Rome. His major concerns in *The Prince* were the acquisition and expansion of political power as the means to restore and maintain order in his time. Late medieval political theorists believed that a ruler was justified in exercising political power only if it contributed to the common good of the people he served. The ethical side of a prince's activity—how a ruler ought to behave based on Christian moral principles—was the focus of many late medieval treatises on politics. Machiavelli bluntly contradicted this approach:

> My hope is to write a book that will be useful, at least to those who read it intelligently, and so I thought it sensible to go straight to a discussion of how things are in real life and not waste time with a discussion of an imaginary world. . . . For the gap between how people actually behave and how they ought to behave is so great that anyone who ignores everyday reality in order to live up to an ideal will soon discover he has been taught how to destroy himself, not how to preserve himself.[10]

Machiavelli considered his approach far more realistic than that of his medieval forebears.

From Machiavelli's point of view, a prince's attitude toward power must be based on an understanding of human nature, which he perceived as basically self-centered: "For of men one can, in general, say this: They are ungrateful, fickle, deceptive and deceiving, avoiders of danger, eager to gain." Political activity, therefore, could not be restricted by moral considerations. The prince acts on behalf of the state and for the sake of the state must be willing to let his conscience sleep. As Machiavelli put it:

> You need to understand this: A ruler, and particularly a ruler who is new to power, cannot conform to all those rules that men who are thought good are expected to respect, for he is often obliged, in order to hold on to power, to break his word, to be uncharitable, inhumane, and irreligious. So he must be mentally prepared to act as circumstances and changes in fortune require. As I have said, he should do what is right if he can; but he must be prepared to do wrong if necessary.[11]

Machiavelli found a good example of the new Italian ruler in Cesare Borgia, the son of Pope Alexander VI, who used ruthless measures to achieve his goal of carving out a new state in central Italy. As Machiavelli said: "So anyone who decides that the policy to follow when one has newly acquired power is to destroy one's enemies, to secure some allies, to win wars, whether by force or by fraud, to make oneself both loved and feared by one's subjects, . . . cannot hope to find, in the recent past, a better model to imitate than Cesare Borgia."[12] Machiavelli was among the first to abandon morality as the basis for the analysis of political activity (see the box on p. 325).

The Intellectual Renaissance in Italy

Individualism and **secularism**—two characteristics of the Italian Renaissance—were most noticeable in the intellectual and artistic realms. Italian culture had matured by the fourteenth century. For the next two centuries, Italy was the cultural leader of Europe. This new Italian culture was primarily the product of a relatively wealthy, urban lay society. The most important literary movement associated with the Renaissance is **humanism.**

Italian Renaissance Humanism

Renaissance humanism was an intellectual movement based on the study of the classical literary works of Greece and Rome. Humanists studied the liberal arts—grammar, rhetoric, poetry, moral philosophy or ethics, and history—all based on the writings of ancient Greek and Roman authors. These are the subjects we call the humanities.

The central importance of literary preoccupations in Renaissance humanism is evident in the professional status or occupations of the humanists. Some of them were teachers of the humanities in secondary schools and universities, where they either gave occasional lectures or held permanent positions, often as professors of rhetoric.

MACHIAVELLI: "IS IT BETTER TO BE LOVED THAN FEARED?"

*I*N 1513, NICCOLÒ MACHIAVELLI wrote a short treatise on political power that, justly or unjustly, has given him a reputation as a political opportunist. In this passage from Chapter 17 of *The Prince*, Machiavelli analyzes whether it is better for a ruler to be loved than to be feared.

✒ Machiavelli, *The Prince*

This leads us to a question that is in dispute: Is it better to be loved than feared, or vice versa? My reply is one ought to be both loved and feared; but, since it is difficult to accomplish both at the same time, I maintain it is much safer to be feared than loved, if you have to do without one of the two. For of men one can, in general, say this: They are ungrateful, fickle, deceptive and deceiving, avoiders of danger, eager to gain. As long as you serve their interests, they are devoted to you. They promise you their blood, their possessions, their lives, and their children, as I said before, so long as you seem to have no need of them. But as soon as you need help, they turn against you. Any ruler who relies simply on their promises and makes no other preparations, will be destroyed. For you will find that those whose support you buy, who do not rally to you because they admire your strength of character and nobility of soul, these are people you pay for, but they are never yours, and in the end you cannot get the benefit of your investment. Men are less nervous of offending someone who makes himself lovable, than someone who makes himself frightening. For love attaches men by ties of obligation, which, since men are wicked, they break whenever their interests are at stake. But fear restrains men because they are afraid of punishment, and this fear never leaves them. Still, a ruler should make himself feared in such a way that, if he does not inspire love, at least he does not provoke hatred. For it is perfectly possible to be feared and not hated. You will only be hated if you seize the property or the women of your subjects and citizens. Whenever you have to kill someone, make sure that you have a suitable excuse and an obvious reason; but, above all else, keep your hands off other people's property; for men are quicker to forget the death of their father than the loss of their inheritance. Moreover, there are always reasons why you might want to seize people's property; and he who begins to live by plundering others will always find an excuse for seizing other people's possessions; but there are fewer reasons for killing people, and one killing need not lead to another.

When a ruler is at the head of his army and has a vast number of soldiers under his command, then it is absolutely essential to be prepared to be thought cruel; for it is impossible to keep an army united and ready for action without acquiring a reputation for cruelty.

Others served as secretaries in the chancelleries of Italian city-states or at the courts of princes or popes. All of these occupations were largely secular, and most humanists were laymen rather than members of the clergy.

The Emergence of Humanism   Petrarch (1304–1374) has often been called the father of Italian Renaissance humanism (see Chapter 11 on his use of the Italian vernacular). Petrarch had rejected his father's desire that he become a lawyer and took up a literary career instead. Although he lived in Avignon for a time, most of his last decades were spent in Italy as the guest of various princes and city governments. With his usual lack of modesty, Petrarch once exclaimed, "Some of the greatest kings of our time have loved me and cultivated my friendship. . . . When I was their guest it was more as if they were mine."[13]

Petrarch did more than any other individual in the fourteenth century to foster the development of Renaissance humanism. He was the first intellectual to characterize the Middle Ages as a period of darkness, promoting the mistaken belief that medieval culture was ignorant of classical antiquity. Petrarch's interest in the classics led him on a quest for forgotten Latin manuscripts and set in motion a ransacking of monastic libraries throughout Europe. In his preoccupation with the classics and their secular content, Petrarch worried at times whether he was sufficiently attentive to spiritual ideals (see the box on p. 326).

His qualms, however, did not prevent him from inaugurating the humanist emphasis on the use of pure classical Latin, making it fashionable for humanists to use Cicero as a model for prose and Virgil for poetry. As Petrarch said, "Christ is my God; Cicero is the prince of the language."

Humanism in Fifteenth-Century Italy   In Florence, the humanist movement took a new direction at the beginning of the fifteenth century when it became closely tied to Florentine civic spirit and pride, giving rise to what one modern scholar has labeled **civic humanism.** Fourteenth-century humanists such as Petrarch had described the intellectual life as one of solitude. They rejected family and a life of action in the community. In the busy civic world of Florence, however, intellectuals began to take a new view of their role as intellectuals. The classical Roman Cicero, who was both a statesman and an intellectual, became their model. Leonardo Bruni (1370–1444), a humanist, Florentine patriot, and chancellor of the city, wrote a biography of Cicero titled *The New Cicero*, in which he waxed enthusiastic about the fusion of political action and literary creation in Cicero's life. From Bruni's time on, Cicero served as the inspiration for the Renaissance ideal that it was the duty of an intellectual to live an active life for one's state. An individual only "grows to maturity—both intellectually and morally—through participation" in the life of the state.

PETRARCH: MOUNTAIN CLIMBING AND THE SEARCH FOR SPIRITUAL CONTENTMENT

*P*ETRARCH HAS LONG BEEN regarded as the father of Italian Renaissance humanism. One of his literary masterpieces was *The Ascent of Mount Ventoux,* a colorful description of an attempt to climb a mountain in Provence in southern France and survey the world from its top. Petrarch's primary interest is in presenting an allegory of his own soul's struggle to achieve a higher spiritual state. The work is addressed to a professor of theology in Paris who had initially led Petrarch to read Augustine. The latter had experienced a vivid conversion to Christianity almost a thousand years earlier.

Petrarch, *The Ascent of Mount Ventoux*

Today I ascended the highest mountain in this region, which, not without cause, they call the Windy Peak. Nothing but the desire to see its conspicuous height was the reason for this undertaking. For many years I have been intending to make this expedition. You know that since my early childhood, as fate tossed around human affairs, I have been tossed around in these parts, and this mountain, visible far and wide from everywhere, is always in your view. So I was at last seized by the impulse to accomplish what I had always wanted to do. . . .

[After some false starts, Petrarch finally achieves his goal and arrives at the top of Mount Ventoux.]

I was glad of the progress I had made, but I wept over my imperfection and was grieved by the fickleness of all that men do. In this manner I seemed to have somehow forgotten the place I had come to and why, until I was warned to throw off such sorrows, for which another place would be more appropriate. I had better look around and see what I had intended to see in coming here. The time to leave was approaching, they said. . . . Like a man aroused from sleep, I turned back and looked toward the west. . . . One could see most distinctly the mountains of the province of Lyons to the right and, to the left, the sea near Marseilles as well as the waves that break against Aigues-Mortes. . . . The Rhône River was directly under our eyes.

I admired every detail, now relishing earthly enjoyment, now lifting up my mind to higher spheres after the example of my body, and I thought it fit to look in the volume of Augustine's *Confessions* which I owe to your loving kindness and preserve carefully, keeping it always in my hands, in remembrance of the author as well as the donor. . . . I opened it with the intention of reading whatever might occur to me first: . . . I happened to hit upon the tenth book of the work. . . . Where I fixed my eyes first, it was written: "And men go to admire the high mountains, the vast floods of the sea, the huge streams of the rivers, the circumference of the ocean, and the revolutions of the stars—and desert themselves." I was stunned, I confess. I bade my brother [who had accompanied him], who wanted to hear more, not to molest me, and closed the book, angry with myself that I still admired earthly things. Long since I ought to have learned, even from pagan philosophers, that "nothing is admirable besides the soul; compared to its greatness nothing is great."

I was completely satisfied with what I had seen of the mountain and turned my inner eye toward myself. From this hour nobody heard me say a word until we arrived at the bottom. These words occupied me sufficiently. I could not imagine that this had happened to me by chance: I was convinced that whatever I had read there was said to me and to nobody else. I remembered that Augustine once suspected the same regarding himself, when, while he was reading the Apostolic Epistles, the first passage that occurred to him was, as he himself relates: "Not in banqueting and drunkenness, not in chambering and wantonness, not in strife and envying; but put you on the Lord Jesus Christ, and make no provision for the flesh to fulfill your lusts."

Civic humanism reflected the values of the urban society of the Italian Renaissance. Humanists came to believe that their study of the humanities should be put to the service of the state. It is no accident that humanists served the state as chancellors, councillors, and advisers.

Also evident in the humanism of the first half of the fifteenth century was a growing interest in classical Greek civilization. One of the first Italian humanists to gain a thorough knowledge of Greek was Leonardo Bruni, who became an enthusiastic pupil of the Byzantine scholar Manuel Chrysoloras, who taught in Florence from 1396 to 1400. Humanists eagerly perused the works of Plato as well as Greek poets, dramatists, historians, and orators, such as Thucydides, Euripides, and Sophocles, all of whom had been ignored by the scholastics of the High Middle Ages as irrelevant to the theological questions they were examining.

By the fifteenth century, a consciousness of being humanists had emerged. This was especially evident in the career of Lorenzo Valla (1407–1457). Valla was brought up in Rome and educated in both Latin and Greek. Eventually, he achieved his chief ambition of becoming a papal secretary. Valla's major work, *The Elegances of the Latin Language,* was an effort to purify medieval Latin and restore Latin to its proper position over the vernacular. The treatise examined the proper use of classical Latin and created a new literary standard. Early humanists had tended to take as classical models any author (including Christians) who had written before the seventh century A.D. Valla identified different stages in the growth of the Latin language and accepted only the Latin of the last century of the Roman Republic and the first century of the empire.

Humanism and Philosophy   In the second half of the fifteenth century, a dramatic upsurge of interest in the works of Plato occurred, especially evident among the members of an informal discussion group known as the Florentine Platonic Academy. Cosimo de' Medici, the de facto ruler of Florence, became its patron and commissioned a translation of Plato's dialogues by Marsilio Ficino (1433–1499), one of the academy's leaders. Ficino dedicated his life to the translation of Plato and the exposition of the Platonic philosophy known as **Neoplatonism.**

In two major works, Ficino undertook the synthesis of Christianity and Platonism into a single system. His Neoplatonism was based on two primary ideas, the Neoplatonic hierarchy of substances and a theory of spiritual love. The former postulated the idea of a hierarchy of substances, or great chain of being, from the lowest form of physical matter (plants) to the purest spirit (God), in which humans occupied a central or middle position. They were the link between the material world (through the body) and the spiritual world (through the soul), and their highest duty was to ascend toward that union with God that was the true end of human existence. Ficino's theory of spiritual or Platonic love maintained that just as all people are bound together in their common humanity by love, so too are all parts of the universe held together by bonds of sympathetic love.

Renaissance Hermeticism   **Hermeticism** was another product of the Florentine intellectual environment of the late fifteenth century. At the request of Cosimo de' Medici, Ficino translated into Latin a Greek work titled *Corpus Hermeticum.* The Hermetic manuscripts contained two kinds of writings. One type stressed the occult sciences, with an emphasis on astrology, alchemy, and magic. The other focused on theological and philosophical beliefs and speculations. Some Hermetic writings espoused **pantheism,** seeing divinity embodied in all aspects of nature and in the heavenly bodies as well as in earthly objects. As Giordano Bruno, one of the most prominent of the sixteenth-century Hermeticists stated, "God as a whole is in all things."[14]

For Renaissance intellectuals, the Hermetic revival offered a new view of humankind. They believed that human beings had been created as divine beings endowed with divine creative power but had freely chosen to enter the material world (nature). Humans could recover their divinity, however, through a regenerative experience or purification of the soul. Thus regenerated, they became true sages or magi, as the Renaissance called them, who had knowledge of God and of truth. In regaining their original divinity, they reacquired an intimate knowledge of nature and the ability to employ the powers of nature for beneficial purposes.

In Italy, the most prominent magi in the late fifteenth century were Ficino and his friend and pupil, Giovanni Pico della Mirandola (1463–1494). Pico produced one of the most famous pieces of writing of the Renaissance, the *Oration on the Dignity of Man.* Pico combed diligently through the works of many philosophers of different backgrounds for the common "nuggets of universal truth" that he believed were all part of God's revelation to humanity. In the *Oration* (see the box on p. 328), Pico offered a ringing statement of unlimited human potential: "To him it is granted to have whatever he chooses, to be whatever he wills."[15] Like Ficino, Pico took an avid interest in Hermetic philosophy, accepting it as the "science of the Divine," which "embraces the deepest contemplation of the most secret things, and at last the knowledge of all nature."[16]

Education in the Renaissance

The humanist movement had a profound effect on education. Renaissance humanists believed that human beings could be dramatically changed by education. They wrote books on education and developed secondary schools based on their ideas. Most famous was the school founded in 1423 by Vittorino da Feltre (1378–1446) at Mantua, where the ruler of that small Italian state, Gian Francesco I Gonzaga, wished to provide a humanist education for his children. Vittorino based much of his educational system on the ideas of classical authors, particularly Cicero and Quintilian.

At the core of the academic training Vittorino offered were the "liberal studies." The Renaissance view of the value of the liberal arts was most strongly influenced by a treatise on education called *Concerning Character* by Pietro Paolo Vergerio (1370–1444). This work stressed the importance of the liberal arts as the key to true freedom, enabling individuals to reach their full potential. According to Vergerio, "We call those studies liberal which are worthy of a free man; those studies by which we attain and practice virtue and wisdom; that education which calls forth, trains, and develops those highest gifts of body and mind which ennoble men."[17] The liberal studies included history, moral philosophy, eloquence (rhetoric), letters (grammar and logic), poetry, mathematics, astronomy, and music. The purpose of a liberal education was thus to produce individuals who followed a path of virtue and wisdom and possessed the rhetorical skills with which to persuade others to do the same. Following the Greek precept of a sound mind in a sound body, Vittorino's school at Mantua also stressed physical education. Pupils were taught the skills of javelin throwing, archery, and dancing and encouraged frequently to run, wrestle, hunt, and swim.

Although a small number of children from the lower classes were provided free educations, humanist schools such as Vittorino's were primarily geared for the education of an elite, the ruling classes of their communities. Also largely absent from such schools were females. Vittorino's only female pupils were the two daughters of the Gonzaga ruler of Mantua. Though these few female students studied the classics and were encouraged to know some history and to ride, dance, sing, play the lute, and appreciate poetry, they were discouraged from learning mathematics and rhetoric. In the educational treatises of the time, religion and morals were thought to "hold the first place in the education of a Christian lady."

PICO DELLA MIRANDOLA AND THE DIGNITY OF MAN

*G*IOVANNI PICO DELLA MIRANDOLA was one of the foremost intellects of the Italian Renaissance. Pico boasted that he had studied all schools of philosophy, which he tried to demonstrate by drawing up nine hundred theses for public disputation at the age of twenty-four. As a preface to his theses, he wrote his famous *Oration on the Dignity of Man,* in which he proclaimed the unlimited potentiality of human beings.

Pico della Mirandola, *Oration on the Dignity of Man*

At last the best of artisans [God] ordained that that creature to whom He had been able to give nothing proper to himself should have joint possession of whatever had been peculiar to each of the different kinds of being. He therefore took man as a creature of indeterminate nature, and assigning him a place in the middle of the world, addressed him thus: "Neither a fixed abode nor a form that is yours alone nor any function peculiar to yourself have we given you, Adam, to the end that according to your longing and according to your judgment you may have and possess what abode, what form, and what functions you yourself desire. The nature of all other beings is limited and constrained within the bounds of laws prescribed by Us. You, constrained by no limits, in accordance with your own free will, in whose hand We have placed you, shall ordain for yourself the limits of your nature. We have set you at the world's center that you may from there more easily observe whatever is in the world. We have made you neither of heaven nor of earth, neither mortal nor immortal, so that with freedom of choice and with honor, as though the maker and molder of yourself, you may fashion yourself in whatever shape you shall prefer. You shall have the power to degenerate into the lower forms of life, which are brutish. You shall have the power, out of your soul's judgment, to be reborn into the higher forms, which are divine."

O supreme generosity of God the Father, O highest and most marvelous felicity of man! To him it is granted to have whatever he chooses, to be whatever he wills. Beasts as soon as they are born bring with them from their mother's womb all they will ever possess. Spiritual beings, either from the beginning or soon thereafter, become what they are to be for ever and ever. On man when he came into life the Father conferred the seeds of all kinds and the germs of every way of life. Whatever seeds each man cultivates will grow to maturity and bear in him their own fruit. If they be vegetative, he will be like a plant. If sensitive, he will become brutish. If rational, he will grow into a heavenly being. If intellectual, he will be an angel and the son of God.

Nevertheless, some women in Italy who were educated in the humanist fashion went on to establish their own literary careers. Isotta Nogarola, born to a noble family in Verona, mastered Latin and wrote numerous letters and treatises that brought her praise from male Italian intellectuals. Cassandra Fedele of Venice, who learned both Latin and Greek from humanist tutors hired by her family, became prominent in Venice for her public recitations of orations. Laura Cereta was educated in Latin by her father, a physician from Brescia. Laura defended the ability of women to pursue scholarly pursuits (see the box on p. 329).

Humanist education was thought to be a practical preparation for life. Its aim was not to create great scholars but rather to produce complete citizens who could participate in the civic life of their communities. As Vittorino said, "Not everyone is obliged to excel in philosophy, medicine, or the law, nor are all equally favored by nature; but all are destined to live in society and to practice virtue."[18] Humanist schools, combining the classics and Christianity, provided the model for the basic education of the European ruling classes until the twentieth century.

Humanism and History

Humanism had a strong impact on the writing of history. Influenced by Roman and Greek historians, the humanists approached the writing of history differently from the chroniclers of the Middle Ages. The humanists' belief that classical civilization had been followed by an age of barbarism (the Middle Ages), which had in turn been succeeded by their own age, with its rebirth of the study of the classics, enabled them to think in terms of the passage of time, of the past as past. Their division of the past into ancient world, dark ages, and their own age provided a new sense of chronology or periodization in history.

The humanists were also responsible for secularizing the writing of history. Humanist historians reduced or eliminated the role of miracles in historical interpretation, not because they were anti-Christian but because they took a new approach to sources. They wanted to use documents and exercised their newly developed critical skills in examining them. Greater attention was paid to the political events and forces that affected their city-states or larger territorial units. Thus Leonardo Bruni wrote the *History of the Florentine People.* The new emphasis on secularization was also evident in the humanists' conception of causation in history. In much medieval historical literature, historical events were often portrayed as being caused by God's active involvement in human affairs. Humanists deemphasized divine intervention in favor of human motives, stressing political forces or the role of individuals in history.

Guicciardini   The high point of Renaissance historiography was achieved at the beginning of the sixteenth century in the works of Francesco Guicciardini (1483–1540).

A Woman's Defense of Learning

S A YOUNG WOMAN, Laura Cereta was proud of her learning but condemned by a male world that found it unseemly for women to be scholars. One monk said to her father, "She gives herself to things unworthy of her—namely, the classics." Before being silenced, Laura Cereta wrote a series of letters, including one to a male critic who had argued that her work was so good it could not have been written by a woman.

Laura Cereta, *Defense of the Liberal Instruction of Women*

My ears are wearied by your carping. You brashly and publicly not merely wonder but indeed lament that I am said to possess as fine a mind as nature ever bestowed upon the most learned man. You seem to think that so learned a woman has scarcely before been seen in the world. You are wrong on both counts. . . .

I would have been silent. . . . But I cannot tolerate your having attacked my entire sex. For this reason my thirsty soul seeks revenge, my sleeping pen is aroused to literary struggle, raging anger stirs mental passions long chained by silence. With just cause I am moved to demonstrate how great a reputation for learning and virtue women have won by their inborn excellence, manifested in every age as knowledge. . . .

Only the question of the rarity of outstanding women remains to be addressed. The explanation is clear: women have been able by nature to be exceptional, but have chosen lesser goals. For some women are concerned with parting their hair correctly, adorning themselves with lovely dresses, or decorating their fingers with pearls and other gems. Others delight in mouthing carefully composed phrases, indulging in dancing, or managing spoiled puppies. Still others wish to gaze at lavish banquet tables, to rest in sleep, or, standing at mirrors, to smear their lovely faces. But those in whom a deeper integrity yearns for virtue, restrain from the start their youthful souls, reflect on higher things, harden the body with sobriety and trials, and curb their tongues, open their ears, compose their thoughts in wakeful hours, their minds in contemplation, to letters bonded to righteousness. For knowledge is not given as a gift, but [is gained] with diligence. The free mind, not shirking effort, always soars zealously toward the good, and the desire to know grows ever more wide and deep. It is because of no special holiness, therefore, that we [women] are rewarded by God the Giver with the gift of exceptional talent. Nature has generously lavished its gifts upon all people, opening to all the doors of choice through which reason sends envoys to the will, from which they learn and convey its desires. The will must choose to exercise the gift of reason. . . .

I have been praised too much; showing your contempt for women, you pretend that I alone am admirable because of the good fortune of my intellect. . . . Do you suppose, O most contemptible man on earth, that I think myself sprung [like Athena] from the head of Jove? I am a school girl, possessed of the sleeping embers of an ordinary mind. Indeed I am too hurt, and my mind, offended, too swayed by passions, sighs, tormenting itself, conscious of the obligation to defend my sex. For absolutely everything—that which is within us and that which is without—is made weak by association with my sex.

He has been called by some Renaissance scholars the greatest historian between Tacitus in the first century (see Chapter 6) and Voltaire and Gibbon in the eighteenth century (see Chapter 17). His *History of Italy* and *History of Florence* represent the beginning of "modern analytical historiography." To Guicciardini, the purpose of writing history was to teach lessons, but he was so impressed by the complexity of historical events that he felt those lessons were not always obvious. From his extensive background in government and diplomatic affairs, he developed the skills that enabled him to analyze political situations precisely and critically. Emphasizing political and military history, his works relied heavily on personal examples and documentary sources.

The Impact of Printing

The Renaissance witnessed the invention of printing, one of the most important technological innovations of Western civilization. The art of printing made an immediate impact on European intellectual life and thought.

Printing from hand-carved wooden blocks had been done in the West since the twelfth century and in China even before that. What was new to Europe in the fifteenth century was multiple printing with movable metal type. The development of printing from movable type was a gradual process that culminated between 1445 and 1450; Johannes Gutenberg of Mainz played an important role in bringing the process to completion. Gutenberg's Bible, completed in 1455 or 1456, was the first true book in the West produced from movable type.

The new printing spread rapidly throughout Europe in the second half of the fifteenth century. Printing presses were established throughout the Holy Roman Empire in the 1460s and within ten years had spread to Italy, England, France, the Low Countries, Spain, and eastern Europe. Especially well known as a printing center was Venice, home by 1500 to almost one hundred printers who had produced almost two million volumes.

By 1500, there were more than one thousand printers in Europe who had published almost forty thousand titles (between eight and ten million copies). Probably 50 percent of these books were religious—Bibles and biblical commentaries, books of devotion, and sermons. Next in importance were the Latin and Greek classics, medieval grammars, legal handbooks, works on philosophy, and an ever-growing number of popular romances.

Printing became one of the largest industries in Europe, and its effects were soon felt in many areas of European life. The printing of books encouraged the development of scholarly research and the desire to attain knowledge. Moreover, printing facilitated cooperation among scholars and helped produce standardized and definitive texts. Printing also stimulated the development of an ever-expanding lay reading public, a development that had an enormous impact on European society. Indeed, without the printing press, the new religious ideas of the Reformation would never have spread as rapidly as they did in the sixteenth century.

The Artistic Renaissance

Leonardo da Vinci, one of the great Italian Renaissance artists, once explained, "Hence the painter will produce pictures of small merit if he takes for his standard the pictures of others, but if he will study from natural objects he will bear good fruit. . . . Those who take for their standard any one but nature . . . weary themselves in vain."[19] Renaissance artists considered the imitation of nature their primary goal. Their search for naturalism became an end in itself: to persuade onlookers of the reality of the object or event they were portraying. At the same time, the new artistic standards reflected a new attitude of mind as well, one in which human beings became the focus of attention, the "center and measure of all things," as one artist proclaimed.

Art in the Early Renaissance

Leonardo and other Italians maintained that it was Giotto in the fourteenth century (see Chapter 11) who began the imitation of nature. But what Giotto had begun was not taken up again until the work of Masaccio (1401–1428) in Florence. Masaccio's cycle of frescoes in the Brancacci Chapel has long been regarded as the first masterpiece of Early Renaissance art. With his use of monumental figures, demonstration of a more realistic relationship between figures and landscape, and visual representation of the laws of perspective, a new realistic style of painting was born. Onlookers become aware of a world of reality that appears to be a continuation of their own world. Masaccio's massive, three-dimensional human figures provided a model for later generations of Florentine artists.

This new Renaissance style was absorbed and modified by other Florentine painters in the fifteenth century. Especially important was the development of an experimental trend that took two directions. One emphasized the mathematical side of painting, the working out of the laws of perspective and the organization of outdoor space and light by geometry and perspective. In the work of Paolo

Masaccio, *Tribute Money.* With the frescoes of Masaccio, regarded by many as the first great works of Early Renaissance art, a new realistic style of painting was born. *Tribute Money* was one of a series of frescoes that Masaccio painted in the Brancacci Chapel of the Church of Santa Maria del Carmine in Florence. In *Tribute Money,* Masaccio illustrated the biblical story of Jesus' confrontation by a tax collector at the entrance to the town of Capernaum (seen at center). Jesus sent Peter to collect a coin from the mouth of a fish from Lake Galilee (seen at left); Peter then paid the tax collector (seen at right). In illustrating this story from the Bible, Masaccio used a rational system of perspective to create a realistic relationship between the figures and their background; the figures themselves are realistic. As one Renaissance observer said, "The works made before Masaccio's day can be said to be painted, while his are living, real, and natural."

Botticelli, *Primavera*. This work reflects Botticelli's strong interest in classical antiquity. At the center of the painting is Venus, the goddess of love. At the right stands Flora, a Roman goddess of flowers and fertility, while the Three Graces dance playfully at the left. Cupid, the son of Venus, aims his arrow at the Three Graces. At the far left of the picture is Mercury, the messenger of the gods. Later in his life, Botticelli experienced a profound religious crisis, leading him to reject his earlier preoccupation with pagan gods and goddesses. He burned many of his early paintings and thereafter produced only religious works.

Uccello (1397–1475), figures became mere stage props to show off his mastery of the laws of perspective. The other aspect of the experimental trend involved the investigation of movement and anatomical structure. *The Martyrdom of Saint Sebastian* by Antonio Pollaiuolo (c. 1432–1498) revels in classical motifs and attempts to portray the human body under stress. Indeed, the realistic portrayal of the human nude became one of the foremost preoccupations of Italian Renaissance art. The fifteenth century, then, was a period of experimentation and technical mastery.

During the last decades of the fifteenth century, a new sense of invention emerged in Florence, especially in the circle of artists and scholars who formed part of the court of the city's leading citizen, Lorenzo the Magnificent. One of this group's prominent members was Sandro Botticelli (1445–1510), whose interest in Greek and Roman mythology was well reflected in one of his most famous works, *Primavera* (Spring). The painting is set in the garden of Venus, a garden of eternal spring. Though Botticelli's figures are well defined, they also possess an otherworldly quality that is far removed from the realism that characterized the painting of the Early Renaissance.

Donatello, *David*. Donatello's *David* first stood in the courtyard of the Medici Palace. On its base was an inscription praising Florentine heroism and virtue, leading art historians to assume that the statue was meant to commemorate the victory of Florence over Milan in 1428. David's pose and appearance are reminiscent of the nude statues of antiquity.

The revolutionary achievements of Florentine painters in the fifteenth century were matched by equally stunning advances in sculpture and architecture. Donato di Donatello (1386–1466) spent time in Rome studying and copying the statues of antiquity. His subsequent work in Florence reveals how well he had mastered the essence of what he saw. Among his numerous works was a statue of David, which is the first known life-size freestanding bronze nude in European art since antiquity. With the severed head of the giant Goliath beneath David's feet, Donatello's statue celebrated Florentine heroism in the triumph of the Florentines over the Milanese in 1428. Like Donatello's other statues, *David* also radiated a simplicity and strength that reflected the dignity of humanity.

Filippo Brunelleschi (1377–1446) was a friend who accompanied Donatello to Rome. Brunelleschi drew much inspiration from the architectural monuments of Roman antiquity, and when he returned to Florence, he poured his new insights into the creation of a new architecture. His first project involved the challenge of building a dome for the unfinished Cathedral of Florence (the Duomo). The cathedral had been started in 1296, but it was Brunelleschi who devised new building techniques and machinery to create a dome, built between 1420 and 1436, that spanned a 140-foot opening.

An even better example of Brunelleschi's new Renaissance architectural style is evident in the Church of San Lorenzo. When the Medici commissioned him to design the church, Brunelleschi, inspired by Roman models, created a church interior very different from that of the great medieval

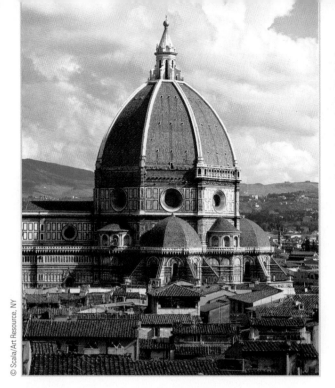

© Scala/Art Resource, NY

Filippo Brunelleschi, Dome of the Duomo. Brunelleschi was first commissioned in 1417 to design the dome for the unfinished Cathedral of Florence. Work did not begin until 1420. Although Brunelleschi would have preferred the Roman hemispheric dome, for practical reasons he was forced to elevate the center of the dome and then lessen the weight of the structure by building a thin double shell around a structure of twenty-four ribs. The most important ribs were placed on the outside of the dome (four of them are visible in this illustration).

cathedrals. San Lorenzo's classical columns, rounded arches, and coffered ceiling created an environment that did not overwhelm the worshiper materially and psychologically, as Gothic cathedrals did, but comforted as a space created to fit human, not divine, measurements. Like painters and sculptors, Renaissance architects sought to reflect a human-centered world.

The new assertion of human individuality, evident in Early Renaissance art, was also reflected in the new emphasis on portraiture. Patrons appeared in the corners of sacred pictures, and monumental tombs and portrait statues honored many of Florence's prominent citizens. By the mid-

fifteenth century, artists were giving an accurate rendering of their subjects' facial features while revealing the inner qualities of their personalities. The portraits of the duke and duchess of Urbino by Piero della Francesca (c. 1410–1492) provide accurate representations as well as a sense of both the power and the wealth of the rulers of Urbino (see p. 321).

The Artistic High Renaissance

By the end of the fifteenth century, Italian painters, sculptors, and architects had created a new artistic environment. Many artists had mastered the new techniques for a scientific observation of the world around them and were now ready to move into individualistic forms of creative expression. This final stage of Renaissance art, which flourished between 1480 and 1520, is called the High Renaissance. The shift to the High Renaissance was marked by the increasing importance of Rome as a new cultural center of the Italian Renaissance.

The High Renaissance was dominated by the work of three artistic giants: Leonardo da Vinci (1452–1519), Raphael (1483–1520), and Michelangelo (1475–1564). Leonardo represents a transitional figure in the shift to

© Scala/Art Resource, NY

Brunelleschi, Interior of San Lorenzo. Cosimo de' Medici contributed massive amounts of money to the rebuilding of the Church of San Lorenzo. As seen in this view of the nave and choir of the church, Brunelleschi's architectural designs were based on the basilica plan borrowed by early Christians from pagan Rome. San Lorenzo's simplicity, evident in its rows of slender Corinthian columns, created a human-centered space.

Leonardo da Vinci, *The Last Supper*. Leonardo da Vinci was the impetus behind the High Renaissance concern for the idealization of nature, moving from a realistic portrayal of the human figure to an idealized form. Evident in Leonardo's *Last Supper* is his effort to depict a person's character and inner nature by the use of gesture and movement. Unfortunately, Leonardo used an experimental technique in this fresco, which soon led to its physical deterioration.

High Renaissance principles. He carried on the fifteenth-century experimental tradition by studying everything and even dissecting human bodies to more clearly see how nature worked. But Leonardo stressed the need to advance beyond such realism and initiated the High Renaissance's preoccupation with the idealization of nature, or the attempt to generalize from realistic portrayal to an ideal form. Leonardo's *Last Supper,* painted in Milan, is a brilliant summary of fifteenth-century trends in its organization of space and use of perspective to depict subjects three-dimensionally in a two-dimensional medium. But it is also more. The figure of Philip is idealized, and there are profound psychological dimensions to the work. The words of Jesus that "one of you shall betray me" are experienced directly as each of the apostles reveals his personality and his relationship to Jesus. Through gestures and movement, Leonardo hoped to reveal a person's inner life.

Raphael blossomed as a painter at an early age; at twenty-five, he was already regarded as one of Italy's best painters. Raphael was acclaimed for his numerous madonnas, in which he attempted to achieve an ideal of beauty far surpassing human standards. He is well-known for his frescoes in the Vatican Palace; his *School of Athens* reveals a world of balance, harmony, and order—the underlying principles of the art of the classical world of Greece and Rome.

Michelangelo, an accomplished painter, sculptor, and architect, was another giant of the High Renaissance. Fiercely driven by his desire to create, he worked with great passion and energy on a remarkable number of projects. Michelangelo was influenced by Neoplatonism, especially evident in his figures on the ceiling of the Sistine Chapel in Rome. In 1508, Pope Julius II had called Michelangelo to Rome and commissioned him to decorate the chapel ceiling. This colossal project was not completed until 1512. Michelangelo attempted to tell the story of the Fall of Man by depicting nine scenes from the biblical book of Genesis. In his *Creation of Adam* (reproduced at the start of this chapter), the well-proportioned figure of Adam awaits the divine spark. Adam, like the other muscular figures on the ceiling, reveals an ideal type of human being with perfect proportions. In good Neoplatonic fashion, the beauty of these figures is meant to be a reflection of divine beauty; the more beautiful the body, the more God-like the figure.

Another manifestation of Michelangelo's search for ideal beauty was his *David,* a colossal marble statue commissioned by the Florentine government in 1501 and completed in 1504. Michelangelo maintained that the form of a statue already resided in the uncarved piece of stone: "I only take away the surplus, the statue is already there."[20] Out of a piece of marble that had remained unused for fifty years, Michelangelo created a 14-foot-high figure, the largest sculpture in Italy since the time of Rome. An awe-inspiring hero, Michelangelo's *David* proudly proclaims the beauty of the human body and the glory of human beings.

The High Renaissance was also evident in architecture, especially in the work of Donato Bramante (1444–1514).

© Erich Lessing/Art Resource, NY

Raphael, *School of Athens.* Raphael arrived in Rome in 1508 and began to paint a series of frescoes commissioned by Pope Julius II for the papal apartments at the Vatican. In *School of Athens,* painted in 1510 or 1511, Raphael created an imaginary gathering of ancient philosophers. In the center stand Plato and Aristotle. At the left is Pythagoras, showing his system of proportions on a slate. At the right is Ptolemy, holding a celestial globe.

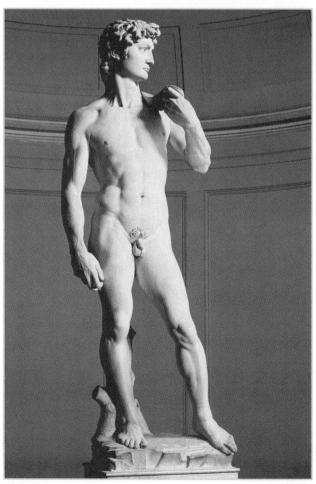

© Scala/Art Resource, NY

He came from Urbino but took up residence in Rome, where he designed a small temple on the supposed site of Saint Peter's martyrdom. The Tempietto, or little temple, with its Doric columns surrounding a sanctuary enclosed by a dome, summarized the architectural ideals of the High Renaissance. Columns, dome, and sanctuary form a monumental and harmonious whole. Inspired by antiquity, Bramante had recaptured the grandeur of ancient Rome. His achievement led Pope Julius II to commission him to design a new basilica for Rome, which eventually became the magnificent Saint Peter's.

Michelangelo, *David.* This statue of David, cut from an 18-foot-high piece of marble, exalts the beauty of the human body and is a fitting symbol of the Italian Renaissance's affirmation of human power. Completed in 1504, *David* was moved by Florentine authorities to a special location in front of the Palazzo Vecchio, the seat of the Florentine government.

THE GENIUS OF LEONARDO DA VINCI

*D*URING THE RENAISSANCE, artists came to be viewed as creative geniuses with almost divine qualities. One individual who helped create this image was himself a painter. Giorgio Vasari was an avid admirer of Italy's great artists and wrote a series of brief biographies of them. This excerpt is taken from his account of Leonardo da Vinci.

Giorgio Vasari, *Lives of the Artists*

In the normal course of events many men and women are born with various remarkable qualities and talents; but occasionally, in a way that transcends nature, a single person is marvelously endowed by heaven with beauty, grace, and talent in such abundance that he leaves other men far behind, all his actions seem inspired, and indeed everything he does clearly comes from God rather than from human art.

Everyone acknowledged that this was true of Leonardo da Vinci, an artist of outstanding physical beauty who displayed infinite grace in everything he did and who cultivated his genius so brilliantly that all problems he studied he solved with ease. He possessed great strength and dexterity; he was a man of regal spirit and tremendous breadth of mind; and his name became so famous that not only was he esteemed during his lifetime but his reputation endured and became even greater after his death. . . .

He was marvelously gifted, and he proved himself to be a first-class geometrician in his work as a sculptor and architect. In his youth Leonardo made in clay several heads of women, with smiling faces, of which plaster casts are still being made, as well as some children's heads executed as if by a mature artist. He also did many architectural drawings both of ground plans and of other elevations, and, while still young, he was the first to propose reducing the Arno River to a navigable canal between Pisa and Florence. He made designs for mills, fulling machines, and engines that could be driven by waterpower; and as he intended to be a painter by profession he carefully studied drawing from life. . . . Altogether, his genius was so wonderfully inspired by the grace of God, his powers of expression were so powerfully fed by a willing memory and intellect, and his writing conveyed his ideas so precisely, that his arguments and reasonings confounded the most formidable critics. In addition, he used to make models and plans showing how to excavate and tunnel through mountains without difficulty, so as to pass from one level to another; and he demonstrated how to lift and draw great weights by means of levers and hoists and ways of cleaning harbors and using pumps to suck up water from great depths.

The Artist and Social Status

Early Renaissance artists began their careers as apprentices to masters in craft guilds. Apprentices with unusual talent might eventually become masters and run their own workshops. As in the Middle Ages, artists were still largely viewed as artisans. Since guilds depended on commissions for their projects, patrons played an important role in the art of the Early Renaissance. The wealthy upper classes determined both the content and purpose of the paintings and pieces of sculpture they commissioned.

By the end of the fifteenth century, a transformation in the position of the artist had occurred. Especially talented individuals, such as Leonardo, Raphael, and Michelangelo, were no longer regarded as artisans but as artistic geniuses with creative energies akin to the divine (see the box above). Artists were heroes, individuals who were praised more for their creativity than for their competence as craftspeople. Michelangelo, for example, was frequently addressed as "Il Divino"—the Divine One. As society excused their

Bramante, Tempietto. Ferdinand and Isabella of Spain commissioned Donato Bramante to design a small building in Rome that would commemorate the place where Saint Peter was purportedly crucified. Completed in 1502, the temple reflected Bramante's increasing understanding of ancient Roman remains.

eccentricities and valued their creative genius, the artists of the High Renaissance became the first to embody the modern concept of the artist.

As respect for artists grew, so did their ability to profit economically from their work and to rise on the social scale. Now welcomed as equals into the circles of the upper classes, they mingled with the political and intellectual elite of their society and became more aware of new intellectual theories, which they then embodied in their art. The Platonic Academy and Renaissance Neoplatonism had an especially important impact on Florentine painters.

The Northern Artistic Renaissance

In trying to provide an exact portrayal of their world, the artists of the north (especially the Low Countries) and Italy took different approaches. In Italy, the human form became the primary vehicle of expression as Italian artists sought to master the technical skills that allowed them to portray humans in realistic settings. The large wall spaces of Italian churches had given rise to the art of fresco painting, but in the north, the prevalence of Gothic cathedrals with their stained-glass windows resulted in more emphasis on illuminated manuscripts and wooden panel painting for altarpieces. The space available in these works was limited, and great care was required to depict each object, leading northern painters to become masters at rendering details.

The most influential northern school of art in the fifteenth century was centered in Flanders. Jan van Eyck (c. 1390–1441) was among the first to use oil paint, a medium that enabled the artist to use a varied range of colors and make changes to create fine details. In the famous *Giovanni Arnolfini and His Bride,* van Eyck's attention to detail is staggering: precise portraits, a glittering chandelier, and a mirror reflecting the objects in the room. Although each detail was rendered as observed, it is evident that van Eyck's comprehension of perspective was still uncertain. His work is truly indicative of northern Renaissance painters, who, in their effort to imitate nature, did so not by mastery of the laws of perspective and proportion but by empirical observation of visual reality and the accurate portrayal of details. Moreover, northern painters placed great emphasis on the emotional intensity of religious feeling and created great works of devotional art, especially in their altarpieces. Michelangelo summarized the difference between northern and Italian Renaissance painting in these words:

> In Flanders, they paint, before all things, to render exactly and deceptively the outward appearance of things. The painters choose, by preference, subjects provoking transports of piety, like the figures of saints or of prophets. But most of the time they paint what are called landscapes with plenty of figures. Though the eye is agreeably impressed, these pictures have neither choice of values nor grandeur. In short, this art is without power and without distinction; it aims at rendering minutely many things at the same time, of which a single one would have sufficed to call forth a man's whole application.[21]

Van Eyck, *Giovanni Arnolfini and His Bride.* Northern painters took great care in depicting each object and became masters at rendering details. This emphasis on a realistic portrayal is clearly evident in this oil painting, supposedly a portrait of Giovanni Arnolfini, an Italian merchant who had settled in Bruges, and his wife, Giovanna Cenami.

By the end of the fifteenth century, however, artists from the north began to study in Italy and were visually influenced by what artists were doing there.

One northern artist of this later period who was greatly affected by the Italians was Albrecht Dürer (1471–1528) from Nuremberg. Dürer made two trips to Italy and absorbed most of what the Italians could teach, as is evident in his mastery of the laws of perspective and Renaissance theories of proportion. He wrote detailed treatises on both subjects. At the same time, as in his famous *Adoration of the Magi,* Dürer did not reject the use of minute details characteristic of northern artists. He did try, however, to integrate those details more harmoniously into his works and, like the Italian artists of the High Renaissance, to achieve a standard of ideal beauty by a careful examination of the human form.

Music in the Renaissance

For much of the fifteenth century, an extraordinary cultural environment was fostered in the domains of the dukes of

Dürer, *Adoration of the Magi*. By the end of the fifteenth century, northern artists had begun to study in Italy and to adopt many of the techniques used by Italian painters. As is evident in this painting, which was the central panel for an altarpiece done for Frederick the Wise in 1504, Albrecht Dürer masterfully incorporated the laws of perspective and the ideals of proportion into his works. At the same time, he did not abandon the preoccupation with detail typical of northern artists. Dürer portrayed himself in the center as the wise man with long hair.

Burgundy in northern Europe. The court of the dukes attracted some of the best artists and musicians of the time. Among them was Guillaume Dufay (c. 1400–1474), perhaps the most important composer of his time. Born in northern France, Dufay lived for a few years in Italy and was thus well suited to combine the late medieval style of France with the early Renaissance style of Italy. One of Dufay's greatest contributions was a change in the composition of the Mass. He was the first to use secular tunes to replace Gregorian chants as the fixed melody that served as the basis for the Mass. Dufay also composed a number of secular songs, an important reminder that during the Renaissance, music ceased to be used chiefly in the service of God and moved into the secular world of courts and cities. In Italy and France, the chief form of secular music was the madrigal.

The Renaissance madrigal was a poem set to music, and its origins were in the fourteenth-century Italian courts. The texts were usually twelve-line poems written in the vernacular, and their theme was emotional or erotic love. By the mid-sixteenth century, most madrigals were written for five or six voices and employed a technique called text painting, in which the music tried to portray the literal meaning of the text. Thus the melody would rise for the word *heaven* or use a wavelike motion to represent the word *water*. By the mid-sixteenth century, the madrigal had also spread to England, where the most popular form was characterized by the *fa-la-la* refrain like that found in the English carol "Deck the Halls."

The European State in the Renaissance

In the first half of the fifteenth century, European states continued the disintegrative patterns of the previous century. In the second half of the century, however, recovery set in,

and attempts were made to reestablish the centralized power of monarchical governments. To characterize the results, some historians have used the label "Renaissance states"; others have spoken of the "**new monarchies**," especially those of France, England, and Spain at the end of the fifteenth century (see Map 12.2). Although monarchs in western Europe succeeded to varying degrees at extending their political authority, rulers in central and eastern Europe were often weak and unable to impose their authority.

The Growth of the French Monarchy

The Hundred Years' War had left France prostrate. Depopulation, desolate farmlands, ruined commerce, and independent and unruly nobles had made it difficult for the kings to assert their authority. But the war had also developed a strong degree of French national feeling toward a common enemy that the kings could use to reestablish monarchical power. The need to prosecute the war provided an excuse to strengthen the authority of the king, already evident in the policies of Charles VII (1422–1461) after he was crowned king at Reims. With the consent of the Estates-General, Charles established a royal army composed of cavalry and archers. He received from the Estates-General the right to levy the *taille,* an annual direct tax usually on land or property, without any need for further approval from the Estates-General. Losing control of the purse meant less power for this parliamentary body.

The process of developing a French territorial state was greatly advanced by King Louis XI (1461–1483), known as the Spider because of his wily and devious ways. By retaining the *taille* as a permanent tax imposed by royal authority, Louis secured a sound, regular source of income. Louis was not, however, completely successful in repressing the French nobility, whose independence posed a threat to his own state building. A major problem was his supposed vassal, Charles the Bold, duke of Burgundy (1467–1477).

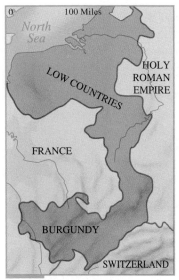

Lands of Charles the Bold

Charles attempted to create a middle kingdom between France and Germany, stretching from the Low Countries to Switzerland. Louis opposed his action, and when Charles was killed in 1477 fighting the Swiss, Louis added part of Charles's possessions, the duchy of Burgundy, to his own lands. Three years later, the provinces of Anjou, Maine, Bar, and Provence were brought under royal control. Many historians believe that Louis created a base for the later development of a strong French monarchy.

England: Civil War and a New Monarchy

The Hundred Years' War had also strongly affected the other protagonist in that conflict. The cost of the war in its final years and the losses in manpower strained the English economy. Moreover, even greater domestic turmoil came to England when the War of the Roses broke out in the 1450s. This civil war pitted the ducal house of Lancaster, whose symbol was a red rose, against the ducal house of York, whose symbol was a white rose. Many aristocratic families of England were drawn into the conflict. Finally, in 1485, Henry Tudor, duke of Richmond, defeated the last Yorkist king, Richard III (1483–1485), at Bosworth Field and established the new Tudor dynasty.

As the first Tudor king, Henry VII (1485–1509) worked to reduce internal dissension and establish a strong monarchical government. Henry ended the private wars of the nobility by abolishing "livery and maintenance," the practice by which wealthy aristocrats maintained private armies

MAP 12.2 Europe in the Second Half of the Fifteenth Century. By the second half of the fifteenth century, states in western Europe, particularly France, Spain, and England, had begun the process of modern state building. With varying success, they reined in the power of the church and nobles, increased the ability to levy taxes, and established effective government bureaucracies. **?** What aspects of Europe's political boundaries help explain why France and the Holy Roman Empire were often at war with each other? **View an animated version of this map or related maps at** http://history.wadsworth.com/spielvogel06/

of followers dedicated to the service of their lord. Since England, unlike France and Spain, did not possess a standing army, the king relied on special commissions to trusted nobles to raise troops for a specific campaign, after which the troops were disbanded. Henry also controlled the irresponsible activity of the nobles by establishing the Court of Star Chamber, which did not use juries and allowed torture to be used to extract confessions.

Henry VII was particularly successful in extracting income from the traditional financial resources of the English monarch, such as the crown lands, judicial fees and fines, and customs duties. By using diplomacy to avoid wars, which are always expensive, the king avoided having to call Parliament on any regular basis to grant him funds. By not overburdening the landed gentry and middle class with taxes, Henry won their favor, and they provided much support for his monarchy. Henry's policies enabled him to leave England with a stable and prosperous government and an enhanced status for the monarchy itself.

The Unification of Spain

During the Middle Ages, several independent Christian kingdoms had emerged in the course of the long reconquest of the Iberian peninsula from the Muslims. Aragon and Castile were the strongest Spanish kingdoms; in the west was the independent monarchy of Portugal; in the north, the small kingdom of Navarre, oriented toward France; and in the south, the Muslim kingdom of Granada (see Map 12.3). Few people at the beginning of the fifteenth century could have predicted the unification of the Iberian kingdoms.

A major step in that direction was taken with the marriage of Isabella of Castile (1474–1504) and Ferdinand of Aragon (1479–1516) in 1469. This was a dynastic union of two rulers, not a political union. Both kingdoms maintained their own parliaments (Cortes), courts, laws, coinage, speech, customs, and political organs. Nevertheless, the two rulers worked to strengthen royal control of government, especially in Castile. The royal council, which was supposed to supervise local administration and oversee the implementation of government policies, was stripped of aristocrats and filled primarily with middle-class lawyers. Trained in the principles of Roman law, these officials operated on the belief that the monarchy embodied the power of the state.

Seeking to replace the undisciplined feudal levies they had inherited with a more professional royal army, Ferdinand and Isabella reorganized the military forces of Spain. The development of a strong infantry force as the heart of the new Spanish army made it the best in Europe by the sixteenth century.

Ferdinand and Isabella recognized the importance of controlling the Catholic church, with its vast power and wealth. They secured from the pope the right to select the most important church officials in Spain, making the clergy virtually an instrument of royal power. Ferdinand and Isabella also pursued a policy of strict religious uniformity. Spain possessed two large religious minorities, Jews and Muslims, both of whom had been largely tolerated in medieval Spain. Increased persecution in the fourteenth century, however, led the majority of Spanish Jews to convert to Christianity. But complaints about the sincerity of these Jewish converts prompted Ferdinand and Isabella to ask the pope to introduce the Inquisition into Spain in 1478. Under royal control, the Inquisition worked with cruel efficiency to guarantee the orthodoxy of the converts but had no authority over practicing Jews. Consequently, in 1492, flush with the success of their conquest of Muslim Granada, Ferdinand and Isabella took the drastic step of expelling all professed Jews from Spain. It is estimated that 150,000 out of possibly 200,000 Jews fled.

Muslims, too, were "encouraged" to convert to Christianity after the conquest of Granada. In 1502, Isabella issued a decree expelling all professed Muslims from her kingdom. To a very large degree, the "Most Catholic" monarchs had achieved their goal of absolute religious orthodoxy as a basic ingredient of the Spanish state. To be Spanish was to be Catholic, a policy of uniformity enforced by the Inquisition.

The Holy Roman Empire: The Success of the Habsburgs

Unlike France, England, and Spain, the Holy Roman Empire failed to develop a strong monarchical authority. After 1438, the position of Holy Roman Emperor remained

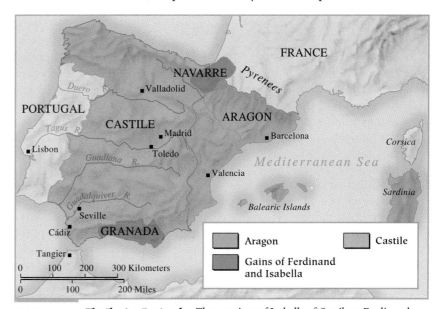

MAP 12.3 **The Iberian Peninsula.** The marriage of Isabella of Castile to Ferdinand of Aragon laid the foundation for the unification of Spain and its rise as a major European power. The two monarchs instituted military and bureaucratic reforms and forced Jews and Muslims to flee the country. ❓ What aspects of Portugal's geography help explain why it became a major seafaring nation, with little overland trade with Europe? 🌎 **View an animated version of this map or related maps at** http://history.wadsworth.com/spielvogel06/

in the hands of the Habsburg dynasty. Having gradually acquired a number of possessions along the Danube, known collectively as Austria, the house of Habsburg had become one of the wealthiest landholders in the empire and by the mid-fifteenth century began to play an important role in European affairs.

Much of the Habsburg success in the fifteenth century was due not to military success but to a well-executed policy of dynastic marriages. As the old Habsburg motto said, "Leave the waging of wars to others! But you, happy Austria, marry; for the realms which Mars [god of war] awards to others, Venus [goddess of love] transfers to you." By marrying his son Maximilian to Mary, the daughter of Duke Charles the Bold of Burgundy, Emperor Frederick III (1440–1493) gained Franche-Comté in east-central France, Luxembourg, and a large part of the Low Countries. The addition of these territories made the Habsburg dynasty an international power and brought it the undying opposition of the French monarchy because the rulers of France feared they would be surrounded by the Habsburgs.

Much was expected of the flamboyant Maximilian I (1493–1519) when he became emperor. Through the Reichstag, the imperial diet or parliament, Maximilian attempted to centralize the administration by creating new institutions common to the entire empire. Opposition from the German princes doomed these efforts, however. Maximilian's only real success lay in his marriage alliances. Philip of Burgundy, the son of Maximilian's marriage to Mary, was married to Joanna, the daughter of Ferdinand and Isabella. Philip and Joanna produced a son, Charles, who, through a series of unexpected deaths, became heir to all three lines, the Habsburg, Burgundian, and Spanish, making him the leading monarch of his age (see Chapter 13).

The Struggle for Strong Monarchy in Eastern Europe

In eastern Europe, rulers struggled to achieve the centralization of their territorial states but faced serious obstacles. Although the population was mostly Slavic, there were islands of other ethnic groups that caused untold difficulties. Religious differences also troubled the area, as Roman Catholics, Greek Orthodox Christians, and pagans confronted each other.

Much of Polish history revolved around a bitter struggle between the crown and the landed nobility until the end of the fifteenth century, when the preoccupation of Poland's rulers with problems in Bohemia and Hungary as well as war with the Russians and Turks enabled the aristocrats to reestablish their power. Through their control of the Sejm or national diet, the magnates reduced the peasantry to serfdom by 1511 and established the right to elect their kings. The Polish kings proved unable to establish a strong royal authority.

Bohemia, Poland's neighbor, was part of the Holy Roman Empire, but distrust of the Germans and close ethnic ties to the Poles and Slovaks encouraged the Czechs of Bohemia to associate with their northeastern Slavic

CHRONOLOGY	Europe in the Renaissance
France	
Charles VII	1422–1461
Louis XI the Spider	1461–1483
England	
War of the Roses	1450s–1485
Richard III	1483–1485
Henry VII	1485–1509
Spain	
Isabella of Castile	1474–1504
Ferdinand of Aragon	1479–1516
Marriage of Ferdinand and Isabella	1469
Introduction of Inquisition	1478
Expulsion of the Jews	1492
Expulsion of the Muslims	1502
Holy Roman Empire	
Frederick III	1440–1493
Maximilian I	1493–1519
Eastern Europe	
Battle of Kosovo	1389
Hungary: Matthias Corvinus	1458–1490
Russia: Ivan III	1462–1505
Fall of Constantinople and Byzantine Empire	1453

neighbors. The Hussite wars (see "The Problems of Heresy and Reform" later in this chapter) led to further dissension and civil war. Because of a weak monarchy, the Bohemian nobles increased their authority and wealth at the expense of both crown and church.

The history of Hungary had been closely tied to that of central and western Europe by its conversion to Roman Catholicism by German missionaries. The church became a large and prosperous institution. Wealthy bishops, along with the great territorial lords, became powerful, independent political figures. For a brief while, Hungary developed into an important European state, the dominant power in eastern Europe. King Matthias Corvinus (1458–1490) broke the power of the wealthy lords and created a well-organized bureaucracy. Like a typical Renaissance prince, he patronized the new humanist culture, brought Italian scholars and artists to his capital at Buda, and made his court one of the most brilliant outside Italy. After his death, Hungary returned to weak rule, and the work of Corvinus was largely undone.

Since the thirteenth century, Russia had been under the domination of the Mongols. Gradually, the princes of Moscow rose to prominence by using their close relationship to the Mongol khans to increase their wealth and expand their possessions. In the reign of the great prince Ivan III (1462–1505), a new Russian state—the principality of Moscow—was born. Ivan III annexed other Russian principalities and took advantage of dissension among the Mongols to throw off their yoke by 1480.

The Ottoman Turks and the End of the Byzantine Empire

Eastern Europe was increasingly threatened by the steadily advancing Ottoman Turks (see Map 12.4). The Byzantine Empire had, of course, served as a buffer between the Muslim Middle East and the Latin West for centuries. It was severely weakened by the sack of Constantinople in 1204 and its occupation by the West. Although the Palaeologus dynasty (1260–1453) had tried to reestablish Byzantine power in the Balkans after the overthrow of the Latin empire, the threat from the Turks finally doomed the long-lasting empire.

Beginning in northeastern Asia Minor in the thirteenth century, the Ottoman Turks spread rapidly, seizing the lands of the Seljuk Turks and the Byzantine Empire. In 1345, they bypassed Constantinople and moved into the Balkans. Under Sultan Murad, Ottoman forces moved through Bulgaria and into the lands of the Serbians, who provided a strong center of opposition under King Lazar.

But in 1389, at the Battle of Kosovo, Ottoman forces defeated the Serbs; both King Lazar and Sultan Murad perished in the battle. Kosovo became a battlefield long revered and remembered by the Serbs. Not until 1480 were Bosnia, Albania, and the rest of Serbia added to the Ottoman Empire in the Balkans.

In the meantime, in 1453, the Ottomans also completed the demise of the Byzantine Empire. With eighty thousand troops ranged against only seven thousand defenders, Sultan Mehmet II laid siege to Constantinople. In their attack on the city, the Turks made use of massive cannons with 26-foot barrels that could launch stone balls weighing up to 1,200 pounds each. Finally, the walls were breached; the Byzantine emperor died in the final battle. Mehmet II, standing before the palace of the emperor, paused to reflect on the passing nature of human glory.

After consolidating their power, the Turks prepared to exert renewed pressure on the West, both in the Mediterranean and up the Danube valley toward Vienna. By the

MAP 12.4 **The Ottoman Empire and Southeastern Europe.** Long a buffer between Christian Europe and the Muslim Middle East, the Byzantine Empire quickly waned in power and territory after Constantinople was sacked by crusaders in 1204. The Ottoman Turks slowly gained Byzantine territory and ended the thousand-year reign with the fall of Constantinople in 1453. **?** Why would the Byzantine Empire have found it difficult to make alliances by 1403? **🐦** **View an animated version** of this map or related maps at http://history.wadsworth.com/spielvogel06/

end of the fifteenth century, they were threatening Hungary, Austria, Bohemia, and Poland. The Holy Roman Emperor, Charles V, became their bitter enemy in the sixteenth century.

The Church in the Renaissance

As a result of the efforts of the Council of Constance, the Great Schism had finally been brought to an end in 1417 (see Chapter 11). The ending of the schism proved to be the council's easiest task; it was much less successful in dealing with the problems of heresy and reform.

The Problems of Heresy and Reform

Heresy was not a new problem, and in the thirteenth century, the church had developed inquisitorial machinery to deal with it. But two widespread movements in the fourteenth and early fifteenth centuries—Lollardy and Hussitism—posed new threats to the church.

Wyclif and Lollardy   English Lollardy was a product of the Oxford theologian John Wyclif (c. 1328–1384), whose disgust with clerical corruption led him to a far-ranging attack on papal authority and medieval Christian beliefs and practices. Wyclif alleged that there was no basis in Scripture for papal claims of temporal authority and advocated that the popes be stripped of their authority and their property. Believing that the Bible should be a Christian's sole authority, Wyclif urged that it be made available in the vernacular languages so that every Christian could read it. Rejecting all practices not mentioned in Scripture, Wyclif condemned pilgrimages, the veneration of saints, and a whole series of rituals and rites that had developed in the medieval church. Wyclif attracted a number of followers who came to be known as Lollards.

Hus and the Hussites   A marriage between the royal families of England and Bohemia enabled Lollard ideas to spread to Bohemia, where they reinforced the ideas of a group of Czech reformers led by the chancellor of the university at Prague, John Hus (1374–1415). In his call for reform, Hus urged the elimination of the worldliness and corruption of the clergy and attacked the excessive power of the papacy within the Catholic church. Hus's objections fell on receptive ears, for the Catholic church, as one of the largest landowners in Bohemia, was already widely criticized. Moreover, many clergymen were German, and the native Czechs' strong resentment of the Germans who dominated Bohemia also contributed to Hus's movement.

The Council of Constance attempted to deal with the growing problem of heresy by summoning John Hus to the council. Granted safe conduct by Emperor Sigismund, Hus went in the hope of a free hearing of his ideas. Instead he was arrested, condemned as a heretic (by a narrow vote), and burned at the stake in 1415. This action turned the unrest in Bohemia into revolutionary upheaval, and the resulting Hussite wars racked the Holy Roman Empire until a truce was arranged in 1436.

Reform of the Church   The reform of the church was even less successful than the attempt to eradicate heresy. Two reform decrees were passed by the Council of Constance. *Sacrosancta* stated that a general council of the church received its authority from God; hence every Christian, including the pope, was subject to its authority. The decree *Frequens* provided for the regular holding of general councils to ensure that church reform would continue. Taken together, *Sacrosancta* and *Frequens* provided for a legislative system within the church superior to the popes.

Decrees alone, however, proved insufficient to reform the church. Councils could issue decrees, but popes had to execute them, and popes would not cooperate with councils that diminished their authority. Beginning as early as Martin V in 1417, successive popes worked steadfastly for thirty years to defeat the conciliar movement. The final blow came in 1460, when Pope Pius II issued the papal bull *Execrabilis,* condemning appeals to a council over the head of a pope as heretical.

By the mid-fifteenth century, the popes had reasserted their supremacy over the Catholic church. No longer, however, did they have any possibility of asserting supremacy over temporal governments as the medieval papacy had. Although the papal monarchy had been maintained, it had lost much moral prestige. In the fifteenth century, the Renaissance papacy contributed to an even further decline in the moral leadership of the popes.

The Renaissance Papacy

The Renaissance papacy refers to the line of popes from the end of the Great Schism (1417) to the beginnings of the Reformation in the early sixteenth century. The primary concern of the papacy is governing the Catholic church as its spiritual leader. But as heads of the church, popes had temporal preoccupations as well, and the story of the Renaissance papacy is really an account of how the latter came to overshadow the popes' spiritual functions.

The manner in which Renaissance popes pursued their interests in the Papal States and Italian politics, especially their use of intrigue and even bloodshed, seemed shocking. Of all the Renaissance popes, Julius II (1503–1513) was most involved in war and politics. The fiery "warrior-pope" personally led armies against his enemies, much to the disgust of pious Christians, who viewed the pope as a spiritual leader. As one intellectual wrote, "How, O bishop standing in the room of the Apostles, dare you teach the people the things that pertain to war?"

To further their territorial aims in the Papal States, the popes needed loyal servants. Because they were not hereditary monarchs, popes could not build dynasties over several generations and came to rely on the practice of **nepotism** to promote their families' interests. Pope Sixtus IV (1471–1484), for example, made five of his nephews cardinals and gave them an abundance of church offices to

Council of Constance	1414–1418
Burning of John Hus	1415
End of the Great Schism	1417
Pius II issues the papal bull *Execrabilis*	1460
The Renaissance papacy	
Sixtus IV	1471–1484
Alexander VI	1492–1503
Julius II	1503–1513
Leo X	1513–1521

A Renaissance Pope: Leo X. The Renaissance popes allowed secular concerns to overshadow their spiritual duties. Shown here is the Medici pope Leo X. Raphael portrays the pope as a collector of books, looking up after examining an illuminated manuscript with a magnifying glass. At the left is the pope's cousin Guilio, a cardinal. Standing behind the pope is Luigi de' Rossi, another relative who had also been made a cardinal.

build up their finances (the word *nepotism* is in fact derived from the Greek *nepos,* meaning "nephew"). Alexander VI (1492–1503), a member of the Borgia family who was known for his debauchery and sensuality, raised one son, one nephew, and the brother of one mistress to the cardinalate. A Venetian envoy stated that Alexander, "joyous by nature, thought of nothing but the aggrandizement of his children." Alexander scandalized the church by encouraging his son Cesare to carve a state for himself in central Italy out of the territories of the Papal States.

The Renaissance popes were great patrons of Renaissance culture, and their efforts made Rome a cultural leader at the beginning of the sixteenth century. For the warrior-pope Julius II, the patronage of Renaissance culture was mostly a matter of policy as he endeavored to add to the splendor of his pontificate by tearing down the Basilica of Saint Peter, which had been built by the emperor Constantine, and beginning construction of the greatest building in Christendom, the present Saint Peter's Basilica.

Julius's successor, Leo X (1513–1521), was also a patron of Renaissance culture, not as a matter of policy but as a deeply involved participant. Such might be expected of the son of Lorenzo de' Medici. Made an archbishop at the age of eight and a cardinal at thirteen, he acquired a refined taste in art, manners, and social life among the Florentine Renaissance elite. He became pope at the age of thirty-seven, supposedly remarking to the Venetian ambassador, "Let us enjoy the papacy, since God has given it to us." Raphael was commissioned to do paintings, and the construction of Saint Peter's was accelerated as Rome became the literary and artistic center of the Renaissance.

CONCLUSION

THE RENAISSANCE WAS a period of transition that witnessed a continuation of the economic, political, and social trends that had begun in the High Middle Ages. It was also a movement in which intellectuals and artists proclaimed a new vision of humankind and raised fundamental questions about the value and importance of the individual. Of course, intellectuals and artists wrote and painted for the upper classes, and the brilliant intellectual, cultural, and artistic accomplishments of the Renaissance were products of and for the elite. The ideas of the Renaissance did not have a broad base among the masses of the people. As Lorenzo the Magnificent, ruler of Florence, once commented: "Only men of noble birth can obtain perfection. The poor, who work with their hands and have no time to cultivate their minds, are incapable of it."

The Renaissance did, however, raise new questions about medieval traditions. In advocating a return to the early sources of Christianity and criticizing current religious practices, the humanists raised fundamental issues about the Catholic church, which was still an important institution. In the sixteenth century, the intellectual revolution of the fifteenth century gave way to a religious renaissance that touched the lives of people, including the masses, in new and profound ways. After the Reformation, Europe would never again be the unified Christian commonwealth it once believed it was.

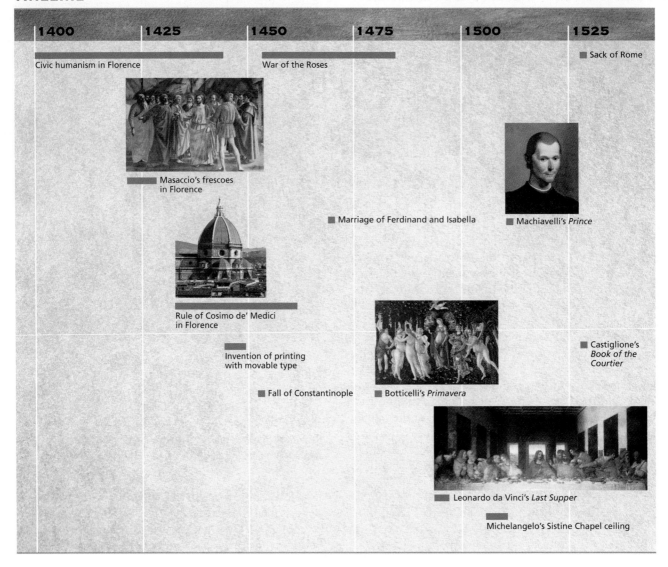

| 1400 | 1425 | 1450 | 1475 | 1500 | 1525 |

Civic humanism in Florence

War of the Roses

■ Sack of Rome

■ Masaccio's frescoes in Florence

■ Machiavelli's *Prince*

■ Marriage of Ferdinand and Isabella

Rule of Cosimo de' Medici in Florence

Invention of printing with movable type

■ Castiglione's *Book of the Courtier*

■ Fall of Constantinople   ■ Botticelli's *Primavera*

■ Leonardo da Vinci's *Last Supper*

Michelangelo's Sistine Chapel ceiling

NOTES

1. Quoted in Jacob Burckhardt, *The Civilization of the Renaissance in Italy,* trans. S. G. C. Middlemore (London, 1960), p. 81.
2. Baldassare Castiglione, *The Book of the Courtier,* trans. Charles S. Singleton (Garden City, N.Y., 1959), pp. 288–289.
3. Quoted in De Lamar Jensen, *Renaissance Europe* (Lexington, Mass., 1981), p. 94.
4. Quoted in Iris Origo, "The Domestic Enemy: The Eastern Slaves in Tuscany in the Fourteenth and Fifteenth Centuries," *Speculum* 30 (1955): 333.
5. Quoted in Gene Brucker, ed., *Two Memoirs of Renaissance Florence* (New York, 1967), p. 132.
6. Quoted in Margaret L. King, *Women of the Renaissance* (Chicago, 1991), p. 3.
7. Quoted in Gene Brucker, ed., *The Society of Renaissance Florence* (New York, 1971), p. 190.
8. Quoted in Garrett Mattingly, *Renaissance Diplomacy* (Baltimore, 1964), p. 42.
9. Ibid., p. 95.
10. Niccolò Machiavelli, *The Prince,* trans. David Wootton (Indianapolis, 1995), p. 48.
11. Ibid., p. 55.
12. Ibid., p. 27.
13. Petrarch, "Epistle to Posterity," *Letters from Petrarch,* trans. Morris Bishop (Bloomington, Ind., 1966), pp. 6–7.
14. Quoted in Frances Yates, *Giordano Bruno and the Hermetic Tradition* (Chicago, 1964), p. 211.
15. Giovanni Pico della Mirandola, *Oration on the Dignity of Man,* in E. Cassirer, P. O. Kristeller, and J. H. Randall Jr., eds., *The Renaissance Philosophy of Man* (Chicago, 1948), p. 225.
16. Ibid., pp. 247, 249.
17. Quoted in W. H. Woodward, *Vittorino da Feltre and Other Humanist Educators* (Cambridge, 1897), p. 102.
18. Quoted in Iris Origo, *The Light of the Past* (New York, 1959), p. 136.
19. Quoted in Elizabeth G. Holt, ed., *A Documentary History of Art* (Garden City, N.Y., 1957), vol.1, p. 286.
20. Quoted in Rosa M. Letts, *The Cambridge Introduction to Art: The Renaissance* (Cambridge, 1981), p. 86.
21. Quoted in Johan Huizinga, *The Waning of the Middle Ages* (Garden City, N.Y., 1956), p. 265.

SUGGESTIONS FOR FURTHER READING

The classic study of the Italian Renaissance is **J. Burckhardt,** *The Civilization of the Renaissance in Italy,* trans. S. G. C. Middlemore (London, 1960), first published in 1860. General works on the Renaissance in Europe include **D. L. Jensen,** *Renaissance Europe* (Lexington, Mass., 1981); **P. Burke,** *The European Renaissance: Centres and Peripheries* (Oxford, 1998); **E. Breisach,** *Renaissance Europe, 1300–1517* (New York, 1973); **J. Hale,** *The Civilization of Europe in the Renaissance* (New York, 1994); and the classic work by **M. P. Gilmore,** *The World of Humanism, 1453–1517* (New York, 1962). Although many of its interpretations are outdated, **W. Ferguson's** *Europe in Transition, 1300–1520* (Boston, 1962), contains a wealth of information. The brief study by **P. Burke,** *The Renaissance,* 2d ed. (New York, 1997), is a good summary of recent literature on the Renaissance. For beautifully illustrated introductions to the Renaissance, see **G. Holmes,** *Renaissance* (New York, 1996), and **M. Aston, ed.,** *The Panorama of the Renaissance* (New York, 1996).

Brief but basic works on Renaissance economic matters are **H. A. Miskimin,** *The Economy of Early Renaissance Europe, 1300–1460* (New York, 1975) and *The Economy of Later Renaissance Europe, 1460–1600* (New York, 1978). For a reinterpretation of economic matters, see **L. Jardine,** *Worldly Goods* (New York, 1996). On family and marriage, see **D. Herlihy,** *The Family in Renaissance Italy* (Saint Louis, Mo., 1974); **C. Klapisch-Zuber,** *Women, Family, and Ritual in Renaissance Italy* (Chicago, 1985); and the well-told story by **G. Brucker,** *Giovanni and Lusanna: Love and Marriage in Renaissance Florence* (Berkeley, Calif., 1986). On women, see **M. L. King,** *Women of the Renaissance* (Chicago, 1991), and **N. Z. Davis and A. Farge, eds.,** *A History of Women: Renaissance and Enlightenment Paradoxes* (Cambridge, Mass., 1993).

The best overall study of the Italian city-states is **L. Martines,** *Power and Imagination: City-States in Renaissance Italy* (New York, 1979); **D. Hay and J. Law,** *Italy in the Age of the Renaissance* (London, 1989), is also a good survey. There is an enormous literature on Renaissance Florence. The best introduction is **G. Brucker,** *Florence: The Golden Age, 1138–1737* (Berkeley, Calif., 1988). On the *condottieri,* see **M. Mallett,** *Mercenaries and Their Masters: Warfare in Renaissance Italy* (Totowa, N.J., 1974). The work by **G. Mattingly,** *Renaissance Diplomacy* (Boston, 1955), remains the basic one on the subject. Machiavelli's life can be examined in **Q. Skinner,** *Machiavelli* (Oxford, 1981).

Brief introductions to Renaissance humanism can be found in **D. R. Kelley,** *Renaissance Humanism* (Boston, 1991); **C. G. Nauert Jr.,** *Humanism and the Culture of Renaissance Europe* (Cambridge, 1995); and **F. B. Artz,** *Renaissance Humanism, 1300–1550* (Oberlin, Ohio, 1966). The fundamental work on fifteenth-century civic humanism is **H. Baron,** *The Crisis of the Early Italian Renaissance,* 2d ed. (Princeton, N.J., 1966). The impact of printing is exhaustively examined in **E. Eisenstein,** *The Printing Press as an Agent of Change,* 2 vols. (New York, 1978).

For brief introductions to Renaissance art, see **R. M. Letts,** *The Cambridge Introduction to Art: The Renaissance* (Cambridge, 1981), and **B. Cole and A. Gealt,** *Art of the Western World* (New York, 1989), ch. 6–8. Good surveys of Renaissance art include **F. Hartt,** *History of Italian Renaissance Art,* 4th ed. (Englewood Cliffs, N.J., 1994); **S. Elliott,** *Italian Renaissance Painting,* 2d ed. (London, 1993); **R. Turner,** *Renaissance Florence: The Invention of a New Art* (New York, 1997); **P. F. Brown,** *Art and Life in Renaissance Venice* (Upper Saddle River, N.J., 1997); and **L. Murray,** *The High Renaissance* (New York, 1967). For studies of individual artists, see **J. H. Beck,** *Raphael* (New York, 1994); **M. Kemp,** *Leonardo da Vinci: The Marvellous Works of Nature and of Man* (London, 1981); and **A. Hughes,**

Michelangelo (London, 1997). For a lively account of the painting of the Sistine Chapel ceiling, see **R. King,** *Michelangelo and the Pope's Ceiling* (New York, 2002).

For a general work on the political development of Europe in the Renaissance, see **J. H. Shennan,** *The Origins of the Modern European State, 1450–1725* (London, 1974). On France, see **R. J. Knecht,** *The Rise and Fall of Renaissance France, 1483–1610,* 2d ed. (Oxford, 2001). Early Renaissance England is examined in **J. R. Lander,** *Crown and Nobility, 1450–1509* (London, 1976). Good coverage of Renaissance Spain can be found in **J. N. Hillgarth,** *The Spanish Kingdoms, 1250–1516,* vol. 2, *Castilian Hegemony, 1410–1516* (New York, 1978). Two good works on eastern Europe include **P. W. Knoll,** *The Rise of the Polish Monarchy* (Chicago, 1972), and **C. A. Macartney,** *Hungary: A Short History* (Edinburgh, 1962). On the Ottomans and their expansion, see **H. Inalcik,** *The Ottoman Empire: The Classical Age, 1300–1600* (London, 1973), and the classic work by **S. Runciman,** *The Fall of Constantinople, 1453* (Cambridge, 1965).

On problems of heresy and reform, see **C. Crowder,** *Unity, Heresy and Reform, 1378–1460* (London, 1977). Aspects of the Renaissance papacy can be examined in **E. Lee,** *Sixtus IV and Men of Letters* (Rome, 1978), and **M. Mallett,** *The Borgias* (New York, 1969). On Rome, see especially **P. Partner,** *Renaissance Rome, 1500–1559: A Portrait of a Society* (Berkeley, Calif., 1976).

History Now™

Enter *HistoryNow* using the access card that is available for *Western Civilization. HistoryNow* will assist you in understanding the content in this chapter with lesson plans generated for your needs. In addition, you can read the following documents, and many more, online:

Giovanni Villani, selections from Books 8 and 9 of *Chronicle*

Two Tractates from Vittorino da Feltre and other Humanist Educators

Giorgio Vasari, Excerpts from *Life of Michelangelo* and *Life of da Vinci*

INFOTRAC SEARCH TERMS

 For additional reading, go to InfoTrac College Edition, your online research library at http://infotrac.thomsonlearning.com

Key Term Search	Subject Guide Search
Leonardo da Vinci	Renaissance
Machiavelli	humanism

WESTERN CIVILIZATION RESOURCES

Visit the *Western Civilization* Companion Web site for resources specific to this book:

http://history.wadsworth.com/spielvogel06/

For a variety of tools to help you succeed in this course, visit the **Western Civilization Resource Center** at

http://history.wadsworth.com/western/

Included are quizzes; images; documents; interactive simulations; maps and timelines; movie explorations; and a wealth of other sources.

GLOSSARY

abbess head of a convent or monastery for women.

abbot head of a monastery.

absolutism a form of government in which the sovereign power or ultimate authority rested in the hands of a monarch who claimed to rule by divine right and was therefore responsible only to God.

Abstract Expressionism a post–World War II artistic movement that broke with all conventions of form and structure in favor of total abstraction.

abstract painting an artistic movement that developed early in the twentieth century in which artists focused on color to avoid any references to visual reality.

aediles Roman officials who supervised the public games and the grain supply of the city of Rome.

Agricultural (Neolithic) Revolution the shift from hunting animals and gathering plants for sustenance to producing food by systematic agriculture that occurred gradually between 10,000 and 4000 B.C. (the Neolithic or "New Stone" Age).

agricultural revolution the application of new agricultural techniques that allowed for a large increase in productivity in the eighteenth century.

anarchism a political theory that holds that all governments and existing social institutions are unnecessary and advocates a society based on voluntary cooperation.

anticlericalism opposition to the power of the clergy, especially in political affairs.

anti-Semitism hostility toward or discrimination against Jews.

apartheid the system of racial segregation practiced in the Republic of South Africa until the 1990s, which involved political, legal, and economic discrimination against nonwhites.

appeasement the policy, followed by the European nations in the 1930s, of accepting Hitler's annexation of Austria and Czechoslovakia in the belief that meeting his demands would assure peace and stability.

Arianism a Christian heresy that taught that Jesus was inferior to God. Though condemned by the Council of Nicaea in 325, Arianism was adopted by many of the Germanic peoples who entered the Roman Empire over the next centuries.

aristocracy a class of hereditary nobility in medieval Europe; a warrior class who shared a distinctive lifestyle based on the institution of knighthood, although there were social divisions within the group based on extremes of wealth.

audiencias advisory groups to viceroys in Spanish America.

Ausgleich the "Compromise" of 1867 that created the dual monarchy of Austria-Hungary. Austria and Hungary each had its own capital, constitution, and legislative assembly but were united under one monarch.

authoritarian state a state that has a dictatorial government and some other trappings of a totalitarian state but does not demand that the masses be actively involved in the regime's goals as totalitarian states do.

auxiliaries troops enlisted from the subject peoples of the Roman Empire to supplement the regular legions composed of Roman citizens.

balance of power a distribution of power among several states such that no single nation can dominate or interfere with the interests of another.

Baroque an artistic movement of the seventeenth century in Europe that used dramatic effects to arouse the emotions and reflected the search for power that was a large part of the seventeenth-century ethos.

benefice in the Christian church, a position, such as a bishopric, that consisted of both a sacred office and the right of the holder to the annual revenues from the position.

bicameral legislature a legislature with two houses.

Black Death the outbreak of plague (mostly bubonic) in the mid-fourteenth century that killed from 25 to 50 percent of Europe's population.

Blitzkrieg "lightning war." A war conducted with great speed and force, as in Germany's advance at the beginning of World War II.

Bolsheviks a small faction of the Russian Social Democratic Party who were led by Lenin and dedicated to violent revolution; they seized power in Russia in 1917 and were subsequently renamed the Communists.

bourgeoisie (burghers) inhabitants (merchants and artisans) of boroughs and burghs (towns).

boyars the Russian nobility.

Brezhnev Doctrine the doctrine, enunciated by Leonid Brezhnev, that the Soviet Union had a right to intervene if socialism was threatened in another socialist state; used to justify moving Soviet troops into Czechoslovakia in 1968.

Burschenschaften student societies in the German states dedicated to fostering the goal of a free, united Germany.

caliph the secular leader of the Islamic community.

capital material wealth used or available for use in the production of more wealth.

cartel a combination of independent commercial enterprises that work together to control prices and limit competition.

Cartesian dualism Descartes's principle of the separation of mind and matter (and mind and body) that enabled scientists to view matter as something separate from themselves that could be investigated by reason.

celibacy complete abstinence from sexual activity. Many early Christians viewed celibacy as the surest way to holiness.

censors Roman officials chosen every five years to assess property holdings to determine taxes, military service, and officeholding.

centuriate assembly the chief popular assembly of the Roman Republic. It passed laws and elected the chief magistrates.

chansons de geste a form of vernacular literature in the High Middle Ages that consisted of heroic epics focusing on the deeds of warriors.

chivalry the ideal of civilized behavior that emerged among the nobility in the eleventh and twelfth centuries under the influence of the church; a code of ethics knights were expected to uphold.

Christian (northern) humanism an intellectual movement in northern Europe in the late fifteenth and early sixteenth centuries that combined the interest in the classics of the Italian Renaissance with an interest in the sources of early Christianity, including the New Testament and the writings of the church fathers.

civic humanism an intellectual movement of the Italian Renaissance that saw Cicero, who was both an intellectual and a statesman, as the ideal and held that humanists should be involved in government and use their rhetorical training in the service of the state.

civil disobedience a policy of peaceful protest against laws or government policies in order to achieve political change.

civilization a complex culture in which large numbers of humans share a variety of common elements, including cities; religious, political, military, and social structures; writing; and significant artistic and intellectual activity.

civil rights the basic rights of citizens, including equality before the law, freedom of speech and press, and freedom from arbitrary arrest.

Cold War the ideological conflict between the Soviet Union and the United States after World War II.

collective farms large farms created in the Soviet Union by Stalin by combining many small holdings into large farms worked by the peasants under government supervision.

collective security the use of an international army raised by an association of nations to deter aggression and keep the peace.

coloni free tenant farmers who worked as sharecroppers on the large estates of the Roman Empire (singular: *colonus*).

Columbian Exchange the reciprocal importation and exportation of plants and animals between Europe and the Americas.

commercial capitalism beginning in the Middle Ages, an economic system in which people invested in trade and goods in order to make profits.

common law law common to the entire kingdom of England; imposed by the king's courts beginning in the twelfth century to replace the customary law used in county and feudal courts that varied from place to place.

commune in medieval Europe, an association of townspeople bound together by a sworn oath for the purpose of obtaining basic liberties from the lord of the territory in which the town was located; also, the self-governing town after receiving its liberties.

conciliarism a movement in fourteenth- and fifteenth-century Europe that held that final authority in spiritual matters resided with a general church council, not the pope; it emerged in response to the Avignon papacy and the Great Schism and was used to justify the summoning of the Council of Constance (1414–1418).

condottieri leaders of bands of mercenary soldiers in Renaissance Italy who sold their services to the highest bidder.

confession one of the seven sacraments of the Catholic church; it provided for the forgiveness of one's sins.

conquistadors "conquerors." Leaders in the Spanish conquests in the Americas, especially Mexico and Peru, in the sixteenth century.

conscription a military draft.

conservatism an ideology based on tradition and social stability that favored the maintenance of established institutions, organized religion, and obedience to authority and resisted change, especially abrupt change.

consuls the chief executive officers of the Roman Republic. Two were chosen annually to administer the government and lead the army in battle.

consumer society Western society that emerged after World War II as the working classes adopted the consumption patterns of the middle class and payment plans, credit cards, and easy credit made consumer goods such as appliances and automobiles affordable.

containment a policy adopted by the United States in the Cold War. Its goal was to use whatever means, short of all-out war, to limit Soviet expansion.

Continental System Napoleon's effort to bar British goods from the Continent in the hope of weakening Britain's economy and destroying its capacity to wage war.

cosmopolitanism the quality of being sophisticated and having wide international experience.

cottage industry a system of textile manufacturing in which spinners and weavers worked at home in their cottages using raw materials supplied to them by capitalist entrepreneurs.

council of the plebs a council only for plebeians. After 287 B.C., however, its resolutions were binding on all Romans.

Crusade in the Middle Ages, a military campaign in defense of Christendom.

Cubism an artistic style developed at the beginning of the twentieth century, especially by Pablo Picasso, that used geometric designs to re-create reality in the viewer's mind.

cultural relativism the belief that no culture is superior to another because culture is a matter of custom, not reason, and derives its meaning from the group holding it.

cuneiform "wedge-shaped." A system of writing developed by the Sumerians that consisted of wedge-shaped impressions made by a reed stylus on clay tablets.

curiales city councilors in Roman cities who played an important role in governing the vast Roman Empire.

Dadaism an artistic movement in the 1920s and 1930s by artists who were revolted by the senseless slaughter of World War I and used their "anti-art" to express contempt for the Western tradition.

dechristianization a policy, adopted in the radical phase of the French Revolution, aimed at creating a secular society by eliminating Christian forms and institutions from French society.

decolonization the process of becoming free of colonial status and achieving statehood; it occurred in most of the world's colonies between 1947 and 1962.

deconstruction (poststructuralism) a system of thought, formulated by Jacques Derrida, that holds that culture is created in a variety of ways, according to the manner in which people create their own meaning. Hence there is no fixed truth or universal meaning.

deism belief in God as the creator of the universe who, after setting it in motion, ceased to have any direct involvement in it and allowed it to run according to its own natural laws.

demesne the part of a manor retained under the direct control of the lord and worked by the serfs as part of their labor services.

denazification after World War II, the Allied policy of rooting out any traces of Nazism in German society by bringing prominent Nazis to trial for war crimes and purging any known Nazis from political office.

depression a very severe, protracted economic downturn with high levels of unemployment.

destalinization the policy of denouncing and undoing the most repressive aspects of Stalin's regime; begun by Nikita Khrushchev in 1956.

détente the relaxation of tension between the Soviet Union and the United States that occurred in the 1970s.

dialectic logic, one of the seven liberal arts that made up the medieval curriculum. In Marxist thought, the process by which all change occurs through the clash of antagonistic elements.

Diaspora the scattering of Jews throughout the ancient world after the Babylonian captivity in the sixth century B.C.

dictator in the Roman Republic, an official granted unlimited power to run the state for a short period of time, usually six months, during an emergency.

diocese the area under the jurisdiction of a Christian bishop; based originally on Roman administrative districts.

direct representation a system of choosing delegates to a representative assembly in which citizens vote directly for the delegates who will represent them.

divination the practice of seeking to foretell future events by interpreting divine signs, which could appear in various forms, such as in entrails of animals, in patterns in smoke, or in dreams.

divine-right monarchy a monarchy based on the belief that monarchs receive their power directly from God and are responsible to no one except God.

domino theory the belief that if the Communists succeeded in Vietnam, other countries in Southeast and East Asia would also fall (like dominoes) to communism; cited as a justification for the U.S. intervention in Vietnam.

Donatism a Christian heresy that argued that the sacraments of the church were not valid if administered by an immoral priest.

dualism the belief that the universe is dominated by two opposing forces, one good and the other evil.

dynastic state a state in which the maintenance and expansion of the interests of the ruling family is the primary consideration.

economic imperialism the process in which banks and corporations from developed nations invest in underdeveloped regions and establish a major presence there in the hope of making high profits; not necessarily the same as colonial expansion in that businesses invest where they can make a profit, which may not be in their own nation's colonies.

economic liberalism the idea that government should not interfere in the workings of the economy.

Einsatzgruppen in Nazi Germany, special strike forces in the SS that played an important role in rounding up and killing Jews.

empiricism the practice of relying on observation and experiment.

enclosure movement in the eighteenth century, the fencing in of the old open fields, combining many small holdings into larger units that could be farmed more efficiently.

encomienda in Spanish America, a form of economic and social organization in which a Spaniard was given a royal grant that enabled the holder of the grant to collect tribute from the Indians and use them as laborers.

encyclical a letter from the pope to all the bishops of the Roman Catholic church.

enlightened absolutism an absolute monarchy in which the ruler follows the principles of the Enlightenment by introducing reforms for the improvement of society, allowing freedom of speech and the press, permitting religious toleration, expanding education, and ruling in accordance with the laws.

Enlightenment an eighteenth-century intellectual movement, led by the philosophes, that stressed the application of reason and the scientific method to all aspects of life.

entrepreneur one who organizes, operates, and assumes the risk in a business venture in the expectation of making a profit.

Epicureanism a philosophy founded by Epicurus in the fourth century B.C. that taught that happiness (freedom from emotional turmoil) could be achieved through the pursuit of pleasure (intellectual rather than sensual pleasure).

equestrians a group of extremely wealthy men in the late Roman Republic who were effectively barred from high office but sought political power commensurate with their wealth; called equestrians because many had gotten their start as cavalry officers (*equites*).

ethnic cleansing the policy of killing or forcibly removing people of another ethnic group; used by the Serbs against Bosnian Muslims in the 1990s.

Eucharist a Christian sacrament in which consecrated bread and wine are consumed in celebration of Jesus' Last Supper; also called the Lord's Supper or communion.

Eurocommunism a form of communism that dropped its Marxist ideology. It was especially favored in Italy.

evolutionary socialism a socialist doctrine espoused by Eduard Bernstein who argued that socialists should stress cooperation and evolution to attain power by democratic means rather than by conflict and revolution.

exchequer the permanent royal treasury of England. It emerged during the reign of King Henry II in the twelfth century.

excommunication in the Catholic church, a censure depriving a person of the right to receive the sacraments of the church.

existentialism a philosophical movement that arose after World War II that emphasized the meaninglessness of life, born of the desperation caused by two world wars.

family allowances one aspect of the welfare state whereby the state provides a minimum level of material assistance for children.

fascism an ideology or movement that exalts the nation above the individual and calls for a centralized government with a dictatorial leader, economic and social regimentation, and forcible suppression of opposition; in particular, the ideology of Mussolini's Fascist regime in Italy.

federates German troops enlisted in groups to fight as allies for the Romans.

feminism the belief in the social, political, and economic equality of the sexes; also, organized activity to advance women's rights.

fief a landed estate granted to a vassal in exchange for military services.

Final Solution the attempted physical extermination of the Jewish people by the Nazis during World War II.

folk culture the traditional arts and crafts, literature, music, and other customs of the people; something that people make, as opposed to modern popular culture, which is something people buy.

free trade the unrestricted international exchange of goods with low or no tariffs.

Führerprinzip in Nazi Germany, a leadership principle based on the belief in a single-minded party (the Nazis) under one leader (Hitler).

functionalism the idea that the function of an object should determine its design and materials.

general strike a strike by all or most workers in an economy; espoused by Georges Sorel as the heroic action that could be used to inspire the workers to destroy capitalist society.

genocide the deliberate extermination of a people.

gentry well-to-do English landowners below the level of the nobility. They played an important role in the English Civil War of the seventeenth century.

geocentric conception the belief that the earth was at the center of the universe and that the sun and other celestial objects revolved around the earth.

glasnost "openness." Mikhail Gorbachev's policy of encouraging Soviet citizens to openly discuss the strengths and weaknesses of the Soviet Union.

good emperors the five emperors who ruled from 96 to 180 (Nerva, Trajan, Hadrian, Antoninus Pius, and Marcus Aurelius), a period of peace and prosperity for the Roman Empire.

Gothic a term used to describe the art and especially architecture of Europe in the twelfth, thirteenth, and fourteenth centuries.

Gothic literature a form of literature used by Romantics to emphasize the bizarre and unusual, especially evident in horror stories.

Great Schism the crisis in the late medieval church when there were first two and then three popes; ended by the Council of Constance (1414–1418).

guest workers foreign workers working temporarily in European countries.

guild an association of people with common interests and concerns, especially people working in the same craft. In medieval Europe, guilds came to control much of the production process and to restrict entry into various trades.

gymnasium in classical Greece, a place for athletics; in the Hellenistic Age, a secondary school with a curriculum centered on music, physical exercise, and literature.

heliocentric conception the belief that the sun, not the earth, is at the center of the universe.

Hellenistic literally, "imitating the Greeks"; the era after the death of Alexander the Great when Greek culture spread into the Near East and blended with the culture of that region.

helots serfs in ancient Sparta who were permanently bound to the land that they worked for their Spartan masters.

heresy the holding of religious doctrines different from the official teachings of the church.

Hermeticism an intellectual movement beginning in the fifteenth century that taught that divinity is embodied in all aspects of nature; it included works on alchemy and magic as well as theology and philosophy. The tradition continued into the seventeenth century and influenced many of the leading figures of the Scientific Revolution.

hetairai highly sophisticated courtesans in ancient Athens who offered intellectual and musical entertainment as well as sex.

hieroglyphics a pictorial system of writing used in ancient Egypt.

high culture the literary and artistic culture of the educated and wealthy ruling classes.

Holocaust the mass slaughter of European Jews by the Nazis during World War II.

home rule in the United Kingdom, self-government by having a separate parliament but not complete independence.

hoplites heavily armed infantry soldiers in ancient Greece who entered battle in a phalanx formation.

Huguenots French Calvinists.

humanism an intellectual movement in Renaissance Italy based on the study of the Greek and Roman classics.

iconoclast member of an eighth-century Byzantine movement against the use of icons (pictures of sacred figures), which it condemned as idolatry.

ideology a political philosophy such as conservatism or liberalism.

imperium In the Roman Republic, the right to command troops that belonged to the chief executive officers (consuls and praetors); a military commander was known as an *imperator*. In the Roman Empire, the title *imperator* (emperor) came to be used for the ruler.

Impressionism an artistic movement that originated in France in the 1870s. Impressionists sought to capture their impressions of the changing effects of light on objects in nature.

indirect representation a system of choosing delegates to a representative assembly in which citizens do not choose the delegates directly but instead vote for electors who choose the delegates.

individualism emphasis on and interest in the unique traits of each person.

indulgence in Christian theology, the remission of part or all of the temporal punishment in purgatory due to sin; granted for charitable contributions and other good deeds. Indulgences became a regular practice of the Christian church in the High Middle Ages, and their abuse was instrumental in sparking Luther's reform movement in the sixteenth century.

infanticide the practice of killing infants.

inflation a sustained rise in the price level.

intendants royal officials in seventeenth-century France who were sent into the provinces to execute the orders of the central government.

interdict in the Catholic church, a censure by which a region or country is deprived of receiving the sacraments.

intervention, principle of the idea, after the Congress of Vienna, that the great powers of Europe had the right to send armies into countries experiencing revolution to restore legitimate monarchs to their thrones.

isolationism a foreign policy in which a nation refrains from making alliances or engaging actively in international affairs.

Janissaries an elite core of eight thousand troops personally loyal to the sultan of the Ottoman Empire.

jihad "striving in the way of the Lord." In Islam, the attempt to achieve personal betterment, although it can also mean fair, defensive fighting to preserve one's life and one's faith.

joint-stock company a company or association that raises capital by selling shares to individuals who receive dividends on their investment while a board of directors runs the company.

joint-stock investment bank a bank created by selling shares of stock to investors. Such banks potentially have access to much more capital than private banks owned by one or a few individuals.

justification the primary doctrine of the Protestant Reformation, teaching that humans are saved not through good works but by the grace of God, bestowed freely through the sacrifice of Jesus.

Kulturkampf "culture conflict." The name given to Bismarck's attack on the Catholic church in Germany, which has come to refer to conflict between church and state anywhere.

laissez-faire "let (them) do (as they please)." An economic doctrine that holds that an economy is best served when the government does not interfere but allows the economy to self-regulate according to the forces of supply and demand.

latifundia large landed estates in the Roman Empire (singular: *latifundium*).

lay investiture the practice in which someone other than a member of the clergy chose a bishop and invested him with the symbols of both his temporal office and his spiritual office; led to the Investiture Controversy, which was ended by compromise in the Concordat of Worms in 1122.

Lebensraum "living space." The doctrine, adopted by Hitler, that a nation's power depends on the amount of land it occupies; thus a nation must expand to be strong.

legitimacy, principle of the idea that after the Napoleonic wars, peace could best be reestablished in Europe by restoring legitimate monarchs who would preserve traditional institutions; guided Metternich at the Congress of Vienna.

Leninism Lenin's revision of Marxism that held that Russia need not experience a bourgeois revolution before it could move toward socialism.

liberal arts the seven areas of study that formed the basis of education in medieval and early modern Europe. Following Boethius and other late Roman authors, they consisted of grammar, rhetoric, and dialectic or logic (the *trivium*) and arithmetic, geometry, astronomy, and music (the *quadrivium*).

liberalism an ideology based on the belief that people should be as free from restraint as possible. Economic liberalism is the idea that the government should not interfere in the workings of the economy. Political liberalism is the idea that there should be restraints on the exercise of power so that people can enjoy basic civil rights in a constitutional state with a representative assembly.

limited liability the principle that shareholders in a joint-stock corporation can be held responsible for the corporation's debts only up to the amount they have invested.

limited monarchy (constitutional monarchy) a system of government in which the monarch is limited by a representative assembly and by the duty to rule in accordance with the laws of the land.

major domus the chief officer of the king's household in the Frankish kingdom.

mandates a system established after World War I whereby a nation officially administered a territory (mandate) on behalf of the League of Nations. Thus France administered Lebanon and Syria as mandates, and Britain administered Iraq and Palestine.

Mannerism a sixteenth-century artistic movement in Europe that deliberately broke down the High Renaissance principles of balance, harmony, and moderation.

manor an agricultural estate operated by a lord and worked by peasants who performed labor services and paid various rents and fees to the lord in exchange for protection and sustenance.

Marshall Plan the European Recovery Program, under which the United States provided financial aid to European countries to help them rebuild after World War II.

Marxism the political, economic, and social theories of Karl Marx, which included the idea that history is the story of class struggle and that ultimately the proletariat will overthrow the bourgeoisie and establish a dictatorship en route to a classless society.

mass education a state-run educational system, usually free and compulsory, that aims to ensure that all children in society have at least a basic education.

mass leisure forms of leisure that appeal to large numbers of people in a society, including the working classes; emerged at the end of the nineteenth century to provide workers with amusements after work and on weekends; used during the twentieth century by totalitarian states to control their populations.

mass politics a political order characterized by mass political parties and universal male and (eventually) female suffrage.

mass society a society in which the concerns of the majority—the lower classes—play a prominent role; characterized by extension of voting rights, an improved standard of living for the lower classes, and mass education.

materialism   the belief that everything mental, spiritual, or ideal is an outgrowth of physical forces and that truth is found in concrete material existence, not through feeling or intuition.

mercantilism   an economic theory that held that a nation's prosperity depended on its supply of gold and silver and that the total volume of trade is unchangeable; its adherents therefore advocated that the government play an active role in the economy by encouraging exports and discouraging imports, especially through the use of tariffs.

Mesolithic Age   the period from 10,000 to 7000 B.C., characterized by a gradual transition from a food-gathering and hunting economy to a food-producing economy.

metics   resident foreigners in ancient Athens who were not permitted full rights of citizenship but did receive the protection of the laws.

Middle Passage   the journey of slaves from Africa to the Americas as the middle leg of the triangular trade.

militarism   a policy of aggressive military preparedness; in particular, the large armies based on mass conscription and complex, inflexible plans for mobilization that most European nations had before World War I.

millenarianism   the belief that the end of the world is at hand and the kingdom of God is about to be established on earth.

ministerial responsibility   a tenet of nineteenth-century liberalism that held that ministers of the monarch should be responsible to the legislative assembly rather than to the monarch.

mir   a peasant village commune in Russia.

mobilization   the organization of troops and supplies for service in time of war.

Modern Devotion   a movement founded by Gerard Groote in the fourteenth century, aimed at a practical mysticism based on leading lives serving the needs of fellow human beings.

Modernism   the artistic and literary styles that emerged in the decades before 1914 as artists rebelled against traditional efforts to portray reality as accurately as possible (leading to Impressionism and Cubism) and writers explored new forms.

monasticism   a movement that began in early Christianity whose purpose was to create communities of men and women who practiced a communal life dedicated to God as a moral example to the world around them.

monk   a man who chooses to live a communal life divorced from the world in order to dedicate himself totally to the will of God.

monogamy   the practice of being married to one person at a time.

monotheism   the doctrine or belief that there is only one God.

mutual deterrence   the belief that nuclear war could best be prevented if both the United States and the Soviet Union had sufficient nuclear weapons so that even if one nation launched a preemptive first strike, the other could respond and devastate the attacker.

mystery religions   religions that involve initiation into secret rites that promise intense emotional involvement with spiritual forces and a greater chance of individual immortality.

mysticism   the immediate experience of oneness with God.

nationalism   a sense of national consciousness based on awareness of being part of a community—a "nation"—that has common institutions, traditions, language, and customs and that becomes the focus of the individual's primary political loyalty.

nationalities problem   the dilemma faced by the Austro-Hungarian Empire in trying to unite a wide variety of ethnic groups (Austrians, Hungarians, Poles, Croats, Czechs, Serbs, Slovaks, and Slovenes, among others) in an era when nationalism and calls for self-determination were coming to the fore.

nationalization   the process of converting a business or industry from private ownership to government control and ownership.

nation in arms   the people's army raised by universal mobilization to repel the foreign enemies of the French Revolution.

nation-state   a form of political organization in which a relatively homogeneous people inhabits a sovereign state, as opposed to a state containing people of several nationalities.

NATO   the North Atlantic Treaty Organization, a military alliance formed in 1949 in which the signatories (Belgium, Canada, Denmark, France, Great Britain, Iceland, Italy, Luxembourg, the Netherlands, Norway, Portugal, and the United States) agreed to provide mutual assistance if any one of them was attacked; later expanded to include other nations.

natural laws   a body of laws or specific principles held to be derived from nature and binding on all human societies even in the absence of written laws governing such matters.

natural rights   certain inalienable rights to which all people are entitled, including the right to life, liberty, and property; freedom of speech and religion; and equality before the law.

natural selection   Darwin's idea that organisms that are most adaptable to their environment survive and pass on the variations that enabled them to survive, while less adaptable organisms become extinct; "survival of the fittest."

Nazi New Order   the Nazis' plan for their conquered territories; it included the extermination of Jews and others considered inferior, ruthless exploitation of resources, German colonization in the east, and the use of Poles, Russians, and Ukrainians as slave labor.

Neoclassicism   a late-eighteenth-century artistic movement that emerged in France. It sought to recapture the dignity and simplicity of the classical style of ancient Greece and Rome.

Neoplatonism   a revival of Platonic philosophy in the third century A.D., associated with Plotinus; a similar revival in the Italian Renaissance, associated with Marsilio Ficino, who attempted to synthesize Christianity and Platonism.

nepotism   the appointment of family members to important political positions; derived from the regular appointment of nephews (Greek, *nepos*) by Renaissance popes.

New Economic Policy   a modified version of the old capitalist system introduced in the Soviet Union by Lenin in 1921 to revive the economy after the ravages of the civil war and war communism.

new imperialism   the revival of imperialism after 1880 in which European nations established colonies throughout much of Asia and Africa.

new monarchies   the governments of France, England, and Spain at the end of the fifteenth century, whose rulers succeeded in reestablishing or extending centralized royal authority, suppressing the nobility, controlling the church, and insisting on the loyalty of all peoples living in their territories.

nobiles   "nobles." The small group of families from both patrician and plebeian origins who produced most of the men who were elected to office in the late Roman Republic.

nominalist   member of a school of thought in medieval Europe that, following Aristotle, held that only individual objects are real and that universals are only names created by humans.

nuclear family   a family group consisting only of a father, a mother, and one or more children.

nuns   female religious monks.

old regime (old order)   the political and social system of France in the eighteenth century before the Revolution.

oligarchy   rule by a few.

optimates   "best men." Aristocratic leaders in the late Roman Republic who generally came from senatorial families and wished to retain their oligarchical privileges.

orders (estates)   the traditional tripartite division of European society based on heredity and quality rather than wealth or economic standing, first established in the Middle Ages and continuing into the eighteenth century; traditionally consisted of those who pray (the clergy), those who fight (the nobility), and those who work (all the rest).

organic evolution   Darwin's principle that all plants and animals have evolved over a long period of time from earlier and simpler forms of life.

Paleolithic Age   the period of human history when humans used simple stone tools (c. 2,500,000–10,000 B.C.).

pantheism   a doctrine that equates God with the universe and all that is in it.

panzer division in the German army under Hitler, a strike force of about three hundred tanks and accompanying forces and supplies.

papal curia the administrative staff of the Catholic church, composed of cardinals who assist the pope in running the church.

pasteurization a process developed by Louis Pasteur for heating a product to destroy the microorganisms that might cause spoilage.

paterfamilias the dominant male in a Roman family whose powers over his wife and children were theoretically unlimited, though they were sometimes circumvented in practice.

patriarchal family a family in which the husband dominates his wife and children.

patriarchy a society in which the father is supreme in the clan or family; more generally, a society dominated by men.

patricians great landowners who became the ruling class in the Roman Republic.

patronage the practice of awarding titles and making appointments to government and other positions to gain political support.

Pax Romana "Roman peace." A term used to refer to the stability and prosperity that Roman rule brought to the Mediterranean world and much of western Europe during the first and second centuries A.D.

Pentateuch the first five books of the Hebrew Bible (Genesis, Exodus, Leviticus, Numbers, and Deuteronomy).

perestroika "restructuring." A term applied to Mikhail Gorbachev's economic, political, and social reforms in the Soviet Union.

perioikoi in ancient Sparta, free inhabitants but not citizens who were required to pay taxes and perform military service.

permissive society a term applied to Western society after World War II to reflect the new sexual freedom and the emergence of a drug culture.

Petrine supremacy the doctrine that the bishop of Rome (the pope), as the successor of Saint Peter (traditionally considered the first bishop of Rome), should hold a preeminent position in the church.

phalanstery a self-sustaining cooperative community, as advocated by Charles Fourier in the early nineteenth century.

phalanx a rectangular formation of tightly massed infantry soldiers.

philosophes intellectuals of the eighteenth-century Enlightenment who believed in applying a spirit of rational criticism to all things, including religion and politics, and who focused on improving and enjoying this world, rather than on the afterlife.

Pietism a movement that arose in Germany in the seventeenth century whose goal was to foster a personal experience of God as the focus of true religious experience.

plebeians the class of Roman citizens that included nonpatrician landowners, craftspeople, merchants, and small farmers in the Roman Republic. Their struggle for equal rights with the patricians dominated much of the Republic's history.

plebiscita laws passed by the council of the plebs.

pluralism the practice of holding several church offices simultaneously; a problem of the late medieval church.

plutocrats members of the wealthy elite.

pogroms organized massacres of Jews.

polis an ancient Greek city-state encompassing both an urban area and its surrounding countryside; a small but autonomous political unit where all major political and social activities were carried out centrally.

political democracy a form of government characterized by universal suffrage and mass political parties.

politiques a group who emerged during the French Wars of Religion in the sixteenth century, placed politics above religion, and believed that no religious truth was worth the ravages of civil war.

polytheism belief in or worship of more than one god.

Pop Art an artistic movement of the 1950s and 1960s in which artists took images of popular culture and transformed them into works of fine art. Andy Warhol's painting of Campbell's soup cans is one example.

popular culture as opposed to high culture, the unofficial written and unwritten culture of the masses, much of which was tradition-

ally passed down orally and centered on public and group activities such as festivals. In the modern age, the term refers to the entertainment, recreation, and pleasures that people purchase as part of the mass consumer society.

populares "favoring the people." Aristocratic leaders in the late Roman Republic who tended to use the people's assemblies in an effort to break the stranglehold of the *nobiles* on political offices.

popular sovereignty the doctrine that government is created by and subject to the will of the people, who are the source of all political power.

populism a political philosophy or movement that supports the rights and power of ordinary people in their struggle against the privileged elite.

portolani charts of landmasses and coastlines made by navigators and mathematicians in the thirteenth and fourteenth centuries.

Post-Impressionism an artistic movement that began in France in the 1880s. Post-Impressionists sought to use color and line to express inner feelings and produce a personal statement of reality.

Postmodernism a term used to cover a variety of artistic and intellectual styles and ways of thinking prominent since the 1970s.

praetor a Roman executive official responsible for the administration of the law.

praetorian guard the military unit that served as the personal bodyguard of the Roman emperors.

predestination the belief, associated with Calvinism, that God, as a consequence of his foreknowledge of all events, has predetermined those who will be saved (the elect) and those who will be damned.

prefect during the reign of Napoleon, an official appointed by the central government to oversee all aspects of a local government.

price revolution the dramatic rise in prices (inflation) that occurred throughout Europe in the sixteenth and early seventeenth centuries.

primogeniture an inheritance practice in which the eldest son receives all or the largest share of the parents' estate.

principate the form of government established by Augustus for the Roman Empire; it continued the constitutional forms of the Republic and consisted of the *princeps* ("first citizen") and the senate, although the *princeps* was clearly the dominant partner.

procurator the head of the Holy Synod, the chief decision-making body for the Russian Orthodox church.

proletariat the industrial working class. In Marxism, the class that will ultimately overthrow the bourgeoisie.

propaganda a program of distorted information put out by an organization or government to spread its policy, cause, or doctrine.

psychoanalysis a method developed by Sigmund Freud to resolve a patient's psychic conflict.

purgatory defined by the Catholic church as the place where souls went after death to be purged of punishment for sins committed in life.

Puritans English Protestants inspired by Calvinist theology who wished to remove all traces of Catholicism from the Church of England.

quadrivium arithmetic, geometry, astronomy, and music; four of the seven liberal arts (the others made up the *trivium*) that formed the basis of medieval and early modern education.

quaestors Roman officials responsible for the administration of financial affairs.

querelles des femmes "arguments about women." A centuries-old debate about the nature of women that continued during the Scientific Revolution as those who argued for the inferiority of women found additional support in the new anatomy and medicine.

rapprochement the rebuilding of harmonious relations between nations.

rationalism a system of thought based on the belief that human reason and experience are the chief sources of knowledge.

Realism a nineteenth-century school of painting that emphasized the everyday life of ordinary people, depicted with photographic accuracy.

realist a subscriber to the medieval European school of thought that held, following Plato, that the individual objects we perceive are not real but merely manifestations of universal ideas existing in the mind of God.

Realpolitik "politics of reality." Politics based on practical concerns rather than theory or ethics.

real wages, income, and prices wages, income, and prices that have been adjusted for inflation.

reason of state the principle that a nation should act on the basis of its long-term interests and not merely to further the dynastic interests of its ruling family.

Reconquista in Spain, the reconquest of Muslim lands by Christian rulers and their armies.

relativity theory Einstein's theory that, among other things, (1) space and time are not absolute but are relative to the observer and interwoven into a four-dimensional space-time continuum and (2) matter is a form of energy ($E = mc^2$).

relics the bones of Christian saints or objects intimately associated with saints that were considered worthy of veneration.

Renaissance the "rebirth" of classical culture that occurred in Italy between c. 1350 and c. 1550; also, the earlier revivals of classical culture that occurred under Charlemagne and in the twelfth century.

rentier a person who lives on income from property and is not personally involved in its operation.

reparations payments made by a defeated nation after a war to compensate another nation for damage sustained as a result of the war; required from Germany after World War I.

revisionism a socialist doctrine that rejected Marx's emphasis on class struggle and revolution and argued instead that workers should work through political parties to bring about gradual change.

revolution a fundamental change in the political and social organization of a state.

revolutionary socialism a socialist doctrine that violent action was the only way to achieve the goals of socialism.

rhetoric the art of persuasive speaking; in the Middle Ages, one of the seven liberal arts.

risorgimento a movement in Italy in the nineteenth century aimed at the creation of a united Italian republic.

Rococo an eighteenth-century artistic movement that emphasized grace, gentility, lightness, and charm.

Romanesque a term used to describe the art and especially architecture of Europe in the eleventh and twelfth centuries.

Romanticism a nineteenth-century intellectual and artistic movement that rejected the emphasis on reason of the Enlightenment. Instead, Romantics stressed the importance of intuition, feeling, emotion, and imagination as sources of knowing.

sacraments rites considered imperative for a Christian's salvation. By the thirteenth century, these consisted of the Eucharist or Lord's Supper, baptism, marriage, penance, extreme unction, holy orders, and confirmation of children; Protestant reformers of the sixteenth century generally recognized only two—baptism and communion (the Lord's Supper).

salons gatherings of philosophes and other notables to discuss the ideas of the Enlightenment; so called from the elegant drawing rooms (salons) where they met.

sans-culottes "without breeches." The common people, who did not wear the fine clothes of the upper classes and played an important role in the radical phase of the French Revolution.

satrap a governor with both civil and military duties in the ancient Persian Empire, which was divided into satrapies, or provinces, each administered by a satrap.

scholasticism the philosophical and theological system of the medieval schools, which emphasized rigorous analysis of contradictory authorities; often used to try to reconcile faith and reason.

scientific method a method of seeking knowledge through inductive principles, using experiments and observations to develop generalizations.

Scientific Revolution the transition from the medieval worldview to a largely secular, rational, and materialistic perspective that began in the seventeenth century and was popularized in the eighteenth.

scriptoria writing rooms for the copying of manuscripts in medieval monasteries.

scutage in the fourteenth century, a money payment for military service that replaced the obligation of military service in the lord-vassal relationship.

secularization the process of becoming more concerned with material, worldly, temporal things and less with spiritual and religious things.

self-determination the doctrine that the people of a given territory or a particular nationality should have the right to determine their own government and political future.

senate the leading council of the Roman Republic; composed of about three hundred men (senators) who served for life and dominated much of the political life of the Republic.

separation of powers a doctrine enunciated by Montesquieu in the eighteenth century that separate executive, legislative, and judicial powers serve to limit and control each other.

serf a peasant who is bound to the land and obliged to provide labor services and pay various rents and fees to the lord; considered unfree but not a slave because serfs could not be bought and sold.

skepticism a doubtful or questioning attitude, especially about religion.

social Darwinism the application of Darwin's principle of organic evolution to the social order; led to the belief that progress comes from the struggle for survival as the fittest advance and the weak decline.

socialism an ideology that calls for collective or government ownership of the means of production and the distribution of goods.

socialized medicine health services for all citizens provided by government assistance.

social security government programs that provide social welfare measures such as old-age pensions and sickness, accident, and disability insurance.

Socratic method a form of teaching that uses a question-and-answer format to enable students to reach conclusions by using their own reasoning.

Sophists wandering scholars and professional teachers in ancient Greece who stressed the importance of rhetoric and tended toward skepticism and relativism.

soviets councils of workers' and soldiers' deputies formed throughout Russia in 1917 that played an important role in the Bolshevik Revolution.

sphere of influence a territory or region over which an outside nation exercises political or economic influence.

squadristi in Italy in the 1920s, bands of armed Fascists used to create disorder by attacking Socialist offices and newspapers.

stagflation a combination of high inflation and high unemployment that was prevalent in the United States and elsewhere from 1973 to the mid-1980s.

Stalinization the adoption by Eastern European Communist countries of features of the economic, political, and military policies implemented by Stalin in the Soviet Union.

Stoicism a philosophy founded by Zeno in the fourth century B.C. that taught that happiness could be obtained by accepting one's lot and living in harmony with the will of God, thereby achieving inner peace.

subinfeudation the practice whereby a lord's greatest vassals subdivided their fiefs and had vassals of their own, who in turn subdivided their fiefs, and so on down to simple knights, whose fiefs were too small to subdivide.

suffrage the right to vote.

suffragists advocates of extending the right to vote to women.

sultan "holder of power." A title taken by Turkish leaders who took command of the Abbasid Empire in 1055.

surplus value in Marxism, the difference between a product's real value and the wages of the worker who produced the product.

Surrealism an artistic movement that arose between World War I and World War II. Surrealists portrayed recognizable objects in unrecognizable relationships in order to reveal the world of the unconscious.

syncretism the combining of different forms of belief or practice, as, for example, when two gods are regarded as different forms of the same underlying divine force and are fused together.

tariffs duties (taxes) imposed on imported goods, usually to raise revenue and to discourage imports and protect domestic industries.

tetrarchy rule by four; the system of government established by Diocletian (284–305) in which the Roman Empire was divided into two parts, each ruled by an "Augustus" assisted by a "Caesar."

theocracy a government ruled by a divine authority.

Third Estate one of the traditional tripartite divisions (orders) of European society based on heredity and quality rather than wealth or economic standing, first established in the Middle Ages and continuing into the eighteenth century; consisted of all who were not members of the clergy or nobility (the first two estates).

three-field system in medieval agriculture, the practice of dividing the arable land into three fields so that one could lie fallow while the others were planted in winter grains and spring crops.

tithe a portion of one's harvest or income, paid by medieval peasants to the village church.

Torah the body of law in Hebrew Scripture, contained in the Pentateuch (the first five books of the Hebrew Bible).

totalitarian state a state characterized by government control over all aspects of economic, social, political, cultural, and intellectual life, the subordination of the individual to the state, and insistence that the masses be actively involved in the regime's goals.

total war warfare in which all of a nation's resources, including civilians at home as well as soldiers in the field, are mobilized for the war effort.

trade union an association of workers in the same trade, formed to help members secure better wages, benefits, and working conditions.

transformism the theory that societies evolve gradually.

transubstantiation a doctrine of the Roman Catholic church that during the Eucharist, the substance of the bread and wine is miraculously transformed into the body and blood of Jesus.

trench warfare warfare in which the opposing forces attack and counterattack from a relatively permanent system of trenches protected by barbed wire; characteristic of World War I.

triangular trade a pattern of trade in early modern Europe that connected Europe, Africa, and the Americas in an Atlantic economy.

tribunes of the plebs beginning in 494 B.C., Roman officials who were given the power to protect plebeians against arrest by patrician magistrates.

trivium grammar, rhetoric, and dialectic or logic; three of the seven liberal arts (the others made up the *quadrivium*) that were the basis of medieval and early modern education.

Truman Doctrine the doctrine, enunciated by Harry Truman in 1947, that the United States would provide economic aid to countries that said they were threatened by Communist expansion.

tyrant in an ancient Greek *polis* (or an Italian city-state during the Renaissance), a ruler who came to power in an unconstitutional way and ruled without being subject to the law.

ultraroyalists in nineteenth-century France, a group of aristocrats who sought to return to a monarchical system dominated by a landed aristocracy and the Catholic church.

uncertainty principle a principle in quantum mechanics, posited by Heisenberg, that holds that one cannot determine the path of an electron because the very act of observing the electron would affect its location.

unconditional surrender complete, unqualified surrender of a belligerent nation.

utopian socialists intellectuals and theorists in the early nineteenth century who favored equality in social and economic conditions and wished to replace private property and competition with collective ownership and cooperation.

vassalage the granting of a fief, or landed estate, in exchange for providing military services to the lord and fulfilling certain other obligations such as appearing at the lord's court when summoned and making a payment on the knighting of the lord's eldest son.

vernacular the everyday language of a region, as distinguished from a language used for special purposes. For example, in medieval Paris, French was the vernacular, but Latin was used for academic writing and for classes at the University of Paris.

viceroy the administrative head of the provinces of New Spain and Peru in the Americas.

volkish **thought** the belief that German culture is superior and that the German people have a universal mission to save Western civilization from "inferior" races.

war communism Lenin's policy of nationalizing industrial and other facilities and requisitioning the peasants' produce during the civil war in Russia.

war guilt clause the clause in the Treaty of Versailles that declared that Germany (with Austria) was responsible for starting World War I and ordered Germany to pay reparations for the damage the Allies had suffered as a result of the war.

Warsaw Pact a military alliance, formed in 1955, in which Albania, Bulgaria, Czechoslovakia, East Germany, Hungary, Poland, Romania, and the Soviet Union agreed to provide mutual assistance.

welfare state a sociopolitical system in which the government assumes primary responsibility for the social welfare of its citizens by providing such things as social security, unemployment benefits, and health care.

wergeld "money for a man." In early Germanic law, a person's value in monetary terms, paid by a wrongdoer to the family of the person who had been injured or killed.

world-machine Newton's conception of the universe as one huge, regulated, and uniform machine that operated according to natural laws in absolute time, space, and motion.

zemstvos local assemblies established in Russia in 1864 by Tsar Alexander II.

ziggurat a massive stepped tower on which a temple dedicated to the chief god or goddess of a Sumerian city was built.

Zionism an international movement that called for the establishment of a Jewish state or a refuge for Jews in Palestine.

Zollverein the customs union of all the German states except Austria, formed by Prussia in 1834.

Zoroastrianism a religion founded by the Persian Zoroaster in the seventh century B.C., characterized by worship of a supreme god, Ahuramazda, who represents the good against the evil spirit, identified as Ahriman.

PRONUNCIATION GUIDE

Abbasid   uh-BAH-sid *or* AB-uh-sid
Abd al-Rahman   ub-duh-rahkh-MAHN
Abu al-Abbas   uh-BOOL-uh-BUSS
Abu Bakr   ah-bu-BAHK-ur
Adenauer, Konrad   AD-uh-now-ur
aediles   EE-dylz
Aeolians   ee-OH-lee-unz
Aeschylus   ESS-kuh-luss
Aetius   ay-EE-shuss
Afrikaners   ah-fri-KAH-nurz
Agesilaus   uh-jess-uh-LAY-uss
Agincourt   AH-zhen-koor
Ahlwardt, Hermann   AHL-vart
Ahuramazda   uh-HOOR-uh-MAHZ-duh
Aix-la-Chapelle   ex-lah-shah-PELL
Akhenaten   ah-kuh-NAH-tun
Akkadians   uh-KAY-dee-unz
Alaric   AL-uh-rik
Alberti, Leon Battista   al-BAYR-tee
Albigensians   al-buh-JEN-see-unz
Albuquerque, Afonso de   AL-buh-kur-kee, ah-FAHN-soh day
Alcibiades   al-suh-BY-uh-deez
Alcuin   AL-kwin
Alemanni   al-uh-MAH-nee
al-Fatah   al-FAH-tuh
al-Hakim   al-hah-KEEM
Alia, Ramiz   AH-lee-uh, rah-MEEZ
al-Khwarizmi   al-KHWAR-iz-mee
Allah   AH-lah
al-Ma'mun   al-muh-MOON
Amenhotep   ah-mun-HOH-tep
Andreotti, Giulio   ahn-dray-AH-tee, JOOL-yoh
Andropov, Yuri   ahn-DRAHP-awf, YOOR-ee
Anjou   AHN-zhoo
Antigonid   an-TIG-uh-nid
Antigonus Gonatus   an-TIG-oh-nuss guh-NAH-tuss
Antiochus   an-TY-uh-kuss
Antonescu, Ion   an-tuh-NESS-koo, YON
Antoninus Pius   an-tuh-NY-nuss PY-uss
Anwar al-Sadat   ahn-wahr-el-suh-DAHT
apella   uh-PELL-uh
Apollonius   ap-uh-LOH-nee-uss
appartement   uh-par-tuh-MUNH
Aquinas, Thomas   uh-KWY-nuss
Arafat, Yasir   ah-ruh-FAHT, yah-SEER
aratrum   uh-RAH-trum
Archimedes   ahr-kuh-MEE-deez
Argonautica   ahr-guh-NAWT-uh-kuh
Aristarchus   ar-iss-TAR-kus
Aristotle   AR-iss-tot-ul
Arsinoë   ahr-SIN-oh-ee
artium baccalarius   ar-TEE-um bak-uh-LAR-ee-uss
artium magister   ar-TEE-um muh-GISS-ter
Aryan   AR-ee-un
Ashkenazic   ash-kuh-NAH-zik

Ashurbanipal   ah-shur-BAH-nuh-pahl
Ashurnasirpal   ah-shur-NAH-zur-pahl
asiento   ah-SYEN-toh
Asoka   uh-SOH-kuh
assignat   ah-see-NYAH
Assyrians   uh-SEER-ee-unz
Astell, Mary   AST-ul
Atahualpa   ah-tuh-WAHL-puh
Attalid   AT-uh-lid
audiencias   ow-dee-en-SEE-uss
Auerstadt   OW-urr-shtaht
augur   AW-gurr
Augustine   AW-guh-steen
Aurelian   aw-REEL-yun
Auschwitz-Birkenau   OWSH-vitz-BEER-kuh-now
Ausgleich   OWSS-glykh
auspices   AWSS-puh-sizz
Austerlitz   AWSS-tur-litz
Australopithecines   aw-stray-loh-PITH-uh-synz
Austrasia   au-STRY-zhuh
Autun   oh-TUNH
Avicenna   av-i-SENN-uh
Avignon   ah-veen-YONH
Azerbaijan   az-ur-by-JAN
Baader-Meinhof   BAH-durr-MYN-huff
Babeuf, Gracchus   bah-BUFF, GRAK-uss
Bach, Johann Sebastian   BAKH, yoh-HAHN suh-BASS-chun
Baden-Powell, Robert   BAD-un-POW-ul
Bakunin, Michael   buh-KOON-yun
Balboa, Vasco Nuñez de   bal-BOH-uh, BAHS-koh NOON-yez day
Ballin, Albert   BAH-leen
Banque de Belgique   BAHNK duh bel-ZHEEK
Barbarossa   bar-buh-ROH-suh
Baroque   buh-ROHK
Barth, Karl   BAHRT
Bastille   bass-STEEL
Batista, Fulgencio   bah-TEES-tuh, full-JEN-see-oh
Bauhaus   BOW-howss
Bayle, Pierre   BELL, PYAYR
Beauharnais, Josephine de   boh-ar-NAY, zhoh-seff-FEEN duh
Beauvoir, Simone de   boh-VWAR, see-MUHN duh
Bebel, August   BAY-bul, ow-GOOST
Beccaria, Cesare   buh-KAH-ree-uh, CHAY-zuh-ray
Bede   BEED
Beguines   bay-GEENZ
Beiderbecke, Bix   BY-der-bek, BIKS
Beijing   bay-ZHING
Belarus   bell-uh-ROOSS
Belgioioso, Cristina   bell-joh-YOH-soh
Belisarius   bell-uh-SAH-ree-uss
benefice   BEN-uh-fiss
Bergson, Henri   BERG-son, AHN-ree
Berlioz, Hector   BAYR-lee-ohz
Berlusconi, Silvio   bayr-loo-SKOH-nee, SEEL-vee-oh
Bernhardi, Friedrich von   bayrn-HAR-dee, FREED-reekh fun

Bernini, Gian Lorenzo   bur-NEE-nee, ZHAHN loh-RENT-zoh
Bernstein, Eduard   BAYRN-shtyn, AY-doo-art
Bethman-Hollweg, Theobald von   BET-mun-HOHL-vek, TAY-oh-bahlt fun
Blanc, Louis   BLAHNH, LWEE
Blitzkrieg   BLITZ-kreeg
Blum, Léon   BLOOM, LAY-ohnh
Boccaccio, Giovanni   boh-KAH-choh, joe-VAH-nee
Bodichon, Barbara   boh-di-SHOHNH
Boer   BOOR *or* BOR
Boethius   boh-EE-thee-uss
Boleyn, Anne   BUH-lin *or* buh-LIN
Bolívar, Simón   buh-LEE-var, see-MOHN
Bologna   buh-LOHN-yuh
Bolsheviks   BOHL-shuh-viks
Bora, Katherina von   BOH-rah, kat-uh-REE-nuh fun
Bosnia   BAHZ-nee-uh
Bossuet, Jacques   baw-SWAY, ZHAHK
Botta, Giuseppe   BOH-tah, joo-ZEP-pay
Botticelli, Sandro   bot-i-CHELL-ee, SAHN-droh
Boulanger, Georges   boo-lahnh-ZHAY, ZHORZH
boule   BOOL
Bracciolini, Poggio   braht-choh-LEE-nee, POH-djoh
Brahe, Tycho   BRAH, TY-koh
Bramante, Donato   brah-MAHN-tay, doh-NAH-toh
Brandt, Willy   BRAHNT, VIL-ee
Brasidas   BRASS-i-duss
Brest-Litovsk   BREST-li-TUFFSK
Brétigny   bray-tee-NYEE
Brezhnev, Leonid   BREZH-neff, lee-oh-NYEET
Briand, Aristide   bree-AHNH, ah-ruh-STEED
Broz, Josip   BRAWZ, yaw-SEEP
Brumaire   broo-MAYR
Brunelleschi, Filippo   BROO-nuh-LESS-kee, fee-LEE-poh
Brüning, Heinrich   BROO-ning, HYN-rikh
Bückeberg   BOOK-uh-bayrk
Bulganin, Nicolai   bool-GAN-yin, nyik-uh-LY
Bund Deutscher Mädel   BOONT DOIT-chuh MAY-dul
Bundesrat   BOON-duhs-raht
Burckhardt, Jacob   BOORK-hart, YAK-ub
Burschenschaften   BOOR-shun-shahf-tuhn
bushido   BOO-shee-doh
Cabral, Pedro   kuh-BRAL
cahiers de doléances   ka-YAY duh doh-lay-AHNSS
Calais   ka-LAY
Calas, Jean   ka-LAH, ZHAHNH
Caligula   kuh-LIG-yuh-luh
caliph   KAY-liff
caliphate   KAY-luh-fayt
Callicrates   kuh-LIK-ruh-teez
Calonne, Charles de   ka-LUNN, SHAHRL duh
Cambyses   kam-BY-seez
Camus, Albert   ka-MOO, ahl-BAYR
Canaanites   KAY-nuh-nytss
Capet, Hugh   ka-PAY, YOO
Capetian   kuh-PEE-shun
Caracalla   kuh-RAK-uh-luh
Caraffa, Gian Pietro   kuh-RAH-fuh, JAHN PYAY-troh
carbonari   kar-buh-NAH-ree
Carolingian   kar-uh-LIN-jun
carruca   kuh-ROO-kuh
Carthage   KAR-thij
Carthaginian   kar-thuh-JIN-ee-un
Cartier, Jacques   kar-TYAY, ZHAK
Cassiodorus   kass-ee-uh-DOR-uss
Castiglione, Baldassare   ka-steel-YOH-nay, bal-duh-SAH-ray

Castro, Fidel   KASS-troh, fee-DELL
Çatal Hüyük   chaht-ul hoo-YOOK
Catharism   KA-thuh-riz-um
Catullus   kuh-TULL-uss
Cavendish, Margaret   KAV-un-dish
Cavour, Camillo di   kuh-VOOR, kuh-MEEL-oh dee
Ceauşescu, Nicolae   chow-SHES-koo, nee-koh-LY
celibacy   SELL-uh-buh-see
cenobitic   sen-oh-BIT-ik
Cereta, Laura   say-REE-tuh, LOW-ruh
Cézanne, Paul   say-ZAHN
Chaeronea   ker-uh-NEE-uh
Chaldean   kal-DEE-un
Chandragupta Maurya   chun-druh-GOOP-tuh MOWR-yuh
chanson de geste   shahn-SAWNH duh ZHEST
Charlemagne   SHAR-luh-mayn
Chateaubriand, François-René de   shah-TOH-bree-AHNH, frahnh-SWAH-ruh-NAY duh
Châtelet, marquise du   shat-LAY, mahr-KEEZ duh
Chauvet   shoh-VAY
Cheka   CHEK-uh
Chiang Kai-Shek   CHANG ky-SHEK
Chirac, Jacques   shee-RAK, ZHAHK
Chrétien, Jean   kray-TYEN, ZHAHNH
Chrétien de Troyes   kray-TYEN duh TRWAH
Cicero   SIS-uh-roh
ciompi   CHAHM-pee
Cistercians   sis-TUR-shunz
Claudius   KLAW-dee-uss
Cleisthenes   KLYSS-thuh-neez
Clemenceau, Georges   kluh-mahn-SOH, ZHORZH
Clovis   KLOH-viss
Codreanu, Corneliu   kaw-dree-AH-noo, kor-NELL-yoo
Colbert, Jean-Baptiste   kohl-BAYR, ZHAHN-bap-TEEST
Colonia Agrippinensis   kuh-LOH-nee-uh uh-grip-uh-NEN-suss
colonus   kuh-LOH-nuss
Columbanus   kah-lum-BAY-nuss
comitia centuriata   kuh-MISH-ee-uh sen-choo-ree-AH-tuh
Commodus   KAHM-uh-duss
Comnenus   kahm-NEE-nuss
Comte, Auguste   KOHNT, ow-GOOST
concilium plebis   kahn-SILL-ee-um PLEE-biss
Concordat of Worms   kun-KOR-dat uv WURMZ *or* VORMPS
Condorcet, Marie-Jean de   kohn-dor-SAY, muh-REE-ZHAHNH duh
condottieri   kahn-duh-TYAY-ree
consul   KAHN-sull
Contarini, Gasparo   kahn-tuh-REE-nee, GAHS-puh-roh
conversos   kohn-VAYR-sohz
Copernicus, Nicolaus   kuh-PURR-nuh-kuss, nee-koh-LOW-uss
Córdoba   KOR-duh-buh
Corinth   KOR-inth
Corpus Hermeticum   KOR-pus hur-MET-i-koom
Corpus Iuris Civilis   KOR-pus YOOR-iss SIV-i-liss
corregidores   kuhr-reg-uh-DOR-ayss
Cortés, Hernán   kor-TAYSS *or* kor-TEZ, hayr-NAHN
Corvinus, Matthias   kor-VY-nuss, muh-THY-uss
Courbet, Gustave   koor-BAY, goo-STAHV
Crassus   KRASS-uss
Crécy   kray-SEE
Crédit Mobilier   kray-DEE moh-bee-LYAY
Croatia   kroh-AY-shuh
Croesus   KREE-suss
cum manu   koom MAH-noo
Curie, Marie   kyoo-REE
Cypselus   SIP-suh-luss
d'Albret, Jeanne   dahl-BRAY, ZHAHN

d'Este, Isabella   DESS-tay, ee-suh-BELL-uh
d'Holbach, Paul   dawl-BAHK
Daimler, Gottlieb   DYM-lur, GUHT-leeb
Dalí, Salvador   dah-LEE or DAH-lee
Danton, Georges   dahn-TAWNH, ZHORZH
Darius   duh-RY-uss
Darmstadt   DARM-shtaht
dauphin   DAW-fin
David, Jacques-Louis   dah-VEED, ZHAHK-LWEE
de Champlain, Samuel   duh sham-PLAYN
de Gaulle, Charles   duh GOHL, SHAHRL
De Rerum Novarum   day RAYR-um noh-VAR-um
Debelleyme, Louis-Maurice   duh-buh-LAYM, LWEE-moh-REESS
Debussy, Claude   duh-bus-SEE, KLOHD
décades   day-KAD
Decameron   dee-KAM-uh-run
decarchies   DEK-ar-keez
decemviri   duh-SEM-vuh-ree
Deffand, marquise du   duh-FAHNH, mar-KEEZ doo
Delacroix, Eugène   duh-lah-KRWAH, oo-ZHEN
Démar, Claire   DAY-mar
Demosthenes   duh-MAHSS-thuh-neez
Denikin, Anton   dyin-YEE-kin, ahn-TOHN
Descartes, René   day-KART, ruh-NAY
Dessau   DESS-ow
dhoti   DOH-tee
Diaghilev, Sergei   DYAHG-yuh-lif, syir-GAY
Dias, Bartholomeu   DEE-ush, bar-toh-loh-MAY-oo
Diaspora   dy-ASS-pur-uh
Diderot, Denis   DEE-droh, duh-NEE
Diocletian   dy-uh-KLEE-shun
Disraeli, Benjamin   diz-RAY-lee
Djoser   ZHOH-sur
Dollfuss, Engelbert   DAHL-fooss
Domesday Book   DOOMZ-day book
Domitian   doh-MISH-un
Donatello, Donato di   doh-nuh-TELL-oh, doh-NAH-toh dee
Donatus   duh-NAY-tus
Donatist   DOH-nuh-tist
Dopolavoro   duh-puh-LAH-vuh-roh
Dorians   DOR-ee-unz
Doryphoros   doh-RIF-uh-rohss
Dostoevsky, Fyodor   dus-tuh-YEF-skee, FYUD-ur
Douhet, Giulio   doo-AY, JOOL-yoh
Dreyfus, Alfred   DRY-fuss
Dubček, Alexander   DOOB-chek
Du Bois, W. E. B.   doo-BOISS
Dufay, Guillaume   doo-FAY, gee-YOHM
Duma   DOO-muh
Dürer, Albrecht   DOO-rur, AHL-brekht
Ebert, Friedrich   AY-bert, FREE-drikh
ecclesia   ek-KLEE-zee-uh
Eckhart, Meister   EK-hart, MY-stur
Einsatzgruppen   YN-zahtz-groop-un
Einstein, Albert   YN-styn or Yn-shtyn
Ekaterinburg   i-kat-tuh-RIN-burk
encomienda   en-koh-MYEN-dah
Engels, Friedrich   ENG-ulz, FREE-drikh
Enki   EN-kee
Enlil   EN-lil
Entente Cordiale   ahn-TAHNT kor-DYAHL
Epaminondas   i-PAM-uh-NAHN-duss
ephor   EFF-ur
Epicureanism   ep-i-kyoo-REE-uh-ni-zum
Epicurus   ep-i-KYOOR-uss
episcopos   i-PIS-kuh-puss

equestrians   i-KWES-tree-unz
equites   EK-wuh-teez
Erasistratus   er-uh-SIS-truh-tuss
Erasmus, Desiderius   i-RAZZ-mus, dez-i-DEER-ee-uss
Eratosthenes   er-uh-TAHSS-thuh-neez
eremitical   er-uh-MIT-i-kul
Erhard, Ludwig   AYR-hart, LOOD-vik
Estonia   ess-TOH-nee-uh
Etruscans   i-TRUSS-kunz
Euclid   YOO-klid
Euripides   yoo-RIP-i-deez
exchequer   EKS-chek-ur
Execrabilis   ek-suh-KRAB-uh-liss
Eylau   Y-low
Falange   fuh-LANJ
fasces   FASS-eez
Fascio di Combattimento   FASH-ee-oh dee com-bat-ee-MEN-toh
Fatimid   FAT-i-mid
Fedele, Cassandra   FAY-duh-lee
Feltre, Vittorino da   FELL-tray, vee-tor-EE-noh dah
Ficino, Marsilio   fee-CHEE-noh, mar-SIL-yoh
Fischer, Joschka   FISH-ur, YUSH-kah
Flaubert, Gustave   floh-BAYR, goo-STAHV
Fleury, Cardinal   floo-REE
Floreal   floh-ray-AHL
fluyt   FLYT
Foch, Ferdinand   FUSH, fayr-di-nawnh
Fontainebleau   fawnh-ten-BLOH
Fontenelle, Bernard de   fawnt-NELL, bayr-NAHR duh
Fouquet, Nicolas   foo-KAY, nee-koh-LAH
Fourier, Charles   foo-RYAY, SHAHRL
Francesca, Piero della   frahn-CHESS-kuh, PYAY-roh del-luh
Frequens   FREE-kwenss
Freud, Sigmund   FROID, SIG-mund or ZIG-munt
Friedan, Betty   free-DAN
Friedland   FREET-lahnt
Friedrich, Caspar David   FREED-rikh, kass-PAR dah-VEET
Frimaire   free-MAYR
Froissart, Jean   frwah-SAR, ZHAHNH
Fronde   FROHND
Fructidor   FROOK-ti-dor
fueros   FWYA-rohss
Führerprinzip   FYOOR-ur-prin-TSEEP
gabelle   gah-BELL
Gaiseric   GY-zuh-rik
Galba   GAHL-buh
Galilei, Galileo   GAL-li-lay, gal-li-LAY-oh
Gama, Vasco da   GAHM-uh, VAHSH-koh dah
Gandhi, Mohandas (Mahatma)   GAHN-dee, moh-HAHN-dus (mah-HAHT-muh)
Garibaldi, Giuseppe   gar-uh-BAHL-dee, joo-ZEP-pay
Gasperi, Alcide de   GAHSS-pe-ree, ahl-SEE-day day
Gatti de Gamond, Zoé   gah-TEE duh gah-MOHNH, zoh-AY
Gaugamela   gaw-guh-MEE-luh
Gelasius   juh-LAY-shuss
Gentileschi, Artemisia   jen-tuh-LESS-kee, ar-tuh-MEE-zhuh
Geoffrin, Marie-Thérèse de   zhoh-FRANH, ma-REE-tay-RAYZ duh
Germinal   jayr-mee-NAHL
gerousia   juh-ROO-see-uh
Gesamtkunstwerk   guh-ZAHMT-koonst-vayrk
Gierek, Edward   GYER-ek
Gilgamesh   GILL-guh-mesh
Giolitti, Giovanni   joh-LEE-tee, joe-VAHN-nee
Giotto   JOH-toh
Girondins   juh-RAHN-dinz
glasnost   GLAHZ-nohst

Gleichschaltung glykh-SHAHL-toonk

Goebbels, Joseph GUR-bulz

Goethe, Johann Wolfgang von GUR-tuh, yoh-HAHN VULF-gahnk fun

Gömbös, Julius GUM-buhsh

Gomulka, Wladyslaw goh-MOOL-kuh, vlah-DIS-lahf

gonfaloniere gun-fah-loh-NYAY-ray

Gonzaga, Gian Francesco gun-DZAH-gah, JAHN frahn-CHES-koh

Gorbachev, Mikhail GOR-buh-chof, meek-HAYL

Göring, Hermann GUR-ing

Gottwald, Clement GUT-vald

Gouges, Olympe GOOZH, oh-LAMP

Gracchus, Tiberius and Gaius GRAK-us, ty-BEER-ee-uss *and* GY-uss

grandi GRAHN-dee

Grieg, Edvard GREEG, ED-vart

Groote, Gerard GROH-tuh

Gropius, Walter GROH-pee-uss, VAHL-tuh

Grossdeutsch GROHS-doich

Groza, Petra GRO-zhuh, PET-ruh

Guicciardini, Francesco gwee-char-DEE-nee, frahn-CHESS-koh

Guindorf, Reine GWIN-dorf, RY-nuh

Guise GEEZ

Guizot, François gee-ZOH, frahnh-SWAH

Gustavus Adolphus goo-STAY-vus uh-DAHL-fuss

Gutenberg, Johannes GOO-ten-bayrk, yoh-HAH-nuss

Guzman, Gaspar de goos-MAHN, gahs-PAR day

Habsburg HAPS-burg

Hadrian HAY-dree-un

Hagia Sophia HAG-ee-uh soh-FEE-uh

hajj HAJ

Hammurabi ham-uh-RAH-bee

Handel, George Friedrich HAN-dul

Hankou HAHN-kow

Hannibal HAN-uh-bul

Hanukkah HAH-nuh-kuh

Harappa huh-RAP-uh

Hardenberg, Karl von HAR-den-berk, KARL fun

Harun al-Rashid huh-ROON ah-rah-SHEED

Hatshepsut hat-SHEP-soot

Haushofer, Karl HOWSS-hoh-fuh

Haussmann, Baron HOWSS-mun

Havel, Vaclav HAH-vul, VAHT-slahf

Haydn, Franz Joseph HY-dun, FRAHNTS YO-zef

hegemon HEJ-uh-mun

Hegira hee-JY-ruh

Heisenberg, Werner HY-zun-bayrk, VAYR-nur

heliaea HEE-lee-ee

Hellenistic hel-uh-NIS-tik

helots HEL-uts

Herculaneum hur-kyuh-LAY-nee-um

Herodotus huh-ROD-uh-tuss

Herophilus huh-ROF-uh-luss

Herzegovina HURT-suh-guh-VEE-nuh

Herzen, Alexander HAYRT-sun

Herzl, Theodor HAYRT-sul, TAY-oh-dor

Hesiod HEE-see-ud

Hesse, Hermann HESS-uh

hetairai huh-TY-ree

Heydrich, Reinhard HY-drikh, RYN-hart

hieroglyph HY-uh-roh-glif

Hildegard of Bingen HIL-duh-gard uv BING-un

Hindenburg, Paul von HIN-den-boork, POWL fun

Hiroshima hee-roh-SHEE-muh

Hitler Jugend HIT-luh YOO-gunt

Ho Chi Minh HOH CHEE MIN

Höch, Hannah HEKH

Hohenstaufen hoh-en-SHTOW-fen

Hohenzollern hoh-en-TSULL-urn

Hohenzollern-Sigmaringen hoh-en-TSULL-urn-zig-mah-RING-un

Holtzendorf HOHLT-sen-dorf

Homo sapiens HOH-moh SAY-pee-unz

Honecker, Erich HOH-nek-uh

Honorius hoh-NOR-ee-uss

hoplites HAHP-lyts

Horace HOR-uss

Horthy, Miklós HOR-tee, MIK-lohsh

Höss, Rudolf HESS

Hoxha, Enver HAW-jah

Huayna Inca WY-nuh INK-uh

Huguenots HYOO-guh-nots

Husák, Gustav HOO-sahk, goo-STAHV

Ibn Sina ib-un SEE-nuh

Ictinus ik-TY-nuss

Ignatius of Loyola ig-NAY-shuss uv loi-OH-luh

Il Duce eel DOO-chay

Île-de-France EEL-de-fronhss

illustrés ee-loo-STRAY

illustrissimi ee-loo-STREE-see-mee

imperator im-puh-RAH-tur

imperium im-PEER-ee-um

intendant anh-tahnh-DAHNH *or* in-TEN-dunt

Isis Y-sis

Issus ISS-uss

ius civile YOOSS see-VEE-lay

ius gentium YOOSS GEN-tee-um

ius naturale YOOSS nah-too-RAH-lay

Jacobin JAK-uh-bin

Jacquerie zhak-REE

Jadwiga yahd-VEE-guh

Jagiello yahg-YEL-oh

Jahn, Friedrich Ludwig YAHN, FREED-rikh LOOD-vik

Jaufré Rudel zhoh-FRAY roo-DEL

Jaurès, Jean zhaw-RESS, ZHAHNH

Jena YAY-nuh

jihad ji-HAHD

Joffre, Joseph ZHUFF-ruh

Journal des Savants zhoor-NAHL day sah-VAHNH

Juana Inés de la Cruz, Sor HWAH-nuh ee-NAYSS day lah KROOZ, SAWR

Judaea joo-DEE-uh

Judas Maccabaeus JOO-dus mak-uh-BEE-uss

Jung, Carl YOONG

Junkers YOONG-kers

Jupiter Optimus Maximus JOO-puh-tur AHP-tuh-muss MAK-suh-muss

Justinian juh-STIN-ee-un

Juvenal JOO-vuh-nul

Ka'ba KAH-buh

Kádár, János KAH-dahr, YAH-nush

kamikaze kah-mi-KAH-zay

Kandinsky, Wassily kan-DIN-skee, vus-YEEL-yee

Kangxi GANG-zhee

Kant, Immanuel KAHNT, i-MAHN-yoo-el

Karlowitz KARL-oh-vits

Karlsbad KARLSS-baht

Kaunitz, Wenzel von KOW-nits, VENT-sul fun

Kemal Atatürk kuh-MAHL ah-tah-TIRK

Kenyatta, Jomo ken-YAHT-uh, JOH-moh

Kerensky, Alexander kuh-REN-skee

Keynes, John Maynard KAYNZ

Khanbaliq khahn-bah-LEEK

Khomeini, Ayatollah khoh-MAY-nee

Khrushchev, Nikita KHROOSH-chawf, nuh-KEE-tuh
Khubilai Khan KOO-bluh KAHN
Kikuya ki-KOO-yuh
Kleindeutsch KLYN-doich
Kohl, Helmut KOHL, HEL-moot
koiné koi-NAY
Kolchak, Alexander kul-CHAHK
Kollantai, Alexandra kul-lun-TY
Königgrätz kur-nig-GRETS
Kornilov, Lavr kor-NYEE-luff, LAH-vur
Kosciuszko, Thaddeus kaw-SHOOS-koh, tah-DAY-oosh
Kosovo KAWSS-suh-voh
Kossuth, Louis KAWSS-uth *or* KAW-shoot
Kostunica, Vojislav kuh-STOO-nit-suh, VOH-yee-slav
kouros KOO-rohss
Koyaanisqatsi koh-YAH-niss-kaht-si
Kraft durch Freude KRAHFT doorkh FROI-duh
Kreditanstalt kray-deet-AHN-shtalt
Kristallnacht kri-STAHL-nahkht
Krupp, Alfred KROOP
Kuchuk-Kainarji koo-CHOOK-ky-NAR-jee
kulaks KOO-lahks
Kulturkampf kool-TOOR-kahmpf
Kun, Béla KOON, BAY-luh
Kundera, Milan koon-DAYR-uh, MEE-lahn
Kursk KOORSK
Kwasniewski, Aleksander kwahsh-NYEF-skee
la belle époque lah BEL ay-PUK
Lafayette, marquis de lah-fay-ET, mar-KEE duh
laissez-faire less-ay-FAYR
Lamarck, Jean-Baptiste lah-MARK, ZHAHNH-bah-TEEST
Lancaster LAN-kas-tur
La Rochefoucauld-Liancourt, duc de lah-RUSH-foo-koh-lee-ahnh-KOOR, dook duh
Las Navas de Tolosa lahss nah-vahss day toh-LOH-suh
latifundia lat-i-FOON-dee-uh
Latium LAY-shee-um
Latvia LAT-vee-uh
Launay, marquis de loh-NAY, mar-KEE duh
Laurier, Wilfred LOR-ee-ay
Lavoisier, Antoine lah-vwah-ZYAY
Lazar lah-ZAR
Lebensraum LAY-benz-rowm
Les Demoiselles d'Avignon lay dem-wah-ZEL dah-vee-NYOHNH
Lespinasse, Julie de less-pee-NAHSS, zhoo-LEE duh
Le Tellier, François Michel luh tel-YAY, frahnh-SWAH mee-SHEL
Lévesque, René luh-VEK, ruh-NAY
Leviathan luh-VY-uh-thun
Leyster, Judith LESS-tur
Licinius ly-SIN-ee-uss
Liebenfels, Lanz von LEE-bun-felss, LAHNts fun
Liebknecht, Karl LEEP-knekht
Liebknecht, Wilhelm LEEP-knekht, VIL-helm
Lindisfarne LIN-dis-farn
Lionne, Hugues de LYUNN, OOG duh
List, Friedrich LIST, FREED-rikh
Liszt, Franz LIST, FRAHNTS
Lithuania lith-WAY-nee-uh
Livy LIV-ee
Li Zicheng lee zee-CHENG
L'Ouverture, Toussaint loo-vayr-TOOR, too-SANH
Louvois loo-VWAH
Lucretius loo-KREE-shus
Luddites LUD-yts
Ludendorff, Erich LOO-dun-dorf
Lueger, Karl LOO-gur

Luftwaffe LOOFT-vahf-uh
l'uomo universale LWOH-moh OO-nee-ver-SAH-lay
Lützen LOOT-sun
Luxemburg, Rosa LOOK-sum-boork
Lyons LYOHNH
Maastricht MAHSS-trikht
Machiavelli, Niccolò mahk-ee-uh-VEL-ee, nee-koh-LOH
Maginot Line MA-zhi-noh lyn
Magna Graecia MAG-nuh GREE-shuh
Magyars MAG-yarz
Maimonides my-MAH-nuh-deez
Maistre, Joseph de MESS-truh
maius imperium MY-yoos im-PEE-ree-um
Malaya muh-LAY-uh
Mallarmé, Stéphane mah-lahr-MAY, stay-FAHN
Malleus Maleficarum mal-EE-uss mal-uh-FIK-uh-rum
Malthus, Thomas MAWL-thuss
Manchukuo man-CHOO-kwoh
Manetho MAN-uh-thoh
Mao Zedong mow zee-DAHNG
Marcus Aurelius MAR-kuss aw-REE-lee-uss
Marcuse, Herbert mar-KOO-zuh
Marie Antoinette muh-REE an-twuh-NET
Marius MAR-ee-uss
Marquez, Gabriel Garcia mar-KEZ
Marseilles mar-SAY
Marsiglio of Padua mar-SIL-yoh uv PAD-juh-wuh
Masaccio muh-ZAH-choh
Masaryk, Thomas MAS-uh-rik
Mästlin, Michael MEST-lin
Matteotti, Giacomo mat-tay-AHT-tee, JAHK-uh-moh
Maxentius mak-SEN-shuss
Maximian mak-SIM-ee-un
Maya MY-uh
Mazarin maz-uh-RANH
Mazzini, Giuseppe maht-SEE-nee, joo-ZEP-pay
Megasthenes muh-GAS-thuh-neez
Mehmet meh-MET
Meiji MAY-jee
Mein Kampf myn KAHMPF
Melanchthon, Philip muh-LANK-tun
Menander muh-NAN-dur
Mendeleyev, Dmitri men-duh-LAY-ef, di-MEE-tree
Mensheviks MENS-shuh-viks
Mercator, Gerardus mur-KAY-tur, juh-RAHR-dus
Merian, Maria Sibylla MAY-ree-un
Merovingian meh-ruh-VIN-jee-un
Mesopotamia mess-uh-puh-TAY-mee-uh
Messiaen, Olivier meh-SYANH, oh-lee-VYAY
Messidor MESS-i-dor
mestizos mess-TEE-ZOHZ
Metaxas, John muh-tahk-SAHSS
Metternich, Klemens von MET-ayr-nikh, KLAY-menss fun
Michel, Louise mee-SHEL
Michelangelo my-kuh-LAN-juh-loh
Mieszko MYESH-koh
Millet, Jean-François mi-YEH, ZHAHNH-frahnh-SWAH
Milŏsević, Slobodan mi-LOH-suh-vich, sluh-BOH-dahn
Miltiades mil-TY-uh-deez
Mirandola, Pico della mee-RAN-doh-lah, PEE-koh DELL-uh
missi dominici MISS-ee doh-MIN-i-chee
Mitterrand, François MEE-tayr-rahnh, frahnh-SWAH
Moctezuma mahk-tuh-ZOO-muh
Mohács MOH-hach
Mohenjo-Daro mo-HEN-jo-DAH-roh
Moldavia mohl-DAY-vee-uh

Moldova   mohl-DOH-vuh
Molière, Jean-Baptiste   mohl-YAYR, ZHAHNH-bah-TEEST
Molotov, Vyacheslav   MAHL-uh-tawf, vyich-chiss-SLAHF
Monet, Claude   moh-NEH, KLOHD
Montaigne, Michel de   mahn-TAYN, mee-SHELL duh
Montefeltro, Federigo da   mahn-tuh-FELL-troh, fay-day-REE-goh dah
Montesquieu   MOHN-tess-kyoo
Montessori, Maria   mahn-tuh-SOR-ee
Morisot, Berthe   mor-ee-ZOH, BAYRT
Mozambique   moh-zam-BEEK
Mozart, Wolfgang Amadeus   MOH-tsart, VULF-gahng ah-muh-DAY-uss
Muawiya   moo-AH-wee-yah
Mudejares   moo-theh-KHAH-rayss
Mughal   MOO-gul
Muhammad   moh-HAM-mud or moo-HAM-mud
Mühlberg   MOOL-bayrk
mulattoes   muh-LAH-tohz
Müntzer, Thomas   MOON-tsur
Murad   moo-RAHD
Muslim   MUZ-lum
Mutsuhito   moo-tsoo-HEE-toh
Myanmar   MYAN-mahr
Mycenaean   my-suh-NEE-un
Nabonidas   nab-uh-NY-duss
Nabopolassar   nab-uh-puh-LASS-ur
Nagasaki   nah-gah-SAH-kee
Nagy, Imry   NAHJ, IM-ray
Nanjing   nan-JING
Nantes   NAHNT
Nasser, Gamal Abdel   NAH-sur, juh-MAHL ahb-DOOL
Navarre   nuh-VAHR
Nebuchadnezzar   neb-uh-kud-NEZZ-ur
Nehru, Jawaharlal   NAY-roo, juh-WAH-hur-lahl
Nero   NEE-roh
Nerva   NUR-vuh
Neumann, Balthasar   NOI-mahn, BAHL-tuh-zahr
Neumann, Solomon   NOI-mahn
Neustria   NOO-stree-uh
Nevsky, Alexander   NYEF-skee
Newcomen, Thomas   NYOO-kuh-mun or nyoo-KUM-mun
Ngo Dinh Diem   GOH din DYEM
Nicias   NISS-ee-uss
Nietzsche, Friedrich   NEE-chuh or NEE-chee, FREED-rikh
Nimwegen   NIM-vay-gun
Ninhursaga   nin-HUR-sah-guh
Nivose   nee-VOHZ
Nkrumah, Kwame   en-KROO-muh, KWAH-may
nobiles   no-BEE-layz
Nogarola, Isotta   NOH-guh-roll-uh, ee-ZAHT-uh
Novalis, Friedrich   noh-VAH-lis, FREED-rikh
Novotny, Antonin   noh-VAHT-nee, AHN-toh-nyeen
novus homo   NOH-vuss HOH-moh
Nystadt   NEE-shtaht
Octavian   ahk-TAY-vee-un
Odoacer   oh-doh-AY-sur
Olivares   oh-lee-BAH-rayss
optimates   ahp-tuh-MAH-tayz
Oresteia   uh-res-TY-uh
Osama bin Laden   oh-SAH-muh bin LAH-dun
Osiris   oh-SY-russ
Ostara   oh-STAH-ruh
Ostpolitik   OHST-paw-li-teek
ostrakon   AHSS-truh-kahn
Ostrogoths   AHSS-truh-gahthss

Ovid   OH-vid
Oxenstierna, Axel   OOK-sen-shur-nah, AHK-sul
Pachakuti   pah-chah-KOO-tee
Paleologus   pay-lee-AWL-uh-guss
Panaetius   puh-NEE-shuss
Pankhurst, Emmeline   PANK-hurst
papal curia   PAY-pul KYOOR-ee-uh
Papen, Franz von   PAH-pun, FRAHNTS fun
Paracelsus   par-uh-SELL-suss
Parlement   par-luh-MAHNH
Parti Québécois   par-TEE kay-bek-KWA
Pascal, Blaise   pass-KAHL, BLEZ
Pasteur, Louis   pas-TOOR, LWEE
paterfamilias   pay-tur-fuh-MEEL-yus
Pensées   pahn-SAY
Pentateuch   PEN-tuh-took
Pepin   PEP-in or pay-PANH
perestroika   per-uh-STROI-kuh
Pergamum   PURR-guh-mum
Pericles   PER-i-kleez
perioeci   per-ee-EE-see
Pétain, Henri   pay-TANH, AHN-ree
Petite Roquette   puh-TEET raw-KET
Petrarch   PEE-trark or PET-trark
Petronius   pi-TROH-nee-uss
phalansteries   fuh-LAN-stuh-reez
philosophe   fee-loh-ZAWF
Phintys   FIN-tiss
Phoenicians   fuh-NEE-shunz
Photius   FOH-shuss
Picasso, Pablo   pi-KAH-soh
Pietism   PY-uh-tiz-um
Pilsudski, Joseph   peel-SOOT-skee
Piscator, Erwin   PIS-kuh-tor, AYR-vin
Pisistratus   puh-SIS-truh-tuss
Pissarro, Camille   pee-SAH-roh, kah-MEEL
Pizan, Christine de   pee-ZAHN, kris-TEEN duh
Pizarro, Francesco   puh-ZAHR-oh, frahn-CHESS-koh
Planck, Max   PLAHNK
Plantagenet   plan-TAJ-uh-net
Plassey   PLA-see
Plato   PLAY-toh
Plautus   PLAW-tuss
plebiscita   pleb-i-SEE-tuh
Pluviose   ploo-VYOHZ
Poincaré, Raymond   pwanh-kah-RAY, ray-MOHNH
polis   POH-liss
politiques   puh-lee-TEEKS
Pollaiuolo, Antonio   pohl-ly-WOH-loh
Poltava   pul-TAH-vuh
Polybius   puh-LIB-ee-uss
Pombal, marquis de   pum-BAHL, mar-KEE duh
Pompadour, madame de   POM-puh-door, ma-DAM duh
Pompeii   pahm-PAY
Pompey   PAHM-pee
pontifex maximus   PAHN-ti-feks MAK-si-muss
populares   PAWP-oo-lahr-ayss
populo grasso   PAWP-oo-loh GRAH-soh
Postumus   PAHS-choo-muss
Potsdam   PAHTS-dam
Poussin, Nicholas   poo-SANH, NEE-koh-lah
Praecepter Germaniae   PREE-sep-tur gayr-MAHN-ee-ee
praetor   PREE-tur
Prairial   pray-RYAL
Pravda   PRAHV-duh
Primo de Rivera   PREE-moh day ri-VAY-ruh

primogeniture   pree-moh-JEN-i-choor
princeps   PRIN-seps
Principia   prin-SIP-ee-uh
Procopius   pruh-KOH-pee-uss
procurator   PROK-yuh-ray-tur
Ptolemaic   tahl-uh-MAY-ik
Ptolemy   TAHL-uh-mee
Pugachev, Emelyan   poo-guh-CHAWF, yim-yil-YAHN
Punic   PYOO-nik
Putin, Vladimir   POO-tin
Pyrrhic   PEER-ik
Pyrrhus   PEER-uss
Pythagoras   puh-THAG-uh-russ
Qianlong   CHAN-lung
Qing   CHING
quadrivium   kwah-DRIV-ee-um
quaestors   KWES-turs
querelle des femmes   keh-REL day FAHM
Quesnay, François   keh-NAY, frahnn-SWAH
Quetzelcoatl   KWET-sul-koh-AHT-ul
Quran   kuh-RAN *or* kuh-RAHN
Racine, Jean-Baptiste   ra-SEEN, ZHAHNH-buh-TEEST
Rahner, Karl   RAH-nur
Rameses   RAM-uh-seez
Raphael   RAFF-ee-ul
Rasputin   rass-PYOO-tin
Rathenau, Walter   RAH-tuh-now, VAHL-tuh
Realpolitik   ray-AHL-poh-lee-teek
Realschule   ray-AHL-shoo-luh
Reichsrat   RYKHSS-raht
Reichstag   RYKHSS-tahk
Rembrandt van Rijn   REM-brant vahn RYN
Renan, Ernst   re-NAHNH
Ricci, Matteo   REE-chee, ma-TAY-oh
Richelieu   REESH-uh-lyoo
Ricimer   RISS-uh-mur
Rikstag   RIKS-tahk
Rilke, Rainer Maria   RILL-kuh, RY-nuh mah-REE-uh
Rimbaud, Arthur   ram-BOH, ar-TOOR
risorgimento   ree-SOR-jee-men-toe
Robespierre, Maximilien   ROHBZ-pyayr, mak-see-meel-YENH
Rococo   ruh-KOH-koh
Rocroi   roh-KRWAH
Röhm, Ernst   RURM
Rommel, Erwin   RAHM-ul
Romulus Augustulus   RAHM-yuh-luss ow-GOOS-chuh-luss
Rossbach   RAWSS-bahkh
Rousseau, Jean-Jacques   roo-SOH, ZHAHNH-ZHAHK
Rurik   ROO-rik
Ryswick   RYZ-wik
Sacrosancta   sak-roh-SANK-tuh
Saint-Just   sanh-ZHOOST
Saint-Simon, Henri de   sanh-see-MOHNH, ahnh-REE duh
Sakharov, Andrei   SAH-kuh-rawf, ahn-DRAY
Saladin   SAL-uh-din
Salazar, Antonio   SAL-uh-zahr
Sallust   SAL-ust
Samnites   SAM-nytss
San Martín, José de   san mar-TEEN, hoh-SAY day
sans-culottes   sahnh-koo-LUT *or* sanz-koo-LAHTSS
Sartre, Jean-Paul   SAR-truh, ZHAHNH-POHL
satrap   SAY-trap
satrapy   SAY-truh-pee
Satyricon   sat-TEER-i-kahn
Schaumburg-Lippe   SHOWM-boorkh-LEE-puh
Schleswig-Holstein   SHLESS-vik-HOHL-shtyn

Schlieffen, Alfred von   SHLEE-fun
Schliemann, Heinrich   SHLEE-mahn, HYN-rikh
Schmidt, Helmut   SHMIT, HEL-moot
Schönberg, Arnold   SHURN-bayrk, AR-nawlt
Schönborn   SHURN-bawn
Schönerer, Georg von   SHURN-uh-ruh, GAY-ork fun
Schröder, Gerhard   SHRUR-duh, GAYR-hahrt
Schuschnigg, Karl von   SHOOSH-nik
Schutzmannschaft   SHOOTS-mun-shahft
Scipio Aemilianus   SEE-pee-oh ee-mil-YAY-nuss
Scipio Africanus   SEE-pee-oh af-ree-KAY-nuss
scriptoria   skrip-TOR-ee-uh
Ségur   say-GOO-uh
Sejm   SAYM
Seleucid   suh-LOO-sid
Seleucus   suh-LOO-kuss
Seljuk   SEL-jook
Seneca   SEN-uh-kuh
Sephardic   suh-FAHR-dik
Septimius Severus   sep-TIM-ee-uss se-VEER-uss
serjents   sayr-ZHAHNH
Sforza, Ludovico   SFORT-sah, loo-doh-VEE-koh
Shalmaneser   shal-muh-NEE-zur
Shang   SHAHNG
Shari'a   shah-REE-uh
Sieveking, Amalie   SEE-vuh-king, uh-MAHL-yuh
Sieyès, Abbé   syay-YESS, ab-BAY
signoria   seen-YOR-ee-uh
sine manu   sy-nee-MAY-noo
Slovenia   sloh-VEE-nee-uh
Société Générale   soh-see-ay-TAY zhay-nay-RAHL
Socrates   SAHK-ruh-teez
Solon   SOH-lun
Solzhenitsyn, Alexander   sohl-zhuh-NEET-sin
Somme   SUM
Sophocles   SAHF-uh-kleez
Sorel, Georges   soh-RELL, ZHORZH
Spartacus   SPAR-tuh-kuss
Spartiates   spar-tee-AH-teez
Speer, Albert   SHPAYR
Speransky, Michael   spyuh-RAHN-skee
Spinoza, Benedict de   spi-NOH-zuh
squadristi   skwah-DREES-tee
Srebrenica   sreb-bruh-NEET-suh
stadholder   STAD-hohl-dur
Staël, Germaine de   STAHL, zhayr-MEN duh
Stakhanov, Alexei   stuh-KHAH-nuf, uh-LEK-say
Stasi   SHTAH-see
Stauffenberg, Claus von   SHTOW-fen-berk, KLOWSS fun
Stein, Heinrich von   SHTYN, HYN-rikh fun
Stilicho   STIL-i-koh
Stoicism   STOH-i-siz-um
Stolypin, Peter   stuh-LIP-yin
strategoi   strah-tay-GOH-ee
Stravinsky, Igor   struh-VIN-skee, EE-gor
Stresemann, Gustav   SHTRAY-zuh-mahn, GOOS-tahf
Strozzi, Alessandra   STRAWT-see
Struensee, John Frederick   SHTROO-un-zay
Sturmabteilung   SHTOORM-ap-ty-loonk
Sudetenland   soo-DAY-tun-land
Suger   soo-ZHAYR
Suharto   soo-HAHR-toh
Sukarno   soo-KAHR-noh
Suleiman   soo-lay-MAHN
Sulla   SULL-uh
Sumerians   soo-MER-ee-unz *or* soo-MEER-ee-unz

Summa Theologica   SOO-muh tay-oh-LOG-jee-kuh
Suppuliumas   suh-PIL-oo-LEE-uh-muss
Suttner, Bertha von   ZOOT-nuh
Symphonie Fantastique   SANH-foh-nee fahn-tas-TEEK
Taaffe, Edward von   TAH-fuh
Tacitus   TASS-i-tuss
taille   TY
Talleyrand, Prince   tah-lay-RAHNH
Tanzania   tan-zuh-NEE-uh
Tenochtitlán   tay-nawch-teet-LAHN
Tertullian   tur-TULL-yun
Thales   THAY-leez
Theocritus   thee-AHK-ruh-tuss
Theodora   thee-uh-DOR-uh
Theodoric   thee-AHD-uh-rik
Theodosius   thee-uh-DOH-shuss
Theognis   thee-AHG-nuss
Thermidor   TAYR-mi-dor
Thermopylae   thur-MAHP-uh-lee
Thiers, Adolphe   TYAYR, a-DAWLF
Thucydides   thoo-SID-uh-deez
Thutmosis   thoot-MOH-suss
Tiberius   ty-BEER-ee-uss
Tiglath-pileser   TIG-lath-py-LEE-zur
Tirpitz, Admiral von   TEER-pits
Tisza, István   TISS-ah, ISHT-vun
Tito   TEE-toh
Titus   TY-tuss
Tlaxcala   tuh-lah-SKAH-lah
Tojo, Hideki   TOH-joh, hee-DEK-ee
Tokugawa Ieyasu   toh-koo-GAH-wah ee-yeh-YAH-soo
Tolstoy, Leo   TOHL-stoy
Topa Inca   TOH-puh INK-uh
Torah   TOR-uh
Tordesillas   tor-day-SEE-yass
Trajan   TRAY-jun
Trevithick, Richard   TREV-uh-thik
Tristan, Flora   TRISS-tun
trivium   TRIV-ee-um
Trotsky, Leon   TRAHT-skee
Troyes   TRWAH
Trudeau, Pierre   troo-DOH, PYAYR
Trufaut, François   troo-FOH, frahnh-SWAH
Tsara, Tristan   TSAHR-rah, TRISS-tun
Tübingen   TOO-bing-un
Tyche   TY-kee
Uccello, Paolo   oo-CHEL-oh, POW-loh
uhuru   oo-HOO-roo
Ulbricht, Walter   OOL-brikkt, VAHL-tuh
Umayyads   oo-MY-adz
Unam Sanctam   OO-nahm SAHNK-tahm
universitas   yoo-nee-VAYR-see-tahss
Uzbekistan   ooz-BEK-i-stan
Valens   VAY-linz
Valentinian   val-en-TIN-ee-un
Valéry, Paul   vah-lay-REE, POHL
Valois   val-WAH
Van de Velde, Theodore   vahn duh VELL-duh, TAY-oh-dor
van Eyck, Jan   vahn YK *or* van AYK, YAHN
van Gogh, Vincent   van GOH *or* vahn GOK
Vasa, Gustavus   VAH-suh, GUSS-tuh-vuss
Vega, Lope de   VAY-guh, LOH-pay day
Vendée   vahnh-DAY

Vendemiaire   vahnh-duh-MYAYR
Venetia   vuh-NEE-shuh
Ventose   vahnh-TOHZ
Verdun   vur-DUN
Vergerio, Pietro Paolo   vur-JEER-ee-oh, PYAY-troh POW-loh
Versailles   vayr-SY
Vesalius, Andreas   vuh-SAY-lee-uss, ahn-DRAY-uss
Vespasian   vess-PAY-zhun
Vespucci, Amerigo   vess-POO-chee, ahm-ay-REE-goh
Vesuvius   vuh-SOO-vee-uss
Vichy   VISH-ee
Vierzehnheiligen   feer-tsayn-HY-li-gen
Virchow, Rudolf   FEER-khoh, ROO-dulf
Virgil   VUR-jul
Visconti, Giangaleazzo   vees-KOHN-tee, jahn-gah-lay-AH-tsoh
Visigoths   VIZ-uh-gathz
Voilquin, Suzanne   vwahl-KANH, soo-ZAHN
Volk   FULK
Volkschulen   FULK-shoo-lun
Voltaire   vohl-TAYR
Wafd   WAHFT
Wagner, Richard   VAG-nur, RIKH-art
Walesa, Lech   vah-WENT-sah, LEK
Wallachia   wah-LAY-kee-uh
Wallenstein, Albrecht von   VAHL-en-shtyn, AWL-brekht
Wannsee   VAHN-zay
Watteau, Antoine   wah-TOH, AHN-twahn
Weill, Kurt   VYL
Weizsäcker, Richard von   VYTS-zek-ur, RIKH-art
wergeld   WURR-geld
Windischgrätz, Alfred   VIN-dish-grets
Winkelmann, Maria   VINK-ul-mahn
Witte, Sergei   VIT-uh, syir-GYAY
Wittenberg   VIT-ten-bayrk
Wojtyla, Karol   voy-TEE-wah, KAH-rul
Wollstonecraft, Mary   WULL-stun-kraft
Würzburg   VOORTS-boork
Wyclif, John   WIK-lif
Xavier, Francis   ZAY-vee-ur
Xerxes   ZURK-seez
Xhosa   KHOH-suh
Ximenes   khee-MAY-ness
Yahweh   YAH-way
Yangtze   YANG tsee
Yeats, William Butler   YAYTS
Yeltsin, Boris   YELT-sun
yishuv   YISH-uv
Zasulich, Vera   tsah-SOO-likh
Zemsky Sobor   ZEM-skee suh-BOR
zemstvos   ZEMPST-vohz
Zeno   ZEE-noh
Zenobia   zuh-NOH-bee-uh
zeppelin   ZEP-puh-lin
Zeus   ZOOSS
Zhenotdel   zhen-ut-DELL
Zhivkov, Todor   ZHIV-kuff, toh-DOR
ziggurat   ZIG-uh-rat
Zimmermann, Dominikus   TSIM-ur-mahn, doh-MEE-nee-kuss
Zinzendorf, Nikolaus von   TSIN-sin-dorf, NEE-koh-LOWSS fun
Zola, Émile   ZOH-lah, ay-MEEL
zollverein   TSOHL-fuh-ryn
Zoroaster   ZOR-oh-ass-tur
Zwingli, Ulrich   TSFING-lee, OOL-rikh